DORLING KINDERSLEY *TRAVEL GUIDES*

GREAT PLACES
TO STAY IN
EUROPE

Main contributors:
FIONA DUNCAN AND LEONIE GLASS

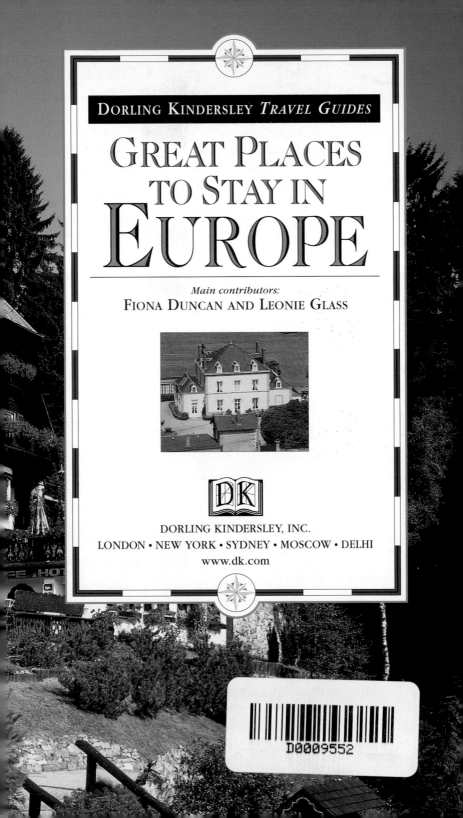

DORLING KINDERSLEY, INC.
LONDON • NEW YORK • SYDNEY • MOSCOW • DELHI
www.dk.com

DORLING KINDERSLEY, INC.

www.dk.com

Edited and produced for Dorling Kindersley by Duncan Petersen
Publishing Ltd, 31 Ceylon Road, London W14 OPY

PROJECT EDITOR Marion Moisy
ASSISTANT EDITORS Nicola Davies, Zoe Ross
DESIGNERS Beverley Stewart, Chris Foley
EDITORIAL ASSISTANT Catherine Iszard
EDITORIAL DIRECTOR Andrew Duncan
ART DIRECTOR Mel Petersen

Dorling Kindersley Ltd
Nick Inman, Nancy Jones, Kate Poole, Dave Pugh

MAIN CONTRIBUTORS
Fiona Duncan and Leonie Glass

CONTRIBUTORS
Philip Lee, Judith Hampson, David Sandhu, Jenny Rees,
Dorine Scherpel, Celia Woolfrey, Sarah Toynbee, Kathy Arnold,
Paul Wade, Robin Gauldie

MAPS
Colourmap Scanning Ltd

Reproduced in England by Colour Zone, London
Printed and bound in Italy by G. Canale & C. S.p.A., Turin

First American Edition, 2000

Published in the United States by
Dorling Kindersley, Inc.
95 Madison Avenue, New York 10016

Copyright 2000 © Dorling Kindersley Limited, London

ISBN 07894 4626x

Library of Congress Cataloging-in-Publication Data

Duncan, Fiona.
  Great places to stay in Europe / main contributors, Fiona
  Duncan and Leonie Glass.
    p.cm. -- (Eyewitness travel guides)
  ISBN 0-7894-4626-x (alk. paper)
    I. Hotels--Europe--Guidebooks. I. Glass, Leonie. II. Title.
  III. Series.

TX907.5.E85 D86 1999
647.944'01--dc21   99-047072

**The information in every
Dorling Kindersley Travel Guide is checked annually**.
Every effort has been made to ensure that this book is as up-to-date as
possible at the time of going to press. Some details, however, such as
telephone numbers, e-mail addresses and prices are liable to change. The
publishers cannot accept responsibility for any consequences arising from the
use of this book. We would be delighted to receive any corrections and
suggestions for incorporation in the next edition; on page 432 you will
find a reader's response form. Or write to:
Editorial Director, Dorling Kindersley Travel Guides,
Dorling Kindersley, 9 Henrietta Street, London WC2E 8PS.

CONTENTS

Facing page 1 Hôtel Cléry, France; 2 The Old Rectory, Great Britain; 3 Castelo Bom Jesus, Portugal;
4 Cley Mill, Great Britain; 5 Hotel Real, Spain; 6 Verbano, Italy; 7 Wald & Schlosshotel Friedrichsruhe,
Germany; 8 Château de Vault de Lugny, France.

◁ Hotel Adler, Germany (large picture)

DK TRAVEL GUIDES

GREAT PLACES TO STAY IN EUROPE

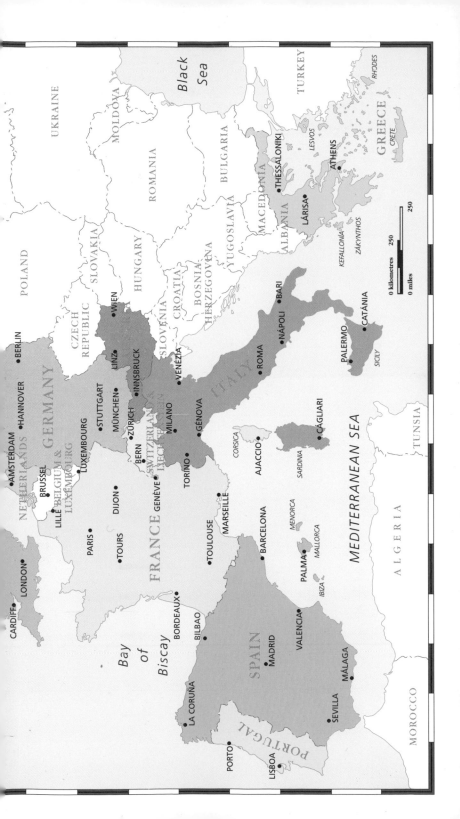

HOW TO USE THIS GUIDE

THIS GUIDE is designed to help you get the most from your travels in Europe. Each place to stay – whether a hotel, a bed-and-breakfast or a country inn – has been chosen because it is in some way special, an experience worth seeking out in its own right and more than just a bed for the night. There are 15 sections, each devoted to a single country. The sections run in loose geographical order, starting in Northern Europe and ending in Southern Europe.

Within each section there are always three parts: introductory pages, describing the accommodation scene overall; maps, showing where the hotels are located; and the hotel entries ('listings') themselves.

OUR EIGHT SELECTION CRITERIA

• *Character - in the buildings, and the interior decoration.*

• *Atmosphere or ambience - often influenced by other guests.*

• *Style and taste not only in the interior decoration but in the details - the placing of furniture, the presentation of menus, and so on.*

• *An interesting, attractive location.*

• *A personal welcome - genuine, not forced - from staff or proprietor.*

• *Bedrooms like real bedrooms, not hotel rooms.*

• *Interesting food, prepared with care from fresh ingredients.*

• *Size: generally not very large, but some large hotels are included - see the qualifications below.*

A Question of Balance

As you would expect, our main entries – the ones illustrated with photographs – tend to score five, six, seven or even eight out of eight on the list described above. *But,* and you will find this clearly stated in the text where appropriate, a significant number of our main selections are especially strong on just one or two of the points, and weak on the others. It is very often the case for example that a lovely old building, in a magical setting, makes a truly special hotel, despite the fact that the bedrooms may be dull, possibly small, and the service not as some would wish. This is especially true of Venice hotels, but you'll find such places throughout the guide.

Generally speaking, our inspectors have rated setting, atmosphere and a personal welcome more important than service, food and sophisticated facilities. But, of course, they have rejected anywhere that doesn't reach their basic standards of comfort. We believe that this philosophy will give our readers more memorable experiences on their travels than a cushioning of standardized comfort and facilities.

Please do use the form on page 432 to let us know your views on the places where you have stayed, or to recommend others for the next edition.

Food

We don't underestimate its importance, and some entries would not have made it in to this guide, were it not for their food. However, it is increasingly true, especially in Britain, France and Italy, that good food is the norm. In these countries, hotels generally need to have more going for them than food alone to be featured in this guide.

Size

A few have less than 15 rooms; most have between 15 and 50; a few have many more than 50. As you might expect, our inspectors favoured the privately-owned, smaller hotels, guesthouses or inns because it's so much easier for them to offer a genuinely personal welcome and an atmosphere in which you feel like an individual, rather than one in a crowd.

Variety

Above all, our contributors have tried to provide variety. There are more than 2,000 entries in the guide, and among them there is every sort of lodging: bed-and-breakfasts in historic private houses; hotels in stately homes and châteaux; self-catering apartments in Venetian palaces; there is even a guest house in a windmill. And if you really need a retreat, try one of the monasteries in Spain that open their door to travellers. We've deliberately mixed the unusual with the more conventional rest-aurants-with-rooms, country inns, smart town houses and crumbling but beautiful farmhouses.

THE COUNTRY INTRODUCTIONS

These pages provide an overview of the country's different types of accommodation, highlight some of the most interesting places to stay, and offer practical information on topics such as tipping and meal times.

Thumb tabs *Each country has a different-coloured thumb tab.*

Highlights *We use this page to single out a few of the outstanding places to stay in each country.*

LOCATOR MAPS

The towns and villages in which our entries are located are shown in a box marked by a star, accompanied by a page number. Simply turn to the page, and you will find the entry for that particular place to stay. You may also find the maps useful for planning holiday routes linking places to stay.

INDEPENDENTLY INSPECTED

Great Places to Stay in Europe has been created by a team of specialist hotel writers, most with many years' experience of inspecting hotels. None of the places featured have paid to be in the guide. Those hotels which we did not already know were visited by inspectors. Most inspection visits were anonymous. For every hotel that appears in the guide, many were rejected.

HOW TO READ THE ENTRIES

THE LISTINGS
These follow in
alphabetical order by
nearest town or city.
Long entries follow their
own alpha order, as do
shorts.

● **The description**
Gives the essential
character of the
place.

● **Regional introduction**
Britain, France, Italy,
Germany and Spain have
been divided into regional
sub-sections, each with a
short introduction. The other
countries in the guide are not
sub-divided.

● **Entries with a photo**
These are our favourite
places. Each conforms to a
large number of our selection
criteria (see panel on page 6).

Don't expect them all to
charge the same price or to
conform to a rigid standard.
In order to make the guide
interesting, many different
types of accommodation have
been included, at every price
level. Not just hotels, but guest
houses, bed-and-breakfasts,
inns and even a few self-
catering places.

● **Short entries
without a photo**
These are all "great places to
stay" – each and every one of
them a useful address – but
for one reason or another our
inspectors could not rate them
as high as the entries with
photos. Don't be surprised to
find some well-known, luxurious places among these
short entries. They may be
top-class hotels, but our
inspectors were briefed to look
for places that offered the
traveller some-thing special,
rather than places that follow
a formula – however
luxurious.

● **The factual information**
All you need to finalize your choice and book. For
an explanation of the symbols, see page 9.

FOR VISITORS FROM OUTSIDE EUROPE

First-time visitors are often
surprised by the following
features of European hotels
and other places to stay:

Adaptors (adapters) The
electricity points vary from
country to country so you
will find it useful to take a
universal adaptor.

Tipping varies widely from
country to country. See the
advice given on the
introductory pages for each
country.

**Face cloths and Kleenex
tissues** are not always
provided.

You'll mostly, but not
always, get a **private
bathroom** with your room.

Floor numbers What
Americans call the first floor
is known as the ground floor
(or "0") in Europe. In Britain,
"elevators" are "lifts".

Breakfasts (especially in
France and Italy) are often

minimal compared with
what's served in the US –
often no more than bread
rolls, butter, jam and possibly
a choice of coffee or tea.

Passport as security Many
of the places featured in this
guide will ask for this when
you check in. It will be
returned when you leave.

**Markings on hot and cold
taps** may be confusing. In
France, for example, 'C'
means hot (*chaud*).

How to Read the Entries

The Longer Entries with Photo

See opposite. The information is always given in the same sequence.

Village, town or city in which, or near which, the entry is located

BROAD CAMPDEN

Photo of hotel

Malt House In a tiny hamlet comprising little more than church and pub, a delightful 17th-century Cotswold house. There are low beamed ceilings and leaded windows overlooking a dream garden. The smart bedrooms include an attractive garden suite. The owners' son, Julian Brown, is the accomplished cook.

Description of hotel

Address

⊠ Broad Campden, Gloucestershire GL55 6UU.

Map p74 A2. 🛈 (01386) 840295. **FAX** (013836) 841334.

Telephone number

Map location

E-mail address

@ nick@the-malt-house.freeserve.co.uk 🍴 b,d.

Fax number

Meals

Number of rooms

Rooms 8. 🌢 ⚫ Christmas. 🗐 AE, DC, MC, V. ⓔⓔ

Garden   When closed   Credit cards   Price band

An Explanation of the Symbols

⊠ **Postal address**

🛈 **Telephone number**

FAX **Fax number**

@ **E-mail address**, if available when we went to press. Many places will have acquired e-mail after this first edition of the guide was printed. Note, too, that many change their e-mail address from time to time. Many hotels on e-mail also have a website – you may find it worthwhile to search for this on the Internet – it is highly convenient to book through the Web.

🍴 **Meals** *generally* served in the establishment's own restaurant or eating area: **b** – breakfast, **l** – lunch, **d** – dinner. Some places serve a light lunch (or even provide a picnic) on request. Remember that restaurants may be closed on certain days of the week – enquire when booking. We do not show whether

room service is available or not.

Number of rooms. We give the total number, including singles, doubles and suites.

🌢 **Garden**, terrace or any outside area.

🗐 **Air conditioning** in most of the rooms, or throughout.

🏊 **Pool** – whether it is indoor, outdoor, heated or without heating.

💪 **Health facilities** – whether exercise machines, fitness room, gymnasium, trainer, sauna, Jacuzzi or whirlpool.

⚫ **Closed**

🗐 **Credit cards** We note only whether American Express (AE), Diners Club (DC), Mastercard (MC) or Visa (V) are accepted. Other cards may be accepted too.

ⓔⓔⓔ **Price bands** in the local currency, referring to the price of a standard double room in high season. These prices were quoted to our contibutors and were correct at time of going to press – there is, however, no guarantee that you will be offered exactly the same prices. (Some hotels in tourist centres will raise their prices when demand looks as if it will exceed space.) The price band is therefore only an indication of the cost of staying in a hotel. Please note that our entries often offer a wide range of rooms, from cheap to expensive: enquire when booking. The price may or may not include breakfast. Depending on the country, breakfast is either included, or an extra, but the price of breakfast rarely makes a significant difference to the price band. The price bands differ for each country, and their actual values are given on the relevant introductory pages.

NORWAY

NORWAY

THERE'S SOMETHING about the pale Norwegian light that makes more southerly climes seem flat and slightly jaded. It gives the landscape a clean, gentle quality, and makes the locations of many of the hotels in this section particularly idyllic. The places themselves are often simple clapboard houses on, say, a harbour front or a spit of land next

to a still fjord. Many are family run – some for as far back as three or four generations. Using our recommendations, you could construct an itinerary taking you from the islands of the south, via Oslo, through the western fjords to north of the Arctic circle, staying in unique places each night, without once having to resort to one of the many bland chain hotels.

Fairytale architecture at The Dalen at Dalen i Telemark, page 17

and weather all toughen up. You cross the Arctic circle between Mo-i-Rana and Bodø, before arriving at the biggest settlement in Northern Norway, the university city of Tromsø. By the time you get to the Northern Cape, and perhaps sail out to Spitsbergen, hotels tend to be functional and cosy, but not, much more.

NORWAY REGION BY REGION

NORWAY CAN be divided into Eastern Norway, Southern Norway, the Western fjords and Northern Norway.

Eastern Norway
Some of Europe's finest museums can be found in Oslo, the capital of Norway, but the city is also stirred by plenty of interesting street life and late night bars. Its 19th-century boulevards are also home to a number of handsome hotels.

Southern Norway
This is Norway's holidayland – an area of flat countryside, long beaches and small islands just off the coast. The town of Kristiansand's water-front is the closest Norway has to a beach resort. It also has a ferry link to Copenhagen, and many small family-run hotels.

The Western Fjords
At the southern end of the Western fjords is Stavanger, an

old town with a maritime feel. In the narrow lanes are attractive tall, white wooden houses where seamen and merchants once lived.

Ferries chugging up the coast take thousands of visitors to the fjords in summer. Many head for Bergen, an old trading centre with restored wooden houses and a lively quayside. There's a wide choice of places to stay here, as well as in the surrounding countryside.

The rail route between Bergen and Oslo goes through great scenery. This is a fine journey at any time, but in winter it offers the bonus of viewing the mountains under snow and waterfalls frozen solid. A branch line – one of the steepest in the world – plunges down to Flåm, on the edge of the serene Sogne Fjord. In this area there are several of the remarkable Norwegian stave churches.

Northern Norway
Around Trondheim, north becomes far north. The landscape, driving conditions

HIGHLIGHTS

PLACES ILLUSTRATED on these introductory pages are by no means the only highlights. Among our other favourites are Hotel Mundal in Fjaerland (page 18), an imposing Victorian building in a great setting; Frogner House Hotel in Oslo (page 21), a smart town hotel with style and individuality; the Kongsvold Fjeldstue inn in Kongsvold (page 19), a 17th century inn formerly used by pilgrims; and the Sygard Grytting near Hundorp (page 19), a beautiful hotel, open for only a couple of months in summer, with a simple wooden interior dating from the 17th century.

FOOD AND DRINK

MUCH NORWEGIAN FOOD is heavy and filling, perfect after a day's cross-country skiing. Some of the best traditional cooking is only available at Christmas, when special dishes like *pinnekjøtt* – smoked mutton steamed over shredded birch bark and served with cabbage – appear on the menu, along with *ribbe, julepølse* and filling *medisterkake* – pork ribs, sausage and dumplings.

Reindeer steaks are available throughout the year, either served with boiled potatoes and cranberry sauce, or as the main component of a rich stew. Venison, elk and seal meat – the latter marinaded until it is almost black and tasting slightly of the sea – are also occasionally offered.

A thick gravy (*brun saus*) seems to be served with anything meaty, but you can get away from this if you opt for fish such as pickled herring or salmon, which are particularly good. *Lutefisk* is preserved cod reconstituted to a jellylike consistency. It is good with potatoes and often served alongside herring dishes as part of a traditional feast. Dried cod fish – soaked to plump it up, but always slightly chewy – is also tasty when served in broth. Some of the simpler foods are the most memorable, and include different kinds of 'black' breads, fresh goat's cheese, and wild cloudberries – from north of the Arctic circle – served with cream.

Beers are classed as I, II or III, III being the strongest and available in bars and shops. Wine and spirits including the local 40 per cent proof *akevitt* can only be bought from the state-controlled Vinmonopol shops, or in bars. All alcoholic drink in Norway is surprisingly expensive.

Drinking is not a mainstream social activity during the week, but at weekends people kick over the traces and indulge in drinking sessions complete with drinking songs and other 'Viking' behaviour. Drinking in Oslo is more urbane, with a fickle bar scene and some 'microbreweries' serving real ale.

BEDROOMS AND BATHROOMS

IF YOU WANT twin beds, ask for them specifically when booking. Doubles are standard size – it's not usual to

Oslo's Nobel House Hotel, page 21

come across king size or extra king size beds. Bathrooms are en-suite and many hotels have shared saunas (mixed-sex).

OTHER PRACTICAL INFORMATION

BREAKFAST IS substantial and typically comprises a help-yourself buffet of different kinds of bread, ham, cheese, pickled fish, sausages, fruit juices and coffee.

Smoking has been banned in all public places (including restaurants and the public areas of hotels) since 1988.

If you are deterred by the price of evening meals, try the lunchtime *koldtbord* that many restaurants offer (the Norwegian rendition of *smörgåsbord*) – all you can eat for a set price. Another good deal is the *dagens rett* – a daily special menu.

During the summer, businesses shut down from July onwards, and hotel prices drop considerably. Between October and June, too, luxury hotels suddenly become much more affordable at the weekends, when substantial discounts (often 40–50 per cent on the usual room rate) come into effect. It is always worth asking what the 'special prices' are.

Language Norwegians have two mother tongues, *Bokmål* (book language) and *Landsmål* or *Nyorsk* (based on Old Norse dialects). *Bokmål* is the commonest, but it's not

something you have to master to get around. English is widely spoken – and, moreover, spoken well.

Currency The Norwegian *krone*, written NKR.

Shops Open 9am–5pm Mon–Wed & Fri; 9am–6pm or 7pm Thu; 9am–2pm or 3pm Sat.

Tipping No extra charge is made for service on the bill, but it's normal to leave a tip of around 10 per cent in restaurants, and 5 to 10 per cent in bars.

Telephoning Inside Norway, dial all 8 digits of a number, wherever you are calling from.
  If you wish to call Norway from the UK, dial 00 47 followed by the number, leaving out the initial 0 from the area code; from the US, dial 011 47.

Public holidays 1 January, Maundy Thursday and Good Friday, Easter Monday, 1 May, 17 May (Constitution Day), Ascension Day, Whit Monday and Tuesday, 15 August, 25 and 26 December.

USEFUL WORDS

Breakfast	*Frokost*
Lunch	*Lunsj*
Dinner	*Middag*
Free room?	*Ledig rom?*
How much?	*Hvor mye?*
Single room	*Enkeltrom*
Double room	*Dobbeltrom*

NORWAY PRICE BANDS

THERE IS NO star (or any other symbol) system to classify the comfort level of Norwegian hotels, so if you are booking a room from a long list of hotels without descriptions, the only thing to go on is price.
  Our price bands as usual refer to the price of a standard double room in high season. Prices quoted by hotels usually include breakfast and all taxes.

ⓚ	under 500NKR
ⓚⓚ	500–1000NKR
ⓚⓚⓚ	1000–1,500NKR
ⓚⓚⓚⓚ	over 1,500NKR

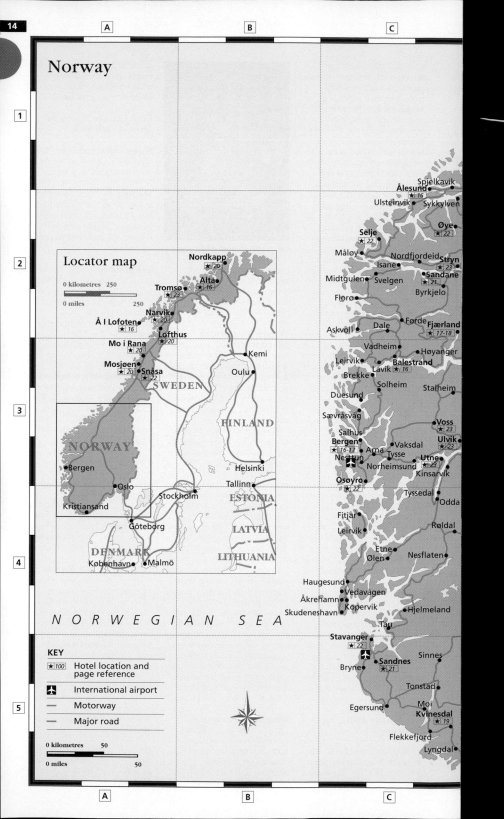

Norway

Locator map

0 kilometres 250

0 miles 250

KEY

★100 Hotel location and page reference

✈ International airport

— Motorway

— Major road

0 kilometres 50

0 miles 50

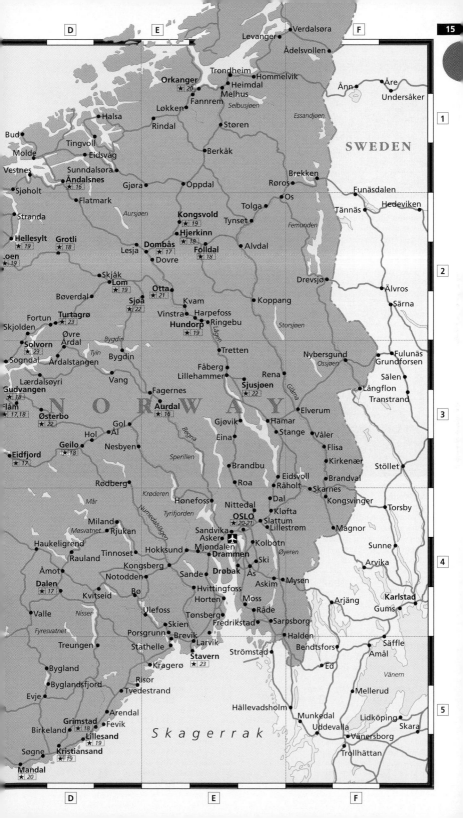

ÅLESUND

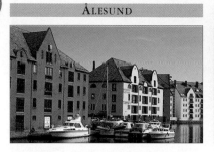

Brosundet Gjestehus One of the most popular places to stay in the Art Nouveau town of Ålesund is this charming hotel-cum-guesthouse, which occupies an old wharfside warehouse down by the main harbour. The rooms boast beamed ceilings, white drapes and pine floors, all part of a bright and cheerful house style.
Apotekergata 5, N-6004 Ålesund. **Map** p14 C1.
70 12 10 00. FAX 70 12 12 95. @ post@ brosundet.no b. **Rooms** 44. Never.
AE, DC, MC, V.

ÅNDALSNES

Grand Hotel Bellevue Despite its austere modern exterior, this long-established hotel has a well-justified reputation as one of the premier places to stay in fjord Norway. Breakfast is a sumptuous feast, the service is efficient and well-meaning, and the public rooms are neat and smart. The best rooms are on the upper floors and offer great views over the Romdalsfjord.
N-6301 Åndalsnes. **Map** p15 D1. 71 22 75 00.
FAX 71 22 60 38. b,l,d. **Rooms** 84. Christmas, Easter. AE, DC, MC, V.

ALTA

Vica Hotell This cosy hotel has been decorated in the style of a mountain lodge, with acres of pine panelling, animal heads on the walls and a scattering of pretty curios. In the restaurant, the waiters wear national costume and serve up a tempting range of Lapland delicacies including cloudberries and caribou, as well as what is probably the best apple pie in town.
Bossekop, N-9500 Alta. **Map** p14 B2.
78 43 47 11. FAX 78 43 42 99. b,l,d. **Rooms** 24.
Never. AE, DC, MC, V.

BALESTARAND

Midtnes Pensjonat Blessed with a lovely location, on the brow of a hill overlooking the Sognefjord, this friendly *pension* is an agreeable base for exploring the fjords. Breakfast, the best meal of the day here, is a sumptuous affair with everything from pickled herring, gherkins and fresh fish through to cornflakes and orange juice. A very popular place for summer weddings.
N-5850 Balestrand. **Map** p14 C3. 05 69 11 33.
FAX 05 69 15 84. b,l,d. **Rooms** 34. Christmas.
Not accepted.

Å I LOFOTEN

Å Rorbu At the southern tip of the Lofoten Islands, the beautiful village of Å boasts this group of old and new fishing huts with stupendous sea views.
Å i Lofoten, N-8392 Sørvågen. **Map** p14 A2.
76 09 11 21 FAX 76 09 12 82 All **Rooms** 28

ALTA

Altafjord Hotell This sprawling modern complex, incorporates traditional turf-roofed buildings and seashore cottages.
Bossekopveien, Postboks 1424, N-9506 Alta.
Map p14 B2. 78 43 70 11. FAX 78 43 70 13.
b,l,d. **Rooms** 30.

AURDAL

Danebu Feriesenter Deep in the countryside with mountain views, the Danebu holiday centre is a great place to unwind. There are rooms in the lodge and in surrounding cabins.
N-2910 Aurdal. **Map** p15 E3. 61 36 52 03.
FAX 61 35 76 01. b,l,d. **Rooms** 32.

BALESTRAND

Kvikne's Hotel This long-established hotel, by the fjord in the resort of Balestrand, is a plush affair distinguished by an ornate dragon woodcarving in the Viking style.
N-5850 Balestrand. **Map** p14 C3. 57 69 11 01.
FAX 57 69 15 02. b,l,d. **Rooms** 210.

BERGEN

Hotel Park Pension Long-established small hotel on the edge of Bergen's town centre, and especially handy for the university. Everything is well-considered, from the attractive façade with its high-pitched gables and iron balconies, through to the pastel colours of the plush interior. It's a very popular place, so book ahead.
Harald Hårfagresgate 35, N-5007 Bergen.
Map p14 C3. 55 54 44 00. FAX 55 54 44 44.
b. **Rooms** 33. Christmas, Easter.
AE, DC, MC, V.

DOMBÅS

Dombås Hotell From the late 19th century, Dombås flourished as a railway junction. Well-heeled travellers were accommodated in this prestigious hotel, whose towers and balconies overlooked the valley. A modern annexe has added nothing to the hotel's charms, but the main building has gracious public rooms, service is attentive and the restaurant first-rate.
N-2660 Dombås. **Map** p15 E2. 61 24 10 01.
FAX 61 24 14 61. b,l,d. **Rooms** 70. Christmas.
AE, DC, MC, V.

DALEN I TELEMARK

Hotel Dalen The fairytale-like Dalen, one of southern Norway's finest country hotels, was built in 1894 in the so-called 'dragon-style' inspired by Norway's medieval stave churches. Outside are gables and galleries, dragon heads and gargoyles; the period interior, with its leather upholstery and stained glass, is splendid too.
Box 123, N-3886, Dalen. **Map** p15 D4.
35 07 70 00. FAX 35 07 70 11. @ DALENHAA@ ONLINE.NO b,l,d. **Rooms** 38. mid-Dec to mid-April. AE, DC, MC, V.

FJÆRLAND

Fjærland Fjordstue Hotell Tiny Fjærland was one of the last of the fjord villages to be connected to the road system. In the unspoiled village is this attractive guesthouse; public rooms are smart and cheerful, the bedrooms equally so. The loggia doubles as a sun-lounge and fjord vantage point. Breakfast features the best of Norwegian ingredients.
N-5855 Fjærland. **Map** p14 C2. 57 69 32 00.
FAX 57 69 31 61. b; d by arrangement. **Rooms** 17.
Nov to March. Not accepted.

BERGEN

Grand Hotel Terminus Charming 1920s hotel by the train station, complete with period furnishings and acres of wood panelling.
Zander Kaaesgate 6, PO Box 1100, N-5001 Bergen.
Map p14 C3. 55 31 16 55. FAX 55 31 85 76.
b,l,d. **Rooms** 131.

BERGEN

Skansen Pensjonat A pretty *pension* in an old townhouse just above the funicular, providing simple accommodation at reasonable rates.
Vetrlidsallmenningen 29, N-5014 Bergen.
Map p14 C3. 55 31 90 80. FAX 55 31 15 27.
@ mail@skansen-pensjonat.no b. **Rooms** 8.

EIDFJORD

Eidfjord Hotel No frills, no fuss, in this smart, modern hotel on a hill in the heart of the fjords. The mountain views are spectacular.
N-5783 Eidfjord. **Map** p15 D3. 53 66 52 64.
FAX 53 66 52 12. @ eidfjordhotel@produktnett.no
b,l,d. **Rooms** 28.

FLÅM

Fretheim Hotell The Flåm railway provides a superb introduction to the fjords; this comfortable hotel is just across from the station.
N-5742 Flåm. **Map** p15 D3. 57 63 22 00.
FAX 57 63 23 03. @ fretheim@bedre.no b,l,d.
Rooms 162.

FJÆRLAND

Hotel Mundal Few hotels can match the instant appeal of the Mundal, whose Victorian façade nestles beside the fjord with the mountains rising steeply behind. Inside are nooks and crannies dripping with antiques and fishing memorabilia. Tasty meals are served in a spacious dining room that appears to have changed little in decades.
✉ N-5855 Fjærland. **Map** p14 C2. 📞 57 69 31 01.
FAX 57 69 31 79. @ hotelmundal@fjordinfo.no
🍴 b,l,d. **Rooms** 35. 🛁 🔘 mid-Sept to mid-May.
💳 AE, DC, MC, V. ⓚⓚ

FOLLDAL

Folldal Fjellstue Norway attracts hill walkers and mountain climbers from the world over. The discerning make their way to this charming mountain lodge by the dramatic landscapes of the Dovre and Rondane national parks. Owners Randi and Jens have refurbished the lodge in classic Scandinavian style and provide superb home-cooked meals.
✉ N-2580 Folldal. **Map** p15 E2. 📞 62 49 01 86.
FAX 62 49 01 86. 🍴 b,d. **Rooms** 17. 🛁 🔘 late Sept to end May. 💳 V. ⓚ

FLÅM

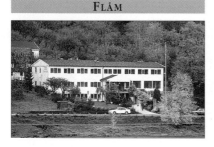

Heimly Pensjonat Twisting its way down the Flåm valley, the narrow-gauge Flåm railway drops 900m (3,000ft) in 20km (14 miles). It's one of Europe's most exhilarating train journeys and, at the bottom in the hamlet of Flåm, is the Heimly Pensjonat. This unassuming and well-maintained pension overlooks the fjord and has an informal, low-key public area.
✉ N-5742 Flåm. **Map** p15 D3. 📞 57 63 23 00.
FAX 57 63 23 40. 🍴 b,d. **Rooms** 25. 🛁 🔘 Never.
💳 AE, DC, MC, V. ⓚ

HJERKINN

Hjerkinn Fjellstue In the remote windswept moors of central Norway is this homely lodge, a comforting place of open fires and cheerfully modern pine furniture. The restaurant serves delicious reindeer steak, culled from local herds, and the seafood is equally tasty. Guides are provided for elk and musk-ox safaris and there's horse-riding too.
✉ N-2661 Hjerkinn. **Map** p15 E2. 📞 61 24 29 27.
FAX 61 24 29 49. 🍴 b,l,d. **Rooms** 38. 🛁 🔘 Christmas.
💳 AE, DC, MC, V. ⓚⓚ

GEILO

Solli Hotel Geilo is Norway's winter sports capital and this neat, modern hotel is a very convenient place to stay – it is sited just 100m from the nearest ski piste.
✉ Skurdalsvegen 25, N-3580 Geilo. **Map** p15 D3.
📞 32 09 11 11. **FAX** 32 09 15 60. 🍴 b,l,d. **Rooms** 24. ⓚ

GRIMSTAD

Grimstad Hotell A clever conversion of several old timber buildings makes this a distinctive hotel. Ibsen worked at the Grimstad chemists'.
✉ Kirkegaten 3, N-4890 Grimstad. **Map** p15 D5.
📞 37 04 47 44. **FAX** 37 04 47 33. 🍴 b,l,d.
Rooms 45. ⓚⓚ

GROTLI

Grotli Høyfjellshotel A mountain lodge with a warm and welcoming pine interior. At 900m (3,000ft) above sea level, there are opportunities for summer skiing, hiking and whitewater rafting.
✉ N-2695 Grotli. **Map** p15 D2. 📞 61 21 39 12.
FAX 61 21 39 40. 🍴 b,l,d. **Rooms** 50. ⓚⓚ

GUDVANGEN

Gudvangen Fjordtell This unusual modern hotel is built in traditional Norwegian style, its huddle of circular buildings constructed of logs and roofed with turf.
✉ N-5717 Gudvangen. **Map** p15 D3. 📞 57 63 39 29.
FAX 57 63 39 80. 🍴 b,l,d. **Rooms** 21. ⓚⓚ

HUNDORP

Sygard Grytting One would not guess this antique farmstead nestling among orchards just north of Hundorp is a guesthouse. The 18th-century farm buildings have survived almost intact and have been carefully modified to accommodate visitors during the summer months. The main house has the best bedrooms.
☒ N-2647 Sør-Fron, Hundorp. **Map** p15 E2.
📞 61 29 85 88. ꜰᴀx 61 29 85 10. @ post@grytting.com
🍴 b; d by arrangement. **Rooms** 7. 🛢 ● mid-Aug to mid-June. 🗟 V. Ⓚ Ⓚ

KRISTIANSAND

Villa Frobusdal Hotel Hidden away beside the town's ring road, this extraordinary hotel occupies an appealing shipowner's mansion built in 1917. The interior boasts a wonderful assortment of antiques and some rare wood panelling alive with dragons and snakes. The light-filled bedrooms are charming.
☒ Frobusdalen 2, N-4613 Kristiansand.
Map p15 D5. 📞 38 07 05 15. ꜰᴀx 38 07 01 15.
@ frobus@online.no 🍴 b. **Rooms** 7. 🛢 ● Dec, Easter.
🗟 AE, DC, MC, V. Ⓚ Ⓚ

KONGSVOLD

Kongsvold Fjeldstue The inn at Kongsvold has been sheltering travellers and pilgrims on the great north road between Oslo and Trondheim since the 1670s. The present incarnation has discretely and very tastefully adapted the old wooden buildings that comprise the complex, even down to the tinkers' hut beyond the picket fence.
☒ Kongsvold, N-7340 Oppdal. **Map** p15 D2.
📞 72 40 43 40. ꜰᴀx 72 40 43 41. 🍴 b,l,d. **Rooms** 35.
🛢 ● Christmas. 🗟 DC, MC, V. Ⓚ Ⓚ

LILLESAND

Hotel Norge One-time haunt of the rich and famous, this glamorous hotel is one of the most celebrated on Norway's peaceful south coast. Decorative highlights include the stained glass, the elegant banqueting hall and the suite where the Spanish King Alfonso XIII stayed in 1931. The restaurant serves the freshest of seafood and breakfasts are lavish banquets.
☒ Strandgaten 3, N-4790 Lillesand. **Map** p15 D5.
📞 37 27 01 44. ꜰᴀx 37 27 30 70. 🍴 b,l,d. **Rooms** 25.
🛢 ● Christmas. 🗟 AE, DC, MC, V. Ⓚ Ⓚ

HELLESYLT
Grand Hotel Built in 1871, the Grand is a well-established favourite of visitors to fjord country. Some rooms are in a modern annexe.
☒ P.O. Box 73, N-6218 Hellesylt. **Map** p15 D2.
📞 70 26 51 00. ꜰᴀx 70 26 52 22. 🍴 b,l,d.
Rooms 29. Ⓚ Ⓚ

KVINESDAL
Rafoss Hotel There has been an inn on this spot since the 1800s. The present incarnation has the old house attached to a modern annexe, where the rooms have river views.
☒ N-4480 Kvinesdal. **Map** p14 C5. 📞 38 35 03 88.
ꜰᴀx 38 35 09 66. 🍴 b; d by arrangement. **Rooms** 18. Ⓚ Ⓚ

LOEN
Hotel Alexandra Within easy striking distance of the Jostedalsbreen glacier, this large, ritzy hotel offers fine dining and ultra-modern rooms.
☒ N-6878 Loen. **Map** p15 D2. 📞 57 87 50 00.
ꜰᴀx 57 87 50 50 @ alex@alexandra.no 🍴 b,l,d.
Rooms 193. Ⓚ Ⓚ Ⓚ

LOM
Fossheim Turisthotell In the small town of Lom is a wonderful stave church. This excellent hotel has rooms in the main lodge and in cabins.
☒ N-2688 Lom. **Map** p15 D2. 📞 61 21 12 05.
ꜰᴀx 61 21 15 10. @ fossheim.lom@online.no 🍴 b,l,d.
Rooms 50. Ⓚ Ⓚ

For key to symbols see backflap. For price categories *see p13*

LOFTHUS

Ullensvang Gjesteheim Rarely does a hotel blend into its surroundings as delightfully as this one, sheltering in a little dell beside a gurgling stream. The main building, a whitewashed wooden lodge, is surrounded by attractive farm buildings. Inside, the public rooms are strewn with antiques and, even though the bedrooms are a little plainer, they are entirely satisfactory.
⊠ N-5774 Lofthus, Hardanger. **Map** p14 A2.
【 53 66 12 36. FAX 53 66 15 19. ▐▐ b,l,d. ✉ Not accepted. ● Christmas Day. ▐ **Rooms** 13. Ⓚ Ⓚ

NORDKAPP

Repvåg Fjord Hotell og Rorbusenter The long road to the northern tip of Norway, Nordkapp, is known to thousands of tourists. Few turn down the country road leading to this remote fishing and trading station, where the ancient wooden shacks have been turned into an atmospheric hotel. There are rooms in the main building and the surrounding cabins.
⊠ N-9778 Repvåg, Nordkapp. **Map** p14 B2.
【 78 47 54 40. FAX 78 47 27 51. ▐▐ b,l,d. **Rooms** 77. ● Nov to March. ✉ AE, DC, MC, V. Ⓚ

MANDAL

Kjøbmandsgaarden Hotel Norway has not got many long sandy beaches; Mandal, a seaside resort on the south coast, has the country's longest. Cosy and intimate, this friendly family-run hotel is squeezed into the narrow streets at the heart of the little town. Rooms are bright and modern, and there is a very good restaurant offering traditional cuisine.
⊠ St Elvegate 57, N-4517 Mandal. **Map** p15 D5.
【 38 26 12 76. FAX 38 26 33 02. ▐▐ b,l,d. **Rooms** 12. ● Christmas. ✉ AE, DC, MC, V. Ⓚ

ORKANGER

Bårdshaug Herregård In the old copper-mining town of Orkanger, the erstwhile manor house of Christian Thams, one of Norway's most successful entrepreneurs, has been turned into the plush Bårdshaug hotel. The finest bedroom, the all-timber 'Royal Room' in which a string of Scandinavian monarchs have spent the night, dates back to Thams.
⊠ N-7300 Orkanger. **Map** p15 E1. 【 72 47 99 00. FAX 72 48 19 23. @ Baardher1@st.telia.no ▐▐ b,l,d. **Rooms** 65. ▐ ● Christmas. ✉ AE, DC, MC, V. Ⓚ Ⓚ

MO-I-RANA
Meyergården Hotell One of northern Norway's most enjoyable hotels: an imaginative mix of old and new, plus fjord views from the upper floors.
⊠ O. T. Olsens gate 24, N-8600 Mo-i-Rana.
Map p14 A3. 【 75 13 40 00. FAX 75 13 40 01.
▐▐ b,l,d. **Rooms** 150. Ⓚ Ⓚ

MOSJØEN
Fru Haugans Hotel Break the journey on the long road to northern Norway at this spacious hotel, parts of which date back to the 1790s.
⊠ N-8651 Mosjøen. **Map** p14 A3. 【 75 17 04 77.
FAX 75 17 05 34. @ fhh-res@fruhaugans.no ▐▐ b,l,d.
Rooms 77. Ⓚ Ⓚ

NARVIK
Breidablikk Gjestehus Narvik is short of good accommodation; this modest but well-tended guesthouse offers great views over the harbour.
⊠ Tore Hundsgate 41, N-8500 Narvik. **Map** p14 A2.
【 76 94 14 18 FAX 76 94 57 86. @ breidablikk@ narviknett.n ▐▐ b. **Rooms** 22. Ⓚ

OSLO
City Hotel This modest but endearing hotel is located above shops and offices in a traditional Oslo apartment block near the train station. Friendly, informal atmosphere; helpful staff.
⊠ Skippergaten 19, N-0106 Oslo. **Map** p15 E4.
【 22 41 36 10. FAX 22 42 24 29. ▐▐ b. **Rooms** 53. Ⓚ Ⓚ

Oslo

Hotel Continental One of Oslo's most prestigious hotels, the Continental boasts sumptuous public rooms furnished in grand style with elegant chandeliers and acres of parquet flooring. It is ideally located, footsteps from Oslo's main street, Karl Johans gate. Of its several bars and restaurants, the Theatercaféen is the most luxurious.

Stortingsgaten 24/26, N-0117 Oslo. **Map** p15 E4. 22 82 40 00. FAX 22 42 96 89. b,l,d. **Rooms** 159. early Dec to early Jan. AE, DC, MC, V. ⓚⓚⓚⓚ

Oslo

Gabelshus Hotel This establishment has been owned by the same family since it was opened in 1912 and is a firm favourite with many regular visitors to Oslo. The hotel's immaculately maintained interior is graced by an eclectic collection of antiques, such as monks' seats, candelabra and ornate fireplaces. Rooms are decorated to a bright, modern standard.

Gabels gate 16, N-0272 Oslo. **Map** p15 E4. 22 55 22 60. FAX 23 27 65 60. b,l,d. **Rooms** 43. Christmas, Easter. AE, DC, MC, V. ⓚⓚⓚ

Oslo

Frogner House Hotel This handsome Victorian building is located in one of Oslo's smartest areas, 2km (1 miles) from the town centre. Stripped wood and thick carpets are the order of the day, but each of the bedrooms is different. The best have balconies overlooking the street; the large attic room is a honeymooners' favourite.

Skovveien 8, N-0257 Oslo. **Map** p15 E4. 22 56 00 56. FAX 22 56 05 00. b; d by arrangement. **Rooms** 60. Christmas, Easter. AE, DC, MC, V. ⓚⓚⓚ

Oslo

Nobel House Hotell It is close to several of the city's best restaurants and museums, and the decor is superb too – a smooth and eye-catching blend of tradition and modernity. Imaginative touches include the magnificent fireplace in the lounge area and the angel painted on the inside of the lift. Lovely roof terrace.

Kongens gate 5, N-0153 Oslo. **Map** p15 E4. 23 10 72 00. FAX 23 10 72 10. @ anne.aanensen@ noblehouse.no b,l,d. **Rooms** 50. Christmas, Easter. AE, DC, MC, V. ⓚⓚⓚⓚ

Oslo

Norum Hotel With its forest of spires and towers, the High Victorian façade of the Norum is splendid. Inside is a modern, efficient hotel.

Bygdøy Allé 53, N-0265 Oslo. **Map** p15 E4. 22 44 79 90. FAX 22 56 05 00. b. **Rooms** 55. ⓚⓚⓚ

Otta

Rondane Høyfjellshotell Hotel-cum-leisure complex in the hills around Otta, and near the treeless steppes of Rondane National Park.

N-2675 Otta. **Map** p15 E2. 61 23 39 33. FAX 61 23 39 52. @ hotel@rondane.no b,l,d. **Rooms** 150. ⓚⓚ

Sandane

Gloppen Hotell Many visitors return to the Gloppen year after year. The 1860s hotel is one of the most attractive in the fjord region.

N-6823 Sandane. **Map** p14 C2. 57 86 53 33. FAX 57 86 60 02. @ glopphot@vestdata.no b,l,d. **Rooms** 30. ⓚⓚ

Sandnes

Kronen Gaard Hotell This venerable hotel prides itself on its scenic fjord country surroundings and intimate atmosphere.

Vatne, N-4309 Sandnes. **Map** p14 C5. 51 66 14 00. FAX 51 62 20 23. b,l,d. **Rooms** 34. ⓚⓚ

For key to symbols see backflap. For price categories *see p13*

Osøyro

Solstrand Fjord Hotel The welcoming Schau-Larsen family run this refined and elegant hotel with an eye to detail. The furnishings are smart and modern, the colours warm and inviting, and the grounds neatly manicured. There's a choice of bathing here too, either in the hotel's swimming pool or in the blue-grey waters of the Bjørnefjorden.

N-5200 Osøyro. **Map** p14 C3. 56 57 11 00. FAX 56 57 11 20. b,l,d. **Rooms** 135. Christmas and New Year. AE, DC, MC, V.

Øye

Hotel Union In the late 19th century, European aristocrats gathered at the Hotel Union to fish for salmon and hike the hills. These halcyon days are recalled by the hotel's interior, in which every room is crammed with carefully chosen antiques. Fans of novelist Karen Blick, author of *Out of Africa*, will enjoy seeing a pair of her lover's boots.

Øye, N-6196 Norangsfjorden. **Map** p14 C2. 70 06 21 00. FAX 70 06 21 16. b,l,d. **Rooms** 27. Oct to Apr. AE, DC, MC, V.

Østerbo

Østerbo Fjellstove This smart, well-maintained mountain lodge lies at the start of the celebrated Aurlandsdal valley walk and is a favourite with hikers. Most of the rooms are in the main lodge; there is additional accommodation in cabins on the grounds, and in an old medieval storehouse. The last is a charming affair of warm wood and narrow bunkbeds.

Østerbo, N-5745 Aurland. **Map** p15 D3. 57 63 11 77. FAX 57 63 11 52. oesterbo@c2i.net b,l,d. **Rooms** 42. Never. V.

Sjoa

Sjoa Gjestehus Whitewater rafters keen to brave the River Sjoa flock to this guesthouse every summer weekend. Some fill the dormitories at the bottom of the hill, others prefer the spacious en suite chalet rooms above. They all meet in the 18th-century farmhouse, where the dinner and breakfast room has an open fire and log walls.

N-2670 Sjoa. **Map** p15 D2. 61 23 62 00. FAX 61 23 60 14. b; d by arrangement. **Rooms** 6, plus 6 dormitories sleeping 6–10 people. Nov to April. MC, V.

Selje

Selje Hotel If it's a remote location you're after, look no further than Selje, a tiny west coast fishing village. This attractive wood and stone hotel is at the heart of the village.

N-6740 Selje. **Map** p14 D2. 57 85 61 07. FAX 57 85 62 72. b,l,d. **Rooms** 49.

Sjusjøen

Sjusjøen Høyfjellshotell Norwegians are fond of the rolling, forest uplands surrounding Sjusjøen and this dapper hotel, with its own indoor pool, is a favourite destination. Smashing food too.

N-2612 Sjusjøen. **Map** p15 E3. 62 36 34 01. FAX 62 36 34 04. b,l,d. **Rooms** 70.

Snåsa

Snåsa Hotell Rural, agricultural Norway is seen to good advantage at the Snåsa, a modern establishment in a fertile valley at the end of a lovely lake. Bedrooms are spacious.

N-7760 Snåsa. **Map** p14 A3. 74 15 10 57. FAX 74 15 16 15. b,l,d. **Rooms** 35.

Stavanger

Skagen Brygge Hotel First-rate hotel in the style of a wharfside warehouse, by the harbour in the oil-rich town of Stavanger. Breakfasts are superb.

Skagen 30, N-4006 Stavanger. **Map** p14 C5. 51 85 00 00. FAX 51 85 00 01. bryggeho@online.no b. **Rooms** 106.

SOLVORN

ULVIK

Walaker Hotell Facing the exquisite Urnes stave church across the narrow Lusterfjord is the little Walaker, owned and operated by the same family since 1690. In summer, the hotel gallery features exhibitions of contemporary art and the delightful garden is awash with roses. Most of the rooms overlook the fjord and the garden.

☒ N-6879 Solvorn, Sognefjord. **Map** p15 D3.
📞 57 68 42 07. FAX 57 68 45 44. @ walaker.hotel@
sf.telia.no 🍴 b,d. **Rooms** 24. 🗐 🛁 ◉ mid-Oct to
mid-Apr. 🖭 AE, DC, MC, V. Ⓚ Ⓚ

Ulvik Fjord Pensjonat There's nothing grand or pretentious about this welcoming family-run guesthouse. The rooms are decorated in simple modern style (the most appealing overlook the Hardangerfjord) and breakfast is served in an open-plan dining room. The best time to visit is the spring when the orchards on the surrounding hills are engulfed by pinky-white apple blossom.

☒ N-5730 Ulvik. **Map** p14 C3. 📞 56 52 61 70.
FAX 56 52 61 60. 🍴 b; d by arrangement. **Rooms** 20.
🛁 ◉ late Sept to Apr. 🖭 V. Ⓚ Ⓚ

TURTAGRØ

VOSS

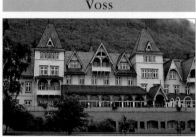

Turtagrø Hotel The modest exterior of the Turtagrø belies its handsome interior, an open affair of solid pine walls decorated with bright modern art and furnished in crisp Scandinavian style. The restaurant deserves its excellent reputation; it's a favourite haunt of mountaineers, who rest up here after climbing the majestic peaks of the Jotunheimen National Park.

☒ N-5834 Fortun. **Map** p15 D2. 📞 57 68 61 16.
FAX 57 68 61 07. @ turtagro@online.no 🍴 b,l,d.
Rooms 29. ◉ late Oct to Easter. 🖭 AE, DC, MC, V. Ⓚ Ⓚ

Fleischer's Hotel One of Norway's premier hotels and an ideal base for exploring the fjords, Fleischer's is a real delight. The lakeside setting is charming and the restaurant outstanding. The modern rooms are extremely comfortable and cheerfully decorated. Supremely helpful and efficient staff make the place even more special.

☒ N-5700 Voss. **Map** p14 C3. 📞 56 52 05 00.
FAX 56 52 05 01. @ fleischr@online.no
🍴 b,l,d. **Rooms** 90. 🚌 🍽 🛁 ◉ Christmas.
🖭 AE, DC, MC, V. Ⓚ Ⓚ

STAVERN

Hotel Wassilioff On the south coast, tiny Stavern is home to this immaculate hotel, founded by a Russian who deserted the Tsar's army in 1844.

☒ Havnegata 1, N-3290 Stavern. **Map** p15 E5.
📞 33 19 83 11. FAX 33 19 97 64. 🍴 b,l,d.
Rooms 31. Ⓚ Ⓚ

STRYN

Walhalla Gjestgiveri Modest, homely lodgings are provided at the Walhalla, an old timber house down by the river in the oldest part of Stryn. Guided glacier walks can be arranged.

☒ Perhusvegen 13, N-6880 Stryn. **Map** p14 C2.
📞 57 87 10 72. FAX 57 87 18 94. 🍴 b. **Rooms** 6. Ⓚ

TROMSØ

Ishavshotel Tromsø's premier hotel, this stylish, ultra-modern establishment sits on the harbour's edge in Tromsø centre. Magnificent fjord views.

☒ Fr Langesgate 2, N-9001 Tromsø. **Map** p14 B2.
📞 77 66 64 00. FAX 77 66 64 44. 🍴 b,l,d.
Rooms 180. Ⓚ Ⓚ Ⓚ

UTNE

Utne Hotel Sitting prettily by the jetty in the Hardangerfjord, this is one of Norway's oldest and quaintest hotels, dating back to 1722. Next door is an excellent folk museum.

☒ N-5797 Utne. **Map** p14 C3. 📞 53 66 69 83.
FAX 53 66 69 50. 🍴 b,l,d. **Rooms** 25. Ⓚ Ⓚ

For key to symbols see backflap. For price categories see *p13*

SWEDEN

SWEDEN

SWEDEN IS traditionally regarded as an expensive country to visit, but recent changes in exchange rates means it is presently more affordable than usual. For many tourists visiting for the first time, it may come as a surprise that the country has so many beautiful hotels. Often these have been converted from historic buildings such as castles, mountain lodges, medieval inns and 18th-century manor houses. They can provide excellent accommodation in beautiful surroundings. Many of the best places are members of two hotel marketing organisations: the Countryside Hotels and the Historiska Hotell groups. In Stockholm – European City of Culture in 1999 – we also have some exceptional entries.

Gripsholms Värdshus, page 33, Mariefred's delightful old inn

SWEDEN REGION BY REGION

SWEDEN CAN be divided into five regions: south, southwest, central, north and far north.

South and Southwest

These regions are relatively flat. Apart from the capital, the main towns are Gothenburg, Malmö and Helsingborg. Gothenburg has an elegant city hotel, a useful first stop before heading for the region's attractive beach resorts, often based around old, fortified towns. The Baltic islands of Öland and Gotland are both popular, relaxed beach holiday places – relatively uncrowded, with attractive seaside hotels.

Stockholm, Sweden's capital, makes a welcome urban interlude. It mixes brutalist modern design with medieval and Beaux-Arts architecture, and its reputation for open-mindedness is well founded. There are woods and water on its doorstep and an archipelago of islands a ferry ride away.

Central and North

The forest and fjords don't begin until you get some way farther north of the capital, and here there are many excellent places to stay – many in beautifully remote settings – served by the main highways or the 'Inland Railroad'. The choice ranges from an inn built on the site of a Carthusian monastery to manor houses dating from the 16th century and country house hotels in peaceful lakeside settings. These last are flourishing concerns, with tremendous atmosphere and very good food. Many have a dual personality: in summer they offer walking, windsurfing, fishing and boating; in winter cross-country skiing. The winter months, especially around Christmas, are a sensible time for breaks if you can put up with the short days, as are May and September, because there are fewer mosquitoes than in July and August.

Far North

The tundra and forest of the far north, above the Arctic Circle, is the home of the nomadic Sami people. In June and July it never properly gets dark. Here hotels are few and far between; among them is the ultimate one-off hotel, the Ice Hotel near Kiruna, which operates in winter, carved each year out of ice. In fact, it's more comfortable than you might imagine and is popular for weddings and christenings. Its phone number is (0980) 668 00.

HIGHLIGHTS

HOTELS ILLUSTRATED on these introductory pages are by no means the only highlights. Other favourites include Stockholm's Mälardrottningen, converted from heiress Barbara Hutton's former yacht (page 35); and Tällberg's Ackerblads (page 36), a much-loved family property run, amazingly, by more than 20 generations of Ackerblads.

FOOD AND DRINK

BOAR AND BERRIES are the traditional staples of Swedish food, the former roasted or made into sausages, the latter (a wild berry called *hjortron*) served with fresh cream or ice cream. Meatballs with gravy and cranberry sauce, and *gravadlax* – raw salmon marinated with dill and served with mustard dressing – are also delicious.

The standard of food in the hotels listed here is generally very high, and will include game in season, along with international dishes.

The only drawback is the expense. You may find that after a few days of hotel dining that stocking up for a picnic lunch becomes a necessity. Lunch at a restaurant is usually not as ex-pensive as dinner, especially if you go for the set menu (*dagens rätt*).

Another economical option is the *smörgåsbord* served at lunchtime in restaurants or hotels – a mouthwatering all-you-can-eat collation of herring, cooked meats, hard-boiled eggs, potato, salads, desserts and fruit.

Alcohol is also notoriously expensive in Sweden. The beer served in bars is classed according to strength. Class III or *starköl* is the strongest, weaker is class II or *folköl*, and the class 1 beer, *lättöl*, is virtually alcohol-free – and great for drivers. There is zero tolerance of drink-driving in this country and a few glasses of wine with dinner followed by a brandy could take you over the limit to drive, even the *following morning*. Outside bars and restaurants, class III beers can only be bought from government liquor stores – whose Swedish name is Systembolage.

Akvavit, a herb-flavoured spirit, is traditionally served ice-cold with beer chasers – a potent combination.

Swedes eat lunch from 11am onwards (generally finishing by 2pm). Dinner starts from around 6pm and restaurants close from around 11pm to midnight.

BEDROOMS AND BATHROOMS

IF YOU WANT twin beds, ask for them specifically when booking. The Swedish have a tradition of being health and environ-ment conscious so some hotels, including larger chains, are switching to anti-allergenic bedding and biodegradeable cleaning products. As well as sparkling bathrooms, many places will have a sauna (usually open to both sexes).

OTHER PRACTICAL INFORMATION

BREAKFAST AT most hotels is lavish – a buffet with cheeses, including the sweet, brown *mesost*, hams, yogurt, muesli, an array of rye and 'black' breads, crispbreads and fruit. The standard of housekeeping is outstanding: everything is immaculately clean, and it works. During the summer business shut-down hotel prices drop considerably. Year-round, luxury hotels become much more affordable at the weekend, when substantial discounts (often 40–50 per cent on the usual room rate) come into effect. Ask what the 'special prices' are.

Language Swedes are true polyglots and often sound like native speakers of whichever language they are using – including English.

Currency The Swedish *krona*, written 'SEK'.

Shops Open 9am–6pm Mon–Fri, and 9am–1pm Sat (department stores till 4pm). Large shops in the cities are sometimes open until 8 or 10pm and on Sunday.

Tipping Hotel room rates and restaurant menu prices are inclusive of service charges. Tipping isn't expected, but if bills come to an odd amount they are often rounded up to

The Grand Hotell, Marstrand, page 34

the nearest 10Kr, or you can leave a tip of around 10 per cent if you want to.

Telephoning As well as the usual call boxes there are Turist Telefon payphones in summer in the major cities, offering half-price calls. To make a phone call within Sweden, dial the full number. To phone Sweden from the UK, dial the international code 00 46, then the phone number, omitting the initial zero; from the US, dial 011 46.

Public holidays 1 January; 6 January; Good Friday and Easter Monday; 1 May; Ascension Day; Whit Monday; Midsummer's Day; 1 November; 25 and 26 December.

USEFUL WORDS

Breakfast	*Frukost*
Lunch	*Lunch*
Dinner/supper	*Middag/ supé*
Free room?	*Ledig rum?*
How much?	*Vad kostar?*
Single room	*Enkel rum*
Double room	*Dubbel rum*

SWEDEN PRICE BANDS

SWEDISH HOTELS are classified by stars, from one to five, but don't be too swayed by this. Our price bands are simpler, and as elsewhere in the guide refer to the price of a standard double room in high season (but don't forget to ask about discounts, which can be substantial). Breakfast is usually included in the room rate; prices include all taxes.

Ⓚ	under 900Kr
ⓀⓀ	900Kr–1,200Kr
ⓀⓀⓀ	1,200Kr–1,600Kr
ⓀⓀⓀⓀ	over 1,600Kr

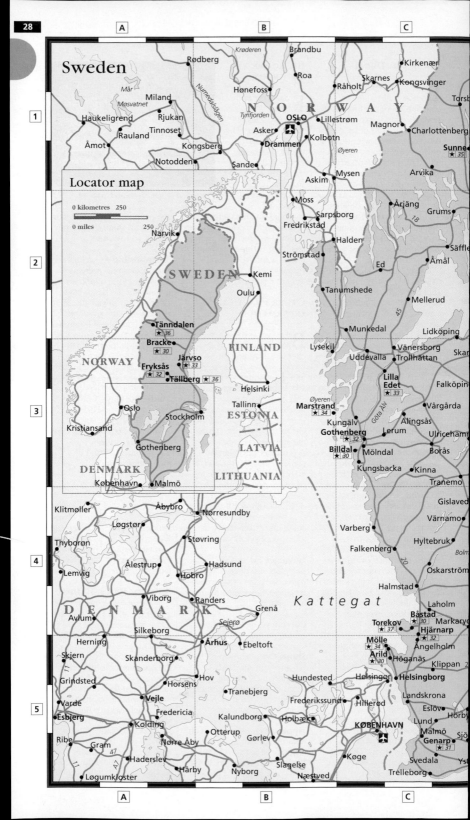

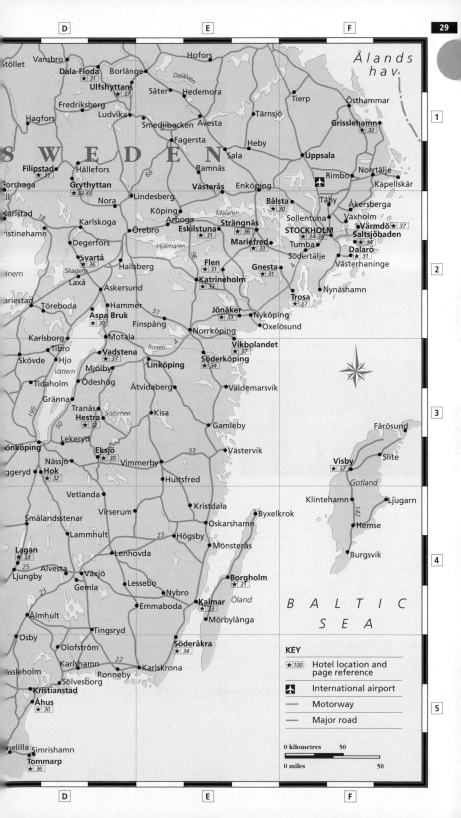

ARILD

BÅLSTA

Rusthållargården This 17th-century inn, set in a little fishing hamlet, enjoys stunning sea views. Inside is a tasteful mixture of modern and old-style elegance; rooms are luxurious, and some have balconies. Recent awards include Best Countryside Hotel, and a place in Sweden's Best Table. Gorgeous sauna suite, jet-stream Jacuzzi.
☒ S-260 43 Arild. **Map** p28 C5. 🄲 (042) 34 65 30. 🄵🄰🄷 (042) 34 67 93. @ receptionen@rusthallargarden.se 🄸🄸 b,l,d. **Rooms** 63. 🅃🄸 🄸 ● Christmas and New Year. 🄴 AE, DC, MC, V. 🄚🄚🄚

Krägga Herrgård Beauty is the keynote of this stylish manor house, filled to the brim with fresh flowers and lovely antiques. In the dining room, seasonal dishes echo the surroundings – each plate is a little masterpiece. Total seclusion, deep in the forest at the lake's edge, yet only 40 minutes' drive from Stockholm and the airport.
☒ S-746 93 Bålsta. **Map** p29 F2. 🄲 (0171) 532 80. 🄵🄰🄷 (0171) 532 65. @ info@kragga.se 🄸🄸 b,l,d. **Rooms** 43. 🄴 🅃🄸 🄸 ● Never. 🄴 AE, DC, MC, V. 🄚🄚🄚

ASPA BRUK

BILLDAL

Aspa Herrgård A casual elegance pervades this unique and exquisitely lovely little manor, which stands in tranquil parkland by Lake Vättern. In the wings of the house, rooms open off cosy lounges. Superb cuisine and fine wines are Aspa's pride, as is attention to every detail for the comfort of its guests.
☒ S-696 93 Aspa Bruk. **Map** p29 D2. 🄲 (0583) 502 10. 🄵🄰🄷 (0583) 501 50. @ info@aspaherrgard.com. 🄸🄸 b,l,d. **Rooms** 28. 🅃🄸 🄸 ● Christmas. 🄴 AE, DC, MC, V. 🄚🄚🄚

Johanneshus It's worth meandering around the country lanes to find this little country house, just 10km (7 miles) outside Gothenburg. It's a real treasure, elegant and restful, and two minutes from the sea. Peter and Rebecca Hägg and their children, give their guests a warm family welcome and take time to sit and chat with them.
☒ Johanneshusvägen 1, 427 36 Billdal. **Map** p28 C3. 🄲 (031) 91 01 25. 🄵🄰🄷 (031) 91 31 41. @ info@countrysidehotels.se 🄸🄸 b,l,d. **Rooms** 6. 🄸 ● Christmas Day, Jan. 🄴 AE, DC, MC, V. 🄚🄚

ÅHUS

Åhus Gestgivaregård The fine food served at this rustic canalside inn goes a long way towards making up for the slight tattiness.
☒ Gamla Skeppsbron 1, 296 21 Åhus. **Map** p29 D5. 🄲 (028) 9050. 🄵🄰🄷 (028) 9250. @ lasse@ahusgastis.com 🄸🄸 b,l,d. **Rooms** 17. 🄚

BÅSTAD

Buena Vista Splendid views over the bay from this stylish old villa, which retains the feel of a private house. Good home cooking.
☒ Tarravägen 5, 269 21 Båstad. **Map** p28 C4. 🄲 (0431) 760 00. 🄵🄰🄷 (0431) 791 00. @ info@hotelbuenavista.nu 🄸🄸 b,l,d. **Rooms** 30. 🄚

BRÄCKE

Björknäsgårdens Quaint hotel in northerly region, rich in history of the old timber trade, 5km (3 miles) from the little town of Bräcke.
☒ Box 188, 840 60 Bräcke. **Map** p28 A3. 🄲 (0693) 160 20. 🄵🄰🄷 (0693) 160 80. @ bjorknasgarden@fc.itz.se 🄸🄸 b,l,d. **Rooms** 27. 🄚

EKSJÖ

Ullinge Wärdshus Traditional style and pretty, with a main building surrounded by cabins. Set in a forest, on a lake with its own jetty.
☒ S-575 96, Eksjö. **Map** p29 D3. 🄲 (0381) 810 60. 🄵🄰🄷 (0381) 810 50. @ info@ ullinge.se 🄸🄸 b,l,d. **Rooms** 34. 🄚🄚

BORGHOLM, ÖLAND

Halltorps Gästgiveri A unique country inn. Each bedroom is designed and decorated by craftsmen from the province it represents and has exquisite hand-made furniture. Enjoy walks by the sea or in the nature reserve. Return to cosy lounges, open fires and local speciality dishes in one of Sweden's finest restaurants.

⊠ S-387 92 Borgholm, Öland. **Map** p29 E4.
C (0485) 85 000. **FAX** (0485) 85 001.
@ halltorps.gastgiveri@mailbox.calypso.net **ⅱ** b,l,d.
Rooms 36. **ⅲ** **⊛** **●** Never. **⊠** AE, DC, MC, V. **Ⓚ**

DALARÖ

Smådalarö Gård Just a 45-minute drive from the city in the Stockholm archipelago, this little gem sits on the edge of the water, offering a family welcome and real home comforts. The modern hotel is traditional Swedish, stylishly simple. Enjoy mouth-watering lunch buffets, picnics and a sauna on the jetty.

⊠ SE-130 54 Dalarö. **Map** p29 F2. **C** (08) 501 532 00.
FAX (08) 501 533 83. **@** info@ smadalarogard.se **ⅱ** b,l,d.
Rooms 61. **ⅲ** **⊛** **●** 22-23 June, Christmas and New Year. **⊠** AE, DC, MC, V. **Ⓚ** **Ⓚ** **Ⓚ**

DALA-FLODA

Vårdshuset i Dala-Floda This wonderful inn has the air of a Provence farmhouse. It boasts its own painting and dance studios while its corners are stuffed full of traditional arts and crafts, and English literature. The owners, who've travelled the world, prepare traditional ethnic dishes with organic local produce – try Cuban Elk.

⊠ Badvägen 6, 780 44 Dala-Floda. **Map** p29 D1.
C (0241) 220 50. **FAX** (0241) 220 38.
@ info@dala-floda.net **ⅱ** b,l,d. **Rooms** 14.
ⅲ **⊛** **●** Never. **⊠** DC, MC, V. **Ⓚ**

FLEN

Yxtaholm This sumptuous manor stands on a strip of land between two lakes. Patrick Arneke has built his reputation on the quality and simplicity of his restaurant. Relax in one of the two elegant salons with a vintage Calvados from his extensive collection, or a refreshing cider, another of the Yxtaholm's specialities.

⊠ 6642 91 Flen. **Map** p29 E2. **C** (0157) 122 65.
FAX (0157) 244 41. **@** info@yxtaholmsslott.se **ⅱ** b,d.
Rooms 46. **ⅲ** **⊛** **●** Christmas and New Year.
⊠ AE, DC, MC, V. **Ⓚ**

ESKILSTUNA
Sundbyholms Slott Old castle with view over the marina. Baronial dining room, picnics by the lake, barbecues; sauna on an island.
⊠ S-635 08 Eskilstuna. **Map** p29 E2. **C** (016) 965 00.
FAX (016) 965 78. **@** hotel.conference@sundbyholms-slott.se **ⅱ** b,l,d. **Rooms** 96. **Ⓚ** **Ⓚ**

FILIPSTAD
Hennickehammars Herrgård Manor house jointly owned by two families, with beautiful grounds and excellent food.
⊠ Box 52, SE-682 22 Filipstad. **Map** p29 D1.
C (0590) 60 85 00. **FAX** (0590) 60 85 05.
@ hotel@hennickehammar.se **ⅱ** b,l,d. **Rooms** 54. **Ⓚ**

GENARP
Häckeberga Slott Real value for money, in a castle with a stupendous setting. Packages include a gourmet dinner.
⊠ SE-240 13 Genarp. **Map** p28 C5. **C** (040) 48 04 40.
FAX (040) 48 04 02. **@** wt@hackebergaslott.se
ⅱ b,l,d. **Rooms** 19. **Ⓚ**

GNESTA
Södertuna Slott Eighteenth-century castle in idyllic lakeside setting. Gorgeous public rooms, afternoon teas and country pursuits.
⊠ 646 91 Gnesta. **Map** p29 F2. **C** (0158) 705 00.
FAX (0158) 705 10. **@** info@sodertuna.se **ⅱ** b,l,d.
Rooms 69. **Ⓚ**

For key to symbols see backflap. For price categories see p27

FRYKSÅS

Fryksås Hotell and Gestgifveri This unspoilt mountain inn sits near the small town of Orsa, on the edge of true wilderness with commanding views over forest and sea. Brown bear, wolves, lynx and elk may all be spotted on arranged treks. Seasonal game, fish and berries feature heavily on the fine menu. Outdoor hot tub.
⊠ Fryksås Fäbod, 794 98 Orsa. **Map** p28 A3.
◖ (0250) 460 20. FAX (0250) 460 90.
@ fryksas.hotell@orsa.mail.utfors.se ▮▮ b,l,d.
Rooms 15. ▼▮ ▮ ● Never. ◪ AE, DC, MC, V. ⓚ

GOTHENBERG

Rederiaktiebolaget Göta Kanal Sail right across Sweden on one of three charming old steamships, through rivers, canals and lakes and out into the Baltic to Stockholm. The oldest boat, *MS Juno*, dates from 1874. So cherished is the original glory, velvet upholstery, Asian carpets, and mahogany, that no one minds the small cabins.
⊠ Hotellplasten 2, Box 272, S-401 24 Göteborg.
Map p28 C3. ◖ (031) 80 63 15. FAX (031) 15 83 11.
@ bookings@gotacanal.se ▮▮ b,l,d. **Rooms** 27-30.
◖ ● mid-Sept to mid-May. ◪ AE, DC, MC, V. ⓚⓚⓚⓚ

GOTHENBERG

Hotel Eggers One of Sweden's oldest hotels, the Eggers still evokes a bygone elegance and remains the stylish place to stay in Gothenberg. Superb old double glazing maintains peace in the spacious rooms, just a stone's throw from the train, tram and bus stations.
⊠ Drottningtorget, Box 323, S-401 25 Göteborg.
Map p28 C3. ◖ (031) 80 60 70. FAX (031) 15 42 43.
@ hotel.eggers@mailbox.swipnet.se ▮ b; l,d (not Sun, Mon). **Rooms** 67. ▮ ● Christmas.
◪ AE, DC, MC, V. ⓚⓚⓚ

GRISSLEHAMN

Havsbaden Grisslehamn This old spa hotel in a fishing village, lovingly restored, offers a very warm welcome. Seasonal local food, such as smoked eel, is a speciality. The sea views, space, and tasteful rooms are a delight. Explore nature, take a ferry to the islands, or enjoy a fishing trip.
⊠ 760 45 Grisslehamn. **Map** p29 F1.
◖ (0175) 309 30. FAX (0175) 330 14.
@ info@hotell-havsbaden.se ▮▮ b,l,d. **Rooms** 50.
▼▮ ▮ ● Christmas; some Suns Nov-Jan.
◪ AE, DC, MC, V. ⓚⓚ

GRYTHYTTAN
Loka Brunn This luxurious 18th-century royal spa is like a little village in the forest, offering total pampering. Museum on spa history.
⊠ S-712 94 Grythyttan. **Map** p29 D1.
◖ (0591) 631 00. FAX (0591) 300 00.
@ loka.brunn@swipnet.se ▮▮ b,l,d. **Rooms** 164. ⓚⓚⓚ

HESTRA
Hestravikens Wärdshus Country lodge with excellent food. Some rooms have river views and verandas. Pool.
⊠ Vik, S-330 27 Hestra. **Map** p29 D3.
◖ (0370) 33 68 00. FAX (0370) 33 62 90.
@ info@hestraviken.se ▮▮ b,l,d. **Rooms** 33. ⓚⓚ

HJÄRNARP
Margretetorps Gästgifvaregård Smart, stylish inn with tasteful rooms off tranquil courtyard with water garden. Noted for its Smörgåsbord.
⊠ S-266 98 Hjärnarp. **Map** p28 C4. ◖ (0431) 45 44 50.
FAX (0431) 45 48 77. @ margretetorp@swipnet.se
▮▮ b,l,d. **Rooms** 60. ⓚⓚⓚ

HOK
Hooks Herrgård Elegant golf and leisure hotel in a manor house where the salons all look out onto the lake. Excellent food.
⊠ 560 13 Hok. **Map** p29 D3. ◖ (0393) 210 80.
FAX (0393) 215 67. @ hook.herrgard@edberg.com
▮▮ b,l,d. **Rooms** 103. ⓚⓚⓚ

GRYTHYTTAN

Grythyttans Gästgivaregård It's one of the most atmospheric old inns in all of Sweden – almost like a little village all by itself, with rooms in several separate buildings and many old salons and cosy parlours. The former dungeon now houses more than 450 fine wines to complement the international gourmet menu.
⊠ Prästgatan 2, S-712 81 Grythyttan. **Map** p29 D1.
☎ (0591) 147 00. ℻ (0591) 141 24.
@ info@grythyttan.com. ⊞ b,l,d. **Rooms** 69.
🌡 ● Never. 🗐 AE, DC, MC, V. Ⓚ Ⓚ Ⓚ

LILLA EDIT

Thorskogs Slott This gorgeous old castle offers a totally homely welcome. Numerous heads of state have enjoyed its exquisite Gustavian salons and dishes from its famous kitchen. After drinks in the flower room, step out onto the terrace for a barbecue, then enjoy boules on the lawn. One of the best breakfasts in Sweden is served here.
⊠ SE-463 93, Västerlanda. **Map** p28 C3.
☎ (0520) 66 10 00. ℻ (0520) 66 18 09.
@ thorskog@netg.se ⊞ b,l,d. **Rooms** 32. 🎄 🌡
● July, Christmas and New Year. 🗐 AE, DC, MC, V. Ⓚ Ⓚ

JÖNÅKER

Wreta Gestgifveri Cancel all other plans in order to visit this delightful little pearl, in a hamlet near Nyköping. You are welcomed into the home of someone who understands the meaning of beauty and comfort. No detail is neglected. Delight in Vivaldi on the CD in your room before drinks and a dinner which lives up to the surroundings.
⊠ Wreta Gård AB, 610 50 Jönåker. **Map** p29 E2.
☎ (0155) 720 22. ℻ (0155) 720 32.
@ wreta@swipnet.se ⊞ b,l,d. **Rooms** 15.
🌡 ● Never. 🗐 AE, MC, V. Ⓚ Ⓚ Ⓚ

MARIEFRED

Gripsholms Värdshus In the tranquil old town of Mariefred, enjoy unashamed luxury and informal hospitality at this divine old inn. Exquisite food, and wine tastings in the old monastery below. In summer, old steam trains and boats from Stockholm stop here; at Christmas there are log fires and skating on the lake.
⊠ Kyrkogatan 1, Box 114, S-647 23 Mariefred.
Map p29 E2. ☎ (0159) 347 50. ℻ (0159) 347 77.
@ info@gripsholms-vardshus.se ⊞ b,l,d. **Rooms** 45.
🗄 🎄 🎄 🌡 ● early Jan. 🗐 AE, DC, MC, V. Ⓚ Ⓚ Ⓚ

JÄRVSÖ

Järvsöbaden A very personal welcome in a charming family-run hotel with lovely gardens. Good, traditional food with Smörgåsbord.
⊠ Box 43, 820 40 Järvsö. **Map** p28 A3.
☎ (0651) 404 00. ℻ (0651) 414 37. ⊞ b,l,d.
Rooms 44. Ⓚ

KALMAR

Slottshotellet A 19th-century seaman's house offering old world charm in historic town with castle. Personal service and good food.
⊠ Slottsvägen 7, S-392 33 Kalmar. **Map** p29 E4.
☎ (0480) 882 60. ℻ (0480) 882 66. @ romantikhotel@ slottshotellet.se ⊞ b,l,d. **Rooms** 44. Ⓚ Ⓚ Ⓚ

KATRINEHOLM

Dufweholms Herrgård The many regular guests attest to the popularity of this lakeside inn. Gourmet food with a Mediterranean slant.
⊠ Herrgårdsvägen 16, 641 92 Katrineholm.
Map p29 E2. ☎ (0150) 785 40. ℻ (0150) 785 60.
@ info@dufweholm.se ⊞ b,l,d. **Rooms** 18. Ⓚ Ⓚ

LAGAN

Toftaholm Herrgård A warm welcome awaits in this pretty, 600-year-old family-run manor house with lake views. Excellent breakfasts.
⊠ Toftaholm, SE-340 14 Lagan. **Map** p29 D4.
☎ (0370) 440 55. ℻ (0370) 440 45. @ frontoffice@ toftaholmherrgard.com ⊞ b,l,d. **Rooms** 45. Ⓚ Ⓚ Ⓚ

For key to symbols see backflap. For price categories see p27

MARSTRAND

Grand Hotell Marstrand Less than an hour from Gothenberg, leave your car behind and take the ferry to this timeless island. The porter collects you on the quay. Sumptuous rooms, some with balconies looking onto the bandstand and harbour beyond. Eat delicious seafood in the popular veranda restaurant. Enchanting.

⊠ SE 440 30 Marstrand. **Map** p28 B3.
📞 (0303) 603 22. FAX (0303) 600 53.
@ info@grandmarstrand.se 🍴 b,l,d. **Rooms** 22. 🍴 🎖
⬤ Christmas and New Year. 💳 AE, DC, MC, V. Ⓚ Ⓚ Ⓚ

SALTSJÖBADEN

Grand Hôtel Saltsjöbaden This stylish hotel, on the edge of the Baltic Sea in the Stockholm archipelago, bathes in 19th-century tranquillity. Original bathing houses still stand on the private island, and a little train built to serve the hotel still does. The piano bar and elegant French dining room have views of the sunset over the marina.

⊠ SE 133 83 Saltsjöbaden, Stockholm. **Map** p29 F2.
📞 (08) 506 170 00. FAX (08) 506 170 01.
🍴 b,l,d. **Rooms** 105. 📖 🍴 🎖 ⬤ Irregular.
💳 AE, DC, MC, V. Ⓚ Ⓚ Ⓚ

MÖLLE

Kullaberg This Neo-Renaissance early 1900s building offers a sojourn into a gracious era long gone. The exquisite dining room affords panoramic views of the harbour. Dine on finest linen, with monogrammed china and hand-blown crystal, on tables covered in white lilies. Some rooms have balconies over the harbour.

⊠ Gyllenstiernas allé 16. Box 43, S-260 42 Mölle.
Map p28 C5. 📞 (042) 34 70 00. FAX (042) 34 71 00.
@ info@hotelkullaberg.se 🍴 b,l,d. **Rooms** 20.
🍴 🎖 ⬤ Never. 💳 AE, DC, MC, V. Ⓚ Ⓚ Ⓚ Ⓚ

SÖDERÅKRA

Stufvenäs Gästgifveri Food and drink are specialities at this family-run inn, beautifully furnished with a homely mix of antique and modern design. Superb dishes are complemented by wines from the extensive, award-winning collection. For a special treat, ask to have your coffee in the lounge-like wine cellar.

⊠ PL 7488, 385 97 Söderåkra. **Map** p29 E5.
📞 (0486) 219 00. FAX (0486) 218 68.
@ stufvenas.gastgifveri@telia.com 🍴 b,l,d. **Rooms** 55.
🍴 🎖 ⬤ Christmas to mid-Jan. 💳 AE, DC, MC, V. Ⓚ Ⓚ

SÖDERKÖPING

Söderköpings Brunn Old spa hotel, with all mod-cons; indoor and outdoor pools.
⊠ Skönbergagatan 35, Box 44 SE-614 21, Soderköping.
Map p29 E3. 📞 (0121) 109 00. FAX (0121) 139 41.
@ info@soderkopingsbrunn.se 🍴 b,l,d.
Rooms 103. Ⓚ Ⓚ

STOCKHOLM

Clas På Hörnet Old-world style and noted food in the heart of the city, courtesy of owner-chef Nils Emil. Busy dining room, quiet terrace.
⊠ Surbrunnsgatan 20, 113 48 Stockholm. **Map** p29 F2.
📞 (08) 16 51 30. FAX (08) 61253 15. @ clas.pa.hornet@telia.com 🍴 b,l,d. **Rooms** 10. Ⓚ Ⓚ Ⓚ

STOCKHOLM

Esplanade Faithfully preserved, this Art Nouveau haven of peace is set back off the main street in a quiet courtyard.
⊠ Strandvägen 7A, S-114 56 Stockholm.
Map p29 F2. 📞 (08) 663 07 40. FAX (08) 662 59 92.
🍴 b. **Rooms** 34. Ⓚ Ⓚ Ⓚ

STOCKHOLM

Lady Hamilton Just a few steps from the royal palace in Stockholm's old town, a friendly atmosphere, and many fine antiques.
⊠ Storkyrkobrinken 5, 111 28 Stockholm. **Map** p29 F2.
📞 (08) 23 46 80. FAX (08) 411 11 48. @ info@lady-hamilton.se 🍴 b. **Rooms**, 34. Ⓚ Ⓚ Ⓚ Ⓚ

STOCKHOLM

Diplomat This long-established family-run hotel sits on Stockholm's most fashionable street, Strandvägen, overlooking an inlet of the Baltic Sea. Inside is all old-style elegance, with tasteful bedrooms and a pleasant streetfront restaurant. International cruise ships dock here and boat trips are available.
⊠ Strandvägen 7C, S-104 40, Stockholm. **Map** p29 F2. 🄲 (08) 663 58 00. ꜰᴀX (08) 459 68 20. @ reservations. sthlm@diplomat-hotel.se 🚻 b,l,d. **Rooms** 128. 🖺 🌢 ⬤ Christmas. 🎫 AE, DC, MC, V. ⓀⓀⓀⓀ

STOCKHOLM

The Victory It's almost like a nautical museum: each sumptuous room is named after a Swedish captain and contains his portrait and model ship. This old-town townhouse is the jewel in the crown of a trio of hotels (with the Lady Hamilton and Lord Nelson, see below). Its Leijontornet Restaurant is one of Stockholm's finest.
⊠ Lilla Nygatan 5, Gamla Stan, S-111 28 Stockholm. **Map** p29 F2. 🄲 (08) 14 30 90. ꜰᴀX (08) 20 21 77. @ info@victory-hotel.se 🚻 b,l,d. **Rooms** 45. 🖺 🌢 ⬤ Christmas and New Year. 🎫 AE, DC, MC, V. ⓀⓀⓀⓀ

STOCKHOLM

Långholmen On an island, close to the city, enjoy a cell in this delightfully converted prison. A museum explains its history.
⊠ Kronohäktet, Box 9116, 102 72 Stockholm. **Map** p29 F2. 🄲 (08) 668 05 00. ꜰᴀX (08) 720 85 75. @ hotel@langholmen.com. 🚻 b,l,d. **Rooms** 101. ⓀⓀ

STOCKHOLM

Lord Nelson In Stockholm's old town, a narrow, nautical theme hotel, built like a ship. Small 'cabins' on the upper decks.
⊠ Västerlånggatan 22, 111 29 Stockholm. **Map** p29 F2. 🄲 (08) 23 23 90. ꜰᴀX (08) 10 10 89. @ hotel@lord-nelson.se 🚻 b. **Rooms** 31. ⓀⓀⓀⓀ

STOCKHOLM

Villa Källhagen It's a delight to discover this exceptionally tasteful modern hotel, only a few minutes' drive from the city centre in a quiet waterside setting. Its large rooms are very light and airy, and the dining terrace is a pleasant place from which to enjoy the delicious food. It's a 15-minute stroll for a boat to the archipelago.
⊠ Djurgårdsbrunnsvägen 10, Stockholm. **Map** p29 F2. 🄲 (08) 665 03 00. ꜰᴀX (08) 665 03 99. @ kallhagen.hotel. restaurant@swipnet.se 🚻 b,l,d. **Rooms** 20. 🖺 🌢 ⬤ Christmas. 🎫 AE, DC, MC, V. ⓀⓀⓀⓀ

SUNNE

Länsmansgården You'll feel at home in minutes in this exceptionally pretty country house, home to the same family since 1840. The comfy parlours are full of family heirlooms, and stories of the house's history abound. It has its own little beach with boats, and is close to both cross-country and downhill skiing. Wonderful regional cooking.
⊠ S-686 93 Sunne. **Map** p28 C1. 🄲 (0565) 140 10. ꜰᴀX (0565) 71 18 05. @ info@lansman.com 🚻 b,l,d. **Rooms** 30. 🖺 🌢 ⬤ Never. 🎫 AE, DC, MC, V. Ⓚ.

STOCKHOLM

The Lydmar This hotel is also a popular music and arts venue. Stylish bedrooms, lively bars.
⊠ Sturegatan 10, S-114 36 Stockholm. **Map** p29 F2. 🄲 (08) 566 113 00. ꜰᴀX (08) 566 113 01. @ info@lydmar.se 🚻 b,l,d. **Rooms** 56. 🌢 ⬤ Never. 🎫 AE, DC, MC, V. ⓀⓀⓀ

STOCKHOLM

Mälardrottningen Anchored in the heart of the city, Barbara Hutton's large yacht offers affordable luxury. Book well ahead.
⊠ Riddarholmen S-111 28 Stockholm. **Map** p29 F2. 🄲 (08) 545 18 780. ꜰᴀX (08) 24 36 76. @ reception@ malardrottningen.se 🚻 b,l,d. **Rooms** 60. ⓀⓀ

SVARTÅ

Svartå Herrgård This little manor house, run by the same family since 1946, is midway between Stockholm and Gothenberg, right on a lake. In summer, the gardens are filled with fragrance and birdsong, and lake pursuits, picnics and country sports are arranged; log fires and skating in winter. Exquisite rooms, many with lake views.
693 93 Svartå. **Map** p29 D2. (0585) 500 03. FAX (0585) 503 03. svarta.herrgard@swipnet.se b,l,d. **Rooms** 38. early Jan; Sun eves (except July, August). AE, DC, MC, V.

TÄLLBERG

Klockargården A unique experience of local culture and tradition are offered here. A handicraft shop in 1937, it has now grown into a little village of crafts studios, and 'living museums' where you can try your hand at baking local breads or smithying. Pretty rooms are dotted throughout the buildings. Music and theatre.
Siljansvägen 6, S-793 70 Tällberg. **Map** p28 A3. (0247) 502 60. FAX (0247) 502 16. hotell@klockargarden.com b,l,d. **Rooms** 40. Never. AE, DC, MC, V.

TÄLLBERG

Åckerblads More than 20 generations of Åckerblads have run this much-loved property, originally a village farm. Quality and an excellent restaurant combine here with real family hospitality. The rooms have won interior design prizes, while the uniquely gorgeous pool is enclosed by hand-painted family 'cottages'.
Sjögattu 2, 793 70 Tällberg. **Map** p28 A3. (0247) 508 00. FAX (0247) 506 52. info@ackerbladstallberg.se b,l,d. **Rooms** 68. Never. DC, MC, V.

TOMMARP

Karlaby Kro A haven of calm, close to fishing villages and sandy beaches. Artists flock here for the special light. At this tastefully renovated farmhouse, hunters, mushroom pickers and fishermen come knocking on the door, ensuring that the six-course, award-winning gourmet dinner is never the same twice.
S-272 93 Tommarp. **Map** p29 D5. (0414) 203 00. FAX (0414) 204 73. reception@karlabykro.se b,l,d. **Rooms** 21. 23-28 Dec. AE, DC, MC, V.

STOCKHOLM

Tre Små Rum A tiny hotel in an arty suburb, very sociable, ecologically conscious and excellent value for money. A home-from-home.
Hogbersgatan 81, 118 54 Stockholm. **Map** p29 F2. (08) 641 2371. FAX (08) 642 8808. info@tresmarum.se **Rooms** 6. b,l,d.

STRÄNGNÄS

Ulvhälls Herrgård Gourmet food in a 17th-century manor looking out onto Lake Mälaren, run by the same family since 1947.
Ulvhälls allé 645 40 Strängnäs. **Map** p29 E2. (0152) 186 80. FAX (0152) 177 97. info@ulvhall.se **Rooms** 42. b,l,d.

TÄLLBERG

Tällbergsgårdens Pensionat The only hotel here with panoramic views over Silyan Lake. Steeped in family history, cosy and friendly.
Holgattu 1, 793 70 Tällberg. **Map** p28 A3. (0247) 508 50. FAX (0247) 502 00. info@tallbergsgarden.se b,l,d. **Rooms** 37.

TÄNNDALEN

Hotel Tänndalen This family-run alpine hotel is popular winter and summer alike. Ideal for nature treks, cross-country and alpine skiing.
S-840 98 Tänndalen. **Map** p28 A2. (0684) 220 20. FAX (0684) 224 24. hotel.tanndalen@tanndalen.se **Rooms** 65. b,l,d.

TOREKOV

Katteghat Gastronomi & Logi The reputation of this 100-year-old restaurant with rooms could not get much higher – it was voted one of Sweden's best in 1998. Watch chefs at work in the open-plan kitchen behind the bar. Rooms are modern, with bright Italian colours. Walk by the sea, play golf, or visit the old spa Bathhouse close by.
☒ Storgatan 46, S-260 93 Torekov. **Map** p28 C4.
🄲 (0431) 36 30 02. FAX (0431) 36 30 03.
@ katteghat@rikardnilsson.com 🍽 b,l,d. **Rooms** 11.
🎔 🌑 Jan-mid March. 🌮 AE, DC. MC, V. Ⓚ Ⓚ Ⓚ Ⓚ

VADSTENA

Vadstena Klosterhotel Recordings of monks singing plainchant welcome you into this atmospheric former monastery, now a protected building. The thick walls shelter cool, quiet rooms. Breakfast is served in an old workroom, under gothic arches. In summer, plays by Shakespeare are performed in the courtyard.
☒ Klosterområdet, S-592 00 Vadstena. **Map** p29 D3.
🄲 (0143) 315 30. FAX (0143) 136 48.
@ hotel@klosterhotel.se 🍽 **Rooms** 29. 🎔
🌑 Christmas and New Year. 🌮 AE, DC, MC, V. Ⓚ Ⓚ

TROSA

Bowman's i Trosa Absolutely no detail is overlooked in this picture-perfect old house right by the River Trosa. The product of years of care lavished by the Bowmans, it is filled with family antiques, mementoes, hand-made furniture and flowers. The small rooms are exquisite, each decorated by the family. Glorious home cooking.
☒ AB, S-619 30 Trosa. **Map** p29 F2. 🄲 (0156) 525 00.
FAX (0156) 525 10. @ info@bomans.se 🍽 b,l,d.
Rooms 31. 🍽 🎔 🌑 22 Dec-10 Jan.
🌮 AE, DC, MC, V. Ⓚ Ⓚ

VISBY, GOTLAND

Toftagården A four-and-a-half-hour ferry trip from Oskarshamn brings you to the enchanting Baltic island of Gotland, a paradise for nature lovers. Toftagården stands in its own wooded park, near a sandy beach. The superb restaurant is famous for the island's lamb and salmon. Very cosy, friendly service and relaxed atmosphere.
☒ Tofta, S-621 98 Visby. **Map** p29 F3.
🄲 (0498) 29 70 00. FAX (0498) 26 56 66.
@ info@toftagarden.se 🍽 b,l,d. **Rooms** 70. 🏊 🍽 🎔
🌑 Christmas. 🌮 AE, DC, DC, MC, V. Ⓚ Ⓚ

TROSA
Trosa Stadshotel This lovely old inn is run by a Swiss owner, who has a talent for making guests welcome. Exellent cooking.
☒ Västra Långgatan 19, Box 18, 619 21 Trosa.
Map p29 F2. 🄲 (0156) 170 70. FAX (0156) 166 96.
@ info@trosastadshotell.se 🍽 b,l,d. **Rooms** 44. Ⓚ Ⓚ

ULFSHYTTANS
Ulfshyttans Herrgård A tiny road leads to this lakeside country house (Borlänge 25km/ 19 miles). Old-style comfort, home cooking.
☒ S-781 96 Borlänge. **Map** p29 D1. 🄲 (0243) 25 13 00.
FAX (0243) 25 11 11. @ info@ulfshyttan.se 🍽 b,l,d.
Rooms 19. Ⓚ

VÄRMDÖ
FågelbroHus Country club style in the Stockholm archipelago 30 minutes' drive from the city, with parkland and golf course.
☒ FågelbroHus AB, SE-139 60 Värmdö. **Map** p29 F2.
🄲 (08) 571 401 00. FAX (08) 571 401 71.
@ info@fagelbrohus.se 🍽 b,l,d. **Rooms** 72. Ⓚ Ⓚ Ⓚ Ⓚ

VIKBOLANDET
Maurtizbergs Slott Most rooms have sea views at this clifftop 16th-century castle. Norrköping international airport 25km (20 miles) away.
☒ S-610 31 Vikbolandet. **Map** p29 E3.
🄲 (0125) 501 00. FAX (0125) 501 04.
@ service@mauritzberg.se 🍽 b,l,d. **Rooms** 44. Ⓚ Ⓚ

For key to symbols see backflap. For price categories *see p27*

DENMARK

DENMARK

ACCOMMODATION IN Denmark, like most things Danish, is usually high quality, spotlessly clean and well-run, albeit at a price. Perhaps Denmark's most characterful form of accommodation is the *kro*, the historic stage-coach inn. Located on main roads (don't worry – Danish traffic is light), the *kro* is ideal for touring the country and it offers value for money. Leaving aside the lights of Copenhagen and other large cities, Denmark remains essentially a rural country. Farmhouse holidays are enduringly popular, and economical. Staying on a farm for a few days as well as in a hotel or inn could make a happy combination.

The elegant retreat of Steensgaard Herregård, Millinge, page 48

DENMARK REGION BY REGION

WE DIVIDE Denmark into three main areas:

Jutland (Jylland)
The bridge between Scandinavia and Europe, this unhurried rural peninsula makes up Denmark's biggest land mass. It is the most attractive part of the country, dotted with lakes, and with a coast lined by windswept dunes. East Jutland is home to Aarhus, Denmark's second-largest city and cultural capital, while southeast Jutland has Legoland. The former has a useful choice of hotel accommodation while Legoland offers a clutch of child-friendly hotels.

Farm accommodation is very popular throughout Jutland, and country cottages and summer houses for rent are particularly common in West Jutland.

Funen (Fyn)
The island-peninsula immediately east of Jutland is known as The Garden of Denmark because of its natural beauty, fruit and vegetable farms and its many flowery gardens. The seaside resorts in the south of Funen feature family holiday centres with a wide range of indoor and outdoor activities and high-quality accommodation. The main cultural draw is the attractive town of Odense, birthplace of the writer Hans Christian Andersen, which has a wide choice of hotels. Elsewhere in this area, accommodation is both simple and relatively cheap.

Many B&Bs have sprung up in recent years, and these are prominently sign-posted along the main roads and elsewhere.

Zealand (Sjaelland)
The larger island east of Funen and nudging Sweden, Zealand is dominated by the bustling city of Copenhagen and has a wide selection of accommodation; from tourist-board-approved private rooms and cheap hostels, to five-star hotels.

Out of town there is the Karen Blixen Museum, Helsingør (Hamlet's Elsinore) and the historic town of Roskilde – all worth a visit.

The island of Bornholm, the 'Jewel of the Baltic', a seven- hour ferry journey from Copenhagen, is a traditional fishing-and-farming settlement, popular for walking and cycling holidays. See our recommendations here on pages 44 and 50.

HIGHLIGHTS

THE PLACES to stay illustrated on these introductory pages are by no means Denmark's only highlights. In Copenhagen, the Admiral (page 46) stands out for having the best location in town, right on the harbour, and for the way it reflects its nautical past. Henne Kirkeby Kro, at Henne (page 46) can rightly claim to have among the best food in Scandinavia. Store Kro, at Fredensborg (page 45) is another favourite – it lives up to its grand setting next to the Danish Royal Family's summer residence. And we especially like the Hotel Dagmar at Ribe (page 49) for retaining, despite great popularity, its historic atmosphere.

FOOD AND DRINK

TRADITIONAL DANISH fare comprises hearty helpings of meat (mostly pork, beef and veal) and fish from the Baltic Sea, North Sea and lakes. The quality is consistently high and so, often, are prices. One home-grown food which you probably will not see is Danish bacon – it is reserved for export.

In Copenhagen there are all manner of ethnic restaurants, many operating on the traditional Danish 'open table' policy: the whole party eats all it can for a fixed price.

At lunchtime, around midday to 2:30pm, look out for the *dagen's ret* (dish of the day). If you are on a tight budget this is the time to eat, as prices at dinner time for similar food in similar establishments are significantly higher.

The local fast food is hot sausages (*pølser*) dispensed by street vendors. The ubiquitous Danish pastry, called *wienerbrød,* (literally, Vienna bread) is standard café fare.

Unlike its Scandinavian neighbours, Denmark is very relaxed in its attitude to alcohol. The Danes are a nation of beer drinkers – Denmark is famous as the home of Carlsberg lager. Tuborg is the alternative. The Danish version of schnapps is *akvavit*. It comes in several forms, most often flavoured with dill or caraway, and is drunk as a chaser or (to the consternation of foreigners) to accompany a meal.

Denmark's best-known culinary institution is

smørrebrød, a selection of open rye sandwiches (*rugbrød*) and trimmings. This term is sometimes also extended to a complete buffet (*det store kolde bord*), including traditional fare such as salmon, crayfish, prawns, herring, hot and cold meats, cheeses and dessert.

OTHER PRACTICAL INFORMATION

BOOK WELL in advance if you are planning to visit Copenhagen or the popular sea-side resorts in Funen during July and August. Note also that many hotels are taken over at weekends all year- for local celebrations such as weddings.

Breakfast is usually a buffet of breads, cheeses, cold meats, fruit and cereals.

Petrol is very expensive by western European standards. Expect high charges for bridge tolls and ferries.

Language English and German are widely understood and most menus are also translated into these two languages.

Currency The Danish *krone* written Kr, usually before the amount, and divided into 100 øre.

Shops Generally open from 9am–5:30pm Mon–Thu, 9am–7 or 8pm Fri, 9am–1 or 2pm Sat (9am–5pm first Sat of the month). Many supermarkets in larger towns open until 7 or 8pm Mon–Fri and some shops also open until 4 or 5pm on Saturdays. Some also open on Sundays.

Tipping This is not required or expected – restaurant bills always include a service charge.

Telephoning To telephone inside Denmark, dial the number, including the first zero of the area code. To

call Denmark from the UK, dial 00 45, then the number, dropping the first zero of the area code; from the US, dial 011 45 and drop the first 0 of the area code.

Public holidays 1 January; Maundy Thursday; Good Friday; Easter Sunday; Easter Monday; Great Prayer Day (fourth Friday after Good Friday); Ascension Day (mid-May); Constitution Day (5 Jun); Whit Sunday; Whit Monday (late May); 24–26 December.

USEFUL WORDS

Breakfast	*Morgenmad*
Lunch	*Frokost*
Dinner	*Aftensmad*
Free room?	*Værelser?*
How much?	*Hvad koster det?*
Single room	*Enkelt værelse*
Double	*Dobbelt værelse*

DENMARK PRICE BANDS

DANISH HOTELS are officially classified by stars, from one to five. A hotel without a restaurant, but with one to three stars, is called a *hotel garni*. Our price bands are simpler and refer, as usual, to the price of a standard double room in high season. Prices quoted usually include breakfast and sales tax. You may, however, encounter a small 'green tax' on your hotel bill in some places.

Ⓚ	below 600Kr
ⓀⓀ	600–900Kr
ⓀⓀⓀ	900–1400Kr
ⓀⓀⓀⓀ	above 1400Kr

Bromølle Kro, Jyderup, page 46

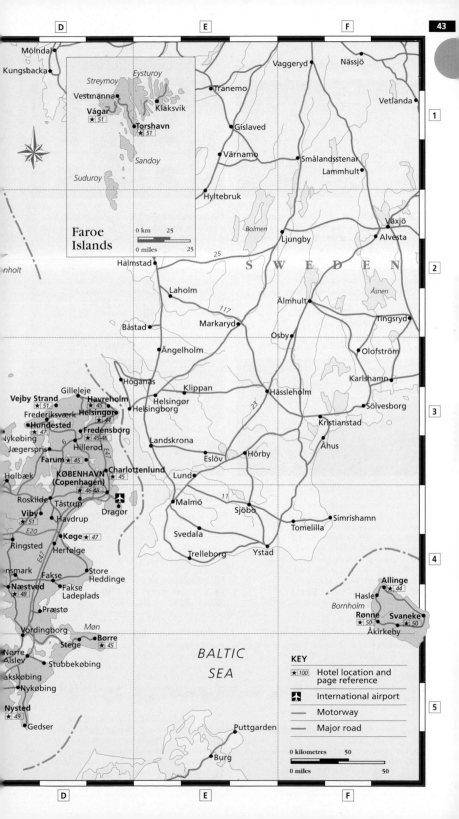

ÅLBORG

Helnan Phønix Since 1853 when Brigadier William von Haling's vast 18th-century residence was converted into a hotel, this has been the smart choice of accommodation in Ålborg, Denmark's fourth city. The heritage of this protected building is reflected within its grand dining halls and plush lounges.
⊠ Vesterbro 77, 9000 Ålborg. **Map** p42 B1.
🔲 98 12 00 11. **FAX** 98 10 10 20. **@** hotel@ helnan-phonix-hotel.dk 🍴 b,l,d. **Rooms** 210.
🍴 ● Never. 💳 AE, DC, MC, V. Ⓚ Ⓚ

DRONNINGLUND

Dronninglund Slot Dronninglund Palace has played an important role in Danish history over the past 800 years. Today, within the pristine whitewashed walls is a luxurious hotel and restaurant in harmony with its heritage. Rooms are exquisite, and are excellent value. The original palace gardens are open to hotel guests.
⊠ Slotsgade 8, 9330 Dronninglund. **Map** p42 C1.
🔲 98 84 33 00. **FAX** 98 84 34 13. **@** slot@ dronninglund-slot.dk 🍴 b,d. **Rooms** 72. 🔵
● Never. 💳 AE, DC, MC, V. Ⓚ Ⓚ

ÅRHUS

Hotel Royal The striking stained glass windows, huge tapestries, and modern art provide an uplifting introduction to this busy city hotel. The attention to aesthetics continues throughout this graceful and sophisticated hotel. The individually appointed rooms are done out in soft hues and sport original artwork on the walls. One of Scandinavia's top casinos is located here.
⊠ Store Torv 4, 8000 Århus. **Map** p42 B3.
🔲 86 12 00 11. **FAX** 86 76 04 04. 🍴 b,l,d.
Rooms 102. 🍴 ● Never. 💳 AE, DC, MC, V. Ⓚ Ⓚ Ⓚ

ESBJERG

Hotel Hjerting Located opposite one of Denmark's most popular beaches at Ho Bugt, this old seaside hotel operates to a particularly high standard. Rooms are modern and stylish, and the restaurant offers both excellent views and good-quality modern Danish cuisine. The hotel's English-style pub gets lively at weekends and throughout the summer.
⊠ Strandpromenaden 1, 6710 Esbjerg. **Map** p42 A4.
🔲 75 11 52 44. **FAX** 75 11 76 77. 🍴 b,l,d. **Rooms** 45.
● Never. 💳 AE, DC, MC, V. Ⓚ Ⓚ

ÅBENRÅ
Sdr Hostrup Kro Super-stylish stopover in the heart of rural South Jutland. Renowned cooking.
⊠ Sdr Hostrup Østergade 21, 6200 Åbenrå.
Map p42 B4. 🔲 74 61 34 46. **FAX** 74 61 30 67.
@ christiessdrhostrupkro@get2net.dk 🍴 b,l,d.
Rooms 28. Ⓚ Ⓚ Ⓚ

ÅBENRÅ
Knapp Unusual and rather formal restaurant-hotel. A grand piano takes pride of place in the ballroom. Rooms are individually furnished.
⊠ Stennevej 79, Stollig, 6200 Åbenrå.
Map p42 B4. 🔲 74 62 00 92. **FAX** 74 62 10 92.
🍴 b,d. **Rooms** 10. Ⓚ Ⓚ Ⓚ

ÅBYBRO
Hotel Søparken Well-equipped modern hotel with a luxurious indoor swimming pool and smart restaurant. A good place for children, and well located for the Fårup Aquapark.
⊠ Søparken 1, 9440 Åbybro. **Map** p42 B1. 🔲 98 24 45 77. **FAX** 98 24 46 76. 🍴 b,l,d. **Rooms** 50. Ⓚ Ⓚ

ALLINGE, BORNHOLM
Strandhotellet Cosy, good-value inn with modern rooms. Beachside recreation area with indoor swimming pool and tennis courts.
⊠ Sandvig, 3770 Allinge, Bornholm. **Map** p43 F4.
🔲 56 48 03 14. **FAX** 56 48 02 09. 🍴 b,l,d.
Rooms 49. Ⓚ Ⓚ

FARUM

Bregnerød Kro A roadside inn has stood in this hamlet, surrounded by deer-filled forests, for centuries. The original was destroyed by Swedish troops in 1700 but was rebuilt five years later, and it has continued to thrive ever since. The extensive use of light and dark woods throughout the thatched building creates a pleasing aesthetic that adds to the sense of comfort.
⊠ Bregnerød Byvej 2, 3520 Farum. **Map** p43 D3.
☎ 44 95 00 57. **FAX** 44 95 06 55. **⟊** b,l,d. **Rooms** 9.
● Sundays. ⊘ DC, V. ⓀⓀ

FREDERICIA

Kryb-I-ly Kro This royal-appointed inn manages to combine informality with opulence under its huge thatched roof. Facilities include a mahogany-panelled library with log fire and a luxury sauna/solarium. Rooms are spacious and staff cheery and helpful. The extensive restaurant menu specializes in fresh fish and game.
⊠ Taulov, 7000 Fredericia. **Map** p42 B4.
☎ 75 56 25 55. **FAX** 75 56 45 14. **@** krybily@krybily.dk
⟊ b,l,d. **Rooms** 42. ▦ ⟊ ◧ ● Never.
⊘ AE, DC, MC, V. ⓀⓀⓀ

FREDENSBORG

Store Kro The palatial establishment was built in 1723 for king Frederick IV. Adjacent to Fredensborg Castle, the Danish royal summer residence, Store Kro's classical architecture is reflected in its regal bedrooms. This is a confident, assured hotel with helpful staff and great attention to detail.
⊠ Slotgade 6, 3480 Fredensborg. **Map** p43 D3.
☎ 48 48 00 47. **FAX** 48 48 45 61.
@ info@storekro.dk **⟊** b,l,d. **Rooms** 49. ◧
● Christmas and New Year. ⊘ AE, DC, MC, V. ⓀⓀⓀ

HAVREHOLM

Havreholm Slot This lakeside manor house near the stylish resort of Hornbæk gives a rather forbidding first impression. This is soon dissolved by the graceful white and turquoise lobby, and the clean lines of Scandinavian design in the rooms. Guests can explore the verdant parkland, which includes a splendid rose garden.
⊠ Kloterrisvej 4, 3100 Havreholm. **Map** p43 D3.
☎ 49 75 86 00. **FAX** 49 75 80 23.
@ havreholm@havreholm.dk **⟊** b,l,d. **Rooms** 29.
▦ ⟊ ◧ ● Never. ⊘ AE, DC, MC, V. ⓀⓀⓀⓀ

ÅRS

Aars Hotel Built in 1897 as a railway inn, now a modern hotel with pool, sauna and disco. Impressive Danish/French menu.
⊠ Himmerlandsgade 111, 9600 Års. **Map** p42 B2.
☎ 98 6216 00. **FAX** 98 62 11 87. **@** aars@aarshotel.dk
⟊ b,d. **Rooms** 27. ⓀⓀ

BØRRE

Liseland Slot Well-preserved lakeside manor house with exquisite interiors and wonderful surrounding parkland. A romantic choice.
⊠ Liseland Slot, 4791 Børre. **Map** p43 D5.
☎ 55 81 20 81. **FAX** 55 81 21 91. **⟊** b,d.
Rooms 22. ⓀⓀⓀⓀ

BROBY

Brobyværk Kro This historic inn, dating back to 1645 and set alongside the Odense River in rural Funen, specializes in traditional fish cuisine. Rooms are clean and modern.
⊠ Marsk-Billesvej 15, 5672 Broby. **Map** p42 B4.
☎ 62 63 11 22. **FAX** 62 63 21 22. **⟊** b,l,d. **Rooms** 20. Ⓚ

CHARLOTTENLUND

Shovshoved A few minutes' drive from chic Charlottenlund, and 20 minutes to Copenhagen. Eclectic, even eccentric, décor; diverse menu.
⊠ Strandvejen 267, 2920Charlottenlund. **Map** p43 D3.
☎ 39 64 00 28. **FAX** 39 64 06 72. **⟊** b,l,d.
Rooms 20. ⓀⓀⓀ

HENNE

Henne Kirkeby Kro Gourmets from the whole of Denmark come here to sample the inventive modern cooking, based on fresh produce from the inn's garden and its own livestock. The former Royal Palace chef Hans Beck Thomsen is regarded as among the nation's best. The homely rooms feature paintings by Danish artist Johannes Larsen, who stayed here to paint the nearby lake.
☒ Strandvejen 234, 6854 Henne. **Map** p42 A3.
█ 75 25 54 00. FAX 75 25 54 99. ██ b,l,d. **Rooms** 6.
● Oct-Apr. ⊠ AE, DC, MC, V. ⓚⓚ

KØBENHAVN (COPENHAGEN)

Ascot This former public bathhouse for Copenhagen's high society was redesigned by architect Martin Nyrop in 1902, utilizing the same Italian Renaissance aesthetic he employed on the city's town hall. The result is a light and airy city retreat, where etchings and a blue-and-white colour scheme evoke building's bathing history.
☒ Studiestræde 61, 1554 København. **Map** p43 D4.
█ 33 12 60 00. FAX 33 14 60 40. @ hotel@ascot-hotel.dk
██ b. **Rooms** 150. ██ █ ● Never.
⊠ AE, DC, MC, V. ⓚⓚ

JYDERUP

Bromølle Kro This thatched highway inn proudly claims to be the oldest in Denmark (dating back to 1198) and is a popular stopover. Pheasant and venison are among the specialities of an excellent kitchen. Compared to the pleasant, subdued tone of the public rooms, the vivid pinks, oranges, lime greens in the bedrooms might seem rather incongruous.
☒ Slagelsevej 78, 4450 Jyderup. **Map** p42 C3.
█ 58 25 00 90. FAX 58 25 02 38. ██ b,l,d.
Rooms 8. ● first 2 weeks Jan. ⊠ DC, MC, V. ⓚⓚ

KØBENHAVN (COPENHAGEN)

Ibsens A quirky use of antique furnishings (single travellers may like to request the four-poster single bed) makes Ibsens an individualistic choice. Room styles range from the romantic through the bohemian to Scandinavian simplicity. Located in the elegant 'Latin Quarter' area, 15 minutes' walk from Copenhagen's centre.
☒ Vendersgade 23, 1363 København.
Map p43 D4. █ 33 13 19 13. FAX 33 13 19 16.
@ hotel@ibsenshotel.dk ██ b. **Rooms** 103.
● Never. ⊠ AE, DC, MC, V. ⓚⓚ

FREDENSBORG

Pension Bondehuset A 180-year-old thatched farmhouse with panoramic views over Lake Esrum and Grib Forest. Salmon fishing, golf.
☒ Sørupvej 14, 3480 Fredensborg. **Map** p43 D3.
█ 48 48 01 12. FAX 48 48 03 01. ██ b,l,d.
Rooms 15. ⓚⓚ

FREDERICIA

Hotel Hybylund Originally a worker's dance hall, now an upmarket beach hotel – but none of the bedrooms has sea views.
☒ Fælledvej 58, 7000 Fredericia. **Map** p42 B4.
█ 75 92 98 00. FAX 75 91 15 81. ██ b,d.
Rooms 12. ⓚⓚⓚ

HADERSLEV

Hotel Harmonien A deceptively modern, smart city hotel: King Frederick VII danced in the banqueting hall in 1863. Friendly staff.
☒ Gåskærgade 19, 6100 Haderslev. **Map** p42 B4.
█ 74 52 37 20. FAX 74 52 44 51. ██ b,d. **Rooms** 28.
● Christmas and New Year. ⓚⓚ

HELSINGØR

Marienlyst Offering an impressive view of Kronborg Castle, this contemporary hotel includes an aquapark, casino, and beach bar.
☒ Nordre Strandvej 2, 3000 Helsingør. **Map** p43 D3.
█ 49 21 40 00. FAX 49 21 49 00. @ gw@marienlyst.dk.
██ b,l,d. **Rooms** 232. ⓚⓚ

KØBENHAVN (COPENHAGEN)

Triton A poorly maintained exterior does little justice to a fashionable hotel located in the heart of town. Marble floors, light wood panelling and steel pillars are incorporated into a contemporary aesthetic. Rooms feature huge windows and are informally stylish. A varied buffet breakfast is served in the hotel's chic café-bar.
⊠ Helgolandsgade 7-11, 1653 København.
Map p43 D4. 📞 33 31 32 66. 📠 33 31 69 70.
@ booking@phg.dk 🍽 b. **Rooms** 123. ● Never.
🅴 AE, DC, MC, V. Ⓚ Ⓚ Ⓚ

KOLDING

Hotel Kolding-Fjord A thoroughly modern hotel with no shortage of style, set in a forest that slopes down to the fjord. Rooms are fashionably neutral and have balconies overlooking the surrounding countryside. A handy location for nearby Legoland, Trapholt Museum of Modern Art, and the Hans Christian Andersen museum.
⊠ Fjordvej 154, 6000 Kolding. **Map** p42 B4.
📞 75 51 00 00. 📠 75 51 00 51. @ hotel@ koldingfjord.dk 🍽 b,l,d. **Rooms** 114. 🎱
● Christmas and New Year. 🅴 AE, DC, MC, V. Ⓚ Ⓚ Ⓚ

KØGE

Vallø Slot Expectations inevitably rise on the long drive up the tree-lined path to the brooding Vallø Castle, and the surroundings within landscaped grounds are certainly regal in this unsurpassable location. But despite the very romantic setting, much of the accommodation here is rather plain and unimaginative; two suites include spa-pools and luxurious four-poster beds.
⊠ Slotsgade 1, Vallø, 4600 Køge. **Map** p43 D4.
📞 56 26 70 20. 📠 56 26 70 71. 🍽 b,l,d. **Rooms** 11.
🎱 ● Never. 🅴 AE, DC, MC, V. Ⓚ Ⓚ Ⓚ

MILLINGE

Falsted Kro It's no wonder that most visitors to this upmarket retreat (originally a 16th-century smuggler's inn) are loyal regulars. The culinary reputation of owner Jean-Louis Lieffroy reaches far beyond Danish borders. Here, the fresh produce of South Funen (the 'Garden of Denmark') is given a classical French twist.
⊠ Assensvej, 5642 Millinge. **Map** p42 B4.
📞 62 68 11 11. 📠 62 68 11 62.
@ Falstedkro@vip.cybercity.dk 🍽 b,l,d.
Rooms 19. 🎱 ● Never. 🅴 AE, DC, MC, V. Ⓚ Ⓚ Ⓚ Ⓚ

HOVBORG
Hovborg Kro A small river runs through the inn's garden; angling opportunities. Traditional cooking. Adventure playground for kids.
⊠ Holmeavej 2, 6682 Hovborg. **Map** p42 A3.
📞 75 39 60 33. 📠 75 39 60 13. 🍽 b,l,d.
Rooms 55. Ⓚ Ⓚ

HUNDESTED
Hundested Kro A lively harbourside hotel in the industrial port of Hundested. The homely bar and restaurant are renowned for delicious locally caught fish specialities. Good value.
⊠ Nørregade 10, 3390 Hundested. **Map** p43 D3.
📞 47 93 75 38. 📠 47 93 78 61. 🍽 b,d. **Rooms** 64. Ⓚ

KERTEMINDE
Tornøes Hotel Popular harbourside hotel. Rooms are quite basic but the Danish cuisine is of a high standard. The café gets lively at weekends.
⊠ Strandgade 2, 5300 Kerteminde. **Map** p42 C2.
📞 65 32 16 05. 📠 65 32 48 40. 🍽 b,l,d.
Rooms 27. Ⓚ Ⓚ

KØBENHAVN (COPENHAGEN)
71 Nyhavn Watch cruise ships dock from this converted 19th-century spice warehouse. Rooms make good use of the original wooden beams.
⊠ Nyhavn 71, 1051 København. **Map** p43 D4.
📞 33 11 85 85. 📠 33 93 15 85. @ 71nyhavnhotel@ arp-hansen.dk 🍽 b,d. **Rooms** 84. Ⓚ Ⓚ Ⓚ

MILLINGE

Steensgaard Herregård This grand manor house dates back to the 14th century. The tone of the elegant retreat is set by touches such as the Louis XIV desk in the sitting room and the Italian rococo furnishings in the 'Yellow Room'. The restaurant menu is surprisingly contemporary. The queen of Denmark often stays here during the autumn hunting season.
⊠ Steensgaard, 5642 Millinge. **Map** p42 B4.
📞 62 61 94 90. 𝐅𝐀𝐗 63 61 78 61. 🍴 b,l,d.
🍽 ● February. 💳 AE, DC, MC, V. Ⓚ Ⓚ Ⓚ

NÆSTVED

Hotel Vinhuset Located in the old town, on the site of a former monastery, this 18th-century inn now makes a characterful yet smart hotel with stylishly modern rooms. There are two restaurants (Les Baraques, specializing in 'nouvelle' French cuisine, and Bytinget, serving traditional Danish dishes) and a vaulted bar where Black Friar monks lived in the 15th century.
⊠ Sct. Peders Kirkeplads 4, 4700 Næstved.
Map p43 D4. 📞 55 72 08 07. 𝐅𝐀𝐗 55 72 03 35. 🍴 b,l,d.
Rooms 58. ● Never. 💳 AE, DC, MC, V. Ⓚ Ⓚ

NÆSTVED

Menstrup Kro A vivacious place, especially at weekends when the large bars and lounges play host to live music and dancing. Other facilities include an indoor pool, a sauna and tennis courts. Rooms feature all mod-cons and the staff always have a smile. There is an interesting memorial to the Danish Hussar Regiment.
⊠ Menstrup Bygade 29, 4700 Næstved. **Map** p43 D4.
📞 55 44 30 03. 𝐅𝐀𝐗 55 44 33 63. @ menstrup@get2net.dk 🍴 b,l,d. **Rooms** 79. 🏊 🍽 ● Never.
💳 AE, DC, MC, V. Ⓚ Ⓚ

NØRRE NEBEL

Nymindegab Kro With its superb views across Jutland's wild western landscape and homely restaurant, this is a perfect example of a traditional Danish inn. It has been run by the Kristensen family since 1849. It's popular with deer hunters in autumn, bird watchers during the summer (bird sanctuary open April to August). Good choice for families: pool, friendly staff.
⊠ Nymindegab 1, 6830 Nørre Nebel. **Map** p42 A3.
📞 75 28 92 11. 𝐅𝐀𝐗 75 28 94 25. 🍴 b,l,d. **Rooms** 42.
🏊 🍽 ● mid-Dec to end Jan. 💳 AE, DC, MC, V. Ⓚ Ⓚ

KØBENHAVN (COPENHAGEN)
Admiral Lots of timbered joists and views of ships gliding into harbour from this converted granary. Staff wear naval uniform.
⊠ Toldbodgade 24-28, 1253 København. **Map** p43 D4.
📞 33 74 14 14. 𝐅𝐀𝐗 33 74 14 16. @ booking@admiral-hotel.dk 🍴 b,l,d. **Rooms** 365. Ⓚ Ⓚ Ⓚ

KØBENHAVN (COPENHAGEN)
Mayfair An ornate, stately hotel furnished in classic English style. Friendly staff reduce the air of formality.
⊠ Helgolandsgade 3, 1653 København.
Map p43 D4. 📞 33 31 48 01. 𝐅𝐀𝐗 33 23 96 86.
@ info@themayfairhotel.dk 🍴 b. **Rooms** 20. Ⓚ Ⓚ

KØBENHAVN (COPENHAGEN)
Sophie Modern harbourside hotel decorated in bold hues. Suites feature floor-to-ceiling windows. Inventive international menu.
⊠ Sankt Annæ Plads 21, 1021 København.
Map p43 D4. 📞 33 13 34 00. 𝐅𝐀𝐗 33 11 77 07.
@ anglehot@remmen.dk 🍴 b,l,d. **Rooms** 134. Ⓚ Ⓚ Ⓚ

KONGENSBRO
Kongensbro Kro Friendly family-run inn. All the rooms have great views across the biggest river in Denmark, the Gudenåen.
⊠ Kongensbro 46, 4424 Kongensbro. **Map** p42 B3.
📞 86 87 01 77. 𝐅𝐀𝐗 86 87 92 17. 🍴 b,d.
Rooms 15. Ⓚ Ⓚ

NYSTED, LOLLAND

The Cottage The chic retreat on the quiet island of Lolland is situated close to a pretty beach and to Nysted, Denmark's oldest harbour. Its English influence stems from the hotel's original owners, two English teachers from a nearby music school, who created a home-from-home in 1920. The food is excellent – landlord Fiari Hodanloo insists on fresh saffron for fish sauce, his speciality.
⊠ Skansevej 19, 4880 Nysted, Lolland. **Map** p43 D5.
📞 54 87 16 00. ℻ 54 87 16 44. 🍴 b,l,d. **Rooms** 22.
⬤ Never. 🛋 AE, DC, MC, V. Ⓚ

ROLD

Rold Gammel Kro A hospitable inn on the outskirts of the Rold Skov, Denmark's biggest forest, the Rold Gammel Kro specializes in organising hunting trips. Rooms are modern and comfortable, and there is an international menu. During the 19th century the inn served as the base for a travelling circus and there is a fascinating circus museum next door.
⊠ Hobrovej 11, 9510 Rold. **Map** p42 B2. 📞 98 56 17 00.
℻ 98 56 11 25. @ rold-gl-kro@nethotel1.dk 🍴 b,l,d.
Rooms 26. ⬤ Never. 🛋 AE, DC, MC, V. ⓀⓀ

RIBE

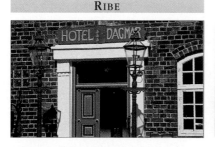

Hotel Dagmar Ribe is Denmark's oldest town, and the tremendously popular Dagmar its oldest hotel (built 1581). The small, unprepossessing house became a protected building in 1963 and there is a genuine respect for its history; many of the floors are uneven and the ceilings low. The two restaurants are majestic – it almost feels like eating within a grand museum.
⊠ Torvet 1, 6760 Ribe. **Map** p42 A4. 📞 75 42 00 33.
℻ 75 42 36 52. 🍴 b,l,d. **Rooms** 48. ⬤ Christmas and New Year. 🛋 AE, DC, MC, V. ⓀⓀⓀ

SKAGEN

Brøndums Hotel Skagen's luminous heath and dune landscape has been inspiring writers and artists since the 1800s, and Brøndums has become *the* place to stay. Hans Christian Andersen was just one of its illustrious guests. The hotel's special atmosphere makes up for its small rooms. The Skagen Museum next door has a fine collection of landscape paintings.
⊠ Anchersvej 3, 9990 Skagen. **Map** p42 C1.
📞 98 44 15 55. ℻ 98 45 15 20. 🍴 b,d. **Rooms** 48.
⬤ end Nov to end Dec. 🛋 AE, DC, MC, V. ⓀⓀⓀ

MUNKEBO

Munkebo Kro Highway inn with a restrained décor under its vast thatched roof and tudor timbering. A good stop-off.
⊠ Fjordvej 56-58, 5330 Munkebo. **Map** p42 C4.
📞 65 97 40 30. ℻ 65 97 55 64. @ munkebo@ munkebokro.dk 🍴 b,l,d. **Rooms** 20. ⓀⓀ

NYKØBING MORS

Sallingsund Færgekro On the enchanting island of Mors, individualistic interiors created by celebrated decorator/florist Jan Munch Lassen.
⊠ Sallingsundvej 104, 7900 Nykøbing Mors.
Map p42 A2. 📞 97 72 00 88. ℻ 97 72 25 40.
🍴 b,l,d. **Rooms** 42. ⓀⓀ

ØLAND

Øland Kroen An unusual mix of the old and new in this converted bakery. Small cottages in the nearby beech wood are also available.
⊠ Hammershøj 29-31, 9460 Øland. **Map** p42 B1.
📞 98 23 61 00. ℻ 98 23 61 20. 🍴 b,l,d.
Rooms 30. ⓀⓀ

RØNDE

Hubertus Kroen Intimate half-timbered inn built in 1710 within a pheasant-hunting area. Rooms are smallish but neat. There is a piano and log fire in the restaurant. Golf and fishing nearby.
⊠ Møllerup Gods, 8410 Rønde. **Map** p42 C3.
📞 86 37 10 03. ℻ 86 37 30 29. 🍴 b,l,d. **Rooms** 7. Ⓚ

For key to symbols see backflap. For price categories see *p41*

SVANEKE, BORNHOLM

Hotel Østersøen Apartment-style comfort in the idyllic island town of Svaneke. Each apartment features a kitchenette, reception room with phone and television, and one, two or three bedrooms. Rooms overlook either the cheerful harbour or the hotel's sheltered back garden and swimming pool. Beach and tennis courts 5 minutes' walk.

☒ Havnebryggen 5, 3740 Svaneke, Bornholm. **Map** p43 F4. ▐ 56 49 60 20. **FAX** 56 49 72 79. ▐▐ b,l,d. **Rooms** 64. 🏖 🎧 ● Never. ▣ AE, DC, MC, V. Ⓚ

SYDALS

Hotel Baltic Understated elegance underpins the Baltic's modish sophistication, and the hotel continually delights the eye. Rooms are individually designed with antique furnishings from across Europe, and most have sea views. Vintage wine-tasting evenings are another classy touch. A real gem.

☒ Havbo 29, 6470 Sydals. **Map** p42 B5. ▐ 74 41 52 00. **FAX** 74 41 53 33. @ info@hotel-baltic.dk ▐▐ b,l,d. **Rooms** 10. ● Christmas and New Year. ▣ DC, MC, V. ⓀⓀ

SVENDBORG

Valdemar Slot This 17th-century treasure, one of Denmark's largest privately owned palaces, enjoys a commanding position within a beachside forest. At night, it's eerily quiet, with only the Baltic wind for company – there is no reception or on-call staff. Each room is furnished with antiques and few modern conveniences (no TV). Lovingly prepared Danish cuisine.

☒ Slotsalleen 100, 5700 Svendborg. **Map** p42 C4. ▐ 62 22 59 00. **FAX** 62 22 69 10. ▐▐ b,l,d. **Rooms** 7. 🎧 ● Jan to March. ▣ AE. ⓀⓀ

THYHOLM

Tambohus Kro This harbourside inn, directly opposite the island of Jegindø, is located on the site of a Viking base. Today, this traditional fishing area is popular with nature-lovers and seafood connoisseurs. Rooms are functional; several have views across the fjord. The restaurant is famous for its speciality, fried eel.

☒ Tambohuse, 7790 Thyholm. **Map** p42 A2. ▐ 97 87 53 00. **FAX** 97 87 51 55. @ tambohus@ post7.tele.dk ▐▐ b,l,d. **Rooms** 29. ● Christmas and New Year. ▣ AE, DC, MC, V. ⓀⓀ

RØNNE, BORNHOLM

Hotel Fredensborg Ideally located near woods and a small beach, and highly regarded Danish cuisine. Smart rooms, some with balconies.

☒ Strandvejen 116, 3700 Rønne, Bornholm. **Map** p43 F4. ▐ 56 95 44 44. **FAX** 56 95 03 14. @ info@hotelfredensborg.dk ▐▐ b,l,d. **Rooms** 120. ⓀⓀ

SILKEBORG

Svostrup Kro Cosy inn by the Gudenå lake with fine views of the Gjern hills. Relaxed company, hearty Danish cuisine. Paddle steamer trips.

☒ Svostrupvej 58-60, 8600 Silkeborg. **Map** p42 B3. ▐ 86 87 70 04. **FAX** 86 87 70 47. ▐▐ b,l,d. **Rooms** 15. ⓀⓀ

SKAGEN

Aalbæk gl. Kro Modern hotel on the site of a 19th-century inn, with a dose of country spirit with a healthy dinner menu. Eco-friendly policies.

☒ Skagensvej 42, 9982 Aalbæk. **Map** p42 C1. ▐ 98 48 90 22. **FAX** 98 48 83 65. @ aalbak@ aalbak.gl.kro.dk ▐▐ b,l,d. **Rooms** 51. ⓀⓀ

SVANEKE, BORNHOLM

Siemsens Gaard Beautifully restored 17th-century merchant's house with stunning views across the harbour. Fine seafood restaurant.

☒ Havnebryggen 9, 3740 Svaneke, Bornholm. **Map** p43 F4. ▐ 56 49 61 49. **FAX** 56 49 61 03. @ hotel@siemsens.dk ▐▐ b,l,d. **Rooms** 51. ⓀⓀ

TÓRSHAVN, STREYMOY

VEJBY STRAND

Hotel Hafnia In the heart of one of the largest town of the Faroes, this traditional, family-run hotel commands a fine view over the harbour and the old town. Rooms feature contemporary design. Excellent Danish/French menu as well as Faroese fish specialities in the restaurant. Good access to both the airport and ferries. The international dialling code for Streymoy is 298.
☒ Áarvegur, FO-110 Tórshavn, Streymoy. **Map** p43 E1. 📞 31 12 70. 📠 31 52 50. @ hafnia@post.olivant.fo 🍴 b,d. **Rooms** 60. ● Never. 🃏 AE, DC, MC, V. Ⓚ Ⓚ Ⓚ

Havgården The emphasis is on relaxation and tranquillity at this old-fashioned farmhouse: rooms have no phones and there is no television. Appreciate the silence of the gardens and nearby secluded beaches, or sample an excellent Danish/French menu utilizing fresh ingredients from the inn's vegetable gardens. The rococo-style rooms are at ground level, by the gardens.
☒ Strandlyvej 1, 3210 Vejby Strand. **Map** p43 D3. 📞 48 70 57 30. 📠 48 70 57 72. 🍴 b,l,d. **Rooms** 11. 🔋 ● Sept-June. 🃏 AE, DC, MC, V. Ⓚ Ⓚ

TYSTRUP

VEJLE

Luneborg Kro This inn owes its eccentric décor (dolls' heads, badger skins, deer skulls) to owner Marianne Kiil, who collects quirky antiques on regular visits to Britain and Germany. Bedrooms are individually furnished in similarly eclectic fashion. The kitchen makes much use of local game; excellent fish buffet (summer) and duck buffet (winter). Sandy beaches 15km (11 miles).
☒ Luneborgvej 310, 9382 Tystrup. **Map** p42 C4. 📞 98 26 51 00. 📠 98 26 51 90. 🍴 b,d. **Rooms** 20. ● mid-Dec to mid-Jan. 🃏 AE, DC, MC, V. Ⓚ

Munkebjerg Hotel High in the hills of the Munkebjerg Forest, this top-class hotel offers everything from a professional golf course and museum to a casino, nightclub, bakery and butcher. Rooms combine clean Danish design with modern comforts. Panorama restaurant with breathtaking views across the fjord.
☒ Munkebjerg 125, 7100 Vejle. **Map** p42 B3. 📞 76 42 85 00. 📠 75 72 08 86. @ reception@ munkebjerg.dk 🍴 b,l,d. **Rooms** 148. ▦ 🍴 ● Christmas. 🃏 AE, DC, MC, V. Ⓚ Ⓚ Ⓚ Ⓚ

TÓRSHAVN, STREYMOY

Hotel Föroyar Arguably the pick of hotels in the Faroes, and the best view. Bright, airy rooms. See Hotel Hafnia above for dialling code to Streymoy.
☒ Vió Oyggjavegin, FO-110 Tórshavn, Streymoy. **Map** p43 E1. 📞 31 75 00. 📠 31 60 19. @ hotel-fo@post.olivant.fo 🍴 b,l,d. **Rooms** 108. Ⓚ Ⓚ Ⓚ

TÓRSHAVN, STREYMOY

Skansin Guesthouse Friendly and clean, but rather basic. Convenient for ferries. See Hotel Hafnia above for dialling code to Streymoy.
☒ Jekaragøta, FO-110 Tórshavn, Streymoy. **Map** p43 E1. 📞 31 22 42. 📠 31 06 57. 🍴 b. **Rooms** 11. Ⓚ

VÁGAR

Hotel Vágar Modern facilities among the natural beauty of the region. Hiking, fishing and sailing trips around the cliffs can be arranged. The international dialling code to Vágar is 298.
☒ FO-380 Sørvágur. **Map** p43 D1. 📞 33 29 55. 📠 33 23 10. 🍴 b,l,d. **Rooms** 26. Ⓚ Ⓚ

VIBY

Viby Kro Located next to the railway station, this traditional town inn comes complete with smoky bar and hearty Scandinavian fare. Rooms are quite basic but homely.
☒ Skolvej 1, 4130 Viby. **Map** p43 D4. 📞 46 19 30 21. 📠 46 19 49 21. 🍴 b,d. **Rooms** 16. Ⓚ

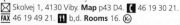

IRELAND

IRELAND

Visiting Ireland is not just about historic sights, dramatic scenery, immersing yourself in great literary and musical traditions, or indulging in a pint or two of the Black Stuff (see under Food and Drink). It's also about meeting the Irish people on their own turf. Their friendly welcome and easy-going way of life may be a well-worn cliché, but as anyone who has visited the Emerald Isle will tell you, it is very much the point of Ireland. An informal atmosphere and personal attention prevail in the plentiful guest-houses, farmhouses and small hotels dotted around Ireland, from traditional cottages in the West, to Georgian townhouses in Dublin.

Ashford Castle and Country Estate, page 60, has a stunning location

IRELAND REGION BY REGION

Ireland divides approximately into six regions.

Northern Ireland
In recent years 'The Troubles' have all but extinguished the Northern Irish overseas tourist economy. In reality, however, you are far safer here than in many other destinations.

The countryside is striking: the lunar landscape of the legendary Giant's Causeway, the nine green Glens of Antrim and the romantic Mountains of Mourne are the area's three highlights.

Northern Ireland's three principal cities, Belfast, Londonderry and Armagh ('the spiritual capital of Ireland'), pack in a wealth of ancient and recent history.

The Northwest and West
The classic West of Ireland verdant valleys and hillscapes are to be found here, particularly in Counties Sligo, Mayo and Galway and the Connemara region. The lively city of Galway is a delight, as are the timeless Aran Islands. County Clare boasts the awesome Cliffs of Moher and the extraordinary limestone landscape of the Burren. Part of 'the South' in name only, dramatic windswept County Donegal is in fact Ireland's northernmost point.

The Midlands
The least-known and visited part of the country comprises large tracts of farmland and bogland, small county towns and a number of historic sites. Perhaps chief of these is Clonmacnoise, which can claim to be Ireland's most important monastic remains.

Dublin
Booming and bustling on a tide of high technology and tourism, the capital city has some top-notch hotels; from U2's post-modern Clarence Hotel to the splendidly old-world Shelbourne (both page 61) and some beautiful Georgian townhouses with every facility and comfort. You'll pay a premium for the privilege of staying here, but it's worthwhile.

The Southeast
Nestled amid the beautiful Wicklow Mountains are two of Ireland's most memorable sights: the atmospheric ruined monastic settlement of Glendalough, and the gardens of Powerscourt. Counties Wexford and Kilkenny are also known for their medieval monastic settlements and the attractive historic towns of Waterford (world-famous for its glass) and Kilkenny.

The Southwest
The Dingle Peninsula is the greenest part of the Emerald Isle and is rich in ancient sites. Nearby, the equally breathtaking landscapes of the Ring of Kerry attract coach parties by the score. County Cork is the home of the Blarney Stone and the enjoyable little town of Cork.

HIGHLIGHTS

Hotels illustrated on these introductory pages are by no means the only highlights. Other favourites include the idyllically secluded St Ernan's House Hotel in Donegal Bay (page 60); the charming, waterfront Narrows in Portaferry (page 64); and Dublin's sleek Fitzwilliam Hotel (page 61).

FOOD AND DRINK

THE TRADITIONAL food of Ireland – potatoes and root vegetables in simple fish and meat dishes – has improved beyond recognition in recent years. The cooking has become lighter, healthier and more cosmopolitan – in fact 'New Irish'.

Old favourites include the ubiquitous Irish stew, a casserole of mutton or lamb and vegetables, and coddle, a mix of pork sausages, bacon, potato and onion. Champ is buttery mashed potatoes with scallions (spring onions). The Irish are also justifiably proud of their fish and shellfish.

The full Irish breakfast is a national institution. Typically it comprises egg, sausage, bacon, black pudding (made from dried blood), tomatoes and toast. The Irish also eat heartily at lunch and dinner.

The best genuine Irish food can be found in pubs. These are also often the most congenial and the cheapest places to eat, but quality can vary enormously.

Few visitors leave Ireland without sampling a drop of smooth, creamy Black Stuff, which is invariably Guinness, a stout or porter-style of beer which derives its distinct flavour and colour from roasted malt and barley and a high hop content. Guinness is always drunk chilled and is allowed to settle for a few minutes. The other national drink is Irish whiskey. This is smoother than Scotch (Scottish whisky) and lacks its smoky flavour. In the pub, asking for a beer by name will get you a pint. If you want a half-pint, ask for a 'glass' of your chosen beer.

OTHER PRACTICAL INFORMATION

BOOK WELL in advance for hotels in Dublin year-round and in other heavily visited spots.

The rules of the road follow those of Great Britain: drive on the left, give way to the right. Road signs are often in both English and Gaelic and it may be useful to

Longueville House, page 63

remember that *An Lár* means town centre. Note too that old signs in miles and new signs in kilometers may (confusingly) both be in use.

Language Although Ireland is officially bilingual, English is the principal language. However, in the parts of Ireland known as the Gaeltacht (principally along the west coast), Gaelic is still the main language. In the remotest parts of the Gaeltacht, English may not be spoken at all.

Currency Republic of Ireland: the Irish *punt,* normally called a pound (£), and divided into 100 pence. The value is usually close to the British pound's. Northern Ireland: the British pound.

Shops Generally open 9am–5:30 or 6pm, Mon– Sat. Smaller towns may have an early closing day, many towns have late shopping on Thursday and/or Friday. In towns and cities, super-markets may open from noon to 6pm on Sundays.

Tipping Ireland is not a tip-conscious society. Where restaurants add a service charge there is no need to tip. Otherwise round up the bill to around 10 per cent. A helpful taxi-driver will expect 10 per cent and porters, tour guides and chamber-maids are also usually tipped.

If you want to show the bartender your appreciation, offer him or her a drink.

Telephoning To make calls inside the Republic of Ireland, dial the whole number, including the initial zero. To call the Irish Republic from the UK, dial 00 353 and omit the first zero; from the US, 011 353.

To call Northern Ireland from the UK, dial the number, including the first zero of the area code; from the US, dial 011 44, omitting the zero of the area code.

Public Holidays Republic of Ireland: 1 January; 17 March (St Patrick's Day); Easter Monday; first Monday in May (May Holiday); first Monday in June (June Holiday); first Monday in August (August Holiday); last Mon-day in October; 25 and 26 December.

Northern Ireland: *See Great Britain, page 71.*

IRELAND PRICE BANDS

IRISH HOTELS are officially classified by stars, from one to five, but don't be too influenced by this. Our price bands refer, as usual, to the price of a standard double room in high season.

Breakfast is often, but not always, quoted within the room rate. Prices quoted for rooms include all taxes and often the service charge.

ⓔ	under £60
ⓔⓔ	£60–£120
ⓔⓔⓔ	£120–£180
ⓔⓔⓔⓔ	over £180

The Kildare Hotel and Country Club, page 65

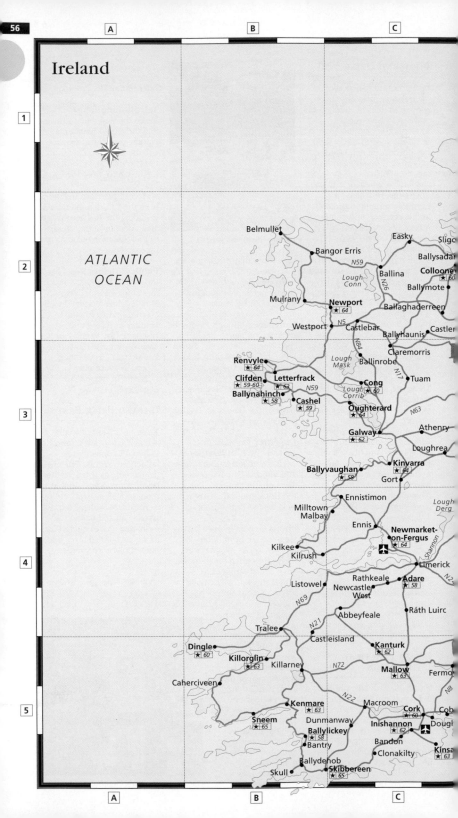

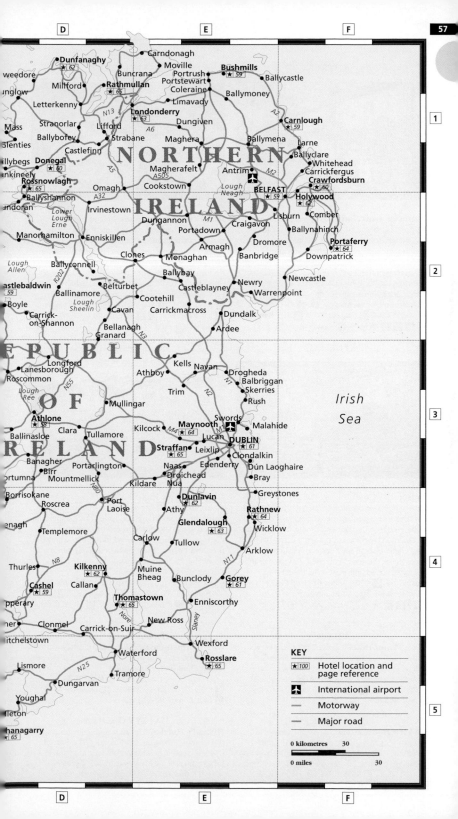

ADARE

Dunraven Arms Hotel Adare is described as the prettiest tourist village in Ireland; this long, low, yellow-fronted inn is in the main street, among thatched cottages and prize-winning gardens. It is smoothly run along traditional lines, yet there is nothing old-fashioned about the extensive facilities: two restaurants, large heated indoor pool, and steam room.
⊠ Adare, Co Limerick. **Map** p56 C4. 【 (061) 396633. FAX (061) 396541. @ dunraven@iol.ie ⑪ b,l,d. **Rooms** 76. ≋ ⑪ 🅾 ⬤ Never. 🖾 AE, DC, MC, V. ⓔⓔⓔ

BALLYLICKEY

Ballylickey Manor House Ireland's veteran Relais and Chateaux establishment is perfectly placed at the head of Bantry Bay, with views of the sea from the front rooms. In the main house are pretty suites; wooden cottages by the pool house tidy rooms. The French restaurant (dinner only) is reached through charming gardens.
⊠ Ballylickey, Bantry Bay, Co Cork. **Map** p56 B5. 【 (027) 50071. FAX (027) 50124. @ ballymh@tinet.ie ⑪ b,d. **Rooms** 12. ≋ 🅾 ⬤ early Nov to late March. 🖾 AE, DC, MC, V. ⓔⓔⓔ

ATHLONE

Hodson Bay Hotel The large white hotel stands by the shores of Lough Ree, in open countryside and next to the golf course, with views of islands in the lake from the bar and dining room. Rooms are smartly co-ordinated; dinner is eaten by candlelight. Superb facilities and reasonable prices make this excellent value. Private marina.
⊠ Roscommon Rd, Athlone, Co Westmeath. **Map** p57 D3. 【 (0902) 92444. FAX (0902) 92688. @ hodson@iol.ie ⑪ b,l,d. **Rooms** 100. ≋ ⑪ 🅾 ⬤ Never. 🖾 AE, DC, MC, V. ⓔⓔ

BALLYVAUGHAN

Gregans Castle High standards of service and an excellent table are assured at this country house hotel, set in a green valley in the limestone Burren area. The dining room has views of Galway Bay; lunch is served in the bar, with turf fires and beams. The largest bedrooms are in a new wing. Good walking country, within easy driving distance of Shannon.
⊠ Ballyvaughan, Co Clare. **Map** p56 C3. 【 (065) 7077005. FAX (065) 7077111. @ res@gregans.ie ⑪ b,l,d. **Rooms** 22. ⬤ mid-Oct to mid-March. 🖾 MC, V. ⓔⓔⓔ

ADARE

Adare Manor Hotel Massive Victorian pile with Gothic façade, formal gardens and vast estate. Style is grand; indoor pool; golf course; riding.
⊠ Adare, Co Limerick. **Map** p56 C4. 【 (061) 396566. FAX (061) 396124. @ reservations@adaremanor.com ⑪ b,l,d. **Rooms** 63. ⓔⓔⓔ

BALLYLICKEY

Sea View House Hotel Owner-run Victorian house with garden and sea views. Legendary hospitality; accomplished country-house cooking.
⊠ Ballylickey, Bantry, Co Cork. **Map** p56 B5. 【 (027) 50073. FAX (027) 51555. @ cmv@indigo.ie ⑪ b,d. **Rooms** 17. ⓔⓔ

BALLYNAHINCH

Ballynahinch Castle A Connemara castle with its own salmon and trout fishery and 13,000-acre shoot. Dine on local produce.
⊠ Recess, Connemara, Co Galway. **Map** p56 B3. 【 (095) 31006. FAX (095) 31085. @ bhinch@iol.ie ⑪ b,l,d. **Rooms** 28. ⓔⓔⓔ

BALLYVAUGHAN

Hyland's Hotel In a small seaside village, among the strange limestone landscape of The Burren, this snug old coaching inn offers good value.
⊠ Ballyvaughan, Co Clare. **Map** p56 C3. 【 (065) 7077037. FAX (065) 7077131. @ hylands@tinet.ie ⑪ b,l,d. **Rooms** 30. ⓔⓔ

BELFAST

McCausland Hotel In the city's commercial heart, two former seed warehouses opened as a stylish luxury hotel in 1998. It retains an ornate Italianate façade, columns and beamed ceilings on the ground floor. Upstairs are businesslike bedrooms with smart bathrooms. Special rooms for women travellers. 'Gourmet' restaurant.
⊠ 34-38 Victoria St, Belfast BT1 3GH. **Map** p57 F2. Ⓒ (01232) 220200. ℻ (01232) 220220. @ info@mccauslandhotel.com 🍴 b,l,d. **Rooms** 60. ⬤ Christmas and New Year. 🗩 AE, DC, MC, V. ⒺⒺⒺ

CASHEL (Co TIPPERARY)

Cashel Palace Hotel At foot of the Rock of Cashel (dramatically lit at night), a lovingly restored and intriguing 18th-century townhouse in delightful walled gardens. Public rooms are panelled in pine; bedrooms have canopied beds and good-sized bathrooms. New rooms in former stables opened in 1999. Historic town.
⊠ Main Street, Cashel, Co Tipperary. **Map** p57 D4. Ⓒ (062) 62707. ℻ (062) 61521. @ reception@ cashel-palace.ie 🍴 b,l,d. **Rooms** 23. 🌡 ⬤ Christmas. 🗩 AE, DC, MC, V. ⒺⒺⒺ

BUSHMILLS

The Bushmills Inn This restored coaching inn is the perfect place to enjoy an evening in front of a turf fire, and a Black Bush from the nearby Bushmills whiskey distillery. The Victorian-style bar (gas lighting) adjoins the original kitchen. Bedrooms in the old inn are smallish; the riverside Mill House annexe houses larger ones.
⊠ 25 Main St, Bushmills, Co Antrim BT57 8QA. **Map** p57 E1. Ⓒ (012657) 32339. ℻ (012657) 32048. @ info@bushmills-inn.com 🍴 b,l,d. **Rooms** 32. 🌡 ⬤ Never. 🗩 AE, MC, V. ⒺⒺ

CASTLEBALDWIN

Cromleach Lodge Country House The small, beautifully appointed hotel is set among hills with views over Lough Arrow. All rooms have lake views. The hotel and its restaurant scoop up awards for their impressive attention to detail and friendly service. The area has peacefulness in abundance and is a walker's paradise.
⊠ Castlebaldwin, Boyle, Co Sligo. **Map** p57 D2. Ⓒ (071) 65155. ℻ (071) 65455. @ cromleac@iol.ie 🍴 b,d. **Rooms** 10. 🌡 ⬤ early Nov to end Jan. 🗩 AE, DC, MC, V. ⒺⒺⒺ

CARNLOUGH

Londonderry Arms Hotel Georgian coaching inn, once bequeathed to Winston Churchill, in an historic fishing village; rooms with harbour views.
⊠ Carnlough, Co Antrim, BT44 0EU. **Map** p57 F1. Ⓒ (01574) 885255. ℻ (01574) 885263. @ lda@ glensofantrim.com 🍴 b,l,d. **Rooms** 35. ⒺⒺ

CASHEL (Co GALWAY)

Cashel House The relaxed country house has winding paths through exotic gardens to its own beach. Antiques, turf fires; tennis, riding.
⊠ Cashel, Co Galway. **Map** p56 B3. Ⓒ (095) 31001. ℻ (095) 31077. @ cashelhh@iol.ie 🍴 b,l,d. **Rooms** 32. ⒺⒺⒺ

CASHEL (Co GALWAY)

Zetland Country House Hotel The 19th-century manor house is garlanded in awards for its food and care. Pretty gardens; sea views; tennis court.
⊠ Cashel Bay, Co Galway. **Map** p56 B3. Ⓒ (095) 31111. ℻ (095) 31117. @ zetland@iol.ie 🍴 b,l,d. **Rooms** 19. ⒺⒺⒺ

CLIFDEN

Ardagh Hotel Purpose-built, family-run hotel, as close to the seashore as could be managed; wonderful sunset views from the dining room.
⊠ Ballyconneely Rd, Clifden, Co Galway. **Map** p56 B3. Ⓒ (095) 21384. ℻ (095) 21314. @ ardaghhotel@tinet.ie 🍴 b,l,d. **Rooms** 17. ⒺⒺ

CLIFDEN

Rock Glen Country House Hotel The 18th-century shooting lodge is one of the most romantic hotels in Ireland. In the extensive grounds, grassy paths lead through a meadow down to the seashore. Inside, sitting rooms are cosy, with turf fires; a large conservatory has views towards the bay. Tennis court.
☒ Clifden, Co Galway. **Map** p56 B3. 📞 (095) 21035/ 21395. 📠 (095) 21737. @ rockglen@iol.ie 🍴 b,l,d.
Rooms 29. 🔵 ◐ mid-Jan to mid-March.
🅰 AE, DC, MC, V. ⓔⓔⓔ

CORK

Arbutus Lodge Hotel The family-owned townhouse (once the home of the Lord Mayor of Cork) is named after the flowering shrub in the prize-winning garden. Inside is an outstanding collection of modern Irish art. The restaurant – a former ballroom with old gaslight fittings – is considered one of the Ireland's best. Fine city views; five minutes from the centre.
☒ Montenotte, Cork, Co Cork. **Map** p56 C5. 📞 (021) 501237. 📠 (021) 502893. @ arbutus@iol.ie 🍴 b,l,d.
Rooms 20. 🔵 ◐ Christmas. 🅰 AE, DC, MC, V. ⓔⓔ

CONG

Ashford Castle and Country Estate The massive mock-Gothic pile, built for the Guinness family in late 1800s, is now American-owned and one of Ireland's most luxurious castle hotels. It has a stunning location on the shores of Lough Corrib, with views of the lake's many islands, and is surrounded by formal gardens. Egon Ronay Best Hotel in Ireland for seven years running.
☒ Cong, Co Mayo. **Map** p56 C3. 📞 (092) 46003. 📠 (092) 46260. @ ashford@ashford.ie 🍴 b,l,d.
Rooms 83. 🎾 🔵 ◐ Never. 🅰 AE, DC, MC, V. ⓔⓔⓔⓔ

DONEGAL

St Ernan's House Hotel The hotel achieves its aim of providing a bolt hole from the pressures of modern life: it is set on a secluded tidal island in Donegal Bay, joined to the mainland by a causeway. The house was built in 1826 by a nephew of the Duke of Wellington; original features remain. Magical views from many rooms.
☒ St Ernan's Island, Donegal, Co Donegal.
Map p57 D1. 📞 (073) 21065. 📠 (073) 22098.
@ info@sainternans.com 🍴 b, d. **Rooms** 12.
◐ end Oct to mid-April. 🅰 MC, V. ⓔⓔⓔ

COLLOONEY

Markree Castle In Yeats country and home of the Cooper family for 350 years, one of the finest castles of its age; magnificent gilded dining room.
☒ Collooney, Co Sligo. **Map** p56 C2. 📞 (071) 67800. 📠 (071) 67840. @ markreecastle@iol.ie 🍴 b,l,d.
Rooms 30. ⓔⓔⓔ

CORK

Maryborough House Hotel A mix of old and new gives charm and character to fine Georgian house. Garden; library; heated indoor pool.
☒ Maryborough Hill, Douglas, Cork, Co Cork.
Map p56 C5. 📞 (021) 365555. 📠 (021) 365662.
@ maryboro@indigo.ie 🍴 b,l,d. **Rooms** 57. ⓔⓔⓔ

CRAWFORDSBURN

The Old Inn One of Ireland's oldest inns, with history going back to 1614; panelling, log fires, canopied beds and modern comfort.
☒ Crawfordsburn, Co Down BT19 1JH. **Map** p57 F1.
📞 (01247) 853255. 📠 (01247) 852775.
@ info@theoldinn.com 🍴 b,l,d. **Rooms** 33. ⓔⓔ

DINGLE

Dingle Skellig Hotel Lively, modern hotel with sea views and pleasant decor. Irish entertainment; heated pool; gardens; local seafood.
☒ Dingle, Co Kerry. **Map** p56 B5. 📞 (066) 9151144.
📠 (066) 9151501. @ dsk@iol.ie 🍴 b,l,d.
Rooms 115. ⓔⓔⓔ

DUBLIN

The Clarence Hotel The 1850s building on the Liffey's 'Left Bank' is now owned by the rock band U2 and one of the most fashionable places to stay and be seen. A makeover in 1996 retained and enhanced the original Arts and Crafts features. Bedrooms have a classy minimalist simplicity; the penthouse has a rooftop hot tub.
⊠ 6-8 Wellington Quay, Dublin 2. **Map** p57 E3.
⟪ (01) 670 9000. **FAX** (01) 670 7800.
@ clarence@indigo.ie 🍴 b,l,d. **Rooms** 50.
● Never. 🗲 AE, DC, MC, V. ££££

DUBLIN

Number 31 City-centre, award-winning guesthouse in a leafy mews (once home of one of Ireland's leading architects, Sam Stephenson) that has spread to an adjacent Georgian house. Californian-style 1970s design extends to the sunken sitting area and the garden. Breakfast is served in the plant-filled conservatory. Good value. New owners took over in 1999.
⊠ 31 Leeson Close, Dublin 2. **Map** p57 E3. ⟪ (01) 676 5011. **FAX** (01) 676 2929. @ number31@iol.ie 🍴 b.
Rooms 19. ● Christmas week. 🗲 AE, MC, V. ££

DUBLIN

The Fitzwilliam Hotel Opened in 1998, the Fitzwilliam is a sleek essay in designer chic by the Conran Group: frosted glass, leather sofas, moody lighting, and everywhere grey. The roof garden, Conrad Gallagher's restaurant, and the hotel's position on St Stephen's Green make this one of the city's most fashionable venues.
⊠ St Stephen's Green, Dublin 2. **Map** p57 E3.
⟪ (01) 478 7000. **FAX** (01) 478 7878.
@ eng@fitzwilliamh.com 🍴 b,l,d. **Rooms** 130.
● Never. 🗲 AE, DC, MC, V. £££££

GOREY

Marlfield House Hotel The magnificent and romantic 1830s country house was once the home of the Earls of Courtown. The hotel has received many accolades and is popular with celebrities. Rooms and bathrooms are suitably luxurious; there are six sumptuous 'state' rooms and a helipad. The vast and beautiful gardens, which include a lake, are a wildlife preserve.
⊠ Gorey, Co Wexford. **Map** p57 E4. ⟪ (055) 21124.
FAX (055) 21572. @ marlf@iol.ie 🍴 b,l,d. **Rooms** 19. ⓘ
● mid-Dec to early Feb. 🗲 AE, DC, MC, V. £££

DONEGAL
Harvey's Point Country Hotel Purpose-built lakeside hotel provides quiet seclusion, attentive staff and a fine table. Tennis, riding, fishing.
⊠ Lough Eske, Donegal, Co Donegal. **Map** p57 D1.
⟪ (073) 22208. **FAX** (073) 22352. @ harveyspoint@ tinet.ie 🍴 b,l,d. **Rooms** 20. ££

DUBLIN
Hibernian Hotel Ornately Victorian and once a nurses' home, this luxury townhouse hotel feels like a private club; well-equipped bedrooms.
⊠ Eastmoreland Pl, Ballsbridge, Dublin 4. **Map** p57 E3.
⟪ (01) 668 7666. **FAX** (01) 660 2655. @ info@ hibernianhotel.com 🍴 b,l,d. **Rooms** 40. £££

DUBLIN
Merrion Hotel Classical elegance and superb interiors in four restored listed Georgian houses with formal gardens. Modern extension; pool.
⊠ Upper Merrion St, Dublin 2. **Map** p57 E3.
⟪ (01) 603 0600. **FAX** (01) 603 0700. @ info@ merrionhotel.com 🍴 b,l,d. **Rooms** 145. ££££

DUBLIN
Shelbourne Hotel The refined charm and traditional style and service are legendary. It's *the* place for afternoon tea. Pool; parking.
⊠ 27 St Stephen's Green, Dublin 2. **Map** p57 E3.
⟪ (01) 676 6471. **FAX** (01) 661 6006. @ shelbourneinfo@ forte-hotel.com 🍴 b,l,d. **Rooms** 169. ££££

Holywood

Culloden Hotel Once a palace of the Bishops of
Down and set in the Holywood Hills overlooking
Belfast Lough and the County Antrim coast, the
Culloden is now a five-star hotel. Facilities
include a health spa with pool and steam room.
Ten suites were refurbished in 1998. Golf nearby;
tennis, squash. Courtesy car service.
⊠ Bangor Rd, Holywood, Co Down BT18 0EX.
Map p57 F20. 🄲 (01232) 425223. **FAX** (01232) 426777.
@ res.cull@hastingshotels.com. 🍴 b,l,d. **Rooms** 79.
🛗🛏🄾◑ Christmas. 🗭 AE, DC, MC, V. ⓔⓔⓔ

Kanturk

Assolas Country House The family-owned,
17th-century greystone house has gained a
reputation for good food and warm hospitality.
The North Cork countryside is extremely
peaceful, and the house stands on the banks of
a small river, in award-winning gardens. The
kitchen makes much use of local cheeses and
the house's own organic vegetables and fruits.
⊠ Kanturk, Co Cork. **Map** p56 C5. 🄲 (029) 50015.
FAX (029) 50795. @ assolas@tinet.ie 🍴 b,d. **Rooms** 9.
🄾◑ end March to 1 Nov. 🗭 AE, MC, V. ⓔⓔⓔ

Innishannon

Innishannon House Hotel The River Brandon
borders the gardens of the country house (built
1720), and there are many walks; boating and
fishing in the grounds. Rooms are imaginatively
furnished, with modern art on the walls and a
growing collection of 'historic' baths. Seafood is
a speciality in the award-winning restaurant.
⊠ Innishannon, Co Cork. **Map** p56 C5. 🄲 (021) 775121.
FAX (021) 775609. @ innishannonhotel@ tinet.ie
🍴 b,l,d. **Rooms** 13. 🎤◑ mid-Jan to mid-March.
🗭 AE, DC, MC, V. ⓔⓔⓔ

Kilkenny

Butler House The large Georgian townhouse
was once the dower house to Kilkenny Castle,
the family seat of the earls of Ormond. The stylish
1970s interior is simple and modern,
with airy, uncluttered rooms and lots of black,
cream and white. Walk through the formal garden
to the castle. Cellar restaurant.
⊠ 16 Patrick St, Kilkenny, Co Kilkenny. **Map** p57 D4.
🄲 (056) 65707. **FAX** (056) 65626. @ res@butler.ie
🍴 b,l; d June to Sept. **Rooms** 14. ◑ 24–29 Dec.
🗭 AE, DC, MC, V. ⓔⓔ

Dunfanaghy

Arnold's Hotel This friendly, family-run
waterside hotel makes a perfect touring base.
Good food; helpful staff; striking bay views.
⊠ Dunfanaghy, Co Donegal. **Map** p57 D1.
🄲 (074) 36208. **FAX** (074) 36352.
@ arnoldshotel@tinet.ie 🍴 b,l,d. **Rooms** 30. ⓔⓔ

Dunlavin

Rathsallagh House Converted Queen Anne
stables with golf course. Luxurious bedrooms and
country house cooking at its best.
⊠ Dunlavin, Co Wicklow. **Map** p57 E4. 🄲 (045) 403112.
FAX (045) 403343. @ info@rathsallagh.com
🍴 b,l,d. **Rooms** 17. ⓔⓔⓔ

Galway

Ardilaun House Hotel Open fires and award-
winning restaurant await at the end of the tree-
lined avenue to this 19th-century house. Sauna.
⊠ Taylor's Hill, Galway, Co Galway. **Map** p56 C3.
🄲 (091) 521433. **FAX** (091) 521546. @ ardilaun@iol.ie
🍴 b,l,d. **Rooms** 89. ⓔⓔⓔ

Galway

Norman Villa The tall stone townhouse B&B
is an inspiring mixture of brass beds, modern art
and polished pine floors. Helpful hosts provide
tea, maps and parking.
⊠ 86 Lower Salthill, Galway, Co Galway. **Map** p56 C3.
🄲 **FAX** (091) 521131. 🍴 b. **Rooms** 5. ⓔⓔ

KINSALE

Blue Haven Hotel This cosy, busy hotel is much loved by Irish and American media folk. Brightly painted in blue and yellow, it features lots of nautical brass and plants; log fires in cold weather. Acclaimed seafood restaurant. The largest bedrooms are in the next-door annexe. New owners took over in 1999.
⊠ 3 Pearse St, Kinsale, Co Cork. **Map** p56 C5. 📞 (021) 772209. **FAX** (021) 774268. @ bluhaven@iol.ie 🍴 b,d. **Rooms** 18. ● Christmas; 3–28 Jan. 💳 AE, DC, MC, V. ⓔⓔⓔ

LONDONDERRY

Beech Hill Country House Hotel In a quiet suburb of Londonderry, within woodland with streams and a small lake, is this gracious late 18th-century house. Food – 'Modern Irish with global overtones' – is taken seriously; formal, elegant restaurant. A leisure centre with sauna, steam room and fitness room opened in 1999.
⊠ 32 Ardmore Rd, Londonderry, Co Londonderry BT47 3QP. **Map** p57 E2. 📞 (01504) 349279. **FAX** (01504) 345366. @ info@beech-hill.com 🍴 b,l,d. **Rooms** 27. 🎾 🌿 ● Christmas. 💳 AE, MC, V. ⓔⓔ

LETTERFRACK

Rosleague Manor The family-owned sugar-pink Georgian country house has a superb position overlooking a small harbour and Ballinakill Bay, and is hidden from the world within vast secluded gardens and woodland. The interiors are charming; rooms at the back of the house have an extra dash of originality. Fresh seafood and homegrown vegetables are a speciality.
⊠ Letterfrack, Co Galway. **Map** p56 B3. 📞 (095) 41101. **FAX** (095) 41168. 🍴 b,l,d. **Rooms** 20. 🌿 ● end Oct to before Easter. 💳 AE, DC, MC, V. ⓔⓔⓔ

MALLOW

Longueville House The O'Callaghan family is back at Longueville after a 300-year absence; from their imposing Georgian manor, the ruins of their former castle can be seen. History blends well with the culinary brilliance of chef William O'Callaghan, who uses produce from the estate's farm, gardens and nearby Blackwater River.
⊠ Mallow, Co Cork. **Map** p56 C5. 📞 (022) 47156. **FAX** (022) 47459. @ info@longuevillehouse.ie 🍴 b,d. **Rooms** 20. 🌿 ● Christmas to mid-Feb. 💳 AE, MC, V. ⓔⓔⓔ

GLENDALOUGH

Glendalough Hotel Family-run hotel beside one of Ireland's most important early monastic ruins, in the Wicklow Mountains. Good traditional cooking and remarkable dining-room views.
⊠ Glendalough, Co Wicklow. **Map** p57 E4. 📞 (0404) 45135. **FAX** (0404) 45142. 🍴 b,l,d. **Rooms** 44. ⓔⓔ

KENMARE

Park Hotel Kenmare Gracious living, world-class cuisine, friendly staff; run with consumate professionalism. Good base on the Ring of Kerry.
⊠ Kenmare, Co Kerry. **Map** p56 B5. 📞 (064) 41200. **FAX** (064) 41402. @ phkenmare@iol.ie 🍴 b,l,d. **Rooms** 49. ⓔⓔⓔⓔ

KENMARE

Sheen Falls Lodge Manor house in a splendid setting, in semi-tropical gardens, within sight and sound of the River Sheen. Heated indoor pool.
⊠ Kenmare, Co Kerry. **Map** p56 B5. 📞 (064) 41600. **FAX** (064) 41386. @ info@sheenfalls.ie 🍴 b,l,d. **Rooms** 61. ⓔⓔⓔⓔ

KILLORGLIN

Ard-na-Sidhe The 'Hill of the Fairies' is a suitably romantic gabled Edwardian house in lakeside gardens. Leisure facilities nearby.
⊠ Caragh Lake, Killorglin, Co Kerry. **Map** p56 B5. 📞 (066) 9769105. **FAX** (066) 9769282. @ khl@iol.ie 🍴 b,l,d. **Rooms** 20. ⓔⓔⓔ

MAYNOOTH

Moyglare Manor Half a mile of avenue leads to this Georgian country house, set in extensive parkland near the historic town and within easy driving distance of Dublin airport. The interior is opulent yet unusual and comfortable, with furniture and fittings of many periods; antiques in the bedrooms. The cosy, intimate bar and dining room are candlelit and have open fires.
Maynooth, Co Kildare. **Map** p57 E3. (01) 6286351. FAX (01) 6285405. @ moyglare@ iol.ie b,d. **Rooms** 17. Christmas. AE, DC, MC, V. ££££

NEWPORT

Newport House Fisherfolk heaven: the owners of the traditionally-run country house have fishing rights on a stretch of the River Newport, which borders the parkland, and the nearby lough. Fish is always on the menu; the house has its own superb whiskey-cured salmon. Lunchtime picnic hampers provided; anglers' tales in the bar in the evening. Four-poster beds in some rooms.
Newport, Co Mayo. **Map** p56 C2. (098) 41222. FAX (098) 41613. @ KJT1@anu.ie b,d. **Rooms** 18. Oct to mid-March. AE, DC, MC, V. ££££

NEWMARKET-ON-FERGUS

Dromoland Castle The ancestral home of the O'Briens, descendants of Brian Boru, 11th-century king of Ireland, is a fairy tale castle. It was turned into Gothic style with turrets and ramparts in the 1800s, and stands beside a lake. Today's luxury hotel has lavish amenities and oak panelling. Jackets and ties to be worn after 7pm.
Newmarket-on-Fergus, Co Clare. **Map** p56 C4. (061) 368144. FAX (061) 363355. @ sales@ dromoland.ie b,d. **Rooms** 73. Never. AE, DC, MC, V. £££££

PORTAFERRY

The Narrows Once through the 18th-century entrance archway, guests might never want to leave this inspiring waterfront courtyard restoration. All rooms have views of Strangford Lough; local artists' work are dotted about the walls; the restaurant looks out on boats and sunsets. Yachtspeople welcome; berths available.
8 Shore Rd, Portaferry, Co Down BT22 1JY. **Map** p57 F2. (012477) 728148. FAX (012477) 28105. @ the.narrows@dial.pipex.com b,d. **Rooms** 13. Feb (occasionally). AE, DC, MC, V. £££

KINVARA

Merriman Inn Although it only opened in 1997, the fishing village hotel has the largest thatched roof in Ireland. There are regular sessions of Irish music and story-telling in the bar.
Main St, Kinvara, Co Galway. **Map** p56 C3. (091) 638222. FAX (091) 637686. b,l,d. **Rooms** 32. ££

OUGHTERARD

Currarevagh House Country house hotel in woodland beside Lough Corrib sets a relaxed tone; fishing, tennis. Superb breakfasts.
Oughterard, Connemara, Co Galway. **Map** p64 C3. (091) 552312. FAX (091) 552731. b,d. **Rooms** 15. £££

RATHNEW

Tinakilly Country House Victorian house with views of the Irish Sea and a celebrated kitchen. Bedrooms have four-poster beds.
Rathnew, Wicklow, Co Wicklow. **Map** p57 E4. (0404) 69274. FAX (0404) 67806. @ wpower@tinakilly.ie b,l,d. **Rooms** 53. £££

RENVYLE

Renvyle House Hotel The grounds of this house with a fascinating history jut out into the Atlantic, with the Connemara countryside all around. Pool.
Renvyle, Connemara, Co Galway. **Map** p56 B3. (095) 43511. FAX (095) 43515. @ renvyle@iol.ie b,l,d. **Rooms** 65. £££

RATHMULLAN

STRAFFAN

Rathmullan House Inside or out, there are glorious views of Lough Swilly and mountains from this large, rambling, informal country house. Its gardens slope down to long, sandy beaches, and the area is ideal for walking. There are three attractive sitting-rooms, with log fires. Excellent facilities include an indoor pool and steam room. ⊠ Rathmullan, Co Donegal. **Map** p57 D1. 📞 (074) 58188/58117. **FAX** (074) 58200. @ rathhse@iol.ie 🍴 b,d. **Rooms** 24. 🛆 🍴 📶 🔊 ● Christmas to mid-Feb. 🗲 AE, DC, MC, V. ⓔⓔⓔ

The Kildare Hotel and Country Club The chateau-style building, complete with a mansard roof, looks like it was transplanted from France, yet it was built in the 1870s as a private home. It is now an unashamedly smart hotel, with views over to the renowned K Club golf course. Some bedrooms overlook the River Liffey. A French restaurant completes the luxury package. ⊠ Straffan, Co Kildare. **Map** p57 E3. 📞 (01) 6017200. **FAX** (01) 6017299. @ hotel@kclub.ie 🍴 b,l,d. **Rooms** 45. 🛆 🍴 📶 🔊 ● Never. 🗲 AE, DC, MC, V. ⓔⓔⓔⓔ

SHANAGARRY

THOMASTOWN

Ballymaloe House First rustled up for guests in the Allens' farmhouse kitchen in the 1960s, Ballymaloe cooking has become the cornerstone of modern Irish country house cuisine. Now there's a cookery school of international repute and an organic farm. But this is still a welcoming family home, with excellent breakfasts. No TV. ⊠ Shanagarry, Midleton, Co Cork. **Map** p57 D5. 📞 (021) 652531. **FAX** (021) 652021. @ bmaloe@iol.ie 🍴 b,d. **Rooms** 33. 🛆 🍴 📶 🔊 ● Christmas. 🗲 AE, DC, MC, V. ⓔⓔⓔ

Mount Juliet Estate A world of its own. The splendid greystone Georgian house sits in a private estate on the River Nore, surrounded by converted outbuildings and cottages. Features include stuccoed ceilings and marble mantelpieces. Riding on trails on the estate; Jack Nicklaus-designed golf course. Super king-sized beds. ⊠ Thomastown, Co Kilkenny. **Map** p57 D4. 📞 (056) 24455. **FAX** (056) 24522. @ info@mountjuliet.ie 🍴 b,l,d. **Rooms** 53 🛆 🍴 📶 🔊 ● Never. 🗲 AE, DC, MC, V. ⓔⓔⓔⓔ

ROSSLARE

Kelly's Resort Hotel Almost an Irish institution. Bill Kelly's cellar and art collection are among his many gifts as an hotelier. Leisure facilities; beach. ⊠ Rosslare, Co Wexford. **Map** p57 E5. 📞 (053) 32114. **FAX** (053) 32222. @ kellyhot@iol.ie 🍴 b,l,d. **Rooms** 99. ⓔⓔⓔ

ROSSNOWLAGH

Sand House Hotel Pink castellated hotel on a popular sandy beach in Donegal Bay. Many rooms have sea views. Award-winning restaurant. ⊠ Rossnowlagh, Co Donegal. **Map** p57 D1. 📞 (072) 51777. **FAX** (072) 52100. @ info@sandhouse-hotel.ie 🍴 b,l,d. **Rooms** 46. ⓔⓔ

SKIBBEREEN

West Cork Hotel This busy family-run establishment was once a railway hotel; it is still a focal point of West Cork life. Courtesy, relaxed hospitality; excellent crab cakes and steaks. ⊠ Ilen St, Skibbereen, Co Cork. **Map** p56 C5. 📞 (028) 21277. **FAX** (028) 22333. 🍴 b,l,d. **Rooms** 36. ⓔⓔ

SNEEM

Great Southern Hotel Parknasilla A spacious Victorian hotel known for welcoming service; subtropical gardens lead down to the shore. P⸱ ⊠ Sneem, Co Kerry. **Map** p56 B5. 📞 (064) 45122. **FAX** (064) 45323. @ res@parknasilla.gsh.ie 🍴 b,l,d. **Rooms** 84. ⓔⓔⓔ

For key to symbols see backflap. For price cate⸱

GREAT BRITAIN

GREAT BRITAIN

BRITAIN'S HOTELS tend to fall into one of two camps: town or country. The metropolitan 'boutique' hotels of London and Glasgow draw a style-conscious and demanding clientele, while the national pastime of the weekend break means that escapees from the city have a wide selection of country hotels to choose from – many of them offering excellent food in beautiful surroundings. As with the other countries in this guide, we include a selection of places to stay across the board, from the best B&Bs (bed & breakfasts) to classic hotels such as Gleneagles, page 111. Many of our listings are in unusual locations, for example, a Kentish oast house, or a croft on a Scottish island. There's as much variety and character in this small country as anywhere.

Inverlochy Castle Hotel, page 113, in magnificent Highland scenery at the foot of Ben Nevis

GREAT BRITAIN REGION BY REGION

IN THIS GUIDE, Britain is divided into five sections: Southern England, Central England, Northern England, Scotland and Wales.

Southern England

In London, recommendations include great places to stay that are also well-placed for shopping, theatres, museums and restaurants. Within easy reach of the capital are the B&Bs of the Weald and down-land of Kent and Sussex, luxurious spa hotels such as Chewton Glen in the New Forest (page 87), and fun places like the traditional beach huts that can be booked at the Hotel Continental, in Whitstable, Kent (page 92). Two hotels in the

Lobby, the Dorchester, page 85

neighbourhood of Bath – the stylish Royal Crescent in Bath itself (page 79), and Babington House in nearby Frome (page 83) – show how British hotel styles are on the move. The Georgian Royal Crescent is one of the new breed of polished townhouse hotel. Babington House is the country offshoot of a Soho club; where the knowing informality is typical of the developing style of the British country-house hotel.

Further west, Devon and Cornwall offer some of the most beautiful stretches of coastline in Britain, plenty of B&Bs, and understated luxury in hotels such as Tresco's Island Hotel (page 90).

Central England

The sandstone villages of the Cotswolds are a plentiful source of guesthouses, coaching inns and manor house hotels. Many offer first-rate service, provide picnic hampers, or transport you to and from great walking country. The old counties of Hereford and Worcester, the university town of Oxford, and the East Anglian counties

West Usk Lighthouse, page 119

of Suffolk and Norfolk also offer some special places to stay, the latter including a B&B in a windmill at Cley-next-the-Sea (page 95).

Northern England

Newcastle is home to one of the Malmaison chain (page 105) – the only hotel chain included in this section – which is noted for its somewhat unconventional ambience and affordable prices. In the northwest, the Lake District is packed out with tourists in summer, but it is easy enough to escape the crowds if you like hill walking or if you visit in autumn when the weather can be clear and warm. There are many B&Bs which don't mind muddy walking boots, and some special country house hotels too, including Old Church at Watermillock on the edge of Ullswater (page 108). Other famous areas of outstanding beauty in the north include the Yorkshire Dales and the Peak District. Nearby are country hotels such as Amerdale House at Arncliffe (page 103), and small hotels with character, among them a former cotton mill.

Scotland

Country hotels in Scotland are memorable for location, character and food: many occupy imposing positions on peaceful lochs, and employ chefs who make full use of the local specialities such as seafood and game, and have a loyal clientele who rearrange their itinerary

to be sure of getting a room. Glasgow and Edinburgh are obvious centres for their art galleries and architecture (and assured townhouse hotels), as well as the annual Edinburgh Festival (and associated Fringe) in August. The High-lands and Islands offer some of the most remote and peaceful places to stay in Britain, one such favourite being the Altnaharrie Inn on Loch Broom (page 115), accessible only by boat, and with perhaps one of the best restaurants in Britain.

Wales

The walking is superb in the Brecon Beacons, Snowdonia and along Offa's Dyke. The Pembrokeshire coastline, with its crumbling medieval castles, and seaside resorts such as Tenby and St David's is well worth a detour. Potential overnight stops include many family-run hotels offering good food –

often with fresh local produce on the menu.

Some hotels in this chapter are Wolsey Lodges – neither hotels, nor just guesthouses. A stay at a Wolsey Lodge is like being at a private house party – except that the host presents you with a bill at the end of your stay.

HIGHLIGHTS

HOTELS ILLUSTRATED on these introductory pages are by no means our only highlights. Other favourites include: Tresanton at St Mawes in Cornwall (page 90) for marrying sophistication with sea-side fun; still in Cornwall, Trebea Lodge at Tintagel (page 91), for an exceptionally warm welcome and personal touch; and Hambleton Hall (page 96), for offering stylish pampering in an away-from-it-all location on Rutland Water, near Oakham in the Midlands. In

Wykham Arms at Winchester, page 92, the archetypal pub-with-

Tanyard at Boughton Monchelsea, page 80, with timber beams dating from the 14th century

London, the Covent Garden (page 85) gets many people's vote for its panache and superb service. And in the north, Amerdale House, in Arncliffe, North Yorkshire (page 103), is extra special because of its stunning setting and good food.

FOOD AND DRINK

Eating has become a form of entertainment for many Londoners, with a hardcore of 'foodie' enthusiasts making – or ruining – the fortunes of restaurants and affording many chefs celebrity status. Sometimes you have to book weeks in advance if you want to dine somewhere in vogue.

However, some of the best British food is served outside the capital, and the 1990s produced some excellent new establishments. As well as the country hotels where food takes pride of place, there are 'restaurants with rooms', which illustrate the 1980s' and 90s' renaissance in British with inventive cooking often uses locally-grown, al produce. The quality game, lamb, and the rsial beef on the

bone is high, and at many hotels chefs have access to a kitchen garden or buy the freshest local produce. Many hotels are at the forefront of the campaign against genetically modified crops, and organically produced food on the menu is now increasingly commonplace.

Modern British cookery is actually an amalgam of many influences and styles, among them provincial Italian and Pacific Rim, with an imaginative use of fresh herbs and spices borrowed from foreign cuisines. Britain is one of the few countries where you can

Tea at the Priory Steps, page 80

be vegetarian and eat well. Classy pub food continues to be excellent value for money, and so is traditional fish and chips, eaten straight from the paper wrapping.

Lunch is generally served from 1–3pm and dinner from 7:30–10:30pm; many pubs stop serving lunch at 2:30pm and dinner at 9 or 9:30pm. Afternoon tea at about 4pm is an old-fashioned institution that city hotels do particularly well. Even better is the West Country (typically Devon and Cornwall) speciality of cream tea – scones eaten with clotted cream and jam – served, of course, with strong traditional English tea.

Britain produces little wine, still less any of note. Beer from the tap is the ubiquitous national drink of the pub or hotel bar, reaching its highest quality in the 'real' ales of independent specialist brewers. It is served by the pint or the half-pint.

Scottish whisky is, of course, renowned. Everyday 'Scotch' is blended. 'Single malts', from one distilling, achieve gourmet status and are accordingly expensive. There are many from which you can choose, and some hotels make a feature of offering a wide range, each with its distinctive style.

BEDROOMS AND BATHROOMS

IF YOU WANT twin beds, ask for them specifically when booking. Even the humblest B&B can have a four-poster bed, a great view or some other interesting feature – it's worth asking beforehand. Some hotels in historic buildings will have a new wing – generally with more spacious rooms and better bathrooms, but less character. You will usually be given the choice when you book, but it is worth making sure that you state which you prefer.

Bathrooms generally mean just a bath – specify if you want a shower.

OTHER PRACTICAL INFORMATION

BRITISH HOTELIERS seem very sensitive about 'no-shows' (people who book a room but don't turn up), and you may be asked for your credit card number or a cheque to secure the booking. Under English law, by making a booking you are entering into a contract. Hotels are within their rights to charge you for the room if you cancel at the last minute, although they must try to re-let the room and are not supposed to profit from your cancellation.

The English cooked breakfast, high in cholesterol, is often a major feature, worth trying at least once.

Language English, and, in Wales, Welsh, tend to be the only languages spoken.

Currency The pound sterling, written '£'.

Shops Generally open from 9:30am–5:30pm Mon–Sat in the country, and until 6 or 7pm in central London. Banks are open Mon–Fri; most closing at 3:30pm, but some staying open until 4:30 or 5:30pm. Supermarkets and shops in tourist areas often open between about noon and 4pm on Sundays.

Tipping A tip of around 15 per cent is the norm for waiters, hairdressers and taxi drivers. A service charge of 10–15 per cent is often added to restaurant bills, in addition to the tip, but the extra rarely goes to the waiting staff. You can negotiate not to pay the service charge (if you have ordered expensive wines, for example, which are already subject to a high mark-up) but be ready for consternation from the management.

In metropolitan bars and cafés the staff may give you your change on a tray, hinting that donations are welcome. In pubs, the terminology of tipping is to say, 'and a drink for yourself' in which case the price of a drink will be added into the total for the round.

Telephoning Hotels are shameless at racking up the phone charges, defending themselves by saying that they publicize their price per unit charges. Some will even charge you for using your own charge card for calls.

Public call boxes are plentiful, accepting coins, phonecards or credit cards (minimum call charge for the latter is 50p). For calls within Britain, dial the zero before the area code. To call Britain from the US, dial 011 44, then the number, dropping the initial zero.

Public holidays England and Wales: 1 January; Good Friday; Easter Monday; first Monday after 1 May; last Monday in May; last Monday in August; 25 and 26 December.

Scotland: 1 and 2 January; 25 December; plus assorted local public holidays.

BRITAIN PRICE BANDS

DON'T BE DISTRACTED by the array of stars, crowns or other symbols of the many hotel awards in Britain. Our price bands are much simpler, referring to the price of a standard double room in high season. Prices usually include breakfast and all taxes.

£	below £60
££	£60–£120
£££	£120–£180
££££	above £180

Lavenham Priory, page 97, in the charming town of Lavenham, Suffolk

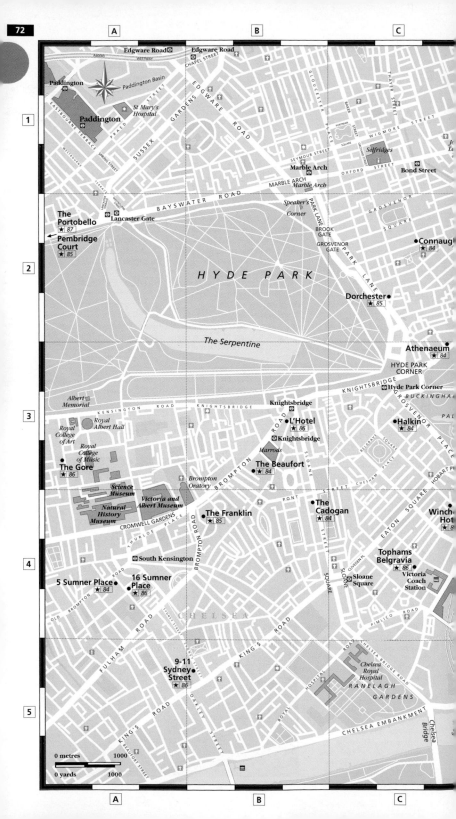

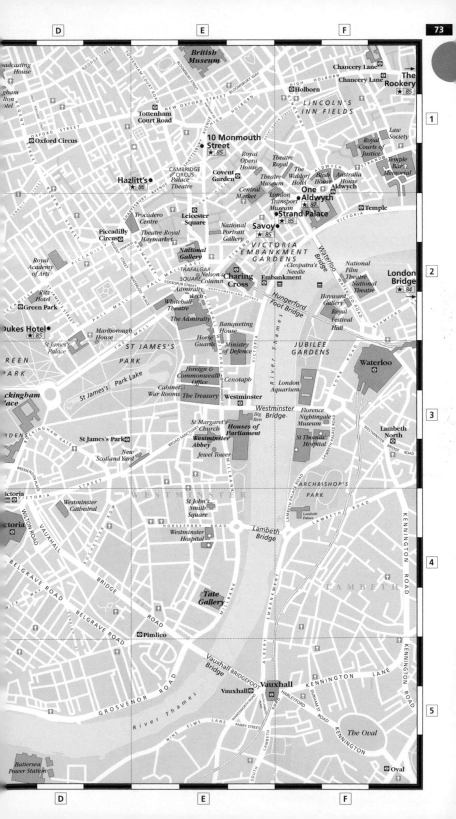

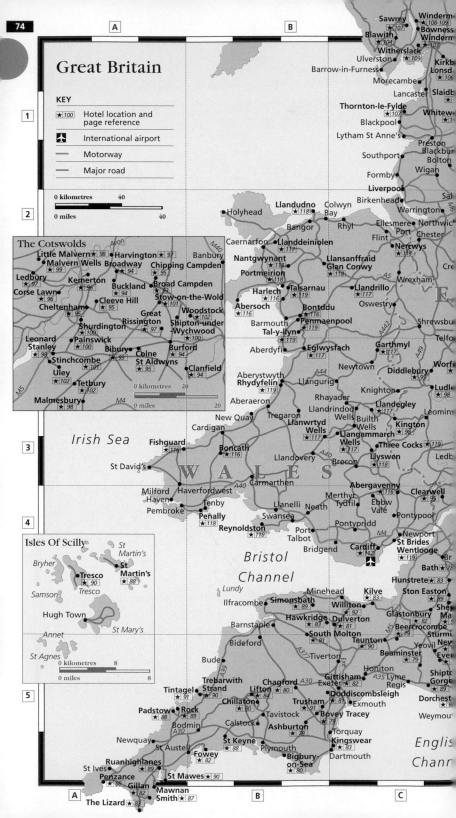

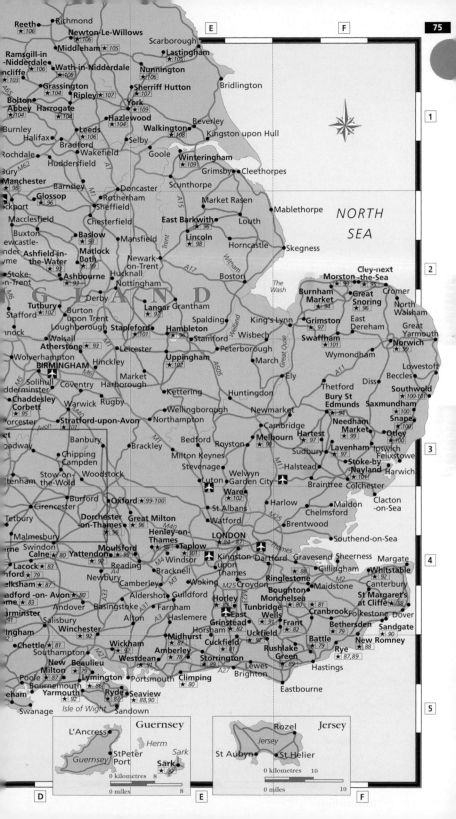

Reeth ★106 • Richmond
Newton-Le-Willows ★106
Middleham ★105
Ramsgill-in -Nidderdale ★106
ncliffe ★103 • Wath-in-Nidderdale ★108
Grassington ★104 • Ripley ★107
Bolton Abbey ★104 • Harrogate ★104
Burnley • Halifax
Leeds ★106
Bradford
Rochdale • Wakefield
Huddersfield
Bury M62
Manchester ★98 • Barnsley
Glossop ★96
ckport • Rotherham
Macclesfield • Sheffield
Buxton • Chesterfield
ewcastle-nder-
yme • Ashfield-in-the-Water ★93
Stoke-n-Trent • Matlock Bath ★99
Ashbourne ★93
Tutbury ★102 • Burton upon Trent
Stafford • Loughborough
nnock • Walsall
Atherstone ★93
Wolverhampton
BIRMINGHAM ✈
Solihull
dderminster • Coventry
Chaddesley Corbett ★95
orcester • Warwick • Rugby
oadway • Stratford-upon-Avon ★101
et • Banbury
Chipping Campden
Stow-on-the-Wold
tenham • Burford • Woodstock
Cirencester • Oxford ★99-100
Tetbury • Dorchester-on-Thames ★96
Malmesbury • Great Milton ★96
rne • Swindon
Calne ★80
Henley-on-Thames
nford ★79 • Lacock ★83
Yattendon ★92 • Moulsford ★99
elksham ★87 • Newbury • Reading
adford-on-Avon ★80 • Bracknell
me ★83 • Andover • Basingstoke
arminster • Camberley
91 • Salisbury • Alton
ingham • Winchester ★92
Chettle ★81
Southampton
New Beaulieu ★79
Milton ★87 • Lymington ★86
Poole • Bournemouth
eham • Yarmouth ★92 • Ryde ★87
Swanage • Isle of Wight • Sandown
Seaview ★88,90

Scarborough
Lastingham ★105
Nunnington ★106
Sherriff Hutton ★107
York ★109
Hazlewood ★104
Walkington ★108
Bridlington
Beverley
Kingston upon Hull
Selby
Goole
Winteringham ★109
Doncaster
Scunthorpe
Grimsby • Cleethorpes
Market Rasen
Mablethorpe
East Barkwith ★96
Louth
Lincoln ★98
Horncastle
Skegness
Newark-on-Trent
Hucknall
Nottingham
Boston
Derby
Langar ★92 • Grantham
Stapleford ★101
Hambleton ★96
Spalding
Stamford
Leicester
Peterborough
Uppingham ★102
March
Market Harborough
Kettering
Wellingborough • Northampton
Huntingdon
Bedford • Royston
Milton Keynes
Stevenage
Brackley
Welwyn Garden City ✈
Luton ✈
Ware ★102
St Albans
Watford
Harlow
Chelmsford
Brentwood

NORTH SEA

Cley-next-the-Sea ★95
Morston ★99
Great Snoring ★96
Burnham Market ★94
Cromer
North Walsham
Great Yarmouth
King's Lynn
Grimston ★97
East Dereham
Swaffham ★101
Wisbech
The Wash
Great Ouse
Ely
Wymondham
Norwich ★99
Lowestoft
Thetford • Diss
Beccles
Southwold ★100-101
Bury St Edmunds ★94
Saxmundham ★100
Needham Market ★99
Snape ★100
Newmarket
Cambridge
Melbourn ★99
Hartest ★97
Otley ★100
Lavenham ★97
Ipswich
Sudbury
Felixstowe
Stoke-by-Nayland ★101
Halstead
Braintree • Colchester
Harwich
Maldon
Clacton-on-Sea
Southend-on-Sea

Gravesend • Sheerness • Margate
Dartford
Kingston upon Thames
Windsor
Woking
Croydon
Aldershot • Guildford
Farnham
Haslemere
Horsham
Midhurst ★87
Amberley ★78
Wickham ★92
Westdean ★91
Climping ★80
Portsmouth
Storrington ★89
Cuckfield ★81
Lewes
Brighton
Eastbourne

Ringlestone ★88
Gillingham
Whitstable ★92
Maidstone
Canterbury
Boughton Monchelsea ★80
St Margaret's at Cliffe ★88
Cranbrook ★81
Folkestone • Dover
Tunbridge Wells ★91
Bethersden ★79
Sandgate
Frant ★82
East Grinstead ★82
Uckfield ★92
Battle ★79
Rye ★87,89
New Romney ★88
Rushlake Green ★89
Hastings

LONDON ★84-87
Taplow ★101
✈

Guernsey
L'Ancress • Herm
StPeter Port • Sark
Guernsey • Sark ★90

0 kilometres 8
0 miles 8

Jersey
Rozel
Jersey
St Aubyn • St Helier

0 kilometres 10
0 miles 10

D • E • F

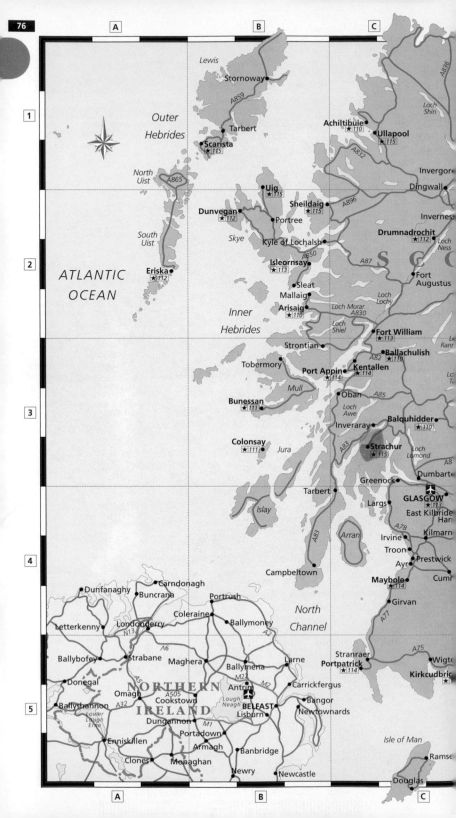

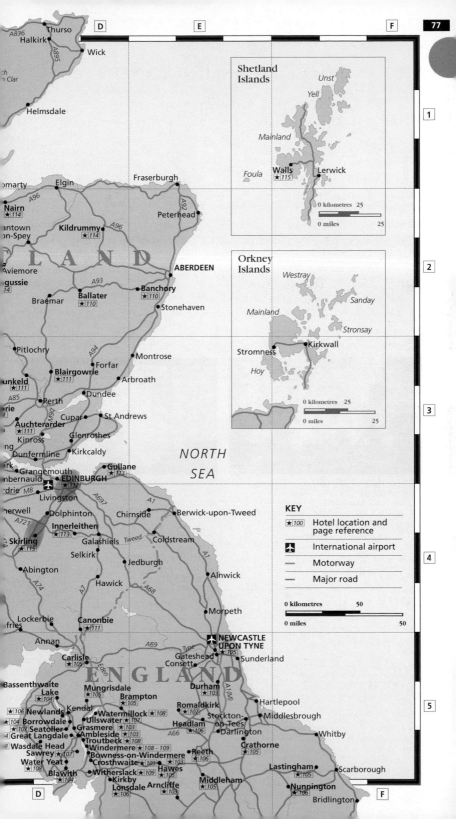

Shetland Islands

Unst

Yell

Mainland

Foula

Walls ★115

Lerwick

0 kilometres 25

0 miles 25

Orkney Islands

Westray

Sanday

Mainland

Stronsay

Stromness

Kirkwall

Hoy

0 kilometres 25

0 miles 25

A836 Thurso
Halkirk
A895
Wick

Helmsdale

marty Elgin
A96
Nairn ★114
Fraserburgh

antown
on-Spey
Kildrummy ★114
A96
Peterhead

Aviemore
ABERDEEN

gussie
14
A93
Ballater ★110
Banchory ★110

Braemar
Stonehaven

Pitlochry
A94
Montrose

unkeld ★111
Blairgowrie ★111
Forfar
Arbroath

A85
Dundee

Perth
Auchterarder ★111
Cupar
St Andrews

Kinross
Glenrothes

ng Dunfermline
Kirkcaldy

irk Grangemouth
Gullane ★113

mbernauld M8 EDINBURGH ★121

drie
Livingston
A697

herwell
Dolphinton
Chirnside
Berwick-upon-Tweed

A721
Innerleithen ★113

Skirling ★115
Galashiels
Tweed
Coldstream

Abington
Selkirk
Jedburgh
Alnwick

A74
Hawick
A68

Lockerbie
Canonbie ★111
Morpeth

fries
A69
Tyne
NEWCASTLE UPON TYNE ★105

Annan
Gateshead
Sunderland

Carlisle ★105
Consett

E N G L A N D
Eden

Bassenthwaite Lake ★104
Mungrisdale ★106
Brampton ★105
Durham ★103
Hartlepool

★106 Newlands
Kendal
Watermillock ★102
Romaldkirk ★107
Stockton-on-Tees
Middlesbrough

★104 Borrowdale
Ullswater ★103
Headlam ★106

★107 Seatoller
Grasmere ★103
Darlington
Whitby

4 Great Langdale
Ambleside ★103
A66

8 Wasdale Head
Troutbeck ★108
Crathorne ★105

Sawrey ★107
Windermere ★108 - 109
Reeth ★106

Water Yeat
Bowness-on-Windermere ★108

★108 Crosthwaite ★103
Hawes ★105
Lastingham ★105
Scarborough

Blawith ★104
Witherslack ★109
Middleham ★105

Kirkby Lonsdale ★106
Arncliffe ★103
Nunnington ★106

Bridlington

NORTH SEA

KEY

★100 Hotel location and page reference

International airport

Motorway

Major road

0 kilometres 50

0 miles 50

SOUTHERN ENGLAND

LONDON • SOUTHEAST • SOUTHWEST
ISLE OF WIGHT • ISLES OF SCILLY • CHANNEL ISLANDS

THE DEEP lanes, hidden valleys and sheltered creeks and coves of Cornwall and Devon make magical settings for a range of charming places to stay, from sophisticated seaside hotels to simple farmhouse B&Bs. In Dorset, Somerset and Avon there are a wealth of gracious mansions and manor houses which have been turned into hotels, perfect choices for a weekend treat. In the southeast, Sussex and Kent are favoured with a crop of delightful traditional buildings, some of them medieval, in which to stay. London had spent many years in the doldrums, but the city and its environs now have an impressive range of beautifully run, highly individual hotels. Note, however, that they are expensive and there are as yet few which stand out in the budget category.

BATH

Bath Priory This is a perfect choice for a weekend treat, combining the seclusion of a country house hotel with the attractions of Bath a stroll away. The bedrooms are luxurious yet homely; the sophisticated drawing room is done out in deep reds and ochre yellow. Smooth service and excellent food (Michelin star).
Weston Rd, Bath, Avon BA1 2XT. **Map** p74 C4.
(01225) 331922. FAX (01225) 448276.
@ 106076.1265@compuserve.com b,l,d. **Rooms** 28.
Never. AE, DC, MC V. ££££

BATH

Queensberry Discreet, quiet and beautifully decorated central Bath haven, with a lift to all levels. Along the characterful maze of corridors are spacious bedrooms with lovely cotton sheets on the (mainly) king-size beds and lavish bathrooms. Two attractive drawing rooms and a popular basement restaurant, the Olive Tree.
Russel St, Bath, Avon BA1 2QF. **Map** p74 C4.
(01225) 447928. FAX (01225) 446065.
@ queensberry@dial.pipex.com b,l,d. **Rooms** 29.
Christmas. DC, MC, V. £££

AMBERLEY

Amberley Castle The real thing, complete with battlements and portcullis in a charming village. Baronial luxury, plus Jacuzzis.
Amberley, Arundel, West Sussex BN18 9ND. **Map** p75 E5. (01798) 831992. FAX (01798) 831998.
b,l,d. **Rooms** 15. ££££

ASHBURTON

Holne Chase Quiet, restful former hunting lodge inside Dartmoor National Park. Perfect for sporting enthusiasts: fishing and shooting on tap.
Ashburton, Devon TQ13 7NS. **Map** p74 B5.
(01364) 631471. FAX (01364) 631453. @ info@holne-chase.co.uk b,l,d. **Rooms** 17. £££

BATH

Brompton House A former rectory is now a good value, well-run B&B. In the city centre, yet set in a large shady garden and churchyard.
St John's Rd, Bath, Avon BA2 6PT. **Map** p74 C4.
(01225) 420972. FAX (01225) 420505. @ brompton_house@compuserve.com b. **Rooms** 18. ££

BATH

Sydney Gardens This large Italianate house overlooking a small park on the edge of town makes a light, attractive and spacious B&B.
Sydney Rd, Bath, Avon BA2 6NT. **Map** p74 C4.
(01225) 464818. FAX (01225) 484347. b.
Rooms 6. ££

BATH

Royal Crescent Occupying the central section of Bath's immaculate Georgian Royal Crescent, the hotel operates to the highest standards and is now one of the country's grandest and most gracious townhouse hotels. It comes complete with secluded garden, pampering health spa, hot air balloon for flights over Bath and river launch.
☒ 16 Royal Crescent, Bath, Avon BA1 2LS.
Map p74 C4. ☎ (01225) 823333. ℻ (01225) 339401.
🍴 b,l,d. **Rooms** 45. 📃 🖾 🔊 ⬤ Never.
🎫 AE, DC, MC, V. ⓔⓔⓔⓔ

BATHFORD

Eagle House In a fine village near Bath, this gracious Georgian mansion is run as a guesthouse by its professional yet informal owners, the Napiers. The house is decorated without pomp, using an eclectic mix of furniture, and has an elegant drawing room overlooking landscaped gardens and beyond.
☒ Church St, Bathford, Avon BA1 7RS. **Map** p75 D4.
☎ (01225) 859946. ℻ (01225) 859430.
@ jonap@eagleho.demon.co.uk 🍴 b. **Rooms** 8.
🔊 ⬤ 10 days Christmas. 🎫 MC, V. ⓔⓔ

BEAMINSTER
Bridge House Originally a 13th-century clergy house, deep in Hardy country with pretty bedrooms and more than adequate food.
☒ Beaminster, Dorset DT8 3AY. **Map** p74 C5.
☎ (01308) 862200. ℻ (01308) 863700. @ enquiries@ bridge-house.co.uk 🍴 b,l,d. **Rooms** 14. ⓔⓔ

BEAULIEU
Montagu Arms In a charming New Forest village, a pleasant, smart, sedate hotel.
☒ Palace Lane, Beaulieu, Hampshire SO42 7ZL.
Map p75 D5. ☎ (01590) 612324. ℻ (01590) 612188.
@ enquiries@montagu-arms.co.uk 🍴 b,d.
Rooms 24. ⓔⓔⓔ

BATTLE

Little Hemingfold This rural haven is hidden away amid farm and woodland yet close to many historic places, including the site of the Battle of Hastings. The rambling house is surrounded by gardens and overlooks a trout lake (fishing, rowing). Inside is cosy (log fires) and full of interesting corners, with plain but individual bedrooms; traditional, satisfying cooking.
☒ Battle, East Sussex TN33 0TT. **Map** p75 F5. ☎ (01424) 774338. ℻ (01424) 775351. 🍴 b,l,d. **Rooms** 14. 🔊
⬤ mid-Jan to mid-Feb. 🎫 AE, DC, MC, V. ⓔ

BETHERSDEN

Little Hodgeham For visitors seeking old-world English charm, this Tudor house with flower-filled garden, leaded windows, inglenook fireplace and three charming bedrooms (one with four-poster) must be a dream come true. Erica Wallace is the dream-maker, very much the ruler of her domain. She serves her pampered guests elegant meals (by arrangement) in her intimate dining room.
☒ Smarden Rd, Bethersden, Ashford, Kent TN26 3HE.
Map p75 F4. ☎ (01233) 850323. 🍴 b,d. **Rooms** 3.
🏊 🔊 ⬤ Sept to mid-Mar. 🎫 Not accepted. ⓔⓔ

BEERCROMBE
Frog Street Farm Hidden, flower-bedecked Somerset longhouse run by friendly farmers and racehorse breeders Veronica and Henry Cole. Log fires, fine Jacobean panelling.
☒ Beercrombe, Taunton, Somerset TA3 6AF. **Map** p74 C4. ☎ ℻ (01823) 480430. 🍴 b,d. **Rooms** 3. ⓔ

BOVEY TRACEY
Bel Alp House On Dartmoor's edge, a sedate Edwardian house with glorious seaward views from the terrace across a patchwork of fields.
☒ Haytor, Bovey Tracey, Devon TQ13 9XX.
Map p74 C5. ☎ (01364) 661217. ℻ (01364) 661292.
🍴 b,d. **Rooms** 8. ⓔⓔⓔ

For key to symbols see backflap. For price categories see p71

BIGBURY-ON-SEA

Burgh Island Board a wheezing sea tractor to the small island that houses this genuine Art Deco hotel. It has been lovingly restored by its owners and is still playing out the Roaring Twenties, when it played host to a string of famous people. It feels a bit flimsy, rather like a film set, but there is a feast of Art Deco furniture and fittings in every room. Fantastic sea and coastal views.
Bigbury-on-Sea, Devon TQ7 4BG. **Map** p74 B5.
(01548) 810514. FAX (01548) 810243. b,l,d.
Rooms 14. Jan, Feb. AE, DC, MC, V. ££££

BRADFORD-ON-AVON

Priory Steps A row of 17th-century weavers' cottages has been sympathetically restored by Carey and Diana Chapman to become both their home and a welcoming small hotel. The bedrooms, carefully decorated with antiques, are surprisingly spacious and light, with sweeping views. Dinner is served at the communal table.
Newtown, Bradford-on-Avon, Wiltshire BA15 1NQ. **Map** p75 D4. (01225) 862230. FAX (01225) 866248.
@ priorysteps@clara.co.uk b,d. **Room**s 5.
Never. MC, V. ££

BOUGHTON MONCHELSEA

Tanyard It is hard to find fault with Tanyard, which especially appeals to those looking for a rural idyll. The 14th-century timber-framed building, amusingly lacking in symmetry and set in a country garden with glorious views, is a delight; the proprietor Jan Davies is a good cook, serving a generous four-course dinner.
Wierton Hill, Boughton Moncheslea, Maidstone, Kent ME17 4JT. **Map** p75 F4. (01622) 744705.
FAX (01622) 741998. b,d. **Rooms** 6.
Christmas to mid-Jan. AE, DC, MC, V. ££

CHAGFORD

Gidleigh Park This luxurious Dartmoor hotel has been run by the Hendersons for the past 25 years, and is still as polished and relaxing as ever. In the oak-panelled sitting room and the bedrooms (some small) a feeling of good living and serenity abounds. The superb food (two Michelin stars) is a highlight. Golf, fishing, tennis, croquet.
Chagford, Devon TQ13 8HH. **Map** p74 B5.
(01647) 432367. FAX (01647) 432574.
@ gidleighpark@gidleigh.co.uk b,l,d. **Rooms** 14, plus 1 cottage. Never. DC, MC, V. ££££

BRADFORD-ON-AVON
Bradford Old Windmill B&B with a delightful difference: an intriguing folly; simple, romantic bedrooms, ethnic curiosities and exotic cooking.
4 Masons Lane, Bradford-on-Avon, Wiltshire BA15 1QN. **Map** p75 D4. (01225) 866842.
FAX (01225) 866848. b,d. **Rooms** 3. ££

CALNE
Chilvester Hill House Elegant family home filled with interesting possessions and presided over by perfect hosts John and Gill Dilley. Dinner is by arrangement, eaten communally.
Calne, Wiltshire SN11 OLP. **Map** p75 D4. (01249) 813981. FAX (01249) 814217. b,d. **Rooms** 3. ££

CHILLATON
Tor Cottage A pool is one of the extras at this award-winning guesthouse hidden in its own valley. Flouncy bedrooms; caring owner.
Chillaton, Devon PL16 OJE. **Map** p74 B5.
(01822) 860248. FAX (01822) 860126.
@ info@torcottage.demon.uk b,d. **Rooms** 4. ££

CLIMPING
Bailiffscourt An astonishingly realistic 1930s' re-creation of a medieval manor houses a slightly corporate luxury hotel, handy for Gatwick.
Climping, Littlehampton, Sussex BN17 5RW.
Map p75 E5. (01903) 723511. FAX (01903) 723107.
b,l,d. **Rooms** 32. £££

CHETTLE

Castleman Chettle is special: the estate village is still owned by one family, the Bourkes, who live in its fine Queen Anne manor house. The former dower house is now a hotel and restaurant, run by Teddy Bourke and Barbara Garnsworthy along informal lines: no frills, but period features and spacious rooms attractively decorated (some with Victorian roll-top baths). Good value.
☒ Chettle, Blandford Forum, Dorset DT11 8DB. **Map** p75 D5. ☏ (01258) 830096. ℻ (01258) 830051. ⊪ b,l,d. **Rooms** 8. ▮ ● Feb. ☒ MC,V. ⓔⓔ

CRANBROOK

Old Cloth Hall Lovely grounds surround this fine 15th-century manor. Its crooked, charming exterior is in perfect keeping with the interior: everywhere are gleaming oak floors and panelling, porcelain, chintz and fresh flowers. This is very much the domain of the charming *châtelaine*, Katherine Morgan, a good cook who often joins her guests at the communal table.
☒ Cranbrook, Kent TN17 3NR. **Map** p75 F4. ☏ ℻ (01580) 712220. ⊪ b,d. **Rooms** 3. ▦ ▯ ● Christmas. ☒ Not accepted. ⓔⓔ

CRANBROOK

Kennel Holt Within easy reach of many houses and gardens open to the public, this is a perfect place in which to unwind after a day's sightseeing. The homely Elizabethan manor has capacious sofas before open fires, an honesty bar, a selection of CDs to choose from, impressive bedrooms and fine food. Secluded setting.
☒ Goudhurst Rd, Cranbrook, Kent TN17 2PT. **Map** p75 F4. ☏ (01580) 712032. ℻ (01580) 715495. ⊪ b,d. **Rooms** 10. ▯ ● 2 weeks Jan. ☒ MC, V. ⓔⓔⓔ

CUCKFIELD

Ockenden Manor Superb views of the South Downs can be had from the grounds of this fine 16th-century manor. The hotel is elegantly furnished; creative English food is served in the atmospheric wood-panelled dining room with painted ceiling and stained-glass windows. Rooms are individual and spacious, service is friendly.
☒ Ockenden Lane, Cuckfield, West Sussex RH17 5LD. **Map** p75 E5. ☏ (01444) 416111. ℻ (01444) 415549. @ info@hshotels.co.uk ⊪ b,l,d. **Rooms** 22. ▯ ● Never. ☒ AE, DC, MC, V. ⓔⓔⓔ

COLERNE

Lucknam Park Stately hotel with aristocratic interior, formal dining and a leisure complex.
☒ Colerne, Wiltshire SN14 8AZ. **Map** p75 D4. ☏ (01225) 742777. ℻ (01225) 743536. @ lucknampark@compuserve.com ⊪ b,l,d. **Rooms** 41. ⓔⓔⓔⓔ

DODDISCOMBSLEIGH

Nobody Inn Quintessential West Country inn with satisfying food and wines; the large rooms are a stroll away in an old house, Town Barton.
☒ Doddiscombsleigh, Exeter, Devon EX6 7PT. **Map** p74 C5. ☏ (01647) 252394. ℻ (01647) 252978. @ inn.nobody@virgin.net ⊪ b,l,d. **Rooms** 7. ⓔⓔ

DORCHESTER

Casterbridge Georgian town-centre hotel with bright rooms (some small); generous breakfasts served in pretty conservatory. Good value.
☒ 49 High East St, Dorchester, Dorset DT1 1HU. **Map** p74 C5. ☏ (01305) 264043. ℻ (01305) 260884. ⊪ b. **Rooms** 14. ⓔⓔ

DULVERTON

Ashwick House Edwardian house on Exmoor. Galleried hall, traditional dining room, bedrooms personally equipped (teddies, binoculars) by host Richard Sherwood.
☒ Dulverton, Devon TA22 9QD. **Map** p74 C4. ☏ ℻ (01398) 323868. ⊪ b,l,d. **Rooms** 6. ⓔⓔ

EAST GRINSTEAD

Gravetye Manor For more than 40 years this serene Elizabethan house has exuded understated luxury – at a price. It is close to London, yet surrounded by natural English gardens and woodland. Standards are unfailingly high, with award-winning cooking and attentive yet unobtrusive service.

☒ Vowels Lane, East Grinstead, West Sussex RH19 4LJ. **Map** p75 E4. 【 (01342) 810567. ℻ (01342) 810080. @ gravetye@relaischateaux.fr ⊞ b,l,d. **Rooms** 18. ◐ ⬤ Never. 🗐 DC, MC, V. ££££

FOWEY

Fowey Hall The grandest of a group of hotels designed specifically for families (see Old Bell, page 98). The facilities for children are endless, yet there is plenty of sophistication for grown-ups too. The setting, overlooking the Fowey estuary and the sea, is an extravagant late 19th-century mansion; modern comforts and leisure activities.

☒ Hanson Drive, Fowey, Cornwall PL23 1ET. **Map** p74 B5. 【 (01726) 833866. ℻ (01726) 834100. ⊞ b,l,d. **Rooms** 25. ▦ ◐ ⬤ Never. 🗐 AE, MC, V. £££

EVERSHOT

Summer Lodge The many devotees of this former dower house in the heart of Dorset love its assets: French windows leading onto flowery gardens; airy bedrooms; good food served in a formal but pretty dining room. Peace, comfort, and a touch of extravagance without intimidation. For exercise there is tennis and croquet.

☒ Summer Lane, Evershot, Dorset DT2 0JR. **Map** p74 C5. 【 (01935) 83424. ℻ (01935) 83005. @ sumlodge@demon.co.uk ⊞ b,l,d. **Rooms** 18. ▦ ◐ ⬤ Never. 🗐 AE, DC, MC, V. ££££

FRANT

Old Parsonage In a charming village, a gracious Georgian country house run as a B&B by Tony and Mary Dakin. Tall, spacious reception rooms are impressively decorated without being overpowering: antiques, Persian rugs, chandeliers, photographs and lithographs on the walls. There is an airy conservatory, and the fresh bedrooms have large bathrooms. Excellent breakfasts.

☒ Church Lane, Frant, Tunbridge Wells, Kent TN3 9DX. **Map** p75 F4. 【 ℻ (01892) 750773. @ oldparson@ aol.com ⊞ b. **Rooms** 3. ◐ ⬤ Never. 🗐 MC, V. ££

GILLAN

Tregildry In a magical setting overlooking a romantic Cornish creek, a vividly decorated hotel with breezy Far Eastern feel.

☒ Gillan, Manaccan, Helston, Cornwall TR12 6HG. **Map** p74 A5. 【 (01326) 231378. ℻ (01326) 231561. @ trgildry@globalnet.co.uk ⊞ b,d. **Rooms** 10. £££

GITTISHAM

Combe House Imposing Elizabethan manor surrounded by woodland. Ornate public rooms, spacious and elegant bedrooms.

☒ Gittisham, Honiton, Devon EX14 OAD. **Map** p74 C5. 【 (01404) 540400. ℻ (01404) 46004. @ stay@ combe-house.co.uk ⊞ b,l,d. **Rooms** 16. £££

GILLINGHAM

Stock Hill House Victorian manor, set in wooded grounds and decorated in the grandly personal style of its owners. Formal dining.

☒ Gillingham, Dorset SP8 5NR. **Map** p75 D4. 【 (01747) 823626. ℻ (01747) 825628. @ reception@ ...hill.net ⊞ b,l,d. **Rooms** 10. ££££

GLASTONBURY

Number 3 Listed Georgian town house B&B with richly decorated public rooms and spacious, carefully coordinated bedrooms.

☒ 3 Magdalene St, Glastonbury, Somerset BA6 9EW. **Map** p74 C4. 【 (01458) 832129. ℻ (01458) 834227. ⊞ b. **Rooms** 4. ££

SOUTHERN ENGLAND **8 3**

FROME

Babington House This contemporary country house hotel offers child-friendly metropolitan chic and unpretentious luxury: cinema, computers, health centre, crêche, tennis, snooker, relaxed but efficient 24-hour service and wonderful bedrooms. In the bathrooms are huge bottles of complimentary lotions – no mean sachets here.
☒ Babington, Frome, Somerset BA11 3RW.
Map p75 D4. ☎ (01373) 812266. FAX (01373) 812112.
@ babhouse@compuserve.com ⏲ b,l,d. **Rooms** 22.
☷ ⏲ ◑ ● Never. ☑ AE, DC, MC, V. ££££

LACOCK

At The Sign of the Angel The epitome of the medieval English inn – half-timbered, with great log fires in cold weather, beamed ceilings, oak panelling, venerable old beds and gleaming antique furniture. The village is owned and cared for by the National Trust. The pleasures are simple, the setting memorable.
☒ 6 Church St, Lacock, Chippenham, Wiltshire SN15 2LB.
Map p75 D4. ☎ (01249) 730230. FAX (01249) 730527.
⏲ b,l,d. **Rooms** 10. ◑ ● Christmas.
☑ AE, DC, MC, V. ££

HORLEY

Langshott Manor Gatwick is only some 2 miles away, and urban sprawl presses on all sides, but this brick-and-timber Elizabethan manor remains at peace in its own landscaped grounds. The expense-account luxury includes swish, well-equipped bedrooms and an intimate dining room; the price includes a week's free airport parking.
☒ Langshott, Horley, Surrey RH6 9LN. **Map** p75 E4.
☎ (01293)786680. FAX (01293) 783905. @ admin@ langshottmanor.com ⏲ b,l,d. **Rooms** 15. ◑ ● Never.
☑ AE, DC, MC, V. £££

THE LIZARD

Landewednack House The family home of Marion and Peter Stanley, this lovely old rectory in a thatched hamlet has an superb headland position. The views across the garden and the church to the sea are heavenly, and the three bedrooms are supremely elegant and luxurious. Guests dine *en famille*; Marion's local seafood dishes, perhaps lobster or crab, are a highlight.
☒ Church Cove, The Lizard, Helston, Cornwall TR12 7PQ.
Map p74 A5. ☎ (01326) 290909. FAX (01326) 290192.
⏲ b,d. **Rooms** 3. ☷ ◑ ● Christmas. ☑ MC, V. ££

HAWKRIDGE
Tarr Steps Set serenely against wooded slopes on the upper reaches of the River Barle, an old-fashioned sporting hotel. No TVs in rooms.
☒ Hawkridge, Dulverton, Somerset TA22 9PY.
Map p74 B4. ☎ (01643) 851293. FAX (01643) 851218.
⏲ b,l,d. **Rooms** 11. ££

HUNSTRETE
Hunstrete House A refined atmosphere fills this mellow, Georgian townhouse. Classy cooking.
☒ Hunstrete, Pensford, Bristol, Somerset BS39 4NS.
Map p74 C4. ☎ (01761) 490490. FAX (01761) 490732.
@ user@hunstretehouse.co.uk ⏲ b,l,d.
Rooms 23. £££

KILVE
Meadow House Former rectory set peacefully between the sea and the Quantock Hills. The spacious rooms are furnished with taste.
☒ Sea Lane, Kilve, Somerset TA5 1EG. **Map** p74 C4.
☎ (01278) 741546. FAX (01278) 741663. ⏲ b,d.
Rooms 10. ££

KINGSWEAR
Nonsuch House The former owners of Langshott (see above) have swapped Surrey for a guest-house with fabulous views across the River Dart.
☒ Church Hill, Kingswear, Dartmouth, Devon TQ6 0BX.
Map p74 C5. ☎ FAX (01803) 752829. ⏲ b,d.
Rooms 5. ££

For key to symbols see backflap. For price categories *see p71*

LONDON

The Athenaeum The West End hotel and apartments have a caring reputation, but lone women are made to feel particularly welcome. Most rooms are comfortable rather than luxurious, with standard bathrooms, but each has a CD and video player and a proper bar. There is also a range of serviced apartments, some sumptuous.
⊠ 116 Piccadilly, London W1V OBJ. **Map** p72 C3. ▐ (020) 7499 3464. **FAX** (020) 7493 1860. @ info@ athenaeumhotel.com ▐ b,l,d. **Rooms** 126, plus 26 apts. ▤ ▐ ● Never. ▨ AE, DC, MC, V. ⓔⓔⓔⓔ

LONDON

The Cadogan This quietly old-fashioned hotel on the borders of Chelsea and Knightsbridge is where Oscar Wilde was arrested (room 118). You can stay here, surrounded by photographs of the playwright. (In Paris, at l'Hotel, you can stay in the room in which he died.) Lilly Langtry's home was also here. Dignified, warm and comforting.
⊠ 75 Sloane St, London SW1X 9SG. **Map** p72 B4. ▐ (020) 7235 7141. **FAX** (020) 7245 0994. @ info@thecadogan.u-net.com ▐ b,l,d. **Rooms** 65. ▤ ● Never. ▨ AE, MC, V. ⓔⓔⓔ

LONDON

The Beaufort Consistently praised and with a high percentage of faithful regulars, this is an exceptional townhouse hotel. It is noted for the friendly attitude of its mainly female staff, the beautiful, enveloping decor, and the wealth of extras included in the rates (airport limo, cream teas, champagne). In a quiet street near Harrods.
⊠ 33 Beaufort Gardens, London SW3 1PP. **Map** p72 B3. ▐ (020) 7584 5252. **FAX** (020) 7589 2834. @ thebeaufort@nol.co.uk ▐ b. **Rooms** 28. ▤ ● Never. ▨ AE, DC, MC, V. ⓔⓔⓔⓔ

LONDON

The Connaught For service – the type of impeccable, deferential service perfected by Jeeves – look no further. Now almost a living time-warp, this bastion of Britishness continues to turn a haughtily blind eye to the modern world; there are few newfangled frills. Mr Bourdin's respected cuisine is produced with solemn ritual.
⊠ Carlos Place, London W1Y 6AL. **Map** p72 C2. ▐ (020) 7499 7070. **FAX** (020) 7495 3262. @ info@ the-connaught.co.uk ▐ b,l,d. **Rooms** 92. ● Never. ▨ AE, DC, MC, V. ⓔⓔⓔⓔ

LIFTON

Arundel Arms Traditional, characterful sporting inn with 20 miles of fishing on the Tamar river and its four tributeries. Log fires, modish food. Tackle shop in rare former cock-fighting pit.
⊠ Lifton, Devon PL16 0AA. **Map** p74 B5. ▐ (01566) 784666. **FAX** (01566) 784494. ▐ b,l,d. **Rooms** 28. ⓔⓔ

LONDON

Five Sumner Place Prettily decorated, fairly priced South Kensington B&B. Airy conservatory breakfast room and cool patio.
⊠ 5 Sumner Place, London SW7 3EE. **Map** p72 A4. ▐ (020) 7584 7586. **FAX** (020) 7823 9962. ▐ b. **Rooms** 13. ⓔⓔⓔ

LONDON

The Halkin Armani-dressed staff deliver seriously good service at this sleek, minimalist yet friendly hotel.
⊠ 5 Halkin St, London SW1X 7DJ. **Map** p72 C3. ▐ (020) 7333 1000. **FAX** (020) 7333 1100. @ res@halkin.co.uk ▐ b,l,d. **Rooms** 41. ⓔⓔⓔⓔ

LONDON

London Bridge Glossy, elegant new business orientated hotel in regenerated area near City.
⊠ 8-18 London Bridge St, London SE1 9SG. **Map** p73 F2. ▐ (020) 7855 2200. **FAX** (020) 7855 2233. @ sales@london-bridge-hotel.co.uk ▐ b,l,d. **Rooms** 119. ⓔⓔⓔⓔ

LONDON

Covent Garden If you are at home in a trendy location and starry company, you will delight in this exceptional hotel. The high-ceilinged former hospital combining inspired design and the latest technology with panache. Stunning drawing room with honesty bar; smiling young staff.
🖂 10 Monmouth St, London WC2H 9HB. **Map** p73 E1. 📞 (020) 7806 1000. **FAX** (020) 7806 1100. @ coventgarden@firmdale.com 🍴 b,l,d. **Rooms** 50. 🖳 🍴 ● Never. 🗲 AE, MC, V; cheques not accepted. ⓔⓔⓔⓔ

LONDON

Dukes Hotel Discreetly set back in its own gas-lit courtyard, this civilized Edwardian hideaway contrives to be both intimate and animated. This is particularly true of the clubby bar where master barman Gilberto Preti concocts his special Dry Martinis. English country house decoration without excess; charming, helpful staff.
🖂 St James's Place, London SW1A 1NY. **Map** p73 D2. 📞 (020) 7491 4840. **FAX** (020) 7493 1264. @ dukeshotel@compuserve.com 🍴 b,l,d. **Rooms** 81. 🖳 🍴 ● Never. 🗲 AE, DC, MC, V. ⓔⓔⓔⓔ

LONDON

The Dorchester Of London's great hotels, this has the edge, sweeping into the lead after its 1990 refurbishment. The 1930s building, looming over Park Lane like an ocean liner, was designed as the perfect grand hotel, and it is. It encompasses corporate events, film star guests, traditional atmosphere, and sumptuous modern luxury.
🖂 Park Lane, London W1A 2HJ. **Map** p72 C2. 📞 (020) 7629 8888. **FAX** (020) 7409 0114. @ reservations@ dorchesterhotel.com 🍴 b,l,d. **Rooms** 248. 🖳 🍴 ● Never. 🗲 AE, DC, MC, V. ⓔⓔⓔⓔ

LONDON

The Franklin This is a top-notch townhouse hotel by any standards, protective and relaxing, but what sets the Franklin apart is the bedrooms. Some are enormous, or look onto beautifully kept communal gardens, full of white roses in summer. Inside are florals and stripes, flounces and swags and huge beds, some canopied.
🖂 28 Egerton Gardens, London SW3 2DB. **Map** p72 B4. 📞 (020) 7584 5533. **FAX** (020) 7584 5449. @ bookings@thefranklin.force9.co.uk 🍴 b. **Rooms** 50. 🖳 🎲 ● Never. 🗲 AE, DC, MC, V. ⓔⓔⓔⓔ

LONDON

Pembridge Court Two ginger cats, a friendly manager and a mass of framed fans are some of the distinguishing features of this cosy hotel.
🖂 34 Pembridge Gardens, London W2 4DX. **Map** p72 A2. 📞 (020) 7229 9977. **FAX** (020) 7727 4982.
@ reservations@pemct.co.uk 🍴 b,l,d. **Rooms** 22. ⓔⓔⓔ

LONDON

The Rookery Created from 18th-century brick buildings and full of clubby period charm.
🖂 12 Peter's Lane, Cowcross St, London EC1M 6DS. **Map** p73 F1. 📞 (020) 7336 0931. **FAX** (020) 7336 0932. @ reservations@rookery.co.uk 🍴 b. **Rooms** 119. ⓔⓔⓔⓔ

LONDON

The Savoy Still charismatic, and a byword for luxury and Art Deco elegance. The Grill Room has a strong draw for the country's elite.
🖂 The Strand, London WC2R 0EU. **Map** p73 F2. 📞 (020) 7836 4343. **FAX** (020) 7240 6040. @ info@ the-savoy.co.uk 🍴 b,l,d. **Rooms** 207. ⓔⓔⓔⓔ

LONDON

Strand Palace Opposite the Savoy, and very different; its pleasant, fresh rooms represent good value. Perfect for theatre visits.
🖂 Strand, London WC2R 0JJ. **Map** p73 F2. 📞 (020) 7836 8080. **FAX** (020) 7257 9402. @ malvinv1@ forte-hotel.com 🍴 b,l,d. **Rooms** 783. ⓔⓔⓔ

London

The Gore With loads of character, including an animated public bar and bistro but a contrastingly quiet sitting room, this makes a delightfully congenial place to stay. Walls are covered in paintings and prints; bedrooms are crammed with antiques and idiosyncracies – ornate beds, a throne loo here, a gallery there.

⊠ 189 Queen's Gate, London SW7 5EX. **Map** p72 A3.
📞 (020) 7584 6601. ꜰᴀx (020) 7589 8127.
@ sales@gorehotel.co.uk 🍴 b,l,d. **Rooms** 54.
● Christmas. 💳 AE, DC, MC, V. ££££

London

L'Hotel Baby sister of, and adjacent to, the suave Capital Hotel, this is an upmarket B&B, well situated for shopping sprees at Harrods. Breakfast is taken in the basement restaurant, Le Metro; there is no sitting room or room service. Bedrooms are mostly quite small, but sophisticated and well-equipped.

⊠ 28 Basil Street, London SW3 1AS. **Map** p72 B3.
📞 (020) 7589 6286. ꜰᴀx (020) 7823 7826.
@ reservations@capitalgrp.co.uk 🍴 b,l,d. **Rooms** 12.
● Never. 💳 AE, DC, MC, V. £££

London

Hazlitt's Visiting authors leave signed copies for literary folk who like their comforts authentic yet stylish. A good Soho base, the three unspoilt Georgian townhouses have retained their sloping floorboards (it can be an uphill walk to bed). They have been decorated with suitable antiques, busts and prints, and Victorian bathroom fittings.

⊠ 6 Frith Street, London W1V 5TZ. **Map** p73 E1.
📞 (020) 7434 1771. ꜰᴀx (020) 7439 1524.
@ reservations@hazlitts.co.uk 🍴 b. **Rooms** 23.
● Christmas. 💳 AE, DC, MC, V. ££££

London

Number Sixteen The elegant South Kensington B&B encompasses four smart terraced houses, and exudes a familial atmosphere of home: richly traditional, harmonious decor, with the bonus of a conservatory and patio garden. The bedrooms are well-proportioned; one has its own terrace. Some bathrooms could be improved.

⊠ 16 Sumner Place, London SW7 3EG. **Map** p72 A4.
📞 (020) 7589 5232. ꜰᴀx (020) 7584 8615.
@ reservations@numbersixteenhotel.co.uk 🍴 b.
Rooms 36. 🔞 ● Never. 💳 AE, DC, MC, V. £££

London

Sydney House Luxury townhouse B&B with 24-hour room service. The rooms are all different, with an international feel.
⊠ 9-11 Sydney St, London SW3 6PU.
Map p72 B5. 📞 (020) 7376 7711. ꜰᴀx (020) 7376 4233.
🍴 b. **Rooms** 21. ££££

London

Tophams Belgravia Cosy family-owned hotel with plenty of personality. Small rooms.
⊠ 28 Ebury St, London SW1W 0LU. **Map** p72 C4.
📞 (020) 7730 8147. ꜰᴀx (020) 7823 5966.
@ tophams_belgravia.compuserve.com 🍴 b,l,d.
Rooms 40. £££

London

Winchester Hotel Stands out among budget options for its neat rooms, excellent house-keeping and en suite facilities (shower only).
⊠ 17 Belgrave Road, London SW1 1RB.
Map p72 C4. 📞 (020) 7828 2972.
ꜰᴀx (020) 7828 5191. 🍴 b. **Rooms** 18. ££

Lymington

Stanwell House Decorated with great flair. Attractive bistro and courtyard.
⊠ High St, Lymington, Hampshire SO41 9AA.
Map p75 D5. 📞 (01590) 677123.
ꜰᴀx (01590) 677756. @ stanwellhouse@virgin.net
🍴 b,l,d. **Rooms** 31. £££

LONDON

One Aldwych Much-hyped hotel whose dramatic lobby has a bar rather than reception desk centre-stage. The best of the soothing bedrooms is the circular suite overlooking Waterloo Bridge. All are filled with state-of-the-art equipment and flowers, though the vacuum plumbing can be anything but restful.
⊠ One Aldwych, London WC2B 4BZ. **Map** p73 F2.
☎ (020) 7300 1000. FAX (020) 7300 1001.
@ sales@onealdwych.co.uk ⑪ b,l,d. **Rooms** 105.
▤ ⌷ ⑪ ① ● Never. ⊠ AE, DC, MC, V. €€€€

MELKSHAM

Shurnhold House This beautifully proportioned stone-built Jacobean house sits close to a main road on the outskirts of an unremarkable town, but is well screened by trees. Inside you will find flagstones, beams, floral fabrics, a room full of books, and spacious bedrooms. The licensed bar is an unusual feature for a B&B. Well placed for touring in several directions.
⊠ Shurnhold, Melksham, Wiltshire, SN12 8DG.
Map p75 D4. ☎ (01225) 790555. FAX (01225) 793147.
⑪ b. **Rooms** 9. ⑧ ● Never. ⊠ AE, MC, V. €€

LONDON

The Portobello The stylish Notting Hill base appeals to people who appreciate its laid-back approach, eclectic Victoriana furnishings, and airy, 24-hour restaurant/bar. Rooms vary from tiny 'cabins' to sybaritic suites (bath in bedroom, mirrors above bed). The best have antique beds and baths – others have showers only.
⊠ 22 Stanley Gardens, London W11 2NG.
Map p72 A2. ☎ (020) 7727 2777. FAX (020) 7792 9641.
⑪ b,l,d. **Rooms** 24. ● Christmas and New Year.
⊠ AE, DC, MC, V. €€€

NEW MILTON

Chewton Glen Once inside this superbly run hotel you are enveloped in an exceptional degree of luxury (with a price tag to match). Rooms and suites are correspondingly faultless, and both service and cuisine are of the highest quality. Many guests come for the golf and the superb, sybaritic health club.
⊠ Christchurch Road, New Milton, Hants BH25 6QS.
Map p75 D5. ☎ (01425) 275341. FAX (014250) 272310.
@ reservations@chewtonglen.com ⑪ b,l,d. **Rooms** 54.
▤ ⌷ ⑪ ⑧ ● Never. ⊠ AE, DC, MC, V. €€€€

MAWNAN SMITH
Nansidwell Arts and Crafts stone-mullioned house in subtropical gardens close to the sea. Cheerful rooms, some small. Ambitious food.
⊠ Mawnan Smith, Falmouth, Cornwall TR11 5HU.
Map p74 A5. ☎ (01326) 250340. FAX (01326) 250 440.
@ bomberob@aol.com ⑪ b,d. **Rooms** 12. €€

MIDHURST
Angel Hotel Coaching inn with Georgian façade and plush, warmly decorated Tudor interior. Many rooms have beams.
⊠ North Street, Midhurst, West Sussex GU29 9DN.
Map p75 E5. ☎ (01730) 812421. FAX (01730) 815928. ⑪ b,l,d. **Rooms** 28. €€

RYDE, ISLE OF WIGHT
Biskra Beach Ryde may be tacky, but this renovated hotel is a colonial-style haven with a stunning terrace (and hot tub) right on the sea.
⊠ 17 St Thomas St, Ryde, Isle of Wight PO33 2DL.
Map p75 D5. ☎ (01983) 567913. FAX (01983) 616976.
@ info@biskra-hotel.com ⑪ b,l,d. **Rooms** 6. €€

RYE
The Old Vicarage Central but peaceful Tudor-Georgian family-run B&B. Breakfast is a highlight: home-made scones and jams.
⊠ 66 Church Square, Rye, East Sussex TN31 7HF.
Map p75 F5. ☎ (01797) 222119. FAX (01797) 227466.
⑪ b. **Rooms** 6. €€

For key to symbols see backflap. For price categories see p71

NEW ROMNEY

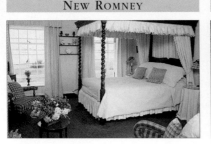

Romney Bay House This remarkable house was designed by Sir Clough Williams-Ellis, creator of Portmeirion (see page 118). It stands on the edge of Romney Marsh, with wonderful sea views (telescope in the first-floor lookout). The rooms are fresh and individually decorated. Tennis, croquet, golf on the doorstep; highly rated food.
☒ Coat Road, Littlestone, New Romney, Kent, TN28 8QY. **Map** p75 F5. ☎ (01797) 364747. ℻ (01797) 367156. ⅋ b,l, d. **Rooms** 10. 🍷 ● Christmas. 🗐 DC MC V. ⓔⓔ

PENZANCE

The Abbey This characterful, rather grand house overlooking the harbour continues to exert its many charms – at times it's a little too laid-back, but it's always relaxed. It is presided over by the charming Mrs Cox (formerly '60s model Jean Shrimpton) and her husband. She has taste and loves buying antiques and curios – both of which are amply evident. Lovely walled garden.
☒ Abbey St, Penzance, Cornwall TR18 4AR. **Map** p74 A5. ☎ (01736) 366906. ℻ (01736) 351163. ⅋ b,d. **Rooms** 7. 🍷 ● Christmas. 🗐 AE, MC, V. ⓔⓔ

PADSTOW

Seafood Restaurant/St Petroc's Hotel/Middle Street Café Choose from one of three places, all friendly and stylish, and all owned by chef Rick Stein. The best rooms (Nos 5 and 6 have estuary views) are above his famous fish restaurant; St Petroc's is a proper hotel; rooms above the Café are the least expensive.
☒ Riverside, Padstow, Cornwall PL28 8BY. **Map** p74 A5. ☎ (01841) 532700. ℻ (01841) 532942. @ seafoodrestpadstow@compuserve.com ⅋ b,l,d. **Rooms** 29. ● Christmas. 🗐 MC, V. ⓔⓔ

RINGLESTONE

Ringlestone Inn An 'ale house' since 1615, Ringlestone Inn is today affably run by Mike Millington Buck and his daughter. They offer comfortable rooms in the converted farmhouse opposite. Hearty pies and English country wines are the specialities of the restaurant, which comprises several intimate dining areas.
☒ Ringlestone, Maidstone, Kent ME17 1NX. **Map** p75 F4. ☎ ℻ (01622) 859900. @ michelle@ringlestone.com ⅋ b,l,d. **Rooms** 5. 🍷 ● Christmas Day. 🗐 AE, DC, MC, V. ⓔⓔ

ST KEYNE

Well House Victorian hill-top house with the plush interior of a much larger establishment. Wine list notable for its clarets; terrace, pool.
☒ St Keyne, Liskeard, Cornwall PL14 4RN. **Map** p74 B5. ☎ (01579) 342001. ℻ (01579) 343891. ⅋ b,l,d. **Rooms** 9. ⓔⓔⓔ

ST MARGARET'S AT CLIFFE

...etts Court Handsome old manor. Smart ...od or more modern bedrooms; pool, spa.
...estcliffe, St Margaret's at Cliffe, Dover, Kent ... 6EW. **Map** p75 F4. ☎ (01304) 852424. ...01304) 853430. @ walletscourt@compuserve.com ...b,d. **Rooms** 17. ⓔⓔ

ST MARTIN'S, ISLES OF SCILLY

St Martin's Welcoming holiday hotel in a superb, remote location. Modern, built of local stone, with comfortable bedrooms. Expensive.
☒ St Martin's, Isles of Scilly TR25 0QW. **Map** p74 A4. ☎ (01720) 422092. ℻ (01720) 422298. ⅋ b,l,d. **Rooms** 30. ⓔⓔⓔⓔ

SEAVIEW, ISLE OF WIGHT

Seaview Hotel Popular seaside hotel and local watering hole, run with care and bonhomie.
☒ High St, Seaview, Isle of Wight PO34 5EX. **Map** p75 E5. ☎ (01983) 612711. ℻ (01983) 613729. @ seaviewhotel@virgin.net ⅋ b,l,d. **Rooms** 16. ⓔⓔ

ROCK

St Enodoc The seaside holiday hotel, with slate roof and pebbledash walls, is no beauty but is typical of the area, and has splendid views across the Camel estuary. Its breezy new interior suits the location perfectly: bright colours, painted furniture, modern art. The Californian-style Bar and Grill is popular with non-residents.
⊠ Rock, Cornwall PL27 6LA. **Map** p74 B5.
[C (01208) 863394. FAX (01208) 863970.
@ enodoc@aol.com ⑪ b,l,d. **Rooms** 18.
≋ ⑪ ⑧ ● Never. ⊠ AE, DC, MC, V. ⓔⓔⓔ

RUSHLAKE GREEN

Stone House Peter and Jane Dunn's ancestral home is a fine 16th-century manor with graceful interior. Of the seven sumptuous bedrooms, two have antique four-posters and huge bathrooms. Jane cooks elegant dinners, and produces picnics for Glyndebourne. Other attractions: log fires, shooting, billiards, woodland walks, croquet.
⊠ Rushlake Green, Heathfield, East Sussex TN21 9QJ.
Map p75 F5. [C (01435) 830553. FAX (01435) 830726.
⑪ b,d. **Rooms** 7. ⑧ ● Christmas to Feb.
⊠ Not accepted. ⓔⓔⓔ

RUANHIGHLANES

Crugsillick Manor Elegant Queen Anne manor in a sheltered hollow on the lovely Roseland Peninsula. Owners the Barstows treat you as their house guests (communal candlelit dinners) but know when privacy is required. The drawing room has a ceiling moulded by Napoleonic prisoners. Picnics hampers available for lunch.
⊠ Ruanhighlanes, Truro, Cornwall TR2 5L.
Map p74 A5. [C (01872) 501214. FAX (01872) 501228.
@ barstow_crugsillick@csi.com ⑪ b,d. **Rooms** 3.
⑧ ● Never. ⊠ MC, V. ⓔⓔ

RYE

Jeake's House The 17th-century building makes a fitting B&B in picture-perfect Rye: beamed bedrooms, furnished with brass or mahogany bedsteads, lace bedspreads and antiques, look out over rooftops or over Romney Marsh. There is a comfortable book-lined sitting room and bar; breakfast is taken in a galleried former chapel.
⊠ Mermaid Street, Rye, East Sussex TN 7ET.
Map p75 F5. [C (01797) 222828. FAX (01797) 222623.
@ jeakeshouse@btinternet.com ⑪ b. **Rooms** 12.
● Never. ⊠ MC, V. ⓔⓔⓔ

SHIPTON GORGE

Innsacre Peaceful, welcoming farmhouse set amongst hills and orchards. French country-style bedrooms; imaginative set dinner and good teas and breakfasts; secluded terrace.
⊠ Shipton Gorge, Bridport, Dorset DT6 4LJ. **Map** p74 C5.
[C FAX (01308) 456137. ⑪ b,d. **Rooms** 4. ⓔⓔ

SIMONSBATH

Simonsbath House Dating from 1654, the first house to be built on Exmoor. Wood panelling and open fires; best rooms have four-posters.
⊠ Simonsbath, Minehead, Somerset TA24 7SH.
Map p74 B4. [C (01643) 831259. FAX (01643)
831557. ⑪ b,d. **Rooms** 7. ⓔⓔ

STON EASTON

Ston Easton House This Palladian mansion has a suitably richly ornamented interior. Excellent service. Formal dining.
⊠ Ston Easton, Bath BA3 4DF. **Map** p74 C4.
[C (01761) 241631. FAX (01761) 241377 @ stoneaston@
cityscape.co.uk ⑪ b,l,d. **Rooms** 21. ⓔⓔⓔⓔ

STORRINGTON

Little Thakenham The chance to stay in one of Lutyens' finest houses, with minstrel's gallery. Furnished in keeping, with vast master suites.
⊠ Merrywood Lane, Storrington, West Sussex RH20 3HE.
Map p75 E5. [C (01903) 744416. FAX (01903) 745022.
⑪ b,l,d. **Rooms** 9. ⓔⓔⓔ

For key to symbols see backflap. For price categories see p71

ST MAWES

Tresanton Owned by Olga Polizzi, daughter of hotelier Lord Forte, this much-vaunted hotel marries cool city sophistication with Cornish character. The cluster of cottages, built on different levels, overlooks the unspoilt town and the sea. Yacht, watersports available. This is a romantic haven, with excellent food and service, but very expensive for an essentially simple hotel.
⊠ St Mawes, Cornwall TR2 5DR. **Map** p74 A5.
((01326) 270055. FAX (01326) 270053. ⅱ b,l,d.
Rooms 26. ⓘ ● Jan. € AE, MC, V. ££££

SARK, CHANNEL ISLANDS

La Sablonnerie A long, low, 16th-century farmhouse at the southern tip of traffic-free Sark, this is the Channel Islands' sweetest hotel, and the one serving the best food. Guests return year after year for utter peace and lovely scenery. There are no phones or TVs in the rooms; instead, each has a vase of flowers and bowl of fruit, and crisp linen on the comfy beds.
⊠ Little Sark, Sark, via Guernsey GY9 0SD. **Map** p75 E5.
((01481) 832061. FAX (01481) 832408. ⅱ b,l,d.
Rooms 22. ⓘ ● Oct to Easter. € AE, MC, V. ££

SANDGATE

Sandgate Hotel As close to France as possible without being there. Ten minutes's drive from the Channel Tunnel, facing the sea, this Gallic hotel/restaurant is owned by Zara Gicqueau and her French husband Samuel, the talented chef. It is staffed by a charming, mainly French team. Try to get a room with sea view, and book dinner.
⊠ The Esplanade, Sandgate, Folkstone, Kent CT20 3DY. **Map** p75 F4. ((01303) 220444. FAX (01303) 220496. ⅱ b,l,d. **Rooms** 15. ● mid-Jan to mid-Feb, first week Oct. € AE, DC, MC, V. ££

SEAVIEW, ISLE OF WIGHT

Priory Bay Stylish decor and contemporary cuisine are successfully married with a relaxed ambience to suit both families and romantic couples. The eclectic house embraces many periods: there are a Georgian muralled dining room and a French Gothic porch. A highlight is the sweep of rare private beach.
⊠ Priory Drive, Seaview, Isle of Wight PO34 5BU. **Map** p75 D5. ((01983) 613146. FAX (01983) 616539.
@ reservations@priorybay.co.uk ⅱ b,l,d. **Rooms** 20, plus 16 cottages. ≋ ⓘ ● Never. € AE, MC, V. £££

STURMINSTER NEWTON
Plumber Manor A relaxed restaurant with cosy rooms, in a handsome Jacobean manor.
⊠ Sturminster Newton, Dorset DT10 2AF.
Map p74 C5. ((01258) 472507.
FAX (01258) 473370. @ plumbermanor@ btinternet.com ⅱ b,d. **Rooms** 16. £££

TAUNTON
Castle Hotel Castellated, wisteria-clad site of Judge Jeffreys' Bloody Assize. Pricey, acclaimed British cooking. Best rooms overlook garden.
⊠ Castle Green, Taunton, Somerset TA1 1NF.
Map p74 C5. ((01823) 272671. FAX (01823) 336066. ⅱ b,l,d. **Rooms** 44. £££

TREBARWITH STRAND
Old Millfloor A steep shady path is the only access to this converted mill, a cosy guesthouse with pretty rooms and good food.
⊠ Trebarwith Strand, Tintagel, Cornwall PL34 0HA.
Map p74 B5. ((01840) 770234.
ⅱ b,l,d. **Rooms** 3. £

TRESCO, ISLES OF SCILLY
Island Hotel Smoothly run, expensive hotel on this charming privately owned island. Public rooms have huge picture windows onto the sea.
⊠ Tresco, Isles of Scilly TR24 0PU. **Map** p74 A4.
((01720) 422883. FAX (01720) 423008. @ islandhotel@ tresco.co.uk ⅱ b,l,d. **Rooms** 45. ££££

SHEPTON MALLET

Bowlish House Exemplary restaurant-with-rooms: despite the august air of this fine Georgian mansion, it is relaxed and homelike. Bob Morley is a warm host, and his wife Linda an award-winning cook; the pale yellow dining room makes an elegant setting for meals. The unobtrusive bedrooms have large bathrooms.
✉ Wells Road, Shepton Mallet, Somerset BA4 5JD. **Map** p74 C4. ☎ FAX (01749) 342022. ⊓ b,d. **Rooms** 3. ⊘ ⬤ 1 week spring, 1 week autumn. ⬛ AE, MC, V. ⓔⓔ

SOUTH MOLTON

Whitechapel Manor A Grade I Elizabethan manor house, surrounded by lawned terraced gardens and overlooking wooded farmland and low hills. Inside are fine William and Mary plasterwork, a Jacobean carved oak screen, and uneven oak floors. The whole is gracious and spacious, with comfortable bedrooms and elegant bathrooms. Serious cooking.
✉ South Molton, Devon EX36 3EG. **Map** p74 B5. ☎ (01769) 573377. FAX (01769) 573797. ⊓ b,d. **Rooms** 10. ⊘ ⬤ Never. ⬛ AE DC, MC, V. ⓔⓔⓔ

TINTAGEL

Trebea Lodge A lovely spot overlooking sea and countryside is the setting for this welcoming, civilized and intimate retreat. The warmly decorated grey stone Georgian house is marked out by panelled walls, flagstones, antiques and personal touches. There is a cosy 'snug' with log fire and honesty bar. At dinner, local produce is a mainstay. Helpful owners.
✉ Trenale, Tintagel, Cornwall PL34 OHR. **Map** p74 A5. ☎ (01840) 770410. FAX (01840) 770092. ⊓ b,d. **Rooms** 8. ⊘ ⬤ Dec to mid-Feb. ⬛ AE, MC, V. ⓔⓔ

TUNBRIDGE WELLS

Hotel du Vin A faded but grand hotel has become the second Hotel du Vin (see page 92). This one has more space and period features but similarly stylish bedrooms and bathrooms. It also has the same friendly, efficient service and buzzing bistro, down to the hop garlands, the sunny food and the world-class sommelier.
✉ Crescent Road, Tunbridge Wells, Kent TN1 2LY. **Map** p75 F4. ☎ (01892) 526455. FAX (01892) 512044. @ reception@hotelduvin.co.uk ⊓ b,l,d. **Rooms** 32. ⊘ ⬤ Never. ⬛ AE, DC, MC, V. ⓔⓔ

TRUSHAM

Cridford Inn Admire a Saxon mosaic in the oldest house in Devon, a cosy thatched inn run by a friendly young pair.
✉ Trusham, Newton Abbot, Devon TQ13 ONR. **Map** p74 B5. ☎ FAX (01626) 853694. ⊓ b,l,d. **Rooms** 4. ⓔⓔ

WAREHAM

The Priory Former nunnery on River Frome. Some bedrooms are in the old boathouse.
✉ Church Green, Wareham, Dorset BH20 4ND. **Map** p75 D5. ☎ (01929) 551666. FAX (01929) 554519. @ reception@theprioryhotel.co.uk ⊓ b,l,d. **Rooms** 19. ⓔⓔⓔ

WARMINSTER

Bishopstrow House Swish Georgian mansion with state-of-the-art health spa and much more. Fantastic suites, but other rooms are small.
✉ Warminster Wilts BA12 9HH. **Map** p75 D4. ☎ (01985) 212312. FAX (01985) 216769. @ bishopstrow_house_ hotel@msn.com ⊓ b,d. **Rooms** 31. ⓔⓔⓔⓔ

WESTDEAN

Old Parsonage Remarkable medieval house, with charming bedrooms, furnished in perfect keeping by its caring, attentive owners.
✉ Westdean, Alfriston, Seaford, East Sussex BN25 4AL. **Map** p75 E5. ☎ FAX (01323) 870432. ⊓ b. **Rooms** 3. ⓔⓔ

UCKFIELD

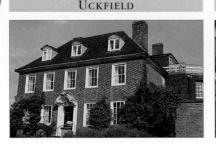

WINCHESTER

Hooke Hall In the centre of Uckfield, this elegant Queen Anne townhouse makes a smart, yet informal hotel. Public rooms and bedrooms (some named after famous lovers) are confidently decorated with designer fabrics by owner Juliet Percy. Despite the homely atmosphere, there are such unexpected accoutrements as minibars and trouser presses. Classy Italian restaurant.
☒ 250 High Street, Uckfield, East Sussex TN22 1EN.
Map p75 E4. ((01825) 761578. FAX (01825) 768025.
b,d. **Rooms** 10. ● ● Christmas. AE, MC, V. ££

Wykham Arms It looks plain, but inside there is a convivial atmosphere, with tables crammed into every available space. Guests tuck into top-notch pub food, washed down by real ales and an impressive selection of wines. Cosy, low-ceilinged bedrooms upstairs; less characterful but smarter ones in the annexe across the road.
☒ 75 Kingsgate Street, Winchester, Hampshire SO23 9PE. **Map** p75 D4. ((01962) 853834.
FAX (01962) 854411. b,l,d. **Rooms** 13. ●
● Christmas Day. AE, DC, MC, V. ££

WINCHESTER

YARMOUTH, ISLE OF WIGHT

Hotel du Vin The owners of this extremely popular modern-day hostelry wrought a miracle when they took over a dowdy town centre hotel. Stylish but unpretentious, its heart is the bustling Bistro (be sure to book), serving zesty food and excellent but affordable wines. The elegant bedrooms are sponsored by wine companies.
☒ Southgate Street, Winchester, Hampshire SO23 9EF. **Map** p75 D4. ((01962) 841414. FAX (01962) 842458.
@ admin@winchester.hotelduvin.co.uk b,l,d.
Rooms 23 ● ● Never. AE, DC, MC, V. ££

George Hotel The carefully restored former 17th-century governor's residence sits in the centre of this breezy and historic little harbour town. It has much to recommend it, including a panelled sitting room and elegant bedrooms. The amiable brasserie is preferable to the sombre dining room, serving well-regarded though variable food.
☒ Yarmouth, Isle of Wight PO41 0PE. **Map** p75 D5.
((01983) 760331. FAX (01983) 760425.
@ res@thegeorge.co.uk b,l,d. **Rooms** 17. ●
● Never. AE, MC, V. £££

WHITSTABLE
Hotel Continental Main hotel decorated in Art Deco style, plus seven simple, gaily decorated fisherman's huts for a bit of seaside fun.
☒ 29 Beach Walk, Whitstable, Kent, CT5 2BP.
Map p75 F4. ((01227) 280280. FAX (01227) 280257.
b,l,d. **Rooms** 30. ££

WICKHAM
Old House In a fine village square, a Georgian house with interesting interior and bedrooms ranging from palatial to cramped. Good food.
☒ The Square, Wickham, Hampshire PO17 5JG.
Map p75 D5. ((01329) 833049. FAX (01329) 833672.
@ riversidehouse@enta.net b,d. **Rooms** 13. ££

WILLITON
White House Comfortable house with pretty courtyard garden run for 30 years by the affable Smiths. They have a passion for good food and wine: their list has won awards.
☒ 11 Long St, Williton, Somerset TA4 4QW. **Map** p74 C4.
((01984) 632306. b,d. **Rooms** 10. ££

YATTENDON
Royal Oak Village pub transformed into a suave, sophisticated and pricey restaurant and buzzing brasserie; attractive bedrooms upstairs.
☒ The Square, Yattendon, Newbury, Berkshire RG18 0UG.
Map p75 D4. ((01635) 201325. FAX (01635) 201926.
b,l,d. **Rooms** 5. £££

CENTRAL ENGLAND
COTSWOLDS • THAMES VALLEY
MIDLANDS • EAST ANGLIA

STRETCHING BETWEEN the Thames Valley in the south and a line drawn east-west from the mouth of the Humber river, Central England encompasses idyllic rural landscapes and great cathedral and university cities such as Lincoln, Manchester and Oxford. In the quintessentially English Cotswolds you will find fine places to stay in every category, from meltingly

beautiful manor houses to enchanting vine-clad inns; the East Anglian counties of Norfolk and Suffolk also have a wide choice. Elsewhere there are smart townhouse hotels, a smattering of stately homes-turned-hotels and a tempting selection of country houses, located in widely differing yet easily accessible settings, and perfect for a restful few days.

BASLOW	BROAD CAMPDEN

Fischer's Baslow Hall A 1907 mock-Elizabethan house has become a Michelin-starred restaurant-with-rooms under the aegis of chef Max Fischer and his wife Susan, an excellent hostess. The food is the point of the place (you can eat more simply in Café Max) but the smart bedrooms make a perfectly good overnight base.
⊠ Calver Rd, Baslow, Derbyshire DE45 1RR.
Map p75 D2. 📞 (01246) 583259. **FAX** (01246) 583818.
🍴 b,l,d. **Rooms** 6. 🔌 ◐ Christmas to early Jan.
💳 AE, DC, MC, V. ⓔⓔⓔ

Malt House In a tiny hamlet comprising little more than church and pub, is this delightful 17th-century Cotswold house. There are low, beamed ceilings and leaded windows overlooking a dream garden. The attractive bedrooms include a garden suite. The owners' son, Julian Brown, is the accomplished cook.
⊠ Broad Campden, Gloucestershire GL55 6UU.
Map p74 A2. 📞 (01386) 840295. **FAX** (01386) 841334.
@ nick@the-malt-house.freeserve.co.uk 🍴 b,d.
Rooms 8. 🔌 ◐ Christmas. 💳 AE, DC, MC, V. ⓔⓔ

ASHBOURNE
Callow Hall Above the Dove valley, a Victorian country house and grounds, lovingly restored. Comfortable and well-run, with good food.
⊠ Mappleton, Ashbourne, Derbyshire DE6 2AA.
Map p75 D2. 📞 (01335) 343403. **FAX** (01335) 343164.
🍴 b,d. **Rooms** 16. ⓔⓔⓔ

ASHFIELD-IN-THE-WATER
Riverside This stone-built, creeper-clad country house has secluded grounds bordering the River Wye. Accommodation is smart.
⊠ Ashford-in-the-Water, Bakewell, Derbyshire DE4 1QF.
Map p75 D2. 📞 (01629) 814275. **FAX** (01629) 812873.
@ riversidehouse@enta.net 🍴 b,l,d. **Rooms** 15. ⓔⓔⓔ

ATHERSTONE
Chapel House A quiet address (church bells excepted) in an old market town. Walled garden, light bedrooms, enjoyable food.
⊠ Friar's Gate, Atherstone, Warwickshire CV9 1EY.
Map p75 D3. 📞 (01827) 718949. **FAX** (01827) 717702.
🍴 b,l,d. **Rooms** 13. ⓔⓔ

BIBURY
Bibury Court Beautiful, affordable Jacobean mansion in idyllic riverside setting (fishing rods available). Atmospheric, if simple, rooms.
⊠ Bibury, Gloucestershire GL7 5NT. **Map** p74 A3.
📞 (01285) 740337. **FAX** (01285) 740660. @ andrew@
biburycourt.co.uk 🍴 b,l,d. **Rooms** 19. ⓔⓔ

BROADWAY

Collin House A haven of peace, in large country gardens tucked away from teeming Broadway. The bar is particularly cosy, with oak beams, armchairs, and an inglenook fireplace where log fires blaze on cool evenings. The pretty, traditional bedrooms and the bathrooms are gradually being upgraded by the new owners.
⊠ Collin Lane, Broadway, Worcestershire WR1 7PB. **Map** p74 A2. 【 (01386) 858354. **FAX** (01386) 858697. @ collin.house@virgin.net **Ⅱ** b,l,d. **Rooms** 7. ⊙ ⬤ Christmas. ⊠ MC, V. ⓕⓕ

BURFORD

The Lamb Most guests agree that the Lamb gets it just right, combining the convivial atmosphere of a cosy traditional pub with the comforts of a hotel. The beamed bedrooms are surprisingly spacious, decorated with floral fabrics and antiques. The daily-changing menus are served in a dining room overlooking a geranium-filled patio. Elsewhere are comfy sofas and log fires.
⊠ Sheep St, Burford, Oxfordshire OX18 4LR. **Map** p74 A3. 【 (01993) 823155. **FAX** (01993) 822228. **Ⅱ** b,l,d. **Rooms** 15. ⊙ ⬤ Christmas. ⊠ MC, V. ⓕⓕ

BURFORD

Burford House In the hands of Jane and Simon Henty, this 15th-century Cotswold stone and timbered building positively gleams with care and attention. The smart bedrooms (some with four-posters) are awash with polished furniture, glossy magazines, flowers, teddies, lotions, sachets and the like. Light lunches and teas (delicious cakes) are served in the adjacent restaurant.
⊠ 99 High St, Burford, Oxfordshire OX18 4QA. **Map** p74 A3. 【 (01993) 823151. **FAX** (01993) 823240. **Ⅱ** b,l. **Rooms** 7. ⊙ ⬤ Never. ⊠ AE, MC, V. ⓕⓕ

BURY ST EDMUNDS

Twelve Angel Hill Georgian to the front, Tudor to the rear, and close to the cathedral, this makes an excellent B&B, especially now that double-glazing has tamed the traffic noise outside. The spacious bedrooms are light, well-maintained, boldly decorated and thoughtfully equipped (if you like trouser presses). The bar is oak-panelled and intimate. Private car park.
⊠ 12 Angel Hill, Bury St Edmunds, Suffolk IP33 1UZ. **Map** p75 F3. 【 (01284) 704088. **FAX** (01284) 72554. **Ⅱ** b. **Rooms** 6. ⊙ ⬤ Jan. ⊠ AE, DC, MC, V. ⓕⓕ

BUCKLAND

Buckland Manor One of the Cotswolds' most exclusive hotels, a rich confection of manicured grounds, lavish bedrooms and formal dining.
⊠ Buckland, Gloucestershire WR12 7LY. **Map** p74 A2. 【 (01386) 852626. **FAX** (01386) 853557. @ buckland-manor-uk@msn.com **Ⅱ** b,l,d. **Rooms** 14. ⓕⓕⓕⓕ

BURNHAM MARKET

Hoste Arms Buzzing, characterful local inn, sometimes very busy, with attractive bedrooms.
⊠ The Green, Burnham Market, Norfolk PE31 8HD. Map p75 F2. 【 (01328) 738777. **FAX** (01328) 730103. @ thehostearms@ compuserve.com **Ⅱ** b,l,d. Rooms 20. ⓕⓕ

BURY ST EDMUNDS

Ounce House Meals are taken round a long table in this elegant Victorian house. It's in the town centre, with a large garden and private parking.
⊠ Northgate St, Bury St Edmunds IP33 1HP. **Map** p75 F3. 【 (01284) 761779. **FAX** (01284) 768315. @ pott@globalnet.co.uk **Ⅱ** b,d. **Rooms** 4. ⓕⓕ

CLANFIELD

Plough A mellow Elizabethan inn with a glossy interior and six bedrooms (two with four-poster beds) which vary in size. Sophisticated cooking.
⊠ Bourton Rd, Clanfield, Bampton, Oxfordshire OX18 2RB. **Map** p74 B3. 【 (01367) 810222. **FAX** (01367) 810596. **Ⅱ** b,l,d. **Rooms** 6. ⓕⓕ

CHADDESLEY CORBETT

CHIPPING CAMPDEN

Brockencote Hall Close to the M5/M42 motorways, this lakeside mansion has a fair proportion of business guests, but Anglo-French owners Alison and Joseph Petitjean ensure a discreetly privileged ambience. This is amply reflected in the decoration, which has distinctly French flourishes. Good food; polite service. ⊠ Chaddesley Corbett, Kidderminster, Worcestershire DY10 4PY. **Map** p75 D3. [(01562) 777876. FAX (01562) 777872. ¶¶ b,l,d. **Rooms** 17. ◑ ● Never. ⊜ AE, DC, MC, V. ⓔⓔⓔ

Cotswold House Each of the scrupulously detailed bedrooms has a different theme, such as regimental souvenirs in 'Military' or lace in 'Aunt Lizzy'. All have impeccable bathrooms. There is a magnificent spiral staircase, a walled garden and two snazzy dining rooms. ⊠ The Square, Chipping Campden, Gloucestershire GL55 6AN. **Map** p74 A2. [(01386) 840330. FAX (01386) 840310. @ reception@cotswold-house. demon.co.uk ¶¶ b,l,d. **Rooms** 15. ◑ ● Christmas. ⊜ AE, DC, MC, V. ⓔⓔⓔ

CHELTENHAM

CLEY-NEXT-THE-SEA

Hotel on the Park Despite some twee touches (two teddies centre stage in the dining room, plastic ducks artfully placed in bathrooms), this is a stylish establishment. The spacious bedrooms are embellished by sumptuous fabrics and antiques, although, at the front, traffic noise can destroy the calm so carefully engendered within. ⊠ Evesham Rd, Cheltenham, Gloucestershire GL52 2AH. **Map** p74 A2. [(01242) 518898. FAX (01242) 511526. @ stay@hotelonthepark.co.uk ¶¶ b,l,d. **Rooms** 12. ◑ ● Never. ⊜ AE, DC, MC, V. ⓔⓔⓔ

Cley Mill Memories of your favourite childrens' adventure stories crowd in as you climb ever higher in this 'real' windmill, finally mounting the ladder to the look-out room. The views over Cley Marshes, a bird-watchers' paradise, are superb. In the pretty, rustic bedrooms, bathrooms are fitted into the most challenging spaces. Good food includes fresh fish and samphire in season. ⊠ Cley-next-the-Sea, Holt, Norfolk NR25 7RP. **Map** p75 F2. [(01263) 740209. ¶¶ b,d. **Rooms** 8. ● Never. ⊜ MC, V. ⓔⓔ

CLEARWELL
Tudor Farmhouse Cosy, neat and simple, with fine oak spiral staircase; breakfast a minor feast. ⊠ Clearwell, Coleford, Gloucestershire GL16 8JS. **Map** p74 C4. [(01594) 833046. FAX (01594) 837093. @ reservations@tudorfarmhse.u-net.com ¶¶ b,d. **Rooms** 12. ⓔⓔ

CLEVE HILL
Cleeve Hill John and Marian Enstone's well-kept Edwardian-style B&B has superb views from the spacious bedrooms. Notable breakfasts. ⊠ Cleeve Hill, Cheltenham, Gloucestershire GL52 3PR. **Map** p74 A2. [(01242) 672052. FAX (01242) 679969. ¶¶ b. **Rooms** 9. ⓔⓔ

COLNE ST ALDWYNS
New Inn The epitome of a creeper-clad 16th-century Cotswold inn, now smart, glossy, sophisticated and highly successful. ⊠ Coln St Aldwyns, Cirencester, Gloucestershire GL7 5AN. **Map** p74 A3. [(01285) 750651. FAX (01285) 750657. @ stay@new-inn.co.uk ¶¶ b,l,d. **Rooms** 14. ⓔⓔ

DIDDLEBURY
Delbury Hall In lovely countryside and grounds, this gracious Georgian mansion overlooking a lake is also a friendly family home. ⊠ Diddlebury, Shropshire SY7 9DH. **Map** p74 C3. [(01584) 841267. FAX (01584) 841441. @ wrigley@ delbury.demon.co.uk ¶¶ b,d. **Rooms** 3. ⓔⓔ

For key to symbols see backflap. For price categories see p71

CORSE LAWN

Corse Lawn House Should you arrive in a coach and four, you could still drive it down the slipway into the pond to water the horses and wash the carriage, as in the days when this was a coaching inn. Instead you will probably be content to enjoy the advantages of this relaxed, long-favourite, if a little jaded country hotel. Bedrooms are large, with antique and modern furniture.
✉ Corse Lawn, Gloucestershire GL19 4LZ. **Map** p74 A2.
☎ (01452)780771. FAX (01452) 780840. ▮ b,l,d.
Rooms 19. ⌂ ▮ ◐ Christmas. ▨ AE, DC, MC, V. ⓔⓔ

HAMBLETON

Hambleton Hall For a sybaritic break in the grandest sort of country hotel, this is a prime contender. A former Victorian shooting lodge, it stands isolated on Rutland Water. It is decorated in glamorous, yet intimate fashion, with stylized bedrooms and a formal dining room serving excellent food. Terrace with views of the lake.
✉ Hambleton, Oakham, Rutland LE15 8TH. **Map** p75 E2.
☎ (01572) 756991. FAX (01572) 724721.
@ hotel@hambletonhall.com ▮ b,l,d. **Rooms** 15. ⌂ ▮
◐ Never. ▨ MC, V. ⓔⓔⓔⓔ.

GREAT SNORING

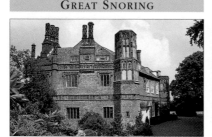

Old Rectory The sleepy village lives up to its name, and this low-key hotel, hidden behind high stone walls beside the church, is easy to miss. It's a quiet, restrained, relaxing sort of place, of mixed vintage, with a hotch-potch of squashy armchairs in the sitting room, comfortable bedrooms and a traditional English menu.
✉ Barsham Rd, Great Snoring, Norfolk NR21 0HP.
Map p75 F2. ☎ (01328) 820597. FAX (01328) 820048.
@ greatsnoringoldrectory@compuserve.com ▮ b,d.
Rooms 6. ▮ ◐ Christmas. ▨ AE, DC, MC, V. ⓔⓔ

KEMERTON

Upper Court The lovely, rather wild grounds of this well-loved family home include a ruined watermill, a lake (fishing, rowing) and a tennis court. The Georgian manor, furnished in country house style, is popular for house parties; accommodation is either in the main house, stables, or self-catering in the coach house.
✉ Kemerton, Tewkesbury, Gloucestershire GL20 7HY.
Map p74 A2. ☎ (01386) 725351. FAX (01386) 725472.
@ uppercourt@compuserve.com ▮ b,d. **Rooms** 10.
⌂ ▮ ◐ Christmas. ▨ MC, V. ⓔⓔ

DORCHESTER-ON-THAMES

George Hotel A spruce 15th-century coaching inn (old beams, open fires), one of the country's oldest, opposite the abbey in a delightful village.
✉ High St, Dorchester-on-Thames, Oxfordshire
OX10 7HH. **Map** p75 D4. ☎ (01865) 340404.
FAX (01865) 341620. ▮ b,l,d. **Rooms** 18. ⓔⓔ

EAST BARKWITH

Bodkin Lodge Walk the wildlife trails on the owners' conservation farm; stay in their light, airy modern home, with views to Lincoln Cathedral.
✉ Grange Farm, Torrington Lane, East Barkwith, Market Rasen, Lincolnshire LN8 5RY. **Map** p75 E2. ☎ (01673)
858249. FAX (01865) 341620. ▮ b. **Rooms** 2. ⓔ

GLOSSOP

Wind in the Willows A welcoming, traditional, family-run establishment. Thoughtful touches in the bedrooms, though some have showers only.
✉ Derbyshire Level, Glossop, Derbyshire SK13 7PT.
Map p75 D2. ☎ (01457) 868001. FAX (01457) 853354.
@ twitwh@aol.com ▮ b,d. **Rooms** 12. ⓔⓔ

GREAT MILTON

Le Manoir aux Quat' Saisons Raymond Blanc's temple of gastronomy, a Cotswold manor with appropriately swish accommodation.
✉ Church Rd, Great Milton, Oxfordshire OX44 7PD.
Map p75 E4. ☎ (01844) 278881. FAX (01844) 278847.
@ lemanoir@blanc.co.uk ▮ b,l,d. **Rooms** 32. ⓔⓔⓔⓔ

LANGAR

LAVENHAM

Langar Hall The owner of this idiosyncratic family home-turned-hotel, Imogen Skirving, has an eye for beautiful things and a taste for fun. Her apricot-coloured house in the Vale of Belvoir has a homely yet uplifting atmosphere. The rather grand restaurant is adorned with classsical statues; the bedrooms are highly individual.
☒ Langar, Nottinghamshire NG13 9HG. **Map** p75 E2.
📞 (01949) 860559. 📠 (01949) 861045.
@ langarhall-hotel@ndirect.co.uk 🍴 b,l,d. **Rooms** 10. 🅾
● Never. 💳 AE, DC, MC, V. ⓔⓔⓔ

Great House This very English building (15th-century, with a Georgian facade) has a French accent, brought to it by its owners, Régis and Martine Crépy, and their largely French staff. The *raison d'être* is the often very busy restaurant, but the rooms are restful and smart, with surprisingly luxurious marble bathrooms.
☒ Market Place, Lavenham, Suffolk CO10 9QZ.
Map p75 F3. 📞 (01787) 247431. 📠 (01787) 248007.
@ greathouse@clara.co.uk 🍴 b,l,d. **Rooms** 5. 🅾
● first 3 weeks Jan. 💳 AE, MC, V. ⓔⓔⓔ

LAVENHAM

LEDBURY

Lavenham Priory The Grade I listed building is one of the finest in this charming half-timbered town. Owners Tim and Gilli Pitt can offer three delightful bedrooms to guests (dinner by arrangement). Choose between a *lit bateau*, a four-poster and a Polonaise bed. Downstairs, the sitting room boasts a huge inglenook fireplace.
☒ Water St, Lavenham, Suffolk CO10 9RW.
Map p75 F3. 📞 (01787) 247404. 📠 (01787) 248472.
@ tim.pitt@btinternet.com 🍴 b,d. **Rooms** 3. 🅾
● Christmas, New Year. 💳 MC, V. ⓔⓔⓔ

Grove House In this manor house-cum-farm, hot water bottles are slipped between crisp cotton sheets on chilly nights in the large bedrooms. In the comfortable sitting room there are cut flowers and an honesty bar; the oak-panelled dining room features a fireplace and a long communal table at which Ellen Ross's highly-rated dinners are served.
☒ Bromsberrow Heath, Ledbury, Herefordshire HR8 1PE.
Map p74 A2. 📞 (01531) 650584. 🍴 b,d. **Rooms** 3.
🅾 ● mid-Dec to early Jan. 💳 Not accepted. ⓔⓔ

GREAT RISSINGTON

Lamb Inn A lovely 300-year-old inn built of Cotswold stone, not luxurious, but run with energy and good humour by its owners.
☒ Great Rissington, Bourton-on-the-Water, Gloucestershire GL54 2LJ. **Map** p74 A2. 📞 (01451) 820388. 📠 (01451) 820724. 🍴 b,l,d. **Rooms** 14. ⓔⓔ

GRIMSTON

Congham Hall Much about this quintessentially English Georgian country house hotel impresses, not least its own cricket pitch and herb garden.
☒ Grimston, King's Lynn, Norfolk PE32 1AH. **Map** 75 F2.
📞 (01485) 600250. 📠 (01485) 601191. 🍴 b,l,d.
Rooms 14. ⓔⓔⓔ

HARTEST

The Hatch The Oatens share their charming, thatched 600-year-old hall house on the Pilgrim's Way (now a country lane) with B&B guests.
☒ Pilgrims Lane, Cross Green, Hartest, Suffolk IP29 4ED. **Map** p75 F3. 📞 (01284) 830226.
🍴 b,d. **Rooms** 3. ⓔⓔ

HARVINGTON

Mill at Harvington Relaxing riverside spot; pool, fishing and boating in summer. Totally redecorated after a disastrous flood in 1998.
☒ Anchor Lane, Harvington, Evesham, Worcestershire WR11 5NR. **Map** p74 A2. 📞 📠 (01386) 870688.
🍴 b,l,d. **Rooms** 21. ⓔⓔ

For key to symbols see backflap. For price categories *see p71*

LEONARD STANLEY

Grey Cottage The stone cottage, dating from 1807 and with a 100ft sequoia in the garden, stands out for the attention to detail paid by its owners, the Reeves. From the carefully prepared dinners to the firm beds, reliable hot water, heated towel rails and fresh fruit in the bedrooms, everything reflects their friendly, helpful, yet unobtrusive attitude.

☒ Leonard Stanley, Stonehouse, Gloucestershire GL10 3LU. **Map** p74 A3. **℡** **FAX** (01453) 822515. **⑪** b,d. **Rooms** 3. **◐ ●** Occasionally. **⊠** Not accepted. **£££**

MALMESBURY

Old Bell One of a small group of hotels (see also Fowey Hall, page 82) dedicated to giving parents and children an equally good time, here set in a 13th-century building. Parents get attractive rooms (Oriental-style in the annexe), children a 'den' liberally endowed with toys and nannies. Both can enjoy above-average food.

☒ Abbey Row, Malmesbury, Wiltshire SN16 0AG. **Map** p74 A3. **℡** (01666) 822344. **FAX** (01666) 825145. **@** woolley@luxury-hotel.demon.co.uk **⑪** b,l,d. **Rooms** 31. **◐ ●** Never. **⊠** AE, DC, MC, V. **£££**

LINCOLN

D'Isney Place This spruce Georgian house is on a busy street close to Lincoln Cathedral. Though it has a garden, which incorporates a 700-year-old tower, it has no public rooms. Breakfast is delivered to guests in their bedrooms – served on bone china and accompanied by a morning paper. Rooms vary; the best have carefully co-ordinated fabrics and whirlpool baths.

☒ Eastgate, Lincoln LN2 4AA. **Map** p75 E2. **℡** (01522) 538881. **FAX** (01522) 511321. **⑪** b. **Rooms** 17. **◐ ●** Never. **⊠** AE, DC, MC, V. **£££**

MANCHESTER

Malmaison This growing chain of city hotels is notable for the value-for-money it offers. The rooms are cool and fresh in a modern, rather masculine style and well-equipped (CD players, in-house movies, good toiletries). Public facilities include a mini-spa and hi-tech gym, a jazzy bar and a French brasserie.

☒ Piccadilly, Manchester M1 3AQ. **Map** p75 D1. **℡** (0161) 278 1000. **FAX** (0161) 278 1002. **@** manchester@malmaison.com **⑪** b,l,d. **Rooms** 112. **⑪ ●** Never. **⊠** AE, DC, MC, V. **£££**

HENLEY-ON-THAMES

Red Lion Long-established town-centre coaching inn fronting the Thames at the busy road bridge. Regatta memorabilia; bedrooms with river views.
☒ Hart St, Henley-on-Thames, Oxfordshire RG9 2AR. **Map** p75 E4. **℡** (01491) 572161. **FAX** (01491) 410039. **⑪** b,l,d. **Rooms** 26. **£££**

KINGTON

Penhros Court An eccentric manor house incorporating a superb medieval cruck hall. Charming bedrooms and inspired organic food.
☒ Kington, Herefordshire HR5 3LH. **Map** p74 C3. **℡** (01544) 230720. **FAX** (01544) 230754. **@** martin@ penhros.kc3ltd.co.uk **⑪** b,d. **Rooms** 12. **££**

LITTLE MALVERN

Holdfast Cottage A Victorian farmhouse with the cosy intimacy of a cottage. Lovely garden.
☒ Marlbank Rd, Little Malvern, Worcestershire WR13 6NA. **Map** p74 A2. **℡** (01684) 310288. **FAX** (01684) 311117. **@** holdcothot@aol.com **⑪** b,d. **Rooms** 8. **££**

LUDLOW

Number 28 In fact three separate buildings make up this excellent B&B – two bedrooms in each. A useful base for visiting attractive Ludlow.
☒ 28 Lower Broad St, Ludlow, Shropshire SY8 1PQ. **Map** p74 C3. **℡** (01584) 876996. **FAX** (01584) 876860. **@** ross.no28@btinternet.com **⑪** b. **Rooms** 6. **££**

MELBOURN

MOULSFORD

Melbourn Bury Lush parkland surrounds this whitewashed and crenallated manor house. Inside are an elegant drawing room and splendid Victorian billiard room, book-lined library and sunny conservatory. Of the three bedrooms, the 'pink room' is particularly delightful, with a large bathroom. Communal dining, dinner-party style.
☒ Melbourn, Hertfordshire SG8 6DE. **Map** p75 E3.
((01763) 261151. **FAX** (01763) 262375. **▮▮** b,d.
Rooms 3. ▮ ◉ Christmas, New Year, Easter.
🖂 AE, MC, V. (£)(£)

Beetle and Wedge A delight in summer when the Thames-side setting comes into its own – Jerome K. Jerome wrote *Three Men in a Boat* here. To eat, choose from the brasserie-style Boathouse or the more formal Dining Room; in fine weather the Watergarden is open. Bedrooms are spacious, interesting, and individually furnished.
☒ Ferry Lane, Moulsford, Wallingford, Oxfordshire OX10 9JF. **Map** p75 D4. **(** (01491) 651381.
FAX (01491) 651376. **▮▮** b,l,d. **Rooms** 10.
▮ ◉ Christmas Day. 🖂 AE, DC, MC, V. (£)(£)(£)

MORSTON

OXFORD

Morston Hall Dominating the ground floor of this brick and flint Norfolk house is the strikingly decorated restaurant, the establishment's main attraction and holder of a Michelin red 'M'. Enjoy a seasonal dinner – perhaps wild mushrooms, fresh fish and samphire – before retiring to one of the (mostly) spacious bedrooms; one is small.
☒ Morston, Holt, Norfolk NR25 7AA. **Map** p75 F2.
((01263) 741041. **FAX** (01263) 740419.
@ reception@morstonhall.demon.co.uk **▮▮** b,d.
Rooms 6. ▮ ◉ Jan. 🖂 AE, DC, MC, V. (£)(£)(£)

Old Parsonage No themed 'olde worlde' charm here, despite the great age of the building. The rather small bedrooms are prettily decorated with pale panelling and unfussy chintz, with marble bathrooms (with telephone). The bar/restaurant has a clubby, cosmopolitan feel. A cool sister hotel, **Old Bank House**, opened in mid-1999.
☒ 1 Banbury Rd, Oxford OX2 6NN. **Map** p75 D4.
((01865) 310210. **FAX** (01865) 311262.
@ oldparsonage@dial.pipex.com **▮▮** b,l,d. **Rooms** 30.
▮ ◉ Christmas. 🖂 AE, DC,MC,V. (£)(£)(£)

MALVERN WELLS
Cottage in the Wood Hardly a cottage, but three buildings, at whose heart is a Georgian dower house. Bedrooms vary; the setting is the key.
☒ Holywell Rd, Malvern Wells, Worcestershire WR14 4LG. **Map** p74 A2. **(** (01684) 575859.
FAX (01684) 560662. **▮▮** b,l,d. **Rooms** 20. (£)(£)

MATLOCK BATH
Hodgkinson's The dull exterior belies a kitsch, amusing interior, filled with eye-catching objects. Eccentric but comfortable, with polite service.
☒ 150 South Parade, Matlock Bath, Matlock, Derbyshire DE4 3NR. **Map** p75 D2. **(** (01629) 582170.
FAX (01629) 584891. **▮▮** b,d. **Rooms** 7. (£)(£)

NEEDHAM MARKET
Pipps Ford Country guesthouse at its best: home produced bread, honey, vegetables and more in a lovely Tudor house with flowery gardens.
☒ Needham Market, Ipswich, Suffolk IP6 8LJ.
Map p75 F3. **(** (01449) 760208. **FAX** (01449) 760561.
▮▮ b,d. **Rooms** 6. (£)(£)

NORWICH
By Appointment A flamboyant, colourful restaurant-with-rooms, filled with Victoriana and other *objets trouvés*. Wonderful breakfasts.
☒ 25-29 St George's St, Norwich, Norfolk NR3 1AB. **Map** p75 F3. **(FAX** (01603) 630730.
▮▮ b,d. **Rooms** 4. (£)(£)

PAINSWICK

Cardynham House Californian artist Carol Keyes has endowed a fine 15th-century Cotswold town house with panache. The bedrooms are beautiful (some have efficient showers, not baths) and are superb value. One has a swimming pool in it! Breakfasts include American specialities. Dinner can be taken in her adjoining Thai restaurant.
⊠ The Cross, Painswick, Stroud, Gloucestershire GL6 6XX. **Map** p74 A3. **C** (01452) 814006. **FAX** (01452) 812321. **ᴵᴵ** b,d. **Rooms** 9. 🚫 ⬤ Christmas. 🗲 Not accepted. ⓔⓔ

SHURDINGTON

The Greenway This formal, traditional hotel (ties must be worn at dinner) is impeccably run and set in gardens and parkland, with the Cotswold Hills in the background. The conservatory dining room, in which elaborate dishes are served, opens onto a sunken garden and lily pond, where drinks can be taken in summer.
⊠ Shurdington, Cheltenham, Gloucestershire GL51 5UG. **Map** p74 A2. **C** (01242) 862352. **FAX** (01242) 862780. @ relax@greenway-hotel.demon.co.uk **ᴵᴵ** b,l,d. **Rooms** 19. 🚫 ⬤ Never. 🗲 AE, DC, MC, V. ⓔⓔⓔⓔ

SHIPTON-UNDER-WYCHWOOD

Lamb Inn A charming and characterful inn in a charming and characterful village – perfection. There are stripped floors and old settles, log fires and a cosy sitting room. The bedrooms are in keeping; two have four-posters. For dinner, you can choose between good pub food in the bar, or more sophisticated dishes in the dining room.
⊠ Upper High St, Shipton-under-Wychwood, Chipping Norton, Oxfordshire OX7 6DQ. **Map** p74 B2. **C** (01993) 830456. **FAX** (01993) 832025. **ᴵᴵ** b,l,d. **Rooms** 5. 🚫 ⬤ Never. 🗲 AE, DC, MC, V. ⓔⓔ

SOUTHWOLD

The Crown Good advice: eat at the Crown but stay at the Swan (see page 101), both owned by Adnam's Brewery. If you can't, fear not: the rooms here, though simple, are pleasing, with well-fitted bathrooms (not all en suite). Downstairs, the brasserie-style bar and popular restaurant add to the informal atmosphere.
⊠ 90 High St, Southwold, Suffolk, IP18 6DP. **Map** p75 F3. **C** (01502) 722275. **FAX** (01502) 727263. @ hotels@adnams.co.uk **ᴵᴵ** b,l,d. **Rooms** 12. ⬤ first week Jan. 🗲 AE, DC, MC, V. ⓔⓔ

OTLEY
Bowerfield House A special B&B: tasteful, elegant 17th-century barn conversion with huge drawing room, billiard room, croquet lawn.
⊠ Otley, Ipswich, Suffolk IP6 9NR. **Map** p75 F3. **C** (01473) 890742. **FAX** (01473) 890059. @ lise@bowerfld.demon.co.uk **ᴵᴵ** b. **Rooms** 4. ⓔ

OXFORD
Cotswold House High standards and attention to detail distinguish this family home B&B. The modern house, built in Cotswold stone, is set in residential north Oxford, 2 miles from the centre.
⊠ 363 Banbury Rd, Oxford OX2 7PL. **Map** p75 D4. **C** **FAX** (01865) 310558. **ᴵᴵ** b. **Rooms** 6. ⓔⓔ

SAXMUNDHAM
Sternfield House Jenny Thornton's home and B&B is a lovely Queen Anne house with luxurious bedrooms. Tennis court, pool and folly.
⊠ Saxmundham, Suffolk IP17 1RS. **Map** p75 F3. **C** (01728) 602252. **FAX** (01728) 604082. **ᴵᴵ** b. **Rooms** 3. ⓔⓔ

SNAPE
Crown Inn An excellent base for visits to the musical Maltings, this is a cosy, characterful pub with good food; pretty, beamed bedrooms (one with four-poster), simple bathrooms.
⊠ Snape, Suffolk IP17 1SL. **Map** p75 F3. **C** (01728) 688324. **ᴵᴵ** b,l,d. **Rooms** 3. ⓔ

SOUTHWOLD

The Swan The finest of breezy Southwold's medieval inns has a thoroughly comfortable interior, with checks and chintzes and open fires creating the country house look. Try to get a room in the main building rather than one of the newer garden rooms. The atmosphere is slightly formal, but staff are friendly and helpful.
☒ Market Place, Southwold, Suffolk IP18 6EG.
Map p75 F3. ☎ (01502) 722186. FAX (01502) 724800.
@ hotels@adnams.co.uk ⅋ b,l,d. **Rooms** 44.
⬛ ◉ Never. ⬛ AE, DC, MC, V. ⓔⓔⓔ

SWAFFHAM

Strattons The Scotts are natural hosts, and have created a very individual hotel from an elegant listed villa in this fine market town. Their taste is decidedly not minimalist: there are possessions everywhere: cushions, objects, books, pictures. Bedrooms are all different (one a luxurious suite). Vanessa's award-winning cooking is cheerfully served by Les in the cosy basement restaurant.
☒ Ash Close, Swaffham, Norfolk PE37 7NH. **Map** p75 F2.
☎ (01760) 723845. FAX (01760) 720458. ⅋ b,l,d.
Rooms 7. ◉ Christmas. ⬛ AE. MC, V. ⓔⓔ

STAPLEFORD

Stapleford Park The stately home experience is taken to extremes here: the finest wines, the most expensive cigars, and bedrooms designed by upmarket companies such as Crabtree & Evelyn and David Hicks. On the sporting front, you can fish, ride, clay pigeon shoot, play golf or practise falconry and archery.
☒ Stapleford, Melton Mowbray, Leicestershire LE14 2EF.
Map p75 D2. ☎ (01572) 787522. FAX (01572) 787651.
@ reservations@stapleford.com ⅋ b,l,d. **Rooms** 51.
⬛ ⬛ ◉ Never. ⬛ AE, DC, MC, V. ⓔⓔⓔⓔ

TAPLOW

Cliveden This stately home was the former residence of dukes and the Astor family (and the setting of the 1960s Profumo scandal). It still exudes a subtle combination of privileged grandeur and faintly louche luxury: elegant restaurants, sporting facilities, vintage boats for river trips. The accommodation includes a cottage hideaway perfect for honeymooners.
☒ Taplow, Berkshire SL6 0JF. **Map** p75 E4. ☎ (01628) 668561. FAX (01628) 661837. ⅋ b,l,d. **Rooms** 38.
⬛ ⬛ ◉ Never. ⬛ AE, DC, MC, V. ⓔⓔⓔⓔ

STINCHCOMBE
Drakestone House For a taste of bygone elegance, try the splendid Edwardian family home of Hugh and Crystal St John-Mildmay. Dinner is by prior arrangement; bring your own wine.
☒ Stinchcombe, Dursley, Gloucestershire GL11 6AS.
Map p74 A3. ☎ (01453) 542140. ⅋ b,d. **Rooms** 3. ⓔ

STOKE-BY-NAYLAND
Angel In the heart of the village, a welcoming inn with well-regarded food and bars buzzing with activity. Bedrooms are homely.
☒ Stoke-by-Nayland, Colchester, Essex CO6 4SA.
Map p75 F3. ☎ (01206) 263245. FAX (01206) 263373.
⅋ b,l,d. **Rooms** 6. ⓔⓔ

STOW-ON-THE-WOLD
Wyck Hill House Manor house with superb views over Windrush Valley (but rooms in the courtyard are cheapest). Formal restaurant.
☒ Burford Rd, Stow-on-the-Wold, Gloucestershire GL54 1HY. **Map** p74 A2. ☎ (01451) 831936.
FAX (01451) 832243. ⅋ b,l,d. **Rooms** 31. ⓔⓔⓔ

STRATFORD-UPON-AVON
Caterham House This centrally located B&B, set in two Georgian houses, is very attractive both inside and out. Stylish and well run.
☒ 58-59 Rother St, Stratford-upon-Avon, Warwickshire CV37 6LT. **Map** p75 D3. ☎ (01789) 267309.
FAX (01789) 414836. ⅋ b. **Rooms** 14. ⓔⓔ

TETBURY

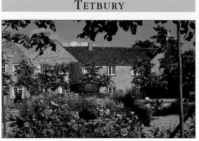

Calcot Manor Various outbuildings surround this old Cotswold manor. The renovated stables house the superb family rooms, with video, fridge, bunks and baby-listening. Children are especially welcome (there is a playroom supervised by a nanny) but adults enjoy the excellent cooking in the cool Conservatory or the Gumstool Inn.
⊠ Tetbury, Gloucestershire GL8 8JY. **Map** p74 A3.
🛈 (01666) 890391. FAX (01666) 890394.
@ reception@calcotmanor.com 🍴 b,l,d. **Rooms** 27.
🏊 🌢 ● Never. 💳 AE, DC, MC, V. ⓔⓔⓔ

UPPINGHAM

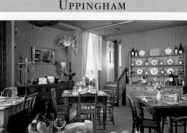

Lake Isle It's a surprise to find something so rustic and countrified in the middle of a busy High Street, even a pretty one like Uppingham's. The family-run restaurant-with-rooms is entered through a flowery courtyard. Bedrooms are cosy, and the bar has a log fire on chilly evenings. The chef/proprietor prepares inventive menus; fine wine cellar.
⊠ 16 High St East, Uppingham, Oakham LE15 9PZ.
Map p75 E3. 🛈 FAX (01572) 822951. 🍴 b,l,d.
Rooms 12. ● Never. 💳 AE, DC, MC, V. ⓔⓔ

ULEY

Owlpen Manor Only superlatives are used to describe Owlpen Manor, hidden in its own little valley. Once seen, the Mander's magical Tudor house is never forgotten. This is luxurious 'serviced' self-catering: stay in a delightful cottage, barn or mill. Eat, if you wish, in the atmospheric restaurant, the Cyder House.
⊠ Owlpen, Nr Uley, Gloucestershire GL11 5BZ.
Map p74 A3. 🛈 (01453) 860261. FAX (01453)
860819. @ sales@owlpen.demon.co.uk 🍴 b,l,d.
Rooms 9 cottages. 🌢 ● Never. 💳 AE, DC, MC, V. ⓔⓔ

WOODSTOCK

Feathers This exceptionally civilized hotel is fashioned from four tall 17th-century townhouses. The place is hard to fault: relaxing upstairs drawing room (with library and open fire); beautifully decorated bedrooms; friendly, unobtrusive service; and excellent food in the lively wood-panelled dining room.
⊠ Market St, Woodstock, Oxfordshire OX20 1SX.
Map p74 B2. 🛈 (01993) 812291. FAX (01993) 813158.
@ enquiries@feathers.co.uk 🍴 b,l,d. **Rooms** 22.
🌢 ● Never. 💳 AE, DC, MC, V. ⓔⓔⓔ

TUTBURY

Mill House A beautifully kept B&B in a pretty spot by an old mill, overlooking Tutbury Castle. Bedrooms are light and spacious.
⊠ Cornmill Lane, Tutbury, Burton upon Trent, Staffordshire DE13 9HA. **Map** p75 D2.
🛈 (01283) 813300. 🍴 b. **Rooms** 3. ⓔ

WARE

Hanbury Manor Owned by the Marriot group, the four-star hotel incorporates modern amenities (health spa, golf) in a grandiose setting.
⊠ Ware, Hertfordshire SG12 0SD. **Map** p75 E4.
🛈 (01920) 487722. FAX (01920) 487692. 🍴 b,l,d.
Rooms 96. ⓔⓔⓔⓔ

WOODSTOCK

Holmwood Two suites in a lovely Queen Anne house, each with lounge and spacious bathroom.
⊠ 6 High St, Woodstock, Oxfordshire OX20 1TF.
Map p74 B2. 🛈 (01993) 812266. FAX (01993)
813233. @ cristina@holm-wood.demon.co.uk
🍴 b. **Rooms** 2. ⓔⓔ

WORFIELD

Old Vicarage Immaculately kept, if pricey, small hotel, Edwardian in character, with mostly large bedrooms and a sunny conservatory.
⊠ Worfield, Bridgnorth, Shropshire WV15 5JZ.
Map p74 C3. 🛈 (01746) 716497. FAX (01746) 716552.
@ admin@pride.u-net.com 🍴 b,l,d. **Rooms** 15. ⓔⓔⓔ

NORTHERN ENGLAND

YORKSHIRE • LANCASHIRE
NORTHUMBERLAND • LAKE DISTRICT

THE LAKE DISTRICT and the Yorkshire Dales are the areas of Northern England which have the largest number of visitors and the greatest concentration of places to stay. Windermere, in particular, offers a bewildering choice; we recommend the best and most secluded. But don't overlook the rest of this region, which stretches north from the mouth of the River Humber to the Scottish borders: not least Northumberland and the North Yorkshire Moors for their rugged beauty, nor the cathedral cities of Durham and York. Wherever our entries are situated, they range from luxurious hideaways to plain, no-nonsense inns and are often in dramatic settings, perfect for walkers and lovers of the great outdoors.

AMBLESIDE

Wateredge Of the myriad hotels around tourist-riven Lake Windermere, this is a long-standing favourite. Family-run, with courteous, willing staff, it's a quiet, traditional holiday hotel situated right on the shores of the lake, its core being two fishermen's cottages (now much extended). Suites in the annexe. Private jetty.
⊠ Waterhead Bay, Ambleside, Cumbria LA22 0EP.
Map p77 D5. 🎜 (015394) 32332. **FAX** (015394) 31878.
@ reception@wateredgehotel.co.uk 🍴 b,l,d. **Rooms** 23.
🛇 ◐ mid-Dec to mid-Jan. 🌊 AE, MC, V. £££

ARNCLIFFE

Amerdale House The setting is one of the most seductive in all the Dales: on the fringe of a pretty village, wide meadows in front, high hills behind. This admirable hotel is distinguished by the warm welcome and exceptional cooking of its owners Paula and Nigel Crapper. Bedrooms are comfortable, if not stylish. Best is the top-floor room with four-poster bed.
⊠ Arncliffe, Littondale, Skipton, North Yorkshire BD23
5QE. **Map** p75 D1, p77 E5. 🎜 **FAX** (01756) 770250. 🍴 b,d.
Rooms 11. 🛇 ◐ Nov to mid-March. 🌊 MC, V. £££

BOWNESS-ON-WINDERMERE

Linthwaite House Glorious lake views and fine grounds. A consummate, pampering hotel.
⊠ Crook Rd, Bowness-on-Windermere, Cumbria
LA23 3JA. **Map** p74 C1, p77 E5. 🎜 (015394) 88600.
FAX (015394) 88601. @ admin@linthwaite.com
🍴 b,l,d. **Rooms** 18. £££££

CROSTHWAITE

Crosthwaite House Handsome Georgian house; kind hosts; honest food served in an attractive dining room. Simple accommodation.
⊠ Crosthwaite, Kendal, Cumbria, LA8 8BP.
Map p77 D5. 🎜 **FAX** (01539) 568264. @ crosthwaite.
house@kencomp.net 🍴 b,d. **Rooms** 6. £

DURHAM

Georgian Town House Town-centre Georgian house decorated with flair (and a profusion of stencils). Breakfasts are taken in the conservatory.
⊠ 10-11 Crossgate, Durham, Co. Durham
DH1 4PS. **Map** p77 E5. 🎜 **FAX** (0191) 386 8070.
🍴 b. **Rooms** 6. £

GRASMERE

White Moss House Renowned for its cuisine, with pretty bedrooms (two in a secluded cottage). In the Wordsworth family until the 1930s.
⊠ Rydal Water, Grasmere, Cumbria LA22 9SE.
Map p77 D5. 🎜 (015394) 35295. **FAX** (015394) 35516.
@ dixon@whitemoss.demon.co.uk **Rooms** 7. £££

For key to symbols see backflap. For price categories see p71

BASSENTHWAITE LAKE

Pheasant Inn The old oak bar, full of dark nooks and crannies, is a gem, little changed from its earliest days. Beyond that are several lounges with generous sitting space. Bedrooms are modern and light, without TV or telephone. The food makes few concessions to fashion – a simple inn, with signs of wear and tear, but characterful.
⊠ Bassenthwaite Lake, Cockermouth, Cumbria CA13 9YE. **Map** p77 D5. 🄲 (017687) 76234. 𝐅𝐀𝐗 (017687) 76002. 🚻 b,l,d. **Rooms** 20. 🛉 ◐ Christmas Day. 🖃 MC, V. ⓔⓔ

BOLTON ABBEY

Devonshire Arms This glossy, go-ahead country hotel is owned by the Duke and Duchess of Devonshire, and furnished largely with objects from Chatsworth House. There are two dining rooms, the formal Burlington Restaurant and the designer Brasserie. Best of the bedrooms are the themed four-poster rooms in the Old Wing.
⊠ Bolton Abbey, Skipton, North Yorkshire BD23 6AJ. **Map** p75 D1. 🄲 (01756) 710441. 𝐅𝐀𝐗 (01756) 710564. @ dev.arms@legend.co.uk 🚻 b,l,d. **Rooms** 41. 🕾 🍽 🛉 ◐ Never. 🖃 AE, DC, MC, V. ⓔⓔⓔ

BLAWITH

Appletree Holme Total seclusion is the setting for this low stone-built house, sympathetically furnished and embellished with pictures, books and open fires on stone hearths. The bedrooms have impressive bathrooms, including two with double-size whirlpool baths. Roy Carlsen's cooking uses local produce to satisfying effect; you could preceed it with a walk to Beacon Tarn.
⊠ Blawith, Ulverston, Cumbria LA12 8EL. **Map** p74 C1, p77 D5. 🄲 (01229) 885618. 🚻 b,d. **Rooms** 4. 🛉 ◐ Never. 🖃 AE, MC, V. ⓔⓔⓔ

BORROWDALE

Leathes Head Owners Patricia Brady and Mark Payne breathed new life into this Edwardian house when they bought it a few years ago, refurbishing it in traditional style but with a bold hand. It has splendid views across the fells. Dinner is a four-course affair with plenty of choice and delicious puddings.
⊠ Borrowdale, Keswick, Cumbria CA12 5UY. **Map** p77 D5. 🄲 (017687) 77247. 𝐅𝐀𝐗 (017687) 77363. @ enq@leatheshead.co.uk 🚻 b,d. **Rooms** 11. 🛉 ◐ Nov to to mid-Feb. 🖃 MC, V. ⓔⓔ

GRASSINGTON

Ashfield House Simple guesthouse (originally three 17th-century cottages) tucked behind the village's main square, with a large walled garden.
⊠ Grassington, Skipton, North Yorkshire BD23 5AE. **Map** p75 D1. 🄲 𝐅𝐀𝐗 (01756) 752584. 🚻 b,d. **Rooms** 7. ⓔⓔ

GREAT LANGDALE

Old Dungeon Ghyll At the heart of the Lake District, a slate-and-stone walkers' hostelry: simple, somewhat worn, with hearty food.
⊠ Great Langdale, Ambleside, Cumbria LA22 9JY. **Map** p77 D5 🄲 𝐅𝐀𝐗 (015394) 37272. 🚻 b,d. **Rooms** 15. ⓔⓔ

HARROGATE

White House Overlooking Harrogate's parkland, The Stray; Italianate exterior; plush interior.
⊠ 10 Park Parade, Harrogate, North Yorkshire HG1 5AH. **Map** p75 D1. 🄲 (01423) 501388. 𝐅𝐀𝐗 (01423) 527973. @ whitehouse-hotel@demon.co.uk 🚻 b,l,d. **Rooms** 10. ⓔⓔⓔ

HAZLEWOOD

Hazlewood Castle A fortified knights' residence is now a luxury hotel equipped with latest accoutrements. Sumptuous interiors; fine food.
⊠ Paradise Lane, Hazlewood, Tadcaster, North Yorkshire LS24 9NJ. **Map** p75 D1. 🄲 (01937) 535353. 𝐅𝐀𝐗 (01937) 530630. 🚻 b,l,d. **Rooms** 21. ⓔⓔⓔ

BRAMPTON

Farlam Hall Though mainly Victorian, the roots of this solid but elegant Border country house are Elizabethan. Set in rolling countryside, it is beautifully furnished with many fine pieces and is imbued with a traditional, discreet atmosphere. In the dining room, superb dinners range from plain country dishes to mild extravagances.

☒ Brampton, Cumbria CA8 2NG. **Map** p77 D5.
🄲 (016977) 46234. FAX (016977) 46683.
@ farlamhall@dial.pipex.com 🍴 b,d. **Rooms** 12.
🛇 ⬤ Christmas. 🗐 MC, V. ⓔⓔⓔ

CRATHORNE

Crathorne Hall The Edwardian stately home, now part of the Virgin hotels group, is set in wooded grounds overlooking River Leven. The trusty English country house school of interior design makes the most of the period features: elegant drawing room, clubby bar and dining room hung with ancestral portraits.

☒ Crathorne, Yarm. North Yorkshire TS15 0AR.
Map p77 E5. 🄲 (01642) 700398. FAX (01642) 700814.
@ reservations@virgin.co.uk 🍴 b,l,d. **Rooms** 37.
🛇 ⬤ Never. 🗐 AE, DC, MC, V. ⓔⓔⓔ

CARLISLE

Number Thirty One A winning combination of hands-on professionalism and imagination mark out this city centre guesthouse. It has just three rooms: Green (Oriental style); Blue, the largest, with walk-in wardrobe; and Yellow, with half-tester. Philip Parker's dinners are based on what's freshest and best that day. As much as possible – breads, preserves and so on – is home-made.

☒ 31 Howard Place, Carlisle, Cumbria CA1D 1LT.
Map p77 D5. 🄲 FAX (01228) 597080. 🍴 b,d. **Rooms** 3.
🛇 ⬤ Dec to March. 🗐 AE, MC, V. ⓔⓔ

HAWES

Simonstone Hall A former hunting lodge (the American owner still takes it over for private shooting parties) with a welcoming, traditional interior. Slump in the elegant drawing room, fraternize in the Game Tavern, or withdraw to your room. The superior and deluxe ones are magnificent: huge and splendidly furnished.

☒ Hawes, North Yorkshire DL8 3LY. **Map** p77 E5.
🄲 (01969) 667255. FAX (01969) 667741.
@ simonstonehall@demon.co.uk 🍴 b,l,d. **Rooms** 19.
🛇 ⬤ Never. 🗐 AE, DC, MC, V. ⓔⓔⓔ

LASTINGHAM

Lastingham Grange Family-run, child-friendly hotel in delightful village with lovely gardens (and play area). Straightforward bedrooms.

☒ Lastingham, York, North Yorkshire YO62 6TH.
Map p75 E1, p77 F1. 🄲 (01751) 417345.
FAX (01751) 417358. 🍴 b,d. **Rooms** 12. ⓔⓔⓔ

MIDDLEHAM

Miller's House Impressive bedrooms at this elegant Georgian house. Friendly owners.

☒ Middleham, Wensleydale, North Yorkshire CL8 4NR.
Map p75 D1, p77 E5. 🄲 (01969) 622630. FAX (01969) 623570. @ millershouse@demon.co.uk 🍴 b,d.
Rooms 7. ⓔⓔ

MUNGRISDALE

Mill A 17th-century former mill cottage in lovely setting, with simple, airy bedrooms and a chintzy sitting room. Vegetarians are well catered for.

☒ Mungrisdale, Penrith, Cumbria CA11 0XR.
Map p77 D5. 🄲 (017687) 79659.
FAX (017687) 79155. 🍴 b,d. **Rooms** 9. ⓔⓔ

NEWCASTLE UPON TYNE

Malmaison The converted warehouse is one in a chain of hotels representing excellent value. Slick rooms are equipped with all the latest requisites.

☒ 104 Quayside, Newcastle upon Tyne, Tyne & Wear NE1 3DX. **Map** p77 E5. 🄲 (0191) 245 5000.
FAX (0191) 245 4545. 🍴 b,l,d. **Rooms** 116. ⓔⓔ

HEADLAM

Headlam Hall The creeper-smothered Jacobean house sits well in its large formal gardens, surrounded by stone walls and massive hedges; in the grounds is a canalized stream. The interior has a refreshingly comfortable ordinariness about it, mixing antique furniture with reproduction. A popular venue for functions.
⊠ Headlam, Gainford, Darlington, Co. Durham DL2 3HA. **Map** p77 E5. ((01325) 730238. FAX (01325) 730790. @ admin@headlamhall.co.uk Ⅱ b,l,d. **Rooms** 36. ≋ ▮ ◉ Christmas. ⊠ AE, DC, MC, V. £££

LEEDS

42 The Calls The converted riverside corn mill is *the* place to stay in Leeds. Stylishly contemporary, amusingly different, it retains original features such as beams, girders, bare brick walls and the odd hoist. Bedrooms and bathrooms are well-equipped. The Brasserie and Pool Court next door make convivial places in which to eat.
⊠ 42 The Calls, Leeds, West Yorkshire LS2 7EW. **Map** p75 D1. ((0113) 244 0099. FAX (0113) 234 4100. @ hotel@42thecalls.co.uk Ⅱ b,l,d. **Rooms** 41. ◉ Christmas. ⊠ AE,DC, MC, V. £££

KIRKBY LONSDALE

Hipping Hall The house-party approach is successfully adopted by Ian and Jos Bryant in their fine house: guests eat communally in the splendid beamed Great Hall with minstrel's gallery. After a day on the fells, sink into sofas around a wood-burning stove at the other end of the Hall. Bedrooms are spacious.
⊠ Cowan Bridge, Kirkby Lonsdale, Cumbria LA6 2JJ. **Map** p74 C1, p77 D5. ((015242) 71187. FAX (015242) 72452. @ hippinghal@aol.com Ⅱ b,d. **Rooms** 5. ▮ ◉ Dec to Feb. ⊠ AE, MC, V. £££

NEWLANDS

Swinside Lodge Immaculately decorated and maintained, with attentive service and agreeable personal touches, this typical Victorian lakeland house makes an excellent country hotel. There is exhilarating walking right from the door. On your return, dinner is a no-choice, four-course, mildly adventurous delight. No drinks licence, so guests must provide their own wine.
⊠ Grange Rd, Newlands, Keswick, Cumbria CA12 5UE. **Map** p77 D5. (FAX (017687) 72948. Ⅱ b,d. **Rooms** 7. ◉ Dec, Jan. ⊠ MC, V. £££

NEWTON-LE-WILLOWS

The Hall The Georgian country house, gracious both inside and out, is made extra-special by the vivacious, sympathetic character of its owner.
⊠ Newton-le-Willows, Bedale, North Yorkshire DL8 1SW. **Map** p75 D1. ((01677) 450210. FAX (01677) 450014. Ⅱ b,d. **Rooms** 3. ££

NUNNINGTON

Ryedale Lodge A former village railway station has been transformed into a well-ordered retreat. New owners have dramatically redecorated.
⊠ Station Rd, Nunnington, York, YO6 5XB. **Map** p75 E1, p77 F5. ((01439) 748246. FAX (01439) 748346. Ⅱ b,l,d. **Rooms** 7. ££

RAMSGILL-IN-NIDDERDALE

Yorke Arms Former shooting lodge with a mellow, countrified interior and good food.
⊠ Ramsgill-in-Nidderdale, Pateley Bridge, Harrogate, North Yorkshire HG3 5RL. **Map** p75 D1. ((01423) 755243. FAX (01423) 755330 . @ enquiries@yorkarms.co.uk Ⅱ b,l,d. **Rooms** 13. ££

REETH

The Burgoyne Within traditional stone walls, a superior base for touring or walking the region. Most bedrooms have fine views over Swaledale.
⊠ On The Green, Reeth, Richmond, North Yorkshire DL11 6SN. **Map** p5 D1, p77 E5. (FAX (01748) 884292. Ⅱ b,d. **Rooms** 8. ££

RIPLEY

Boar's Head Opened in the late 1980s by the present resident at Ripley Castle, Sir Thomas Ingilby, this former inn has much to recommend it. Not least is its elegant, even sumptuous interiors, augmented by ancestral portraits and ornaments. The candlelit dining room is romantic, and the cooking takes itself very seriously.
⊠ Ripley Castle Estate, Harrogate HG3 3AY.
Map p75 D1. ☎ (01423) 771888. ☎ (01423) 771509.
@ boarshead@ripleycastle.co.uk ⌗ b,l,d. **Rooms** 25.
● Never. ☑ AE, DC, MC, V. ⓔⓔⓔ

SEATOLLER

Seatoller House This is not a run-of-the-mill hotel, but, if you are convivial, it is a delight. Guests eat communally at set times, and, to get the best out of the place, should take part in its social life. A guesthouse for more than 100 years, standing at the foot of Honister Pass, it has simple bedrooms, a low-ceilinged sitting room, plain country dining room and good food.
⊠ Seatoller, Borrowdale, Keswick, Cumbria CA12 5XN.
Map p77 D5. ☎ FAX (017687) 77218. ⌗ b,d.
Rooms 9. ☷ ● Dec to Feb. ☑ Not accepted. ⓔ

ROMALDKIRK

Rose and Crown This thriving former coaching inn, set on the village inn, is noted for the modish English food. Eat in the wood-panelled, candlelit dining room, then withdraw to the rustic bars, dotted with log fires, old photographs and much brass. Courtyard rooms are modern; those in the main building more characterful.
⊠ Romaldkirk, Barnard Castle, Co. Durham DL12 9EB.
Map p77 E5. ☎ (01833) 650213. ☎ (01833) 650828.
@ hotel@rose-and-crown.co.uk ⌗ b,l,d. **Rooms** 12.
● Christmas. ☑ MC, V. ⓔⓔ

ULLSWATER

Sharrow Bay For more than 50 years, Sharrow Bay has been famed for its food, service, luxury and lakeside setting. Its founder Francis Coulson has died, but co-owner Brian Sack remains involved and little has changed – including the fussy decoration which now seems amusingly old-hat, except to its many regulars.
⊠ Ullswater, Penrith, Cumbria CA10 2LZ. **Map** p77 D5.
☎ (017684) 86301. ☎ (017684) 86349.
@ enquiries@sharrow-bay.com ⌗ b,l,d. **Rooms** 26.
☷ ● Dec to March. ☑ DC, MC, V. ⓔⓔⓔⓔ

SAWREY

Ees Wyke In a glorious spot above Esthwaite Water; grand views. Old-fashioned in the best sense, and lovingly cared for. Welcoming owners.
⊠ Near Sawrey, Hawkshead, Ambleside, Cumbria LA22 0JZ. **Map** p74 C1, p77 D5. ☎ (015394) 36393.
⌗ b,d. **Rooms** 8. ⓔⓔ

SHERRIFF HUTTON

Rangers House The converted stables have been idiosyncratically decorated by their down-to-earth owners. Children welcome.
⊠ Sherriff Hutton Park, Sherriff Hutton, York, North Yorkshire YO60 6RH. **Map** p75 E1.
☎ FAX (01347) 878397. ⌗ b,d. **Rooms** 6. ⓔⓔ

SLAIDBURN

Parrock Head This beautifully sited 17th-century farmhouse has a beamed upstairs sitting room; bedrooms are plain but comfortable.
⊠ Slaidburn, Clitheroe, Lancashire BB7 3AH.
Map p74 C1. ☎ (01200) 446614. ☎ (01200) 446313.
⌗ b,d. **Rooms** 9. ⓔⓔ

THORNTON-LE-FYLDE

River House The characterful hotel, set on the banks of a tidal creek, reflects owner Bill Scott's personality. Two hooded 19th-century baths.
⊠ Skippool Creek, Thornton-le-Fylde, Blackpool, Lancashire FY5 5LF. **Map** p74 C1. ☎ (01253) 883497.
☎ (01253) 892083. ⌗ b,l,d. **Rooms** 5. ⓔⓔ

For key to symbols see backflap. For price categories *see p71*

WASDALE HEAD

Wasdale Head In a site unrivalled even in the Lake District, this robust old inn stands above deep, dramatic Wastwater. There are convivial bars, a comfortable lounge, a panelled dining room decorated with china and pewter. Most bedrooms are simple and small; there are also eight self-catering apartments.
✉ Wasdale Head, Gosforth, Seascale CA20 1EX. **Map** p77 D5. ☎ (019467) 26229. ℻ (019467) 26334. @ wasdaleheadinn@msn.com ⑪ b,l,d. **Rooms** 11. 🔌 ● Never. ⬛ AE, MC, V. ⓔⓔ

WATERMILLOCK

Old Church The whitewashed 18th-century house on the shores of Ullswater has been in the care of owners Mr and Mrs Whitemore since the late 1970s. Maureen has created bold interiors, with a confident but harmonious use of colour in the bedrooms, which all have lake views. Kevin is the cook, producing satisfying menus. Boating.
✉ Watermillock, Penrith, Cumbria CA11 0JN. **Map** p77 D5. ☎ (017684) 86204. ℻ (017684) 86368. @ info@oldchurch.co.uk ⑪ b,d. **Rooms** 10. 🔌 ● Nov to March. ⬛ AE, MC, V. ⓔⓔⓔ

WATH-IN-NIDDERDALE

Sportsman's Arms The village, near Gouthwaite Reservoir, is as enchanting as its name suggests. The accommodation at this inn is modest but spotlessly clean. Not all the bedrooms are ensuite. Ray Carter's restaurant is popular, with a lively menu embracing both local and more adventurous dishes.
✉ Wath-in-Nidderdale, Pateley Bridge, Harrogate, North Yorkshire HG3 5PP. **Map** p75 D1. ☎ (01423) 711306. ℻ (01423) 712524. ⑪ b,l,d. **Rooms** 13. 🔌 ● Christmas Day. ⬛ MC, V. ⓔⓔ

WHITEWELL

Inn at Whitewell Just the right note is struck at this mellow Forest of Bowland inn. The owners ensure a relaxed, unstuffy atmosphere, extending an equally warm welcome to adults, children and pets. The decoration is full of good taste, particularly in the bedrooms – some of which have peat fires. Most have videos, CD players and impressive bathrooms. Excellent value.
✉ Whitewell, Clitheroe BB7 3AT. **Map** p74 C1. ☎ (01200) 448222. ℻ (01200) 448298. ⑪ b,l,d. **Rooms** 15. 🔌 ● Never. ⬛ AE, DC, MC, V. ⓔⓔ

TROUTBECK

Mortal Man Glorious views of Windermere from this friendly Lakeland inn. The bedrooms are functional; traditional bars, hearty food.
✉ Troutbeck, Windermere, Cumbria LA23 1PL. **Map** p77 D5. ☎ (015394) 33193. ℻ (015394) 31261. ⑪ b,l,d. **Rooms** 12. ⓔⓔ

WALKINGTON

Manor House Late-Victorian house in tranquil position, opulently decorated with standard bedrooms. Elaborate food; long wine list.
✉ Northlands, Walkington, East Yorkshire HU17 8RU. **Map** p75 E1. ☎ (01482) 881645. ℻ (01482) 866501. ⑪ b,d. **Rooms** 7. ⓔⓔ

WATER YEAT

Water Yeat Jill Labat has gained an impressive reputation for her inspired cooking at this 17th-century farmhouse. The decoration is simple and countrified; the welcome warm.
✉ Water Yeat, Ulverston, Cumbria LA12 8DJ. **Map** p77 D5. ☎ ℻ (01229) 885306. ⑪ b,d. **Rooms** 5. ⓔ

WINDERMERE

The Archway Superior B&B with high standards. It is cosy and well-furnished with high quality beds; breakfasts are excellent.
✉ 13 College Rd, Windermere, Cumbria LA23 1BU. **Map** p74 C1, p77 D5. ☎ (015394) 45613. @ archway@btinternet.com ⑪ b,d. **Rooms** 4. ⓔ

WINDERMERE

Gilpin Lodge Notable for its high standards and attention to detail, Edwardian Gilpin Lodge presents a fresh, white, flower-bedecked exterior. Its immaculate, cosy yet smart interior is embellished with many ornaments and flower arrangements. The bedrooms do not disappoint; some have four-posters and whirlpool baths.
⊠ Crook Rd, Windermere, Cumbria LA23 3NE. **Map** pp74 C1, p77 D5. ((015394) 88818. FAX (015394) 88058. @ hotel@gilpin-lodge.co.uk ⁕ b,l,d. **Rooms** 14. ⊙ ● Never. ⊜ AE, DC, MC, V. ££££

WITHERSLACK

Old Vicarage The building, though not exceptional, is hidden in a large wooded garden, and the owners have invested it with an easy-going atmosphere. The straightforward decoration combines new with old; five of the bedrooms have private terraces. Dinner is a highlight, using local ingredients in fresh and thoughtful ways.
⊠ Church Rd, Witherslack, Grange-over-Sands, Cumbria LA11 6RS. **Map** p74 C1, p77 D5. ((015395) 52381. FAX (015395) 52373. @ hotel@old-vic.demon.co.uk ⁕ b,d. **Rooms** 14. ⊙ ● Never. ⊜ MC, V. ££££

WINDERMERE

Holbeck Ghyll The set-back position of this classic Victorian lakeland hotel provides welcome privacy from the bustle of Windermere, as well as grand lake views from the immaculate gardens. Traditional and rather formal in style, with a professional, friendly staff, it has mostly very spacious bedrooms and bathrooms.
⊠ Holbeck Lane, Windermere, Cumbria LA23 1LU. **Map** pp74 C1, p77 D5. ((015394) 32375. FAX (015394) 34743. @ accommodation@holbeck-ghyll.co.uk ⁕ b,l,d. **Rooms** 20. ⁘ ⊙ ● Never. ⊜ AE, DC, MC, V. ££££

YORK

Middlethorpe Hall The magnificent William III house, once home of diarist Lady Mary Wortley Montagu, is now part of Historic House Hotels, which transforms important buildings into places to stay. One feels special just walking in, yet the atmosphere is not intimidating; it feels almost like staying in a private home. Extremely expensive.
⊠ Bishopthorpe Rd, York YO23 2GB. **Map** p75 E1. ((01904) 641241. FAX (01904) 620176. @ info@middlethorpe.u-net.com ⁕ b,l,d. **Rooms** 30. ≋ ⁘ ⊙ ● Never. ⊜ MC, V. £££££

WINDERMERE
Storrs Hall This handsome Georgian mansion has emerged from a change of ownership bedecked in opulent country house finery.
⊠ Windermere, Cumbria LA23 3LG. **Map** pp74 C1, p77 D5. ((015394) 47111. FAX (015394) 47555. ⁕ b,l,d. **Rooms** 18. £££

WINTERINGHAM
Winteringham Fields The name is bleak but not the house, whose owners have created an alluring formula: highly praised food, lovely bedrooms.
⊠ Winteringham, North Lincolnshire DN15 9PF. **Map** p75 E1. ((0724) 733096. FAX (01724) 733898. @ euroannie@aol.com ⁕ b,l,d. **Rooms** 6. £££

YORK
The Grange Handsome Regency townhouse with a richly decorated interior and a sedate ambience. Elegant dining room; helpful service
⊠ 1 Clifton, York, North Yorkshire YO30 6AA. **Map** p75 E1. ((01904) 644744. FAX (01904) 612453. @ grangehotel.co.uk ⁕ b,l,d. **Rooms** 30. £££

YORK
Holmwood House Very comfortable B&B about 15 minutes' walk from the centre of the city.
⊠ 114 Holgate Rd, York, North Yorkshire YO2 4BB. **Map** p75 E1. ((01904) 626183. FAX (01904) 670899. @ holmwood.house@ dial.pipex.com ⁕ b. **Rooms** 11. ££

SCOTLAND

BORDERS • LOWLANDS • SOUTHWESTERN SCOTLAND
HIGHLANDS AND ISLANDS

FROM PASTORAL *border country to the raw, majestic scenery of the Highlands and Islands, Scotland's landscape never ceases to amaze, and presents endless opportunities for outdoor pursuits – notwithstanding the rain and the summer midges. On the following pages you will find some of the most remote hotels in Europe, as well as ones fashioned from buildings as diverse as castles* *and crofts. The vast majority are in superb locations and are wonderfully secluded, perhaps overlooking a quiet loch with a view of distant mountains, or with lawns running down to a deserted swathe of golden beach. Of Scotland's cities, Edinburgh is well-served with fine hotels, and we include several useful addresses in Glasgow.*

ACHILTIBUIE

Summer Isles The very remote, cottage-like hotel has a Michelin star for its impressive cookery, which makes much use of fresh local fish; the cheeseboard is justly famous. Only three of the fairly simple but satisfactory rooms have a TV. If possible, go for the suite: it has a spiral staircase, huge bathroom and breathtaking views.
⊠ Achiltibuie, Ullapool, Ross-shire IV26 2YG.
Map p76 C1. 📞 (01854) 622282. 📠 (01854) 622251.
@ smilehotel@aol.com 🍴 b,l,d. **Rooms** 13.
● mid-Oct to Easter. 💳 MC, V. ⓔⓔⓔ

ARISAIG

Arisaig House With glorious grounds filled with rhododendrons and stunning views across the Sound of Arisaig to the distant Morven Hills, this is a polished, dignified and extremely comfortable retreat (Relais et Chateaux). The spacious bedrooms are fresh and neat, with well-equiped bathrooms. Billiards, croquet; good food.
⊠ Beasdale, Arisaig, Inverness-shire PH39 4NR.
Map p76 B2. 📞 (01687) 450622. 📠 (01687) 450626.
@ ArisaiGHSE@aol.com 🍴 b,l,d. **Rooms** 12. 🛇
● Nov to Easter. 💳 MC, V. ⓔⓔⓔⓔ

BALLACHULISH .

Ballachulish House Peaceful old country house with stunning views of Loch Linnhe and the Morven Hills. Gourmet dinners. Billiards; croquet.
⊠ Ballachulish, Argyll PA39 4JX. **Map** p76 C3.
📞 (01855) 811266. 📠 (01855) 811496. 🍴 b,d.
Rooms 8. ⓔⓔ

BALLATER

Darroch Learg An imposing Victorian country house hotel, splendidly situated and easy-going. Noted for its inventive food and excellent wines.
⊠ Braemar Rd, Ballater, Aberdeenshire AB35 5UX.
Map p77 D2. 📞 (013397) 55443. 📠 (013397) 55252.
🍴 b,d. **Rooms** 23. ⓔ

BALQUHIDDER

Monachyle Mhor Rustic, cosy former farmhouse by Loch Voil. It is run with verve by the Lewis family, with splendid cooking from son Tom.
⊠ Balquhidder, Lochearnhead, Stirling FK19 8PQ.
Map p76 C3. 📞 (01877) 384622. 📠 (01877) 384305.
🍴 b,l,d. **Rooms** 10. ⓔⓔ

BANCHORY

Tor-na-Coille This grey granite, ivy-clad Victorian mansion has been a hotel for most of its life, and is furnished in keeping. Quiet atmosphere.
⊠ Inchmarlo Rd, Banchory, Aberdeenshire AB31 4AB.
Map p77 E2. 📞 (01330) 822242. 📠 (01330) 824012.
@ tornacoille@btinternet.com 🍴 b,l,d. **Rooms** 22. ⓔⓔ

AUCHTERARDER

Gleneagles This spectacular Art Deco hotel was built in the 1920s as the 'playground of the gods'. Intimate it is not; occupied you will certainly be, with a raft of activities, both leisure and sporting, now on offer (including, of course, the world-class golf which made the hotel's name). Suites and 'Estate Rooms' are nicest, but very expensive.
☒ Auchterarder, Perthshire PH3 1NF. **Map** p77 D3.
☎ (01764) 662231. FAX (01764) 662134.
@ resort.sales@gleneagles.com 🍴 b,l,d. **Rooms** 230.
🏊 🍴 📶 ◉ Never. 🅖 AE, DC, MC, V. ⓔⓔⓔⓔⓔ

COMRIE

Royal Hotel In an endearing village, well placed for touring, this 18th-century former coaching inn became 'royal' when Queen Victoria stayed. Today it is a beautifully presented, traditional hotel with an eye for modern tastes and a cool yet homely ambience: heavy iron bedsteads are offset by pale walls and gleaming wooden floors.
☒ Melville Square, Comrie, Perthshire PH6 2DN.
Map p77 D3. ☎ (01764) 679200. FAX (01764) 679219.
@ reception@royalhotel.co.uk 🍴 b,l,d. **Rooms** 11.
📶 ◉ Never. 🅖 AE, MC, V. ⓔⓔⓔⓔ

BLAIRGOWRIE

Kinloch House The early Victorian country house, adorned with a neatly trimmed creeper on the outside and pincushion-neat inside, is set in wooded parkland and has a fine walled garden. The atmosphere is quiet, the staff traditionally dressed, the rooms furnished with antiques. Bar for cocktails or a wee dram; conservatory.
☒ Blairgowrie, Perthshire PH10 6SG. **Map** p77 D3.
☎ (01250) 884237. FAX (01250) 884333.
@ kinlochhouse@compuserve.com 🍴 b,l,d. **Rooms** 21.
🏊 🍴 📶 ◉ Christmas. 🅖 AE, DC, MC, V. ⓔⓔⓔⓔⓔ

DUNKELD

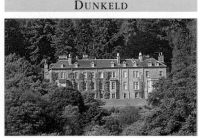

Kinnaird This Edwardian mansion harks back to a more gracious age, with modern requirements subtly blended in: the dining room is decorated with frescoes, bedrooms are spacious and luxurious. The River Tay (fishing possible) flows through the estate. Also self-catering cottages.
☒ Kinnaird Estate, Dunkeld, Perthshire PH8 0LB.
Map p77 D3. ☎ (01796) 482440. FAX (01796) 482289.
@ enquiry@kinnairdestate.com 🍴 b,l,d.
Rooms 9, plus 9 cottages. 📶 ◉ Mon-Wed in Jan and Feb. 🅖 MC, V. ⓔⓔⓔⓔⓔ

BUNESSAN, ISLE OF MULL

Ardfenaig House Originally the Duke of Argyll's factor's house, standing at the head of a narrow sea loch and with views in the other direction of splendid moorland. Traditional, comfortable.
☒ Bunessan, Isle of Mull, Argyll PA67 6DX. **Map** p76 B3.
☎ FAX (01681) 700210. 🍴 b,d. **Rooms** 5. ⓔⓔ

BUNESSAN, ISLE OF MULL

Assapol House The home of the Robertson family, a remote white-painted manse by a loch, is friendly yet dignified. The dinners are excellent.
☒ Bunessan, Isle of Mull, Argyll PA67 6DW.
Map p76 B3. ☎ (01681) 700258. FAX (01681) 700445.
🍴 b,d. **Rooms** 5. ⓔⓔ

CANONBIE

Riverside Inn Country-style decor and ambitious food characterize this black-and-white village inn, which faces a public park and overlooks the River Esk (fishing available).
☒ Canonbie, Dumfries and Galloway DG14 0UX. **Map** p77 D4. ☎ (013873) 71512. 🍴 b,l,d. **Rooms** 7. ⓔⓔ

COLONSAY, ISLE OF

Isle of Colonsay Hotel Perfect island life: away from it all in a warmly civilized house serving good fresh food. Cycling, fishing, golf, sailing.
☒ Isle of Colonsay, Argyll PA61 7YP. **Map** p76 B3.
☎ (01951) 200316. FAX (01951) 200353. @ colonsay.
hotel@pipemedia.co.uk 🍴 b,l,d. **Rooms** 11. ⓔⓔ

DUNVEGAN, ISLE OF SKYE

Harlosh House Londoner Peter Elford makes every effort for his guests and is an accomplished self-taught cook, specializing in seafood. The guesthouse is set on the shores of Loch Bracadale and is a very peaceful place. None of the six simple, thoughtfully equipped rooms has a phone or television. Breakfast is served until 11.30am.
🖂 Dunvegan, Isle of Skye, Highland IV55 8ZG.
Map p76 B2. 🄲 **FAX** (01470) 521367.
@ harlosh.house@ virgin.net 🍴 b,d. **Rooms** 6.
● Oct to Easter. 🗲 MC, V. ⓔⓔ

EDINBURGH

The Howard The most luxurious of three Edinburgh hotels in the same stable (see also The Bonham, below left), The Howard is a made up of three richly decorated terraced townhouses. Original features include romantic Italianate frescoes in the breakfast room. The hotel's minimalist restaurant, 36, is well known.
🖂 34 Great King St, Edinburgh EH3 6QH. **Map** p77 D3.
🄲 (0131) 557 3500. **FAX** (0131) 557 6515.
@ reserve@thehoward.com 🍴 b,l,d. **Rooms** 15.
● Christmas. 🗲 AE, DC, MC, V. ⓔⓔⓔⓔ

EDINBURGH

The Bonham In the same ownership as the Howard (see this page), the townhouse hotel is situated in a leafy side street close to the city centre. It has been equipped for the 21st century, with communications technology installed in the calm, contemporary bedrooms; these also feature original paintings by young Scottish artists.
🖂 35 Drumsheugh Gardens, Edinburgh EH3 7RN.
Map p77 D3. 🄲 (0131) 226 6050. **FAX** (0131) 226 6080.
@ reserve@thebonham.com 🍴 b,l,d. **Rooms** 48.
● Christmas. ⓔⓔⓔ

ERISKA

Isle of Eriska Close to Oban and connected to the mainland by a road bridge, Eriska feels a world away, and the family-run baronial house is a pleasant echo of the Victorian age. High tea is served at 6pm in old-fashioned public rooms. The bedrooms are light and mainly spacious. Families can expect a warm welcome. Private golf course.
🖂 Eriska, Ledaig, Oban, Argyll PA37 1SD.
Map p76 A2. 🄲 (01631) 720371. **FAX** (01631) 720531.
@ reserve@eriska-hotel.co.uk 🍴 b,d. **Rooms** 17.
🏊 🍴 🄾 ● Jan. 🗲 AE, MC, V. ⓔⓔⓔⓔ

DRUMNADROCHIT
Polmaily House Secluded hotel near Loch Ness; both adults and children are well taken care of.
🖂 Drumnadrochit, Inverness-shire IV3 6XT.
Map p76 C2. 🄲 (01456) 450343. **FAX** (01456) 450813.
@ pomailyhousehotel@btinternet.com
🍴 b,l,d. **Rooms** 14. ⓔⓔ

EDINBURGH
The Balmoral A highly prestigious new address in the heart of the city, mixing baronial grandeur with the very latest in luxury and fine dining.
🖂 1 Princes St, Edinburgh EH2 2EQ. **Map** p77 D3.
🄲 (0131) 556 2414. **FAX** (0131) 557 3747.
🍴 b,l,d. **Rooms** 186. ⓔⓔⓔⓔ

EDINBURGH
Albany Peaceful Georgian terrace close to Princes Street. Pleasant bedrooms, sparkling bathrooms.
🖂 39 Albany St, Edinburgh EH1 3QY. **Map** p77 D3.
🄲 (0131) 556 0397. **FAX** (0131) 557 6633.
@ centuryhousehotel@compuserve.com
🍴 b,l,d. **Rooms** 21. ⓔⓔⓔ

EDINBURGH
Drummond House An insight into life behind the façade of a grand 1819 home, complete with moulded ceilings, pillared hallway, cantilevered stone staircase, and slightly faded elegance.
🖂 17 Drummond Pl, Edinburgh EH3 6LP. **Map** p77 D3.
🄲 **FAX** (0131) 557 9189. 🍴 b. **Rooms** 4. ⓔⓔ

FORT WILLIAM

Inverlochy Castle The hotel in which Conservative Party leader William Hague chose to spend his stag night, walking off the effects on Ben Nevis. You can understand his choice: the Scottish Baronial pile is neither intimidating nor stuffy, at the same time being deeply, elegantly luxurious. Superb food; tennis, billiards, fishing.
⊠ Torlundy, Fort William, Inverness-shire PH33 6SN.
Map p76 C2. 〖 (01397) 702177. ℻ (01397) 702953.
@ info@inverlochycastle.co.uk 👖 b,l,d. **Rooms** 17.
🔌 ● mid-Jan to mid-Feb. 🗩 MC, V. ⓔⓔⓔⓔ

GLASGOW

One Devonshire Gardens Even among London's myriad town house hotels One Devonshire Gardens would stand out; in Glasgow it positively glows. In fact it comprises three handsome houses, not interconnecting, on a busy road close to the city centre. Step inside, and the effect is one of richly coloured opulence.
⊠ One Devonshire Gardens, Glasgow G12 0UX.
Map p76 C4. 〖 (0141) 339 2001. ℻ (0141) 337 1663.
@ markcalpin@btconnect.com 👖 b,l,d. **Rooms** 27.
🔌 ● Never. 🗩 AE, DC, MC, V. ⓔⓔⓔ

GLASGOW

Malmaison This was the second of the Malmaison chain of city hotels (the first was in Edinburgh), noted for their contemporary image and good value. It created a much-appreciated new address in Glasgow, with stylish, well-equipped bedrooms, a suave reception foyer, brasserie-style dining room, and Italian Café Mal.
⊠ 278 West George St, Glasgow G2 4LL. **Map** p76 C4.
〖 (0141) 572 1000. ℻ (0141) 572 1002.
@ glasgow@malmaison.com 👖 b,l,d. **Rooms** 72.
👔 ● Never. 🗩 AE, DC, MC, V. ⓔⓔ

GULLANE

Greywalls An obvious choice for golfers, since it overlooks the 10th green of the Muirfield course, this immaculate honey-stoned, crescent-shaped building was designed by Sir Edwin Lutyens. The feel is still one of an elegant private house; the panelled library is particularly appealing. Refined dinners and hearty breakfasts.
⊠ Muirfield, Gullane, East Lothian EH31 2EG.
Map p77 D3. 〖 (01620) 842144. ℻ (01620) 842241.
@ greywalls@hotel17.freeserve.co.uk 👖 b,l,d. **Rooms** 23.
🔌 ● Nov to March. 🗩 AE, DC, MC, V. ⓔⓔⓔⓔ

FORT WILLIAM
The Grange Jessica Lange stayed in this B&B while filming *Rob Roy*. Maybe she had the Turret Room, but all are charming with lovely views.
⊠ Grange Rd, Fort William, Inverness-shire PH33 6JF.
Map p76 C2. 〖 (01397) 705516. ℻ (01397) 701595.
👖 b. **Rooms** 3. ⓔⓔ

GLASGOW
Babbity Bowster An original name for an original little restaurant-with-rooms with a lively ambience. Bedrooms are small and simple.
⊠ 16-18 Blackfriars St, Glasgow G1 1PE. **Map** p76 C4.
〖 (0141) 552 5055. ℻ (0141) 552 7774. 👖 b,d.
Rooms 6. ⓔⓔ

INNERLEITHEN
The Ley A guesthouse with quiet hosts, well-appointed rooms, good dinners (by request) and memorable Scottish breakfasts, as well as seclusion and natural beauty all around.
⊠ Innerleithen, Peebleshire EH44 6NL. **Map** p77 D4.
〖 ℻ (01896) 830240. 👖 b,d. **Rooms** 3. ⓔⓔ

ISLEORNSAY
Eilean Iarmain Traditional 19th-century seaside inn with a Gaelic feel. Wonderful views from the comfy bedrooms and public rooms.
⊠ Isleornsay, Sleat, Isle of Skye, Highland IV43 8QR.
Map p76 B2. 〖 (01471) 833332. ℻ (01471) 833275.
👖 b,l,d. **Rooms** 16. ⓔⓔ

MAYBOLE

PORT APPIN

Culzean Castle On a windswept clifftop, Robert Adam's last masterpiece (c.1785). The top floor was given by Scotland to the late ex-US President Eisenhower for his lifetime, and is now a small hotel. It includes a wonderful circular sitting room with views to Arran and Mull of Kintyre. Or you can rent the entire apartment for a private party.

Culzean Castle, Maybole, Ayrshire KA19 8LE. **Map** p76 C4. (01655) 760274. FAX (01655) 760615. @ culzean@nts.org.uk b,d. **Rooms** 6. Nov to March. AE, MC, V. ££££

Airds Hotel In a pretty waterfront village, Airds is an old ferry inn with lovely views across Loch Linnhe to the hills beyond. It's a sophisticated place, in the same family for 22 years, with a flower-filled conservatory and Michelin-starred kitchen. Four much less expensive rooms are available in an annexe in the village.

Port Appin, Appin, Argyll PA38 4DF. **Map** p76 C3. (01631) 730236. FAX (01631) 730535. @ airds@airds-hotel.com b,d. **Rooms** 16. Christmas, Jan. MC, V. £££

NAIRN

PORTPATRICK

Clifton House Though it's not unusual to find hotels with a theatrical touch, this is in a different league: it *is* a theatre, staging plays and recitals in the dining room during winter months. The Victorian house is richly furnished, the bedrooms with a mix of antiques and assorted painted pieces. Relaxed atmosphere, good food and wine.

Viewfield St, Nairn, Nairnshire IV12 4HW. **Map** p77 D2. (01667) 453119. FAX (01667) 452836. @ macintyre@clara.net b,l,d. **Rooms** 12. mid-Dec to mid-Jan. AE, DC, MC, V. ££

Knockinaam Lodge This is a most comfortable place to get away from the hurly burly, or perhaps take a break en route to the Stranraer ferry. Set in a remote wooded glen, its lawned garden runs down to a sandy cove. Peace reigns, both in the smart public rooms and the large, dignified bedrooms. Dinner is compulsory.

Portpatrick, Wigtownshire, Dumfries and Galloway DG9 9AD. **Map** p76 C5. (01776) 810471. FAX (01776) 810435. b,l,d. **Rooms** 10. Never. AE, DC, MC, V. £££

KENTALLEN

Ardsheal House Set above Loch Linnhe, with stunning views. Hospitable, slightly old-fashioned; guest rooms are decorated with family antiques.

Kentallen of Appin, Argyll PA38 4BX. **Map** p76 C3. (01631) 740227. FAX (01631) 740342. @ info@ardsheal.co.uk b,d. **Rooms** 6. ££

KILDRUMMY

Kildrummy Castle Large, rather stately Victorian castellated building, set in lovely gardens overlooking a castle ruin. Traditional interiors.

Kildrummy, Alford, Aberdeenshire AB33 8RA. **Map** p77 D2. (019755) 71288. FAX (019755) 71345. b,l,d. **Rooms** 17. £££

KINGUSSIE

The Cross Former tweed mill, well-known for its gourmet food. Very pleasant bedrooms.

Tweed Mill Brae, Kingusssie, Inverness-shire PH211TC. **Map** p77 D2. (01540) 661166. FAX (01540) 661080. @ fabulousfood@thecross.co.uk b,d. **Rooms** 9. £££

KIRKUDBRIGHT

Gladstone House Excellent B&B in an appealing town. It is decorated with taste and makes a civilized place to stay, with plentiful breakfasts.

48 High St, Kirkcudbright, Dumfries and Galloway DG6 4JX. **Map** p76 C5. (01557) 331734. b. **Rooms** 3. £

SCARISTA, ISLE OF HARRIS

Scarista House The manse stands alone on a windswept slope overlooking tidal sands. The decoration is quite formal, but the atmosphere is relaxed and, by the open peat fires, conversation replaces television. Most bedrooms are in a separate single-storey building. A great attraction, as well as the solitude, is the mostly organic food.
⊠ Scarista, Isle of Harris, Western Isles HS3 3HX.
Map p76 B1. ☎ (01859) 550238. FAX (01859) 550277.
@ ian@scaristahouse.demon.co.uk ☷ b,l,d. **Rooms** 5.
● Oct to Apr. ☒ MC, V. ££

ULLAPOOL

Altnaharrie Inn First prize for the best hotel in the most out-of-the-way location. Having reached Ullapool in the northwestern extremity of the British Isles, you then take the hotel's boat to the far shore of Loch Broom. Here you will find complete seclusion in a wild, grand landscape, a warmly decorated house and the widely acclaimed cooking of Gunn Eriksen. At a price.
⊠ Ullapool, Inverness-shire IV26 2SS. **Map** p76 C1.
☎ (01854) 633230. ☷ b,l,d. **Rooms** 8. 🔌
● Nov to Easter. ☒ AE, MC, V. ££££

STRACHUR

Creggans Inn Run by Sir Charles Maclean, son of writer and traveller Sir Fitzroy Maclean and cookery expert Lady Maclean, this friendly, refined inn is part of their Strachur estate on the shores of Loch Fyne. Public rooms and bedrooms are charmingly decorated. Good food, wines and rare malts, including their own Old MacPhunn.
⊠ Strachur, Argyll PA27 8BX. **Map** p76 C3.
☎ (01369) 860279. FAX (01369) 860637.
@ info@creggans-inn.co.uk ☷ b,l,d. **Rooms** 17.
🔌 ● Never. ☒ AE, DC, MC, V. ££

WALLS, SHETLAND ISLANDS

Burrastow House A long, single-track road through Burrastow's spacious grounds ends at a remote spot by a rocky shore. In this isolated setting, the calm, solid stone house exudes a genuinely friendly and welcoming ambience. After a day in the open, everyone appreciates Bo Simmons's comforting food.
⊠ Walls, Shetland ZE2 9PD. **Map** p77 F1.
☎ (01595) 809307. FAX (01595) 809213.
@ burr.hs.hotel@zetnet.co.uk ☷ b,l,d. **Rooms** 5.
🔌 ● Christmas Day, Jan, Feb. ☒ AE, MC, V. ££

SHEILDAIG
Tigh an Eilean Easily mistaken for an ordinary village house, this is an excellent small hotel in one of the most beautiful regions of Scotland.
⊠ Sheildaig, Strathcarron, Ross-shire IV54 8XN.
Map p76 B2. ☎ (01520) 755251. FAX (01520) 755321.
☷ b,l,d. **Rooms** 11. ££

SKIRLING
Skirling House A fascinating Arts-and-Crafts house surrounded by lovely gardens. Superb dinner party-style food; sympathetic hosts.
⊠ Skirling, Biggar, Lanarkshire ML12 6HD. **Map** p77 D4.
☎ (01899) 860274. FAX (01899) 860255.
@ skirlinghouse@dial.pipex.com ☷ b,d. **Rooms** 3. ££

UIG, ISLE OF LEWIS
Baile-na-Cille The relaxed, beautifully set 18th-century manse makes a special guesthouse.
⊠ Timsgarry, Uig, Isle of Lewis, Outer Hebrides PA86 9JD. **Map** p76 B2. ☎ (01851) 672242.
FAX (01851) 672241. @ RandJGollin@compuserve.com
☷ b,l,d. **Rooms** 14. ££

ULLAPOOL
Ceilidh Place Happy centre of music and song. Budget bunk-bed accommodation also available.
⊠ West Argyle St, Ullapool, Ross-shire IV26 2TY.
Map p76 C1. ☎ (01854) 612103.
FAX (01854) 612886. @ reservations@
ceilidh.demon.co.uk ☷ b,l,d. **Rooms** 23 ££

For key to symbols see backflap. For price categories see p71

WALES

BORDER COUNTRY • NORTH WALES
SOUTH WALES

ALTHOUGH WALES NOW *has its first cutting edge five-star hotel, on Cardiff's waterfront, this is a land best suited to the traditional country house establishment: warm, welcoming and above all, restful. Many places take advantage of the superb landscape of Wales, with views across tidal estuaries or of distant mountains. Some of the hotels we list – including a smattering of fine historic mansions – are in rolling border country. Others are along the beautiful coastline; others by the peaks of Snowdonia. Accommodation in Wales ranges from private ancestral homes, with a mere handful of rooms set aside for guests, to sophisticated retreats. Hearty Welsh breakfasts and good local cooking (with Welsh cheese a speciality) are often a feature.*

ABERSOCH

Porth Tocyn For 50 years, the Fletcher-Brewer family have run this excellent family-orientated hotel with magnificent views across Cardigan Bay and Snowdonia. The plain building was fashioned from a group of lead-miners' cottages. Inside is a series of homely sitting rooms, and simple bedrooms, some interconnecting.

🗺 Abersoch, Gwynedd LL53 7BU. **Map** p74 B2.
📞 (01758) 713303. ℻ (01758) 713538. 🍴 b,l,d.
Rooms 17. 🛏 🚭 ● mid-Nov to week before Easter.
🛋 MC, V. ££

BONCATH

Llancych With an enchanting setting on the river Cych (trout fishing available), this is a most endearing house, a white-walled, slate-roofed confection of styles. Sarah and Tony Jones-Lloyd are warm, relaxed hosts, and their antique-filled home, from the book-lined library to the huge, impressive dining room and the traditional bedrooms, reflects their personality.

🗺 Boncath, Pembrokeshire SA37 0LJ. **Map** p74 B3.
📞 (01239) 698378. ℻ (01239) 698686. 🍴 b. **Rooms** 3.
🚭 ● early Nov to early March. 🛋 MC, V. ££

ABERGAVENNY

Llanwenarth House The Weatherill's home has spacious bedrooms and displays a love of horse and hound. Dinner party-style dining.

🗺 Govilon, Abergavenny, Monmouthshire NP7 9SF.
Map p74 C4. 📞 (01873) 830289. ℻ (01873) 832199.
🍴 b,d. **Rooms** 5. ££

BONTDDU

Borthwynog Hall Regency house in superb site on Mawddach Estuary; an elegant home run on hotel lines. The library is an art gallery.

🗺 Bontddu, Dolgellau, Gwynedd LL40 2TT.
Map p74 B2. 📞 (01341) 430271. ℻ (01341) 430682.
@ borthall@enterprise.co.net 🍴 b,d. **Rooms** 3. ££

FISHGUARD

Tregonyn Farmhouse Cosy retreat with one bedroom in the 16th-century stone farmhouse, the others in adjacent cottages.

🗺 Gwaun Valley, Fishguard, Pembrokeshire SA65 9TU.
Map p74 A3. 📞 (01239) 820531. ℻ (01239) 820808.
@ tregonyn@uk-holidays.co.uk 🍴 b,d. **Rooms** 6. ££

HARLECH

Castle Cottage The plain exterior belies the traditional beamed interior of this friendly little hotel in the shadow of Harlech's mighty castle. Small, practical bedrooms; well-regarded food.

🗺 Pen Llech, Harlech, Gwynedd LL46 2YL. **Map** p74 B2.
📞 ℻ (01766) 780479. 🍴 b,d. **Rooms** 6. £

CARDIFF

St David's Spa This swish waterfront establishment, which features a hydrotherapy centre and spa, is a five-star oasis, particularly for businessmen. The imposing structure is topped by an extraordinary flying tail fin; the interior is suitably nautical, cool and curvacious. Every room has a private bay-view deck.
☒ Havannah St, Cardiff CF10 5SD. **Map** p74 C4. 🕻 (029) 2045 4045. **FAX** (029) 2048 7056. @ reservations@ fivestar-htl-wales.com **11** b,l,d. **Rooms** 136.
▤ ⛲ 🍴 ● Never. 🗲 AE, DC, MC, V. ⓔⓔⓔⓔ

GARTHMYL

Garthmyl Hall Designers Tim and Nancy Morrow have brought youthful, affordable flair to this handsome red-brick Georgian house. The velvety drawing room retains its ornate ceiling; there is a cosy library, and the bedrooms are cool, contemporary and perfectly judged. The food is simple but good, the ambience informal.
☒ Garthmyl, Montgomery, Powys SY15 6RS.
Map p74 C3. 🕻 (01686) 640550. **FAX** (01686) 640609.
11 b,d. **Rooms** 10. ▯ ● Never. 🗲 MC, V. ⓔⓔ

EGLWYSFACH

Ynyshir Hall The house stands in glorious gardens next to the Ynyshir Bird Reserve and Dovey estuary. Its boldly coloured interior is the creation of owner Rob Reen, as are the striking paintings which adorn the walls. The zesty cooking is similarly adventurous. Bedrooms are named and furnished after famous artists.
☒ Eglwysfach, Machynlleth, Ceredigion SY20 8TA.
Map p74 B3. 🕻 (01654) 781209. **FAX** (01654) 781366. **11** b,l,d. **Rooms** 10. ▯ ● Never.
🗲 AE, DC, MC, V. ⓔⓔⓔ

LLANDRILLO

Tyddyn Llan The warm and welcoming ambience is the mark of a country house hotel which gets it just right: no intrusive reception desk; spacious sitting rooms furnished with style; and elegant dining room where imaginative dishes are served. The well-equipped bedrooms are enhanced by original pieces of furniture.
☒ Llandrillo, Corwen, Denbighshire LL21 0ST.
Map p74 C2. 🕻 (01490) 440264. **FAX** (01490) 440414. @ tyddynllanhotel@compuserve.com **11** b,l,d.
Rooms 10. ● 2 weeks Jan. 🗲 AE, DC, MC, V. ⓔⓔⓔ

LLANDDEINIOLEN

Ty'n Rhos A quiet, traditional, well-run country hotel. Excellent Welsh breakfasts.
☒ Seion, Llanddeiniolen, Caernarfon, Gwynedd LL55 3AE. **Map** p74 B2. 🕻 (01248) 670489.
FAX (01248) 670079. @ tynrhos@netcomuk.co.uk
11 b,l,d. **Rooms** 14. ⓔⓔ

LLANDEGLEY

The Ffaldau An endearingly beamed and buckled 16th-century guesthouse, owned by a Methodist minister and a relaxation therapist.
☒ Llandegley, Llandrindod Wells, Powys LD1 5UD. **Map** p74 C3. 🕻 (01597) 851421.
11 b,d. **Rooms** 4. ⓔⓔ

LLANGAMMARCH WELLS

The Lake A grand country house hotel, with polished service and plenty of activities.
☒ Llangammarch Wells, Powys LD4 4BS.
Map p74 C3. 🕻 (01591) 620202. **FAX** (01591) 620457. @ lakehotel@ndirect.co.uk **11** b,l,d.
Rooms 4. ⓔⓔⓔ

LLANWRTYD WELLS

Lasswade Country House Edwardian house overlooking fields on the outskirts of town. Light and airy bedrooms, well-kept bathrooms.
☒ Station Rd, Llanwrtyd Wells, Powys LD5 4RW.
Map p74 B3. 🕻 (01591) 610515. **FAX** (01591) 610611.
11 b,d. **Rooms** 8. ⓔⓔ

For key to symbols see backflap. For price categories see p71

LLANDUDNO

LLANSANFFRAID GLAN CONWY

Bodysgallen Hall At the core of this 17th-century Grade I listed house is a 13th-century tower, which should be climbed for the view. There are impressive formal gardens, including a walled rose garden and a knot garden. Inside, the atmosphere is one of traditional and rather formal elegance, with corresponding – pricey – cuisine.
Llandudno, Conwy LL30 1RS. **Map** p74 B2.
(01492) 584466. FAX (01492) 582519. info@ bodysgallen.u-net.com b,l,d. **Rooms** 35.
Never. MC, V. ££££

Old Rectory The glorious sweeping view across the Conwy estuary is the most memorable asset of this pretty Georgian rectory. A close second is the delicious cooking of Wendy Vaughan and her husband's intelligent wine list. Relax in the elegant wood-panelled sitting room. Bedrooms feel old-fashioned, with grandiose beds.
Llansanffraid Glan Conwy, Colwyn Bay, Conwy LL28 5LF. **Map** p74 C2. (01492) 580611.
FAX (01492) 584555. oldrect@aol.com b,d.
Rooms 6. mid-Dec to Feb. MC, V. ££

LLANDUDNO

PORTMEIRION

St Tudno With 26 years at the helm, the Blands are meticulous in attending to every detail of this Victorian seafront hotel. Period charm is balanced with modern facilities, plus a long list of thoughtful extras which add to the sense of comfort. The food is right on target in the inviting dining room; the staff are young and willing.
Promenade, Llandudno, Conwy LL30 2LP.
Map p74 B2. (01492) 874411. FAX (01492) 860407.
sttudnohotel@btinternet.com b,l,d. **Rooms** 20.
Never. AE, DC, MC, V. £££

Portmeirion Hotel 'Magical' is the most apposite word to describe the hotel at the centre of Clough Williams-Ellis's enchanting fantasy village. The heady ensemble mixes Wales (bilingual staff and menus, harpist), Capri (Italianate gardens, statues, columns) and Rajasthan (Indian fabrics, paintings, objects). Improving reports of the food.
Portmeirion, Gwynedd LL48 6ET. **Map** p74 B2.
(01766) 770000. FAX (01766) 771331. hotel@ portmeirion.wales.com b,l,d. **Rooms** 39.
Christmas Day. AE, DC, MC, V. ££££

LLYSWEN

Llangoed Hall Luxury, beautifully decorated hotel created by Bernard Ashley (Laura's widower) in a Clough Williams-Ellis mansion.
Llyswen, Powys LD3 0YP. **Map** p74 C3. (01874) 754525. FAX (01874) 754545. 101543.3211@ compuserve.com **Rooms** 23. ££££

NANTGWYNANT

Pen-y-Gwryd Hotel Set high in the desolate heart of Snowdonia, a plain, old-fashioned inn revered by mountaineers. Sauna, natural swimming pool (strictly for the hardy).
Nantgwynant, Gwynedd LL55 4NT. **Map** p74 B2.
(01286) 870211. b,l,d. **Rooms** 16. £

NERCWYS

Tower B&B in historic castellated border house, the ancestral home of the owners. Baronial rooms, and a dining room hook from which the Mayor of Chester was hung in 1465.
Nercwys, Mold, Flintshire CH7 4ED. **Map** p74 C2.
FAX (01352) 700220. b. **Rooms** 3. £

PENALLY

Penally Abbey The setting is the key attraction of this Victorian Gothic house. Elegant dining by candlelight; many rooms with four-posters.
Penally, Pembrokeshire SA70 7PY. **Map** p74 B4
(01834) 843033. FAX (01834) 844714. penally. abbey@btinternet.com b,d. **Rooms** 13. ££

REYNOLDSTON

Fairyhill A quiet and civilized retreat (the bedrooms include CD players) in the heart of the Gower Peninsula. Set in vast grounds – much of it still semi-wild – it features a walled garden, orchard, trout stream and lake. A series of spacious public rooms lead to the dining room, where fine food might include Penclawdd cockles, Welsh lamb and laverbread.
Reynoldston, Swansea SA3 1BS. **Map** p74 B4.
(01792) 390139. FAX (01792) 391358. b,l,d.
Rooms 8. Christmas. AE, MC, V. ££££

TAL-Y-LLYN

Minffordd One dreams of stumbling across this sort of place unexpectedly: an old drover's inn tucked under the mighty Cader Idris peak, with a genuinely warm welcome, cosy rooms, open fires and well-kept bedrooms (all shapes and sizes; no TVs). At its heart is the beamed, candlelit dining room, where chef Jenny Carpenter's mainly Welsh recipes go down a treat.
Tal-y-llyn, Tywyn, Gwynedd LL36 9AJ. **Map** p74 B2.
(01654) 761665. FAX (01654) 761517. b,d.
Rooms 6. Dec-Feb. MC, V. ££

ST BRIDES WENTLOOGE

West Usk Lighthouse A B&B to visit for novelty value, and for very good breakfasts. You will have spent the night in a wedge-shaped portion of an unusual 1821 lighthouse. You may also have slept in a waterbed, showered in a red telephone box, had an aromatherapy massage and soaked away your cares in a flotation tank. Not to mention the Dalek.
Lighthouse Rd, St Brides Wentlooge, Newport NP1 9SF.
Map p74 C4. (01633) 810126. FAX (01633) 815582.
b. **Rooms** 4. Never. AE,DC, MC, V. ££

THREE COCKS

Old Gwernyfed The public rooms are the most memorable: an oak-panelled sitting room overlooked by a minstrel's gallery, a dining room whose vast fireplace has a wood-burning stove. Modern life is kept at bay (no TVs in the bedrooms); instead the historic character of the place is allowed to shine. Period music at dinner.
Felindre, Three Cocks, Brecon, Powys LD3 0SU.
Map p74 C3. (01497) 847376. FAX (01497) 897767. b,d. **Rooms** 10. Jan, Feb.
AE, DC, MC, V. ££

PENMAENPOOL
Penmaenuchaf Hall Wood-panelled walls, log fires, luxurious bedrooms and vast grounds.
Penmaenpool, Dolgellau LL40 1YB.
Map p74 B2. (01341) 422129. FAX (01341) 422787.
FAX (01352) 700220. @ penhall@tinyonline.co.uk
b. **Rooms** 3. £

RHYDYFELIN
Nanteos Mansion A fine Georgian house with a magnificent hall and spacious rooms.
Rhydyfelin, Aberystwyth, Ceredigion SY23 4LU.
Map p74 B3. (01970) 624363).
FAX (01970) 626332. @ nanteos@btinternet.com.
b,d. **Rooms** 6. ££

TALSARNAU
Maes-y-Neuadd 600-year-old granite manor house with panelled walls, comfortable public rooms and luxurious bedrooms.
Talsarnau, Gwynedd LL47 6YA. **Map** p74 B2.
(01766) 780200. FAX (01766) 780211. @ myn@ wales-snowdonia.com. b,l,d. **Rooms** 16. £££

THREE COCKS
Three Cocks Hotel Characterful inn with a palpable Belgian influence supplied by its Belgian-born owner and her chef husband.
Three Cocks, Brecon, Powys LD3 0SL. **Map** p74 C3.
(01497) 847215. FAX (01497) 847339. b,d.
Rooms 7. ££

THE NETHERLANDS

THE NETHERLANDS

DUTCH HOTELS offer some interesting contrasts. In Amsterdam you'll find rows of canalhouses knocked through to make one hotel. Decorated with great panache, these places mix antiques with contemporary urban style. Away from the big cities, you'll find smart rusticity: old box beds, or flagged floors and candlelight, and great cooking. The level of hospitality is high, with some hotels prepared to set up the Jacuzzi or light a log fire for your arrival. If your taste is for gritty realism, head instead for the bustling port of Rotterdam, where the 'left bank' has been revitalized with bars and cafés, presided over by the Hotel New York (page 131), a stylish hotel in a landmark port building.

The graceful Château St Gerlach, at Valkenburg, page 131

THE NETHERLANDS, REGION BY REGION

THE NETHERLANDS is not a big country, but it divides conveniently into west, north, east and south.

The West
This region includes the cities of Amsterdam, The Hague, Utrecht and Rotterdam – known as *De Randstad* or 'rim towns'. Each offers distinctive townhouse hotels. Amsterdam's attractions include its canals and three big museums (namely the Rijksmuseum, the Van Gogh and the Stedelijk). The palace city of The Hague is the seat of government.

Smaller cities with equally attractive places to stay include Maastricht, home to a flamboyant carnival in February and a gourmet food festival in August; and Delft, known as the Prinsenstad (city of princes). Three other attractive towns worth a visit include Utrecht, with its pretty canals, alleyways, and specialist shops in the streets around the old centre; Leiden, an historic university town; and Gouda, famous for its cheese.

The North
Friesland is an intriguing area of farms, lakes and black-and-white cows, with its own language and cultural identity. There's a grand hotel in Leeuwarden, a town of small canals and shopping streets. In the otherwise rural province of Groningen you can stay in an old guardhouse on the former toll bridge in the university city capital (also called Groningen).

The East
The provinces of Flevoland, Gelderland and Overijssel were created from reclaimed land. This is the site of the Hoge Veluwe National Park, the principal national park of the Netherlands and one in which you can stay, in a 'cottage' hotel at Otterlo (page 129). In this area of canals and fertile farmland, there are many other relaxing country hotels offering excellent food.

The South
The region encompasses Limburg, Noord-Brabant and Zeeland, the delta province. This is a pleasure-loving area and the food here is said to be the best in the Netherlands. Limburg's Geul Valley is really special, overlooked by a beautiful hotel at Valkenburg (see above).

HIGHLIGHTS

HOTELS ILLUSTRATED on these introductory pages are only a few of our favourites. Others include the Jachtslot de Mookerheide castle hotel in Molenhoek, with its Art Nouveau interior (page 129);

and the half-timbered Winselerhof, a 17th-century farmhouse serving good food at Landgraaf (page 128).

FOOD AND DRINK

CLASSIC DUTCH cooking is generally brasserie-style food in generous portions, with especially good grilled meat and fish. There are plentiful fresh supplies of mussels (*mosselen*), eel (*paling*), served smoked, and herring (*haring*). Traditional standbys include a pea soup thick enough to stand your spoon up in (*erwtensoep*) and mashed vegetable dishes (*stamppotten*), many of them incorporating lard.

Perhaps more enticing are the pancakes, sweet mini pancakes (*poffertjes*) and hard waffles (*stroopwafel*), of traditional Dutch cooking.

International cuisine is the order of the day in city restaurants, and many hotels offer a Dutch-French hybrid. Vegetarians won't do too badly, especially if they don't mind fish. Holland's colonial past means there's a wide choice of Indonesian and Chinese restaurants, where the *rijsttafel* ('rice table') is a feast of many dishes.

Amsterdam is home to the atmospheric *bruine kroeg* ('brown cafés'), warm bolt-holes (named due to colour of decoration) that are some-times literary cafés, and sometimes simply a venue for enjoying a cup of coffee, a glass of wine or a beer. There are also modernist white cafés which tend to be more popular with a younger crowd. You'll also find the occasional *proeflokalen* (tasting house) bar which traditionally used to serve only spirits such as the national drink *jenever* (gin) made from juniper berries.

Lunch is often just a snack or a cold collation known as *koffietafel* which can be had from 11am to 2:30 or 3pm.

Many restaurants do not open for lunch, but open for dinner from about 5:30pm; most shut at about 10pm in the provinces, 11pm or later in cities. The traditional day

of closure for restaurants is Monday, and sometimes Tues-day as well. Restaurants with rooms may be shut on one or both of these days, too.

BEDROOMS AND BATHROOMS

ROOMS IN canalhouse hotels are often at the top of narrow rickety wooden stairs and it's the exception rather than the rule for these small hotels to have lifts – so while there will be someone to help you with your bags when you arrive, they might not suit those who have restricted mobility. Rooms in these historic hotels are often small, or narrow, but of course what they lack in space they make up for in character.

OTHER PRACTICAL INFORMATION

BREAKFAST IS usually an ex-tensive buffet of different kinds of bread, cheese, cold meats, hard-boiled eggs, yog-hurt, muesli and stewed fruit.

Language English is widely spoken and understood, so too is German and, in some places, French.

Currency The Dutch *guilder* often written as 'Fl' or 'DFl'.

Shops Generally open 8:30 or 9am–5:30 or 6pm Mon–Sat; many close on Monday mornings, and from 4 or 5pm on Saturdays. Late-night shopping is on Thursday and Friday evenings. In Amsterdam many shops stay open until 10pm. Banks are open 9am–4 or 5pm Mon– Fri; in some places they are open until 9pm on Thursday evenings and open on Saturday mornings.

Tipping Generally, you'll find a 15 per cent service charge added to restaurant bills. Otherwise, it's normal practice to round up the total to the nearest five guilders, the tip being

left in cash, not added to the total on the cheque or card.

Telephoning Public call boxes take mainly phonecards and credit cards, though a few still take coins. Post offices have booths where you can pay the amount due after your call. Inside the country, dial the full area code. To call the Netherlands from the UK or US, dial 00 31, then the number, omitting the initial zero; from the US, 011 31.

Public holidays 1 January; Good Friday and Easter Sunday and Monday; 30 April (Queen's Day); 5 May (Liberation Day); Ascension Day; Whit Sunday (Pentecost) and Monday; 15 August; 25 and 26 December.

USEFUL WORDS

Breakfast	*Ontbijt*
Lunch	*Lunch*
Dinner	*Diner*
Free room?	*Kamer vrij?*
How much?	*Wat kost?*
Single	*Een eenpersoons kamer*
Double	*Een tweepersoons kamer*

NETHERLANDS PRICE BANDS

OUR PRICE bands refer to the price of a standard room in high season, and usually include breakfast. Most prices quoted include all taxes, but you may encounter local taxes in some places.

ⓕ	up to Fl200
ⓕⓕ	Fl200–Fl500
ⓕⓕⓕ	Fl500–Fl1,000
ⓕⓕⓕⓕ	over Fl1,000

The Canal House, Amsterdam, page 126

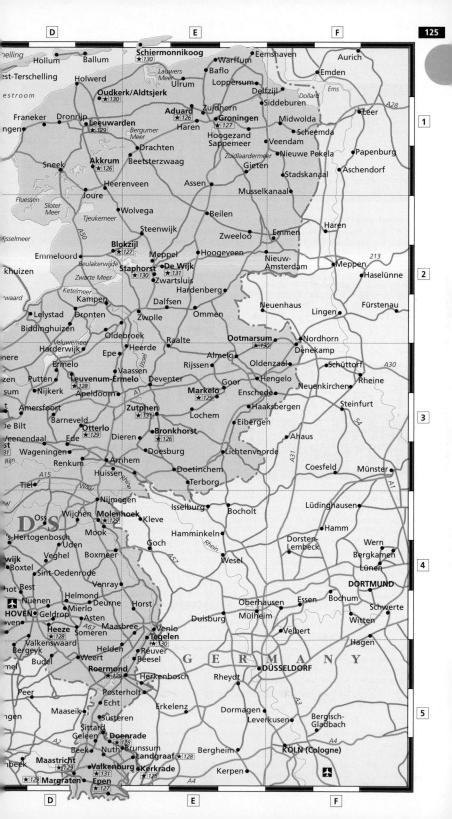

ADUARD

Herberg Onder de Linden In an inn dating back to 1735 is this Michelin-starred restaurant with rooms, serving enticing French and Dutch specialities. The old building is well maintained and free of historic tweeness; rooms are decorated in restful, contemporary style.
⊠ Burg. van Barneveldweg 3, 9831 RD Aduard.
Map p125 E1. █ (050) 403 1406. ꜰꜱ (050) 403 1814.
@ herberg@alliance.nl 🍴 b,l,d. **Rooms** 5. 🛁
● Sun, Mon; 1 week July; Christmas and New Year.
▨ AE, DC, MC, V. Ⓕ

AMSTERDAM

Canal House An American couple own and run this 17th-century house with narrow winding stairs, beautifully executed period decoration, and an old-fashioned bar where guests meet to chat. Breakfast is served in the salon, where guests are welcome to play the grand piano. Ask for a room facing the canal or the garden.
⊠ Keizersgracht 148, 1015 CX Amsterdam.
Map p124 C3. █ (020) 622 5182. ꜰꜱ (020) 624 1317.
@ canalhousehotel@compuserve.com 🍴 b. **Rooms** 26.
🛁 ● Never. ▨ AE, DC, MC, V. ⒻⒻ

AMSTERDAM

Ambassade The atmosphere is quiet, and service solicitous in this hotel occupying a series of elegant canalside houses. Books by many of the writers who have stayed here adorn the Louis XVI lounge. Bedrooms are decorated in a mixture of French classical and English country style. The hotel has its own massage centre nearby.
⊠ Herengracht 341, 1016 AZ Amsterdam.
Map p124 C3. █ (020) 626 2333. ꜰꜱ (020) 555 0277.
@ info@ambassade-hotel.nl 🍴 b. **Rooms** 59.
● Never. ▨ AE, DC, MC, V. ⒻⒻ

AMSTERDAM

The Grand This well-loved hotel lives up to its name. A former convent, it was turned into a hotel for royal guests in the 16th century, becoming the Town Hall in the early 1900s. The beautiful courtyard is used for outdoor dining from a mainly French menu. Locals pack out the hotel's Café Roux.
⊠ Oudezijds Voorburgwal 197, 1012 EX Amsterdam.
Map p124 C3. █ (020) 555 3111. ꜰꜱ (020) 555 3222.
@ hotel@thegrandwestern.nl 🍴 b,l,d. **Rooms** 182.
▦ 🍴 🛁 ● Never. ▨ AE, DC, MC, V. ⒻⒻⒻ

AKKRUM
De Oude Schouw A hotel-restaurant in a rural waterfront setting, with pool and boats for hire. The restaurant specializes in game.
⊠ Oude Schouw 6, 8491 MP Akkrum. **Map** p125 D1.
█ (0566) 652125. ꜰꜱ (0566) 652102. @ bostbus@
oudeschouw.nl 🍴 b,l,d. **Rooms** 15. Ⓕ

BRONKHORST
De Gouden Leeuw This 17th-century inn has an extensive seasonal menu, and simple rooms with wooden floors, fresh flowers and box beds.
⊠ Bovenstraat 2, 7226 LM Bronkhorst. **Map** p125 E3.
█ (0575) 451231. ꜰꜱ (0575) 452566. @ oechies@
worldonline.nl 🍴 b,l,d. **Rooms** 13. Ⓕ

DELFT
Museumhotel The name refers to the Delftware specially commissioned for this elegant canalside hotel. Bedrooms are modern.
⊠ Oude Delft 189, 2611 HD Delft. **Map** p125 C3.
█ (015) 214 0930. ꜰꜱ (015) 214 0935.
@ dmh@bestwestern.nl 🍴 b. **Rooms** 51. ⒻⒻ

DRUNEN
De Duinrand On the edge of a wooded heath, a stylish hotel with wood-block floors and open fires, sybaritic suites, and excellent food.
⊠ Steegerf 2, 5151 RB Drunen. **Map** p124 C4.
█ (0416) 372498. ꜰꜱ (0416) 374919.
🍴 b,l,d. **Rooms** 15. ⒻⒻⒻ

AMSTERDAM

Pulitzer Sunday opera brunches, a sculpture garden, and a restaurant in a former pharmacy are all part of this unusual city-centre hotel. It consists of 24 neighbouring canalside houses, each with their own character. A walkway linking the houses contains an art gallery. Bedrooms are furnished with classic fabrics and good furniture.
⊠ Prinsengracht 315–331, 1016 GZ Amsterdam.
Map p124 C3. 📞 (020) 523 5235.
☎ (020) 627 6753. ﯼ b,l,d. **Rooms** 224.
▮ ● Never. 💳 AE, DC, MC, V. ⒻⒻⒻ

AMSTERDAM

Toro This patrician townhouse is a short taxi ride from the city centre but is close to the Rijksmuseum, and its location in a residential area overlooking the Vondelpark ensures tranquillity. The terrace is a relaxing place to enjoy the view of the facing lake, and the birdsong that fills the garden. Inside are stained-glass windows, tasteful antiques and a wonderful Art Nouveau ceiling.
⊠ Koningslaan 64, 1075 AG Amsterdam.
Map p124 C3. 📞 (020) 673 7223. ☎ (020) 675 0031.
ﯼ b. **Rooms** 22. ● Never. 💳 AE, DC, MC, V. ⒻⒻ

AMSTERDAM

Seven One Seven Men's fashion stylist Kees van der Valk has created a glossy canalhouse hotel in the city centre. There are log fires, candles and art books in the lounge, and the breakfast room leads out to patios. Glasses of wine and afternoon tea are on the house. Each of the individual suites has CD player and VCR.
⊠ Prinsengracht 717, 1017 JW Amsterdam.
Map p124 C3. 📞 (020) 427 0717.
☎ (020) 423 0717. ﯼ b. **Rooms** 7. ▮ ● Never.
💳 AE, DC, MC, V. ⒻⒻⒻ.

BLOKZIJL

Kaatje bij de Sluis This townhouse hotel stands either side of the harbour drawbridge, and there are good views of boats passing by and of the old town from the terraces and garden room. Decoration is modern, the atmosphere relaxed. The restaurant serves regional dishes. Choice of ordinary or 'Emperor's' gourmet breakfast.
⊠ Brouwerstraat 20, 8356 DS Blokzijl.
Map p125 D2. 📞 (0527) 291833. ☎ (0527) 291836.
@ kaatje.bij@wxs.nl ﯼ b,l,d. **Rooms** 8.
● Mon, Tue; Dec 29-Jan 7; Feb. 💳 AE, DC, V. ⒻⒻ

EDAM

De Fortuna A row of old step-gabled houses now makes a popular restaurant-with-rooms, decked in pine and patchwork quilts.
⊠ Spuistrat 3, 1135 AV Edam. **Map** p124 C2.
📞 (0299) 371671. ☎ (0299) 371469.
@ fortuna2@wxs.nl ﯼ b,d. **Rooms** 26. Ⓕ

EPEN

De Smidse Clapboard-clad guesthouse with simple rooms, good home cooking and quite old-fashioned atmosphere. Walkers welcome.
⊠ Molenweg 9, 6285 NJ Epen. **Map** p125 D5.
📞 (043) 455 1253. @ smidse@worldonline.nl
ﯼ b,l,d. **Rooms** 10. Ⓕ

GRONINGEN

Corps de Garde Bedrooms are in military guards' former sleeping quarters in this relaxed hotel. The restaurant is exceptionally good.
⊠ Oude Boteringestraat 74, 9712 GN Groningen.
Map p125 E1. 📞 (050) 314 5437. ☎ (050) 313 6320.
@ info@corpsdegarde.nl ﯼ b,l,d. **Rooms** 26. Ⓕ

GRONINGEN

Hotel de Ville Oriental carpets and modern art are well mixed in this fine 19th-century building, as are the cocktails in the conservatory.
⊠ Oude Boteringestraat 43, 9712 GD Groningen.
Map p125 E1. 📞 (050) 318 1222. ☎ (050 318 1777.
@ hotel@deville.nl ﯼ b,l,d. **Rooms** 45. ⒻⒻ

DOENRADE

Kasteel Doenrade This informal hotel in a turreted castle dating back to 1118 will appeal to collectors: armour and stained-glass windows decorate the former chapel, and a farmer's cart from 1780 graces the walls of the restaurant. Food is rich and well prepared, but you can cycle it off in the surrounding countryside.

☒ Limpensweg 20, 6439 BE Doenrade. **Map** p125 D5.
☎ (046) 442 4141. FAX (046) 442 4030.
@ doenrade@silencehotel.nl ⊞ b,l,d. **Rooms** 24.
🍴 🕭 ● Never. 🅮 AE, DC, MC, V. ⓕⓕ

KRUININGEN-YERSEKE

Inter Scaldes Exceptional food is produced by Maartje Boudeling in this 'manoir restaurant'. Host Kees Boudeling created the cottage-style garden, a fine backdrop for summer dining. The rooms and suites – some split-level or with Jacuzzi and balcony – feature antiques and fresh colours.

☒ Zandweg 2, 4416 NA Kruiningen-Yerseke.
Map p124 B4. ☎ (0113) 381753. FAX (0113) 381763.
@ interscaldes@alliance.nl ⊞ b;l,d (not Mon, Tue).
Rooms 12. 🕭 ● Jan, 1week Oct.
🅮 AE, DC, MC, V. ⓕⓕ

DEN HAAG (THE HAGUE)

Corona It was a coffee house in the 1700s and then a gentlemen's club until 1919. Today it's a city-centre hotel whose conservatory brasserie attracts guests and hungry shoppers alike. The foyer is all swirling marble and revolving doors. Veneered furniture reflects the Art Deco feel of the rooms. Suites are more Louis XVI in style.

☒ Buitenhof 39–42, 2513 AH Den Haag. **Map** p124 B3.
☎ (070) 363 7930. FAX (070) 361 5785.
@ info@corona.nl ⊞ b,l,d. **Rooms** 26. ● Never.
🅮 AE, DC, MC, V. ⓕⓕ

LANDGRAAF

Winselerhof Good food characterizes a stay at this half-timbered 17th-century farmhouse. A full breakfast is served in the conservatory in the morning sun, and there's a vast vaulted cellar for pre-dinner drinks. The Pirandello restaurant, decorated with *trompe l'oeil* murals of Tuscany, serves imaginative Italian dishes.

☒ Tunnelweg 99, 6372 XH Landgraaf.
Map p125 E5. ☎ (045) 546 4343.
FAX (045) 535 2711. ⊞ b,l,d. **Rooms** 49.
🕭 ● Never. 🅮 AE, MC, DC, V. ⓕⓕ

DEN HAAG (THE HAGUE)

Carlton Ambassador Choose between Old Dutch (chintzy) or Old English (Tudor) style bedrooms. Restaurant, bar-bistro and live jazz.

☒ Sophialaan 2, 2514 JP Den Haag. **Map** p124 B3.
☎ (070) 363 0363. FAX (070) 360 0535.
@ ambassador@carlton.nl ⊞ b,l,d. **Rooms** 80. ⓕⓕⓕ

HEEZE

Van Gaalen Welcoming restaurant-with-rooms run by chef and Harley-Davidson rider Jules van Gaalen and his wife Josephine.

☒ Kapelstraat 48, 5591 HE Heeze. **Map** p125 D4.
☎ (040) 226 3515. FAX (040 226 3876.
@ van.gaalen@alliance.nl ⊞ b,l,d. **Rooms** 14. ⓕ

KERKRADE

Brughof Stately 18th-century castle hotel with rooms in the farmhouse opposite. Romantics will enjoy the restaurant's candle-lit entrance.

☒ Oud Erensteinerweg 6, 6468 PC Kerkrade.
Map p125 E5. ☎ (045) 546 1333. FAX (045) 546 0748.
⊞ b,l,d. **Rooms** 44. ⓕⓕ

LEUVENUM-ERMELO

Het Rooder Koper An English-style Edwardian villa transplanted to the Gelderland countryside. Some bedrooms are in outbuildings.

☒ Sandbergweg 82, 3852 PV Leuvenum-Ermelo.
Map p125 D3. ☎ (0577) 407393. FAX (0577) 407561.
⊞ b,l,d. **Rooms** 26. ⓕⓕ

LEEUWARDEN

Het Stadhouderlijk Hof The services akin to a much larger hotel are on offer at this stately palace in the old city: covers are turned down at night, the weather forecast is slipped under your door first thing. The atmosphere is relaxed, however, with a choice of à la carte dining in the courtyard garden or a buffet in the vaulted cellars.
Hofplein 29, 8911 HJ Leeuwarden. **Map** p125 D1.
(058) 216 2180. FAX (058) 216 3890.
@ info@stadhouderlijkhof.nl b,l,d. **Rooms** 22.
27 Dec–1 Jan. AE, DC, MC, V. (F)(F)

MARGRATEN

Groot Welsden It's worth opting for the deluxe rooms in this spa hotel – among other treats, they have their own whirlpool baths. The hotel is done out in the style of an English country house. Many people come to Margraten for thermal treatments and stay on half-board basis, but the Groot Welsden is also wonderful for a shorter stay and for trips into the Ardennes countryside.
Groot Welsden 27, 6269 Margraten. **Map** p125 D5.
(043) 458 1394. FAX (043) 458 2355. b,l,d.
Rooms 16. Carnival week. AE, V. (F)

MAASTRICHT

Hotel Botticelli A passion for Renaissance art, bold colours and contemporary furniture sets the style for this townhouse hotel. Hosts Louis Hendriks and Pierre Janssens treat guests as if they were personal friends. The back bedrooms and the courtyard are very quiet, despite being a few steps from Vrijthof Square. Lavish breakfasts.
Papenstraat 11, 6211 LG Maastricht. **Map** p125 D5.
(043) 352 6300. FAX (043) 352 6336.
@ botticelli.hotel@wxs.nl b. **Rooms** 18. Never.
AE, DC, MC, V. (F)(F)

MOLENHOEK

Jachtslot de Mookerheide The tall tower of this castle hotel – once a hunting lodge for the Baron of Luden – gives wide views of the wooded estate. Hennie and Anne van Hout have created dramatic bedrooms in the original Art Nouveau interior. Game features on the menu of both the restaurants, in the castle and the coach house.
Heumensebaan 2, 6584 CL Molenhoek.
Map p125 D4. (024) 358 3035.
FAX (024) 358 4355. b,l,d. **Rooms** 21.
Never. AE, DC, MC, V. (F)(F)

MAASTRICHT
Hotel d'Orangerie Friendly city-centre hotel with mosaic floors and ornate friezes, owned and run by Jolanda Lutgens. Comfortable and relaxed.
Kleine Gracht 4, 6211 CB Maastricht.
Map p125 D5. (043) 326 1111. FAX (043) 326 1287.
b. **Rooms** 33. (F)

MARKELO
In de Kop'ren Smorre Rustic farmhouse restaurant with waitresses in regional costume. Small and medium-sized bedrooms next door.
Holterweg 20, 7475 AW Markelo. **Map** p125 E3.
(0547) 361344. FAX (0547) 362201.
@ markelo@koprensmorre.nl b,l,d. **Rooms** 8. (F)

OTTERLO
Carnegie Cottage Hotel with conservatory restaurant in the heart of the De Hoge Veluwe national park. Smallish, colourful bedrooms.
Onderlands 35, 6731 BK Otterlo.
Map p125 D3. (0318) 591220. b,l,d.
Rooms 12. (F)

ROERMOND
Kasteeltje Hattem Castle hotel with suites with Jacuzzis and waterbeds, a Gothic bar, and covered dining terrace (heated in cold weather).
Maastrichterweg 25, 6041 NZ Roermond.
Map p125 E5. (0475) 319222. FAX (0475) 319292.
b,l,d. **Rooms** 11. (F)

For key to symbols see backflap. For price categories *see p123*

OISTERWIJK

De Swaen A village inn which serves imaginative gourmet meals in a formal restaurant or in a younger, more relaxed bistro. Bedrooms are in a mix of styles; the most lavish, a suite, is in a new wing built in 1997. The suite contains a beautiful antique walnut bed, a large Jacuzzi and an open fire lit for guests' arrival.
De Lind 47, 5061 HT Oisterwijk. **Map** p125 D4. (013) 523 3233. FAX (013) 528 5860. @ swaen@ swaen.nl **b,l,d. Rooms** 24. 2 days before Ash Wed, 2 weeks July. AE, DC, MC, V. ⓕⓕⓕ

OUDERKERK AAN DE AMSTEL

't Jagershuis This well-known restaurant with rooms has a dozen bedrooms and suites, all with a view over the Amstel river. The international food includes some Thai dishes. Activities revolve around the river: watching the yachts from the terrace, or skating on the Amstel when it freezes, then warming up next to the open fire.
Amstelzijde 2–4, 1184 VA Ouderkerk aan de Amstel. **Map** p124 C3. (020) 496 2020.
FAX (020) 496 4541. **b,l,d. Rooms** 12. New Year. AE, DC, MC, V. ⓕⓕ

OOTMARSUM

De Wiemsel Guests come to De Wiemsel to be pampered: hosts Ton and Barbara provide club sandwiches and glasses of wine round the pool, sweets in the bedrooms, and other thoughtful extras from umbrellas to the next day's weather forecast. The hotel's 'Beautyworld' is a fully equipped spa. There are two restaurants.
Winhofflaan 2, 7631 HX Oostmarsum. **Map** p125 F2. (0541) 292155. FAX (0541) 293295.
@ toba.holdeng@yxs.nl **b,l,d. Rooms** 49. Never. AE, DC, MC, V. ⓕⓕ

OUDKERK/ALDTSJERK

De Klinze The owner of this stucco-clad country hotel, Gert Snijders, has been known to give spur of the moment rides to guests in his horsedrawn carriage or Rolls-Royce. The house dates from the 17th century but the rooms are modern; Andrew Fox's management ensures a relaxed atmosphere. There's classic Italian food in the restaurant.
Van Sminiaweg 32–36, 9064 KC Oudkerk/Aldtsjerk. **Map** p125 D1. (058) 256 1050. FAX (058) 256 1060. @ klinze@wxs.nl **b,l,d. Rooms** 27. Never. AE, DC, MC, V. ⓕⓕ

SCHIERMONNIKOOG

Van der Werff On a small island with few cars, this is a peaceful hotel with modest but comfortable rooms, friendly bar and pool room.
Reeweg 2, 9166 PX Schiermonnikoog. **Map** p125 E1. (0519) 531203. FAX (0519) 531748. **b,l,d. Rooms** 56. ⓕ

STAPHORST

Het Boerengerecht A 17th-century farmhouse hotel; the 'best room' is the restaurant. One suite has a huge wooden bathtub, now a Jacuzzi.
Middenwolderweg 2, 7951 EC Staphorst.
Map p125 E2. (0522) 461967. FAX (0522) 461166. **b,l,d. Rooms** 2. ⓕ

TEGELEN

Château Holtmühle Beautiful pitched-roof castle furnished in English style and guarded by enthusiastic geese. Spa centre and indoor pool.
Kasteellaan 10, 5932 AG Tegelen. **Map** p125 E4. (077) 373 8800. FAX (077) 374 0500.
@ holtmuehle@bilderberg.nl **b,l,d. Rooms** 66. ⓕⓕ

VEERE

De Campveerse Toren Ancient castle-like inn and hotel on the town fortifications, overlooking the harbour and the Veerse Meer. Bright rooms.
Kade 2, 4351 AA Veere. **Map** p124 B4. (0118) 501291. FAX (0118) 501695.
b,l,d. Rooms 10. ⓕ

ROTTERDAM

Hotel New York This landmark hotel occupies a prime position in the rejuvenated port area. The building was the former headquarters of the Holland America shipping line, and the hotel retains the feel of a busy port hotel. There are harbour views from most rooms, and bedrooms have CD players and videos. The restaurant specializes in fish dishes; additional oyster bar.
⊠ Koninginnenhoofd 1, 3072 AD Rotterdam.
Map p124 C3. ☎ (010) 439 0500. FAX (010) 484 2701.
🍴 b,l,d. **Rooms** 72. ◯ Never. 🅴 AE, DC, MC, V. Ⓕ

VALKENBURG

Château St Gerlach Accommodation is in a series of beamed outbuildings, decorated in rich fabrics and colours, on the estate of this grand château. Dining is in the formal restaurant with its crystal chandeliers or in the old kitchen, done out like a 19th-century Liège pub. The breakfast room overlooks the herb garden and the Geul valley.
⊠ Joseph Corneli Allée 1, 6301 KK Valkenburg a/d Geul.
Map p125 D5. ☎ (043) 608 8888.
FAX (043) 604 2883. 🍴 b,l,d. **Rooms** 97.
🌊 🍴 🎤 ◯ Never. 🅴 AE, DC, MC, V. ⒻⒻ

SCHOORL

Merlet The informal atmosphere of this family-run hotel is enhanced by the Mediterranean feel of its restaurant, with red tiled floors and sunny colours. Suites are similarly bright, the standard doubles whiter and more floral. Diners eat in view of the open kitchen, where both 'traditional' and 'creative' menus are prepared.
⊠ Duinweg 15, 1871 AC Schoorl. **Map** p124 C2.
☎ (072) 509 3644. FAX (072) 509 1406.
@ merlet@worldonline.nl 🍴 b,l,d. **Rooms** 18.
🌊 🍴 🎤 ◯ 10 days early Jan. 🅴 AE, DC, MC, V. Ⓕ

DE WIJK

De Havixhorst Bedrooms are unusually spacious at this rural chateau hotel and restaurant, and those in the attic have beamed ceilings. The hotel's own kitchen garden supplies many of the ingredients for the elaborate cuisine. To work off the calories, bicycles can be hired for exploring the local lanes and nature reserves.
⊠ Schiphorsterweg 34–36, 7957 NV De Wijk.
Map p125 E2. ☎ (0522) 441487.
FAX (0522) 441489. **Rooms** 8. 🍴 b,l,d. ◯ Sundays.
🅴 AE, DC, MC, V. ⒻⒻ

VOLENDAM

Spaander This lively hotel-café-restaurant is packed with paintings and knick-knacks in the Dutch equivalent of High Victorian style.
⊠ Haven 15-19, 1131 EP Volendam. **Map** p124 C2.
☎ (0299) 363595. FAX (0299) 369615. 🍴 b,l,d.
Rooms 80. Ⓕ

VREELAND AAN DE VECHT

De Nederlanden Country-house hotel on the River Vecht, with a terrace overlooking the waterway, busy with yachts.
⊠ Duinkerken 3, 3633 EM Vreeland aan de Vecht.
Map p124 C3. ☎ (0294) 232326. FAX (0294) 231407.
@ nederland@euronet.nl 🍴 b,l,d. **Rooms** 7. ⒻⒻ

ZEIST

Kasteel 't Kerkebosch Baronial 1904 mansion in the woods with a lively atmosphere, busy restaurant and informal garden.
⊠ Arnhemse Bovenweg 31, 3708 AA Zeist.
Map p125 D3. ☎ (030) 691 4734. FAX (030) 691 3114.
@ info@bilderberg.nl 🍴 b,l,d. **Rooms** 30. ⒻⒻ

ZUTPHEN

Museumhotel A hotel of murals and sculpture. Bedrooms have designer furniture; suites in the wooden 'attic' are all decorated individually.
⊠ 's-Gravenhof 6, 7201 DN Zutphen. **Map** p125 E3.
☎ (0575) 546111. FAX (0575) 545999.
@ info@bestwestern.nl 🍴 b,d. **Rooms** 65. ⒻⒻ

For key to symbols see backflap. For price categories *see p123*

BELGIUM & LUXEMBOURG

BELGIUM AND LUXEMBOURG

BELGIUM AND ITS diminutive neighbour have much in common: they fall naturally into the same section. Many of their old castles and pretty half-timbered mansions have been converted into luxury hotels, and everywhere you will find an emphasis on food. Some hotels do two rounds of breakfast (the second starting at 11am). Expect generous portions.

Simple soup can turn out to be a 'relay race' of several different flavours; a humble *espresso* may be elaborated with a side order of whipped cream and pralines. If the eating gets too much, you could try resting your liver at a 'thermal centre', such as one of those found in the Belgian town of Spa – parent of 'health farms' worldwide.

Shamrock, Maarkedal, page 141, great food and landscaped gardens

BELGIUM AND LUXEMBOURG REGION BY REGION

BELGIUM DIVIDES neatly into north and south, along the so-called 'language divide' (see below), formalised constitutionally in 1962. In the southeastern corner, on the border with Germany, is the 999-sq mile (2,600 sq km) Grand Duchy of Luxembourg.

The North
The Flemish north and the Walloon south of Belgium have different languages, communities and indeed administrations. The capital, Brussels, is on the dividing line separating the two. In the north are the provinces of West and East Flanders, Antwerp, Limburg and the upper reaches of Brabant. The region is flat and very similar to Holland. Antwerp mixes sleaze and wealth in equal measure, is Europe's second largest port and centre of the world diamond trade.

Some wonderful places to stay here include a town-house hotel dating from the 16th century, and an Art Deco villa. In Flanders, to the southwest, there's the chance to stay in a couple of quay-side hotels in Bruges, and visit Ghent, with its artistic and architectural treasures.

The South
The Walloon south begins at the province of Hainaut. To the east are the Ardennes, an area of thickly forested hills which also spill over into Luxembourg and northeastern France. Whereas the French Ardennes are industrialised, the Belgian Ardennes are largely unspoilt, and some of the region's most beautiful hill-top castles have been converted into hotels. The Ardennes town of Spa was noted in Roman times by Pliny the Elder as a health resort, and there are some interesting places to stay in and around the town. If the

treatments don't appeal, then make your way to Namur, the gastronomic capital of Belgium.

Luxembourg
Luxembourg has two aspects: the hilly Ardennes in the north and the farmland of the south – called the Bon Pays or Gutland (Good Land). The Grand Duchy (population about 400,000) has its own steel industry which is concentrated in the southwest. The rest of the country is covered in vineyards, particularly the slopes on either side of the Moselle river.

HIGHLIGHTS

THE PLACES to stay illustrated on these introductory pages are by no means the only highlights of this section. Other favourites include: Le Val d'Amblève at Stavelot (page 141), a half-timbered house in the Liège countryside, combining understated but smart decoration with great food; and De Witte Lelie in Antwerp (page 138), three 16th-century houses knocked together to make an unusual B&B hotel – grand and spacious, with high ceilings, but an informal atmosphere.

FOOD AND DRINK

BELGIANS ARE keen to point out that their country contains more Michelin-starred restaurants than France. Dishes are similar in style to French cuisine and specialities include *foie gras*, fine cheeses, snails served with herb butter, and fresh trout, pike, perch and crayfish from the rivers. Beef from Herve and lamb from Hainaut are particularly good. In Brussels, café snacks include mussels and chips, shrimp croquettes, chips and mayonnaise or *stoemp* (steak tartare). Vegetarians are not particularly well catered for: in fact, vegetarian restaurants are rare – the notable exception being Lombardia (03 233 6819) in Antwerp.

Sweets and pastries are on sale everywhere. As any chocoholic knows, Belgium and chocolate go together as readily as Plastic Bertrand and Europop. There is a Chocolat Jacques 'kingdom of chocolate' at Eupen, 30km (18 miles) from Liège, but if you don't make it there, look out for their chocolates on sale everywhere, or those of Galler Manufacture, Léonidas or Godiva, who are the other top chocolate producers.

There are more than 400 types of Belgian beer, including three strong beers brewed in the traditional way by the Trappist monks at Chimay, Rochefort and Orval. It's also worth trying the equally lively fruit beers. Brussels' famous beers are Faro, Gueuze, Lambic and Kriek.

Luxembourg's specialities include mussels, Ardennes ham, pastries and trout. Its Moselle wines are similar in style if not in quality to those over the border in Germany.

BEDROOMS AND BATHROOMS

Rooms usually have double beds. If you would like twin or single beds, these must be requested when booking. It's very rare for any of the hotels listed here not to have en suite bathrooms, but a bathroom with a bath costs more than one with a shower.

OTHER PRACTICAL INFORMATION

In northern Belgium, breakfasts are like Dutch breakfasts; in the south, they are more like the French. Luxembourg breakfasts are a mixture of Dutch and French.

Many of the restaurants with rooms offer reductions for half board or *demi-pension* (a per person rate for the room, dinner and breakfast). These are often good value.

Language About 60 per cent of Belgians are Flemish speakers; the rest (the Walloons) speak French. There are also some German speakers in the eastern provinces.

In Luxembourg, the two official languages are French and Letzeburgesch. The latter is a Germanic language which most of the population speaks. Road signs are written in both.

Currency The Belgian franc, written as BEF or FB; and the Luxembourg franc – LUF.

Shops 9am–5:30pm Mon–Fri. Some shops are closed on Monday mornings and for lunch. On Saturdays shops open for half a day or all day and are closed on Sunday.

Tipping In hotels, service is included in the bill, and a 16 per cent service charge is usually added to restaurant bills. A further tip is only required for exceptional service. As in France, cinema usherettes are given a small tip (about BEF20).

Telephones Public phones in Belgium take 5 or 20 BEF coins, or telecards, which are on sale at post offices, newsstands and stations.

Luxembourg has two types of call box taking either coins or cards. But with local calls costing just LUF5 for unlimited time, and the cheapest phone card costing LUF250, phoning from a hotel may, unusually for Europe, be a relatively economical option.

To make phone calls inside Belgium, dial the whole number including the initial 0. To telephone Belgium (or Luxembourg) from the UK, dial 00 32 (00 352), then the number omitting the initial 0 from the area code; from the US, dial 011 32 (00 352), also omitting the initial zero from the area code.

Public holidays Carnival time (the week around Shrove Tuesday) sees many businesses shut, and the grape harvest in Luxembourg's Moselle Valley is another occasion for holidays. The official holidays are, Belgium: January 1; Easter Sunday and Monday; 1 May; Ascension Day; Whit Sunday and Monday; 21 July; 15 August; 1 November; 11 November (Armistice Day); 15 November (King's Birthday); 25 and 26. December. Luxembourg: As above, but with the addition of Good Friday; 23 June (National Day).

USEFUL WORDS

See France, page 217; and Germany, page 147.

PRICE BANDS

Price bands refer to the price of a standard room in high season, and usually include breakfast. Prices quoted for rooms include all taxes.

Ⓕ	up to 3,599 BEF
ⒻⒻ	3,600–9,599 BEF
ⒻⒻⒻ	9,600–18,899 BEF
ⒻⒻⒻⒻ	above 18,900+BEF

We give no separate price bands for the Luxembourg hotels since the two currencies usually have the same value, and both sets of bank notes are interchangeable.

Oud-Huis Amsterdam in Brugge, page 138

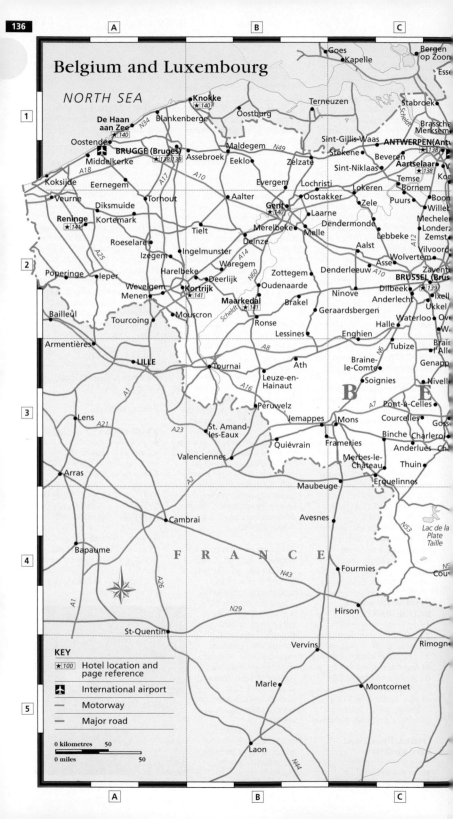

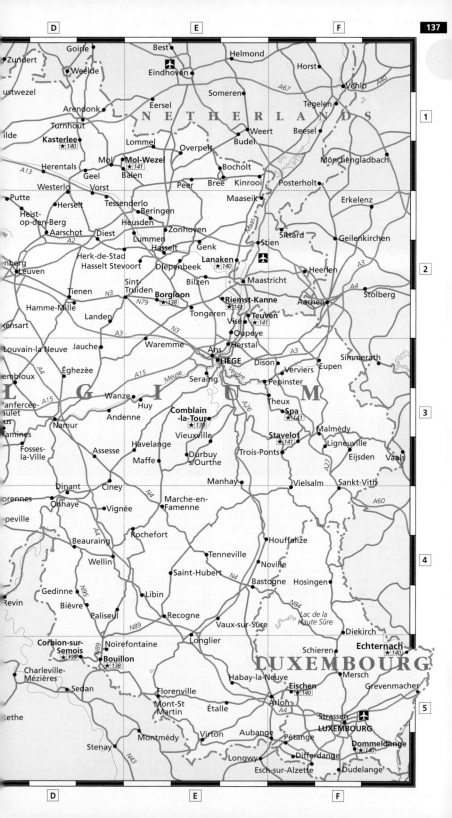

AARTSELAAR

Kasteel Cleydael The excellent food at this turreted castle-hotel next to a lake is the major attraction; the menu is imaginative and includes a 'relay race' of soups. All rooms are large and well-equipped, but the Hellemans room in the hexagonal tower is an exceptionally spacious suite (book well in advance).
✉ Cleydaellaan 36, 2630 Aartselaar. **Map** p136 C1.
📞 (03) 887 0504. FAX (03) 877 2018. @ mail@kasteel-cleydael.be ▮▮ b,l,d. **Rooms** 7. 📺 ◐ mid-July to mid-Aug, Christmas and New Year. 💳 AE, DC, MC, V. Ⓕ Ⓕ Ⓕ

BORGLOON

Kasteel van Rullingen Chef Pieter Pieterman often takes time out to greet his guests at his serene lakeside castle. Public rooms have grand chandeliers and pastoral wall paintings; bedrooms are simpler affairs but with beautiful casement windows. On summer weekends the chapel is a popular place for weddings.
✉ Rullingen 1, 3840 Borgloon. **Map** p137 E2.
📞 (012) 743 146. FAX (012) 745 486. @ rullingen@ping.be ▮▮ b,l,d. **Rooms** 11. 🔋 ◐ first week Jan, 2 weeks July. 💳 Not accepted. Ⓕ Ⓕ

ANTWERPEN

De Witte Lelie This modish yet restfully decorated B&B hotel occupies three interconnecting 16th-century houses in the oldest street in Antwerp, and is run by two sisters. High ceilings emphasize the spaciousness of the bedrooms. In the morning, a filling breakfast is accompanied by the day's newspapers.
✉ Keizerstraat 16–18, 2000 Antwerpen. **Map** p136 C1.
📞 (03) 226 1966. FAX (03) 234 0019. @ hotel@dewittelelie.be ▮▮ b. **Rooms** 10. 🔋 ◐ Christmas and New Year. 💳 AE, DC, MC, V. Ⓕ Ⓕ

BRUGGE (BRUGES)

Oud-Huis Amsterdam Antique collectors Caroline and Philip Traen run this quayside hotel packed with treasures. Córdoba leather covers some walls, and there are original 18th-century chimneypieces and staircases. Bedrooms are richly furnished. There's a bar in the old kitchen, a crackling fire in the breakfast room in winter, and a courtyard terrace for summer drinks.
✉ Spiegelrei 3, 8000 Brugge. **Map** p136 A1.
📞 (050) 341 810. FAX (050) 338 891. @ info@oha.be ▮▮ b. **Rooms** 32. 🔋 ◐ Never. 💳 AE, DC, MC, V. Ⓕ Ⓕ

ANTWERPEN

Firean In a quiet suburb a ten-minute tram ride from the centre, Firean is in a 1920s' mansion decorated with warm colours and Persian rugs.
✉ Karel Oomsstraat 6, 2018 Antwerpen. **Map** p136 C1.
📞 (03) 237 0260. FAX (03) 238 1168. @ hotel.firean@skynet.be ▮▮ b. **Rooms** 15. Ⓕ Ⓕ

ANTWERPEN

't Sandt A former spice merchant's house in the city centre, now Neo-Classical in style. One suite has a roof terrace with a view of the cathedral.
✉ Zand 17, 2000 Antwerpen. **Map** p136 C1.
📞 (03) 232 9390. FAX (03) 232 5613.
@ sandt@villageuunet.be ▮▮ b. **Rooms** 15. Ⓕ Ⓕ

BOUILLON

Hostellerie la Pommeraie At this grand hotel, dine on the terraces in sight of Bouillon's floodlit medieval castle in summer.
✉ rue de la Poste 2, B6830 Bouillon. **Map** p137 D5.
📞 (061) 469 017. FAX (061) 469 083. ▮▮ b,l,d. **Rooms** 9. Ⓕ Ⓕ Ⓕ

BRUGGE (BRUGES)

De Orangerie Wrought-ironwork and leaded windows gives this canalside hotel a medieval feel. Leather sofas and open fires in the lounge.
✉ Kartuizerinnenstraat 10, 8000 Brugge.
Map p136 A1. 📞 (050) 341 649. FAX (050) 333 016.
@ orangerie@innet.be ▮▮ b. **Rooms** 19. Ⓕ Ⓕ

BRUGGE (BRUGES)

Pandhotel The six Ralph Lauren suites set the style for this hotel in the city centre. The designer's signature furnishings, plus four-poster beds, piles of leather-bound books and oil paintings make this a comforting bolt-hole. The calm drawing rooms are great places to relax and read a book after a day exploring the streets of the old town.
☒ Pandreitje 16, 8000 Brugge. **Map** p136 A1. ☎ (050) 340 666. ℻ (050) 340 556. @ info@pandhotel.com ⊪ b. **Rooms** 24. ◉ Never. ◪ AE, DC, MC, V. ⒻⒻ

BRUSSEL (BRUSSELS)

Stanhope A Brighton Pavilion theme dominates at the Stanhope. A portrait of King George IV, builder of that fantasy Oriental palace, hangs in the restaurant – called Brighton – and Chinoiserie extends into the bedrooms and suites. The garden, with a magnolia tree strung with lights, is a lovely place to dine in summer.
☒ rue du Commerce 9, 1000 Brussels. **Map** p136 C2. ☎ (02) 506 9111. ℻ (02) 512 1708. @ summithotel@ stanhope.be ⊪ b;l,d (not Sat, Sun). **Rooms** 50.
▤ ⊪ ◐ ◉ Never. ◪ AE, DC, MC, V. ⒻⒻⒻ

BRUGGE (BRUGES)

Die Swaene Originally the chambers for the guild of tailors, Die Swaene has a drawing room which dates back to 1779, but the three canalhouses the hotel occupies are a few hundred years older still. Much remains of the original buildings. The large bedrooms are decorated in modern Baroque style. Service is good and the welcome friendly.
☒ Steenhouwersdijk (Groene Rei), 8000 Brugge. **Map** p136 A1. ☎ (050) 342 798. ℻ (050) 336 674. @ dieswaene@unicall.be ⊪ b,l,d. **Rooms** 22. ▨ ⊪ ◐ Never. ◪ AE, DC, MC, V. Ⓕ

COMBLAIN-LA-TOUR

L'Hostellerie Saint-Roch An old post house is now a solid, ivy-clad hotel on the edge of the Ardennes; its decking terrace overlooks the River Ourthe. Rooms are decorated with tapestry fabrics, some chintz, and warm subdued colours. The restaurant serves seasonal country cuisine.
☒ Vallée de l'Ourthe, B4180 Comblain-la-Tour. **Map** p137 E3. ☎ (04) 369 1333. ℻ (04) 369 3131. @ hostelleriesaintroch@skynet.be ⊪ b,l,d. **Rooms** 15. ⊪ ◐ ◉ early Jan to mid-March; Mon, Tue except July, Aug. ◪ AE, DC, V. ⒻⒻⒻ

BRUGGE (BRUGES)
De Snippe Long renowned for its seafood, the elegant De Snippe also has a small number of similarly smart bedrooms.
☒ Nieuwe Gentweg 53, 8000 Brugge. **Map** p136 A1. ☎ (050) 337 070. ℻ (050) 337 662. ⊪ b,l,d. **Rooms** 9. ⒻⒻ

BRUSSEL (BRUSSELS)
Le Dixseptième A chic 18th-century residence decorated in hot colours, with 12 studios and 12 spacious suites, most with kitchenettes.
☒ rue de la Madeleine 25, 1000 Brussel. **Map** p136 C2. ☎ (02) 502 5744. ℻ (02) 502 6424. @ ledixseptieme@ net7.be ⊪ b. **Rooms** 24. ⒻⒻ

BRUGGE (BRUGES)
de Tuilerieën Choose between chintzy rooms overlooking the canal or quieter ones at the back. Swimming pool in the conservatory.
☒ Dijver 7, 8000 Brugge. **Map** p136 A1. ☎ (050) 343 691. ℻ (050) 340 400. @ tuilerieen@unicall.be ⊪ b. **Rooms** 26. ⒻⒻⒻ

CORBION-SUR-SEMOIS
Hotel des Ardennes This family-run hotel run in wooded countryside has two excellent restaurants, a pool table and games for children.
☒ rue de la Hate 1, 6838 Corbion. **Map** p137 D5. ☎ (061) 466 621. ℻ (061) 467 730. @ contact@ hoteldesardennes.be ⊪ b,l,d. **Rooms** 30. ⒻⒻ

ECHTERNACH, LUXEMBOURG

Hotel Bel-Air This smooth four-star hotel is set just outside the medieval town of Echternach, surrounded by a vast private park and forests, with splendid views to the Sûre valleys. The original mansion house is practically hidden by modern extensions, but inside all is deeply soothing. Fine dining in the elegant dining room.
⊠ route de Berdorf, 6409 Echternach, Luxembourg. **Map** p137 F5. **C** 72 93 83. **FAX** 72 86 94. **@** belair@pt.lu **11** b,l,d. **Rooms** 39. **◖** **●** Never. **⊘** AE, DC, MC, V. **Ⓕ Ⓕ Ⓕ**

EISCHEN, LUXEMBOURG

Hotel de La Gaichel Behind the pink façade of this 19th-century building stretch vast grounds bordered by a little river. The bedrooms all face the park, and the restaurant is bordered by a large, tree-shaded dining terrace. Guests can choose between activities such as golf and tennis, or simply enjoying the peace of this rural spot.
⊠ 8469 Eischen, Luxembourg. **Map** p137 F5. **C** 39 01 29. **FAX** 39 00 37. **@** Gaichel@pt.lu **11** b,l,d. **Rooms** 13. **◖** **●** Sun nights; 10 days end Aug, 1 month Jan-Feb. **⊘** AE, DC, MC, V. **Ⓕ Ⓕ Ⓕ**

KNOKKE

Manoir du Dragon The wide views of the Royal Zoute Golf Course suggest that this might appeal to couples where one is not a golfer. While one partner raises divots of turf beyond, the other can enjoy a late breakfast of crêpes, French cheeses and pâtés served on silver platters. The bedrooms are all well equipped and have video players and kitchenettes.
⊠ Albertlaan 73, 8300 Knokke. **Map** p136 B1. **C** (050) 630 580. **FAX** (050) 630 590. **11** b. **Rooms** 13. **目** **◖** **●** Never. **⊘** AE, DC, MC, V. **Ⓕ Ⓕ**

LANAKEN

La Butte Aux Bois De-stress in the Shiseido and Thalgo beauty centres, cycle through the woods, or simply unwind in this calm 1920s mansion complete with lawns and lake. There's a choice of 'castle' rooms in the main building, or romantic bedrooms in the house opposite. The second round of breakfasts begins at 11am.
⊠ Paalsteenlaan 90, 3620 Lanaken. **Map** p137 E2. **C** (089) 721286. **FAX** (089) 721647. **@** info@labutteauxbois.be **11** b,l,d. **Rooms** 39. **♨** **🍴** **◖** **●** Never. **⊘** AE, DC, MC, V. **Ⓕ Ⓕ**

DOMMELDANGE, LUXEMBOURG
Hostellerie du Grunewald Gently old-fashioned hotel done out with Oriental carpets and button-backed chairs. Gourmet restaurant.
⊠ 10-14 route d'Echternach, 1453 Dommeldange, Luxembourg. **Map** p137 F5. **C** 43 18 82. **FAX** 42 06 46. **11** b. **Rooms** 28. **Ⓕ Ⓕ**

GENT
St Jorishof This guesthouse claims to be in Europe's oldest building (1298). Flemish specialities on the menu; helpful service.
⊠ Botermarkt 2, 9000 Gent. **Map** p136 B2. **C** (09) 224 2424. **FAX** (09) 224 2640. **@** courstgeorges@ skynet.be **11** b,l,d. **Rooms** 41. **Ⓕ Ⓕ**

DE HAAN AAN ZEE
Carpe Diem Seaside summer villa; simple three-course dinners and honesty bar.
⊠ Prins Karellaan 12, 8420 De Haan aan Zee. **Map** p136 A1. **C** (059) 233220. **FAX** (059) 233396. **@** manoir.carpe.diem.r@skynet.be **11** b,d. **Rooms** 15. **Ⓕ Ⓕ**

KASTERLEE
De Watermolen A watermill turned hotel and restaurant serving traditional French cuisine. Bedrooms are modern and spacious.
⊠ Houtum 61, 2460 Kasterlee. **Map** p137 D1. **C** (014) 852 374. **FAX** (014) 852 370. **@** hotel.de. watermolen@village.uunet.be **11** b,l,d. **Rooms** 18. **Ⓕ Ⓕ**

MAARKEDAL

Shamrock The half-timbered country house was built as a summer residence in 1928, and the gardens were landscaped by the internationally known designer Jacques Wirtz. It's now a gourmet *hostellerie* owned and run by Claude and Livine Debeyter, with an ambitious menu and florally decorated bedrooms.

⊠ Ommegangstraat 148, 9680 Maarkedal.
Map p136 B2. ☎ (055) 215 529. 📠 (055) 215 683.
@ host@shamrock@unicall.be 🔢 b,l,d. **Rooms** 5. 🔹
● 2 weeks Jan, 2 weeks July. 💳 AE, DC, MC, V. ⒻⒻ

RENINGE

't Convent Chef Rudi De Volder is a truffle enthusiast, and it is not unknown for guests to fly in by helicopter to savour the Périgordian speciality in his regional and Italian-based cuisine. The style of the bedrooms varies widely, from Venetian through rustic to modern. The stone and timber-built farm and manor house has its own vineyard.

⊠ Halve Reningestraat 1, 8647 Reninge. **Map** p136 A2.
☎ (057) 400 771. 📠 (057) 401 127. 🔢 b,l,d. **Rooms** 15.
🏨 🍴 🔹 ● Feb. 💳 AE, DC, MC, V. ⒻⒻⒻⒻ

MOL-WEZEL

Manoir Hippocampus The food at this manor house is particularly good, with owner-chef Francis Scheyvaerts planning his daily menu around what's best at market that day. In summer, tables are set out next to the white house overlooking the lily pond. The three bedrooms are named after puddings: *tarte tatin*, *sabayon* and *javanais*.

⊠ Sint Jozeflaan 79, 2400 Mol-Wezel. **Map** p137 E1.
☎ (014) 810 808. 📠 (014) 814 590. 🔢 b,l,d. **Rooms** 3.
🔹 ● 2 weeks Aug. 💳 AE, DC, MC, V. Ⓕ.

STAVELOT

Le Val d'Amblève '*Carpe diem*' is the motto of the owners of this half-timbered hotel in the Liège countryside; you would be hard-pressed to find more elegant surroundings in which to enjoy the pleasures of the moment. The style is in the detail, from the cool 'garden room' restaurant to the copper baths in some of the bedrooms.

⊠ route de Malmedy 7, B4970 Stavelot.
Map p137 F3. ☎ (080) 862 353. 📠 (080) 864 121.
@ leval.dambleve@gate71.be 🔢 b,l,d. **Rooms** 14.
🍴 🔹 ● 3 weeks Jan. 💳 AE, DC, V. ⒻⒻⒻ

KORTRIJK

Damier An old coaching inn now furnished in English country-house style, and popular with business people. Breakfast is in the orangery.
⊠ Grote Markt 41, 8500 Kortrijk. **Map** p136 B2.
☎ (056) 221547. 📠 (056) 228631. 🔢 b,d.
Rooms 49. ⒻⒻ

RIEMST-KANNE

Huize Poswick This relaxed hotel's bedrooms have wood floors, 1920s' or antique furniture, beamed ceilings and bright walls.
⊠ Muizenberg 7, 3770 Riemst-Kanne.
Map p137 E2. ☎ (012) 457127. 📠 (012) 458105.
🔢 b. **Rooms** 6. Ⓕ

SPA

Villa des Fleurs A town-centre mansion built in 1880, characterized by yards of draped and swagged curtains and crystal-drop chandeliers.
⊠ rue Albin Body 31, 4900 Spa. **Map** p137 F3.
☎ (087) 795 050. 📠 (087) 795 060. @ paul.geelen@ skynet.be 🔢 b. **Rooms** 12. ⒻⒻ

TEUVEN

Hof De Draeck A very popular hotel in what was once a feudal manor house, with creaking stairs and a park with deer. Dinner is good value.
⊠ Hoofdstraat 6, 3793 Teuven. **Map** p137 E2.
☎ (04) 381 1017. 📠 (04) 381 1188. 🔢 b,l,d.
Rooms 10. Ⓕ

For key to symbols see backflap. For price categories *see p135*

GERMANY

GERMANY

Germany has plenty of family-run hotels of character and style, but the successful ones tend to grow in size. The really small hotel (say, five to ten rooms) is uncommon – as are hotel chains; some hotels group together for joint promotion, such as the Romantik chain, Silencehotels, renowned for their secluded settings, and Gast im Schloss, a group of converted castles, some still run by their ancestral owners. Our selection offers places to suit all tastes, from simple country inns, picturesque *Gasthöfe* (guesthouses) and town hotels to palatial mansions and *Kur-hotels* (located in spas or health resorts).

Schlosshotel Hugenpoet at Essen-Kettwig, page 172, has style on a grand scale

GERMANY REGION BY REGION

In this guide, we have divided the country into three areas: Northern Germany, Central Germany and Southern Germany.

Northern Germany

This comprises the states of Lower Saxony, Schleswig-Holstein and Mecklenburg-West Pomerania. It also includes the two great Baltic seaports of Hamburg and Bremen (each is almost a semi-autonomous state on its own), and numerous historic towns and seaside resorts where the handsome and spacious mansions of wealthy merchants and seafarers now make magnificent hotels.

In Mecklenburg-West Pomerania, a low-lying, rural region of lakes, meadows, forests and beaches, are hidden country guesthouses and small family-run hotels. Alternatively, log-cabin-style inns and hunting lodges in the picturesque Harz mountains make for a perfect year-round sporting getaway, with plenty of opportunities for skiing, cycling and hiking.

Central Germany

The region stretches from the sprawling cityscapes of Düsseldorf, Dortmund and Frankfurt in the west, to the new capital, Berlin, in the east. It includes the former capital, Bonn, many of Germany's best wine-growing regions, the states of Hesse,

Thuringia and Brandenburg and Saxony, and the newly-fashionable, one-time eastern cities of Dresden and Leipzig.

Most hotels in the former German Democratic Republic (GDR, or East Germany) are now moving closer to standards of service, food and comfort found in the rest of Germany, although their prices tend to be marginally cheaper. The city hotels tend to be efficient but sometimes rather large and impersonal. Look out for the smaller, family-run hotels, called *Pensionen*, friendlier in character but usually lacking full hotel facilities. Alternatively, head to the vineyard *Gasthöfe* of the Rhine and its various tributaries, or splash out on one of several castle-hotels here. In the little-known Erzgebirge mountains by the Czech border, Sächsische Schweiz (Saxony's 'Little Switzerland'), you will find reasonably-priced, quaint chalet-style accommodation.

Southern Germany

The southern part of the country boasts more than its fair share of sensational scenery, from the dreamy landscapes of the Black Forest and the Swabian Jura, to the chocolate-box villages and lakes of Bavaria, where country excursions frequently end with a warm welcome at a typically rustic country inn.

The region also includes some of the country's finest cities – Heidelberg, Konstanz, Nürnber, Regensburg and Ulm – with their magnificent half-timbered houses and accommodation to suit all pockets, not to mention the bustling metropolis of Munich, Germany's most popular city, which also has some of its finest hotels.

To the south, the snow-capped Alps, with their numerous mountain inns and sophisticated sports hotels, make a majestic backdrop to the entire region.

HIGHLIGHTS

H OTELS ILLUSTRATED on these introductory pages are just a selection. Other favourites include the romantic Malerwinkel, a tiny lakeside hotel in Seebruck, at the foot of the Alps (page 166); Zum Krug in Eltville-Hattenheim, at the heart of the Rheingau

The garden restaurant at the Residence, Essen-Kettwig, page 172

wine region (page 172); the palatial castle-hotels Burg Colmberg (page 156), with its four-poster beds, log fires and private chapel, and Schloss Kronberg (page 175), with its antique furnishings, golf course and rose gardens; Munich's Insel-Mühle (page 162), a fine converted watermill; and, in Konstanz, Seehotel Siber (page 161) with its renowned gourmet restaurant and magnificent rooms with views over Lake Constance to keep you entranced all day.

FOOD AND DRINK

G ERMAN CUISINE is reputedly simple and solid, and it is an undeniable fact that heavy foods such as sausages, sauerkraut, potatoes, beer and huge cream cakes frequently feature on the menu.

However, from the lowland Dutch borders and Baltic seaboard in the north to the Alpine fringes of the south, German food and drink is as varied as its landscapes. Also, the country's restaurant scene has recently been transformed by *Neue Deutsche Küche*, the German answer to *nouvelle cuisine*, with an innovative new range of light, creative dishes based on traditional German ingredients.

Breakfast is something of a German speciality and, except in the smallest hotels, is generally served as a buffet of yoghurt and muesli, platters of cheese, cold cuts and bread. Germans can consume a truly staggering amount of bread, and the variety of breads in bakeries is

Parkhotel Wehrle at Triberg im Schwarzwald, page 167

Berlin's Brandenburger Hof, page 169, a successful mix of new and old

astounding. Traditionally, lunch is the main meal of the day, and normally consists of meat in large portions, vegetables, potatoes and sauces and is usually accompanied by beer.

Regional specialities worth looking out for include Rhine salmon prepared with steamed plums; *Sauerbraten* (marinated beef in vinegar and herb gravy); snails in herb butter from Baden; Bavarian *Weisswürste* (white sausages, customarily eaten before midday); and *Leberkäs* ('livercheese'), a chunky meat-loaf which, despite its name, contains neither cheese nor liver. German desserts are usually fruit or cream-based; perhaps the best-known is the Black Forest gâteau.

Germany is also famous for its beer. It is found in a variety of forms, from Pils and Kölsch to the dark brown Düssel ale, popular in Düsseldorf, and Berlin's light, foamy Weisse, containing a sweet raspberry syrup.

German beers vary greatly in their alcohol content. While a normal brew contains around 5.5 per cent alcohol, *Starkbier* (especially popular in Southern Germany) can contain up to 16 per cent or more. Beer is usually ordered in one-litre mugs, and perhaps best en-joyed in the legendary and often atmospheric *Bierkeller* and *Biergarten*.

Wine is drunk less often than beer, but can be a welcome and refreshing addition to a solid German meal. The main wine-growing areas follow the valleys of the Rhine and its tributaries, the Mosel, Main, Nahe and Neckar, although there are also some lesser-known but equally notable vineyards, particularly around Naumburg and Dresden.

Most German wine is white, produced mainly from Riesling, Müller-Thurgau and Silvaner grapes. Only about one-eighth of the total production is red. All wines are divided into three qualities: *Tafelwein* (table wine), *Qualitätswein* (quality wine) and *Qualitätswein mit*

Prädikat (quality wine with distinctive features). These are printed on the label. Some of the finest wines include the golden coloured and sweet whites from late-harvested grapes (labelled *Spätlese* or *Auslese*).

BEDROOMS AND BATHROOMS

IN MOST HOTELS, duvets (*Federbetten*) rather than sheets and blankets are the norm. Asking for a double room does not necessarily mean you will get a double bed: usually it is two single mattresses in a 'double' frame, topped with two single duvets. If you require twin beds, ask for them specifically when booking.

As a friendly gesture, many hotels will leave a chocolate or sweet on the pillow as a small goodnight gift.

Many hotels have showers rather than baths, so if you would prefer a room with a bath remember to request this when booking. Some of the hotels in the lower price bands have shared bath-rooms. If you require an en suite bathroom, be sure to specify this when making your reservation.

The 300-year-old Hotel Adler in Eichstätt, page 156

Bülow Residenz, page 171, a Baroque house in the old part of Dresden

OTHER PRACTICAL INFORMATION

Reservations should be made as far ahead as possible, especially during holiday seasons, and in cities, which often get fully booked in advance for trade fairs and popular festivals. These include the Oktoberfest in Munich (late September–early October), the Cologne Carnival (late February–early March) or the Bayreuth opera festival (June–July).

There has recently been a move in Germany towards environmentally conscious 'eco-tourism' (*Ökotourismus*). Coincidentally, German hotels and restaurants have become more tolerant of smokers, and are now less prepared to prohibit smoking in certain rooms or areas. However, at the other extreme, some hotels offer special *Antiallergica* rooms, for those prone to such allergies as household dust.

Many hotels contain top-class restaurants where you can eat even if you are not a resident. Note that it is customary in some restaurants to share your table with other diners, especially if the table is marked *Stammtisch*. Note also that you will be charged for each piece of bread consumed.

Language *Hochdeutsch,* 'High German', is the official language, but regional dialects, often with strong local accents, are spoken in many areas.

Saxony, Bavaria and Swabia have particularly pronounced local dialects, while Berlin and Cologne retain their own 'city dialects' which even visitors from nearby areas may find hard to understand. In the north, *Plattdeutsch* is another regional variation.

Currency The *Deutsche Mark,* (written 'DM' before the amount), made up of 100 *Pfennigs*.

Shops As a rule, shops open from 9am–6:30pm Mon–Fri (some remain open until 8:30pm on Thursdays), and 8:30am–2pm Sat – except for the first Saturday of each month, when they open until 4pm.

Tipping Prices in hotels and restaurants are always inclusive of service. You therefore need leave nothing extra for room service; in restaurants it is customary to round up the bill to the nearest DM5 or DM10.

Telephoning For calls within Germany, dial the initial zero of the area code. To call Germany from the UK, dial 00 49, then the number, omitting the initial zero; from the US, 011 49, again without the initial zero.

Public holidays 1 January; Good Friday and Easter Monday; 1 May; Ascension Day; Whit Monday; Corpus Christi; 3 October (Unification Day); 25 and 26 December.

USEFUL WORDS

Breakfast	*Frühstück*
Lunch	*Mittagessen*
Dinner	*Abendessen*
Free room?	*Zimmer frei?*
How much?	*Wieviel?*
Single room	*Einzelzimmer*
Double room	*Doppelzimmer*

GERMANY PRICE BANDS

Germany does not have a hotel classification system with star ratings. Instead, hotels and guesthouses are differentiated and described according to their type – *Hotel Garni, Kur-hotel, Hotel Pension,* and so on.

Our price bands, as elsewhere in the guide, refer to the price of a standard double room in high season. Breakfast is usually, but not always, included in the room price. VAT, *Mehrwertsteuer,* is always included in the prices quoted by hotels.

ⓓ	under DM110
ⓓⓓ	DM110–DM210
ⓓⓓⓓ	DM210–310
ⓓⓓⓓⓓ	over DM310

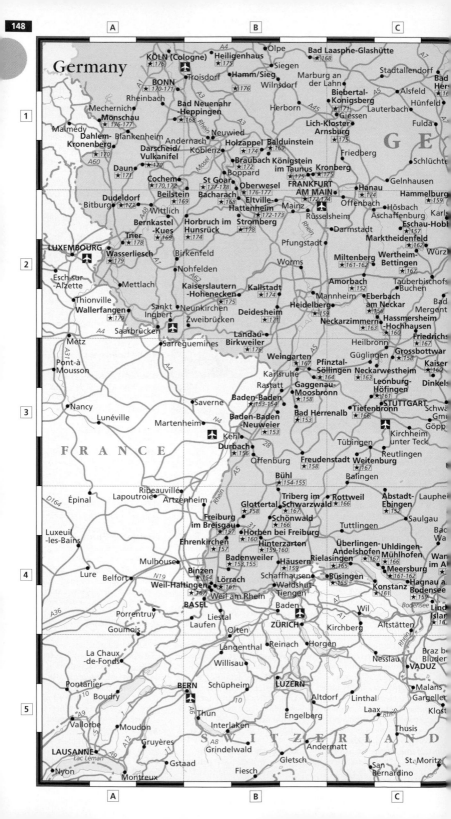

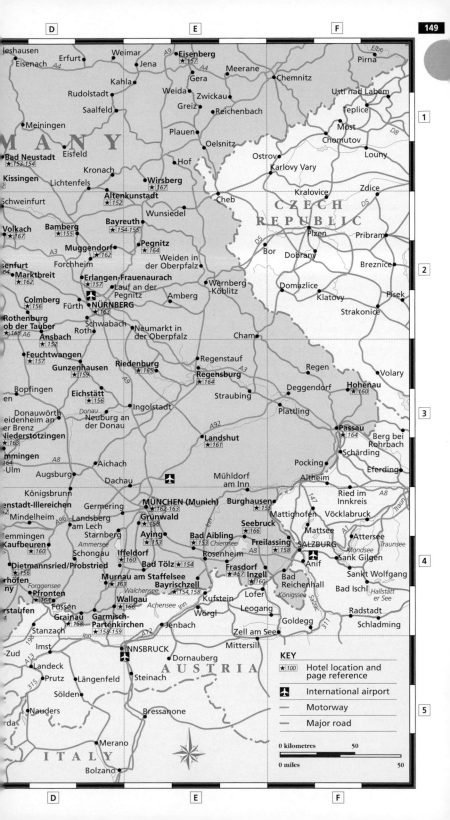

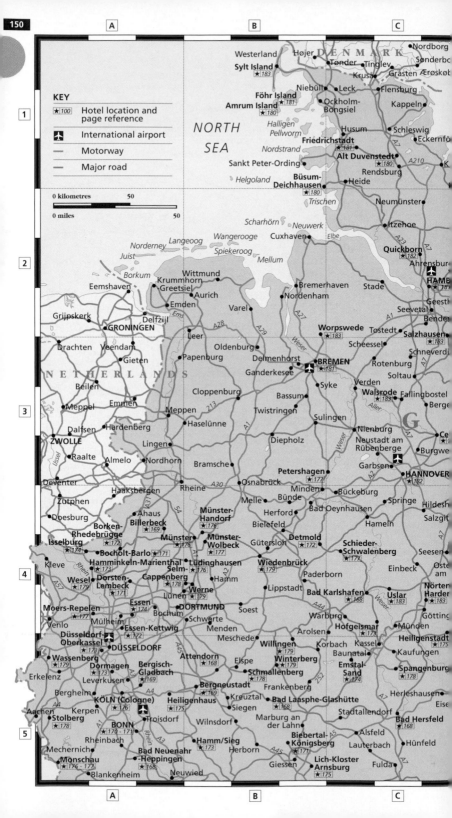

KEY

★100	Hotel location and page reference
✈	International airport
—	Motorway
—	Major road

0 kilometres   50

0 miles   50

NORTH

SEA

DENMARK

Nordborg
Westerland
Højer
Tønder
Tinglev
Sønderbo
Sylt Island ★183
Krusa
Grasten
Ærøskøb
Niebüll
Leck
Flensburg
Föhr Island ★181
Ockholm-Bongsiel
Kappeln
Amrum Island ★180
Husum
Schleswig
Halligen
Pellworm
Eckernfö
Nordstrand
Friedrichstadt ★181
Alt Duvenstedt ★180
A210
K
Sankt Peter-Ording
Rendsburg
Helgoland
Büsum-Deichhausen ★180
Heide
Neumünster
Trischen
Scharhörn
Neuwerk
Itzehoe
Wangerooge
Cuxhaven
Elbe
Norderney
Langeoog
Spiekeroog
Quickborn ★182
A23
A7
Juist
Mellum
Ahrensbur
HAMB ★18
Borkum
Wittmund
Krummhorn
Greetsiel
Bremerhaven
Stade
Seevetal
Geest
Eemshaven
Aurich
Nordenham
Bendes
Grijpskerk
Emden
Varel
A1
Salzhausen ★183
Ems
Worpswede ★183
Tostedt
Schnevardi
Delfzijl
Leer
Oldenburg
Scheessel
GRONINGEN
A28
A29
Papenburg
Delmenhorst
BREMEN ★181
Rotenburg
Drachten
Veendam
Gieten
Ganderkesee
Soltau
Beilen
Cloppenburg
Bassum
Syke
Verden
Walsrode ★183
Fallingbostel
Meppel
Emmen
Meppen
Haselünne
Twistringen
Sulingen
Nienburg
Berge
G
Dalfsen
Hardenberg
Diepholz
Neustadt am Rübenberge
Ce ★
ZWOLLE
Lingen
Weser
Burgwe
Raalte
Almelo
Nordhorn
Bramsche
Garbsen
HANNOVER ★182
Deventer
Haaksbergen
Rheine
A30
Osnabrück
Minden
Bückeburg
Springe
Hildesh
Zutphen
Melle
Bünde
Bad Oeynhausen
Hameln
Salzgit
Doesburg
Ahaus
Billerbeck ★169
Münster-Handorf ★176
Herford
A7
Borken-Rhedebrügge ★172
Bielefeld
Detmold ★172
Schieder-Schwalenberg ★177
Seesen
Isselburg ★174
Bocholt-Barlo ★171
Münster ★176
Münster-Wolbeck ★177
Gütersloh
Oste am
Hamminkeln-Marienthal ★173
Lüdinghausen
Wiedenbrück ★179
Einbeck
Kleve
Wesel ★179
Dorsten-Lembeck ★171
Selm-Cappenberg ★178
Hamm
Paderborn
Bad Karlshafen ★168
Uslar ★183
Nörten Harder ★183
Moers-Repelen ★177
Essen ★174
Lünen
Werne ★179
Lippstadt
Venlo
Mülheim
Bochum
DORTMUND
Soest
Warburg
Hofgeismar ★173
Münden
Göttin
Düsseldorf-Oberkassel ★172
Essen-Kettwig ★172
Schwerte
Menden
Arolsen
Heiligenstadt ★175
Wassenberg ★179
DÜSSELDORF
Meschede
Willingen ★179
Korbach
Kassel
Kaufungen
Erkelenz
Dormagen ★173
Bergisch-Gladbach ★169
Attendorn ★168
Elspe
Winterberg ★179
Baunatal
Spangenburg ★178
Bergheim
Leverkusen
Bergneustadt ★169
Schmallenberg ★178
Frankenberg
Emstal-Sand ★174
Aachen
Kerpen
KÖLN (Cologne) ★176
Heiligenhaus ★175
Kreuztal
Bad Laasphe-Glashütte ★168
Herleshausen
Stolberg ★178
Troisdorf
Siegen
Marburg an der Lahn
Stadtallendorf
Eise
BONN ★170-171
Wilnsdorf
Bad Hersfeld ★168
Mechernich
Rheinbach
Rhein
A3
Hamm/Sieg ★173
Herborn
Biebertal-Königsberg ★171
Alsfeld
Monschau ★176-177
Bad Neuenahr-Heppingen ★168
A45
Lich-Kloster Arnsburg ★175
Lauterbach
Hünfeld
Blankenheim
Neuwied
Giessen
Fulda

A
B
C

SOUTHERN GERMANY

NORTHERN BAVARIA • SOUTHERN BAVARIA
BADEN-WÜRTTEMBERG AND THE BLACK FOREST

*F*OR MANY VISITORS, *Southern Germany is a microcosm of the whole country, with its stereotypical brass bands, beer halls and locals clad in* Lederhosen. *The whole region brims with good-quality hotels and represents Germany at its most picturesque. Choose between the wooded hills and tranquil valleys of the Black Forest to the west, with its smart spa hotels and* Gasthöfe *(guesthouses) that could have come straight from a picture postcard, and Bavaria's lush rolling countryside and snow-capped Alps, dotted with half-timbered inns, rustic* Landhaus *(farmhouses) and chalet-style hostelries – not forgetting the converted castles and top-notch townhouse hotels of some of Germany's most majestic cities.*

ALTENSTADT-ILLEREICHEN

Landhotel Schlosswirtschaft Eberhard Aspacher is one of the best chefs in Germany, and he serves modern and artistically presented food in his Michelin-starred restaurant. The hotel is small but well run. The decor is pleasant, and there is some really charming furniture in the bedrooms. But be warned: expect to at least treble your bill when you eat.
☒ 89281 Illereichen, Kirchpl 2. **Map** p149 D4.
[(08337) 74100. **FAX** (08337) 741020. ⊪ b,l,d.
Rooms 11. ● Never. ⬛ AE, DC, MC, V. ⓂⓂⓂ

AMORBACH

Der Schafhof The red sandstone house, surrounded by meadows, is a perfect retreat. It feels virtually self-sufficient, with almost all the food coming from the estate or the local market. There are snug attic bedrooms and slightly grander ones on the first floor. Peaceful terraces, with views over the countryside.
☒ 63916 Amorbach, Schafhof 1. **Map** p148 C2.
[(09373) 97330. **FAX** (09373) 4120.
@ Der.Schafhof.Amorbach@t-online.de ⊪ b,l,d.
Rooms 23. ⧆ ● Never. ⬛ AE, DC, MC, V. ⓂⓂⓂ

ABSTADT-EBINGEN

Hotel Linde Half-timbered exterior, meticulously maintained inside; some bedrooms are lavish. The restaurant is well-known for its lobster.
☒ 72458 Albstadt 1, Untere Vorstadt 1. **Map** p148 C4.
[(07431) 1341400. **FAX** (07431) 1341430. ⊪ b,l,d.
Rooms 23. ⓂⓂ

ALTENKUNSTADT

Hotel Gondel The Jahn family have run this cheerful white-and-timber village inn for some hundred years. Neat, unassuming bedrooms.
☒ 96264 Altenkunstadt, Marktplatz 7. **Map** p148 D1.
[(09572) 3661. **FAX** (09572) 4596. ⊪ b,l,d.
Rooms 38. ⓂⓂ

ANSBACH

Hotel Bürger Palais Lavishly renovated baroque townhouse hotel: chandeliers, silk furnishings, marble-tiled bathrooms. Garden and terrace.
☒ 91522 Ansbach, Neustadt 48. **Map** p149 D2.
[(0981) 95132. **FAX** (0981) 95600. ⊪ b,l,d.
Rooms 12. ⓂⓂ

BAD KISSINGEN

Laudensacks Parkhotel Elegant townhouse spa hotel with first-rate food and sophisticated modern design. Surrounded by beautiful gardens.
☒ 97688 Bad Kissingen, Kurhausstr. 28. **Map** p149 D1.
[(0971) 72240. **FAX** (0971) 722444. ⊪ b,l,d.
Rooms 19. ⓂⓂⓂ

AYING

Brauereigasthof Hotel Aying The village is famous for its Bavarian beer, and this vine-smothered inn is right next door to the brewery. Its beer garden and halls are the perfect place to sample the local brew from the huge choice on offer. Inside are rooms large enough to host banquets, as well as intimate dining rooms. The bedrooms are spacious and well appointed.
⊠ 85653 Aying, Zornedinger Str 2. **Map** p149 E4.
((08095) 705. **FAX** (08095) 906566. 🍴 b,l,d. **Rooms** 28.
🕯 🌑 23 and 24 Dec. 🖰 AE, DC, MC, V. 📀📀📀

BAD HERRENALB

Mönchs Posthotel Behind its half-timbered façade with cheerful green and white shutters, lies a stylish blend of traditional atmosphere and modern luxury. Rooms are lavishly furnished with antiques and bouquets of flowers; bedrooms at the back are quietest. Fine food in the beamed gourmet restaurant; additional bistro in summer.
⊠ 76328 Bad Herrenalb. **Map** p148 B3.
((07083) 7440. **FAX** (07083) 744122.
@ MoenchsPosthotel@t-online.de 🍴 b,l,d. **Rooms** 32.
🌊 🎭 🕯 🌑 Never. 🖰 AE, DC, MC, V. 📀📀📀📀

BAD AIBLING

Hotel Lindner A stylish exterior of yellow-washed walls and smart striped shutters hints at the building's thousand-year history. Inside, the association continues, with vaulted ceilings, crystal chandeliers and oil paintings. But the spacious bedrooms are up to date; some are across the courtyard in a modern annexe.
⊠ 83043 Bad Aibling, Marienplatz 5. **Map** p149 E4.
((08061) 90630. **FAX** (08061) 30535.
@ lindner@romantik.de 🍴 b,l,d. **Rooms** 32.
🕯 🌑 Never. 🖰 AE, DC, MC, V. 📀📀

BAD NEUSTADT

Kur- & Schlosshotel Indulge yourself at modest cost at this little 18th-century baroque castle, set in a popular spa town. Public rooms include two glorious dining rooms, serving 'anti-stress' food, and a comfy bar. Bedrooms are large and bright, furnished with silks, and have gleaming, marble-lined bathrooms.
⊠ 97616 Bad Neustadt an der Saale, Kurhausstr. 37.
Map p149 D1. ((09771) 61610. **FAX** (09771) 2533.
🍴 b,l,d. **Rooms** 14. 🕯 🌑 Never.
🖰 AE, DC, MC, V. 📀📀

BADEN-BADEN
Hotel am Markt Simple hotel on cobbled square in the old town. Good sightseeing base.
⊠ 76530 Baden-Baden, Marktplatz 18. **Map** p148 B3.
((07221) 27040. **FAX** (07221) 270444.
@ Hotel.Am.Markt@t-online.de 🍴 b,l,d.
Rooms 26. 📀📀📀

BADEN-BADEN-NEUWEIER
Gasthaus zum Lamm Hospitable, simple country guesthouse south of Baden-Baden, with leafy terrace and rustic dining room.
⊠ 76534 Baden-Baden, Mauerbergstr. 34. **Map** p148 B3.
((07223) 57038. **FAX** (07223) 52612. 🍴 b,l,d.
Rooms 12. 📀📀

BADENWEILER
Hotel Schössle A neat villa houses a guesthouse with a personal touch and cosy bedrooms. Pretty terrace, garden; swimming pool.
⊠ 79410 Badenweiler, Kanderner Str. 4. **Map** p148 B4.
((07632) 240. **FAX** (07632) 821031. 🍴 b,l,d.
Rooms 14. 📀📀

BADENWEILER
Villa Hedwig The no-through road by a park ensures a peaceful atmosphere at the Arts and Crafts town villa. Fine dining to classical music.
⊠ 79410 Badenweiler, Römerstr. 10. **Map** p148 B4.
((07632) 82000. **FAX** (07632) 820031. 🍴 b,d.
Rooms 15. 📀📀📀

For key to symbols see backflap. For price categories see p147

BAD NEUSTADT

BADEN-BADEN

Schwan & Post This bustling hotel is set by Bad Neustadt's old town gate, an area of narrow cobbled streets and inviting little shops. Outside is a tiny, tree-shaded terrace; inside, a dining room and vaulted cellar bar. A grand staircase leads to the older bedrooms, others are in an annexe. Sauna, fitness room and whirlpool complex add to the attractions.
✉ 97616 Bad Neustadt, Hohnstr 35. **Map** p149 D1.
☎ (09771) 91070. **FAX** (09771) 910767. **⑪** b,l,d.
Rooms 30. **⑪** ● Never. **⑤** AE, DC, MC, V. ⓓⓜ ⓓⓜ ⓓⓜ

Bad Hotel Zum Hirsch The cheerful Zum is in the pedestrianized centre of this busy spa town, offering plenty of opportunity for people-watching from its terrace. The delightful bedrooms – some with balconies – are spacious and beautifully furnished with antiques. Taps in the bathrooms are connected to Baden-Baden's famous thermal water.
✉ 76530 Baden-Baden, Hirschstrasse 1. **Map** p148 B3.
☎ (07221) 9390. **FAX** (07221) 38148. **⑪** b,l,d.
Rooms 58. ● Never. **⑤** AE, DC, MC, V. ⓓⓜ ⓓⓜ ⓓⓜ

BAD TÖLZ

BADEN-BADEN

Altes Fahrhaus The old ferry boathouse on the river Isar, which separates the old town of Bad Tölz from the spa town, makes an attractive location for this smart restaurant with rooms. Elly Reisser's classical cooking features much fish and game; breakfasts with parma ham and marinated salmon are a highlight. The bedrooms all have balconies over the river.
✉ 83646 Bad Tölz, An der Isarlust 1. **Map** p149 E4.
☎ (08041) 6030. **FAX** (08041) 72270. **⑪** b,l,d. **Rooms** 5.
● Occasionally. **⑤** Not accepted. ⓓⓜ ⓓⓜ

Der Kleine Prinz An elegant, central hotel, close to the public gardens, the baths and the festival house. A solid, unremarkable exterior hides an extremely individual interior. Each of the stylish bedrooms has its own feature, be it a fireplace, a balcony or even a whirlpool. The restaurant serves French and regional cuisine.
✉ 76530 Baden-Baden, Lichtentaler Str. 36.
Map p148 B3. ☎ (07221) 346600. **FAX** (07221) 3466059.
@ info@derkleineprinz.de **⑪** b,l,d. **Rooms** 33.
● Never. **⑤** AE, DC, MC, V. ⓓⓜ ⓓⓜ ⓓⓜ

BAYREUTH

Hotel Konigshof Conveniently located close to the station and theatre, this chic hotel has a terrific mix of bedrooms at a wide price range.
✉ 95444 Bayreuth, Bahnhofstr. 23. **Map** p149 E2.
☎ (0921) 24094. **FAX** (0921) 12264. **⑪** b,l,d.
Rooms 35. ⓓⓜ ⓓⓜ ⓓⓜ

BINZEN

Mühle Old mill done up with lush fabrics and pretty antiques; well-designed rooms, good food.
✉ 79589 Binzen, Mühlenstr. 26. **Map** p148 B4.
☎ (07621) 6072. **FAX** (07621) 65808.
@ Hotel.Muehle.Binzen@t-online.de **⑪** b,l,d.
Rooms 22. ⓓⓜ ⓓⓜ

BAYRISCHZELL

Die Meindelei Informal and welcoming family-run chalet hotel in glorious Alpine valley. Extra chalet bungalows are dotted around the garden.
✉ 83735 Bayrischzell, Michael-Meindl Str. 13.
Map p149 E4. ☎ (08023) 80890. **FAX** (08023) 1480.
⑪ b,d. **Rooms** 12. ⓓⓜ ⓓⓜ

BÜHL

Grüne Bettlad In the centre of the Black Forest town, an ancient building housing a French-influenced restaurant with romantic rooms.
✉ 77815 Bühl, Blumenstr. 4. **Map** p148 B3. ☎ (07223)
931310. **FAX** (07223) 931317. @ gruene.bettlad@
t-online.de **⑪** b,l,d. **Rooms** 6. ⓓⓜ ⓓⓜ ⓓⓜ

BADENWEILER

Hotel Sonne You are guaranteed a warm welcome at this pretty hotel in the centre of a small spa town. The Fischer family run this place with great thought for detail – there are fresh flowers everywhere and it is sparklingly clean. The bedrooms are comfortable; some have chic modern bathrooms.
79405 Badenweiler, Moltkestr. 4. **Map** p148 B4.
(07632) 75080. FAX (07632) 750865. @ hotel@zur-sonne.de b,l,d. **Rooms** 41.
Never. AE, DC, MC, V.

BAMBERG

Weinhaus Messerschmitt A wine-house began trading on this spot in the 15th century. It was transformed into a restaurant in 1832 and has remained in the same family ever since. Tiled floors and polished wood predominate. Eel and sage is one of the regional specialities served in the restaurant. The Gothic cathedral is close by.
96047 Bamberg, Lange Str. 41. **Map** p149 D2.
(0951) 27866. FAX (0951) 26141.
@ Hotel-Messerschmitt@t-online.de b,l,d.
Rooms 17. Christmas. AE, DC, MC, V.

BAMBERG

Barock Hotel am Dom An ornate Baroque façade envelops this tidy little hotel in the centre of the old town. Inside are unfussy, modern rooms, impeccably kept by a team of friendly staff. Sympathetic modernization has retained the ancient vaulted breakfast room. Breakfast is a hearty affair. The hotel has its own parking spaces outside – unusual in this busy town.
96049 Bamberg, Vorderer Bach 4. **Map** p149 D2.
(0951) 54031. FAX (0951) 54021. b.
Rooms 17. Feb. AE, DC, MC, V.

BAYREUTH

Schlosshotel Thiergarten Despite its proximity to the motorway, this late-Baroque hunting lodge just 6km (4 miles) from Bayreuth is a wonderfully peaceful place. The impressive public rooms have huge oil paintings, sparkling chandeliers and stucco walls by Domenico Caddenazi. Most of the spacious bedrooms have rural views.
95448 Bayreuth, Oberthiergärtner Str. 36.
Map p149 E2. (09209) 9840. FAX (09209) 98429.
@ schlosshotel-thiergarten@t-online.de b,l,d.
Rooms 8. Never. AE, DC, MC, V.

BÜHL

Plättig Hotel Large, late 18th-century building in beautiful country, with elegant furnishings. Pretty terrace, garden and indoor swimming pool.
77815 Bühl/Baden. **Map** p148 B3. (07226) 530.
FAX (07226) 53444. @ plaetttig@t-online.de b,l,d.
Rooms 57.

BÜHL

Wehlauer's Badischer Hoff A waterside terrace draws diners to this attractive 17th-century house named after its famed chef. Modern bedrooms.
77815 Buhl, Haupstr. 36. **Map** p148 B3.
(07223) 93350. FAX (07223) 933550. b,l,d.
Rooms 25.

BURGHAUSEN

Klostergasthof Raitenhaslach The extremely popular, large vaulted dining rooms ensure a lively atmosphere at this former monastery.
84489 Burghausen, Raitenhaslach 9. **Map** p149 F4.
(08677) 9730. FAX (08677) 66111. b,l,d.
Rooms 14.

BÜSINGEN

Alte Rheinmühle Set right on the banks of the Rhine, a beautifully converted old mill. Beamed restaurant by the river; log fires in cool weather.
78266 Büsingen, Junkerstr. 93. **Map** p148 C4.
(07734) 93190. FAX (07734) 931926. b,l,d.
Rooms 14.

BAYRISCHZELL

Postgasthof Rote Wand This plain but welcoming village inn has a glorious location – a valley surrounded by Alps – and caring service. It has a large terrace, and is very popular with hikers and skiers who appreciate the hearty food. The kitchen closes at 8pm. There are no TVs in the rooms. Children and dogs welcome.
83735 Bayrischzell, Geitau 15.
Map p149 E4. (08023) 9050. **FAX** (08023) 656.
@ GasthofRoteWand@t-online.de b,l,d. **Rooms** 30.
mid-Nov to mid-Dec. AE, MC, V.

DURBACH

Hotel Ritter An extremely well-run hotel in the centre of the little wine town of Durbach. It has been carefully decorated to keep its country style, but with luxurious touches too. Bedrooms in the main house are traditional, but there are also some modern apartments with their own terraces. The restaurant is Michelin-starred.
77770 Durbach, Talstr 1. **Map** p148 B3.
(0781) 93230. **FAX** (0781) 9323100.
@ Ritter-Durbach@t-online.de b,l,d. **Rooms** 62.
Never. AE, DC, MC, V.

COLMBERG

Burg Colmberg The massive castle comes complete with stone staircases, a private chapel and huge beamed rooms with open fires. The bedrooms are magnificent, with vast carved wooden beds (some four-posters) and beautiful furniture. Some of the rooms have stunning views. Children are welcome: there's a playground and an animal park. Golf course.
91598 Colmberg, An der Burgenstr. **Map** p149 D2.
(09803) 91920. **FAX** (09803) 262. b,l,d.
Rooms 27. Jan. MC.

EICHSTÄTT

Hotel Adler A 300 year-old building with a wonderful baroque exterior, set on the town marketplace. Inside it has been completely modernized to make a thoroughly pleasant hotel. The bedrooms are large and plainly decorated. There are two dining rooms. Good buffet breakfast.
85072 Eichstätt, Markplatz 22-24. **Map** p149 D3.
(08421) 676769. **FAX** (08421) 8283. b.
Rooms 38. mid-Dec to mid-Jan.
AE, DC, MC, V.

DIETMANNSRIED/PROBSTRIED
Landhaus Henze Chalet hotel and restaurant, with large, well-designed bedrooms. Book ahead for the restaurants – one formal, one rustic.
87463 Dietmannsried/Probstried, Wolhmutser Weg 2.
Map p149 D4. (08374) 58320. **FAX** (08374) 583222.
b,l,d. **Rooms** 8.

DINKELSBÜHL
Deutsches Haus The welcoming ancient town inn is crammed full with wall paintings, painted ceilings and doors, and antique furniture.
83 Dinkelsbühl, Weinmarkt 3. **Map** p148 C3.
(09851) 6058. **FAX** (09581) 7911. b,l,d.
Rooms 8.

DINKELSBÜHL
Gasthof zum Goldenen Anker Family-run town inn, a peaceful haven away from the busy streets; traditional public rooms, spacious bedrooms.
91550 Dinkelsbühl, Untere Schmiedsgasse 22.
Map p148 C3. (09851) 57800. **FAX** (09851) 578080.
@ Goldener.Anker@t-online.de b,l,d. **Rooms** 16.

EBERBACH AM NECKAR
Altes Badhaus Town hotel in which traditional beamed bedrooms have been successfully modernized with a touch of high-tech.
69412 Eberbach am Neckar, Am Lindenplatz 1.
Map p148 C2. (06271) 92300. **FAX** (06271) 923040.
b,l,d. **Rooms** 13.

EISENBERG

Magnushof Not only is this delightful place in a beautiful rural location at the foot of the Alps, but there is also a pool and a fitness room. Inside, the mish-mash of styles works well, and the effect is charming. The bedrooms are spacious and are equipped with books and games. Breakfasts are hearty. The restaurant offers regional food with an excellent wine list.
⊠ 87637 Eisenberg, Unterreuten 51. **Map** p149 E1, p151 E5. ☎ (08363) 91120. FAX (08363) 911250.
🍴 b,l,d. **Rooms** 10. 🏊 🚹 ● Never. 🗲 MC, V. ⓂⓂ

FEUCHTWANGEN

Hotel Greifen-Post Great sensitivity has been shown in renovating this ancient marketplace inn. Look for the lovely frescoes in one of the four dining rooms. Each bedroom is different, some furnished in Laura Ashley, others in Biedermeier; some have four-poster beds. Superb swimming pool in the old stables.
⊠ 91555 Feuchtwangen, Marktplatz 8. **Map** p149 D3.
☎ (09852) 6800. FAX (09852) 68068. @ Greifen@romantik.de 🍴 b,l,d. **Rooms** 41. 🏊 ● Never.
🗲 AE, DC, MC, V. ⓂⓂⓂ

ERLANGEN-FRAUENAURACH

Schwarzer Adler The industrial town of Erlangen is close by yet this feels a million miles away. The old inn is truly rustic, but beautifully and unfussily decorated. Each delightful bedroom is named after a bird and has both lovely old furniture and all the modern conveniences. Snacks and drinks are available in the evenings.
⊠ 91056 Erlangen-Frauenaurach, Herdegenpl 1.
Map p149 D2. ☎ (09131) 992051. FAX (09131) 993195.
🍴 b. **Rooms** 15. ● mid-May to June, mid-Aug to Sept.
🗲 AE, DC, V. ⓂⓂ

FRIEDRICHSRUHE

Wald & Schlosshotel Friedrichsruhe This elegant and rather formal hotel is home to one of the best chefs in Germany, Lothar Eiermann. The lavishly furnished dining room does justice to the menu. The bedrooms, both in the main house and in the adjoining hunting lodge, are appropriately luxurious and tranquil.
⊠ 74639 Friedrichsruhe. **Map** p148 C2.
☎ (07941) 60870. FAX (07941) 61468.
@ Schlosshotel_friedrichsruhe@t-online.de 🍴 b,l,d.
Rooms 43. 🏊 🎱 ● Never. 🗲 AE, DC, MC, V. ⓂⓂⓂ

EHRENKIRCHEN

Gasthaus zur Krone Inspiring regional wine tastings and well-prepared food marks out this whitewashed country inn.
⊠ 79238 Ehrenkirchen, Herrenstr. 5. **Map** p148 B4.
☎ (07633) 5213. FAX (07633) 83550. @ info@gasthaus-krone.de 🍴 b,l,d. **Rooms** 9. Ⓜ

ESCHAU-HOBBACH

Gasthof Engel This 200-year-old country inn is tucked away on the edge of the Spessart nature reserve. Modern bedroom extension.
⊠ 63863 Eschau-Hobbach, Bayernstrasse 47.
Map p148 C2. ☎ (09374) 388. FAX (09374) 7831.
🍴 b,l,d. **Rooms** 24. ⓂⓂ

FRASDORF

Landgasthof Karner Extremely popular and stylish country hotel, with a wonderful garden terrace. The restaurant is Michelin-starred.
⊠ 83112 Frasdorf, Nussbaumstr. 6. **Map** p149 E4.
☎ (08052) 4071. FAX (08052) 4711. @ info@landgasthof-karner.de 🍴 b,l,d. **Rooms** 23. ⓂⓂ

FREIBURG IM BREISGAU

Zum Roten Bären In the centre of the old town, this has been a hostelry since the early 12th century. Cleverly modernized inside.
⊠ 79098 Freiburg im Breisgau, Oberlinden 12.
Map p148 B4. ☎ (0761) 387870. FAX (0761) 3878717.
@ info@roter-baeren.de 🍴 b,l,d. **Rooms** 25. ⓂⓂⓂ

GLOTTERTAL

Gasthause zum Adler Home-made black pudding is one of the highlights of the unusual menu offered at this guesthouse, set in a tranquil valley in the south of the Black Forest. There is also a menu for child gourmets. The decor is simple and unfussy, and the bedrooms full of colour and character.
⊠ 79286 Glottertal, Talstr 11. **Map** p148 B4.
[(07684) 1081. **FAX** (07684) 1083.
@ Adler.Glottertal@t-online.de ⏍ b,l,d. **Rooms** 13.
● Never. ⊞ DC, MC, V. ⊛⊛

GROSSBOTTWAR

Stadtschänke Grossbottwar, in the Württenberg wine-growing area, is an old town of cobbled streets. This 15th-century building is in keeping with its half-timbered neighbours on the marketplace; timbered rooms with rustic furniture retain a medieval atmosphere. The five bedrooms are cosy and carefully decorated. The menu is strong on fish; wine tastings are encouraged.
⊠ 71723 Grossbottwar, Hauptstr 36. **Map** p148 C3.
[(07148) 8024. **FAX** (07148) 4977. ⏍ b,l,d. **Rooms** 5.
● first 2 weeks Sept. ⊞ AE, DC, MC, V. ⊛⊛

GRAINAU

Alpenhof This modern chalet hotel stands out for its restrained use of traditional styles, with muted fabrics and antique furnishings softening the large, white-painted rooms. The indoor pool looks out onto the lush garden, where theme evenings are held in summer. The mountain train to the Zugspitze peak passes through the village.
⊠ 82491 Grainau, Alpspitzstr 34. **Map** p149 D4.
[(08821) 9870. **FAX** (08821) 98777.
@ alpenhof@grainau.de ⏍ b,l,d. **Rooms** 36.
⊞ ⏍ ● mid-Nov to mid-Dec. ⊞ DC, MC, V. ⊛⊛

GRÜNWALD

Alter Wirt This friendly and welcoming place is handily located just off the road into Munich, and offers larger, brighter rooms than many city-centre hotels. It has also got a particularly pretty terrace, canopied by trees, where snacks and drinks are served, and a pleasant garden. Some of the public rooms are wood-panelled.
⊠ 82039 Grünwald, Marktpl 1. **Map** p149 E4.
[(089) 641 9340. **FAX** (089) 641 93499.
@ AlterWirt@Landidyll.de ⏍ b,l,d. **Rooms** 50.
⏍ ● Christmas Eve. ⊞ AE, MC, V. ⊛⊛

FREILASSING
Gasthof Moosleitner Elegantly simple furnishings enhance the atmosphere of this country hotel, set in a 700-year-old building.
⊠ 883395 Freilassing, Wasserburger Str. 52.
Map p149 F4. [(08654) 2081. **FAX** (08654) 62010.
⏍ b,l,d. **Rooms** 50. ⊛⊛

FREUDENSTADT
Langenwaldsee A large pool, small lake and vast forest attract sporty types to this country hotel just outside of town. Bedrooms are modern.
⊠ 72250 Freudenstadt, Strassburger Str. 99. **Map** p148 B3.
[(07441) 88930. **FAX** (07441) 88936. @ langenwaldsee@
t-online.de ⏍ b,l,d. **Rooms** 53. ⊛⊛

GAGGENAU-MOOSBRONN
Mönchof Renovated in the 1980s, this 18th-century half-timbered house makes a smart yet cosy country hotel retaining beams, tiled floors and rustic furniture. Iceland ponies for hire.
⊠ 76571 Gaggenau-Moosbronn. **Map** p148 B3.
[(07204) 619. **FAX** (07204) 1256. ⏍ b. **Rooms** 16. ⊛⊛

GARMISCH-PARTENKIRCHEN
Hotel Garmischer A chic chalet hotel in the centre of town, with stunning views of the Alps from the delightful garden.
⊠ 82467 Garmisch-Partenkirchen, Chamonixstr 10.
Map p149 D4. [(08821) 9110. **FAX** (0881) 51440.
⏍ b,l,d. **Rooms** 59. ⊛⊛⊛

HAMMELBURG

Halbritter's Landgasthaus Despite its traditional appearance and its location in deepest Bavaria, there's nothing rustic about this country hotel. Halbritter's is boldly and stylishly decorated, with individual, luxurious bedrooms. Food in the dining room is modern too; more hearty food is served in the *Grill-Stube*.
⊠ 97797 Hammelburg, Hauptstr 4, Wartmannsroth. **Map** p148 C2. 🄲 (09737) 890. 🄵🄰🄇 (09737) 8940. @ landhotelhalbritter@t-online.de 🍴 b,l,d. **Rooms** 11. 🎙 ⬤ Never. 🄶 AE, MC, V. 🄾🄼🄾🄼🄾🄼

HEIDELBERG

Hirschgasse A total refurbishment in 1989 has made a real gem of this city hotel. Mark Twain once stayed here. Each of the charming suites is different – the Chinoiserie suite has lacquered walls and Chinese lamps – and has a lavish bathroom to match. The cosy 'Le Gourmet' restaurant lives up to its name; booking essential.
⊠ 69120 Heidelberg 1, Hirschgasse 3. **Map** p148 C2. 🄲 (06221) 4540. 🄵🄰🄇 (06221) 454111. @ ekraft@compuserve.com 🍴 b,d. **Rooms** 20 suites. ⬤ Never. 🄶 AE, DC, MC, V. 🄾🄼🄾🄼

HÄUSERN

Hotel Adler Modern, Michelin-starred cuisine is one of the highlights of this village hotel. The place has been beautifully spruced up, with mellow wood panelling and deeply coloured rugs on the tiled floors. The modern bedrooms have handsome furniture; many have balconies.
⊠ 79838 Häusern, Fridolin Str 15. **Map** p148 B4. 🄲 (07672) 4170. 🄵🄰🄇 (07672) 417150. @ Hotel-Adler-Schwarzwald@t-online.de 🍴 b,l,d. **Rooms** 44. 🏊 ⬤ mid-Nov to mid-Dec. 🄶 AE, DC, MC, V. 🄾🄼🄾🄼

HINTERZARTEN

Sassenhof This welcoming hotel is set right on the village green of the little Black Forest resort village of Hinterzarten. It is pleasantly furnished in a more sophisticated way than is usual in this rural area. Bedrooms differ in size – those in the attic can be small. The breakfasts are hearty and delicious; there is no restaurant, but there are plenty of options in the village.
⊠ 79856 Hinterzarten Adlerweg 17. **Map** p148 B4. 🄲 (07652) 1515. 🄵🄰🄇 (07652) 484. 🍴 b. **Rooms** 26. 🏊 🎙 ⬤ mid-Nov to mid-Dec. 🄶 Not accepted. 🄾🄼🄾🄼

GARMISCH-PARTENKIRCHEN
Posthotel Partenkirch A beautifully maintained 16th-century coaching inn, with rich wood panelling in some bedrooms. Five restaurants.
⊠ 82467 Garmisch-Partenkirchen, Ludwigstrasse 49. **Map** p149 D4. 🄲 (08821) 51067. 🄵🄰🄇 (08821) 78568. 🍴 b,l,d. **Rooms** 59. 🄾🄼🄾🄼🄾🄼

GUNZENHAUSEN
Hotel zur Post A modern hotel occupies this old post-house, where guests lounge in panelled public rooms. Well-presented, ambitious cooking.
⊠ 91710 Gunzenhausen, Bahnhofstr. 7. **Map** p149 D3. 🄲 (09831) 67470. 🄵🄰🄇 (09831) 6747222 🍴 b,d. **Rooms** 26. 🄾🄼🄾🄼

HAGNAU AM BODENSEE
Erbguth's Landhaus Tiny, immaculately clean hotel with a personal touch, right on the shores of Lake Constance. Verandas, garden, swimming.
⊠ 88709 Hagnau am Bodensee. **Map** p148 C4. 🄲 (07532) 43130. 🄵🄰🄇 (07532) 6997. @ Erbguth@villa-am-see.de 🍴 b. **Rooms** 6. 🄾🄼🄾🄼

HAGNAU AM BODENSEE
Der Löwen This 17th-century house has a private lake foreshore a few minutes away. Bright rooms.
⊠ 88709 Hagnau am Bodensee, Hansajakobstr. 2. **Map** p148 C4. 🄲 (07532) 433980. 🄵🄰🄇 (07532) 43398300. @ Loewen-hagnau@t-online.de 🍴 b,d. **Rooms** 17. 🄾🄼🄾🄼

For key to symbols see backflap. For price categories *see p147*

HOHENAU

Die Bierhütte Both the hearty food and the rural seclusion (close to the Czech border) attract visitors to this informal village hotel. Terrace tables overlook the hotel pond; inside, the stylish *Stube* has a marvellous painted ceiling. Traditional rooms in the main building and a chalet annexe; ultra-modern in a third house.
✉ 94546 Hohenau, Bierhütte 10. **Map** p149 F3.
📞 (08558) 96120. **FAX** (08558) 961270.
@ bierhuette@t-online.de 🍴 b,l,d. **Rooms** 43.
🌡 ● Never. 💳 AE, DC, MC, V. ⓄⓄ

KAISERBACH

Schassberger's Ebnisee This thriving complex of chalet-type buildings by the Ebnisee offers plenty of opportunities for leisure activities. Swimming, tennis, squash, lakeside and rural walks, fishing, boating and cycling are all available. What with two restaurants (creative-classic and regional), some visitors never leave the grounds.
✉ 73667 Kaiserbach, am Ebnisee. **Map** p148 C3.
📞 (07184) 2920. **FAX** (07184) 292204. @ Schassbergers-Ebnisee@t-online.de 🍴 b,l,d. **Rooms** 49. 🌡 ● Never.
💳 AE, MC, V. ⓄⓄⓄ

INZELL

Zur Post This traditional Bavarian hotel is located in the middle of the village, by the church, and is a popular place. The public rooms are welcoming and elegant, the bedrooms spacious and rather luxurious. There are lots of health and sporting activities on offer, and the swimming pool is terrific.
✉ 83334 Inzell, Reichenhaller Str 2. **Map** p149 E4.
📞 (08665) 9850. **FAX** (08665) 985100.
@ kontakt@post-inzell.de 🍴 b,l,d. **Rooms** 45.
♨ 🍴 ● mid-Nov to mid-Dec. 💳 DC, MC, V. ⓄⓄ

KAUFBEUREN

Goldener Hirsch The 17th-century house is Kaufbeuren's main hotel, and has been sensitively modernized to retain some old features. It makes an ideal base for visiting the famous castles built by King Ludwig II – all under an hour's drive away. The public rooms are light and airy and the bedrooms plainly but comfortably furnished.
✉ 87600 Kaufbeuren, Kasier-Max Str 39-41.
Map p149 D4. 📞 (08341) 43030. **FAX** (08341) 430375.
@ Hotel-Goldenerhirsch@llgaeu.de 🍴 b,l,d.
Rooms 40. ● Never. 💳 AE, DC, MC, V. ⓄⓄⓄ

HASSMERSHEIM-HOCHHAUSEN

Schloss Hochhausen Manor house hotel set within a deer park. Lots of open fires; spacious Biedemeier-furnished bedrooms. Meals feature meat and vegetables from the park and garden.
✉ 74855 Hassmersheim-Hochhausen. **Map** p148 C2.
📞 (06261) 893142. 🍴 b,l,d. **Rooms** 18. ⓄⓄ

HINTERZARTEN

Hotel Reppert Lake, woods and meadows are the backdrop for this family-run country hotel. Smart bedrooms; health treatments.
✉ 79856 Hinterzarten, Adlerweg 21-23.
Map p148 B4. 📞 (07652) 12080. **FAX** (07652) 120811.
@ wellnesshotel@reppert.de 🍴 b,l,d. **Rooms** 39. ⓄⓄⓄ

HORBEN BEI FREIBURG

Zum Engel Set in magnificent hilly countryside, the traditional four-storey country hotel offers well-appointed, provincial-style bedrooms. There is a pretty garden and a shady terrace.
✉ 79289 Horben-Langackern. **Map** p148 B4. 📞 (0761) 29111. **FAX** (0761) 290627. 🍴 b,l,d. **Rooms** 22. ⓄⓄ

IFFELDORF

Landgasthof Osterseen Grand views over the lake from the terraces of this popular chalet hotel, beautifully run by the Link family.
✉ 82393 Iffeldorf, Hofmark 9. **Map** p149 D4.
📞 (08856) 92860. **FAX** (08856) 928645. 🍴 b,l,d.
Rooms 24. ⓄⓄⓄ

KONSTANZ

MEERSBURG

Seehotel Siber Chef Berthold Siber opened his 19th-century lakeside villa as a hotel and restaurant in 1984; both his gourmet cooking and the accommodation are highly regarded. The best of the restrained bedrooms have lake views, as does the dining room terrace. The casino is next door, central Konstanz a short walk away.
✉ 78464 Konstanz, Seestr 25. **Map** p148 C4.
📞 (07531) 63044. **FAX** (07531) 64813.
@ seehotel.siber@t-online.de 🍴 b,l,d. **Rooms** 11.
🅿 ⬤ 1 week Feb. 💳 AE, DC, MC, V. ⒹⓂ ⒹⓂ

Zum Bären This is all you could want of an inn in a lakeside town like old Meersburg. It's on the marketplace, parts of the gabled building date back to 1250, and it's been run by the Gilowsky family for five generations. It's a homely place, with carefully furnished rooms; some are rather grand. Good, simple food.
✉ 88709 Meersburg, Marktplatz 11. **Map** p148 C4.
📞 (07532) 43220. **FAX** (07532) 432244.
🍴 b;l,d (restaurant closed Dec, Jan). **Rooms** 19.
💳 Not accepted. ⬤ Never. ⒹⓂ

LANDSHUT

MILTENBERG

Hotel Fürstenhof The care and attention Hertha Sellmair lavishes on her establishment more than makes up for its unremarkable location on the outskirts of Landshut. Her flair for decor is apparent, from the stylish dining rooms and sitting room to the tasteful bedrooms. Food in the three dining rooms is modern German.
✉ 84034 Landshut, Stethaimer Str 3. **Map** p149 E3.
📞 (0871) 92550. **FAX** (0871) 925544.
@ fuerstenhof@romantik.de 🍴 b,l,d. **Rooms** 24.
🅿 ⬤ Never. 💳 AE, DC, MC, V. ⒹⓂ ⒹⓂ

Jagd Hotel Rose The exterior of this town inn is marvellously welcoming, with stripey red and white shutters and wisteria dripping over the entrance. It is attractive inside, too: plain but cosy bedrooms and unfussy public rooms, all with a light airy atmosphere, with natural woods and tiled floors. There is an attractive terrace.
✉ 63897 Miltenberg, Hauptstr 280. **Map** p148 C2.
📞 (09371) 40060. **FAX** (09371) 400617.
@ jagd-hotel-rose@t-online.de 🍴 b,l,d.
Rooms 23. ⬤ Never. 💳 AE, DC, MC, V. ⒹⓂ ⒹⓂ

LEONBERG-HÖFINGERN
Schloss Höfingen A carefully renovated, airy castle hotel with kitchens run by renowned Franz Feckl. Bedrooms are relatively plain but spacious.
✉ 71229 Leonberg-Höfingern, Am Schlossberg 17.
Map p148 C3. 📞 (07152) 21049. 🍴 b,l,d.
Rooms 9. ⒹⓂ ⒹⓂ

LINDAU ISLAND
Lindauer Hof Old building with a contemporary feel, perfectly located above the harbour of the island, with Lake Constance beyond.
✉ 88105 Lindau/Insel, An der Seepromenade. **Map** p148 C4.
📞 (08382) 4064. **FAX** (08382) 24203. @ Lindauer.Hof@
t-online.de 🍴 b,l,d. **Rooms** 25. ⒹⓂ ⒹⓂ

LÖRRACH
Villa Elben A tranquil Art Deco town hotel with its own grounds and a galleried reception area. Thoughtfully decorated bedrooms. No restaurant.
✉ 75939 Lörrach, Hünerbergweg 26. **Map** p148 B4.
📞 (07621) 2066. **FAX** (07621) 43820. 🍴 b.
Rooms 44. ⒹⓂ ⒹⓂ

MAIERHÖFEN BEI ISNY
Gasthof zur Grenze Traditional chalet hotel: lots of flowers and murals. Most rooms have balcony views over the hills. Cheerful dining room.
✉ 88167 Maierhöfen bei Isny, Schanz 103.
Map p149 D4. 📞 (07562) 975510. **FAX** (07562) 9755129.
🍴 b,l,d. **Rooms** 16. ⒹⓂ ⒹⓂ

For key to symbols see backflap. For price categories *see p147*

MILTENBERG

Hotel zum Riesen This small guesthouse – claimed to be the oldest in Germany – is right in the pedestrianized centre of Miltenberg. Proprietor Werner Jöst trained as an architect and has used his skills wisely. Each room has a different style; one has its own roof terrace. Hearty breakfasts are served in a room under the eaves. Separate *Stube* downstairs.
☒ 63897 Miltenberg, Haupstr. 97. **Map** p148 C2. ☎ (09371) 3644. ⊟ b. **Rooms** 14. ● mid-Dec to mid-March. ⬛ DC, MC. ⓓⓜ

MUGGENDORF

Hotel Feiler This solid village building houses spacious rooms above its fine restaurant, which no visitor should pass up. Horst Feiler, whose family have run the establishment for more than 100 years, is a mushroom expert; summer truffles are a highlight of the gourmet menu. The terrace is heavenly. Informal but beautifully run.
☒ 91346 Muggendorf, Oberer Markt 4. **Map** p149 D2. ☎ (09196) 92950. **FAX** (09196) 362. @ info@hotel-feiler.de ⊟ b,l,d. **Rooms** 15. ● ● Never. ⬛ AE, MC, V. ⓓⓜ

MÜNCHEN (MUNICH)

Acanthus Choose your preferred style at this central city hotel: antique furniture and 'English-style' furnishings on the Alba-Rose floor, or a cleaner, more modern look (and cheaper prices) on the Rustikana floors. All are tastefully done out. There is a wide range of tempting buffet dishes for breakfast. The bar is open day and night for drinks and snacks.
☒ 80331 München, An der Hauptfeuerwache 14. **Map** p149 E4. ☎ (089) 231880. **FAX** (089) 2607364. ⊟ b. **Rooms** 36. ● Christmas. ⬛ AE, MC, V. ⓓⓜ

MÜNCHEN (MUNICH)

Insel-Mühle Perfectly situated by the river, this old watermill has been tastefully converted in an elegant Bavarian rustic style. The bedrooms are pretty, the best ones being under the eaves, and the bathrooms are modern. The riverside beer garden makes the most of the hotel's location, and is a popular local meeting place.
☒ 80999 München, Von-Kahr-Str 87. **Map** p149 E4. ☎ (089) 81010. **FAX** (089) 8120571. @ INSEL-MUEHLE@t-online.de ⊟ b,l,d. **Rooms** 37. ● Never. ⬛ DC, MC, V. ⓓⓜ

MARKTBREIT

Hotel Löwen A magnificent 15th-century half-timbered building with a high-ceilinged dining room. Some of the bedrooms are fantastic too.
☒ 97340 Marktbreit, Markstr. 8. **Map** p149 D2. ☎ (09332) 50540. **FAX** (09332) 9438. ⊟ b,l,d. **Rooms** 25. ⓓⓜ

MARKTHEIDENFELD

Anker The modern town hotel is not strong on style but is hospitable, very effficiently run and comfortable. Michelin-starred restaurant.
☒ 97828 Marktheidenfeld, Obertorstr. 6-8. **Map** p148 C2. ☎ (09391) 60040. **FAX** (09391) 600477. @ info@hotel-anker.de ⊟ b,l,d. **Rooms** 39. ⓓⓜ

MEERSBURG

Weinstube Löwen A cheerful old town inn on the marketplace. The dining rooms are snug and popular, the bedrooms comfortable and simple.
☒ 88709 Meersburg, Marktpl 2. **Map** p148 C4. ☎ (07532) 43040. **FAX** (07532) 430410. ⊟ b,l,d. **Rooms** 21. ⓓⓜ

MÜNCHEN (MUNICH)

Hotel Splendid Traditional, central hotel with large bedrooms. There is no dining room but snacks and drinks are served on the terrace.
☒ 80538 München 22, Maximilianstr. 54. **Map** p149 E4. ☎ (089) 296606. **FAX** (089) 2913176. ⊟ b. **Rooms** 40. ⓓⓜ

MÜNCHEN (MUNICH)

Hotel Rafael The roof terrace with pool, right in the city centre, gives a hint of what to expect at this large, professional hotel. The place has been carefully furnished with a blend of modern and traditional elements, and cosy public areas include a piano bar. Bedrooms are large and sumptuous, with bathrooms to match.
⊠ 80331 München, Neuturmstr. 1. **Map** p149 E4.
☎ (089) 290980. ℻ (089) 222539.
@ info@hotelrafael.com ⊪ b,l,d. **Rooms** 74.
≋ ● Never. 🛋 AE, DC, MC, V. ⒹⓂⒹⓂ

MÜNCHEN (MUNICH)

Schrenkof This seemingly ordinary town chalet on the southern outskirts of Munich is unexpectedly lavish inside. A great deal of marquetry and paintwork is used throughout, and each room is furnished in a different historical style. The breakfast room is delightful, with a Renaissance tiled stove.
⊠ 82008 München, Leonhardsweg 6, Unterhaching.
Map p149 E4. ☎ (089) 6100910. ℻ (089) 61009150.
⊪ b. **Rooms** 25. ● 20 Dec to 8 Jan. 🛋 AE, DC, MC, V.
ⒹⓂⒹ

MÜNCHEN (MUNICH)
Hotel Prinzregent Riverside hotel with marvellous panelling and interesting bedrooms.
⊠ 81675 München, Ismaninger Str. 42-44.
Map p149 E4. ☎ (089) 416050. ℻ (089) 41605466.
@ rezeption2@prinzregent.de ⊪ b.
Rooms 66. ⒹⓂⒹⓂ

MURNAU AM STAFFELSEE
Alpenhof Murnau A smart chalet hotel with rural views across to the Alps and understated decor. The food is modern and imaginative.
⊠ 82418 Murnau am Staffelsee, Ramsachstr. 8. **Map** p149 D4. ☎ (08841) 4910. ℻ (08841) 5438. @ info@alpenhof-murnau.com ⊪ b,l,d. **Rooms** 44. ⒹⓂⒹ

NECKARWESTHEIM

Schlosshotel Liebenstein Impeccably renovated in the 1980s, this 16th-century hilltop castle provides a wonderfully historic atmosphere as well as great comfort. A highlight is the huge vaulted dining room. For snacks and drinks, there is a tavern with a terrace. The large bedrooms are decorated with taste. Golf course.
⊠ 74382 Neckarwestheim. **Map** p148 C3.
☎ (07133) 98990. ℻ (07133) 6045.
@ info@Liebenstein.com ⊪ b,l,d. **Rooms** 24.
❶ ● 24 Dec. 🛋 AE, DC, MC, V. ⒹⓂⒹ

NIEDERSTOTZINGEN

Schlosshotel Oberstotzingen It's a manor house rather than a castle, but the 700-year-old building in the flat countryside near the Danube makes a stylish hotel. Food in the elegant vaulted dining room is imaginative, with a regional slant. Bedrooms make good use of bold colour schemes; some of the prettiest are in the tower.
⊠ 89166 Niederstotzingen, Stettener Str. 35-37.
Map p149 D3. ☎ (07325) 1030. ℻ (07325) 10370.
⊪ b,l,d. **Rooms** 17. ● Never.
🛋 AE, DC, MC, V. ⒹⓂⒹ

NECKARZIMMERN
Burg Hornberg This converted castle is also partly a museum, so is bustling with people. Beautiful position above the river Neckar.
⊠ 74865 Neckarzimmern. **Map** p148 C2. ☎ (06261) 92460. ℻ (06261) 924644.@ info@castle-hotel-hornberg.com ⊪ b,l,d. **Rooms** 24. ⒹⓂⒹ

NÜRNBERG
Hotel Zirbelstube In an enchanting position on the Ludwig canal. Charming bedrooms, attractive terrace and smart dining room.
⊠ 90455 Nürnberg-Worzeldorf 60, Friedrich-Overbeck-Str. **Map** p149 D2. ☎ (0911) 998820. ℻ (0911) 9988220. ⊪ b,d. **Rooms** 8. ⒹⓂ

OBERSTAUFEN

Hotel zum Löwen This is a spa hotel, with fitness rooms and treatments, but you can ignore all that and enjoy yourself anyway – the food is delicious, the bedrooms vast and stylish, and the indoor pool is stunning. All the bedrooms have balconies with views onto the hills. Choice of three dining rooms, and a long wine list.
⊠ 87534 Oberstaufen, Kirchplatz 8.
Map p149 D4. 📞 (08386) 4940. FAX (08386) 494222.
@ kurlaub@t-online.de 🍴 b,l,d. **Rooms** 30.
〰 🍴 ● Never. 🗲 AE, DC, V. ⓄⓄⓄ

PEGNITZ

Pflaums Posthotel It looks like a typical inn, with a flower-bedecked exterior; inside it is anything but. Wagner is the theme here, with films of his operas shown in the foyer. The theme recurs in the quirky bedrooms. The taste for the dramatic extends to the ambitious food. Breakfasts are not to be missed.
⊠ 91257 Pegnitz, Nürnbergerstrasse 12-16.
Map p149 E2. 📞 (09241) 7250. FAX (09241) 80404.
@ info@ppp.com 🍴 b,l,d. **Rooms** 50. 🍴
● Never. 🗲 AE, DC, MC, V. ⓄⓄⓄ

PASSAU

Hotel Wilder Mann This beautifully preserved rococo-style hotel occupies a prime position in the centre of Passau. Elegance and a faded grandeur characterize the interior, and the restaurant is Michelin-starred. Choice of the bedrooms are the quieter ones overlooking the garden. Terrace for drinks. Also in the building is a small glass museum.
⊠ 94032 Passau, am Rathausplatz. **Map** p149 F3.
📞 (0851) 35071. FAX (0851) 31712. 🍴 b,l,d.
Rooms 49. ● Never. 🗲 AE, DC, MC, V. Ⓞ

PFINZTAL-SÖLLINGEN

Villa Hammerschmiede This 19th-century villa on the edge of the Black Forest is best described as a restaurant with rooms – chef Markus Nagy has won it a Michelin star. Two dining rooms: one in the conservatory, the other in the wine cellar. Chic, large bedrooms, plush bathrooms.
⊠ 76327 Pfinztal-Söllingen, Hauptstrasse 162.
Map p148 B3. 📞 (07240) 6010. FAX (07240) 60160.
@ info@villa-hammerschmiede.de 🍴 b,l,d.
Rooms 26. 🛁 〰 ● 24 Dec (restaurant only).
🗲 AE, DC, V. ⓄⓄⓄ

OCHSENFURT

Polisina A welcoming atmosphere in this sporty hotel, a stone-and-wood building with tennis courts and a first-rate indoor pool.
⊠ 97199 Ochsenfurt, Markbreiter Str. 265.
Map p149 D2. 📞 (09331) 8440. FAX (09331) 7603.
@ Polisina@landidyll.de 🍴 b,l,d. **Rooms** 93. ⓄⓄⓄ

PFRONTEN

Hotel Bavaria At the head of a tranquil valley is this lavishly comfortable hotel, with open fires, pools, solarium and sauna.
⊠ 87459 Pfronten-Dorf, Kienbergstr. 62. **Map** p149 D4.
📞 (08363) 9020. FAX (08363) 6815. 🍴 b,l,d.
Rooms 48. ⓄⓄⓄ

RAMMINGEN

Landgasthaus Adler Village guesthouse with a large informal garden. Charming bedrooms, generous and modern bathrooms. Hearty meals.
⊠ 89192 Rammingen, Riegestr 15. **Map** p149 D3.
📞 (07345) 96410. FAX (07345) 964110. 🍴 b,l,d.
Rooms 14. ⓄⓄ

REGENSBURG

Bischofshof am Dom An old bishops' palace makes a very attractive hotel with a charming courtyard. Lavish furnishings, fine cuisine.
⊠ 93047 Regensburg, Krauterermarkt 3. **Map** p149 E3.
📞 (0941) 5941010. FAX (0941) 594101171. 🍴 b,l,d.
Rooms 54. ⓄⓄ

RIEDENBURG

Schloss Eggersberg This solid 15th-century castle combines warm welcome, stylish interiors and fabulous sporting opportunities: guests can boat, fish and bicycle on the vast estate, and there's even stabling for horses. There is good skiing too. Bedrooms do not disappoint. Accomplished international cooking. There is also a theatre in the granary.
⊠ 93339 Riedenburg. **Map** p149 E3. 📞 (09442) 91870. **FAX** (09442) 918787. 🍴 b,l,d. **Rooms** 15. 🅸
● Christmas, Jan, Feb. 🅰 AE, DC, MC, V. 🆂🆂

ROTHENBURG OB DER TAUBER

Kloster-Stüble This 16th-century inn is tucked away from the crowds in a side street off the marketplace. It's a traditional place, peaceful and cool. The delightful dining room has French windows out onto the terrace. Bedrooms at the back have views of the wooded Tauber valley.
⊠ 91541 Rothenburg ob der Tauber, Heringsbronnengasse 5. **Map** p149 D2.
📞 **FAX** (09861) 6774. 🅰 Hotel@klosterstueble. rothenburg.de 🍴 b,l,d. **Rooms** 20. ● restaurant only, Jan and Feb. 🅰 V. 🆂🆂

ROTHENBURG OB DER TAUBER

Burg-Hotel The severe exterior of this little hotel, set in old monastery grounds on the edge of the medieval town, hides a stylish little hotel with plush furnishings. The terrace is set into the city walls – views are stunning. Some of the bedrooms are really quite large: try to get one with views of the Tauber river.
⊠ 91541 Rothenburg ob der Tauber, Klostergasse 3. **Map** p149 D2. 📞 (09861) 94890. **FAX** (09861) 948940. [1 🅰 Burghotel.rothenburg@t-online.de 🍴 b. **Rooms** 15.
● Never. 🅰 AE, DC, MC, V. 🆂🆂🆂

ROTHENBURG OB DER TAUBER

Hotel Markusturm The core of this central hotel is a 12th-century building, once the town's customs house, and the place became an inn in 1488. The traditional interior features lots of dried flowers and knick-knacks. The chef is a keen mushroom hunter; other specialities include game, and fish from the hotel's ponds.
⊠ 91541 Rothenburg ob der Tauber, Rödergasse 1. **Map** p149 D2. 📞 (09861) 94280. **FAX** (09861) 2692. 🅰 markusturm@t-online.de 🍴 b,l,d. **Rooms** 28.
● Never. 🅰 AE, DC, MC, V. 🆂🆂🆂

RIELASINGEN
Zur Alten Mühle Pretty little rustic inn, formerly a mill. Imaginative food from the split-level bar/ dining room; charming terrace for outside eating.
⊠ 78239 Rielasingen, Singener Str 3. **Map** p148 C4.
📞 (07731) 52055. **FAX** (07731) 52057. 🍴 b,l,d.
Rooms 6. 🆂

ROTHENBURG OB DER TAUBER
Hotel Baren Plushy and stylish, in a quiet side street – unusual in this busy tourist town. Very good modern cooking.
⊠ 91541 Rothenburg ob der Tauber, Hofbronnengasse 9.
Map p149 D2. 📞 (09861) 94410. **FAX** (09861) 944160.
🍴 b,d. **Rooms** 35. 🆂🆂🆂

ROTHENBURG OB DER TAUBER
Eisenhut This charming hotel in the heart of the medieval town dates from the 15th century. Comfortable, with an historic atmosphere.
⊠ 91541 Rothenburg ob der Tauber, Herrngasse 3-7.
Map p149 D2. 📞 (09861) 7050. **FAX** (09861) 70545.
🅰 hotel@eisenhut.com 🍴 b,l,d. **Rooms** 79. 🆂🆂🆂

ROTHENBURG OB DER TAUBER
Hotel Reichs-Küchenmeister A 14th-century inn in the centre of the old town.
⊠ 91541 Rothenburg ob der Tauber, Kirchpl 8-10.
Map p149 D2. 📞 (09861) 9700. **FAX** (09861) 86965.
🅰 hotel@reichskuechmeister.com 🍴 b,l,d.
Rooms 50. 🆂🆂🆂

For key to symbols see backflap. For price categories *see p147*

ROTTWEIL

SEEBRUCK

Haus zum Sternen Rottweil is one of Germany's oldest fortified towns; this 14th-century building is one of the town's oldest. The welcoming hotel has a marvellously historic atmosphere, with beamed ceilings and antique furniture beautifully set off by plain carpets and white walls. Choice of regional food or modern German.
☒ 78628 Rottweil, Hauptstr 60. **Map** p148 C4.
☏ (0741) 53300. FAX (0741) 533030.
@ sternen@romantik.de 🛏 b,l,d. **Rooms** 12.
🌶 ● Never. 🅰 AE, MC, V. ⓄⓄ

Malerwinkel A lakeside position overlooking the Chiemsee, with stunning views to the Alps beyond, and the warmth of the welcome, make the Malerwinkel a real gem. First-rate food is served from the dining room, which in summer opens out to the terrace and hotel jetty. Bedrooms are tastefully furnished; the best have views of the lake. Friendly staff.
☒ 83358 Seebruck, Lambach 23. **Map** p149 E4.
☏ (08667) 88800. FAX (08667) 888044. 🛏 b,l,d.
Rooms 20. ● Never. 🅱 🅰 MC. ⓄⓄ

SCHÖNWALD

TIEFENBRONN

Hotel Dorer This charming little place, deep in the Black Forest, is untypical of the rural inns of the area both in its restrained decor and its imaginative cuisine. Most of the uncluttered bedrooms have a balcony or shared terrace. Look out for the amazing ancient gramophone on the first floor. Solarium, indoor pool, tennis court.
☒ 78137 Schönwald, Franz-Schubertstr 20.
Map p148 B4. ☏ (07722) 95050. FAX (07722) 950530.
@ hotel-dorer-schoenwald@t-online.de 🛏 b,l,d.
Rooms 15. 🎴 🅱 ● Never. 🅰 AE, DC, MC, V. ⓄⓄ

Ochsen Post The village inn looks the image of a traditional establishment, with its half-timbered façade and lush flower-boxes; inside, the Michelin-starred restaurant is noted for its *nouvelle cuisine* with a regional slant. Some of the bedrooms feature timbered walls, some are plainer, but all have luxurious bathrooms.
☒ 75333 Tiefenbroon, Franz-Josef-Gall-Str.
Map p148 C3. ☏ (07234) 8030.
FAX (07234) 9545145. 🛏 b,l,d. **Rooms** 19. ● Never.
🅰 AE, DC, MC, V. ⓄⓄ

SCHÖNWALD
Hotel zum Ochsen Good food and comfortable bedrooms in the Black Forest country.
☒ 78141 Schönwald, Ludwig-Uhland-Str 18.
Map p148 B4. ☏ (07722) 1045. FAX (07722) 3018.
@ ringhotel@ochsen.com 🛏 b,l,d.
Rooms 33. ⓄⓄⓄ

UHLDINGEN-MÜHLHOFEN
Hotel Fischerhaus Picture-postcard hotel by Lake Constance, with its own private beach.
☒ 88690 Uhldingen-Mühlhofen 1, Seefelden am Bodensee. **Map** p148 C4. ☏ (07556) 8563. FAX (07556) 6063. @ fischerhaus.seefeldon@t-online.de 🛏 b,l,d.
Rooms 27. ⓄⓄⓄ

WALLGAU
Parkhotel Wallgau Richly ornate public rooms, plainer bedrooms (some with balconies). Terrace, large garden, indoor pool.
☒ 82499 Wallgau, Barmseestr 1. **Map** p149 D4.
☏ (08825) 290. FAX (08825) 366. 🛏 b,l,d.
Rooms 52. ⓄⓄⓄ

WANGEN IM ALLGÄU
Hotel Alte Post Stylishly furnished, central inn with countrified bedrooms. Same ownership as more opulent Hotel Postvilla nearby.
☒ 88239 Wangen im Allgäu, Postpl 2. **Map** p148 C4.
☏ (07522) 97560. FAX (07522) 22604.
@ altepost@t-online.de 🛏 b,l,d. **Rooms** 30. ⓄⓄ

TRIBERG IM SCHWARZWALD

Parkhotel Wehrle This country resort hotel has been run by the same family for hundreds of years, and despite the renowned food and luxurious fittings it is a relaxed place. It is furnished in traditional style, with several further buildings dotted around the landscaped garden. Indoor and outdoor heated pools.

⊠ 78094 Triberg im Schwarzwald, Gartenstr 24. **Map** p148 B4. 🄲 (07722) 86020. 𝐅𝐀𝐗 (07722) 860290. @ Parkhotel.Wehrle@t-online.de 🍽 b,l,d. **Rooms** 56. 🎿 🎤 🟢 Never. 🎫 AE, DC, MC, V. ⓓⓜⓓⓜ

VOLKACH

Zur Schwane The courtyard restaurant makes a charming entrance to this family-run inn (founded 1404). Inside are two further dining rooms. The area is one of vine-covered hills, and the Pfaff family produce award-winning wines from their own vineyards. The imaginative food has a regional slant. The bedrooms are well equipped.

⊠ 97332 Volkach, Haupstrasse 12. **Map** p149 D2. 🄲 (09381) 80660. 𝐅𝐀𝐗 (09381) 806666. @ schwane@romantik.de 🍽 b,l,d. **Rooms** 29. 🟢 early Feb; Mon (restaurant only). 🎫 AE, DC, MC, V. ⓓⓜⓓⓜ

ÜBERLINGEN-ANDELSHOFEN

Johanniter Kreuz It started as a village guest house in the early 1900s; the black-and-white timbered building still in the same family, but has matured into a comfortable and attractive inn. It's a cosy place, with agreeably plain rooms, a large garden and a pretty terrace used for dining in the summer. Regional food, fish is the speciality.

⊠ 88662 Überlingen-Andelshofen, Johanniterweg 11. **Map** p148 C4. 🄲 (07551) 61091. 𝐅𝐀𝐗 (07551) 67336. @ johanniter-kreuz@romantik.de 🍽 b,l,d. **Rooms** 25. 🎤 🟢 Never. 🎫 AE, DC, MC, V. ⓓⓜⓓⓜ

WERTHEIM-BETTINGEN

Schweizer Stuben This country hotel in the Main valley was a single hotel-restaurant building in 1971; it's now a cluster of buildings set in a park. Facilities include pool and tennis courts; bicycles are available. Accommodation ranges from rooms and suites to apartments. Three fine restaurants: French, Italian and Swiss.

⊠ 97877 Wertheim-Bettingen, Geiselbrunnweg 11. **Map** p148 C2. 🄲 (09342) 3070. 𝐅𝐀𝐗 (09342) 307155. @ stuben@relaischateaux.fr 🍽 b,l,d. **Rooms** 33. 🎿 🍽 🎤 🟢 Never. 🎫 AE, DC, MC, V. ⓓⓜⓓⓜⓓⓜ

WEIL-HALTINGEN

Zum Hirschen Good value for money: a simple, family-run village inn with understated stylish rooms; charming garden for summer eating.

⊠ 75976 Weil-Haltingen, Grosse Gass 1. **Map** p148 B4. 🄲 (07621) 9407860. 𝐅𝐀𝐗 (07621) 9407880. 🍽 b,l,d. **Rooms** 9. ⓓⓜⓓⓜ

WEINGARTEN

Walk'sches Haus Rustic inn whose owner Dietmar Rüenbaker is a keen cook. The dining rooms are carved and panelled; plainer bedooms.

⊠ 76356 Weingarten, Marktplatz 7. **Map** p148 B3. 🄲 (07244) 70370. 𝐅𝐀𝐗 (07244) 703740. 🍽 b,l,d. **Rooms** 14. ⓓⓜⓓⓜ

WEITENBURG

Schloss Weitenburg Historic castle with stunning location above the Neckar river. Rooms are in keeping. Sporting facilities include indoor pool, riding school and 18-hole golf course.

⊠ 72181 Weitenburg. **Map** p148 C3. 🄲 (07457) 9330. 𝐅𝐀𝐗 (07457) 933100. 🍽 b,l,d. **Rooms** 34. ⓓⓜⓓⓜⓓⓜ

WIRSBERG

Posthotel Attractive village hotel with a superb indoor pool and lovely gardens.

⊠ 95339 Wirsberg, Marktplatz 11. **Map** p149 E1. 🄲 (09227) 2080. 𝐅𝐀𝐗 (09227) 5860. @ posthotelwirsberg@t-online.de 🍽 b,l,d. **Rooms** 44. ⓓⓜⓓⓜⓓⓜ

For key to symbols see backflap. For price categories see p147

CENTRAL GERMANY

RHINE VALLEY • HESSE AND THURINGIA • SAXONY
SAXONY-ANHALT • BERLIN • BRANDENBURG

THERE'S SOMETHING to suit all tastes and budgets in Central Germany: from simple country inns and smart townhouse hostelries, to log cabin-style hunting lodges, mountain chalets, lakeside villas, converted water mills, monasteries and fanciful fairytale castles. What's more, the region's scenery is as diverse as its accommodation. This section covers the popular wine-growing Rhine Valley region in the west, through Hesse and Thuringia (often called the 'green heart' of Germany) to Berlin, the flat lake-lands of Brandenburg, and Saxony. The latter, the most densely populated region of eastern Germany, is divided from the Czech Republic by the delightful, little-known Erzgebirge mountains.

ATTENDORN

Burg Schnellenberg High on a hill, deep in the forest, is this dramatic castle dating from the 13th century, complete with its own chapel. It is lavishly done up without being intimidating, and has a cosy bar and a peaceful garden to lounge around in. Some of the bedrooms are huge, with stunning views over the woods.
⊠ 57439 Attendorn. **Map** p150 B5. **C** (02722) 6940.
FAX (02722) 694169. **⑪** b,l,d. **Rooms** 42.
⑧ ● Christmas and three weeks Jan.
⊘ AE, DC, MC, V. ⓂⓂⓂ

BAD NEUENAHR-HEPPINGEN

Zur Alten Post The epitome of a restaurant with rooms – or rather two adjoining restaurants. Choose between Hans-Stefan Steinheuer's impressive new German cooking and a range of 400 wines, or more traditional regional dishes in an informal setting. Very modern bedrooms with up-to-the-minute bathrooms.
⊠ 53474 Bad Neuenahr-Heppingen,
Landskronerstr 110. **Map** p148 A1, p150 A5.
C (02641) 94860. **FAX** (02641) 948610. **⑪** b,l,d.
Rooms 10. **●** Never. **⊘** AE, DC, MC, V. ⓂⓂⓂ

BACHARACH
Altkölnischer Hof This family-run town inn dates from the 11th century, and has a large restaurant and cosy bar.
⊠ 55422 Bacharach, Am Marktpl. **Map** p148 B2.
C (06743) 1339. **FAX** (06743) 2793.
@ tscherba@sparkasfe.net **⑪** b,l,d. **Rooms** 19. ⓂⓂ

BAD HERSFELD
Zum Stern A delightful, flower-decked hotel and restaurant in the marketplace of this spa town. Swimming pool and sauna.
⊠ 36251 Bad Hersfeld, Linggpl 11. **Map** p148 C1, p150 C5. **C** (06621) 1890. **FAX** (06621) 189260.
@ zum-stern@romantik.de **⑪** b,l,d. **Rooms** 45 ⓂⓂⓂ

BAD KARLSHAFEN
Haus Schöneck Understated elegance at this late-19th-century villa, surrounded by tree-shaded terraces and rolling grounds. Indoor pool.
⊠ 34381 Bad Karlshafen, C D Stunweg 10.
Map p150 C4. **C** (05672) 925010. **FAX** (05672) 925011.
⑪ b. **Rooms** 18. ⓂⓂ

BAD LAASPHE-GLASHÜTTE
Jaghof Glashütte A wonderfully comfortable, family-run former hunting lodge with an amazing swimming pool built into the rock.
⊠ 57334 Bad Laasphe-Glashütte, Glashütter Str. 20.
Map p148 B1, p150 B5. **C** (02754) 3990. **FAX** (02754)
399222. **⑪** b,l,d. **Rooms** 29. ⓂⓂⓂ

BERGISCH GLADBACH

Schlosshotel Lerbach This is a place for spoiling yourself – a truly luxurious manor house hotel, set in its own beautiful park with a fishing lake, tennis courts and pool. Chef Dieter Muller's cooking is Michelin-starred, and the wine list is excellent. Bedrooms are richly furnished; some have four-poster beds. Pretty terrace and cosy bar.
☒ 51465 Bergisch Gladbach, Lerbacher Weg.
Map p150 A5. ☎ (02202) 2040. FAX (02202) 204940.
@ Lerbach@t-online.de ⏰ b,l,d. **Rooms** 54.
🏊 🍴 🎿 ⬤ Never. 💳 AE, DC, MC, V. (DM)(DM)(DM)(DM)

BERLIN

Brandenburger Hof Wonderfully central yet tranquil, this historic hotel has been luxuriously decorated with a successful mix of old and modern styles. The bedrooms are lavish and designed in the Bauhaus style. There is a large conservatory with a Japanese garden, and a courtyard. The restaurant is Michelin-starred.
☒ 10789 Berlin, Eislebener Str. 14. **Map** p151 F3.
☎ (030) 214050. FAX (030) 21405100.
@ info@brandenberger-hof.com. ⏰ b,l,d.
Rooms 82. ⬤ Never. 💳 AE, MC, DC, V. (DM)(DM)(DM)(DM)

BERNKASTEL-KUES

Zur Post On the main riverside road of Bernkastel-Kues, one of the main tourist towns of the Mosel, is this cheerful, geranium-bedecked inn. The modest 19th-century building is one of the smartest hotels, with a busy restaurant; the warm welcome makes up for the slighty plain bedrooms. There are some family apartment-style rooms in the annexe next door.
☒ 54463 Bernkastel-Kues, Gestade 17. **Map** p148 A2.
☎ (06531) 96700. FAX (06531) 967050. ⏰ b,l,d.
Rooms 42. ⬤ Jan. 💳 AE, DC, MC, V. (DM)(DM)

BILLERBECK

Domschenke Hard by Billerbeck's cathedral, in the pedestrianized town centre, is this long-established inn – an expanded 17th-century building run by the Groll family for more than 130 years. Ancient beams in the bar and dining room, which specializes in Westphalian dishes. Bedrooms are neat, if not stylish.
☒ 48727 Billerbeck, Markt 6. **Map** p150 A4.
☎ (02543) 93200. FAX (02543) 932030.
@ domschenke@t-online.de ⏰ b,l,d. **Rooms** 25.
⬤ Never. 💳 AE, DC, MC, V. (DM)(DM)

BALDUINSTEIN
Zum Bären Ambitious food in the two marvellous dining rooms, cooked by Walter Buggle whose family have been here since 1827. .
☒ 65558 Balduinstein, Bahnhofstr. 24. **Map** p148 B1.
☎ (06432) 81091. FAX (06432) 83643. ⏰ b,l,d.
Rooms 10. (DM)(DM)

BEILSTEIN
Haus Lipmann In a delightful village, a simple guesthouse owned by the same family since 1795. Charming dining room; terrace with great views.
☒ 56814 Beilstein, Marktplatz 3. **Map** p148 B1.
☎ (02673) 1573. FAX (02673) 1521. ⏰ b,l,d.
Rooms 5. (DM)(DM)

BERGISH GLADBACH
Romantik Waldhotel Mangold Peaceful, family-run country hotel only a short drive from Cologne.
☒ 51429 Bergisch Gladbach-Bensberg, Am Milchborntal 39-43. **Map** p150 A5. ☎ (02204) 95550.
FAX (02204) 955560. @ mangold@waldhotel.de
⏰ b,d. **Rooms** 21. (DM)(DM)(DM)

BERGNEUSTADT
Rengser Mühle Delightful little restored mill, tucked away in lovely countryside. Traditional food; waffles and cakes in the garden.
☒ 51702 Bergneustadt, Niederrengse 4. **Map** p150 B5.
☎ (02763) 91450. FAX (02763) 914520. @ info@ rengser-muehle.de ⏰ b,l,d. **Rooms** 4. (DM)(DM)

For key to symbols see backflap. For price categories see p147

BONN

Schlosshotel Kommende Ramersdorf The castle this hotel is named after is now a museum; the hotel occupies the converted stable block. Downstairs are a snug bar and a stylish Italian restaurant, considered to be one of the best in the country. A collection of restored antiques furnishes the bedrooms; some are for sale.
⊠ 53227 Bonn, Oberkasseler Str 10. **Map** p148 A1, p150 A5. 【 (0228) 440734. ⅢAX (0228) 444400. Ⅱ b,l,d. **Rooms** 18. 🔌 ● 4 weeks July-Aug; 2 weeks Dec-Jan. 🛒 AE, MC, V. ⊙⊙

DAHLEM-KRONENBERG

Schlosshotel Das Burghaus Stunning views of the hilltop medieval village reward guests to this manor house hotel. It's a lived-in place, with the setting and the warm welcome making up for the homely rooms. Heavy antique furniture and old flagged floors dominate the ground floor. Dine to the smell of woodsmoke in the original kitchen, or in the high-ceilinged baronial hall.
⊠ 53949 Dahlem-Kronenburg, Burgbering 1-4. **Map** p148 A1. 【 (06557) 265. ⅢAX (06557) 1397. Ⅱ b,l,d. **Rooms** 13. ● Tue. 🛒 DC, MC, V. ⊙⊙

COCHEM

Alte Thorschenke Right in the centre of Cochem's old town, by the medieval city wall, is the 14th-century Alte Thorschenke. With its gables, towers and timbers, it has a truly historic ambiance. Bedrooms at the front have the most character – the Napoleon suite has a huge four-poster bed. Good regional fish and game dishes.
⊠ 56812 Cochem, Brückenstr 3. **Map** p148 A1. 【 (02671) 7059. ⅢAX (02671) 4202. @ altethorschenke@t-online.de Ⅱ b,l,d. **Rooms** 43. ● Jan to early Mar. 🛒 AE, DC, MC, V. ⊙⊙⊙

DARSCHEID/VULKANEIFEL

Kucher's Landhotel Run with great enthusiasm by the young Heidi and Martin Kucher, this hotel has a gourmet restaurant and lovely gardens and terrace to sit out on. The bedrooms are charming – some have four-poster beds – and the bathrooms are bright and modern. All in all, Kucher's represents excellent value for money. A good place for walks on the Eifel hills.
⊠ 54552 Darscheid/Vulkaneifel, Karl-Kaufmann-Str 2. **Map** p148 A1. 【 (06592) 629. ⅢAX (06592) 3677. Ⅱ b,l,d. **Rooms** 15. 🔌 ● Jan. 🛒 AE, MC. ⊙⊙

BERLIN

Forsthaus Paulsborn A strange but rather enchanting 19th-century hunting lodge in wooded park, suitably decorated with hunting trophies.
⊠ 14193 Berlin 33, Am Grunewaldsee. **Map** p151 F3. 【 (030) 8181910. ⅢAX (030) 81819150. Ⅱ b,l,d. **Rooms** 10. ⊙⊙⊙

BERLIN

Landhaus Schlachtensee A large, cool villa in an area of woods and lake, yet only a short underground train-ride from the centre.
⊠ 14163 Berlin, Bogotastr. 9. **Map** p151 F3. 【 (030) 8099470. ⅢAX (030) 80994747. @ hotel-landhaus-schlachtensee@t-online.de Ⅱ b. **Rooms** 19. ⊙⊙⊙

BERLIN

Hecker's Hotel Choose classic or modern design for your room at this chic hotel in the centre of town. Noted regional food in the restaurant.
⊠ 10623 Berlin 12, Grolmanstr. 35. **Map** p151 F3. 【 (030) 88900. ⅢAX (030) 8890260. @ info@heckers-hotel.com Ⅱ b,l,d. **Rooms** 72. ⊙⊙⊙

BERLIN

Hotel Residenz A superb dining room and first-rate bedrooms mark out this attractive large hotel, set on a quiet but central street.
⊠ 10719 Berlin, Meinekestr. 9. **Map** p151 F3. 【 (030) 884430. ⅢAX (030) 8824726. @ info@hotelresidenz.com Ⅱ b,l,d. **Rooms** 88. ⊙⊙⊙

DAUN

Kurfürstliches Amtshaus The manor house hotel boasts a bed that was slept in by more than 50 visiting heads of state when it was in the government residence in Bonn. The terrace has superb views over the village. Inside, rooms have all modern comforts, with a scattering of antiques. Italian-influenced cooking; good wine list.
✉ D-54550 Daun, Auf dem Burgberg. **Map** p148 A1.
🄲 (06592) 9250. FAX (06592) 925255. @ kurfuerstliches. amtshaus@t-online.de 🍴 b,l,d. **Rooms** 42. 🏊
● 2-3 weeks Jan. 🅱 DC, MC, V. ⓓⓜⓓⓜⓓⓜ

DORSTEN-LEMBECK

Schlosshotel Lembeck A magical 17th century castle, surrounded by a moat and with its own ravishing grounds – guests are welcome to explore the park. Meals can be eaten on the terrace, with its magnificent views, or in the huge cellar bar with its extraordinary domed ceiling. The bedrooms are vast and furnished with antique furniture; some have four-poster bed.
✉ 46286 Dorsten-Lembeck, Schloss 1. **Map** p150 A4.
🄲 (02369) 7213. FAX (02369) 77370. 🍴 b,l,d.
Rooms 10. ● Never. 🅱 AE, DC, MC, V. ⓓⓜⓓⓜⓓⓜ

DEIDESHEIM

Deidesheimer Hof This luxurious inn located in the centre of the village was a favourite with Chancellor Kohl. Choose between a smart gourmet restaurant, a less formal flowery terrace, and *weinstube* with regional food. The spacious bedrooms are decorated in a traditional style.
✉ 67146 Deidesheim, Am Marktplatz 1. **Map** p148 B2.
🄲 (06326) 96870. FAX (06326) 7685.
@ deidesheimer_Hof_Hotelbet.GmbH@t-online.de
🍴 b,l,d. **Rooms** 20. ● first week Jan.
🅱 AE, DC, MC, V. ⓓⓜⓓⓜⓓⓜ

DRESDEN

Bülow Residenz Located in the old part of Dresden, this beautiful Baroque house offers large lavish rooms and bathrooms, and an elegant but intimate restaurant with an impressive wine list. The cosy bar downstairs is a popular rendezvous. There is also a delightful courtyard for quiet drinks or quiet times.
✉ 01097 Dresden, Rähnitzgasse 19. **Map** p151 F5.
🄲 (0351) 80030. FAX (0351) 8003100.
@ info@buelow-residenz.de 🍴 b,l,d. **Rooms** 31.
● Never. 🅱 AE, DC, MC, V. ⓓⓜⓓⓜⓓⓜⓓⓜ

BIEBERTAL-KÖNIGSBERG

Berghof Reehmühle A delightful little hotel covered in creepers, with fantastic rural views. The bedrooms are charmingly rustic.
✉ 35444 Biebertal-Königsberg, Bergstr. 47.
Map p148 C1, p150 B5. 🄲 FAX (06446) 360. 🍴 b,l,d.
Rooms 8. ⓓⓜⓓⓜ

BOCHOLT-BARLO

Schloss Diepenbrock The twin-turreted castle, still a family home, houses four bedrooms. Restaurant and most bedrooms in modern house.
✉ 46397 Bocholt-Barlo, Schlossallee 5. **Map** p150 A4.
🄲 (02871) 21740. FAX (02871) 217433. 🍴 b,l,d.
Rooms 23. ⓓⓜⓓⓜⓓⓜ

BONN

Domicil A slick, modern hotel with lots of glass and chrome and minimalist decoration.
✉ 53111 Bonn, Thomas-Mann-Str. 24. **Map** p148 A1, p150 A5. 🄲 (0228) 729090. FAX (0228) 691207
@ info@domicil-bonn.bestwestern.de 🍴 b,l,d.
Rooms 42. ⓓⓜⓓⓜ

BONN

Kaiser Karl The smart town house hotel is conveniently situated for the airport. Bathrooms are opulent. Terrace; French bistro.
✉ 53119 Bonn, Vorgebirgsstrasse 56. **Map** p148 A1, p150 A5. 🄲 (0228) 650933. FAX (0228) 637899.
🍴 b,l,d. **Rooms** 42. ⓓⓜⓓⓜⓓⓜⓓⓜ

For key to symbols see backflap. For price categories *see p147*

ELTVILLE-HATTENHEIM

Zum Krug Eltville-Hattenheim is right in the middle of the wine-growing area of Rheingau, and this peaceful inn is ideal for serious wine drinkers. Rooms are comfy, but the real point of this place is the wine; the restaurant offers a four-course gourmet menu with a specially chosen glass of local wine to go with each.
☒ 65347 Eltville-Hattenheim, Hauptstr 34.
Map p148 B2. ☎ (06723) 99680. ☎ (06723) 996825.
🍴 b,l,d. **Rooms** 10. ● 20 Dec to 20 Jan; 10 days July.
🅫 AE, DC, MC, V. ⓂⓂ

ESSEN-KETTWIG

Schloss Hugenpoet There's nothing gloomy or claustrophobic about the interior of this striking moated castle, now a smart and luxurious hotel. The reception rooms are marvellously done out with great style and panache. The large bedrooms are lavishly decorated and furnished with antiques.
☒ 45219 Essen-Kettwig 18, August-Thyssen-Str 51.
Map p150 A4. ☎ (02054) 12040. 𝔽𝔸𝕏 (02054) 120450.
@ hugenpoet@relaischateaux.fr 🍴 b,l,d. **Rooms** 25. 🛈
● Christmas, one week Jan. 🅫 DC, MC, V. ⓂⓂⓂⓂ

ESSEN-KETTWIG

Residence Guests are cossetted at this (extremely pricey) Michelin-starred restaurant with rooms. The efficiently run white villa, surrounded by its leafy landscaped garden, is hidden away in a quiet suburb. The bedrooms are small but chic. Book well ahead
☒ 45219 Essen-Kettwig, Auf der Forst 1.
Map p150 A4. ☎ (02054) 95590. 𝔽𝔸𝕏 (02054) 82501.
@ info@hotel-residence.de 🍴 b,d. **Rooms** 18.
🛈 ● 1 week Jan, 3 weeks July-Aug.
🅫 DC, MC, V. ⓂⓂⓂ

FRANKFURT AM MAIN

Hotel Westend The great bonus in this peaceful haven, close to the centre of Frankfurt, is its delightful walled garden. The 18th-century building is beautifully preserved, with some wonderful furniture and oil paintings, and retains the feel of a private house. Cosy bedrooms. Cold snacks are offered in the evening.
☒ 60325 Frankfurt 1, Westendstr 15. **Map** p148 C2.
☎ (069) 746702. 𝔽𝔸𝕏 (069) 745396. 🍴 b.
Rooms 20. 🛈 ● Christmas to New Year.
🅫 AE, DC, MC, V. ⓂⓂⓂ

BORKEN/RHEDEBRUGGE
Grüneklee An attractive little village inn with nice food (served on the garden terrace in fine weather) and comfortable, rustic rooms.
☒ 46325 Borken 1/Rhedebrugge, Rhedebrugger Str 16.
Map p150 A4. ☎ (02872) 1818. 𝔽𝔸𝕏 (02872) 2716.
🍴 b,d. **Rooms** 5. ⓂⓂ

BRAUBACH
Zum Weissen Schwanen Half-timbered old inn right by the town walls, with lively public rooms. The best bedrooms are in the old watermill.
☒ 56338 Braubach, Brunnenstr. 4. **Map** p148 B1.
☎ (02627) 9820. 𝔽𝔸𝕏 (02627) 8802. @ zum-weissen-schwanen@t-online.de 🍴 b,d. **Rooms** 16. ⓂⓂ

COCHEM
Weissmühle Secluded chalet-style hotel near the busy Mosel and Rhine valleys. The Alpine exterior hides thouroughly modern rooms.
☒ 56812 Cochem, Enderttal. **Map** p148 A1.
☎ (02671) 8955. 𝔽𝔸𝕏 (02671) 8207. @ weissmuehle-cochem@t-online.de 🍴 b,l,d. **Rooms** 36. ⓂⓂ

DETMOLD
Detmolder Hof Pleasant townhouse hotel on the main pedestrian street. Charming bar and bright bedrooms; attractive outdoor terrace.
☒ 32756 Detmold, Lange Strasse 19. **Map** p150 B4.
☎ (05231) 99120. 𝔽𝔸𝕏 (05231) 991299. @ DetmolderHof@t-online.de 🍴 b,l,d. **Rooms** 36. ⓂⓂⓂ

HAMM/SIEG

Hotel Alte Vogtei An ancient half-timbered hotel set in the middle of a small village, surrounded by woods. Beautifully preserved old furniture makes the most of the simple decor. Markus Wortelkamp, the son of the proprietors, has spent several years in France and England, and his excellent cuisine reflects this.
57577 Hamm/Sieg, Lindenalle 3. **Map** p148 B1, p150 B5. (02682) 259. FAX (02682) 8956.
@ alte-vogtei@romantik.de. b,l,d. **Rooms** 16.
Never. AE, DC, MC, V.

HERLESHAUSEN

Hotel Hohenhaus A quiet setting in wooded countryside, and proximity to the former East German border and E40 motorway, make this a very popular hotel. The building is not new, but the bright rooms have been thoughtfully designed in contemporary style; bedrooms retain a traditional feel. Imaginative food.
37293 Herleshausen 7, Holzhausen.
Map p150 C5. (05654) 680. FAX (05654) 1303.
@ hohenhaus@t-online.de b,l,d. **Rooms** 26.
Never. AE, MC, V.

HAMMINKELN-MARIENTHAL

Haus Elmer Efficiency and professionalism are the bywords at this hotel, situated in a village near the Dutch border. The best bedrooms are the new ones in one of the old buildings, with modern furniture and exposed beams. The popular restaurant serves hearty meals. Perfect cycling country – bikes are available for guests.
46499 Hamminkeln-Marienthal, An der Klosterkirche 12. **Map** p150 A4. (02856) 9110. FAX (02856) 91170.
@ hauselmer@romantik.de b,l,d. **Rooms** 31.
Never. DC, MC, V.

HOFGEISMAR

Dornroschenschloss Sababurg It's nicknamed 'Sleeping Beauty Castle'; visitors are greeted by Sleeping Beauty herself and can buy themed gifts. But don't be put off. It's a very romantic place, with fantastic views, and the hotel part of the castle has been beautifully furnished. Peaceful evenings, excellent food.
34369 Hofgeismar, Hofgeismar-Sababurg.
Map p150 C4. (05671) 8080. FAX (05671) 808200.
@ reception@sababurg.de b,l,d. **Rooms** 18.
Never. AE, DC, MC, V.

DORMAGEN

Hotel Hottche The town hotel has a guesthouse feel and similarly warm welcome. Excellent cuisine is served in the panelled dining rooms.
41539 Dormagen 1, Krefelder Str. 14-18.
Map p150 A5. (02133) 2530. FAX (02133) 10616.
b,l,d. **Rooms** 56.

DUDELDORF

Zum alten Brauhaus Beautifully decorated former brewery, with fine antiques and prints. Delightful bedrooms; outdoor terrace and garden.
54647 Dudeldorf, Herrengasse 2. **Map** p148 A2.
(06565) 92750. FAX (06565) 927555. @ brauhaus@ romantik.de. b,l,d. **Rooms** 15.

DÜSSELDORF-OBERKASSEL

Hotel Hanseat An elegantly furnished townhouse just across the Rhine from the city. Tasteful bedrooms; tranquil public rooms.
40545 Düsseldorf 11-Oberkassel, Belsenstr. 6.
Map p150 A5. (0211) 575069. FAX (0211) 589662.
b. **Rooms** 37

ELTVILLE-HATTENHEIM

Kronen Schlösschen In the cobbled town, with its own grounds. Bedrooms all differ and have plush bathrooms. Two popular restaurants.
65347 Eltville-Hattenheim, Rheinallee. **Map** p148 B2.
(06723) 640. FAX (06723) 7663. @ info@ kronenschloesschen.de b,l,d. **Rooms** 18.

HOLZAPPEL

Herrenhaus zum Bären This enchanting village inn, a lavishly timbered 17th-century building fronted by a tree-shaded terrace, was formerly the official residence of the Count of Holzappel. Inside, the mixture of furniture works well. The bedrooms are extremely comfortable, with marble-tiled bathrooms. The food is enterprising.
☒ 56379 Holzappel, Am Alten Markt 15.
Map p148 B1. 【 (06439) 91450. 𝗙𝗔𝗫 (06439) 914511.
@ herrenhaus.holzappel@t-online.de 𝗜𝗜 b,l,d.
Rooms 20. 🚲 ● Jan. 🅮 AE, DC, MC, V. ⓂⓂⓂ

HORBRUCH IM HUNSRÜCK

Historiche Schlossmühle Thick walls, a water wheel and stream are evidence of the building's original purpose as a mill. It is now a smart yet extremely hospitable hotel. Walls covered in books and paintings give the reception rooms a homely feel, and bedrooms are tastefully furnished. Excellent French-influenced food.
☒ 55483 Horbruch im Hunsrück. **Map** p148 B2.
【 (06543) 4041. 𝗙𝗔𝗫 (06543) 3178. @ historiche@ schlossmuehle.com 𝗜𝗜 b,d. **Rooms** 10. ● Never.
🅮 MC, V. ⓂⓂⓂ

ISSELBURG

Wasserburg Anholt One of central Germany's most impressive castles: the massive red-brick building seems to be floating on its lake. One part is open to the public; another has been converted into an attractive hotel. A highlight is the ground-floor café, with a terrace overlooking the water. The bedrooms are mainly unexceptional.
☒ 46419 Isselburg, Kleverstr 2. **Map** p150 A4.
【 (02874) 4590. 𝗙𝗔𝗫 (02874) 4035.
@ wasserburg-anholt@t-online.de 𝗜𝗜 b,l,d. **Rooms** 30.
🚲 ● 2 weeks Jan. 🅮 AE, DC, MC, V. ⓂⓂⓂ

KALLSTADT

Weinkastell 'Zum Weissen Ross' Modern refurbishment has not spoiled the ancient atmosphere of this eye-catching village hotel. At its heart is the pine-panelled *Stube*, used for breakfast and evening drinking, and an ambitious restaurant. The bedrooms are relatively plain; the honeymoon room has a huge four-poster bed.
☒ 67169 Kallstadt, an der Weinstr. 80-82. **Map** p148 B2.
【 (06322) 5033. 𝗙𝗔𝗫 (06322) 66091. 𝗜𝗜 b,l,d.
Rooms 13. ● 4 weeks Jan-Feb, 1 week July-Aug.
🅮 AE, MC. ⓂⓂ

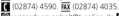

EMSTAL-SAND

Grischäfer A peaceful country guesthouse set in a collection of buildings, only a few miles from the busy town of Kassel.
☒ 34308 Bad Emstal, Kasseler Str. 27. **Map** p150 C5.
【 (05624) 354. 𝗙𝗔𝗫 (05624) 8778. 𝗜𝗜 b,l,d.
Rooms 17. ⓂⓂ

ESSEN

Parkhause Hügel Handsome hotel, originally a casino. Grand terrace with wonderful views on to the lake and the surrounding countryside.
☒ 45133 Essen 1, Freiherr-vom-Stein Str 209.
Map p150 A4. 【 (0201) 471091. 𝗙𝗔𝗫 (0201) 444207.
𝗜𝗜 b,l,d. **Rooms** 13. ⓂⓂ

FRANKFURT AM MAIN

Hotel Palmenhof A perfect refuge from the city with lavish bedrooms and a good restaurant.
☒ 60325 Frankfurt am Main 1, Bockenheimer Landstr. 89-91. **Map** p148 C2. 【 (069) 7530060. 𝗙𝗔𝗫 (069) 75300666. @ hotel.palmenhof@t-online.de 𝗜𝗜 b,l,d.
Rooms 46. ⓂⓂⓂ

HANAU

Hotel Birkenhoff Pretty villa in landscaped gardens, close to castle, church and restaurants.
☒ 63456 Hanau-Steinheim, von Eiff-Str. 37-41.
Map p148 C1. 【 (06181) 64880. 𝗙𝗔𝗫 (06181) 648839.
@ khfichtne@rhein-main.netsurf.de 𝗜𝗜 b,d.
Rooms 23. ⓂⓂ

KLEIN-BRIESEN

Parkhotel Juliushof The log-cabin-type former hunting lodge is deep in the pine woods, and is popular with outdoor types; hunting and fishing are available. But it's also an extremely civilized place to stay, with suites in the main building and double rooms in a separate cabin. This is not the best place for vegetarians – the menu is strong on wild boar, venison and local trout.
⊠ 14806 Klein-Briesen (Kreis Belzig). **Map** p151 E4.
📞 (033846) 40056. FAX (033846) 40245. 🍴 b,l,d.
Rooms 14. ⬤ Never. 🖃 AE, MC. ⓄⓄ

KRONBERG

Schlosshotel Kronberg This extraordinary place was built by a daughter of Queen Victoria. It is stuffed full of wonderful furniture and pictures and still has the atmosphere of a superb and friendly country house. Set in a splendid park it has a golf course and rose garden too. The food is excellent.
⊠ 61476 Kronberg, Hainstr 25. **Map** p148 B1.
📞 (06173) 70101. FAX (06173) 701267.
@ info@schlosshotel.de 🍴 b,l,d. **Rooms** 59. 🔋
⬤ Never. 🖃 AE, DC, MC, V. ⓄⓄⓄⓄ

KÖNIGSTEIN IM TAUNUS

Hotel Sonnenhof A former palace of the Rothschilds now makes a marvellously peaceful and quiet country house hotel, only 20 minutes' drive from Frankfurt. Inside are elegant public rooms and beautifully decorated bedrooms (some with balconies). Outside are a pretty terrace, vast grounds and some good walks. Fine food.
⊠ 61462 Königstein im Taunus, Falkensteinerstr 9.
Map p148 B1. 📞 (06174) 29080. FAX (06174) 290875.
🍴 b,l,d. **Rooms** 45. 🎪 🍽 🔋 ⬤ Never.
🖃 AE, DC, MC, V. ⓄⓄⓄ

LICH-KLOSTER ARNSBURG

Alte Klostermühle A mill, brewery and monastery once occupied the ancient buildings that make up this charming country hotel. Vast grounds and a welcoming beer garden continue to ensure a mix between seclusion and sociability. The bedrooms are large, with some beautiful antiques, and public rooms are inviting. Choice of several countrified dining rooms.
⊠ 35423 Lich-Kloster Arnsburg. **Map** p148 C1, p150 B5.
📞 (06404) 91900. FAX (06404) 919091. 🍴 b,l,d.
Rooms 25. 🔋 ⬤ Never. 🖃 AE, DC, MC, V. ⓄⓄⓄ

HEILIGENHAUS
Waldhotel This steep-roofed country hotel is furnished with taste and confidence in modern style. Attractive terrace looking out onto woods.
⊠ 42579 Heiligenhaus, Parkstr. 38. **Map** p148 B1, 150 A5.
📞 (02056) 5970. FAX (02056) 597260. @ waldhotel-heiligenhaus@t-online.de 🍴 b,l,d. **Rooms** 78. ⓄⓄⓄ

HEILIGENSTADT
Traube An inn with turrets and half-timbering, on the main road out of the town. Pristinely clean and good, plentiful food.
⊠ 91332 Heiligenstadt/Eichsfeld, Bahnhofstr. 2.
Map p150 C4. 📞 (03606) 612253. FAX (03606) 604509.
🍴 b,l,d. **Rooms** 11. Ⓞ

HESSEN
Schlosshotel Rettershof A sturdy Victorian building in the Taunus mountains. The public rooms are charming and some of the bedrooms are large and elegant.
⊠ 65779 Kelkheim. **Map** p151 D4. 📞 (06174) 29090.
FAX (06174) 25352. 🍴 b,l,d. **Rooms** 35. ⓄⓄⓄ

KAISERLAUTERN-HOHENECKEN
Burgschänke An attractive inn with a cheerful beer garden and cosy bar. Bedrooms are simple but chic, with good furniture and ornaments.
⊠ 67661 Kaiserlautern 32-Hohenecken, Schlossstr 1.
Map p148 B2. 📞 (0631) 56041. FAX (0631) 56301.
🍴 b,l,d. **Rooms** 15. ⓄⓄ

For key to symbols see backflap. For price categories see p147

MONSCHAU

Haus Vecqueray This tall, delicately timbered guesthouse with window boxes full of flowers, was built in 1716. The bedrooms, at the top of a spiral staircase, are delightful, with pretty rugs on the wood floors, antiques and views over the attractive old town. There is limited room to sit downstairs but you will get a substantial breakfast in cosy surroundings.

☒ 52156 Monschau, Kirchstr 5. **Map** p148 A1, p150 A5. 📞 (02472) 3179. 📠 (02472) 4320. 🍴 b. **Rooms** 13. ● Never. 🗐 DC, MC, V. ⃝

MÜNSTER-HANDORF

Hof zur Linde The Lofken family have run their ancient farmhouse as a hotel for several generations now, creating a sophisticated rural retreat. Inside, trophies and paintings reflect Otto Lofken's passion for hunting. Bedrooms range from country style through Victorian to modern. Beautifully served food in the rustic restaurant.

☒ 48175 Münster-Handorf, Am Handorfer Werseufer 1. **Map** p150 B4. 📞 (0251) 32750. 📠 (0251) 328209. @ hofzurlinde@t-online.de 🍴 b,l,d. **Rooms** 51. ● Never. 🗐 AE, DC, MC, V. ⃝⃝⃝

MÜNSTER

Schloss Wilkinghege A formal garden with a tiny private chapel is the introduction to this grand 18th-century moated mansion. Inside are a lofty hallway and spacious rooms with period furniture; those at the back have views of the moat and open countryside. Some bedrooms are in the old stables. Tennis, golf course.

☒ 48159 Münster, Steinfurter Str 374. **Map** p150 B4. 📞 (0251) 213045. 📠 (0251) 212898. @ schloss_wilkinghege@t-online.de 🍴 b,l,d. **Rooms** 34. 🔵 ● Christmas. 🗐 AE, DC, MC, V. ⃝⃝⃝⃝

OBERWESEL

Burghotel Auf Schönburg The ruins of an ancient castle high on a ridge above the Rhine shelter this newer Gothic building. Each room in this quirky hotel is different – some round, some tiny, some with magnificent views – but all blend comfort with romance. Good regional food and friendly service from the Huttl family.

☒ 55430 Oberwesel. **Map** p148 B1. 📞 (06744) 93930. 📠 (06744) 1613. @ huett@hotel-schoenburg.com 🍴 b,l,d. **Rooms** 22. ● Never. 🗐 AE, DC, MC, V. ⃝⃝⃝

KÖLN (COLOGNE)

Atrium A few miles from the city centre, this slick 'designer' hotel has a restrained colour scheme and elegant furniture.

☒ 50996 Köln, Karlstr. 2-10. **Map** p148 A1, p150 A5. 📞 (0221) 935720. 📠 (0221) 93572222. 🍴 b,l,d. **Rooms** 68. ⃝⃝⃝

KÖLN (COLOGNE)

Hotel Viktoria Chic villa hotel by the left bank of the Rhine (some of the rooms have views), with some effective Art Nouveau. Great breakfasts.

☒ 50668 Köln, Worringer Str 23. **Map** p148 A1, p150 A5. 📞 (0221) 9731720. 📠 (0221) 727067. @ hotel@hotelviktoria.com 🍴 b. **Rooms** 47. ⃝⃝⃝

LANDAU-BIRKWEILER

St Laurentius Hof A quaint little village inn with a charming vine-smothered courtyard and good country food, such as suckling pig.

☒ 768131 Landau-Birkweiler, Haupstr. 21. **Map** p148 B2. 📞 (06345) 8945. 📠 (06345) 8946. 🍴 b,l,d. **Rooms** 12.

LÜDINGHAUSEN

Hotel Borgmann An attractive little townhouse, run with great care by the Borgmann family. Rooms vary. Pretty terrace and hearty food.

☒ 59348 Lüdinghausen, Munsterstr. 17. **Map** p150 B4. 📞 (02591) 91810. 📠 (02591) 918130. 🍴 b,l,d. **Rooms** 7. ⃝⃝

OBERWESEL

Römerkrug This delightful 15th-century inn, right on the cobbled market square of this Rhine Valley village, has kept all its traditional charm. The interior has been very carefully renovated – in fact, much of it has been left well alone – and it is extremely cosy. Attractive little pavement terrace; heartily satisfying food. Nearby there are wine-tastings and boat trips.

⊠ 55430 Oberwesel, Marktpl 1. **Map** p148 B1.
📞 (06744) 7091. **FAX** (06744) 1677. 🍴 b,l,d. **Rooms** 7.
● 24 Dec, Jan. 🅴 AE, MC, V. ⓄⓄ

POTSDAM

Schloss Cecilienhof This castle was built as a retreat for the Crown Prince Wilhelm and his wife Cecilie in 1914, and now combines museum and public gardens with modern hotel. The interior retains its old elegance, with spacious rooms offering with stunning views over the English gardens, known locally as Neuer Garten.

⊠ 14469 Potsdam, Neuer Garten. **Map** p151 E3.
📞 (0331) 37050. **FAX** (0331) 292498.
@ cecilienhof@t-online.de 🍴 b,l,d. **Rooms** 42.
🔵 🎵 ● Never. 🅴 AE, DC, MC, V. ⓄⓄⓄ

PETERSHAGEN

Schloss Petershagen The riverside castle, built in the 14th century as a local stronghold, was transformed into a elegant hotel 25 years ago. Rooms are cool, peaceful and richly furnished, and the park invites relaxation. Choice of riverview restaurant offering imaginative modern dishes, or medieval room with traditional cuisine.

⊠ 32469 Petershagen 1, Schlosst 5-7. **Map** p150 C3.
📞 (05707) 93130. **FAX** (05707) 2373.
@ schloss-petershagen@t-online.de 🍴 b,l,d. **Rooms** 12.
🔀 🎵 ● Never. 🅴 DC, MC, V. ⓄⓄⓄ

SCHIEDER-SCHWALENBERG

Burghotel Schwalenberg This 13th-century fortress, perched up on a wooded hill above the town, is the real thing. Towers and turrets outside; inside, creaky corridors, suits of armour, boars' heads on the walls and huge old sofas. Bedrooms are spacious. Regional cookery from a modern extension with panoramic windows.

⊠ 32816 Schieder-Schwalenberg 2. **Map** p150 C4.
📞 (05284) 98000. **FAX** (05284) 980027.
@ schwalenberg@wesercastles.com 🍴 b,l,d.
Rooms 24. ● Jan, Feb. 🅴 DC, MC, V. ⓄⓄⓄ

MOERS-REPELEN

Welling Hotel zur Linde The old inn has a lively beer garden, several bars and dining rooms; a modern wing houses the large bedrooms.

⊠ 47445 Moers-Repelen, An der Linde 2. **Map** p150 A4.
📞 (02841) 9760. **FAX** (02841) 97666. @ info@hotel-zur-linde.de 🍴 b,l,d. **Rooms** 30. ⓄⓄⓄ

MONSCHAU

Burghotel Monschau Traditional townhouse in the centre of medieval Monschau, full of character and charm.

⊠ 52156 Monschau. **Map** p148 A1, p150 A5.
📞 **FAX** (02472) 2332. @ info@Burg-Hotel-Monschau.de
🍴 b,l,d. **Rooms** 13. Ⓞ

MÜNSTER-WOLBECK

Thier-Hülsmann This converted farmhouse has been decorated with panache: old beams contrast with bright colours. Modern rooms in annexe.

⊠ 48167 Münster-Wolbeck, Münsterstr. 33.
Map p150 B4. 📞 (02506) 83100. **FAX** (02506) 831035.
@ info@thier-huelsmann.de 🍴 b,l,d. **Rooms** 37. ⓄⓄ

ST GOAR

Landsknecht Beautifully positioned on the banks of the Rhine with valley views and charming terrace. Food hearty, bedrooms plush.

⊠ 56325 St Goar, Rheinuferstrasse. **Map** p148 B1.
📞 (06741) 2011. **FAX** (06741) 7499. @ landsknecht-st-goar@t-online.de 🍴 b,l,d. **Rooms** 14. ⓄⓄⓄ

For key to symbols see backflap. For price categories see p147

SPANGENBERG

Schloss Spangenberg Not only is this 13th-century converted castle wonderfully peaceful, but it also has stunning hilltop views, a moat and a drawbridge. The charming dining room looks out on to wooded hills; venison is one of the specialities. Of the characterful rooms, perhaps the best is the family apartment in the gatehouse.
⊠ 34286 Spangenberg. **Map** p150 C5.
📞 (05663) 866. 📠 (05663) 6174. @ hotel-schloss@t-online.de ⏶ b,l,d. **Rooms** 27. ● Christmas.
💳 AE, DC, MC, V. ⓂⓂⓂ

STROMBERG

Burghotel Stromberg A castle was first built here, at the heart of what is now the Nahe wine region, in the 11th century, but the present building is a 19th-century reconstruction. It makes a suitable backdrop to the fine food served in its two restaurants, one modern, one traditional. Lavish bedrooms include a suite in the tower.
⊠ 55442 Stromberg. **Map** p148 B2.
📞 (06724) 93100. 📠 (06724) 931090. @ johannlafer@germany.net ⏶ b,d. **Rooms** 14. ● Never.
💳 AE, DC, MC, V. ⓂⓂⓂ

STOLBERG

Altes Brauhaus Burgkeller A series of ancient riverside buildings, built around Stornber's oldest house (1594), make up this rambling inn. Despite modernization, many of the rooms retain great character; bedrooms are modern. The riverside terrace is a delight. Under the same ownership as the modern Parkhotel nearby.
⊠ 52222 Stolberg, Klatterstr 8-12. **Map** p150 A5.
📞 (02402) 27272. 📠 (02402) 27270.
@ burgkeller@romantik.de ⏶ b,l,d. **Rooms** 29.
● Few days in Feb (carnival). 💳 AE, DC, MC, V. ⓂⓂ

TRIER

Hotel Petrisberg Large picture windows make the most of this hillside hotel's views over the old city. It's a modern building, yet rooms are anything but anonymous: some have murals and painted ceilings, some are in Scandinavian style, all are cosy. There are larger suites in the small annexe. Evening meals can be arranged. It's a hard 20-minute walk back from town.
⊠ 54296 Trier, Sickingenstr. 11-13. **Map** p148 B2.
📞 (0651) 4640. 📠 (0651) 46450. ⏶ b.
Rooms 30. ● Never. 💳 Not accepted. ⓂⓂ

ST GOAR
Schlosshotel & Villa Rheinfels A comfortable, well-kept hotel with good food and wine.
⊠ 56329 St Goar, Schlossberg 47. **Map** p148 B1.
📞 (06741) 8020. 📠 (06741) 802802.
@ rheinfels.st.goar.@t-online.de ⏶ b,l,d.
Rooms 56. ⓂⓂⓂ

SCHMALLENBERG
Landhotel Gasthof Schutte A peaceful hotel with a wonderful swimming pool. Good food, smart rooms and sports facilities offered.
⊠ 57392 Schmallenberg-Oberkirchen. **Map** p150 B5.
📞 (02975) 820. 📠 (02975) 82522. @ Landhotel@schuette.sou.de ⏶ b,l,d. **Rooms** 59. ⓂⓂⓂ

SELM-CAPPENBERG
Kreutzkamp Traditional, brick-built country hotel with two lovely, old-fashioned dining rooms. Neat, functional bedrooms.
⊠ 59379 Selm-Cappenberg, Cappenberger Damm 3.
Map p150 A4. 📞 (02306) 750410. 📠 (02306) 7504110.
@ hotelkreutzkamp@t-online.de ⏶ b,l,d. **Rooms** 15. ⓂⓂ

TRIER
Villa Hügel The beautifully decorated early 1900s villa, in a leafy residential area close to the centre of town, has a rooftop terrace, indoor pool and solarium. Modern bedroom extension.
⊠ 54295 Trier, Bernhardstr. 14. **Map** p148 B2. 📞 (0651)
33066. 📠 (0651) 37958. ⏶ b. **Rooms** 34. ⓂⓂ

WALLERFANGEN

Villa Fayence For fine dining followed by a luxurious night, look no further than this elegant pink-washed villa. French influenced food is served in style, accompanied by a formidable wine list. In the winter guests consider the menu with a drink in the Baroque drawing room, in the summer in the conservatory by the park.

✉ 66798 Wallerfangen, Haupstr. 12. **Map** p148 A2.
📞 (06831) 96410. **FAX** (06831) 62068. 🍴 b,l,d.
Rooms 4. ● Mon (restaurant only).
💳 AE, DC, MC, V. ⑳⑳⑳

WESEL

Waldhotel Tannenhäuschen Very plush, with good antique and reproduction furniture, deep carpets and spacious rooms, this comfortable hotel is set in its own large, pleasant grounds. The bedrooms are generous, some with four-poster beds. There is a pretty terrace, indoor swimming pool and cosy bars. Delicious breakfasts, lavish food.

✉ 46487 Wesel, Am Tannenhäuschen 7. **Map** p150 A4.
📞 (0281) 96690. **FAX** (0281) 64153. 🍴 b,l,d.
Rooms 46. ● Never. 💳 AE, DC, MC, V. ⑳⑳⑳

WERNE

Baumhove The low, rough-beamed bar and dining room characterize this ancient house in the cobbled old town. The inn is divided into cosy sections, with a smarter gallery area reached by an open staircase. Dark corridors lead to rooms which are surprisingly modern; some overlook the marketplace. Good, hearty food.

✉ 59368 Werne, Markt 2. **Map** p150 B4. 📞 (02389) 989590. **FAX** (02389) 98959120.
@ hotelamkloster@baumhove.de 🍴 b,l,d. **Rooms** 17.
● Never. 💳 AE, DC, MC, V. ⑳⑳⑳

WIEDENBRÜCK

Ratskeller Wiedenbrück Right in the centre of the historic town of Wiedenbruck is this prettily timbered and decorated town inn, dating from 1560. It has been run by five generations of the Surmann family, who have done a fine restoration job of the panelled bar and the beamed dining room. Unfussy bedrooms.

✉ 33378 Rheda-Wiedenbrück, Lange Strasse am Markpl. **Map** p150 B4. 📞 (05242) 9210. **FAX** (05242) 921100.
@ ratskeller@romantik.de 🍴 b,l,d. **Rooms** 34.
● Christmas. 💳 AE, DC, MC, V. ⑳⑳⑳

WASSENBERG

Burg Wassenberg Ancient but sensitively modernized house with many original features.

✉ 41849 Wassenberg, Kirchstr 17. **Map** p150 A5.
📞 (02432) 9490. **FAX** (02432) 949100.
@ BurgWassenberg@t-online.de 🍴 b,l,d.
Rooms 28. ⑳⑳

WASSERLIESCH

Scheid Hubert Scheid's classical French cuisine (Michelin-starred) is the draw at this restaurant-with-rooms. Scheid's patisserie is in nearby Trier.

✉ 54332 Wasserliesch, Reinigerstr 48. **Map** p148 A2.
📞 (06501) 13958. **FAX** (06501) 13959. 🍴 b,l,d.
Rooms 13. ⑳

WILLINGEN

Stryckhaus The elegant country hotel in woodland setting is a wonderful place to relax by the pool. Good food and well-priced wines.

✉ 34508 Willingen. **Map** p150 B5. 📞 (05632) 9860.
FAX (05632) 69961. @ stryckhaus@t-online.de
🍴 b,l,d. **Rooms** 61. ⑳⑳

WINTERBERG

Berghotel Astenkrone A wonderfully plush country hotel. Superb swimming pool, golf.

✉ 59955 Winterberg-Altastenberg, Astenstr 24.
Map p150 B5. 📞 (02981) 8090. **FAX** (02981) 809198.
@ Astenkrone.winterberg@eurohotel.com 🍴 b,l,d.
Rooms 43 ⑳⑳⑳

NORTHERN GERMANY

LOWER SAXONY • THE NORTH COAST
NORTHEAST GERMANY

NORTHERN GERMANY, which stretches from Lower Saxony on the Dutch frontier to Mecklenburg-West Pomerania bordering Poland, offers a wide variety of scenery, from the windswept landscapes of pancake-flat Schleswig-Holstein in the north to the densely forested Harz Mountains in the south. Most of our entries are located in and around the major seaport of Hamburg, such as in the historic towns of Bremen, Hannover and Lübeck, and in popular seaside resorts, ideal for family holidays. There are also a few off-the-beaten-track addresses on the North Frisian islands of Sylt and Föhr, off the mainland in the North Sea, where you can find some of Europe's finest beaches.

ALT DUVENSTEDT

Töpferhaus Set in tranquil grounds close to the shores of the Bistensee, the Töpferhaus has wide views over the garden to the lake. The bedrooms are nicely furnished and modern, with marble-tiled bathrooms, and some have their own balcony or terrace. The simply decorated beamed restaurant serves international and regional food.
24791 Alt Duvenstedt, Am Bistensee.
Map p150 C1. (04338) 99710. **FAX** (04338) 997171.
info@toepferhaus.de b,l,d. **Rooms** 52. Never.
AE, DC, MC, V.

BAD DOBERAN

Kurhotel This pleasant and stylish establishment, facing the shady park in the middle of town, was built in the late 18th century as a guesthouse for the local duke. The uncluttered bedrooms are beautifully decorated in English country-house style, while the public rooms are classical Biedemeier with historical prints on the delicately painted walls. The food is on the heavy side.
18209 Bad Doberan, Am Kamp. **Map** p151 D2.
(038203) 63036. **FAX** (038203) 62126. b,l,d.
Rooms 60. Never. AE, MC, V.

AMRUM ISLAND
Ual Öömrang Wiartshüs A pretty, thatched hotel with a nautical flavour. It's not fancy, but is charmingly decorated and has a pretty garden.
25946 Nordseeheilbad Norddorf, Insel Amrum.
Map p150 B1. (04682) 836. **FAX** (04682) 1432.
b,l,d. **Rooms** 10.

BRAUNSCHWEIG
Ritter St Georg This city hotel has some lovely painted ceilings in the restaurant and bar. Plain but chic bedrooms, some quite large.
38100 Braunschweig, Alte Knochenhauerstr 12-13.
Map p151 D4. (0531) 13039. **FAX** (0531) 13038.
b,l,d. **Rooms** 22.

BÜSUM-DEICHHAUSEN
Der Rosenhof Near the sea. The Swiss owners have made this a chic and comfortable hotel, with sauna and beauty parlour.
25761 Büsum-Deichhausen, To Wurth 12.
Map p150 B1. (0171) 3803362. b,l,d.
Rooms 23.

FRIEDRICHSTADT
Holländische Stube A charming set of terraced houses on the canal, pleasantly decorated.
25840 Friedrichstadt, Am Mittelburgwall 24-26.
Map p150 C1. (04881) 93900. **FAX** (04881) 939022.
Klaus-Peter-Willhoeftt@t-online.de b,l,d.
Rooms 8.

BREMEN

Park Hotel Sheltered within a beautiful park, this sumptuous hotel provides the peace of the countryside combined with proximity to the town centre. The wonderful *trompe-l'oeil* ceiling in the hall and the Art Deco bar set the tone for the impeccable bedrooms. Breakfast by the lake; dine on French cuisine.
☒ 28209 Bremen, Im Bürgerpark.
Map p150 B3. ((0421) 34080. FAX (0421) 340 8602. @ relax@park-hotel-bremen.de ⅰ b,l,d. **Rooms** 149. 〰 ● Never. ⊜ AE, DC, MC, V. ⑩⑩⑩⑩

FÖHR ISLAND

Landhause Altes Pastorat A perfect place for rest and recuperation: away from the bustle of the small island's port, a long brick building dating from the 17th and 18th centuries, filled with flowers, antiques and books. Upstairs, bedroom windows poke through the thatch to look out over the lush garden.
☒ 25938 Insel Föhr, Süderende. **Map** 150 B1.
((04683) 4747. FAX (04681) 250.
@ ikn@inselfoehr.de ⅰ b. **Rooms** 5. ▯
● Oct to mid-March. ⊠ Not accepted. ⑩⑩⑩

CELLE

Utspann The former tannery makes a delightful little inn, tucked away by the north end of the city wall in the old part of the town, and is well located for sightseeing from the doorstep. Its 18 bedrooms have been imaginatively decorated in a lively rustic style, and all have baths. A cobbled courtyard and a wine cellar add to the charm.
☒ 29221 Celle, Im Kreise 13. **Map** p150 C3.
((05141) 92720. FAX (05141) 927252. ⅰ b,l,d.
Rooms 23. ● Never. ⊜ AC, DC, MC, V. ⑩⑩⑩

HAMBURG

Hotel Hanseatic The town villa feels more like a smart English club than a hotel. There is no sign outside; inside, each of the elegant and well-equipped bedrooms has a decanter of sherry. Home-made jams and a choice of 15 different teas, poured from silver teapots, are offered for breakfast. Close to the city centre and to the Alster ferry.
☒ 22299 Hamburg-Winterhude, Sierichstr. 150.
Map p150 C2. ((040) 485772. FAX (040) 485773.
ⅰ b. **Rooms** 13. ● Never. ⊠ Not accepted. ⑩⑩⑩

HAMBURG

Hotel Vier Jahreszeiten Stylish and quiet yet central; luxurious bedrooms, Art Deco restaurant, Euro-Asiatic restaurant and coffee house.
☒ 20354 Hamburg, Neuer Jungfernstieg 9-14. **Map** p150 C2. ((040) 34940. FAX (040) 34942600. @ vier-jahreszeiten@hvj.de ⅰ b,l,d. **Rooms** 158. ⑩⑩⑩⑩

HAMBURG

Hotel Wedina A pretty building in a quiet street close to the station. It is wonderfully spacious and airy, with terrific, bold interior design.
☒ 20099 Hamburg, Gurlittstrasse 23. **Map** p150 C2.
((040) 243011. FAX (040) 2803894.
@ wedina@aol.com ⅰ b. **Rooms** 28. ⑩⑩⑩

HERINGSDORF

Diana The late-19th-century villa offers gorgeous sea-views from rooms in the main house; plainer annexe bedrooms. Simply delicious breakfasts.
☒ 17424 Heringsdorf, Delbrückstr. 14. **Map** p151 F2.
((038378) 31952. FAX (038378) 31953. ⅰ b.
Rooms 10. ⑩⑩⑩

KÜHLUNGSBORN

Residenz Waldkrone In a lovely position by sea and sand, the Waldkrone has a fresh style that masks its origins as a works holiday home.
☒ 18225 Kühlungsborn, Tannestr 4. **Map** p148 A1.
((038293) 4000. FAX (038293) 40011 ⅰ b,l,d.
Rooms 21. ⑩⑩⑩

For key to symbols see backflap. For price categories see *p147*

HAMBURG

Strandhotel Blankanese The area is now a smart residential suburb, but when this delightful Art Nouveau hotel was built by the estuary of the Elbe in the early 1900s, the Blankensee area was a fishing village. The lovely bedrooms are furnished with antiques and modern art, and there is a beach terrace for peaceful drinks. Good food in the snug dining room.
✉ 22587 Hamburg 55, Strandweg 13. **Map** p150 C2.
((040) 861344. FAX (040) 864936. ⫟ b,l,d. **Rooms** 15.
● Christmas and New Year. ⊞ AE, DC, MC, V. ⓜⓜⓜ

HANNOVER

Landhaus Ammann A combination of country-house atmosphere and city convenience, and, to top it all, a Michelin-starred kitchen and superlative cellar. The first-class food can be enjoyed either in the stylishly decorated dining room or on the terrace, which looks onto the garden and woods. Spacious, sleek bedrooms.
✉ 30173 Hannover, Hildesheimer Str 185. **Map** 150 C3.
((0511) 830818. FAX (0511) 843 7749.
@ mail@landhaus-ammann.de ⫟ b,l,d. **Rooms** 14.
● Never. ⊞ AE, DC, MC, V. ⓜⓜⓜ

HANNOVER

Georgenhof The heart of this wonderfully peaceful place, close to the Herrenhausen Gardens, is its much-acclaimed restaurant. Food here is modern, unfussy and expensive, served in a simple, almost austere beamed room. The bedrooms are similarly uncluttered, with little touches of ornamentation. Outside are a pleasant terrace next to a pond with a fountain.
✉ 31067 Hannover 1, Herrenhauser Kirchweg 20.
Map 150 C3. ((0511) 702244. FAX (0511) 708559.
⫟ b,l,d. **Rooms** 14. ● Never. ⊞ AE, DC, MC, V. ⓜⓜⓜ

LÜBECK

Kaiserhof Two period mansions in a residential part of the city were lovingly renovated to produce this smart hotel. The beautifully decorated public rooms invite guests to linger. Bedrooms are spacious and stylish; many have their own balcony. There is also an attractive terrace and superb swimming pool.
✉ 23560 Lübeck, Kronsforder Allee 11.
Map p151 D2. ((0451) 703301.
FAX (0451) 795083. ⫟ b,l,d. **Rooms** 65.
⊞ ● Never. ⊞ Not accepted. ⓜⓜⓜ

MALENTE-GREMSMUHLEN
Weisser Hof A lovely garden with ponds surrounds this black-and-white hotel. The bedrooms are large and comfortable.
✉ 23714 Malente-Gremsmuhlen, Vosstr. 45.
Map p151 D1. ((04523) 99250. FAX (04523) 6899.
⫟ b,l,d. **Rooms** 18. ⓜⓜⓜ

MORAAS
Heidehof The popular thatched hotel has a peaceful setting next to the village pond. Wood-panelled *stube* for informal dining and drinking.
✉ 19230 Moraas, Hauptstr. 15. **Map** p151 D2.
((03883) 722140. FAX (03883) 729118. ⫟ b,l,d.
Rooms 11. ⓜⓜ

QUICKBORN
Jagdhaus Waldfrieden Hunting lodge-type villa in an enchanting park. Enterprising food. Hamburg is less than 30 minutes' drive away.
✉ 25451 Quickborn, Kieler Str. **Map** p150 C2.
((04106) 61020. FAX (04106) 69196. @ waldfrieden@ romantik.de ⫟ b,l,d. **Rooms** 24. ⓜⓜⓜ

RUGEN
Baumhaus The unassuming former woodcutter's lodge is situated on the edge of the Jasmund national park, and makes a pleasant place from which to investigate the local wildlife.
18551 Hagen auf Rugen. **Map** p151 F1.
(FAX (038392) 22310. ⫟ b. **Rooms** 8. ⓜ

NÖRTEN-HARDENBERG

Burghotel Hardenberg For some 300 years this long timbered building, set in woods on the edge of the village, has offered refreshment and shelter to visitors. Modern standards of comfort do not spoil the traditional atmosphere. Two popular restaurants: the Novalis with enterprising modern food, and the more traditional Bürgmuhlen.
⊠ 37176 Nörten-Hardenberg, Im Hinterhaus 11a. **Map** p150 C4. **(** (05503) 9810. ⅲ (05503) 981666. ⅲ b,l,d. **Rooms** 45. ● Never. ⅲ AE, DC, MC, V. ⓓⓓⓓ

SYLT ISLAND

Hamburger Hof With a ravishing location right next to the sea, there is plenty for the energetic to do here but it's also a great place to get away from it all. The pretty little hotel is light and airy throughout. The bedrooms are unfussy and beautifully decorated in creams and pastel shades, and have first-rate modern bathrooms. Light lunches can be arranged. Evening bar.
⊠ 25999 Kampen-Sylt, Kurhausstr 3. **Map** p150 B1. **(** (04651) 94600. ⅲ (04651) 43975. ⅲ b. **Rooms** 15. ● Never. ⅲ Not accepted. ⓓⓓ

SYLT ISLAND

Benen-Diken-Hof One of the smarter hotels on the island, this solid thatched house dates from 1841, with a very clever extension added in the 1980s. Inside, it is a plain but striking mix of antiques and modern furniture, with flower arrangements and paintings dotted about. Bedrooms are bright and uncluttered.
⊠ 25980 Keitum-Sylt, Süderstr 3. **Map** p150 B1. **(** (04651) 93830. ⅲ (04651) 938383. @ benen-diken-hof-sylt@t-online.de ⅲ b; d for guests only. **Rooms** 37. ⅲ Never. ⅲ AE, DC, V. ⓓⓓⓓ

WALSRODE

Landhaus Walsrode A tranquil stopover for travellers along the nearby motorways. Set in its own parkland, the 400-year-old farmhouse has been tastefully decorated to create an elegant guesthouse. In the evenings, drinks are served in the large drawing room or cosy reading room. A simple evening meal can be provided.
⊠ 29664 Walsrode, Oskar-Wolff-Str 1. **Map** p150 C3. **(** (05161) 98690. ⅲ (05161) 2352. @ LandhausWa@aol.com ⅲ b. **Rooms** 19. ⅲ mid-Dec to mid-Jan. ⅲ AE, MC. ⓓⓓ

SALZHAUSEN

Josthof A totally unmodernized farmhouse hotel: warm welcome, hearty meals and impressive wine list. Some of the bedrooms are very large.
⊠ 21376 Salzhausen, Am Lindenberg 1. **Map** p150 C2. **(** (04172) 90980. ⅲ (04172) 6225. @ josthof@romantik.de ⅲ b,l,d. **Rooms** 16. ⓓⓓ

SYLT ISLAND

Jörg Müller Attached to a very pretty tiled gourmet restaurant, seven beautifully decorated rooms with much attention paid to detail.
⊠ 25980 Westerland/Sylt, Süderstrasse 8. **Map** p150 B1. **(** (04651) 27788. ⅲ (04651) 201471. ⅲ b,l,d. **Rooms** 7. ⓓⓓⓓ

USLAR

Menzhausen Attractive 16th-century building with modern annexe opposite. Lovely dining room with regional food and good wine list.
⊠ 37170 Uslar, Lange Str 12. **Map** p150 C4. **(** (05571) 2051. ⅲ (05571) 92230. @ menzhausen@romantik.de ⅲ b,l,d. **Rooms** 40. ⓓⓓ

WORPSWEDE

Eichenhof In the middle of the town but surprisingly rural, with ponds, fields and trees. Pristine bright bedrooms and breakfast rooms.
⊠ 27726 Worpswede, Ostendorfer Str 13. **Map** p150 B2. **(** (04792) 2676. ⅲ (04792) 4427. ⅲ b. **Rooms** 18. ⓓⓓ

For key to symbols see backflap. For price categories see *p147*

AUSTRIA

AUSTRIA

For visitors to Austria, one of the most striking things about the country is the sheer number of small hotels which have been run by the same family for generations: a fact reflected in the warm welcome and friendly atmosphere you encounter in so many of our entries. The hotels are as diverse as the countryside and you can find something to suit every taste; establishments range from simple mountain inns and smart winter sports hotels to lakeside hostelries, plush city-centre hotels and imposing castles. The heart of most Austrian lodgings is the *Stube*, a room which is usually wood-panelled, with huge tables and bench seats and warmed by a stove – an informal setting for a drink and a chat.

Hotel Spielmann, Ehrwald, page 191, a text-book Tyrolean chalet

AUSTRIA REGION BY REGION

Austria is not a large country, but it divides neatly into five regions:

Western Austria
This comprises the states of Vorarlberg, Tyrol and Salzburgland. Vorarlberg is the classic Alpine province, practically cut off from the rest of the country by the Arlberg mountains. As you would expect, it has fine skiing hotels, but they brush shoulders with delightful family-run inns.

The Tyrol, with its dramatic mountains and picture-postcard villages, has many a country hotel set amidst breathtaking lake or mountain scenery.

Some of the simpler hotels may strike you as surprisingly inexpensive for such a sought-after area.

Historic Salzburgland has some charming town hotels, with marvellous lakes and mountains within easy reach.

Northwestern Austria
Known as Oberösterreich, this is the home of the dumpling. It has a varied landscape, with mountains, lush valleys and lakes, and has some very attractive hotels in its medieval towns as well as some lovely country ones.

Northeastern Austria
Known as Niederösterreich, this includes Vienna, the capital of Austria. There are some lovely hotels in the famous Vienna woods – still popular with the Viennese for a day out – and a wide variety of inns and castle hotels. Vienna itself has plenty of smart hotels, but there is no shortage of less expensive *pensions* either. Obviously, any establishment outside the city centre (the area bounded by the Ringstrasse) will be cheaper.

Eastern Austria
Burgenland is the least typical state in the country – it was part of Hungary until 1921. It has a pleasantly mild climate, suitable for vines and fruit trees, which you will see in abundance.

Accommodation here is cheaper and simpler than in the rest of Austria. Goose with red cabbage is the ubiquitous (and filling) local dish.

Southern Austria
Kärnten is a popular tourist region and the hotels are of a particularly high standard. The Tauern mountains and clean, warm lowland lakes provide plenty of outdoor life.

Steiermark, the second largest state, has diverse country with fine skiing on the Dachstein range, gentle vine-covered hills in the south, and flat plains in the east. There are lakeside and castle hotels, and many attractive small inns.

HIGHLIGHTS

HOTELS ILLUSTRATED on these introductory pages are by no means the only highlights. Other favourites include the Parkhotel Tristachersee, set on a secluded lake (page 195); the Hotel König von Ungarn, right in the centre of Vienna (page 197); and Deuring Schlössle (page 191), in a breathtaking 17th-century castle with fine views over Lake Constance.

FOOD AND DRINK

AUSTRIA SHARES borders with six countries, so the food has many interesting influences and variations – rich pasta dishes from Italy, goulash from Hungary and dumplings from Bohemia – but, on the whole, it is dominated by meat. Don't overlook the renowned *Wiener Schnitzel* (an escalope of veal in breadcrumbs) and, of course, the wonderful cakes and pastries, many topped with cream.

Increasingly, however, you'll find places to stay where there is an emphasis on healthy eating. '*Bio*' signs indicate the use of wholefood or organic products, while '*Bio* rooms' are furnished in natural materials.

Austrian-grown wine is mainly white – there are approximately 40,000 hectares (98,850 acres) of vineyards. There are some notable dry whites. Try also the intense, fruity Rieslings from the Wachau region and the attractive sweet wine of the Neusiedlersee region.

The beer is excellent, with each region producing its own brew. Obviously there are huge regional differences and it is wise to go for the local speciality – Stiegl Bier in Salzburg and Gösser Bier from Steiermark, for instance.

The Austrians treat lunch, usually starting at about 12:30pm, as their main meal: they'll eat their way through soup, a main course, and dessert. Supper or dinner is eaten in the early evening, and is usually cold meats, cheese and bread. Mid-

morning and mid-afternoon snacks are also common.

No stay in Austria is complete without a visit to one of the coffee houses. With wonderful rich smells of croissant, coffee and chocolate, they are great places to visit any time of the day.

BEDROOMS AND BATHROOMS

IF YOU WANT twin beds, ask for them specifically when booking. A 'double' bed is usually two single mattresses in a 'two-mattress' frame, covered with two single duvets. It you require an en suite bathroom, be sure to specify this when you make your reservation.

OTHER PRACTICAL INFORMATION

BOOK AHEAD for hotels in Vienna, and for others in peak times, and state any particular requirements. It is always worth confirming check-out times too. Breakfast is typically a buffet of breads, cheese, fruit and cold meats. Tourism is big business, and the standard of hotels and guesthouses is usually high.

Language German is spoken by 98 per cent of the population, but since most have good English it is easy to get by, especially in cities.

Currency The Austrian *schilling*, written 'Sch' or, less commonly, 'ATS'.

Shops Generally open 8:30am–6pm Mon to Fri (many close for lunch), and until noon on Saturdays.

Tipping It is customary to round-up the bill to the nearest 5Sch or 10Sch, making it close to 10 per cent, even if the service charge is included. Don't leave it on the table: tell the waiter how much you are paying, including the tip. For example, if the bill is 75Sch

Breakfast room, Landhaus Veronika, page 194

and you want to give him 10Sch, handing him a 100Sch note you say '85Sch'.

Telephoning To phone within Austria, dial the full number, including the initial zero. To call Austria from the UK, dial 00 43; then the number, omitting the initial zero. from the US, 011 43.

Restaurants Note that you will be charged for each piece of bread you eat.

Public holidays 1 January; 6 January; Easter Monday; 1 May; Ascension Day; Whit Monday; Corpus Christi; 15 August; 26 October; 1 November; 8 December; 25 and 26 December.

USEFUL WORDS

See page 147.

AUSTRIA PRICE BANDS

AUSTRIAN HOTELS are officially classified by stars, from one to five, but don't be too swayed by this. Our price bands are much simpler to use, referring simply to the price of a standard double room in high season.

Breakfast is often, but not always, included in room prices quoted by hotels. In some areas you may be charged a local tax.

Ⓢ	below 500Sch
ⓈⓈ	500–1,500Sch
ⓈⓈⓈ	1,500–2,500Sch
ⓈⓈⓈⓈ	above 2,500Sch

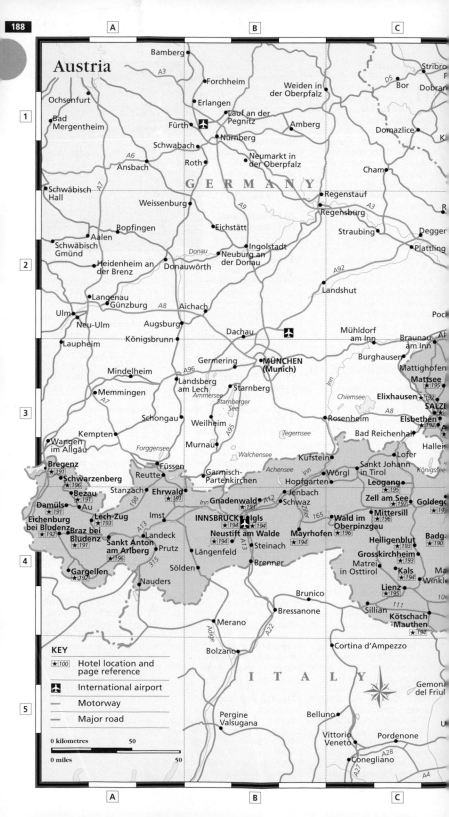

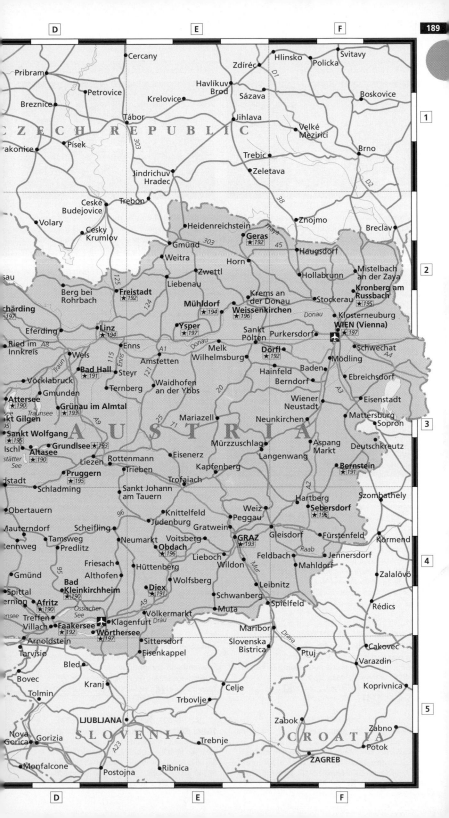

ALTAUSSEE

Hubertushof Crammed with hunting trophies, this hilltop inn was built in 1894 for the present owner's grandparents and retains the atmosphere of a private house, with a grandfather clock and an open fire in the sitting room. The bedrooms are beautifully decorated and there are stunning views of lake and mountains from the terrace.
⊠ 8992 Altaussee, Puchen 86. **Map** p189 D3.
🄲 (03622) 71280. ̄FAX (03622) 7128080. 🍴 b.
Rooms 9. 🎱 ● mid-Oct to 26 Dec; Jan, March, April; open at Easter. 🅲 AE, DC, MC, V. Ⓢ Ⓢ

ATTERSEE

Gasthof Häupl Run by the Häupl family for seven generations, this large hotel with stunning views over the Attersee – the largest lake in the Austrian Alps – is noted for its first-rate restaurant. Interesting antiques are dotted about, and there are cosy places for reading or conversation. Most bedrooms are simple. Book early.
⊠ 4863 Seewalchen am Attersee, Haupstr 20-22.
Map p189 D3. 🄲 (07662) 63630. ̄FAX (07662) 636362.
@ haupl@haupl.co.at 🍴 b,l,d. **Rooms** 33.
● Never. 🅲 AE, DC, MC, V. Ⓢ Ⓢ Ⓢ

ANIF

Romantik Hotel Schlosswirt Originally the guesthouse to a nearby castle, this is now a lively inn, only 20 minutes' drive from Salzburg. There is a feeling of history about the place; both food and ambience are traditional. Each bedroom is decorated in a different style. There is a 15th-century annexe opposite.
⊠ 5081 Anif bei Salzburg. **Map** p188 C3.
🄲 (06246) 72175. ̄FAX (06246) 721758.
@ info@schlosswirt-anif.com 🍴 b,l,d. **Rooms** 28.
● 2 weeks Feb, 2 weeks Oct. 🅲 AE, V. Ⓢ Ⓢ

BADGASTEIN

Haus Hirt Here is a wonderful mixture of modern and traditional, with some split-level bedrooms and William Morris prints, and a fully equipped health farm. The delicious breakfast buffet features home-made jams, herbal teas and bread so popular that some guests go home with a loaf in their baggage.
⊠ 5640 Badgastein, Kaiserpromenade. **Map** p188 C4.
🄲 (06434) 2797. ̄FAX (06434) 279748. @ info@ haus-hirt.com 🍴 b,l,d. **Rooms** 30. 🏊 🍴 ● Apr to mid-May, mid-Oct to mid-Dec. 🅲 AE, DC, MC, V. Ⓢ Ⓢ Ⓢ

AFRITZ

Hotel Lärchenhof Run by a sporting family, this mountain hotel caters for the same. There are three tennis courts and a pool; skiing in winter.
⊠ 9542 Afritz-Verditz. **Map** p189 D4.
🄲 (04247) 2134. ̄FAX (04247) 213411. 🍴 b,l,d.
Rooms 23. Ⓢ Ⓢ

ATTERSEE

Villa Langer This quiet lakeside villa is informal and suitable for families. Each suite has a kitchenette, but dinner is available five nights a week. Private boathouse; windsurfers for hire.
⊠ 4854 Weissenbach. **Map** p189 D3. 🄲 (07663) 242.
̄FAX (07663) 24236. 🍴 b,l,d. **Rooms** 19. Ⓢ Ⓢ

BADGASTEIN

Villa Solitude Stuffed full of antiques and silks, this charming villa overlooking the Gastein falls is peaceful and comfortable.
⊠ 5640 Badgastein, Kaiser Franz Joseph Str 16.
Map p188 C4. 🄲 (06434) 5101. ̄FAX (06434) 51013.
🍴 b. **Rooms** 6. Ⓢ Ⓢ Ⓢ

BAD KLEINKIRCHHEIM

Hotel Romerbad Delicious wholefood cookery, many health treatments available, and skiing nearby. Most bedrooms have a balcony.
⊠ 9546 Bad Kleinkirchheim. **Map** p189 D4. 🄲 (04240) 84540. ̄FAX (04240) 823457. @ hotel.romerbad@ carinthia.co.at 🍴 b. **Rooms** 28. Ⓢ Ⓢ

Bad Hall

Schloss Feyregg As befits a castle (built 1720), this hotel is wonderfully quiet and secluded, and it retains the feel of the private residence it was. Each bedroom has its own small sitting room. Rooms look over the village church, or over the wonderful gardens – which include an avenue lined with statues, a courtyard, and wild garden beyond. There is an inn just below the castle, where guests can migrate for lunch or dinner.
✉ 4540 Bad Hall. **Map** p189 D3. ☎ (07258) 2591. 🍴 b. **Rooms** 11. ● Christmas. 💳 Not accepted. ⓈⓈⓈ

Bregenz

Deuring Schlössle 'Breathtaking' is the word for this 17th-century castle overlooking Lake Constance. The reception rooms are huge; the bedrooms large, and furnished with antiques and silks. The hotel was taken over by chef Ernst Huber in 1989. The food he and his son prepare is light and fresh, using mainly local produce.
✉ 6900 Bregenz, Ehre-Guta-Platz 4. **Map** p188 A3. ☎ (05574) 47800. FAX (05574) 4780080. @ deuring@schloessle.vol.at 🍴 b,l,d. **Rooms** 15. ● Christmas. 💳 AE, DC, MC, V. ⓈⓈⓈ

Bernstein

Burg Bernstein Everything you could wish for in a castle: towers, fortifications, a dungeon, and a Knights' Hall with a stuccoed ceiling which is now a restaurant. The staircase is thought to be by Fischer von Erlach, the great Viennese baroque architect. The bedrooms are vast, and each is furnished with antiques; no two are alike. No telephones, televisions or minibars.
✉ 7434 Bernstein. **Map** p189 F3. ☎ (03354) 6382. FAX (03354) 6520. @ bergeralmfay@netway.at 🍴 b,d. **Rooms** 11. ≋ ● Nov to end April. 💳 AE, MC, V. ⓈⓈ

Ehrwald

Hotel Spielmann Meadows surround this old Tyrolean chalet, and every bedroom has a balcony from which to admire the jagged mountain peaks. The food is cooked by the Spielmann father and son, both top-rated chefs and noted mountaineers. Near the Sonnenhang ski-lifts, and good hiking; facilities for children.
✉ 6632 Ehrwald. **Map** p188 B4. ☎ (05673) 22250. FAX (05673) 22255. @ info@hotelspeilman.com 🍴 b,l,d. **Rooms** 38. ≋ 🌾 ● mid-Oct to mid-Dec; after Easter to late May. 💳 AE, DC, MC, V. ⓈⓈⓈ

Bezau

Gasthof Sonne Geranium-filled window boxes and painted shutters greet you at this edge-of-village inn. Health spa, cross-country skiing.
✉ 6870 Bezau. **Map** p188 A4. ☎ (05514) 2262. FAX (05514) 2912. @ sonne-bezou@aon.at 🍴 b,l,d. **Rooms** 30. ⓈⓈ

Braz bei Bludenz

Gasthof Traube Braz There is a permanent nanny here, so it is popular with skiing families. Plain bedrooms, attractive public rooms.
✉ 6751 Braz bei Bludenz, Klostertalerstr. **Map** p188 A4. ☎ (0552) 281830. FAX (0552) 2810340. 🍴 b,l,d. **Rooms** 26. ⓈⓈ

Damüls

Berghotel Madlener The Madlener is a fine example of a chalet-style hotel, with open fires and bedrooms panelled in pale wood.
✉ 6884 Damüls, Haus 22. **Map** p188 A4. ☎ (05510) 2210. FAX (05510) 22115. @ berghotel.madlener@aon.at 🍴 b,l,d. **Rooms** 26. ⓈⓈ

Diex

Berggasthof Jesch A working farm with home-grown produce for the table. Simple and suitable for families; horse-riding available.
✉ 9103 Diex, Wandelitzen 10. **Map** p189 E4. ☎ (04232) 7196. FAX (04232) 719620. @ jesch@carinthia.com 🍴 b,l,d. **Rooms** 22. ⓈⓈ

ELIXHAUSEN

Romantik Hotel Gmachl In the family since 1538, and totally refurbished in 1987, the Gmachl is a profusion of old prints and dried flower decorations. The hotel's own butcher's shop sells its renowned Bratwurst to the locals as well as to guests. An annexe has 22 pleasantly done-out double bedrooms. Tennis and horse-riding.
✉ 5161 Salzburg-Elixhausen. **Map** p188 C3.
☎ (0662) 4802120. [FAX] (0662) 48021272.
@ rgmachl@salzburg.co.at 🍴 b,l,d. **Rooms** 34.
🏊 🌿 ● 2 weeks mid-June. 💳 Not accepted. [S][S]

GARGELLEN

Alpenhotel Heimspitze This hotel feels remote, tucked away across the river from the small ski resort of Gargellen. It's a homely place, with woven rugs and painted furniture, and an adventure playground for children. The award-winning kitchen produces a daily-changing menu; home-made jams and cakes.
✉ 6787 Gargellen. **Map** p188 A4. ☎ (05557) 6319. [FAX] (05557) 631920. @ hotel@heimspitze.com 🍴 b,l,d. **Rooms** 20. 🍸 🌿 ● mid-Oct to mid-Dec; mid-Apr to June. 💳 AE, DC, MC, V. [S][S][S]

ELSBETHEN

Hotel Schwaitlalm With wonderful views across a valley to the hills of Germany, this ancient shingled farmhouse is only 15 minutes' drive from Salzburg. It was taken over in 1991 by the Austro-Italian Birenti family, and the food reflects this, with ravioli and carpaccio as well as traditional Austrian dishes. Large indoor pool.
✉ 5061 Elsbethen bei Salzburg. **Map** p188 C3.
☎ (0662) 6259270. [FAX] (0662) 6296063.
@ birenti@sbg.at 🍴 b,l,d. **Rooms** 17. 🏊 🍸
● early Jan to early March. 💳 Not accepted. [S][S]

GERAS

Alter Schüttkasten Geras The huge 17th-century building, once a granary belonging to a local monastery, has been perceptively and unfussily converted. The atmosphere is peaceful, the style simple. Two dining rooms offer local fish and game. There is good hiking in the woods of the Waldviertel; summer painting courses can be arranged through the hotel.
✉ 2093 Geras, Vorstadt 11. **Map** p189 E2. ☎ (02912) 332. [FAX] (02912) 33233. @ hotel.schuettkasten@telecom.at 🍴 b,l,d. **Rooms** 26. ● Never. 💳 DC. [S][S]

DÖRFL

Pedro's Landhaus Extravagant and luxurious furnishings characterize Pedro's, a lavish joint venture by opera star Jose Carreras and Pedro Massana. Set in a park in the Vienna Woods.
✉ 3072 Dörfl, Kasten. **Map** p189 F3. ☎ (02744) 7387. [FAX] (02744) 7389. 🍴 b,l,d. **Rooms** 11. [S][S][S]

EICHENBERG BEI BLUDENZ

Hotel Schönblick Dazzling views across Lake Constance lure both locals and visitors. There is a good restaurant and an indoor swimming pool.
✉ 6911 Eichenberg bei Bregenz. **Map** p188 A4.
☎ (05574) 45965. [FAX] (05574) 459657. @ hotel.schoenblick@schoenblick.at 🍴 b,l,d. **Rooms** 22. [S][S]

FAAKERSEE

Inselhotel Informal hotel set on a small island; guests park by the shore and cross by private launch. Tennis, sailing; nanny in July, August.
✉ 9583 Faakersee, Faak am See. **Map** p189 D4.
☎ (04254) 2145. [FAX] (04254) 213677. 🍴 b,l,d.
Rooms 32. [S][S]

FREISTADT

Gasthof Zum Goldenen Hirschen In the centre of this fine medieval town, a guesthouse with large bedrooms and imaginative cuisine.
✉ 4240 Freistadt, Böhmergasse 8-10. **Map** p189 D2.
☎ (07942) 722580. [FAX] (07942) 7225840. @ deim@upperaustria.or.at 🍴 b,l,d. **Rooms** 18. [S][S]

GNADENWALD

Gasthof Michaelerhof Louis Schiestl took over this former farmhouse more than 30 years ago, and turned it first into a restaurant, then into an hotel. Having worked all over the world, Schiestl provides food which is truly international, with curries and Scandanavian fish dishes alongside traditional Austrian food. Bedrooms are pleasant. Only ten minutes' drive from central Innsbruck. ✉ 6060 Gnadenwald. **Map** p188 B4. 🄲 (05223) 48128. ℻ (05223) 481284. 🍴 b,l,d. **Rooms** 12. ⬤ Nov to mid-Dec; 2 weeks after Easter. 🅴 AE, DC. 💲💲

HEILIGENBLUT

Haus Senger This small hotel, owned by the former Olympic sportsman Hans Senger, was rebuilt in 1966, but beams, stone-flagged floors and open fires make for a perfect atmosphere. Some of the country-style bedrooms have a kitchenette. A separate wing houses a health and fitness area; there is skiing from the door. ✉ 9844 Heiligenblut. **Map** p188 C4. 🄲 (04824) 2215. ℻ (04824) 22159. @ sengerja@magnet.at 🍴 b,d. **Rooms** 13. 🎯 ⬤ Oct to mid-Dec; after Easter to mid-June. 🅴 AE, DC, MC, V. 💲💲💲

GOLDEGG

Hotel Seehof The village of Goldegg is beautifully preserved, with cobbled streets and old houses. The Seehof, an inn since 1727, has been run by the Schellhorns for four generations. Bedrooms are cheerful, some featuring painted furniture. Lovely strudels by son Sepp; skiing (downhill and cross-country) with father, Franz. Skate on the lake in winter, swim in summer. ✉ 5622 Goldegg am See. **Map** p188 C4. 🄲 (06415) 81370. ℻ (01645) 8276. @ seehof@saltzburg.co.at 🍴 b,l,d. **Rooms** 27. ⬤ Apr; Nov. 🅴 DC, V. 💲💲

LECH-ZUG

Hotel Rote Wand This is a perfect place for health and fitness enthusiasts: as well as winter sports, there is a wide year-round choice of exercise programmes, including water gymnastics and weight training. The restaurant is very traditional, while the bedrooms are designer-fresh, with the beds up on split-level galleries. ✉ 6764 Lech-Zug am Arlberg. **Map** p188 A4. 🄲 (05583) 34350. ℻ (05583) 343540. @ gafthof@rotewand.com 🍴 b,l,d. **Rooms** 34. 🎯 ⬤ Sept to early Dec; after Easter to July. 🅴 DC. 💲💲💲

GRAZ
Schlossberg Hotel Stuffed full with lovely antiques. Comfortable bedrooms and a roof garden with views over the town. ✉ 8010 Graz, Kaiser-Franz-Josef-Kai 30. **Map** p189 E4. 🄲 (0316) 80700. ℻ (0316) 807070. @ office@schlossberg-hotel.at 🍴 b. **Rooms** 45. 💲💲💲

GROSSKIRCHHEIM
Nationalparkhotel Schlosswirt Wildlife and flowers abound around this inn. Good, straightforward food and cheerful bedrooms. ✉ 9843 Grosskirchheim-Döllach. **Map** p188 C4. 🄲 (04825) 411. ℻ (04825) 411165. @ schlosswirt@eunet.at 🍴 b,l,d. **Rooms** 28. 💲💲

GRÜNAU IM ALMTAL
Romantik Hotel Almtalhof Alpine air, a river, trees and flowers make this hotel special. Good food and fine wine list. ✉ 4645 Grünau im Almtal. **Map** p189 D3. 🄲 (07616) 8204. ℻ (07616) 820466. @ almtalhof@romantik.at 🍴 b,l,d. **Rooms** 21. 💲💲

GRUNDLSEE
Gasthof Ladner A 200-year-old inn on the shore of the Grundlsee lake, close to the Totes Gebirge mountains and the cable-car up to the Appelhaus. ✉ 8993 Grundlsee Gössl 1. **Map** p189 D3. 🄲 (03622) 8211. ℻ (03622) 82114. @ ladner@eunet.at 🍴 b,l,d. **Rooms** 6. 💲💲

For key to symbols see backflap. For price categories *see p187*

Linz

Wolfinger It may once have been a monastery, but little is spartan here. It's a tasteful city hotel, the walls covered in old mirrors and photographs, public rooms and bedrooms displaying much Biedermeier and Art Nouveau furniture. Most bedrooms overlook the quiet courtyard. Good views of the Hauptplatz from the breakfast room.
✉ 4020 Linz, Hauptplatz 19. **Map** p189 D2. ☎ (0732) 7732910. [FAX] (0732) 77329155. [@] wolfinger@austria-classic-hotels.at 🍴 b,l,d. **Rooms** 30. ● Never. 💳 AE, DC, MC, V. [€][€]

Mühldorf

Burg Oberrana High up on a hill above the Danube valley, this white-walled castle has great views all around. More than 900 years old, it also has the oldest Romanesque chapel crypt in Austria, some 200 years older than the castle itself. The well-restored bedrooms are furnished with antiques. Delicious home-made brandies.
✉ 3622 Mühldorg bei Spitz/Donau. **Map** p189 E2. ☎ (02713) 8221. [FAX] (02713) 8366. [@] hotel-gutenbrunn@netway.at 🍴 b. **Rooms** 12. 🍃 ● Nov to end Apr. 💳 AE, V. [€][€]

Mayrhofen

Landhaus Veronika Set in meadows just five minutes' walk from the centre of the popular resort village of Mayrhofen, the Veronika is luxurious but cosy too. It has spacious aparments where guests can relax when bad weather makes outings difficult. There is no restaurant, but there are plenty in the village; guests can have breakfast brought to their rooms.
✉ 6290 Mayrhofen 250b. **Map** p188 B4. ☎ (05285) 63347. [FAX] (05825) 63819. [@] bh13@netway.at 🍴 b. **Rooms** 9. 🏋 🍃 ● Never. 💳 Not accepted. [€][€]

Neustift am Walde

Landhaus Fuhrgassl-Huber Located in a wine-producing village and backing on to a vineyard, this homely *pension* has a fresh, spacious feel and big, comfortable bedrooms. You can taste the famous Fuhrgass-Huber from the nearby vineyard. The area is peaceful and rural, yet Vienna is only half an hour's bus and tram ride away.
✉ 1190 Wien, Neustift am Walde, Rathstr 24. **Map** p188 B4. ☎ (01) 4403033. [FAX] (01) 4402714. [@] f-huber@hotels.or.at 🍴 b. **Rooms** 22. 🍃 ● 2 weeks Feb. 💳 MC, V. [€][€]

Igls

Schlosshotel Igls Small castle hotel with a luxurious indoor pool, a formal drawing room, and a cosy bar. Golf, ski areas nearby.
✉ 6080 Igls. **Map** p188 B4. ☎ (0512) 377217. [FAX] (0512) 377217198. [@] schlosshotel-Igls@netway.at 🍴 b,l,d. **Rooms** 19. [€][€][€]

Innsbruck

Weisses Rössl This establishment, set in a townhouse in central Innsbruck, is popular with the locals too for its well-priced restaurant.
✉ 6020 Innsbruck, Kiebachgasse 8 in der Altstadt. **Map** p188 B4. ☎ (0512) 583057. [FAX] (0512) 5830575. 🍴 b,l,d. **Rooms** 14. [€][€]

Kals

Gasthof Taurerwirt Overlooking a beautiful valley, the homely Taurerwirt is perfect for open-air types: hiking, fishing and skiing close by.
✉ 9981 Kals am Grossglockner. **Map** p188 C4. ☎ (04876) 8226. [FAX] (04876) 822611. [@] taurerwirt@tirol.com 🍴 b,l,d. **Rooms** 30. [€][€]

Kötschach-Mauthen

Sissy Sonnleitner's Kellerwand Owner Sissy Sonnleitner, a self-taught cook, was Austria's 'Chef of the Year' in 1990. First-rate bedrooms.
✉ 9640 Kötschach-Mauthen. **Map** p188 C4. ☎ (04715) 269. [FAX] (04715) 26916. [@] sonnl@netway.at 🍴 b. **Rooms** 12. [€][€]

PRUGGERN

Farmreiterhof Wake up to the sound of cowbells in this archetypal Alpine hotel set up above the village, in the middle of the countryside. The building dates from 1872, and has been in the Gerharter family for five generations. People return here year after year. Homely food such as *Kasnockerln* (cheese noodles); winter sports, riding and hiking.
⊠ 8965 Pruggern 65. **Map** p189 D3. █ (03685) 22692. **FAX** (03685) 2333377. ██ b,d. **Rooms** 5. ▨ ▮ ⬤ Christmas. ▨ Not accepted. Ⓢ Ⓢ

ST GILGEN

Gasthof Zur Post This charming inn was built in 1415, and its exterior is decorated with a fine painted frieze of a boar hunt. Oak beams and dark stone floors give it a wonderfully historic atmosphere. The comfortable bedrooms have views onto the streets. Mozart's mother was born in the village, and a fountain and statue in the square honours the composer.
⊠ 5340 St Gilgen, Mozartplatz 8. **Map** p189 D3. █ (06227) 2157. **FAX** (06227) 2157600. ██ b,l,d. **Rooms** 19. ⬤ Never. ▨ AE, DC, MC, V. Ⓢ Ⓢ

SALZBURG

Hotel Schloss Mönchstein Sitting on the Monschsberg crag above Salzburg, this elegant but friendly castle hotel is popular with both businesspeople and people on holiday. The rooms are well equipped; half have views of the city, and half of the gardens. You can get down to the city by Mönchsberg-Lift.
⊠ 5020 Salzburg, Mönchsberg Park 26. **Map** p188 C3. █ (0662) 8485550. **FAX** (0662) 848559. @ saltzburg@monchstein.at ██ b,l,d. **Rooms** 17. ▮ ⬤ Never. ▨ AE, DC, MC, V. Ⓢ Ⓢ Ⓢ Ⓢ

ST WOLFGANG

Seehotel Appesbach A wonderful contrast to the busy lakeside resort of St Wolfgang, this elegant villa hotel has garden, lake and woods to keep it secluded. At first glance, the house has changed little since the Duke of Windsor stayed here in 1937, but it has been sympathetically modernized; facilities include tennis courts and sauna
⊠ 5360 St Wolfgang am see. **Map** p189 D3. █ (06138) 2209. **FAX** (06138) 220914. @ landhaus@ping.at ██ b,l,d. **Rooms** 26 , plus 9 suites. ▮ ⬤ Nov to Easter. ▨ AE, DC, MC, V. Ⓢ Ⓢ

KRONBERG AM RUSSBACH
Landhaus Kronberghof Ideal for horse-riding foodies: there are 70 horses and an indoor school, and the excellent food is mainly local.
⊠ 2123 Kronberg am Rossbach 3. **Map** p189 F2. █ (02245) 4304. **FAX** (02245) 43044. @ kronberghof@netway.at ██ b,l,d. **Rooms** 5.

LEOGANG
Hotel Rupertus Jolly holiday hotel with supervised children's activities in summer. Adults appreciate the sauna, steam bath and gym.
⊠ 5771 Leogang. **Map** p188 C3. █ (06583) 84660. **FAX** (06583) 846655. @ rupertus@eunet.at ██ b,l,d. **Rooms** 27. Ⓢ Ⓢ

LIENZ (TRISTACHERSEE)
Parkhotel Tristachersee Wonderfully spacious, this retreat has a conservatory right on the lake. Luxurious rooms and award-winning restaurant.
⊠ 9900 Lienz, Tristachersee. **Map** p188 C4. █ (04852) 67666. **FAX** (04852) 67699. ██ b,l,d. **Rooms** 42. Ⓢ Ⓢ

MATTSEE
Iglhauser Bräu Ancient, comfortable family-run hostelry. Guests can windsurf in the nearby lake, sail in the hotel's dinghies, and row in their boats.
⊠ 5163 Mattsee, Schlossbergweg 4. **Map** p188 C3. █ (06217) 5205. **FAX** (06217) 520533. ██ b,l,d. **Rooms** 20. ▨ MC, V. Ⓢ Ⓢ

SCHWARZENBERG

Gasthof Hirschen The distinctive 18th-century wooden-shingled inn, set in the centre of the village, has something for everyone. Families come for skiing, locals drop in for a drink, and in the summer it is popular with couples. The old house is traditional, but the annex very modern. The restaurant is popular with locals.
✉ 6867 Schwarzenberg. **Map** p188 A3. ☎ (05512) 29440. ℻ (05512) 294420. @ romantikhotel@hirschen.vol.at ⅈ b,l,d. **Rooms** 32. ⬤ Never. 🗠 AE, DC, MC, V. Ⓢ Ⓢ

WALD IM OBERPINZGAU

Hotel Schöneben A quintessential Austrian country inn: in summer the balconies groan with geraniums; in winter you crunch through thick white snow to toast by a comforting open fire. Inside is done out in 'modern rustic' style, with lots of flowers and books. The bedrooms are small but nicely furnished.
✉ 5742 Wald im Pinzgau. **Map** p188 C4. ☎ (06565) 82890. ℻ (06565) 8419. @ schoeneben@magnet.at ⅈ b,l,d. **Rooms** 24. ⬤ Nov to mid-Dec; after Easter to mid-May. 🗠 Not accepted. Ⓢ Ⓢ

SEBERSDORF

Schlosshotel Obermayerhofen In the family of the proprietors, the Counts Kottulinksy, since 1777, this fine castle has been a hotel only since the mid-1980s. Accommodation is wonderfully luxurious, with four-poster beds and huge lavish bathrooms. Chandeliers, a marvellous 18th-century jungle fresco and a private chapel add to the opulence of this hilltop haven.
✉ 8272 Sebersdorf. **Map** p189 F4. ☎ (03333) 2503. ℻ (03333) 250350. ⅈ b,l,d. **Rooms** 20. ⬤ early Jan to end Feb. 🗠 AE, DC, MC, V. Ⓢ Ⓢ Ⓢ

WEISSENKIRCHEN

Raffelsbergerhof Smothered in wisteria and vines, this village inn used to be a ship-master's house, and the horses that pulled the barges up the Danube were stabled here. It is full of intriguing objects collected by the present owner's father, and even the light-fittings are worth a second look. Of the charming bedrooms, two have views of the great river.
✉ 13610 Weissenkirchen. **Map** p189 E2. ☎ (02715) 2201. ℻ (02715) 220127. @ raffelsberger@magnet.at ⅈ b. **Rooms** 13. ⬤ Nov to end Apr. 🗠 MC. Ⓢ Ⓢ

MITTERSILL
Nationalparkhotel Felben Children's activities, a profusion of farm animals, large bedrooms and heated pool make this perfect for families.
✉ 5730 Mittersill. **Map** p188 C4. ☎ (06562) 4407. ℻ (06562) 440772. @ info@felben.at ⅈ b,l,d. **Rooms** 31. Ⓢ Ⓢ

OBDACH
Judenburger Hütte Sports lovers flock to this mountain haven near the small town of Obdach: it has the highest tennis courts in Styria, large swimming pools and skiing from the door.
✉ 8742 St Wolfgang am Zirbitz. **Map** p189 E4. ☎ ℻ (03578) 8202. ⅈ b,l,d. **Rooms** 15. Ⓢ Ⓢ

SALZBURG
Hotel Zistelalm High on the Gaisberg crag and with walls covered in antlers, crackling log fires in winter and year-round views over the city.
✉ 5020 Saltzburg, Gaisberg. **Map** p188 C3. ☎ (0662) 641067. ℻ (0662) 642618. @ zistelalm@eunet.at ⅈ b,l,d. **Rooms** 24. Ⓢ Ⓢ

ST ANTON AM ARLBERG
St Antoner Hof Four-poster beds, painted furniture, and an indoor pool cleverly mix the lavish with the traditional. New Austrian cuisine.
✉ 6580 St Anton am Arlberg. **Map** p188 A4. ☎ (05446) 2910. ℻ (05446) 3551. @ ahof@tirol.com ⅈ b,l,d. **Rooms** 31. Ⓢ Ⓢ

Wien (Vienna)

Altstadt Vienna This spacious hotel in Josefstadt, an unspoilt baroque part of the city, is only ten minutes by bus from central Vienna. Owner Otto Ernst Wiesenthal, a seasoned traveller, has decorated the place according to his own definite tastes: a happy mix of antique and modern pieces. Friendly and helpful service; rooftop views over the city.
✉ 1070 Wien, Kirchengasse 41. **Map** p189 F2. ☎ (01) 52633990. FAX (01) 5234901. @ hotel@alstadt.at 🍴 b. **Rooms** 30. ⚫ Never. 💳 AE, DC, MC, V. [S][S]

Wien (Vienna)

Hotel König von Ungarn Right in the centre of the old city, very close to St Stephen's Cathedral, and extremely popular. The building dates from the 18th century; inside, chandeliers, portraits and an enclosed courtyard all add to its charm. The bedrooms are comfortable but not over-grand. The restaurant serves traditional Austrian cuisine.
✉ 1010 Wien, Schulerstr 10. **Map** p189 F2. ☎ (01) 515840. FAX (01) 515848. 🍴 b,l,d. **Rooms** 33. ⚫ Never. 💳 DC, MC, V. [S][S][S][S]

Wien (Vienna)

Altwienerhof Although located in an unfashionable part of Vienna, the Altwienerhof is special. Its restaurant is visited by gourmets from all over the world (closed 1-21 Jan). The wine list is very good too. The rooms are sumptuous, and breakfast can be taken in the conservatory or the garden. Bargain prices with half-board.
✉ 1150 Wien, Herklotzgasse 6. **Map** p189 F2. ☎ (01) 8926000. FAX (01) 89260008. @ altwienerhof@netway.at 🍴 b,l,d. **Rooms** 23. 🍃 ⚫ Jan. 💳 AE, DC, MC, V. [S][S][S]

Ysper

Zum Grünen Baum The Rotter family have been running their coaching inn since 1648. The village is unspoilt, and ancient agricultural implements cover the white-washed walls. The atmosphere is warm and informal; children are very welcome. The food is traditional, with vegetables and herbs from the inn's garden. Bedrooms in a new wing are light and airy.
✉ 3683 Ysper. **Map** p189 E2. ☎ (07415) 7218. FAX (07415) 721849. 🍴 b,l,d. **Rooms** 35. ⚫ 2 weeks Feb, 1 week Nov. 💳 Not accepted. [S][S]

Scharding

Förstingers Wirtshaus The 17th-century tavern retains old beams and vaulted ceilings.
✉ 4780 Scharding am Inn, Unterer Stadtplatz 3. **Map** p189 D2. ☎ (07712) 23020. FAX (07712) 23023. @ romantikhotel-forstinger@magnet.at 🍴 b,l,d. **Rooms** 16. [S][S][S]

Wien (Vienna)

Hotel am Schubertring A central hotel, near the Staatsoper and Konzerthaus, this is a favourite of visiting artists and musicians. Quiet bedrooms.
✉ 1010 Wien, Schubertring 11. **Map** p189 F2. ☎ (01) 717020. FAX (01) 7139966. @ hotel.amschubertring@teleweb.at 🍴 b. **Rooms** 39. [S][S][S]

Wörthersee

Schloss Hallegg This huge 800-year-old castle offers wonderful views, vast bedrooms and a 40m (120ft) long hall. Breakfast on the ramparts is a must. Open in summer only.
✉ 9201 Krumpendorf am Wörthersee, Halleggerstr 131. **Map** p189 D4. ☎ (0463) 49311. 🍴 b. **Rooms** 15. [S][S]

Zell am See

Hotel 'Der Metzgerwirt' The main building is more than 500 years old. Rooms in the new annexe look onto a courtyard and rose garden.
✉ 5700 Zell am See, Saalfeldnerstr 5. **Map** p188 C4. ☎ (06542) 725200. FAX (06542) 7252034. 🍴 b,l,d. **Rooms** 31. [S][S]

For key to symbols see backflap. For price categories *see p187*

SWITZERLAND

SWITZERLAND

THE MOUNTAINOUS GEOGRAPHY of Switzerland divides this small country into a number of self-contained localities. In the past, communication, even between neighbouring valleys, was minimal. Local differences are reinforced by the fact that four languages are spoken: French, German, Italian and Romansch, a Latinised form of Swiss German.

Switzerland has always been a highly popular European tourist destination, and, not surprisingly, its hoteliers are famous for their excellent and enthusiastic house-keeping. It is all too easy to think of Switzerland as mountains, lush valleys – and chalet hotels. But it has some smart town hotels, too, and some beautiful lakeside ones.

The Walserhof, page 207, fine food in the seemingly ever-fashionable ski resort of Klosters

SWITZERLAND REGION BY REGION

WE DIVIDE Switzerland into five regions: Western, Northern, Central, Eastern and Southern. (In fact, the country is sub-divided into 26 cantons.)

Western Switzerland
This comprises Suisse Romande and Bern. Suisse Romande is the French-speaking area of the country and, in Geneva, which is culturally more French than the rest of the country, there are some very sophisticated hotels. But you can also find charming rural retreats and country house hotels nearby. Perhaps the best-known Alpine holiday region, the Bernese Alps, offers everyone's idea of mountain scenery and chic resorts.

Northern Switzerland
Separated from Germany and Austria by the Rhine and Lake Constance, this region encompasses Basel and the surrounding cantons. The main language is German, but there are French influences. Basel itself has its share of good hotels and

Villa Principe Leopoldo, page 208

there is no shortage of enchanting places to stay on beautiful Lake Constance.

Central Switzerland
This is William Tell country, and takes in Lucerne, perhaps the country's most visited city. It has beautiful scenery and a wide choice of inns and hotels.

Eastern Switzerland
The least densely populated area of the country, Eastern Switzerland boasts some 360 sq km (140 sq miles) of glacier, and the fashionable ski resorts of Klosters and St Moritz. Apart from many charming winter sports hotels, there are some lovely country inns, too.

Southern Switzerland
This includes Valais and Ticino. Valais contains some

of the most dramatic and famous mountain scenery in the country: here, for example, is the village of Zermatta, dominated by the famous pyramid-shaped peak of the Matterhorn. It is also a very productive wine-growing region.

Magical Ticino, with its sunshine, lakes, mountains and flowers, has a number of beguiling lakeside inns.

HIGHLIGHTS

THE HOTELS pictured on these introductory pages are by no means the only highlights. Other favourites include the welcoming chalet hotel of Aux Milles Etoiles (page 209), which is good for skiing and wonderfully peaceful; and the Chesa Salis at Bever (page 205), a charming village hotel with a warm welcome and first-rate food.

FOOD AND DRINK

CHEESE AND chocolate are synonymous with Switzerland, but each region has its own particular specialities. There are more than a hundred different varieties of cheese made in individual dairies, and the national dish is fondue. Lake fish are often on the menu; so also is *Rösti*, a delicious fried potato cake, and *raclette*, shavings of melted cheese. If you are feeling particularly hungry, try the *Berneplatte*, the classic dish of Bern which consists typically of a huge pile of sauerkraut (pickled cabbage) topped with sausages, ham and other ingredients. In the south, risotto and polenta are very popular. All over the country you will find delicious patisseries. The commonest delicacy is the cream-filled *gugelhopf*.

The first chocolate factory in Switzerland opened in 1819. Swiss chocolate is considered to be the best in the world and, perhaps not surprisingly, the Swiss eat and drink more chocolate per capita than any other nation. In 1875, milk

chocolate was invented here, and in 1879 the first chocolate bar was made.

Most of the wine produced in the country is white, and is best drunk when young. There are more than 300 small wine-growing areas spread over the country. In the French-speaking part, try Fendant or Johannisberg. In the German-speaking there are some good dry reds. The beer is good, too. *Helles* is light, *Dunkles* dark.

Kirsch is the national 'hard' drink, made from cherry stones, with a variety of flavourings. In the south you will find Grappa.

OTHER PRACTICAL INFORMATION

BREAKFAST is usually a help-yourself buffet and consists of breads, cold meats, cereals, fruit and cheeses. In most hotels the 'double bed' is in fact two single beds pushed together with two single duvets.

In the German-speaking regions, the *stube*, or bar, is the focal point of many of the hotels and inns; in the Italian speaking area *grottos* are the equivalent.

Language English is spoken by most of the population as a second language.

Currency The Swiss *franc*, written 'F' or 'SF'.

Shops Normal shop hours are from 8am–12pm and 1:30–6:30pm. Saturday closing is at 11am except in the large cities.

Tipping A 15 per cent service charge is added to all hotel and restaurant bills. You only need leave more if you feel that the service has been unusually good.

Telephoning If you wish to make a phone call from within Switzerland,

dial the full area code. To call Switzerland from the UK, first dial the international code, 00 41 (from the US, 011 41), as usual omitting the first zero of the country area code.

Public holidays 1 January; Good Friday; Easter Monday; Ascension Day; Whit Monday; 1 August; 25 and 26 December.

USEFUL WORDS

FRENCH, German and Italian are spoken. See pages 217, 147 and 333.

SWITZERLAND PRICE BANDS

SWISS HOTELS are officially classified by stars, one to five. Our price bands are much simpler and, as elsewhere in the guide, refer to the cost of a standard double room in high season. Prices are normally quoted inclusive of breakfast and tax. However, in some places, a guest tax may be charged. In this event, a discount card is sometimes offered, giving reduced price entry to certain local attractions.

Ⓕ	Below 100 SF
ⒻⒻ	100–200 SF
ⒻⒻⒻ	200–300SF
ⒻⒻⒻⒻ	Over 300SF

Guarda Val, page 208, sits above Lenzerheide

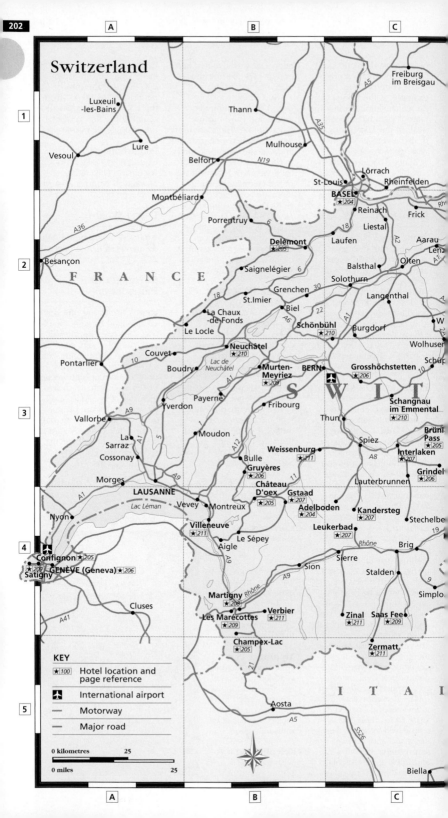

202

Switzerland

Luxeuil-les-Bains

Lure

Vesoul

Thann

Mulhouse

Belfort

N19

Freiburg im Breisgau

St-Louis

Lörrach

Rheinfelden

BASEL
★204

Reinach

Frick

Montbéliard

Porrentruy

6

Delémont
★205

Laufen

Liestal

Aarau

Lenz

Besançon

F R A N C E

Saignelégier

6

Balsthal

Olten

Grenchen

30

Solothurn

Langenthal

St.Imier

Biel

22

Schönbühl
★210

Burgdorf

Wolhuser

La Chaux-de-Fonds

A6

Le Locle

Couvet

Neuchâtel
★210

Lac de Neuchâtel

Murten-Meyriez
★209

BERN

Grosshöchstetten
★206

Schüp

Pontarlier

10

Boudry

S W I T

Payerne

A1

Fribourg

Thun

Schangnau im Emmental
★210

Yverdon

Vallorbe

A9

1

Moudon

A12

Weissenburg
★211

Spiez

A8

Brüni Pass
★205

Interlaken
★207

La Sarraz

Bulle

Gruyères
★206

Grindel
★206

Cossonay

Château D'oex
★205

Gstaad
★207

Lauterbrunnen

Morges

LAUSANNE

Vevey

Montreux

Adelboden
★204

Kandersteg
★207

Stechelbe

Nyon

Lac Léman

Villeneuve
★211

Leukerbad
★207

Brig

19

Confignon ★205

Aigle

Le Sépey

Rhône

Stalden

9

GENÈVE (Geneva) ★206

Sion

Sierre

Satigny ★209

A9

Simplo

Cluses

A41

Martigny
★208

Rhône

Les Marécottes
★209

Verbier
★211

Zinal
★211

Saas Fee
★209

Champex-Lac
★205

Zermatt
★211

I T A I

Aosta

A5

S526

Biella

Vesoul

Pontarlier

Vallorbe

La Sarraz

Cossonay

Morges

Nyon

Confignon

Satigny

Cluses

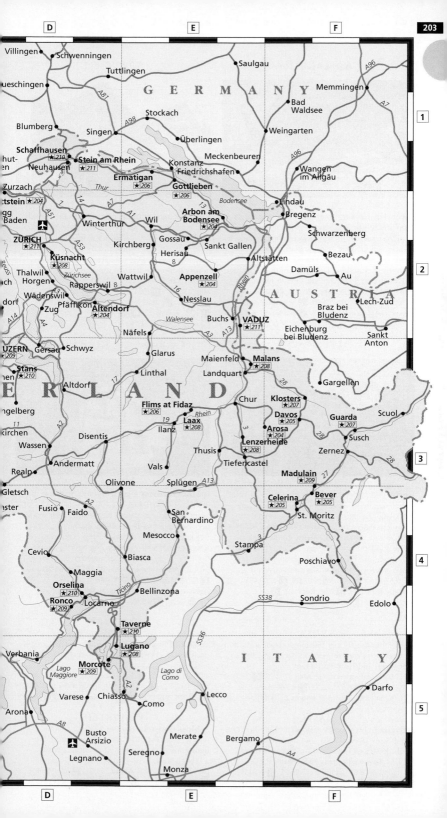

ADELBODEN

Bären The building dates from 1500, but it has been a hotel for only ten years. The proprietor, a local, has made it thoroughly comfortable, and it is especially popular with families. All the bedrooms are differently done out – one has a four-poster waterbed. Delicious *Rösti* and a range of French and German dishes in the restaurant. ✉ 3715 Adelboden BE. **Map** p202 C4. 📞 (033) 673 21 51. 🆎 (033) 673 21 90. @ hotelbaeren@ bluewin.ch 🍴 b,l,d. **Rooms** 13. ● end Nov to mid-Dec; mid-May to mid-June. 🅿 AE, DC, MC, V. Ⓕ Ⓕ

APPENZELL

Säntis Colourful folk patterns adorn the outside of this lively inn, much enlarged since the Heeb family took it over in 1919. The restaurant serves local cheeses and wines, but the specialities are lake fish and sausages. Of the bedrooms, No.242 is very popular – it has a frilly four-poster. ✉ am Landsgemeindeplatz, 9050 Appenzell AI. **Map** p203 E2. 📞 (071) 788 11 11. 🆎 (071) 788 11 10. @ romantikhotelsaentis@bluewin.ch 🍴 b,l,d. **Rooms** 32. 🅿 ● Never. 🅿 AE, DC, MC, V. Ⓕ Ⓕ

ALTENDORF

Hecht This popular place on the shores of Lake Zurich has been an inn since the 15th century. Today, the Hecht's seafood cuisine, served in a modern extension and outdoor terrace, draws people from all around – many come by boat. Accommodation is in the older part of the house. Bathrooms are basic, but the seven simple, wood-panelled bedrooms are attractive. ✉ 8852 Altendorf SZ. **Map** p203 D2. 📞 (055) 451 01 00. 🆎 (055) 451 01 01. 🍴 b,l,d. **Rooms** 7. 🅿 ● 2 weeks Jan. 🅿 AE, DC, MC, V. Ⓕ Ⓕ

ARBON AM BODENSEE

Gastof Frohsinn A beer drinkers' paradise: the three-storied building is a brewery as well as an hotel. The basement is a beer cellar, with wooden benches and a vaulted ceiling. Some 500 litres (110 gal) of lager are produced twice a week, with a stronger brown beer in winter. Rooms are plain and neat; vegetarian dishes. ✉ 9320 Arbon, Romanshornerstr 15 TG. **Map** p203 E2. 📞 (071) 447 84 84. 🆎 (071) 446 41 42. @ frohsinn@tele-net.ch 🍴 b,l,d. **Rooms** 11. 🅿 ● Never. 🅿 AE, DC, MC, V. Ⓕ Ⓕ

AROSA

Belri From this former finishing school at the top of Arosa, you can 'ski out, ski back'. The lifts to Weisshorn and Hornli are close. ✉ 7050 Innerarosa, Arosa GR. **Map** p203 F3. 📞 (081) 377 21 97. 🆎 (081) 377 40 75. @ belri@bluewin.ch 🍴 b (summer); b,l,d (winter). **Rooms** 25. Ⓕ Ⓕ

BASEL

Helvetia Known for its seafood and the Red Ox Bar. It's not overly pretty, but the bedrooms are sleek. It is close to the station and air terminal. ✉ 4051 Basel, Küchengasse 13 BS. **Map** p202 C2. 📞 (061) 272 06 88. 🆎 (061) 272 06 22. 🍴 b,l,d. **Rooms** 17. Ⓕ Ⓕ

BASEL

Teufelhof Run by theatre people. Each room is designed by a different artist, and changed every two years. Comfortable. 4051 Basel, Leonhardsgraben 47/Heuberg 30 BS. **Map** p202 C2. 📞 (061) 261 10 10. 🆎 (061) 261 10 04. @ info@teufelhof.com 🍴 b,l,d. **Rooms** 33. Ⓕ Ⓕ Ⓕ

BÖTTSTEIN

Schloss Böttstein Built in 1250, this castle was refurbished in 1974 and has comfortable bedrooms. The menu is international, with a French slant. ✉ 5315 Böttstein AG. **Map** p203 D2. 📞 (056) 269 16 16. 🆎 (056) 269 16 66. 🍴 b,l,d. **Rooms** 20. Ⓕ Ⓕ

BEVER

Chesa Salis The fine 16th-century house was remodelled in the 1870s, and many rooms look like part of a giant doll's house. One room, for private parties, is completely wood-panelled, with tiny windows; one bedroom is painted like a music box, another has very low beams. Classic French and Italian cuisine, as well as local dishes.
⊠ 7502 Bever GR. **Map** p203 F4. 📞 (081) 852 48 38. FAX (081) 852 47 06. @ chesa.salis@compunet.ch 🍴 b,l,d. **Rooms** 20. 🚿 ⬤ mid-Oct to mid-Dec; after Easter to mid-June. 💳 AE, DC, MC, V. ⒻⒻⒻ

CHAMPEX-LAC

Hotel Belvédère Eccentric and informal, but comfortable, with a mish-mash of artifacts hanging from the ceilings and walls. The owner has several fighting cows, called Queens, to be found only in this area, and he has a video to tell you all about it. The mountain inn is popular with people from Geneva. Fine country cooking and glorious views from the bar's stone terrace.
⊠ 1938 Champex-Lac VS. **Map** p202 B4.
📞 (027) 783 11 14. FAX (027) 783 25 76. 🍴 b,l,d.
Rooms 9. 🚿 ⬤ Never. 💳 MC, V. ⒻⒻ

CELERINA

Stüvetta Veglia Choosing a room at this extraordinary hotel is an aesthetic challenge: each has been decorated by a different Swiss artist. Room 8 has Carigiet landscapes, and there are two Gimmi nudes in No.5. Bathrooms are luxurious. The gourmet restaurant is well known; people travel from St Moritz to sample specialities such as beef marinated in hay and herbs.
⊠ 7505 Celerina GR. **Map** p203 F4. 📞 (081) 833 80 08. FAX (081) 833 45 42. 🍴 b,l,d. **Rooms** 18. ⬤ Nov to mid-Dec; after Easter to late June. 💳 AE, DC, MC, V. ⒻⒻⒻ

CONFIGNON

Auberge de Confignon Combine rural peace with city sightseeing. The traffic-free village of Confignon is so close to Geneva that you can get into the city on the trolley-bus; there are views over the town and the Salève mountains. The simple inn is also an animated village bar. Italian-based food is cooked by the owner. The bedrooms are unfussy, the bathrooms utilitarian.
⊠1232 Confignon, Place de l'Eglise 6 GE. **Map** p202 A4.
📞 (022) 757 19 44. FAX (022) 757 18 89. 🍴 b,l,d.
Rooms 14. 🚿 ⬤ Never. 💳 MC, V. ⒻⒻ

BRÜNIG PASS

Brünig Kulm At about 1,000m (3,330ft), the views from this simple mountain inn are fantastic. It is much favoured by skiers and walkers. Meals are substantial.
⊠ 6082 Brunig BE. **Map** p202 C3. 📞 (033) 971 17 08. FAX (033) 971 17 49. 🍴 b,l,d. **Rooms** 8. ⒻⒻ

CHÂTEAU-D'OEX

Bon Accueil A typical Swiss chalet with open fires, good food and stunning views over the fields and mountains. Good for walking holidays.
⊠ 1837 Château-d'Oex VD. **Map** p202 B4. 📞 (026) 924 63 20. FAX (026) 924 51 26. @ host-bon-accueil@ bluewin.ch 🍴 b,l,d. **Rooms** 21. ⒻⒻ

DAVOS

Hotel Larix This peaceful chalet hotel is furnished with the owners' possessions. The location is convenient for the Jakobshorn ski lifts. 7270 Davos-Platz, Albertistr 9 GR. **Map** p203 F4.
📞 (081) 413 11 88. FAX (081) 413 33 49. @ hotel-larix@ bluewin.ch 🍴 b,l,d. **Rooms** 20. ⒻⒻ

DELÉMONT

Du Midi This award-winning hotel provides excellent food in a brasserie, a restaurant and a gourmet dining room; Mediterranean influences. The bedrooms are pleasant.
⊠ 2800 Delémont JU. **Map** p202 B2. 📞 (032) 422 17 77. FAX (032) 423 19 89. 🍴 b,l,d. **Rooms** 4. ⒻⒻ

GOTTLIEBEN

Krone This restful hotel is set in the gloriously pretty village of Gottlieben, which dates from the 12th century; a short stroll along little lanes on the banks of the Rhine takes you past half-timbered houses and a monastery. Inside, there are some well-furnished bedrooms at the front with a view of the river streaming past outside; those in the back extension are plainer.
✉ 8274 Gottlieben TG. **Map** p203 E1. 🕻 (071) 666 80 60. 📠 (071) 666 80 69. @ krone@romantikhotel.ch 🍴 b,l,d. **Rooms** 25. ● Never. 💳 AE, DC, MC, V. ⒻⒻⒻ

GROSSHÖCHSTETTEN

Sternen This old farmhouse has been a village inn since the early 19th century, and it's still a classic, complete with a bowling alley. Its traditional decor make it a popular place with the diplomatic set from Bern, only 25km (19 miles) away. Home-cured ham is one of the specialities of the restaurant, along with large portions of regional specialities. Pleasant, simple bedrooms.
✉ 3506 Grosshöchstetten BE. **Map** p202 C3.
🕻 (031) 710 24 24. 📠 (031) 710 24 25. 🍴 b,l,d. **Rooms** 10. ● Never. 💳 MC, V. ⒻⒻ

GRINDELWALD

Fiescherblick Grindelwald is the only one of this region's resorts accessible by car, so walkers and skiers flock to this hotel; many return regularly. Packed lunches are provided, and staff can advise on trails and mountain guides. In the lively restaurant, second helpings always offered. Most bedrooms are spacious.
✉ 3818 Grindelwald BE. **Map** p202 C3.
🕻 (033) 853 44 53. 📠 (033) 853 44 57. @ hotel@ fiescherblick.ch 🍴 b,l,d. **Rooms** 25. ● late Nov to early Dec; after Easter to mid-May. 💳 AE, DC, MC, V. ⒻⒻ

GRUYÈRES

Hostellerie des Chevaliers Having been away for 20 years, the Corbot family took over their mountain inn again in 1998. Their son-in-law runs the kitchen, where he provides a gourmet menu as well as more traditional food. The bedrooms have magnificent views of the meadows and mountains around this medieval town; bathrooms are functional.
✉ 1663 Gruyères FR. **Map** p202 B3. 🕻 (026) 921 19 33.
📠 (026) 921 25 52. @ hotel_chevaliers@bluewin.ch
🍴 b,l,d. **Rooms** 32. 🅿 ● Jan. 💳 AE, DC, MC, V. ⒻⒻ

ERMATIGEN

Adler Dating from 1270 (rebuilt 1500), this tall, half-timbered building is the oldest inn in Thurgau. Try the innovative fish dishes in the wood-panelled dining room.
✉ Dorfplatz, 8272 Ermatigen TG. **Map** p203 E1. 🕻 (071) 664 11 33. 📠 (071) 664 30 11. 🍴 b,l,d. **Rooms** 4. Ⓕ

ERMATIGEN

Hirschen A charming old lakeside inn where you can eat delicious fish and game while watching the boats on Lake Constance, shaded beneath white parasols and sycamore trees.
✉ 8272 Ermatigen TG. **Map** p203 E1.
🕻 (071) 664 10 03. 🍴 b,l,d. **Rooms** 4. ⒻⒻ

FLIMS AT FIDAZ

Fidazerhof You can have a seriously healthy time in this ancient inn, with massage, reflexology, and vegetarian meals provided.
✉ 7017 Flims-Fidaz GR. **Map** p202 E3. 🕻 (081) 911 35 03. 📠 (081) 911 21 75. @ fidazerhof@kns.ch
🍴 b,l,d. **Rooms** 14. ⒻⒻ

GENEVA

Tiffany This is a warm and well-liked hotel, close to the Stock Exchange. Decorations very Art Nouveau; the best bedrooms are at the top.
✉ Rue de l'Arquebuse 18, 1204 Geneva GE.
Map p202 A4. 🕻 (022) 329 33 11. 📠 (022) 320 89 91.
@ info@hotel-tiffany.ch 🍴 b,l,d. **Rooms** 28. ⒻⒻⒻ

GUARDA

Meisser Built in 1645 as a farmhouse, this was converted to an inn by the present owner's great-grandfather. Although tiny, Guarda is a popular tourist spot due to its decorated houses and local craftsmen. You can enjoy sweeping views while eating gastronomic food on the terrace, or simpler grills in the garden. All the rooms are different.
✉ 7545 Guarda GR. **Map** p203 F3. ☎ (081) 862 21 32.
FAX (081) 862 24 80. @ meisser@mirus.ch 🍴 b,l,d.
Rooms 22. 🛏 ● Nov to mid-Dec (some apartments available). 🅿 AE, DC, MC, V. Ⓕ Ⓕ Ⓕ

INTERLAKEN

Hirschen Despite modern renovation, many ancient timbers survive at this very welcoming, traditional inn; modern furniture blends well with antiques. The inn's vast overhanging roof shelters a pavement terrace. Inside is a popular restaurant and a snug sitting room, and three upper stories of pleasantly decorated bedrooms. Some have balconies with views of the Jungfrau peak.
✉ 3800 Interlaken-Matten BE. **Map** p202 C3.
☎ (033) 822 15 45. FAX (033) 823 37 45. 🍴 b,l,d.
Rooms 22. 🛏 🛏 ● Nov. 🅿 AE, DC, MC, V. Ⓕ Ⓕ

GSTAAD
Hotel Olden Farmers and jetsetters alike love this place. Local specialities as well as international dishes. The bedrooms are charming. Large, quiet garden.
✉ 3780 Gstaad BE. **Map** p202 B4. ☎ (033) 744 34 44.
FAX (033) 744 61 64. 🍴 b,l,d. **Rooms** 15. Ⓕ Ⓕ Ⓕ

KANDERSTEG
Ruedihus Like a living museum, in the meadows beneath the mountains. Four-poster beds, 'Grandma's' jam, and no Coca-Cola – heavenly.
✉ 3718 Kandersteg BE. **Map** p202 C4.
☎ (033) 675 81 82. FAX (033) 675 81 85. @ voldenhorn@compuserve.com 🍴 b,l,d. **Rooms** 9. Ⓕ Ⓕ

KLOSTERS

Chesa Grischuna Very close to the Gotschnagrat-Parsenn cable car, this was originally a railway hotel. Now it swarms with visitors. It is a natural *après-ski* meeting place, with a bar, a sitting room with games, and a restaurant serving local food as well as caviar; afternoon tea is popular. Bedrooms are cosy.
✉ 7250 Klosters Platz GR. **Map** p203 F3.
☎ (081) 422 22 22. FAX (081) 422 22 25.
@ chesagrischuna@bluewin.ch 🍴 b,l,d. **Rooms** 24.
● 6 weeks after Easter. 🅿 AE, DC, MC, V. Ⓕ Ⓕ Ⓕ

KLOSTERS

Walserhof Although the hotel is on the main road, all the bedrooms look out on to fields. Chef Beat Bolliger, one of Switzerland's finest, provides a wide range of fine foods in the pretty restaurant, including his famous stuffed ravioli. The bedrooms are comfortable and the bathrooms luxurious.
✉ 7250 Klosters Platz GR. **Map** p203 F3. ☎ (081) 410 29 29. FAX (081) 410 29 39. @ walserhof@bluewin.ch 🍴 b,l,d. **Rooms** 13. ● late Oct to early Dec; mid-Apr to mid-June. 🅿 AE, DC, MC, V. Ⓕ Ⓕ Ⓕ

KLOSTERS
Rätia Originally a farmhouse and now a relaxed hotel. Some of the bedrooms look out on to rolling fields by Klosters.
✉ 7252 Klosters Dorf. **Map** p203 F3. ☎ (081) 422 47 47. FAX (081) 422 47 49. @ mail@hotelraetia.ch 🍴 b,l,d. **Rooms** 22. Ⓕ Ⓕ

LEUKERBAD
Les Sources des Alpes A marvellously luxurious place: delicious unfattening food, thermal spring-water swimming pools and lots of spa treatments. Peaceful, well-designed and large bedrooms.
✉ 3954 Leukerbad VS. **Map** p202 C4. ☎ (027) 470 51 51. FAX (027) 470 35 33. 🍴 b,l,d. **Rooms** 30. Ⓕ Ⓕ Ⓕ

For key to symbols see backflap. For price categories *see p201*

KÜSNACHT

LENZERHEIDE

Ermitage You can hardly believe you are just seven minutes' drive from the centre of Zurich when you sit in the serene gardens of this 300-year-old lakeside house. The spacious reception area, with antiques and paintings, feels like the private house it was some 40 years ago. Massive beds and white marble bathrooms.
⊠ 8700 Kusnacht-Zurich, Seestr 80 ZH.
Map p203 D2. ⒸⒾ (01) 914 42 42. FAX (01) 914 42 43.
ⓐ ermitage@bluewin.ch 🅝 b,l,d. **Rooms** 26. 🅑
⬤ Never. 🅔 AE, DC, MC, V. ⒻⒻⒻ

Guarda Val Standing in the middle of the pastures above Lenzerheide, this unique inn was created out of abandoned farmbuildings in the late 1960s. It now has many faithful regulars who return throughout the year and expect to stay in the same room. Bedrooms are stylishly decorated in pale colours. Local dishes in the restaurant.
⊠ 7078 Lenzerheide/Sporz CR. **Map** p203 E3. ⒸⒾ (081) 385 85 85. FAX (081) 385 85 95. ⓐ hotel@guardaval.ch
🅝 b,l,d. **Rooms** 34. 🅘 🅑 ⬤ Nov to mid-Dec; after Easter to mid-June. 🅔 AE, DC, MC, V. ⒻⒻⒻ

LAAX

LUGANO

Pöstli A charming stone building with green shutters in the delightful upper Rhine village of Laax. In 1978, marketing man Peter Panier came home and did what many dream of: he created this inn because he wanted 'the kind of hotel that I always wanted to stay in'. Food is traditional Swiss, and each bedroom is different – one of the singles has a sleigh bed.
⊠ 7031 Laax GR. **Map** p203 E3. ⒸⒾ (081) 921 44 66.
FAX (081) 921 34 00. 🅝 b,l,d. **Rooms** 6. 🅑
⬤ May, June, 3 weeks Sept. 🅔 MC, V. ⒻⒻ

Villa Principe Leopoldo This former holiday home of Leopold of Hapsburg has stunning views of Lugano, the mountains and the lake, and a scented, flower-covered terrace. It is well preserved, and decorated with portraits, busts and sporting prints. The bedrooms (all junior suites) are luxurious. Imaginative food.
⊠ 6900 Lugano, Via Montalbano 5, TI.
Map p203 D5. ⒸⒾ (091) 985 88 55. FAX (091) 985 88 25.
ⓐ info@leopoldo.ch 🅝 b,l,d. **Rooms** 37. 🅢 🅘 🅑
⬤ Never. 🅔 AE, DC, MC, V. ⒻⒻⒻⒻ

LUGANO

Romantik Hotel Ticino 'Art and Gastronomy' is the motto of the owner of this 400 year-old palazzo. All bedrooms have top quality beds.
⊠ 6901 Lugano, Piazza Cioccaro 1 TI. **Map** p203 D5.
ⒸⒾ (091) 922 77 72. FAX (091) 923 62 78. 🅝 b,l,d.
Rooms 20. ⒻⒻⒻⒻ

LUZERN (LUCERNE)

Baslertor An unexpected bonus in this pleasant spot is the outdoor swimming pool. There is a cocktail bar and a cosy restaurant.
⊠ 6000 Luzern, Pfistergasse 17 LU. **Map** p203 D3.
ⒸⒾ (041) 240 09 18. FAX (041) 240 20 30.
ⓐ info@baslertor.ch 🅝 b,l,d. **Rooms** 30. ⒻⒻ

MALANS

Weisskreuz The charming traditional inn is popular with locals and visitors. Good regional food. Modern bedrooms; excellent bathrooms.
⊠ 7208 Malans GR. **Map** p203 E3. ⒸⒾ (081) 322 81 61.
FAX (081) 322 81 62. ⓐ gtinguely@weisskreuz.com
🅝 b,l,d. **Rooms** 11. ⒻⒻ

MARTIGNY

Le Forum A popular stop-over from Italy to France. The food is first-rate and the welcome so warm you won't notice the uninspiring building.
⊠ 1920 Martigny, Av du Grand-St-Bernard VS.
Map p202 B4. ⒸⒾ (027) 722 18 41. FAX (027) 722 79 25.
🅝 b,l,d. **Rooms** 29. ⒻⒻ

LUZERN (LUCERNE)

Zum Rebstock Each room is different in this 600-year-old hotel. Owner and art-collector Claudia Moser has covered the place in pictures. The three very different, but equally excellent restaurants serve local specialities. The breakfast buffet, featuring ten different kinds of bread and piles of fruit, is a dream.
⊠ 6006 Luzern, St Leodegarstr 3. **Map** p203 D3.
🄲 (041) 410 35 81. 𝗙𝗔𝗫 (041) 410 39 17.
@ hotel-rebstock@bluewin.ch 🍴 b,l,d. **Rooms** 28.
● Never. 🖪 AE, DC, MC, V. ⒻⒻⒻ

LES MARÉCOTTES

Aux Mille Etoiles This is very much a family hotel – among the 25 rooms is a good selection of junior suites and family rooms. Jan Mol, one of the extended family who run the place, produces a newsletter every day with suggestions for ski trips, hikes and a weather report. The indoor swimming pool opens on to the garden.
⊠ 1923 Les Marécottes VS. **Map** p202 B4.
🄲 (027) 761 16 66. 𝗙𝗔𝗫 (027) 761 16 00. 🍴 b,l,d.
Rooms 25. 🏊 🍴 🛇 ● Nov to mid-Dec; 4 weeks after Easter. 🖪 MC, V. ⒻⒻ

MADULAIN

Stüva Colani Set in the middle of a village, this 200-year-old building has been opened up and beautifully modernised. The bright, airy Tavolini restaurant has a pasta menu perfect for children; for gastronomes, there is a separate gourmet restaurant. The hotel decoration blends old and new, with slate floors and pastel furnishings.
⊠ 7523 Madulain GR. **Map** p203 F3.
🄲 (081) 854 17 71. 𝗙𝗔𝗫 (081) 854 14 85. 🍴 b,l,d.
Rooms 16. 🛇 ● Nov to mid Dec; after Easter to early June. 🖪 AE, DC, MC, V. ⒻⒻ

MURTEN-MEYRIEZ

Le Vieux Manoir au Lac A French general built this lakeside manor house about a century ago. Each of the elegant bedrooms has a sitting area; two hexagonal suites in the old tower overlook the hotel's park and lake. There is a conservatory restaurant, and a beautiful breakfast room. The medieval town of Murten is a short drive away.
⊠ 3280 Murten-Meyriez FR. **Map** p202 B3.
🄲 (026) 678 61 61. 𝗙𝗔𝗫 (026) 678 61 62.
@ vieuxmanoir@bluewin.ch 🍴 b,l,d. **Rooms** 30. 🛇
● mid-Dec to mid-Feb. 🖪 AE, DC, MC, V. ⒻⒻⒻⒻ

MORCOTE

Carina Carlton In this charming location on the Lugano, you can have dinner sitting over the water. The terraced garden has a swimming pool. Church bells ring 66 times at 6am.
⊠ 6922 Morcote TI. **Map** p203 D5. 🄲 (091) 996 11 31.
𝗙𝗔𝗫 (091) 996 19 29. 🍴 b,l,d. **Rooms** 21. ⒻⒻ

RONCO

Albergo Ronco Fantastic views over Lake Maggiore. The home-made pasta is delicious; cakes can be eaten on the vine-covered terrace.
⊠ 6622 Ronco s/Ascona TI. **Map** p203 D4.
🄲 (091) 791 52 65. 𝗙𝗔𝗫 (091) 791 06 40.
@ hotel-ronco@ticino.com 🍴 b,l,d. **Rooms** 20. ⒻⒻ

SAAS FEE

Fletschhorn Stunning views (the hotel is located at around 1,800m/5,900ft) and splendid French cuisine. Delightful traditional bedrooms.
⊠ 3906 Saas Fee VS. **Map** p202 C4. 🄲 (027) 957 21 31.
𝗙𝗔𝗫 (027) 957 21 87. @ hotel.fletschhorn@saasfee.ch
🍴 b,l,d. **Rooms** 15. ⒻⒻ

SATIGNY

Domaine de Châteauvieux Sample wonderful food and local wines in this popular old farmhouse. Plain bedrooms; generous breakfasts.
⊠ 1242 Satigny, Peney-Dessus GE. **Map** p202 A4.
🄲 (022) 753 15 11. 𝗙𝗔𝗫 (022) 753 19 24.
@ chateauvieux@bluewin.ch 🍴 b,l,d. **Rooms** 19. ⒻⒻ

NEUCHÂTEL

La Maison du Prussien The name of this hotel and restaurant, a converted brewery by a spectacular gorge, refers to the time when the region was part of Prussia. The 18th-century building has been sympathetically restored, with plain stone walls and exposed beams; romantic bedrooms with modern, luxurious bathrooms.
⊠ Au Gor du Vauseyon, 2006 Neuchâtel NE. **Map** p202 B3. 🄲 (032) 730 54 54. ⅎᴬˣ (032) 730 21 43. @ info@hotel-prussien.ch 🔢 b,l,d. **Rooms** 10. 🔋 ● Never. 🄴 AE, DC, MC, V. Ⓕ Ⓕ Ⓕ

PORTO RONCO

La Rocca The Rocca's garden offer unbeatable views of Lake Maggiore from its hillside position by Porto Ronco, a writers' and artists' colony. The hotel is cosy, with a bar and terrace area, and holds occasional themed evenings with accordion music and barbecues. The simple bedrooms are bright and airy; some have balconies.
⊠ 6613 Porto Ronco, Ascona TI. **Map** p203 D4. 🄲 (091) 791 53 44. ⅎᴬˣ (091) 791 40 64. @ Hotel@la-rocca.ch 🔢 b,l,d. **Rooms** 21. 🏊 🔋 ● Never. 🄴 DC, MC, V. Ⓕ Ⓕ Ⓕ

ORSELINA

Hotel Mirafiori It looks like many other holiday hotels in the popular Locarno area, high above Lake Maggiore. Yet the Mirafiori stands out for its warm welcome, its lush garden with swimming pool (superb views), and its excellent regional cooking. Some bedrooms are in hillside annexes; one is in its own, miniature cottage.
⊠ 6644 Locarno-Orselina, Via Al Parco TI. **Map** p203 D4. 🄲 (091) 743 18 77. ⅎᴬˣ (091) 743 77 39. 🔢 b,l,d. **Rooms** 25. 🏊 🔋 ● early Nov to mid-March. 🄴 AE, DC, MC, V. Ⓕ Ⓕ Ⓕ

SCHANGNAU IM EMMENTAL

Kemmeriboden-Bad Set in a beautiful valley, this was originally built over a century ago for people coming to the sulphur springs. Now visitors come for much more, including fishing, walking, skiing and mountain climbing. The bedrooms are traditional, and some can sleep up to six. Lots of things for children to do.
⊠ 6197 Schangnau im Emmental. **Map** p202 C3. 🄲 (034) 493 77 77. ⅎᴬˣ (034) 493 77 70. @ hotel@kemmeriboden.com 🔢 b,l,d. **Rooms** 29. 🔋 ● Dec. 🄴 AE, DC, MC, V. Ⓕ Ⓕ

SCHAFFHAUSEN

Rheinhotel Fischerzunft Has one of the most acclaimed restaurants in the country. A perfect mix of East and West. The bedrooms are chic.
⊠ 8200 Schaffhausen, Rheinquai 8 SH. **Map** p203 D1. 🄲 (052) 632 05 05. ⅎᴬˣ (052) 632 05 13. @ info@ fischerzunft.ch 🔢 b,l,d. **Rooms** 10. Ⓕ Ⓕ Ⓕ

SCHÖNBÜHL BEI BERN

Schönbühl A typical village hotel, with wood-panelled walls and a happy mix of antique and modern furniture.
⊠ 3322 Schönbühl bei Bern BE. **Map** p203 C2. 🄲 (031) 859 69 69. ⅎᴬˣ (031) 859 69 05. @ gasthof.schoenbuehl@ swissonline.ch 🔢 b,l,d. **Rooms** 12. Ⓕ Ⓕ

STANS

Engel At this no-nonsense inn set between a lake and a mountain, you get plain bedrooms and substantial helpings of food.
⊠ 6370 Stans, am Dorfplatz NW. **Map** p203 D3. 🄲 (041) 619 10 10. ⅎᴬˣ (041) 619 10 11. @ engelstans@bluewin.ch 🔢 b,l,d. **Rooms** 9. Ⓕ Ⓕ

TAVERNE

Ristorante Motto del Gallo In an industrial area near a motorway, but stupendous food. Worth staying a night.
⊠ 6807 Taverne-Lugano TI. **Map** p203 D4. 🄲 (091) 945 28 71. ⅎᴬˣ (091) 945 27 23. 🔢 b,l,d. **Rooms** 3. Ⓕ Ⓕ

STEIN AM RHEIN

Rheinfels This ancient hostelry is by the river next to the bridge, with the terrace restaurant jutting out over the water. There is a medieval atmosphere: creaky wooden stairs, full-sized suits of armour, and old beams. Edi Schwegler's food is very popular, especially his fish and game in season. Bedrooms are functional.
⊠ 8260 Stein am Rhein SH. **Map** p203 D1. 🌓 (052) 741 21 44. **FAX** (052) 741 25 22. @ rheinfels@bluewin.ch
🍴 b,l,d. **Rooms** 17. ⬤ mid-Dec to early March.
🅯 AE, DC, MC, V. Ⓕ Ⓕ

ZERMATT

Romantik Hotel Julen A proper family hotel, with resident children and a working sheepdog who minds the cash register as a sideline. The bedrooms are lavish; some at the top have their own sitting area. Don't miss the *Schaeferstube* (sheep room). The garden is large, and there are marvellous views of the Matterhorn. Adventure pool and many fitness facilities.
⊠ 3920 Zermatt VS. **Map** p202 C5. 🌓 (027) 966 76 00. **FAX** (027) 966 76 76. @ hotel.julen@zermatt.ch 🍴 b,l,d.
Rooms 36, 🛏 🍴 🛁 ⬤ Never. 🅯 AE, DC, MC, V. Ⓕ Ⓕ

VILLENEUVE

Les Marines The modern, two-storey hotel by the lake was designed to merge into the surrounding landscape. The bedrooms are huge, with windows looking out on to the lake, and each has a kitchenette which can be opened if required. There is a manicured lawn on the roof, and an outside dining area on the terrace.
⊠ 1844 Villeneuve, Montreux VD. **Map** p202 B4.
🌓 (021) 960 39 06. **FAX** (021) 960 39 34.
@ suissemajestic@bluewin.ch 🍴 b,l,d. **Rooms** 23.
🛁 ⬤ End Oct to Easter. 🅯 AE, DC, MC, V. Ⓕ Ⓕ Ⓕ

ZURICH

Tiefenau The discreet 19th-century house is on a tree-lined street near the university and is much favoured by actors and musicians. It's got a homely feel, with plants and comfy sofas in the bar and library. Rooms vary in style; bathrooms are small but luxurious. Local dishes are a speciality in the restaurant; summer dining terrace.
⊠ 8032 Zurich, Steinwiesstr 8-10 ZH. **Map** p203 D2.
🌓 (01) 267 87 87. **FAX** (01) 251 24 76. @ info@
tiefenau.ch 🍴 b,l,d. **Rooms** 18. 🛁 ⬤ Christmas and
New Year. 🅯 AE, DC, MC, V. Ⓕ Ⓕ Ⓕ

VADUZ

Gasthof Löwen See the 400-year-old fresco in this historic inn. Beautiful carpets, antiques and luxurious bathrooms. Quiet rooms at the back.
⊠ Herrengasse 35, 9490 Vaduz FL. **Map** p203 E2.
🌓 (075) 238 11 44. **FAX** (075) 238 11 45.
@ loewen@hotels.li 🍴 b,l,d. **Rooms** 7. Ⓕ Ⓕ Ⓕ

VERBIER

Golf Hotel Unpretentious golfing hotel, friendly if a little old-fashioned. French cooking. Stunning views of Mont Blanc and the Trient.
⊠ 1936 Verbier VS. **Map** p202 B4. 🌓 (027) 771 65 15.
FAX (027) 771 14 88. @ golfotel@axiom.ch
🍴 b,l,d. **Rooms** 30. Ⓕ Ⓕ Ⓕ

WEISSENBURG

Alte Post Set by the river, this characterful inn has open fires and wood-panelled bedrooms. Popular with skiers and canoeists. Good food.
⊠ 3764 Weissenburg Dorf BE. **Map** p202 B3.
🌓 (033) 783 15 15. **FAX** (033) 783 15 78. 🍴 b,l,d.
Rooms 9. Ⓕ Ⓕ

ZINAL

Le Besso Old inn at the top of the Val d'Anniviers. The proprietor likes taking guests out on hikes. Stunning views of the Matterhorn and glacier.
⊠ 3961 Zinal VS. **Map** p202 C4. 🌓 (027) 475 31 65.
FAX (027) 475 49 82. @ besso@bluewin.ch 🍴 b,l,d.
Rooms 10. Ⓕ Ⓕ

For key to symbols see backflap. For price categories *see p201*

FRANCE

FRANCE

FRENCH HOTELS are beginning to enjoy a reputation as the point of your journey, rather than somewhere to be endured along the way. This is not a universal trend, but individual hoteliers have been adding personal attention, style and comfort to their existing culinary reputations. If you have a complaint or a compliment, this new breed of hands-on owner will be there to listen to you – with interest. Such hotels are typically family-run and housed in sympathetically-restored and furnished historic buildings – part of the landscape rather than modern intrusions. Often they are proud to proclaim their unique regional identity.

Château du Domaine St-Martin, at Vence, page 264, one of the most expensive hotels in France

FRANCE REGION BY REGION

IN THIS GUIDE the country has been divided into Northern France, Central France and Southern France.

Northern France
The plains of Picardy, with their traditional inns and converted châteaux, are bordered to the north by the Ardennes forests and to the east by the mountains and hills of Vosges. Paris and its surroundings dominate the centre of the region, its hotels ranging from chic townhouses to the grand buildings of the large hotels.

The Channel coast has its share of heavy industry and oil refineries, concentrated round Le Havre and Rouen, but close by lie the beautiful port of Honfleur, Bayeux

with its memories of William the Conqueror's invasion of England (and the more recent D-Day landings), and the lush farmland of the Pays d'Auge and La Suisse Normande, with châteaux, mills and half-timbered inns. To the west of the Channel port of Cherbourg lies the monastery island of Le Mont-St-Michel; here begins the more rugged landscape of Celtic Brittany, with its manors and seaside hotels.

Central France
We define this region as beginning to the south of the Ile de France, and stretching from Nantes at the mouth of the Loire in the west, to the Jura mountains in the east. The great châteaux of the Loire Valley, many of which were re-modelled during the

Renaissance, are almost always breathtaking, and not all just for looking at: two exquisite examples of places to stay are the Château de Noirieux at Briollay, (page 239) and the Hostellerie du Château de Bellecroix at Chagny (page 240).

Burgundy stands out for the rustic buildings of the fragmented vineyards of the Côte d'Or; the religious showpieces at Vézelay, Fontenay and Cluny, and the splendid palaces of Dijon. Further east is Franche-Comté, with its alpine highlands, crystal rivers, and rolling farmland in the Saône valley.

Southern France
Poitou, to the north of the city of Bordeaux, and Aquitaine, stretching down to the western end of the

Pyrenees at Biarritz, make up the final section of France's Atlantic coastline. Mile upon mile of sandy beaches are backed by dunes and pine forests. The Romans left their imperial mark here – the great arch of Germanicus and the amphitheatre at Saintes are both worth a detour.

Medieval pilgrims travelling to the shrine of St James at Santiago de Compostela left a legacy of Romanesque churches such as those at Poitiers and Parthenay. The vineyards of Bordeaux have kept the city prosperous for centuries. A number of the château hotels in this region, (such as the one at Pauillac, page 257), run their own wine appreciation courses.

To the east lie the green, rolling hills, farms and manors of the Dordogne Valley and the caves and culinary delights of Périgord. The cave paintings at Lascaux are probably the most important in France – but if you prefer *foie gras*, walnuts and truffles, try Sarlat's fabulous Saturday market. In the far south-west, the French Pyrenees take you into Basque country, offering spectacular scenery – and mountain activities as tiring or thrilling as anybody could want. Returning to your Basque inn, or perhaps to the Hôtel du Vieux Pont at Sauveterre-de-Béarn (page 263), with its spectacular position on medieval arches above the Gave d'Oloron river, will make you glad you survived the day intact.

Languedoc-Roussillon is squeezed in between the Mediterranean shore and the Massif Central range. Roussillon was Spanish until 1659, and the Fort de Salses still stands at the old border. Carcassonne is an amazingly well-restored medieval town and Nîmes still has much of the Roman about it.

The Massif Central is an enigmatic area, wild and hard on the Grands Causses, gentle in the Limousin and

spectacular where the Lot, Aveyron and Tarn leave the Aubrac mountains through rugged gorges.

To the east lies the Rhône Valley and beyond are the French Alps with some traditional chalet hotels.

Provence is nowadays almost too familiar to need much description. The salt-marshes of the Camargue and the resorts of the Côte d'Azur have, as a back-drop, a highly-coloured and scented hinterland, where the Romans who built the theatre (still in use) at Vaison-la-Romaine may well have found Bronze Age remains. Hotels have found their way into *mas* – the Provençal farmhouses – and into villas originally built for private pleasure.

HIGHLIGHTS

THE HOTELS ILLUSTRATED on these introductory pages are just a taste of what you will find in the listings that

follow. Fans of the quaint will love the topsy-turvy Auberge du Vieux Puits in Pont-Audemer (page 235). Champagne buffs will gravitate to the Château des Crayères in Reims (page 235), or to the Château de Courcelles (page 228), where the cellars house outstanding champagnes. Those who navigate principally by menu are unlikely to pass up a chance to stay at Jean-Marc Reynaud's eponymous restaurant at Tain l'Hermitage (page 246) or at Alain Ducasse's La Bastide de Moustiers (page 257). Those for whom a holiday without a beach is unthinkable will take a close look at the reasonably-priced and child-friendly Ti Al-Lannec at Trébeurden (page 237). Mountain air and a stunning view of Mont Blanc are both on offer at the Auberge du Bois Prin's classic chalet at Chamonix (page 240). Further south there are more panoramic views from the

The Paris Ritz, page 234, opulence on a lavish scale

Château de Brélidy at Brélidy in Brittany, page 227, a severe exterior, but relaxing inside

beautifully converted medieval Le Cagnard at Haut-de-Cagnes (page 253).

FOOD AND DRINK

FRENCH COOKING is probably the subtlest, most varied and most imaginative in the world. It is not necessarily elaborate, but the care taken to choose, season and flavour the principal ingredients can lift dishes into the realms of the extraordinary.

In the late 1980s and early 1990s, some gastronomes felt that French food had lost its edge, at any rate compared with the new cuisines of Britain, Australia and the US Pacific Rim. Nowadays, our impression is that French food is re-inventing itself.

The range of styles is stupendous – in the north the coastal waters yield huge platters of *fruits de mer*, and travelling eastwards you find the ham,

Marceau Hôtel, page 242

sausages, stout stews and tangy cheeses of Alsace. In the west the pork, cream and calvados of Normandy are neighbours to the Breton crêpes, seafood and lamb raised on the coastal salt marshes.

Moving southwest the *foie gras,* truffles, *confits* and walnut oil of Périgord, the wine-based cookery of Bordeaux, and the shellfish and lobsters of Arcachon and Marennes eventually give way to the robust and often highly-spiced dishes of the Basque southwest.

Lyon can claim to be the gastronomic centre of France: in this fortunate city, Bresse chicken, Charolais beef, wild fowl from the Dombes, smoked sausage and freshwater fish from Franche-Comté and the Jura join forces with a host of local cheeses such as Vacherin, Cantal, and Fourme d'Ambert.

The south of France has the brightest palette of colours: in the markets, aubergines, courgettes, asparagus, huge tomatoes, peppers, peaches and cherries contrast with black olives, walnuts, braids of garlic and wild mushrooms. The basis of many a dish is lamb from the Camargue, or red mullet and red snapper – combined with conger eel and monkfish

to make *bouillabaisse*, the king of fish soups.

Entire books have been devoted to the wine of single French vineyards. All that can be said here is that prices range from the stratospheric to rock-bottom; and that it is a matter of pride for most restaurateurs to offer excellent value house wine (*vin du patron*) from the lower end of the scale. Do try them, if only to give your purse a rest.

France has been listing and classifying wine production areas for nearly 200 years. There are three principal classifications: *appellation contrôlée (AC)* which guarantees origin and a certain standard, *vin délimité de qualité supérieure (VDQS)*, which distinguish good wines of local interest; and *vin de pays* which is the humblest grade of all.

Virtually all the best wine-producing areas are dominated by their rivers. The Marne and the topmost reaches of the Seine flow through Champagne; the Loire through the vineyards producing the dry whites of Muscadet in the west, and of Pouilly and Sancerre in the east, and the sweeter wines of Touraine and Anjou at the centre. The Charente cuts Cognac in half; the Dordogne graces

Bergerac and then, like the Garonne, empties into the Gironde estuary near Bordeaux, where the great wines of the Médoc, St Émilion, Pomerol and Graves are produced. From east of the Burgundian capital of Beaune, the Saône flows almost due south through the Mâconnais to join the Rhône, which itself continues south through the rich red wine-producing areas between the cities of Lyon and Avignon.

BEDROOMS AND BATHROOMS

U NLESS OTHERWISE specified, a double room has a double bed (*grand lit*). If you want twin beds (*deux lits*) be sure to ask for them – there may be an extra charge. Specify clearly if you want your own bathroom (*avec salle de bain en suite*).

Bathrooms may not have a bath (*une baignoire*). If a shower (*une douche*) will not do, be sure to say so when booking.

OTHER PRACTICAL INFORMATION

W EEKEND WEDDING parties can go on very noisily till dawn. It is worth asking if your booking will coincide with *un mariage* – and well worth revising your plans if it does.

The national summer holidays start around 14 July and end on 31 August; if possible, avoid travelling around these dates.

Language Most hotels have an English-speaker, or can find one, but no matter how bad your French, you will collect some goodwill by trying it. In Alsace-Lorraine if you don't know the word in French, try German.

Currency The French *franc* (written 'F', 'FF' or 'Fr'), is divided into 100 *centimes*. The decimal point is shown as a comma. Some traditionalists may baffle you with huge numbers –

Château de Noirieux, page 239

they are still reckoning in 'old' francs (last used many years ago).

Shops Food shops tend to open at about 7am, close around noon for lunch, and reopen in the late afternoon until 7pm. Food shops often open on Sunday mornings but stay closed on Monday mornings. Other shops usually open 9am–6pm Mon–Sat, and, except for the supermarkets and hypermarkets, take a lunch break.

Tipping A service charge is usually added in cafés and restaurants, but most French people leave a few francs at bars and 5 per cent at restaurants.

Telephoning Phoning abroad from hotels can be very expensive. Some public telephones take 1F to 10F coins, others take *télécartes* (50 or 120 unit phonecards from post offices, *tabacs* and some cafés). Post offices have *cabines* –

booths where you can call first and pay afterwards.

All French telephone numbers have ten digits: a two-figure area prefix, followed by an eight-digit number. If phoning from within France, always include the full area prefix. To phone France from the UK, dial 00 33, then the phone number, omitting the initial zero from the area prefix; from the US, 011 33.

Public holidays 1 January; Easter Sunday and Monday; Ascension Day (sixth Thursday after Easter); Whit Monday (second Monday after Ascension Day); 1 May; 8 May; 14 July; 1 November; 11 November; 25 December.

USEFUL WORDS

Breakfast	*Petit déjeuner*
Lunch	*Déjeuner*
Dinner	*Dîner*
Free room?	*Chambre libre?*
How much?	*Combien?*
A single	*Une chambre pour une personne*
A double	*Une chambre pour deux personnes*

FRANCE PRICE BANDS

O UR PRICE BANDS refer to the price of a standard double room in high season *including* breakfast. (However, French hotels usually quote room prices excluding breakfast.)

Ⓕ	under 500F
ⒻⒻ	500F–900F
ⒻⒻⒻ	900F–1,300F
ⒻⒻⒻⒻ	over 1,300F

Château de Nieuil, at Nieuil page 243, a former royal hunting lodge

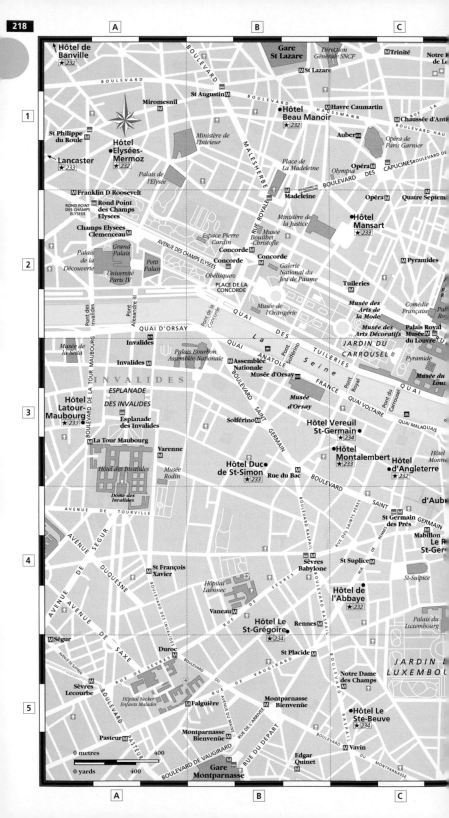

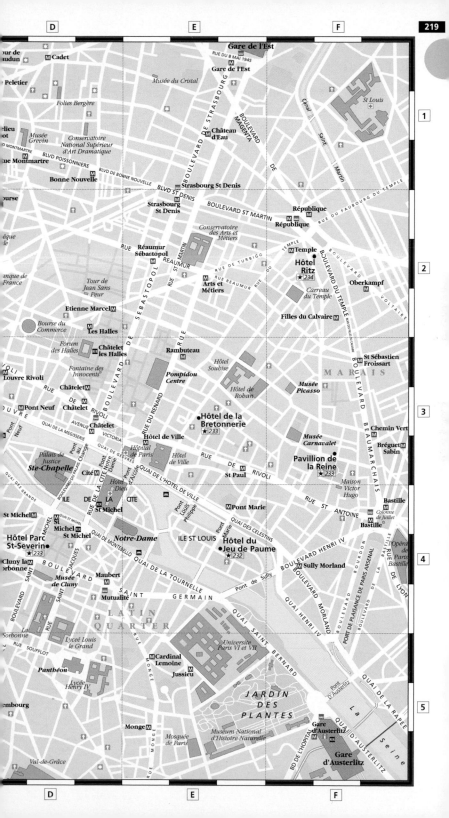

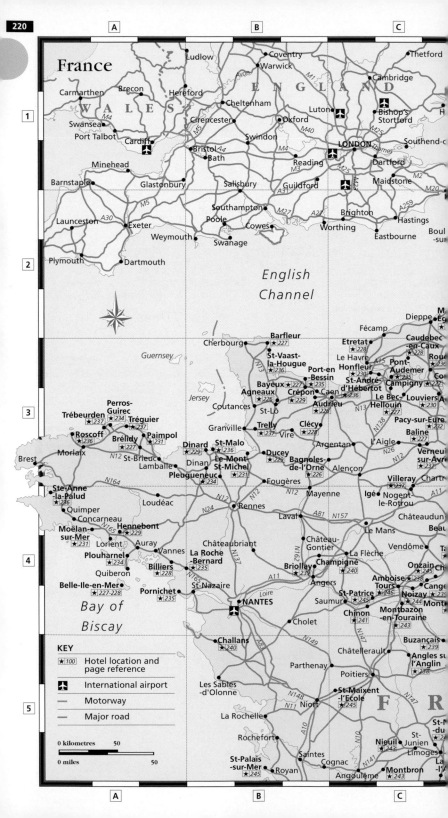

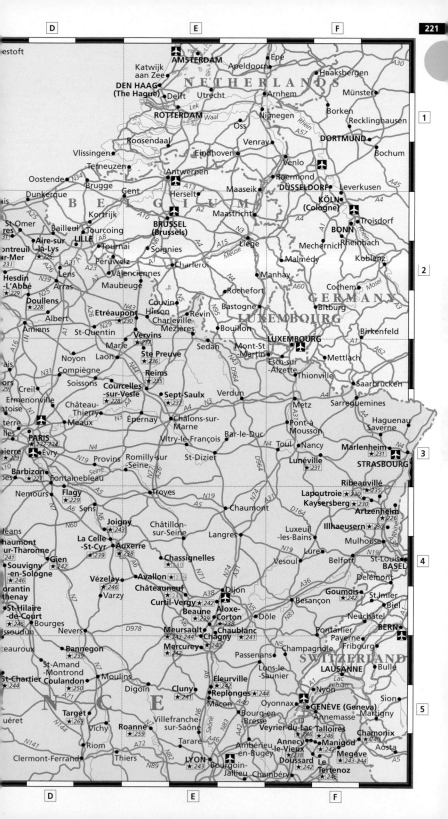

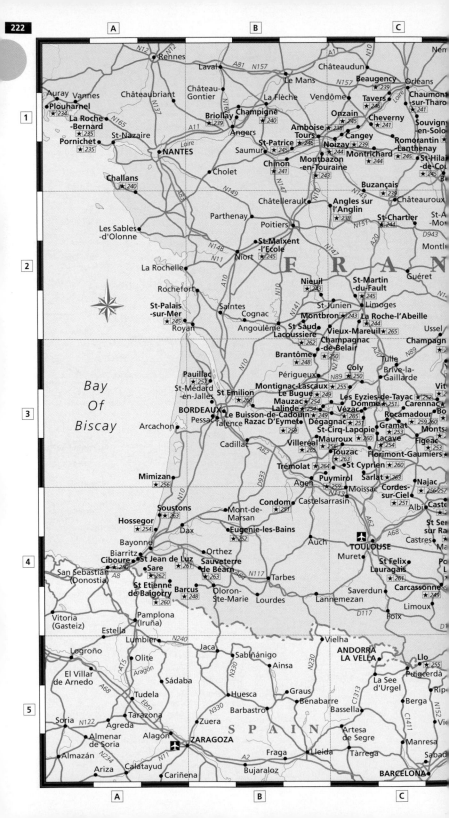

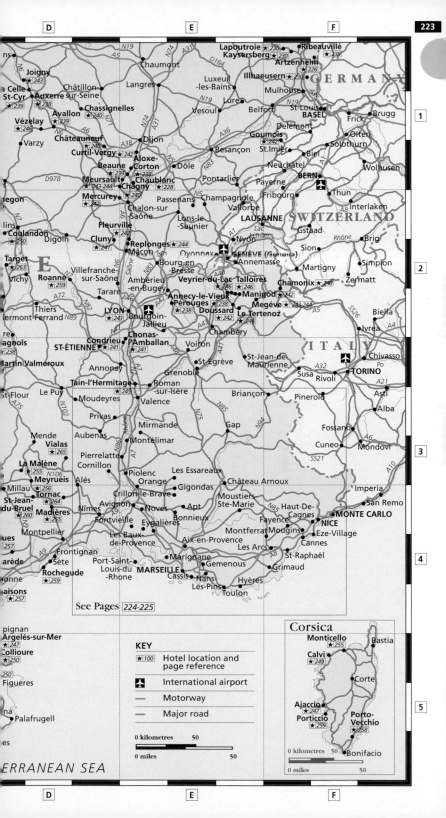

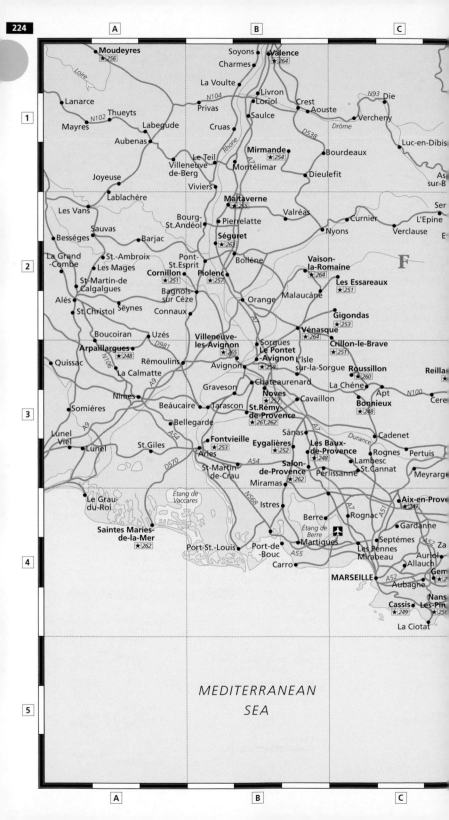

NORTHERN FRANCE

NORMANDY • BRITTANY • PICARDY AND PAS-DE-CALAIS
PARIS • CHAMPAGNE-ARDENNE • ALSACE-LORRAINE

ORTHERN FRANCE offers travellers an almost infinite array of choices in scenery and accommodation. The region stretches southwards from the plains of Picardy, through the apple orchards, lush countryside and converted mills of Normandy to rugged Brittany, with its austere granite chateaux and perfect seaside hotels for family holidays. Paris, at the heart of Northern France, is one of the most romantic cities in the world. It also boasts a large collection of very chic hotels. Pas-de-Calais, the rolling countryside behind the Channel ports of Calais and Boulogne, is ideal for weekend breaks from Britain. Wine lovers with more time to spare can go further east to Champagne.

AGNEAUX

Château d'Agneaux The rather austere exterior of this 13th-century château hides a comfortable hotel with attractive but not over-decorated rooms. Try for one in the turret. Though only just outside the town of Saint-Lô, this is a peaceful spot in hilly countryside. The restaurant serves fine food.
☒ Avenue Ste-Marie, 50180 St-Lô-Agneaux, Manche. **Map** p220 B3. ☎ 02 33 57 65 88. ☎ 02 33 56 59 21. @ chateau.agneaux@wanadoo.fr ⊓ b,l,d. **Rooms** 12. ⊓ ◐ ◉ Never. ☒ AE, DC, MC, V. ⒻⒻ

AIRE-SUR-LA-LYS

Hostellerie des Trois Mousquetaires If the gracious rooms at this cheerful family-run hotel in a mock Tudor house don't charm you, the large wooded garden with its ponds and streams might well do the trick. Despite the grand furnishings, this is an informal place. Vast portions of regional food for meals, and a vegetarian menu.
☒ Château du Fort de la Redoute, 62120 Aire-sur-la-Lys, Pas-de-Calais. **Map** p221 D2. ☎ 03 21 39 01 11. ☎ 03 21 39 50 10. ⊓ b,l,d. **Rooms** 33. 🗐 ◐ ◉ mid-Dec to mid-Jan. ☒ AE, MC, V. ⒻⒻ

LES ANDELYS

Hôtel de la Chaîne d'Or Books and paintings give this 18th-century inn a homely feel. An unrivalled position, hugging a loop in the Seine.
☒ 27 rue Grande, 27700 Les Andelys, Eure. **Map** p220 C3. ☎ 02 32 54 00 31. ☎ 02 32 54 05 68. ⊓ b,l,d. **Rooms** 10. ⒻⒻ

ARTZENHEIM

Auberge d'Artzenheim Brimming with rustic charm, an inn with a cosy beamed restaurant. Summer dining on the flower-filled terrace.
☒ 30 rue du Sponeck, 68320 Artzenheim, Haut-Rhin. **Map** p221 F4. ☎ 03 89 71 60 51. ☎ 03 89 71 68 21. ⊓ b,l,d. **Rooms** 10. Ⓕ

AUDRIEU

Château d'Audrieu Ancestral pile of the Livry-Level family, transformed into a Relais et Château with huge rooms and an impressive wine list.
☒ 14250 Audrieu, Calvados. **Map** p220 B3. ☎ 02 31 80 21 52. ☎ 02 31 80 24 73. @ audrieu@relaischateaux.fr ⊓ b,l,d. **Rooms** 30. ⒻⒻⒻ

BAGNOLES-DE-L'ORNE

Manoir du Lys A geranium-bedecked hunting lodge with pool and Michelin-starred cuisine.
☒ La Croix Gauthier, Route de Juvigny, 61140 Bagnoles-de-l'Orne, Orne. **Map** p220 B3. ☎ 02 33 37 80 69. ☎ 02 33 30 05 80. @ manoirdulys@lemel.fr ⊓ b,l,d. **Rooms** 28. ⒻⒻ

BALINE

Moulin de Balisne A 10 ha (25 acre) park protects this carefully restored water mill from sight and sound of the nearby N12 highway. Fishing enthusiasts can take boats out into a lake and fish two rivers. The hotel is crammed with antiques, and has charming bedrooms and a congenial bar/dining room.
☒ RN 12 Baline, 27130 Verneuil-sur-Avre, Eure.
Map p220 C3. 🔾 02 32 32 03 48.
🅵🅰🅷 02 32 60 11 22. 🄸🄸 b,l,d. **Rooms** 12. 🔾
🔾 Never. 🔾 AE, DC, MC, V. Ⓕ Ⓕ

BRÉLIDY

Château de Brélidy Don't be put off by the severe granite walls, which are typical of 16th-century Breton architecture. Those who venture in will find a welcoming family-run hotel, with relaxing bedrooms named after flowers. Added attractions are a billiard room, a Jacuzzi beneath an arbour in the garden, and an unspoilt setting.
☒ Brélidy, 22140 Bégard, Côtes-d'Armor. **Map** p220 A3.
🔾 02 96 95 69 38. 🅵🅰🅷 02 96 95 18 03. 🄸🄸 b,d. **Rooms** 14.
🔾 🔾 🔾 Nov to Easter. 🔾 AE, DC, MC, V. Ⓕ Ⓕ

BARBIZON

Hostellerie Les Pléiades Millet and other Barbizon painters stayed at this reliable 19th-century hostelry, set back from the road. Today it blends traditional charm with contemporary comforts: bedrooms are blessed with both character and new bathrooms. It has a snug bar and a stylish, well-respected restaurant.
☒ 21 Grande-Rue, 77630 Barbizon, Seine-et-Marne.
Map p221 D3. 🔾 01 60 66 40 25. 🅵🅰🅷 01 60 66 41 68.
＠ les.pleiades.barbizon@wanadoo.fr 🄸🄸 b,l,d.
Rooms 24. 🔾 🔾 Never. 🔾 AE, DC, MC, V. Ⓕ

CAMPIGNY

Le Petit Coq aux Champs The large thatched house – mostly 19th-century with a modern extension – blends the rustic, chic and eccentric. It is tucked away among the rolling meadows and forests of the Risle valley. All the rooms are differently done out; some have balconies over the garden. Impressive cooking.
☒ Campigny, 27500 Pont-Audemer, Eure. **Map** p220 C3.
🔾 02 32 41 04 19. 🅵🅰🅷 02 32 56 06 25.
＠ le.petit.coq.aux.champs@wanadoo.fr 🄸🄸 b,l,d.
Rooms 14. 🄸 🄸 🔾 🔾 Jan. 🔾 AE, DC, MC, V. Ⓕ Ⓕ

BARFLEUR
Le Conquérant Abundant ivy softens the grey granite façade of this manor house with a walled garden, fresh new bedrooms and a *salon de thé*.
☒ 16-18 rue St-Thomas Becket, 50760 Barfleur, Manche.
Map p220 B3. 🔾 02 33 54 00 82. 🅵🅰🅷 02 33 54 65 25.
🄸🄸 b,d. **Rooms** 13. Ⓕ

BAYEUX
Hôtel d'Argouges Friendly, central yet quiet B&B in an 18th-century mansion with flower garden, dignified sitting room and a period feel.
☒ 21 rue St-Patrice, 14400 Bayeux, Calvados.
Map p220 B3. 🔾 02 31 92 88 86. 🅵🅰🅷 02 31 92 69 16.
🄸🄸 b. **Rooms** 25. Ⓕ

LE BEC-HELLOUIN
Auberge de l'Abbaye Polished tiled floors and furniture, high-cholesterol cooking and heaps of atmosphere in a quintessential country inn.
☒ Le Bec-Hellouin, 27800 Brionne, Eure.
Map p220 C3. 🔾 02 32 44 86 02. 🅵🅰🅷 02 32 46 32 23.
🄸🄸 b,l,d. **Rooms** 11. Ⓕ

BELLE-ILE-EN-MER
Castel Clara Modern but tasteful retreat on this quiet island. Pricey but with salt-water pool, sea views and sublime *fruits de mer*.
☒ Goulphar, Belle-Ile-en-Mer, 56360 Bangor, Morbihan.
Map p220 A4. 🔾 02 97 31 84 21. 🅵🅰🅷 02 97 31 51 69.
🄸🄸 b,l,d. **Rooms** 43. Ⓕ Ⓕ Ⓕ Ⓕ

For key to symbols see backflap. For price categories see *p217*.

CLÉCY

Hostellerie du Moulin du Vey This creeper-clad former water mill is in a stunning part of the Orne Valley at the heart of La Suisse Normande, within a short drive of Caen. In summer, local dishes are served on a riverbank terrace among the willows; in winter, in a barn of a restaurant. The simple bedrooms are all differently done out, with stylish touches; some are in annexes. ⊠ Le Vey, 14570 Clécy, Calvados. **Map** p220 B3. **(** 02 31 69 71 08. **FAX** 02 31 69 14 14. **ᴦ** b,l,d. **Rooms** 19. **⊗ ◯** Dec, Jan. **∅** AE, DC, MC, V. **ⒻⒻ**

DOULLENS

Château de Remaisnil This lovely 18th-century house was once home to designer Laura Ashley, whose style still dominates the plush bedrooms, even though it now belongs to a dedicated American couple. Despite its vast grounds and rococo interior, it retains a homely feel. There are nine cheaper rooms in the coach house. ⊠ 80600 Doullens, Somme. **Map** p221 D2. **(** 03 22 77 07 47. **FAX** 03 22 77 41 23. **@** adriandoull@ compuserve.com **ᴦ** b,l,d. **Rooms** 20. **⊞ ⊗ ◯** late Feb to early March. **∅** AE, DC, MC, V. **ⒻⒻⒻⒻ**

COURCELLES-SUR-VESLE

Château de Courcelles A 17th-century château where Racine and Napoleon laid their heads. The landscaped garden setting is magical, and the hotel strikes all the right chords: huge bedrooms enlivened by colourful fabrics, friendly staff, *haute cuisine* presented in an airy dining room, and a cellar of phenomenal champagnes. ⊠ 02220 Courcelles-sur-Vesle, Aisne. **Map** p221 D3. **(** 03 23 74 13 53. **FAX** 03 23 74 06 41. **@** courcelles@ relaischateaux.fr **ᴦ** b,l,d. **Rooms** 18. **⊞ ⊗ ◯** Never. **∅** AE, DC, MC, V. **ⒻⒻⒻ**

ETRETAT

Le Donjon Perched on a hill above the cliffs of Etretat, is this ancient castle with historical associations and a secret underground passage to the sea. It has been elegantly converted by a Parisian, who has created ten highly original bedrooms. Views from the romantic mirrored dining room are spectacular. Half board only. ⊠ Chemin de St Clair, 76790 Etretat, Seine-Maritime. **Map** p220 C3. **(** 02 35 27 08 23. **FAX** 02 35 29 92 24. **@** ledonjon@wanadoo.fr **ᴦ** b,l,d. **Rooms** 10. **⊞ ⊗ ◯** Never. **∅** AE, V. **ⒻⒻ**

BELLE-ILE-EN-MER

Le Clos Fleuri Near the picturesque island port of Le Palais, simple but chic, with lawns, fresh bedrooms and a delicious daily brunch. ⊠ Bellevue, Route de Sauzon, Belle-Ile-en-Mer, 56360 Le Palais, Morbihan. **Map** p220 A4. **(** 02 97 31 45 45. **FAX** 02 97 31 45 57. **ᴦ** b,l,d. **Rooms** 20. **ⒻⒻ**

BILLIERS

Domaine de Rochevilaine Cluster of buildings on rocky headland, filled with Breton antiques. ⊠ Pointe de Pen Lan-Sud, 56190 Billiers, Morbihan. **Map** p220 A4. **(** 02 97 41 61 61. **FAX** 02 97 41 44 85. **@** domaine@domainederochevilaine.com **ᴦ** b,l,d. **Rooms** 28. **ⒻⒻⒻ**

CAUDEBEC-EN-CAUX

Le Normandie A good position on the Seine marks out this friendly and well maintained hotel. ⊠ 19 Quai Guilbaud, 76490 Caudebec-en-Caux, Seine-Maritime **Map** p220 C3. **(** 02 35 96 25 11. **FAX** 02 35 96 68 15. **@** lle-normandie@planete-b.fr **ᴦ** b,l,d. **Rooms** 16. **Ⓕ**

CONNELLES

Le Moulin de Connelles Mill enjoying perfect Seine-side setting, mature park and plush interior. ⊠ 40 route d'Amfreville-sur-les-Monts, 27430 Connelles, Eure. **Map** p220 C3. **(** 02 32 59 53 33. **FAX** 02 32 59 21 83. **@** moulindeconnelles@cofrase.com **ᴦ** b,l,d. **Rooms** 13. **ⒻⒻ**

FLAGY

Hostellerie du Moulin A half-timbered flour mill with cob walls and tremendous character, where the original workings are still operational and provide a focal point in the rustic sitting room. It enjoys a perfect setting too, beside the millstream set in fields. Pretty bedrooms with low rafters are tucked away in nooks and crannies.
⊠ 2 rue du Moulin, 77940 Flagy, Seine-et-Marne.
Map p221 D4. 📞 01 60 96 67 89. 📠 01 60 96 69 51.
🍴 b,l,d. **Rooms** 10. 🛢 ⬤ late Sept.
💳 AE, DC, MC, V. Ⓕ Ⓕ

HENNEBONT

Château de Locguénolé A vast lawn extends from the château down to the Blavet estuary, popular for sailing, and the park hugs 2km (1 mile) of coast. Inside, wood-panelled rooms are filled with tapestries and antiques. Sweat off a fine seafood dinner in the Turkish bath.
⊠ Route de Port-Louis en Kervignac, 56700 Hennebont, Morbihan. **Map** p220 A4. 📞 02 97 76 76 76.
📠 02 97 76 82 35. @ locguenole@relaischateaux.fr
🍴 b,l,d. **Rooms** 22. 🏊 🍴 🛢 ⬤ Never.
💳 DC, MC, V. Ⓕ Ⓕ Ⓕ Ⓕ

GISORS

Château de la Râpée The decoration inside this 19th-century Gothic mansion is slightly eccentric (lots of antlers, carpets as wallcoverings), and public rooms can be a bit dark. But the location is tranquil, with fine country views, furnishings are tasteful and bedrooms are light and spacious. There are grounds to wander round, and a flower garden. Serious classic regional cooking.
⊠ Bazincourt-sur-Epte, 27140 Gisors, Eure. **Map** p221 D3.
📞 02 32 55 11 61. 📠 02 32 55 95 65. 🍴 b,l,d.
Rooms 13. 🛢 ⬤ Feb. 💳 AE, DE, MC, V. Ⓕ Ⓕ Ⓕ

HESDIN-L'ABBÉ

Hôtel Cléry The young owners of this small 18th-century chateau are dedicated hoteliers, enthusiastic and welcoming. A tree-lined drive leads up to the elegant white façade but, despite the splendid Louis XV wrought-iron staircase, there is no formality in the pale, simply furnished interior. Some of the bedrooms are in annexes.
⊠ 62360 Hesdin-l'Abbé, Pas-de-Calais.
Map p221 D2. 📞 03 21 83 19 83. 📠 03 21 87 52 59.
🍴 b,d. **Rooms** 22. 🛢 ⬤ mid-Dec to end Jan.
💳 AE, DC, MC, V. Ⓕ Ⓕ

CRÉPON

Ferme de la Rançonnière Tapestries and fine furniture are scattered about this fortified old farmhouse. Huge breakfasts of eggs and cream.
⊠ Route d'Arromanches, 14480 Crépon, Calvados.
Map p220 C3. 📞 02 31 22 21 73. 📠 02 31 22 98 39.
🍴 b,l,d. **Rooms** 35. Ⓕ

DAMPIERRE

Auberge du Château Purpose-built in 1650 in rural surroundings just 30 minutes' drive from Paris. Low rafters and undulating floors.
⊠ 1 Grande Rue, 78720 Dampierre, Yvelines.
Map p221 D3. 📞 01 30 47 56 56. 📠 01 30 47 51 75.
🍴 b,l,d. **Rooms** 20. Ⓕ Ⓕ

DINARD

Hôtel Roche Corneille Faultless housekeeping and gastronomic menus at this sophisticated seaside villa built in the late 19th century.
⊠ 4 rue G Clémenceau, 35800 Dinard, Ille-et-Vilaine.
Map p220 B3. 📞 02 99 46 14 47. 📠 02 99 46 40 80.
🍴 b. **Rooms** 28. Ⓕ Ⓕ

DUCEY

Auberge de la Sélune Crab pie is the most acclaimed dish in this modest inn. There is some unfortunate new decoration, but a pretty garden.
⊠ 2 rue St-Germain, 50220 Ducey, Manche.
Map p220 B3. 📞 02 33 48 53 62. 📠 02 33 48 90 30.
@ girres@club.internet.fr 🍴 b,l,d. **Rooms** 21. Ⓕ

For key to symbols see backflap. For price categories see p217

HONFLEUR

La Chaumière Just outside the colourful little port, this timbered farmhouse is typical of the region. Set amid orchards, it is now a Relais et Château hotel boasting sea views, a friendly staff, well-decorated bedrooms, and good honest Norman cooking. In the same ownership is the nearby La Ferme Saint-Siméon.
⊠ Route du Littoral, Vasouy, 14600 Honfleur, Calvados. **Map** p220 C3. ☎ 02 31 81 63 20. FAX 02 31 89 59 23. @ chaumiere@relaischateaux.fr ⑪ b,l,d. **Rooms** 8.
🔘 ⬤ Never. 🗲 AE, MC, V. ⑥⑥⑥⑥

ILLHAEUSERN

Hôtel des Berges One of the most highly regarded restaurants in the country, L'Auberge de l'Ill, has a number of select and beautifully furnished rooms, with a lush garden on the banks of the River Ill. Run with verve by several generations of the Haeberlin family, the *auberge* takes the cuisine of Alsace to new heights.
⊠ 68970 Illhaeusern, Haut-Rhin. **Map** p221 F4, p223 F1. ☎ 03 89 71 87 87. FAX 03 89 71 87 88.
⑪ b,l,d. **Rooms** 18. 🔘 ⬤ Feb.
🗲 AE, DC, MC, V. ⑥⑥⑥⑥

HONFLEUR

Le Manoir du Butin This classic 18th-century half-timbered Norman manor is outside town, in shady grounds within spitting distance of the sea. The rustic, heavily beamed interior is warm and comfy, especially on chilly evenings when the fires are lit. Great regional cuisine and a large selection of *Calvados vieux*.
⊠ Phare du Butin, 14600 Honfleur, Calvados. **Map** p220 C3. ☎ 02 31 81 63 00.
FAX 02 31 89 59 23. ⑪ b,d. **Rooms** 9. 🔘
⬤ Never. 🗲 AE, MC, V. ⑥⑥⑥⑥

MARTIN-ÉGLISE

Auberge du Clos Normand This calm retreat is in an idyllic setting just outside the port of Dieppe. The wisteria-covered inn is backed by a garden and a stream, over which agreeably old-fashioned rooms have a view. Classic Norman cuisine, served in generous portions, appeals to gourmands and gourmets alike.
⊠ 22 rue Henri IV, Martin Église, 76370 Neuville-les-Dieppe, Seine-Maritime. **Map** p220 C2.
☎ 02 35 04 40 34. FAX 02 35 04 48 49. ⑪ b,l,d.
Rooms 8. 🔘 ⬤ mid-Nov to mid-Dec. 🗲 AE, MC, V. ⑥

ETRÉAUPONT
Le Clos du Montvinage The red-brick town hotel is cheerful and spacious, with well-equipped bedrooms; pleasant walled garden.
⊠ RN 2, 02580 Etréaupont, Aisne. **Map** p221 E2.
☎ 03 23 97 91 10. FAX 03 23 97 48 92. ⑪ b,l,d.
Rooms 19, plus one apartment. ⑥⑥

KAYSERSBERG
Hôtel Résidence Chambard Two ancient buildings house an upmarket traditional-style restaurant with large, pleasantly furnished rooms.
⊠ 13 rue de Général de Gaulle, 68240 Kaysersberg, Haut-Rhin. **Map** p221 F4, p223 F1. ☎ 03 89 47 10 17.
FAX 03 89 47 35 03. ⑪ b,l,d. **Rooms** 20. ⑥⑥

LAPOUTROIE
Les Alisiers Great views from this modest farmhouse. Small but snug bedrooms. The kitchen specializes in Alsatian dishes.
⊠ 5 Faudé, 68650 Lapoutroie, Haut-Rhin. **Map** p221 F4, p223 E1. ☎ 03 89 47 52 82. FAX 03 89 47 22 38.
⑪ b,l,d. **Rooms** 13. ⑥

LOUVIERS
Hôtel La Haye-le-Comte Sporty types will enjoy a spell here: tennis, *pétanque*, croquet, a golf range and mountain bikes are all on offer.
⊠ 4 route de La Haye-le-Comte, 27400 Louviers, Eure.
Map p220 C3. ☎ 02 32 40 00 40. FAX 02 32 25 03 85.
⑪ b,l,d. **Rooms** 16. ⑥⑥

MOËLAN-SUR-MER

Manoir de Kertalg Forest walks, tennis, fly fishing, riding and sandy beaches are all within easy reach of this miniature chateau. It has all the qualifications: stone-built, with steep slate roofs and dormer windows, and set in a vast park. Decoration is refined, and, though it's officially a B&B, you can book a seafood supper.

☒ Route de Riec-sur-Belon, 29350 Moëlan-sur-Mer, Finistère. **Map** p220 A4. 📞 02 98 39 77 77.
📠 02 98 39 72 07. 🍴 b. **Rooms** 10. 📶 🔋
⬤ Nov to Apr. 🅵 MC, V. Ⓕ Ⓕ

MONTREUIL-SUR-MER

Château de Montreuil The kind of luxury you would expect of a Relais et Châteaux is presented here with real flair, from captivating bedrooms – each one different – and elegant public rooms to the private English gardens. The cooking uses garden vegetables and herbs.

☒ 4 Chaussée des Capucins, 62170 Montreuil-sur-Mer, Pas-de-Calais. **Map** p221 D2. 📞 03 21 81 53 04.
📠 03 21 81 36 43. @ montreuil@relaischateaux.fr
🍴 b,l,d. **Rooms** 17. 🔋 ⬤ mid-Dec to Feb.
🅵 AE, DC, MC, V. Ⓕ Ⓕ Ⓕ

MONTREUIL-SUR-MER

Auberge de la Grenouillère Nicknamed 'the Froggery' by its fans (the restaurant walls are lined with froggy caricatures), a Michelin-starred riverside restaurant with rooms. The food, served on the outdoor terrace in good weather, is not only excellent but good value too, and the farmhouse rooms are enchanting.

☒ La Madelaine-sous-Montreuil, 62170 Montreuil-sur-Mer, Pas-de-Calais. **Map** p221 D2. 📞 03 21 06 07 22.
📠 03 21 86 36 36. 🍴 b,l,d. **Rooms** 4. 🔋
⬤ mid-Dec to end Jan. 🅵 AE, DC, MC, V. Ⓕ

PAIMPOL

Le Repaire de Kerroc'h This quayside house built in 1793 has a romantic past, having once belonged to a pirate. Bedrooms differ in style. Old ones have a faded elegance, new ones are decorated in bright vivid colours. All are comfortable. Chef Louis Le Roy runs a kitchen with a Michelin star.

☒ 29 Quai Morand, Port de Plaisance, 22500 Paimpol, Côtes-d'Armor. **Map** p220 A3. 📞 02 96 20 50 13.
📠 02 96 22 07 46. @ kerroch@infonie.fr 🍴 b,l,d.
Rooms 13. 📶 🔋 ⬤ Never. 🅵 AE, V. Ⓕ Ⓕ

LUMBRES

Moulin de Mombreux A mill that blends old and new: a homely *salon* displays the original wheels; a new annexe houses the bedrooms.
☒ Route de Bayenghem, 62380 Lumbres, Pas-de-Calais. **Map** p221 D2. 📞 03 21 39 62 44. 📠 03 21 93 61 34.
🍴 b,l,d. **Rooms** 24. Ⓕ Ⓕ

LUNÉVILLE

Château d'Adoménil Moated château with turrets and hall, where a convivial air prevails.
☒ Rehainvillier, 54300 Lunéville, Meurthe-et-Moselle. **Map** p221 F3. 📞 03 83 74 04 81.
📠 03 83 74 21 78. @ adomenil@relaischateaux.fr
🍴 b,l,d. **Rooms** 12. Ⓕ Ⓕ Ⓕ

MARLENHEIM

Le Cerf Picture-postcard-pretty inn, known for gastronomic Alsatian food. Modest rooms; for drinks, a courtyard that is a riot of colour.
☒ 30 rue du Général-de-Gaulle, 67520 Marlenheim, Bas-Rhin. **Map** p221 F3. 📞 03 88 87 73 73.
📠 03 88 87 68 08. 🍴 b,l,d. **Rooms** 20. Ⓕ Ⓕ

LE MONT-ST-MICHEL

Auberge St-Pierre In the best hotel on the mount's main street, you'll find honest home cooking and pleasing rooms.
☒ BP 16, 50116 Le Mont-St-Michel, Manche.
Map p220 B3 📞 02 33 60 14 03. 📠 02 33 48 59 82.
🍴 b,l,d. **Rooms** 20. Ⓕ Ⓕ

PARIS

Hôtel de l'Abbaye This beautifully converted former abbey has quite a following for its faultless service, stylish rooms and calm ambience. Double rooms can be small; if you can afford it, go for a duplex. On fine days breakfast can be taken in a little paved courtyard bordered by flowering shrubs.
⊠ 10 rue Casette, 75006 Paris. **Map** p218 C4.
📞 01 45 44 38 11. FAX 01 45 48 07 86.
@ hotel.abbaye@wanadoo.fr 🍴 b. **Rooms** 46.
🗐 🎴 ● never. 🗲 AE, MC, V. Ⓕ Ⓕ Ⓕ

PARIS

Hôtel d'Aubusson The entrance to this fine hotel is through immense double doors, used for coaches in the 17th century when the honey-stone building was built. Inside are a lovely beamed *salon* and a breakfast room hung with tapestries. Restrained luxury defines the pale bedrooms. Although it is quite pricey, the Aubusson is at the lower end of this price band.
⊠ 33 rue Dauphine, 75006 Paris. **Map** p218 C4.
📞 01 43 29 43 43. FAX 01 43 29 12 62. 🍴 b. **Rooms** 12.
🗐 🎴 ● Never. 🗲 AE, DC, MC, V. Ⓕ Ⓕ Ⓕ Ⓕ

PARIS

Hôtel d'Angleterre Some people say the elegance is a bit faded, but this former British embassy near the boulevard Saint-Germain is still a winner for its feeling of spacious calm and its relatively low prices. Echoes of former glories include fine mantelpieces and *trompe l'oeil* murals. All the rooms are differently done out and most are very roomy. Delightful courtyard garden.
⊠ 44 rue Jacob, 75006 Paris. **Map** p218 C3.
📞 01 42 60 34 72. FAX 01 42 60 16 93. 🍴 b.
Rooms 27. 🗐 🎴 ● Never. 🗲 AE, DC, MC, V. Ⓕ Ⓕ

PARIS

Hôtel de Banville The elegance doesn't stop at the furnishings in this 1930s town house north of Etoile. The hotel is strong on the personal touch: fresh flowers in the individually decorated bedrooms, beds turned down at night and ever-cheerful staff. A pianist is a regular feature in the comfortable bar/sitting area in the evenings.
⊠ 166 bd Berthier, 75017 Paris. **Map** p218 A1.
📞 01 42 67 70 16. FAX 01 44 40 42 77.
@ hotelbanville@wanadoo.fr 🍴 b. **Rooms** 42.
🗐 ● Never. 🗲 AE, MC, V. Ⓕ Ⓕ Ⓕ

PACY-SUR-EURE

Château de Brécourt Splendid Louis XIII château, complete with moat and wooded park, boasting frescoed ceilings and fine furniture.
⊠ Douains, 27120 Pacy-sur-Eure, Eure. **Map** p220 C3.
📞 02 32 52 40 50. FAX 02 32 52 69 65. 🍴 b,l,d.
Rooms 33. Ⓕ Ⓕ

PARIS

Hôtel Beau Manoir The clue is in the name: this hotel styles itself on a rural manor, with damask drapes and tapestries on wood-panelled walls.
⊠ 6 rue de l'Arcade, 75008 Paris. **Map** p218 B1.
📞 01 42 66 03 07. FAX 01 42 68 03 00. @ bm@
parishotel.charm.com 🍴 b. **Rooms** 32. Ⓕ Ⓕ Ⓕ

PARIS

Hôtel Elysées-Mermoz Attractive and fresh-looking, it has a conservatory-style foyer and well-designed bedrooms with Pierre Frey fabrics.
⊠ 30 rue Jean-Mermoz, 75008 Paris. **Map** p218 A1.
📞 01 42 25 75 30. FAX 01 45 62 87 10.
@ elymermoz@ worldnet.fr 🍴 b. **Rooms** 16. Ⓕ Ⓕ Ⓕ

PARIS

Hôtel du Jeu de Paume Avant-garde conversion of a 17th-century tennis court by the architect owner, creating an atrium inside the old timbers.
⊠ 54 rue St-Louis-en-l'Ile, 75004 Paris. **Map** p219 E4.
📞 01 43 26 14 18. FAX 01 40 46 02 76. 🍴 b.
Rooms 32. Ⓕ Ⓕ Ⓕ Ⓕ

PARIS

Hôtel de la Bretonnerie The busy streets of the picturesque Marais and Pompidou Centre area surround this 17th-century townhouse, yet inside all is calm and comfort. Beams, tiled floors and hardwood furniture are offset by rich furnishings and wallcolourings. Bedrooms are surprisingly spacious; some have a mezzanine gallery.
⊠ 22 rue Ste-Croix-de-la-Bretonnerie, 75004 Paris. **Map** p219 E3. ☎ 01 48 87 77 63. **FAX** 01 42 77 26 78. ⤙ b. **Rooms** 85. 🖥 🌊 🍴 🌡 ⍟ Aug. 🖸 MC, V. ⓕⓕⓕⓕ

PARIS

Lancaster Swiss hotelier Emile Wolf opened the Lancaster back in 1930, and it quickly attracted the glitterati of the day. The present owner has restored furniture and rooms to their former glory, incorporating into her elegant decorative scheme the hotel's collection of Boris Pastoukhoff paintings (he used them to pay his bills).
⊠ 7 rue de Berri, 75008 Paris. **Map** p218 A1. ☎ 01 40 76 40 76. **FAX** 01 40 76 40 00. @ pippaona@ hotel-lancaster.fr ⤙ b,l,d. **Rooms** 60. 🖥 🍴 🌡 ⍟ Never. 🖸 AE, DC, MC, V. ⓕⓕⓕⓕ

PARIS

Hôtel Duc de St-Simon From the elegant courtyard, the first glimpse of this gorgeous, if pricey, little hotel through two sets of French doors is pure magic. The *salon* is deliciously furnished with upholstered and antique pieces, pictures and ornaments, and has the private-house feel that the Swedish proprietor intended. Bedrooms manage to be both stylish and cosy.
⊠ 14 rue de St-Simon, 75007 Paris. **Map** p218 B3. ☎ 01 44 39 20 20. **FAX** 01 45 48 68 25. ⤙ b. **Rooms** 34. 🌡 ⍟ Never. 🖸 AE, DC, MC, V. ⓕⓕⓕⓕ

PARIS

Pavillon de la Reine Its location on the most harmonious square in the city is ideal and one of this handsome 17th-century mansion's main draws. Anne of Austria's home now has the air of a baronial hall, complete with huge hearth and wood panelling. You couldn't call it cosy, but it's precisely run and supremely comfortable.
⊠ 28 place des Vosges, 75003 Paris. **Map** p219 F3. ☎ 01 40 29 19 19. **FAX** 01 40 29 19 20. @ pavillon@ club-internet.fr ⤙ b. **Rooms** 55. 🖥 🌡 ⍟ Never. 🖸 AE, DC, MC, V. ⓕⓕⓕⓕ

PARIS

Hôtel Latour-Maubourg The warmth of the owner/managers and the private-house feel make this a really special place to stay.
⊠ 150 rue de Grenelle, 75007 Paris. **Map** p218 A3. ☎ 01 47 05 16 16. **FAX** 01 47 05 16 14. @ victor@ worldnet.fr ⤙ b. **Rooms** 10. ⓕⓕ

PARIS

Hôtel Montalembert Choose between rooms furnished with antiques or smart high-tech pieces in this sleek modern hotel.
⊠ 3 rue Montalembert, 75007 Paris. **Map** p218 C3. ☎ 01 45 49 68 68. **FAX** 01 45 49 69 49. ⤙ b,l,d. **Rooms** 56. ⓕⓕⓕⓕ

PARIS

Hôtel Mansart Beyond the modern lobby are immense, stately bedrooms with large mirrors and panelling picked out in gold.
⊠ 5 rue des Capucines, 75001 Paris. **Map** p218 C2. ☎ 01 42 61 50 28. **FAX** 01 49 27 97 44. @ espfranc@ micronet.fr ⤙ b. **Rooms** 57. ⓕⓕⓕ

PARIS

Hôtel Parc St-Severin This hotel is included for its penthouse suite: chic, bright and surrounded by a fabulous roof terrace with spectacular views.
⊠ 22 rue de la Parcheminerie, 75005 Paris. **Map** p219 D4. ☎ 01 43 54 32 17. **FAX** 01 43 54 70 71. @ st.hotelparc@wanadoo.fr ⤙ b. **Rooms** 27. ⓕⓕⓕ

PARIS

Le Relais St-Germain Cleverly mirrored and sleekly furnished as it is, the ground floor of this luxurious little hotel is cramped, so the spacious bedrooms come as an especially welcome surprise. These are offset by solid country antiques, deep sofas and rich fabrics. Breakfast is in a café that was a haunt of Hemingway and Picasso.

✉ 9 carrefour de l'Odéon, 75006 Paris. **Map** p218 C4. 📞 01 43 29 12 05. FAX 01 46 33 45 30. 🍴 b. **Rooms** 22. 📋 ⬤ Never. 💳 AE, DC, MC, V. ⒻⒻⒻⒻ

PARIS

Hôtel Le St-Grégoire The interior of this tall townhouse has been designed with great flair, reflecting the passion of the owner's wife, who scoured antique shops and markets for *objets d'art*. These furnish the pretty sitting room, from where the restful colour scheme leads upstairs to comfortable bedrooms.

✉ 43 rue de l'Abbé-Grégoire, 75006 Paris. **Map** p218 C5. 📞 01 45 48 23 23. FAX 01 45 48 33 95. @ hotel@saintgregoire.com 🍴 b. **Rooms** 20. ⬤ Never. 💳 AE, DC, MC, V. ⒻⒻⒻ

PARIS

Hôtel Ritz Since César Ritz opened his hotel in 1898, its sumptuous luxury has attracted devotees as diverse as Proust, Hemingway and royalty. The spirit of opulence lives on in each of the eight magnificent *salons* and in the ornate bedrooms. A superb new health club and cookery school ensure that it's no anachronism.

✉ 15 place Vendôme, 75001 Paris. **Map** p219 F2. 📞 01 43 16 30 30. FAX 01 43 16 36 68. @ resa@ritzparis.com 🍴 b,l,d. **Rooms** 175. 📋 ♨ 🛢 ⬤ Never. 💳 AE, DC, MC, V. ⒻⒻⒻⒻ

PARIS

Hôtel Le Ste-Beuve This friendly hotel just off Boulevard Montparnasse is not luxurious, but likes to cosset its guests and has a policy of upgrading them to a better room if one is free. Another draw is the delicious breakfast; it is served at any time of the day or night, either in the refined, cream-painted *salon* where a fire blazes on wintry days, or in the bedrooms.

✉ 9 rue Ste-Beuve, 75006 Paris. **Map** p218 B4. 📞 01 45 48 20 07. FAX 01 45 48 67 52. 🍴 b. **Rooms** 23. ⬤ Never. 💳 AE, MC, V. ⒻⒻⒻ

PARIS

Hôtel Verneuil St-Germain In a charming street and with a zany foyer, a successful mix of beams, mirrored walls, statues and vivid pictures.

✉ 8 rue de Verneuil, 75007 Paris. **Map** p218 C3. 📞 01 42 60 82 14. FAX 01 42 61 40 38. @ verneuil@ cybercable.fr 🍴 b. **Rooms** 22. ⒻⒻⒻ

PERROS-GUIREC

Le Manoir du Sphinx The cliffside garden of this lofty hotel leads down to the rocky shore. Some bedrooms have sea view.

✉ 67 chemin de la Messe, 22700 Perros-Guirec, Côtes-d'Armor. **Map** p220 A3. 📞 02 96 23 25 42. FAX 02 96 91 26 13. 🍴 b,l,d. **Rooms** 20. ⒻⒻ

PLEUGUENEUC

Château de la Motte Beaumanoir It's only a B&B, but this 15th-century château with lake and landscaped garden is a great place for a break.

✉ 35720 Pleugueneuc, Ille-et-Vilaine. **Map** p220 B3. 📞 02 99 69 46 01. FAX 02 99 69 42 49. 🍴 b. **Rooms** 8. ⒻⒻ

PLOUHARNEL

Les Ajoncs d'Or Cottagey, granite-built *logis* that seems frozen in time. Run by a mother and daughter, who prepare good Breton country fare.

✉ Kerbachique, 56340 Plouharnel, Morbihan. **Map** p220 A4, p222 A1. 📞 02 97 52 32 02. FAX 02 97 52 40 36. 🍴 b,d. **Rooms** 17. Ⓕ

PONT-AUDEMER

Auberge du Vieux Puits This is not just another half-timbered Norman inn but the archetypal one. Everywhere are topsy-turvy beams, serpentine stairs and leaded windows, and the rooms are suitably furnished with antiques and burnished copper. Some of the pretty bedrooms are smallish; some are in a new wing.
⊠ 6 rue Notre-Dame-du-Pré, 27500 Pont-Audemer, Eure. **Map** p220 C3. 02 32 41 01 48. **FAX** 02 32 42 37 28. @ vieux.puits@wanadoo.fr b,l,d. **Rooms** 13. ⬤ late Dec to Feb. AE, MC, V. ⒻⒻ

PORT-EN-BESSIN

La Chenevière In summer the lawns are dotted with sun loungers, and tables and chairs, shaded by parasols, are set out on the terrace. But this refined Norman mansion will not only appeal to hedonists; the airy rooms are aesthetically pleasing too. Everywhere you look are paintings, architectural prints, ancient seals or *objets d'art*.
⊠ Escures-Commes, 14520 Port-en-Bessin, Calvados. **Map** p220 B3. 02 31 51 25 25. **FAX** 02 31 51 25 20. @ la.cheneviere@wanadoo.fr b,l,d. **Rooms** 21. ⬤ Dec to mid-Feb. AE, MC, V. ⒻⒻⒻ

REIMS

Château des Crayères A champagne buff's paradise: the park of this graceful Louis XVI mansion is bordered by the cellars of all the great vineyards. Decoration of the grand interior is skilfull and sympathetic, retaining a sweeping staircase, marble columns and wood panelling.
⊠ 64 bd Henry-Vasnier, 51100 Reims, Marne. **Map** p221 E3. 03 26 82 80 80. **FAX** 03 26 82 65 52. @ crayeres@relaischateaux.fr b,l,d. **Rooms** 19. ⬤ 3 weeks Christmas/New Year. AE, DC, MC, V. ⒻⒻⒻⒻ

LA ROCHE-BERNARD

Auberge Bretonne Home-grown fruit and vegetables feature large in Jacques Thorel's cooking, which has earned two Michelin stars for this Breton-style Relais et Chateaux inn. The cellar is equally impressive. Tasteful bedrooms. You must book months ahead.
⊠ 2 place Duguesclin, 56130 La Roche-Bernard, Morbihan. **Map** p220 B4, p222 A1. 02 99 90 60 28. **FAX** 02 99 90 85 00. @ aubbretonne@relaischateaux.fr b,l,d. **Rooms** 8. ⬤ mid-Nov to early Dec, 2 weeks Jan. AE, MC, V. ⒻⒻ

PONT-AUDEMER
Belle-Isle-sur-Risle With a large island garden, it's hard to imagine a more romantic setting for this late 19th-century mansion.
⊠ 112 route de Rouen, 27500 Pont-Audemer, Eure. **Map** p220 C3. 02 32 56 96 22. **FAX** 02 32 42 88 96. b,l,d. **Rooms** 19. ⒻⒻⒻ

PORNICHET
Hôtel Sud Bretagne A family-run four-star with an eye-catching blue and white façade. Facilities include indoor pool, billiards and its own ketch.
⊠ 42 bd de la République, 44380 Pornichet, Loire-Atlantique. **Map** p220 A4, p222 A1. 02 40 11 65 00. **FAX** 02 40 61 73 70. b,l,d. **Rooms** 30. ⒻⒻ

RIBEAUVILLÉ
Le Clos Saint-Vincent An essential stopover on the Riesling wine route. Excellent cuisine.
⊠ Route de Bergheim, 68150 Ribeauvillé, Haut-Rhin. **Map** p221 F3, p223 F1. 03 89 73 67 65. **FAX** 03 89 73 32 20. @ clos.saintvincent@wanadoo.fr b,l,d. **Rooms** 15. ⒻⒻ

LA ROCHE-BERNARD
Domaine de Bodeuc Welcoming touches await guests at this handsome house in large grounds. Dinner is not served in summer.
⊠ 56130 La Roche-Bernard, Morbihan. **Map** p220 B4. 02 99 90 89 63. **FAX** 02 99 90 90 32. b,d. **Rooms** 8. ⒻⒻ

St-André-d'Hébertot

Auberge du Prieuré Be warned, dinner here is costly in comparison with the good-value rooms. These are split between a new but sympathetic annexe and the house, a 13th-century priory of honey stone, no less lovely inside than out, furnished with solid antiques and mellow fabrics. Beyond the leafy garden with a heated pool, lie orchards and fields.
⊠ St-André-d'Hébertot, 14130 Pont-l'Évêque, Calvados. **Map** p220 C3. ▌ 02 31 64 03 03. FAX 02 31 64 16 66. ▐▌ b,l,d. **Rooms** 13. ▦ ▮ ● Never. ▣ MC, V. Ⓕ Ⓕ

Ste-Anne-la-Palud

Hotel de la Plage With the sea and sandy beach on its doorstep, this hotel is ideal for families if a touch pricey. It combines chic with Breton simplicity; some bedrooms are all white with the odd antique. The dining room offers superb seafood and views from floor-to-ceiling windows.
⊠ Ste-Anne-la-Palud, 29127 Plonévez-Porzay, Finistère. **Map** p220 A4. ▌ 02 98 92 50 12. FAX 02 98 92 56 54. @ laplage@relaischateaux.fr ▐▌ b,l,d. **Rooms** 30. ▦ ▜ ▮ ● mid-Nov to Apr. ▣ AE, DC, MC, V. Ⓕ Ⓕ Ⓕ Ⓕ

St-Malo

La Korrigane Staying in this fine-looking town house near the harbour is like being a guest in an elegant home. The pale drawing room is furnished with books, photographs and ornaments, and in the bedrooms are easy chairs, antique mirrors and oil paintings. Too refined for children just back from the beach.
⊠ 39 rue Le Pomellec, 35400 St-Malo, Ille-et-Vilaine. **Map** p220 B3. ▌ 02 99 81 65 85. FAX 02 99 82 23 89. ▐▌ b. **Rooms** 12. ▮ ● Never. ▣ AE, DC, MC, V. Ⓕ Ⓕ Ⓕ

Ste-Preuve

Château de Barive A short drive from Reims, Laon and Liesse, this impressive 17th-century hunting lodge is the perfect place to stay for cathedral touring, as well as sampling first-class cuisine. Public rooms are gracious and formal, though you can dine in a more casual garden room. There is a vast estate to explore.
⊠ Ste-Preuve, 02350 Liesse, Aisne. **Map** p221 E3. ▌ 03 23 22 15 15. FAX 03 23 22 08 39. ▐▌ b,l,d. **Rooms** 14. ▦ ▜ ▮ ● mid-Dec to mid-Jan. ▣ AE, DC, MC, V. Ⓕ Ⓕ

Roscoff
Le Brittany From this well-furnished stone manor the next stop is Newfoundland. Huge bay windows take advantage of the light and views.
⊠ Bd Sainte-Barbe, 29680 Roscoff, Finistère. **Map** p220 A3. ▌ 02 98 69 70 78. FAX 02 98 61 13 29. ▐▌ b,l,d. **Rooms** 25. Ⓕ Ⓕ

Rouen
Hôtel de la Cathédrale Off a quiet lane, a warren of rooms in faded yet elegant style. Some overlook a courtyard overflowing with flowers.
⊠ 12 rue St-Romain, 76000 Rouen, Seine-Maritime. **Map** p220 C3. ▌ 02 35 71 57 95. FAX 02 35 70 10 54. ▐▌ b. **Rooms** 24. Ⓕ

St-Malo
Le Valmarin Handsome grey-stone B&B in tree-filled grounds close to the harbour, run by the friendly Pollitzers. Children welcome.
⊠ 7 rue Jean XXIII, 35400 St-Malo, Ille-et-Vilaine. **Map** p220 B3. ▌ 02 99 81 94 76. FAX 02 99 81 30 03. ▐▌ b. **Rooms** 12. Ⓕ Ⓕ

St-Vaast-la-Hougue
Hôtel de France et des Fuchsias The *raison d'être* of this congenial hotel is its restaurant, serving seafood and home-farm produce.
⊠ 18 rue Maréchal Foch, 50550 St-Vaast-la-Hougue, Manche. **Map** p220 B3. ▌ 02 33 54 42 26. FAX 02 33 43 46 79. ▐▌ b,l,d. **Rooms** 33. Ⓕ

TRÉBEURDEN

Manoir de Lan-Kerellec A Relais et Château manor yet nonetheless unpretentious and intimate, standing on a grassy hillside above the rocky pink granite coast. Not surprisingly seafood is *de rigueur* in the nautical dining room. There are several beautiful bays a short walk away.
⊠ Allée Centrale, 22560 Trébeurden, Côtes d'Armor. **Map** p220 A3. ☎ 02 96 15 47 47. 𝗙𝗔𝗫 02 96 23 66 88. @ lankerellec@relaischateaux.fr ⊪ b,l,d. **Rooms** 20. 🗕 ▨ ◉ mid-Nov to mid-March. ⊡ AE, DC, MC, V. ⒻⒻⒻⒻ

VERNEUIL-SUR-AVRE

Hostellerie le Clos A jokey exterior of chequerboard and trellis-patterned brickwork, reminiscent of a Disneyland castle, masks a gorgeous little hotel. In the dining room *trompe l'oeil* garden scenes divide windows looking out to the real thing. Half-board only at weekends.
⊠ 98 rue de la Ferté-Vidame, 27130 Verneuil-sur-Avre, Eure. **Map** p220 C3. ☎ 02 32 32 21 81. 𝗙𝗔𝗫 02 32 32 21 36. @ leclos@relaischateaux.fr ⊪ b,l,d. **Rooms** 10. ▨ ▨ ◉ mid-Dec to mid-Jan. ⊡ AE, DC, MC, V. ⒻⒻⒻⒻ

TRÉBEURDEN

Ti Al-Lannec Child-friendly and good value, with steps down to the beach from its eyrie position, this is a hotel with a heart, run with loving care. Guests find books and fresh flowers placed in bedrooms, many of which have verandas. The sitting room is stunning, as are the garden and the views over the bay of Lannion.
⊠ Allée de Mezo-Guen, BP 3, 22560 Trébeurden, Côtes d'Armor. **Map** p220 A3. ☎ 02 96 15 01 01. 𝗙𝗔𝗫 02 96 23 62 14. @ ti.al.lannec@wanadoo.fr ⊪ b,l,d. **Rooms** 29. 🗕 ▨ ◉ mid-Nov to mid-March. ⊡ AE, MC, V. ⒻⒻⒻⒻ

VILLERAY

Moulin de Villeray The Eelsens, who rescued this old mill from dereliction, have transformed it into an idyllic rural retreat, with quiet bedrooms and a pleasant *salon* where pre-prandial drinks are served. The hub is the restaurant with its beams and massive fireplace. Half-board is obligatory in high season.
⊠ Villeray, 6110 Condeau, Orne. **Map** p220 C3. ☎ 02 33 73 30 22. 𝗙𝗔𝗫 02 33 73 38 28. @ moulin.de.villeray@wanadoo.fr ⊪ b,l,d. **Rooms** 25. ▨ ◉ Never. ⊡ AE, DC, MC, V. ⒻⒻ

SEPT-SAULX

Le Cheval Blanc Without spoiling this old *auberge*, the owners make more improvements inside and out every year. It has outstanding food and a lush garden.
⊠ 51400 Sept-Saulx, Marne. **Map** p221 E3. ☎ 03 26 03 90 27. 𝗙𝗔𝗫 03 26 03 97 09. ⊪ b,l,d. **Rooms** 25. ⒻⒻ

TRÉGUIER

Kastell Dinec'h An old stone farmhouse with a leafy garden shaded by conifers, a heated pool and small but appealing bedrooms.
⊠ Route de Lannion, 22220 Tréguier, Côtes-d'Armor. **Map** p220 A3. ☎ 02 96 92 49 39. 𝗙𝗔𝗫 02 96 92 34 02. ⊪ b,d. **Rooms** 14. ⒻⒻ

TRELLY

La Verte Campagne Roses cover a farmhouse where bedrooms take second place to food; chef Pascal Bernou has won a Michelin star.
⊠ Hameau Chevalier, 50660 Trelly, Manche. **Map** p220 B3. ☎ 02 33 47 65 33. 𝗙𝗔𝗫 02 33 47 38 03. ⊪ b,l,d. **Rooms** 7. Ⓕ

VERVINS

La Tour du Roy This atmospheric inn on the town ramparts bristles with turrets outside and attractive features inside.
⊠ 45 rue du Général Leclerc, 02140 Vervins, Aisne. **Map** p221 E2. ☎ 03 23 98 00 11. 𝗙𝗔𝗫 03 23 98 00 72. @ chatotel@chatotel.com ⊪ b,l,d. **Rooms** 18. ⒻⒻ

CENTRAL FRANCE

LOIRE VALLEY • POITOU-CHARENTES • LIMOUSIN • AUVERGNE
BOURGOGNE • FRANCHE-COMTÉ • RHÔNE-ALPES

*T*HE CHATEAU-HOTEL *comes into its own in the Loire Valley. Although it is possible to stay in castles all over Europe, there is a special charm about sleeping in a fairytale French Renaissance chateau with its turrets, steep roofs, dormer windows, formal garden and park. But there are chateau-hotels in other regions of Central France, such as the Limousin and Périgord.*

Many are old, solid bourgeois residences, flat-fronted, shuttered mansions with mansard roofs. There are also converted mills, and country and village inns full of character. To the east, in the upland regions of the Jura and Alp mountains, chalet-style hotels with steeply sloping roofs, shutters and wooden balconies, are prevalent.

ALOXE-CORTON

Villa Louise On the edge of a village that is a Mecca for lovers of white wine, is this low 17th-century house. Inside, original timberwork and fireplaces are offset with an avant-garde interior and Art Deco furnishings. The tasteful bedrooms have swish bathrooms; breakfast is a feast of cheese, eggs and fruit.
✉ 21420 Aloxe-Corton, Côte-d'Or. **Map** p221 E4, p223 E1. 📞 03 80 26 46 70. 📠 03 80 26 47 16.
@ villalou@iafrica.com 🍴 b. **Rooms** 10.
🔊 🅿 Never. 🅴 MC, V. ⒻⒻ

AUXERRE

Parc des Maréchaux The best bedrooms are those looking on to the park from which the hotel takes its name, though all are spacious, in restful colours and furnished traditionally with wooden beds and antique chests. A large, dignified townhouse, it makes an exceedingly upmarket yet value-for-money B&B. There is a comfortable *salon* and a congenial bar.
✉ 6 avenue Foch, 89000 Auxerre, Yonne. **Map** p221 D4, p223 D1. 📞 03 86 51 43 77. 📠 03 86 51 31 72. 🍴 b.
Rooms 24. 🔊 🅿 Never. 🅴 AE, DC, MC, V. ⒻⒻ

AMBOISE
Château de Pray The 13th-century fortress is well placed to visit some of the great chateaux. Splendid vantage point above the Loire.
✉ 37400 Amboise, Indre-et-Loire. **Map** p220 C4, p222 C1. 📞 02 47 57 23 67. 📠 02 47 57 32 50.
@ chateau.depray@wanadoo.fr 🍴 b,l,d. **Rooms** 19. ⒻⒻ

ANGLES SUR L'ANGLIN
Le Relais du Lyon d'Or In a contender for the prettiest village in France, a former royal tythe depot with terracotta floors and wooden beams.
✉ 4 rue d'Enfer, 86260 Angles sur l'Anglin, Vienne. **Map** p220 C5, p222 C2. 📞 05 49 48 32 53. 📠 05 49 84 02 28. @ lyondor.com 🍴 b,l,d. **Rooms** 10. Ⓕ

ANNECY-LE-VIEUX
L'Abbaye Idiosyncratic abbey hotel in a suburb, with a stunning vaulted restaurant and attractive bedrooms. Opt for one on the garden side.
✉ 15 chemin de l'Abbaye, 74940 Annecy-le-Vieux, Haute-Savoie. **Map** p221 F5, p223 E2. 📞 04 50 23 61 08.
📠 04 50 27 77 65. 🍴 b,d. **Rooms** 18. ⒻⒻ

BAGNOLS
Château de Bagnols Restored medieval fortress with sumptuous, frescoed rooms. Devotées claim it's worth every *centime*.
✉ 69620 Bagnols, Rhône. **Map** p223 D3.
📞 04 74 71 40 00. 📠 04 74 71 40 49.
@ bagnols@relaischateaux.fr 🍴 b,l,d. ⒻⒻⒻⒻ

AVALLON

Château de Vault de Lugny From the moment you arrive at the iron gates of this elegant home, you feel like a guest at an exclusive house party. Peacocks wander on the lawn along the drive, and at the front door a butler relieves you of your bags. The decoration is tasteful and not too grand; guests dine at one single long table.

☒ 11 rue du Château, 89200 Avallon, Yonne.
Map p221 E4, p223 D1. 📞 03 86 34 07 86. **FAX** 03 86 34 16 36. @ lugny@transeo.fr 🍴 b,l,d. **Rooms** 12. �e
⬤ mid-Nov to early Apr. 💳 AE, MC, V. ⒻⒻⒻ

BRIOLLAY

Château de Noirieux On the western reaches of the Loire château trail, this 17th-century manor house with 1920s additions eclipses all the local competition. Service is courteous with just the right amount of pampering. Rooms have some stunning antiques, and the garden is shady and well-kept.

☒ 26 route du Moulin, 49125 Briollay, Maine et Loire.
Map p222 B1. 📞 02 41 42 50 05. **FAX** 02 41 37 91 00.
@ noirieux@relaischateaux.fr 🍴 b,l,d. **Rooms** 19.
🎱🍴�e⬤ Feb, Nov. 💳 AE, DC, MC, V. ⒻⒻⒻ

BANNEGON

Auberge du Moulin de Chaméron A mixture of water-mill museum and restaurant in deep country. In summer, meals can be taken on the dining terrace by the mill stream. A swimming pool and quiet wooded gardens amply make up for the comfortable but dull rooms, which are housed in modern buildings across the garden.

☒ Bannegon, 18210 Charenton-du-Cher, Cher.
Map p221 D5, p223 D2. 📞 02 48 61 83 80. **FAX** 02 48 61 84 92. 🍴 b,l,d. **Rooms** 14. 🎱�e⬤ mid-Nov to early March; Tue in low season. 💳 AE, MC, V. ⒻⒻ

CANGEY

Le Fleuray Peter and Hazel Newington took over an almost derelict house in the early 1990s, and have restored it with flair and imbued it with an intimate atmosphere. Bedrooms are fresh, light and blissfully quiet. Hazel is in charge of the splendid kitchen; half-board is obligatory at times.

☒ Cangey, 37530 Amboise, Indre-et-Loire.
Map p220 C4, p222 C1. 📞 02 47 56 09 25.
FAX 02 47 56 93 97. @ LEFLEURAYHOTEL@wanadoo.fr
🍴 b,d. **Rooms** 11. �e⬤ late Feb; late Oct to early Nov; Christmas and New Year. 💳 MC, V. Ⓕ

BEAUGENCY

L'Abbaye The former Augustine convent, set by an old bridge across the Loire, now makes a fine hotel. Period rooms and fine cuisine.

☒ 2 quai de l'Abbaye, 45190 Beaugency, Loiret.
Map p220 C4, p222 C1. 📞 02 38 44 67 35.
FAX 02 38 44 87 92. 🍴 b,l,d. **Rooms** 18. ⒻⒻ

BEAUNE

Château de Challanges The setting for this late 18th-century mansion is a park of lawns and paths, minutes from the historic city.

☒ Rue des Templiers, Challanges, 21200 Beaune, Côte-d'Or. **Map** p221 E4, p223 D1. 📞 03 80 26 32 62.
FAX 03 80 26 32 52. 🍴 b. **Rooms** 14. ⒻⒻ

BUZANÇAIS

L'Hermitage Owner-chef Claude Sureau runs a superior Logis de France, a small manor in a mature garden with a pavilion for summer dining. Well-priced menus feature home-grown produce.

☒ 36500 Buzançais, Indre. **Map** p222 C1. 📞 02 54 84 03 90. **FAX** 02 54 02 13 19. 🍴 b,l,d. **Rooms** 14. Ⓕ

LA CELLE-ST-CYR

La Fontaine aux Muses A creeper-covered country inn, with modest rooms leading on to a garden and a lovely pool. Fish-biased cooking.

☒ Route de la Fontaine, 89116 La Celle-St-Cyr, Yonne.
Map p221 D4, p223 D1. 📞 03 86 73 40 22.
FAX 03 86 73 48 66. 🍴 b,l,d. **Rooms** 17. Ⓕ

For key to symbols see backflap. For price categories *see p217*

CHAGNY

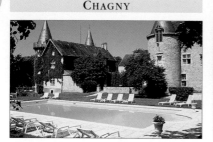

Hostellerie du Château de Bellecroix A former command post of the Knights of Malta, this turreted, creeper-clad castle was built in the 12th century with 18th-century additions. Both architecture and location in parkland are superb. Annexe rooms are larger than those in the chateau, though the ones in the turrets are fun.
✉ Route Nationale 6, 71150 Chagny, Saône-et-Loire. **Map** p221 E5, p223 E1. 📞 03 85 87 13 86. 📠 03 85 91 28 62. 🍴 b,l,d. **Rooms** 21. 🛏 🔌 ⬤ end Dec to mid-Feb. 💳 AE, DC, MC, V. ⒻⒻⒻ

CHAMONIX

Hôtel du Jeu de Paume Parisian style arrives in the Alps with the opening of the sister hotel of the Ile St-Louis Jeu de Paume. It follows the lines of a classic chalet, with wood dominating inside and out. In winter the hotel lays on a car to take guests to the ski lifts. Dinner on their return is superb.
✉ 705 route du Chapeau, Le Lavancher, 74400 Chamonix, Haute-Savoie. **Map** p221 F5, p223 F2. 📞 04 50 54 03 76. 📠 04 50 54 10 75. 🍴 b,l,d. **Rooms** 22. 🛏 🍽 🔌 ⬤ mid-May to mid-June; mid-Oct to mid-Dec. 💳 AE, DC, MC, V. ⒻⒻⒻ

CHAMONIX

Auberge du Bois Prin To wake up to a breathtaking vista of Mont Blanc is reason enough to stay in this traditional-style mountain chalet. But it's also exceptionally well run without being stuffy. The terrific food includes a particularly fine cheeseboard. Large terrace.
✉ 69 chemin de l'Hermine, Les Moussoux, 74400 Chamonix, Haute-Savoie. **Map** p221 F5, p223 F2. 📞 04 50 53 33 51. 📠 04 50 53 48 75. @ boisprin@ relaischateaux.fr 🍴 b,l,d. **Rooms** 11. 🔌 ⬤ mid-Apr to early May; late Oct, Nov. 💳 AE, DC, MC, V. ⒻⒻⒻ

CHAMPIGNÉ

Château des Briottières English gardens surround the de Valbray's gracious family seat. The present young owners have opened their elegant doors to guests, who find public rooms, furnished with Louis XV pieces and portraits, plus harmonious bedrooms. The de Valbrays join their guests for dinner, which usually features regional dishes.
✉ 49330 Champigné, Maine-et-Loire. **Map** p220 B4, p222 B1. 📞 02 41 42 00 02. 📠 02 41 42 01 55. @ briottieres@wanadoo.fr 🍴 b,d. **Rooms** 10. 🛏 🔌 ⬤ Feb. 💳 AE, DC, MC, V. ⒻⒻⒻ

CHAGNY

Hôtel Lameloise One of the great restaurants (three Michelin stars) in a calm, shuttered house.
✉ 36 place d'Armes, 71150 Chagny, Saône-et-Loire. **Map** p221 E5, p223 E1. 📞 03 85 87 65 65. 📠 03 85 87 03 57. @ lameloise@relaischateaux.fr 🍴 b,l,d. **Rooms** 17. ⒻⒻⒻ

CHALLANS

Château de la Vérie The beaches are just a short walk away from this lavishly furnished manor house. Spacious gardens, tennis court and pool.
✉ Route de St-Gilles-Croix-de-Vie, 85300 Challans, Vendée. **Map** p220 B5, p222 A1. 📞 02 51 35 33 44. 📠 02 51 35 14 84. 🍴 b,l,d. **Rooms** 23. ⒻⒻ

CHASSIGNELLES

Hôtel de l'Ecluse A row of cottages on a canal – *écluse* refers to the lock – contain seven colourful, modestly priced bedrooms with smart bathrooms, a country-style dining room and bar.
✉ 89160 Chassignelles. **Map** p221 E4. 📞 03 86 75 18 51. 📠 03 86 75 02 04. 🍴 b,l,d. **Rooms** 7. Ⓕ

CHÂTEAUNEUF

Hostellerie du Château A 15th-century former presbytery in a medieval village. Quiet rooms overlook terraced gardens; regional cooking.
✉ Châteauneuf, 21320 Pouilly-en-Auxois, Côte-d'Or. **Map** p221 E4, p223 D1. 📞 03 80 49 22 00. 📠 03 80 49 21 27. 🍴 b,l,d. **Rooms** 17. ⒻⒻ

CHAUBLANC

Moulin d'Hauterive Rustic chic, bright, romantic bedrooms and the inventive cooking of owner Mme Moille make a stay at this large converted mill an unusual blend of rural seclusion and good living. In the large lawn behind are a little pool and tennis courts; there are also a sauna, fitness room and solarium – and even a heliport.

⊠ Chaublanc, 71350 St-Gervais-en-Valière, Saone et Loire. **Map** p223 E1. ☎ 03 85 91 55 56. FAX 03 85 91 89 65. @ hauterive1@aol.com ⊞ b,l,d. **Rooms** 19. ▤ ≋ ⛟ ⛴ ● Christmas, Jan. ⤵ AE, DC, MC, V. ⒻⒻⒻ

CHINON

Hôtel Diderot Jolly French Cypriots own this white-shuttered town house in a pleasant courtyard, and run it as a down-to-earth B&B. Some of the spotless, no-frills bedrooms have beams and fine views; some lead on to a terrace. Breakfasts are scrumptious, due to Madame Kazamias' home-made jams.

⊠ 4 rue Buffon, 37500 Chinon, Indre-et-Loire. **Map** p220 C4, p222 B1. ☎ 02 47 93 18 87. FAX 02 47 93 37 10. ⊞ b. **Rooms** 22. ⛴ ● mid-Dec to mid-Jan. ⤵ AE, DC, MC, V. Ⓕ

CHAUMONT-SUR-THARONNE

La Croix Blanche de Sologne The simple *logis* has a 200-year-old tradition of employing female chefs, and they have acquired a lofty reputation for their mainly Périgordian cuisine. The building dates back to 1424 and its rustic style is fitting: rooms are full of country antiques, and hunting trophies are displayed on the walls.

⊠ 41600 Chaumont-sur-Tharonne, Loir-et-Cher. **Map** p221 D4, p222 C1. ☎ 02 54 88 55 12. FAX 02 54 88 60 40. ⊞ b,l,d. **Rooms** 18. ⛴ ● Never. ⤵ AE, DC, MC, V. ⒻⒻ

CLUNY

Hôtel de Bourgogne Guests of this 19th-century town hotel are assured a warm welcome from the friendly Gosse family. The place has a very French provincial air about it, and delightfully old-fashioned bedrooms are arranged around a calm courtyard garden. The restaurant specializes in Burgundian dishes.

⊠ Place de l'Abbaye, 71250 Cluny, Saône-et-Loire. **Map** p221 E5, p223 D2. ☎ 03 85 59 00 58. FAX 03 85 59 03 73. ⊞ b,l,d. **Rooms** 15. ⛴ ● mid-Nov to March. ⤵ AE, DC, MC, V. ⒻⒻ

CHEVERNY

Château du Breuil Polished antiques in pale rooms and a sumptuous *salon* characterize this 18th-century chateau; vast parkland.

⊠ Route de Fougères-sur-Bièvre, 41700 Cheverny, Loir-et-Cher. **Map** p220 C4, p222 C1. ☎ 02 54 44 20 20. FAX 02 54 44 30 40. ⊞ b,l,d. **Rooms** 18. ⒻⒻⒻ

CHONAS-L'AMBALLAN

Domaine de Clairefontaine The Giradons own two hostelries in the village; this one has simpler rooms and a Michelin star for Philippe's cuisine.

⊠ Chonas-l'Amballan, 38121 Reventin-Vaugris, Isère. **Map** p223 E3. ☎ 04 74 58 81 52. FAX 04 74 58 80 93. ⊞ b,l,d. **Rooms** 16. Ⓕ

CHONAS-L'AMBALLAN

Hostellerie Le Marais St-Jean The Giradons' farmhouse combines character with creature comforts; simple food and hordes of fans.

⊠ Chonas-l'Amballan, 38121 Reventin-Vaugris, Isère. **Map** p223 E3. ☎ 04 74 58 83 28. FAX 04 74 58 81 96. ⊞ b,l,d. **Rooms** 10. ⒻⒻ

CONDRIEU

Hôtellerie Beau Rivage On the bank, or *rivage*, of the Rhône river; many rooms share the view. Friendly staff and Michelin-starred food.

⊠ 2 rue du Beau Rivage, 69420 Condrieu, Rhône. **Map** p223 D3. ☎ 04 74 56 82 82. FAX 04 74 59 59 36. ⊞ b,l,d. **Rooms** 24. ⒻⒻ

DOUSSARD

Marceau Hôtel Don't judge this B&B from its rather ordinary exterior; its attractions lie within. Friendly and family-run, it is blissfully quiet, and has panoramas of the mountains and nearby Lake Annecy. Fine furniture fills the snug *salon* and the large bedrooms, and in summer guests can sit out on the terrace or in the rambling garden.
◻ 115 chemin de la Chapelliere, 74210 Doussard, Haute-Savoie. **Map** p223 E2. ◖ 04 50 44 30 11. FAX 04 50 44 39 44. ▮▮ b. **Rooms** 15. ▯ ● Never. ◪ AE, DC, MC, V. ⒻⒻ

MANIGOD

Chalet Hôtel de la Croix-Fry Enthusiasts return year after year, as a spell in this archetypal mountain chalet, built of dark wood, its terrace a sea of flowers, is a truly relaxing experience. The interior is simple and rustic, and it's no hardship that a minimum of three nights is required.
◻ Route du Col de la Croix-Fry, Manigod, 74230 Thônes, Haute Savoie. **Map** p221 F5, p223 E2. ◖ 04 50 44 90 16. FAX 04 50 44 94 87. ▮▮ b,l,d. **Rooms** 12. ▦ ▯▯ ▯ ● mid-Sep to mid-Dec; mid-Apr to mid-June. ◪ AE, MC, V. ⒻⒻⒻ

FLEURVILLE

Château de Fleurville Just 17km (12 miles) north of the wine centre of Mâcon is this chateau hotel that is neither luxurious nor intimidating. Many rooms retain 16th-century features and their decoration has been kept agreeably simple and in character. This, together with a caring staff, creates a relaxed, informal air. Prices are reasonable too.
◻ 71260 Fleurville, Saône-et-Loire. **Map** p223 E2. ◖ 03 85 33 12 17. FAX 03 85 33 95 34. ▮▮ b,l,d. **Rooms** 15. ▦ ▯ ● Nov to Feb. ◪ DC, MC, V. ⒻⒻⒻ

MERCUREY

Hostellerie du Val d'Or This early 19th-century coaching inn in the wine village of Mercurey makes a pleasant contrast with the many formal and extremely expensive establishments of the region. Devotees come here to savour Jean-Claude Cogny's Michelin-starred cooking; many return to stay in the neatly decorated bedrooms. Friendly service; attractive gravelled garden.
◻ Grande-Rue, 71640 Mercurey, Saône-et-Loire. **Map** p223 D2. ◖ 03 85 45 13 70. FAX 03 85 45 18 45. ▮▮ b,l,d. **Rooms** 13. ▯ ● Mon. ◪ MC, V. ⒻⒻ

CURTIL-VERGY

Hôtel Le Manassès Strictly for lovers of Burgundy: the hotel is in a vineyard and there's a wine museum in a barn. Bedrooms are modern, public rooms are furnished with antiques.
◻ 21220 Curtil-Vergy, Côte d'Or. **Map** p221 E4. ◖ 03 80 61 43 81. FAX 03 80 61 42 79. ▮▮ b. **Rooms** 12. Ⓕ

GIEN

Hôtel du Rivage The hotel is contemporary and stylish, but the real draw is Christian Gaillard's cuisine. Rooms at the front have the view.
◻ 1 Quai de Nice, 45500 Gien, Loiret. **Map** p000 00. ◖ 02 38 37 79 00. FAX 02 38 38 10 21. ▮▮ b,l,d. **Rooms** 19. ⒻⒻ

GOUMOIS

Hôtel Taillard In the same family for four generations, this hotel in the Jura, close to the Swiss border, is efficiently run. There are comfy rooms, a pretty garden and a breakfast terrace.
◻ 25470 Goumois, Doubs. **Map** p221 F4. ◖ 03 81 44 20 75. FAX 03 81 44 26 15. ▮▮ b,l,d. **Rooms** 24. Ⓕ

IGÉ

Château d'Igé The medieval castle comes close to perfection, with ivy-clad turrets and a flower garden. A huge hearth warms diners.
◻ 71960 Igé, Saône-et-Loire. **Map** p220 C4. ◖ 03 85 33 33 99. FAX 03 85 33 41 41. ＠ ige@ relaischateaux.fr ▮▮ b,l,d. **Rooms** 13. ⒻⒻⒻ

MEURSAULT

Les Magnolias This old winegrower's house in peaceful surroundings has been converted into a B&B with great flair and is owned by a genial half-English man. Antiques pepper communal rooms and bedrooms; the ones in the eaves, with dormer windows are most appealing. On fine days the substantial breakfasts can be eaten in a courtyard.
⊠ 8 rue Pierre Joigneaux, 21190 Meursault, Côte-d'Or. **Map** p221 E4, p223 D1. 📞 03 80 21 23 23. 📠 03 80 21 29 10. 🍴 b. **Rooms** 12. 🔘 ⬤ Dec to mid-Mar. 🅔 AE, MC, V. Ⓕ Ⓕ

MONTBRON

Hostellerie Château Ste-Catherine At the end of a long drive through verdant gardens, stands a severe-looking stone manor house built around 1800 for the Empress Joséphine. First impressions are not reinforced by the warmth and charm of the interior, where walls are hung with tapestries and fires blaze in the hearths.
⊠ Route de Marthon, 16220 Montbron, Charente. **Map** p220 C5, p222 B2. 📞 05 45 23 60 03. 📠 05 45 70 72 00. 🍴 b,l,d. **Rooms** 18. 🈂 🔘 ⬤ Never. 🅔 AE, DC, MC, V. Ⓕ Ⓕ

MONTBAZON-EN-TOURAINE

Domaine de la Tortinière Its hillside position in vast grounds lends this fairytale castle panoramas over the Indre valley. Built in 1861 in Renaissance style, it is smartly furnished, and offers an impressive array of activities including boating, tennis and mountain biking.
⊠ Route de Ballan-Miré - Les Gués de Veigné, 37250 Montbazon-en-Touraine, Indre-et-Loire. **Map** p220 C4, p222 B1. 📞 02 47 34 35 00. 📠 02 47 65 95 70. @ domaine.tortiniere@wanadoo.fr 🍴 b,l,d. **Rooms** 21. 🈂 🔘 ⬤ late Dec to March. 🅔 MC, V. Ⓕ Ⓕ Ⓕ

NIEUIL

Château-Hôtel de Nieuil François I's former hunting lodge is a Renaissance castle with turrets, formal garden and magnificent rooms. But its charm lies in the warmth of the owners. Monsieur Bodinaud is an exuberant man, responsible for managing a collection of fine cognacs. Madame is the chef, responsible for a Michelin star.
⊠ Route de Fontafie, 16270 Nieuil, Charente. **Map** p220 C5. 📞 05 45 71 36 38. 📠 05 45 71 46 45. @ nieuil@relaischateaux.fr 🍴 b,l,d. **Rooms** 14. 🈂 🔘 ⬤ early Nov to late Apr. 🅔 AE, DC, MC, V. Ⓕ Ⓕ Ⓕ Ⓕ

JOIGNY

La Côte St-Jacques On the banks of the Yonne river avant-garde decor is coupled with tip-top cuisine – three Michelin stars.
⊠ 14 fbg de Paris, 89304 Joigny, Yonne. **Map** p221 D4. 📞 03 86 62 09 70. 📠 03 86 91 49 70. @ cotestjacques@calvacom.fr 🍴 b,l,d. **Rooms** 29. Ⓕ Ⓕ Ⓕ Ⓕ

LYON

La Tour Rose In old Lyon, a Michelin-starred restaurant with amazing rooms, each one reflecting a different period in the history of silk.
⊠ 22 rue du Boeuf, 69005 Lyon, Rhône. **Map** p221 E5, p223 D2. 📞 04 78 37 25 90. 📠 04 78 42 26 02. @ chavent@asi.fr 🍴 b,l,d. **Rooms** 12. Ⓕ Ⓕ Ⓕ Ⓕ

LYON

Villa Florentine A luxurious mix of Renaissance style with contemporary Italian design.
⊠ 25 montée St-Barthélémy, 69005 Lyon, Rhône. **Map** p221 E5, p223 D2. 📞 04 72 56 56 56. 📠 04 72 40 90 56. @ florentine@relaischateaux.fr 🍴 b,l,d. **Rooms** 19. Ⓕ Ⓕ Ⓕ Ⓕ

MEGÈVE

Chalet du Mont d'Arbois Old pine furniture, log fires and fresh bedrooms in a traditional chalet.
⊠ 447 chemin de la Rocaille, 74120 Megève, Haute-Savoie. **Map** p221 F5, p223 E2. 📞 04 50 21 25 03. 📠 04 50 21 24 79. @ montarbois@relaischateaux.fr 🍴 b,l,d. **Rooms** 21. Ⓕ Ⓕ Ⓕ Ⓕ

NOIZAY

Château de Noizay Formal French gardens
stretch away from this substantial 16th-century
chateau. Inside, sturdy wooden stairs lead from
the black and white tiled hall to the bedrooms,
many of them furnished with four poster beds.
The food and local Vouvray wines are excellent.
⊠ Route de Chançay, 37210 Noizay, Indre-et-Loire.
Map p220 C4, p222 C1. ☎ 02 47 52 11 01.
FAX 02 47 52 04 64. @ noizay@relaischateaux.fr
⊪ b,l,d. **Rooms** 14. ⊠ ⊗ ● mid-Jan to mid-March.
⊘ AE, DC, MC, V. ⒻⒻⒻ

LA ROCHE-L'ABEILLE

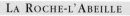

Moulin de la Gorce Two main reasons for a visit
to this flour mill are the peace it enjoys and the
food it produces. Built in the 1500s in an enviable
position by a lake, it is now run by pastry chefs.
Decoration varies: some country, some period,
but the chintzy bedrooms look a touch out of
place. Exceptional cuisine.
⊠ 87800 La Roche-l'Abeille, Haute-Vienne.
Map p220 C5. ☎ 05 55 00 70 66. FAX 05 55 00 76 57.
@ moulingorce@relaischateaux.fr ⊪ b,l,d. **Rooms** 10.
⊗ ● Jan. ⊘ AE, DC, MC, V. ⒻⒻⒻ

REPLONGES

La Huchette The Gualdieri family have restored
and enlarged this old inn and smartened it up
considerably in the process. The bold decoration
includes a colourful mural of country scenes in
the beamed dining room, which specializes in
regional dishes. The best and quietest bedrooms
are those facing the large garden.
⊠ 01750 Replonges, Ain. **Map** p221 E5, p223 E2.
☎ 03 85 31 03 55. FAX 03 85 31 10 24.
@ lahuchette@wanadoo.fr ⊪ b,l,d. **Rooms** 12.
⊠ ⊗ ● Nov. ⊘ AE, DC, MC, V. ⒻⒻ

ST-CHARTIER

Château de la Vallée Bleue The Gasquets have
owned and run this mini chateau since 1985, and
more committed hoteliers would be hard to find.
Flowers brighten the rooms; on chilly days a log
fire blazes in the hall; service is caring; and an
easy air pervades the hotel. It is surrounded by
garden, giving every room a pleasing outlook.
⊠ Route de Verneuil, St-Chartier, 36400 La Châtre, Indre.
Map p221 D5, p222 C2. ☎ 02 54 31 01 91.
FAX 02 54 31 04 48. ⊪ b,l,d. **Rooms** 18. ⊠ ⊤ ⊗
● mid-Nov to mid-Dec, Jan to March. ⊘ MC, V. ⒻⒻ

MEGÈVE
Le Fer à Cheval Hansel and Gretel wood chalet
with gleaming furniture and fresh fabrics, plus
pool and health centre. Half board obligatory.
⊠ 36 route du Crêt-d'Arbois, 74120 Megève, Haute-
Savoie. **Map** p221 F5, p223 F2. ☎ 04 50 21 30 39.
FAX 04 50 93 07 60. ⊪ b,d. **Rooms** 41. ⒻⒻⒻ

MEURSAULT
Hôtel les Charmes Secluded grounds with tall
trees surround this civilized 18th-century *maison
bourgeoise*. The pool is a plus.
⊠ 10 place du Murger, 21190 Meursault, Côte-d'Or.
Map p221 E4, p223 D1. ☎ 03 80 21 63 53.
FAX 03 80 21 62 89. ⊪ b. **Rooms** 14. ⒻⒻ

MONTRICHARD
Château de Chissay Some rooms in this plush
fairytale-style castle are vast, but the smaller ones
are good value. Great views and a pool.
⊠ Chissay-en-Touraine, 41400 Montrichard, Loir-et-Cher.
Map p220 C4, p222 C1. ☎ 02 54 32 32 01.
FAX 02 54 32 43 80. ⊪ b,l,d. **Rooms** 31. ⒻⒻ

MONTRICHARD
Château de la Menaudière A small, beautifully
furnished chateau with a snug bar, pretty
courtyard and lawns, and a warm heart.
⊠ 41401 Montrichard, Loir-et-Cher. **Map** p220 C4,
p222 C1. ☎ 02 54 71 23 45. FAX 02 54 71 34 58.
⊪ b,l,d. **Rooms** 25. ⒻⒻ

St-Hilaire-de-Court

Château de la Beuvrière Dedicated chateau-hoppers can enjoy a night in the genuine medieval article without having to dip too far into their pockets. On a huge estate in the Cher valley, it has been carefully renovated, its lovely rooms full of family furniture. The pool is rather too close to the house – but that's just a quibble.
⊠ St-Hilaire-de-Court, 18100 Vierzon, Cher.
Map p221 D4, p222 C1. (02 48 75 14 63.
FAX 02 48 75 47 62. 🍴 b,l,d. **Rooms** 15. 🏊 🔘
🔘 mid-Dec to mid-March. 🅐 AE, DC, MC, V. Ⓕ

St-Martin-du-Fault

La Chapelle-St-Martin The trim and tidy manor house stands proud within its equally trim and tidy grounds with small lake and mature trees. Inside is decorated to the hilt, mixing antiques, modern conveniences and rich fabrics; bedrooms are equally impressive. Yet the ambience is relaxed. Fine swimming pool, tennis courts.
⊠ St-Martin-du-Fault, 87510 Nieul, Haute-Vienne.
Map p220 C5, p222 C2. (05 55 75 80 17.
FAX 05 55 75 89 50. @ chapelle@relaischateaux.fr
🍴 b,l,d. **Rooms** 14. 🔘 Jan. 🅐 AE, MC, V. ⒻⒻⒻ

St-Maixent-L'Ecole

Le Logis Saint-Martin Once you're ensconced in this pretty Relais du Silence, surrounded by woods, it seems impossible that the A10 motorway is so close. Built in the 17th century of pale stone, it has a tower converted into a smart split-level suite. Bertrand Heintz is a welcoming host, and the classic cuisine uses only organic produce.
⊠ Chemin de Pissot, 79400 St-Maixent-L'Ecole,
Deux-Sèvres. **Map** p220 C5, p222 B2. (05 49 05 58 68.
FAX 05 49 76 19 93. 🍴 b,l,d. **Rooms** 11.
🔘 🔘 Jan. 🅐 AE, DC, MC, V. ⒻⒻ

St-Patrice

Château de Rochecotte A vast park and formal garden enclose the grand family-run stately home; inside gorgeous furnishings enhance the classical rooms. Yet it retains the feel of a private home – the family could not be more welcoming nor the staff more attentive. Madame Pasquier serves consistently elegant cuisine.
⊠ St-Patrice, 37130 Langeais, Indre-et-Loire.
Map p220 C4. (02 47 96 16 16. FAX 02 47 96 90 59.
@ chateau.rochecotte@wanadoo.fr 🍴 b,l,d. **Rooms** 32.
🏊 🔘 🔘 Feb. 🅐 AE, DC, MC, V. ⒻⒻⒻ

Onzain

Domaine des Hauts de Loire Characterful 19th-century hunting lodge. Michelin-starred cuisine.
⊠ Route de Herbault, 41150 Onzain, Loir-et-Cher.
Map p220 C4, p222 C1. (02 54 20 72 57.
FAX 02 54 20 77 32. @ hauts-loire@relaischateaux.fr
🍴 b,l,d. **Rooms** 35. ⒻⒻⒻ

Pérouges

Ostellerie du Vieux Pérouges In the centre of the medieval town. Excellent traditional cooking; bedrooms are in four separate houses.
⊠ Place du Tilleul, Pérouges, 01800 Meximieux, Ain.
Map p223 E2. (04 74 61 00 88. FAX 04 74 34 77 90.
🍴 b,l,d. **Rooms** 29. ⒻⒻ

Romorantin-Lanthenay

Grand Hôtel du Lion d'Or Gastronomic food in a flamboyant villa in this undiscovered town.
⊠ 69 rue Georges Clemenceau, 41200 Romorantin-Lanthenay, Loir-et-Cher. **Map** p221 D4, p222 C1.
(02 54 94 15 15. FAX 02 54 88 24 87. @ liondor@relaischateaux.fr 🍴 b,l,d. **Rooms** 16. ⒻⒻⒻ

St-Palais-sur-Mer

Hôtel Primavera Elaborate yet serene late 18th-century villa in private grounds. Its kitchen inclines towards fish. Indoor swimming pool.
⊠ 12 rue Brick, St-Palais-sur-Mer, Charente-Maritime.
Map p220 B5, p222 A2. (05 46 23 20 35.
FAX 05 46 23 28 78. 🍴 b,l,d. **Rooms** 45. ⒻⒻ

For key to symbols see backflap. For price categories see p217

TAVERS

La Tonnellerie The internal garden of this 19th-century wine-merchant's house is glorious in summer, when tables are set out beneath the chestnuts. The modern regional cuisine is always a draw. The hotel is kept in pristine order by the delightful Marie-Christine Pouey; among the pretty floral bedrooms are four apartment suites. ✉ 12 rue des Eaux, Tavers, 45190 Beaugency, Loiret. **Map** p220 C4. ☎ 02 38 44 68 15. ℻ 02 38 44 10 01. @ tonelri@club-internet.fr 🍴 b,l,d. **Rooms** 20. 🛏 🔊 ● early Jan to March. 🄰 AE, MC, V. ⒡⒡

TOURS

Jean Bardet Sitting in a wicker chair inside the colonnade, sipping a cocktail and savouring the landscaped garden is just one of the treats at the Jean Bardet. Luxurious bedrooms and delectable food are others. A refined 19th-century villa in Touraine stone, the hotel has the bonus of being only 2km (about 1 mile) from the city centre. ✉ 57 rue Groison, 37100 Tours, Indre-et-Loire. **Map** p220 C4. ☎ 02 47 41 41 11. ℻ 02 47 51 68 72. @ sophie@jeansbardet.com 🍴 b,l,d. **Rooms** 21. 🛏 🔊 ● Never. 🄰 AE, DC, MC, V. ⒡⒡⒡⒡

VEYRIER-DU-LAC

La Demeure de Chavoire For a spell of total peace, look no further than this hotel on the shores of Lake Annecy. It forges a winning combination of classic elegance and modern luxury, with artistic decoration and romantic bedrooms named after local writers and beauty spots. Basically a B&B, but snacks are available. ✉ 71 route d'Annecy-Chavoire, 74290 Veyrier-du-Lac, Haute-Savoie. **Map** p221 F5, p223 E2. ☎ 04 50 60 04 38. ℻ 04 50 60 05 36. 🍴 b. **Rooms** 13. 🔊 ● Never. 🄰 AE, DC, MC, V. ⒡⒡⒡

VÉZELAY

Le Pontot The only hotel within the town walls of old Vézelay, this special B&B occupies an ancient, sprawling house, fortified and rebuilt over the centuries. Bedrooms range from ones with stone floors, rafters and rustic furniture to a suite in Louis XVI style. In winter breakfast is served in front of a splendid log fire; in summer, in the pretty walled garden. ✉ Place du Pontot, 89450 Vézelay, Yonne. **Map** p221 D4, p223 D1. ☎ 03 86 33 24 40. ℻ 03 86 33 30 05. 🍴 b. **Rooms** 10. 🔊 ● Nov to Easter. 🄰 DC, MC, V. ⒡⒡

SOUVIGNY-EN-SOLOGNE

Auberge de la Croix Blanche A genial brick-and-timber inn. The kitchen serves vast portions of good, regional fare. ✉ Rue Eugenie Labiche, Souvigny-en-Sologne, 41600 Lamotte-Beuvron, Loir-et-Cher. **Map** p221 D4. ☎ 02 54 88 40 08. ℻ 02 54 88 91 06. 🍴 b,l,d. **Rooms** 9. ⒡

TAIN L'HERMITAGE

Reynaud Fine restaurant-with-rooms, the accent is on fish and home-grown vegetables. Glorious terrace beside the Rhône river. ✉ 82 avenue President-Roosevelt, 26600 Tain-l'Hermitage, Drôme. **Map** p223 D3. ☎ 04 75 07 22 10. ℻ 04 75 08 03 53. 🍴 b,l,d. **Rooms** 10. ⒡

TALLOIRES

Auberge du Père Bise Swanky inn on the lake, run by *mère et fille* Bise, exalted for their cuisine. ✉ Route du Port, 74290 Talloires, Haute-Savoie. **Map** p221 F5, p223 E2. ☎ 04 50 60 72 01. ℻ 04 50 60 73 05. @ bise@relaischateaux.fr 🍴 b,l,d. **Rooms** 34. ⒡⒡⒡⒡

LE TERTENOZ

Au Gay Séjour A simple white and wood chalet with spectacular alpine views and hearty food; the muzak is not to everyone's taste. ✉ Le Tertenoz de Seythenex, 74210 Faverges, Haute-Savoie. **Map** p221 F5. ☎ 04 50 44 52 52. ℻ 04 50 44 49 52. 🍴 b,l,d. **Rooms** 12. ⒡⒡

SOUTHERN FRANCE

DORDOGNE AND AQUITAINE • MASSIF CENTRAL • PYRENÉES
LANGUEDOC-ROUSSILLON • PROVENCE-CÔTE D'AZUR

THE DORDOGNE and the Lot, the fertile valleys in the southwest, are popular holiday spots. They offer a wealth of attractive small hotels and B&Bs in old mills, stables, manors and farmhouses. Further west is Bordeaux, with its incomparable vineyards, and the tree-bordered beaches of the Landes. The Massif Central, arguably the least spoilt part of France, has a range of hotels, from farmsteads and chalets to medieval stone-built inns and elegant restaurants with rooms. Many are very good value for money. To the southeast of the region, in Provence, whitewashed walls and tiled roofs, and shady courtyards with wrought-iron furniture, are typical.

AIX-EN-PROVENCE

Mas d'Entremont A cool courtyard lies at the heart of the hotel, a cluster of low, modern buildings. Their red roofs were constructed from old materials, giving them a softer, more rustic look. Wood pillars and beams abound in both the public rooms and the bedrooms, which are furnished with country pieces.
☒ Montée d'Avignon, 13090 Aix-en-Provence.
Map p224 C4. ☎ 04 42 17 42 42. **FAX** 04 42 21 15 83.
@ entremont@wanadoo.fr ⑪ b,l,d. **Rooms** 17.
▤ ☷ ⑧ ● Nov to mid-Mar. ⓔ MC, V. ⑤⑤⑤

AIX-EN-PROVENCE

Villa Gallici From the terrace with its deep-cushioned seats shaded by plane trees, to the glamorous bedrooms with fabric-draped beds, the villa is perfect – interior-decorated to the last tie-back. Perhaps it's a little too perfect to put you completely at ease, but the restaurant excels.
☒ Avenue de la Violette, 13100 Aix-en-Provence, Bouches-du-Rhône. **Map** p224 C4. ☎ 04 42 23 29 23.
FAX 04 42 96 30 45. @ gallici@relaischateaux.fr
⑪ b,l,d. **Rooms** 19. ▤ ☷ ⑧ ● Never.
ⓔ AE, DC, MC, V. ⑤⑤⑤⑤

AIX-EN-PROVENCE
Hôtel des Quatre Dauphins Painted furniture graces the reception room and simple, tasteful bedrooms in this good-value *maison bourgeoise*.
☒ 54 rue Roux Alphéron, 13100 Aix-en-Provence, Bouches-du-Rhône. **Map** p224 C4. ☎ 04 42 38 16 39.
FAX 04 42 38 60 19. ⑪ b. **Rooms** 13. ⑤

AJACCIO, CORSICA
Hôtel Dolce Vita The glossy hotel has an acclaimed restaurant specializing in fish, and a glorious covered dining terrace.
☒ Route des Sanguinaires, 20000 Ajaccio, Corse-du-Sud. **Map** p223 F5. ☎ 04 95 52 42 42. **FAX** 04 95 52 07 15.
⑪ b,l,d. **Rooms** 32. ⑤⑤⑤⑤

LES ARCS
Le Logis du Guetteur From the outside the 11th-century fort has barely changed; inside, calm modern rooms enjoy incomparable views.
☒ Place du Château, 83460 Les Arcs, Var.
Map p225 E4. ☎ 04 94 99 51 10.
FAX 04 94 99 51 29. ⑪ b,l,d. **Rooms** 11. ⑤⑤

ARGELÈS-SUR-MER
Le Cottage Logis de France seaside hotel with pleasant garden and pool. Innovative cuisine; simple bedrooms.
☒ 21 rue Arthur-Rimbaud, 66700 Argelès-sur-Mer, Pyrénés-Orientales. **Map** p223 D5. ☎ 04 68 81 07 33.
FAX 04 68 81 59 69. ⑪ b,l,d. **Rooms** 32. ⑤⑤⑤

LES BAUX-DE-PROVENCE

Auberge de la Benvengudo With its shuttered façade almost hidden by creepers, the *auberge* looks older than its 20-odd years. A large garden and pool, prepossessing bedrooms, a snug *salon* and a talented chef (the owner's son) make this a most inviting choice.

⊠ Vallon de l'Arcoule, 13520 Les Baux-de-Provence, Bouches-du-Rhône. **Map** p224 B3. 🄲 04 90 54 32 54. 🅵🅰🅇 04 90 54 42 58. 🄰 benvengudo@aol.com
🕮 b,l,d. **Rooms** 20. 🎴 🄰 🌑 end Oct to early March. 🅔 AE, MC, V. Ⓕ Ⓕ

LES BAUX-DE-PROVENCE

L'Oustau de Baumanière The hotel makes the most of its splendid position high in the craggy Alpilles. You can swim with a view in the glorious pool, almost carved out of rock, and eat with one too on the panoramic terrace; the food is first-class. A few of the bedrooms are baronial, all are well-equipped.

⊠ 13520 Les Baux-de-Provence, Bouches-du-Rhône. **Map** p224 B30. 🄲 04 90 54 33 07. 🅵🅰🅇 04 90 54 40 46. 🄰 oustau@relaischateaux.fr 🕮 b,l,d. **Rooms** 20. 🎛 🎴 🄰 🌑 mid-Jan to Mar. 🅔 AE, DC, MC, V. Ⓕ Ⓕ Ⓕ Ⓕ

BRANTÔME

Le Chatenet The Laxtons' dog may bound out to greet you at this friendly B&B. A fine, low stone manor tucked away from the hurly-burly down a country track off the main riverside road, its interior is graciously but comfortably furnished. In the garden, deckchairs are placed temptingly in shady spots. There's also an honesty bar and a barbecue for the use of guests.

⊠ 24310 Brantôme, Dordogne. **Map** p222 B3. 🄲 05 53 05 81 08. 🅵🅰🅇 05 53 05 85 52. 🕮 b. **Rooms** 12. 🎴 🄰 🌑 occasionally, Nov to Apr. 🅔 MC, V. Ⓕ Ⓕ

BRANTÔME

Moulin de l'Abbaye Its riverside situation makes this delectable former mill a magical place. A superb outlook across the Dronne river to the old town is shared by the flowery terrace and some of the smart, variously styled bedrooms. Housekeeping is flawless, the Michelin-starred food imaginative and the staff courteous.

⊠ 1 route de Bourdeilles, 24310 Brantôme, Dordogne. **Map** p222 B3. 🄲 05 53 05 80 22. 🅵🅰🅇 05 53 05 75 27. 🄰 moulin@relaischateaux.fr 🕮 b,l,d. **Rooms** 19. 🄰 🌑 Nov to May. 🅔 AE, DC, MC, V. Ⓕ Ⓕ Ⓕ

ARPAILLARGUES

Hôtel Marie d'Agoult The rural retreat was once home to Franz Liszt's mistress. It now makes a civilized and secluded retreat.

⊠ Château d'Arpaillargues, Arpaillargues, 30700 Uzès, Gard. **Map** p224 A3. 🄲 04 66 22 14 48. 🅵🅰🅇 04 66 22 56 10. 🕮 b,l,d. **Rooms** 28. Ⓕ Ⓕ Ⓕ

BARCUS

Hôtel Chilo A village hotel with views of the countryside that has been in the same family for three generations. Outstanding food; pool.

⊠ 64130 Barcus, Pyrénées-Atlantiques. **Map** p222 A4. 🄲 05 59 28 90 79. 🅵🅰🅇 05 59 28 93 10. 🄰 martine.chilo@wanadoo.fr 🕮 b,l,d. **Rooms** 10. Ⓕ

BOISSET

Auberge de Concasty Cheerful house and lawns on a family farm. Build up an appetite in the pool: Martine Causse's delicious local dishes are filling.

⊠ 15600 Boissy, Cantal. **Map** p222 C3. 🄲 04 71 62 21 16. 🅵🅰🅇 04 71 62 22 22. 🕮 b,l,d. **Rooms** 16. Ⓕ Ⓕ

BONNIEUX

L'Hostellerie du Prieuré A chef from Maxim in Paris provides a fine Provençal table at this old *hôtel-Dieu* which retains all its original details: hefty oak doors and grand tiled staircase.

⊠ 84480 Bonnieux, Vaucluse. **Map** p224 C3. 🄲 04 90 75 80 78. 🅵🅰🅇 04 90 75 96 00. 🕮 b,l,d. **Rooms** 10. Ⓕ Ⓕ

LE BUISSON-DE-CADOUIN

Manoir de Bellerive This handsome manor overlooking the Dordogne was renovated by interior designers, who created some striking paint effects and stylish rooms. A magnificent colonnaded entrance has an elegant double staircase. Set in private parkland, the place is as calm as the leisurely river.
⊠ Route de Siorac, 24480 Le Buisson-de-Cadouin, Dordogne. **Map** p222 C3. █ 05 53 22 16 16. ᴀ̃ 05 53 22 09 05. ▮▮ b,l,d. **Rooms** 25. 🏊 ⷮ █ ● Nov to mid-Apr. ☕ MC, V. ⓕⓕ

CARENNAC

Hostellerie Fénelon The little hotel, a cluster of red roofs and window boxes in a captivating village, represents excellent value for money. It's not fancy, but the welcoming hostess, Mme Raynal, offers a warm welcome, good honest cooking and a little swimming pool, at low cost. In good weather, meals can be taken on the dining terrace. Friendly, unobtrusive staff.
⊠ 46110 Carennac, Lot. **Map** p222 C3. █ 05 65 10 96 46. ᴀ̃ 05 65 10 94 86. ▮▮ b,l,d. **Rooms** 16. 🏊 ⷮ █ ● early Jan to mid-March. ☕ MC, V. ⓕ

CALVI, CORSICA

Auberge Relais de la Signora Candlelit dinner on the palm-shaded terrace by the seductive pool is one of the joys of staying here, a simple but stylish 17th-century house with an exotic garden. When cool, meals are served in an attractive ochre-washed dining room. If you can, opt for a room in the main house not the annexe.
⊠ Route de la Fôret de Bonifato, 20260 Calvi, Haute-Corse. **Map** p223 F5. █ 04 95 65 93 00. ᴀ̃ 04 95 65 38 77. ▮▮ b,l,d. **Rooms** 10. 🖿 🏊 ⷮ █ ● mid-Oct to Apr. ☕ AE, MC, V. ⓕⓕⓕ

CASTELPERS

Château de Castelpers The present owner's great-grandfather built the house in the 19th century on the ruins of an earlier mill. Visitors today find a reflective place, a rambling country house filled with old paintings, antiques and four-poster beds. Enveloping the building is a garden of rivers and tall trees. And all this at modest cost.
⊠ Castelpers, 12170 Léderques, Aveyron. **Map** p222 C4. █ 05 65 69 22 61. ᴀ̃ 05 65 69 25 31. ▮▮ b,l,d. **Rooms** 8. █ ● Oct to March. ☕ AE, DC, MC, V. ⓕ

LE BUGUE

Domaine de la Barde An elegant shuttered manor house, mill and old forge, in a garden bounded by streams, fields and woods.
⊠ Route de Périgueux, 24260 Le Bugue, Dordogne. **Map** p222 B3. █ 05 53 07 16 54. ᴀ̃ 05 53 54 76 19. ▮▮ b,l,d. **Rooms** 18. ⓕⓕ

CARCASSONNE

Domaine d'Auriac Golf, tennis and swimming are a few attractions of this plush country house. Fine dining on a splendid terrace.
⊠ Route de St-Hilaire, 11009 Carcassonne, Aude. **Map** p224 C4. █ 04 68 25 72 22. ᴀ̃ 04 68 47 35 54. @ auriac@relaischateaux.fr ▮▮ b,l,d. **Rooms** 24. ⓕⓕⓕ

CASSIS

Le Clos des Arômes A 50-year-old hotel jazzed up by the young, hospitable Bonnets. Bedrooms are small but pretty; not all have bathrooms.
⊠ 10 rue Paul Mouton, 13260 Cassis, Bouches-du-Rhône. **Map** p222 C4. █ 04 42 01 71 84. ᴀ̃ 04 42 01 31 76. ▮▮ b,l,d. **Rooms** 8. ⓕⓕ

CÉRET

Le Mas Trilles A delightful 17th-century former farmhouse with pool in a verdant landscape. Rooms are big and stylish but not elaborate.
⊠ Le Pont de Reynès, 66400 Céret, Pyrénées-Orientales. **Map** p223 D5. █ 04 68 87 38 37. ᴀ̃ 04 68 87 42 62. ▮▮ b,d. **Rooms** 10. ⓕⓕⓕ

For key to symbols see backflap. For price categories see p217

CÉRET

La Terrasse au Soleil This luxurious ranch-like manor has an individual style and intimacy that is reflected in its warm colour schemes. The restaurant has a reputation for serious food, but serves brasserie-style lunches too. Bedrooms are in annexes, some with verandas.
✉ Route de Fontfrède, 66400 Céret, Pyrénées-Orientales. **Map** p223 D5. ☎ 04 68 87 01 94. FAX 04 68 87 39 24. @ terrasseausoleil.hotel@wanadoo.fr ⬛ b,l,d. **Rooms** 25. ▤ ≋ ◗ ● Nov to March. ⬛ AE, MC, V. ⓕⓕⓕⓕ

COLY

Manoir d'Hautegente This 13th-century manor has been through several incarnations: first it was a forge, then a mill, before becoming a private house. The hotel's charm is that it keeps the feel of home intact with fresh-coloured, antique-filled rooms. The menu features the Hamelins' home-produced *foie gras*.
✉ Coly, 24120 Terrasson, Dordogne. **Map** p223 C3. ☎ 05 53 51 68 03. FAX 05 53 50 38 52. @ manoir.d.hautegente@wanadoo.fr ⬛ b,d. **Rooms** 15. ≋ ◗ ● Nov to Easter. ⬛ AE, MC, V. ⓕⓕ

CHAMPAGNAC-DE-BELAIR

Le Moulin du Roc This former walnut mill has a heavenly setting on the banks of the Dronne river, encircled by a fertile garden. The interior is a delightful clutter of carved furniture, sumptuous fabrics, huge pictures and mill paraphernalia. The kitchen prepares delicate regional food.
✉ 24530 Champagnac-de-Belair, Dordogne. **Map** p222 C2. ☎ 05 53 02 86 00. FAX 05 53 54 21 31. @ moulin_du_roc@horeca-tm.fr ⬛ b,l,d. **Rooms** 14. ≋ ◗ ● early Jan to early March. ⬛ AE, DC, MC, V. ⓕⓕ

COULANDON

Le Chalet The chalet-style *logis*, deep in the Bourdonnais countryside, is an unsophisticated, traditional place: rooms are colourful and jolly rather than stylish. But for simple pleasures, the place is idyllic. In the wooded grounds are a pool and a large pond where guests can fish, and the little raised dining terrace has fine rurual views.
✉ 03000 Coulandon, Allier. **Map** p221 D5, 223 D2. ☎ 04 70 44 50 08. FAX 04 70 44 07 09. ⬛ b,l,d. **Rooms** 19. ≋ ◗ ● mid-Dec to end Jan. ⬛ AE, DC, MC, V. ⓕⓕ

CHAMPAGNAC
Château de Lavendès Auvergne specialities feature on Madame Gimmig's menu at this modest *logis* set in tranquil, rolling landscape.
✉ 15350 Champagnac, Cantal. **Map** p222 C3. ☎ 04 71 69 62 79. FAX 04 71 69 65 33. ⬛ b,l,d. **Rooms** 8. ⓕⓕ

CHÂTEAU-ARNOUX
La Bonne Etape Imaginative cuisine in a hushed setting with a pool. The rooms are stunning.
✉ Chemin du Lac, 04160 Château-Arnoux, Alpes-de-Haute-Provence. **Map** p225 D2. ☎ 04 92 64 00 09. FAX 04 92 64 37 36. @ bonneetape@relaischateaux.fr ⬛ b,l,d. **Rooms** 19. ⓕⓕⓕ

CIBOURE
Lehen Tokia Children are not permitted in this 1920s Basque villa, embellished with Art Deco details and heirlooms. Meals by arrangement.
✉ Chemin Achotarreta, 64500 St-Jean-de-Luz, Pyrénées-Atlantiques. **Map** p222 A4. ☎ 05 59 47 18 16. FAX 05 59 47 38 04. ⬛ b,l,d. **Rooms** 6. ⓕⓕ

COLLIOURE
Hôtel Casa Païral An exotic enclosed garden, with pine trees and a 100-year-old palm, lies at the heart of this alluring old Catalan-style B&B.
✉ 66190 Collioure, Pyrénées-Orientales. **Map** p223 D5. ☎ 04 68 82 05 81. FAX 04 68 82 52 10. ⬛ b. **Rooms** 28. ⓕⓕ

CONDOM

Hôtel des Trois Lys The elegance of this white-shuttered honey-stone house extends from the outside in. An immense stone staircase leads to the bedrooms, some of which are huge and wood-panelled, with deep-pile carpet and pristine bathrooms. There is a pool at the back and a restaurant, Le Dauphin, next door.
⊠ 38 rue Gambetta, 32100 Condom, Gers.
Map p222 B4. █ 05 62 28 33 33. **FAX** 05 62 28 41 85.
@ hoteltroislys@minitel.net ▮ b. **Rooms** 10.
▦ ▮ ● Feb. ⊘ AE, MC, V. ⒻⒻ

CRILLON-LE-BRAVE

Hostellerie de Crillon-le-Brave A substantial former vicarage of ochre stone, set on a hilltop in Italianate gardens, houses a hotel that is luxurious and precisely run without forfeiting its character. The interior is all worn flagged floors, stone walls, rustic furniture, old books and comfy sofas.
⊠ Place de l'Eglise, 84410 Crillon-le-Brave, Vaucluse.
Map p224 C2. █ 04 90 65 61 61. **FAX** 04 90 65 62 86.
@ crillonbrave@relaischateaux.fr ▮ b,d. **Rooms** 24.
▦ ▮ ● Jan to March. ⊘ AE, MC, V. ⒻⒻⒻ

CORNILLON

La Vieille Fontaine Built within the walls of a ruined castle in the medieval village of Cornillon, this hotel is the baby of the Auberts. He is *patron* and talented chef; she is in charge of decoration. Her style is Provençal and unfussy, with touches of panache like the outside staircase encased in glass. Steep steps lead through terraced gardens to a hilltop pool.
⊠ 30630 Cornillon, Gard. **Map** p224 A2.
█ 04 66 82 20 56. **FAX** 04 66 82 33 64. ▮ b,l,d.
Rooms 8. ▦ ▮ ● Jan to March. ⊘ AE, MC, V. ⒻⒻ

LES ESSAREAUX

Hostellerie La Manescale Surrounded by woodland walks, this serene former shepherd's cottage will delight nature lovers. Thoughtful hosts, the Warlands provide all sorts of extras, from novels to swimming towels for the pool. Drinks on the terrace in the evening are accompanied by classical music.
⊠ Route de Faucon, Les Essareaux, 84340 Entrechaux, Vaucluse. **Map** p224 C2. █ 04 90 46 03 80.
FAX 04 90 46 03 89. ▮ b,d. **Rooms** 5. ▦ ▮
● Nov to Easter. ⊘ AE, DC, MC, V. ⒻⒻ

CORDES-SUR-CIEL
Le Grand Ecuyer Michelin-starred cuisine, courtesy of pastry cook Yves Thuriès, in an old hunting lodge in this perfect medieval village.
⊠ Rue Voltaire, 81170 Cordes-sur-Ciel, Tarn.
Map p222 C4. █ 05 63 53 79 50. **FAX** 05 63 53 79 51.
▮ b,l,d. **Rooms** 13. ⒻⒻ

DÉGAGNAC
Auberge sans Frontière The simple village inn in sleepy Dégagnac offers superb value for its hearty cuisine and trim bedrooms. The dining room also serves as a bar and sitting room.
⊠ Dégagnac, 46340 Salviac, Lot. **Map** p222 C3.
█ 05 65 41 52 88. ▮ b,l,d. **Rooms** 8. Ⓕ

DOMME
Hôtel de l'Esplanade The area is busy with visitors, but the hotel's breathtaking position on a cliff-edge above the Dordogne, superb food and pretty rooms make you forget the crowds.
⊠ 24250 Domme, Dordogne. **Map** p222 C3. █ 05 53 28 31 41. **FAX** 05 53 28 49 92. ▮ b,l,d. **Rooms** 25. ⒻⒻ

EYGALIÈRES
Auberge Provençale Owner/chef Didier Pézeril creates culinary works of art in his characterful inn. The bedrooms are sweet and simple with colour-washed walls.
⊠ Place de la Mairie, 13810 Eygalières. **Map** p224 B3.
█ 04 90 95 91 00. ▮ b,l,d. **Rooms** 7. Ⓕ

EUGÉNIE-LES-BAINS

Le Couvent aux Herbes In a refined spa town, this B&B, part of a small empire owned by Michel Guérard, is run with warmth and flair by his wife Christine. Rooms in the 18th-century former nunnery are all beautifully furnished. Meals are taken across the garden in the renowned Les Prés d'Eugénie restaurant.
☒ 40320 Eugénie-les-Bains, Landes. **Map** p222 B4.
📞 05 58 05 06 07. 🖷 05 58 51 10 10.
@ guerard@relaischateaux.fr 🍴 b. **Rooms** 8. ♨ ▮
● Dec to mid-Feb. 🅥 AE, DC, MC, V. Ⓕ Ⓕ Ⓕ Ⓕ

FAYENCE

Moulin de la Camandoule A seductively charming place: a converted olive mill with a Roman aqueduct in the garden. The atmosphere is relaxed. Madame Rilla's deliciously simple lunches can be taken beside the pool or on the glorious terrace overlooking cherry orchards. Bedrooms vary in standard.
☒ Chemin Notre-Dame-des-Cyprès, 83440 Fayence, Var.
Map p225 E34. 📞 04 94 76 00 84. 🖷 04 94 76 10 40.
@ moulin.camandoule@wanadoo.fr 🍴 b,l,d. **Rooms** 12.
♨ ▮ ● Never. 🅥 MC, V. Ⓕ

LES EYZIES-DE-TAYAC

Hôtel Les Glycines The hotel is named after the wisteria that has practically engulfed a pergola in the lush garden. It is set on the outskirts of a village that draws the crowds to explore its famous caves. There's a swimming pool, an open terrace for *apéritifs* and, if it rains, a covered terrace and plenty of space to sit inside.
☒ 24620 Les Eyzies-de-Tayac, Dordogne.
Map p222 C3. 📞 05 53 06 97 07. 🖷 05 53 06 92 19.
🍴 b,l,d. **Rooms** 25. ♨ ▮ ● mid-Oct to mid-Apr.
🅥 AE, MC, V. Ⓕ

FLORIMONT-GAUMIERS

La Daille British ex-pats Derek and Barbara Brown have been in charge of this red-roofed farmhouse in rolling grounds for more than 20 years. There used to be a restaurant here; now it's a congenial B&B, but their weekend afternoon teas have become a local institution. The bedrooms are in a separate, modern building; there is a minimum stay of three days.
☒ 24250 Florimont-Gaumiers, Dordogne. **Map** p222 C3.
📞 05 53 28 40 71. 🍴 b. **Rooms** 3. ♨ ▮
● Oct to May. 🅥 Not accepted. Ⓕ Ⓕ

EYGALIÈRES
Hostellerie Mas dou Pastré Exquisite Provençal furnishings in a *mas* looking out to the Alpilles. Light lunches on a terrace; pool in the garden.
☒ Route d'Organ, 13810 Eygalières, Bouches-du-Rhône.
Map p224 B3. 📞 04 90 95 92 61. 🖷 04 90 90 61 75.
🍴 b,l. **Rooms** 12. Ⓕ

LES EYZIES-DE-TAYAC
Moulin de la Beune An oasis of calm at the heart of the tourist trail, with bright bedrooms and a Périgordian restaurant in the garden.
☒ 24620 Les Eyzies-de-Tayac, Dordogne. **Map** p222 C3.
📞 05 53 06 94 33. 🖷 05 53 06 98 06. 🍴 b,l,d.
Rooms 20. Ⓕ

EZE-VILLAGE
Château de la Chèvre d'Or Smart hotel perched on a clifftop, where every bedroom has a view.
☒ Rue du Barri, Eze-Village, Alpes-Maritimes.
Map p225 F3. 📞 04 92 10 66 66. 🖷 04 93 41 06 72.
@ chevredor@relaischateaux.fr 🍴 b,l,d.
Rooms 29. Ⓕ Ⓕ Ⓕ Ⓕ

EZE-VILLAGE
Château Eza Tapestries on stone walls and utter luxury, 400m (1,300ft) above the sea.
☒ Rue de la Pise, 06360 Eze-Village, Alpes-Maritimes. **Map** p225 F3. 📞 04 93 41 12 24.
🖷 04 93 41 16 64. @ chateza@webstore.fr
🍴 b,l,d. **Rooms** 10. Ⓕ Ⓕ Ⓕ Ⓕ

FONTVIEILLE

Auberge La Régalido An idyllic garden and Jean-Pierre Michel's incomparable Provençal meals are two reasons to stay at this converted old mill. Friendly staff, individually decorated bedrooms with lots of extras, and an atmosphere of well-being complete the picture.
⊠ Rue Frédéric-Mistral, 13990 Fontvieille, Bouches-du-Rhône. **Map** p224 B3. 📞 04 90 54 60 22. 📠 04 90 54 64 29. @ regalido@relaischateaux.fr 🍴 b,l,d. **Rooms** 15. 🛏 🔧 ⭘ Jan. 💳 AE, DC, MC, V. Ⓕ Ⓕ Ⓕ

GRAMAT

Château de Roumégouse This castle hotel is a rarity: a flawless Relais et Châteaux establishment with prices that are not sky-high. The style changes from one bedroom to another, but fresh flowers appear in each, as well as in the airy reception rooms. In summer, meals are taken on the panoramic terrace.
⊠ Rignac, 46500 Gramat, Lot. **Map** p222 C3. 📞 05 65 33 63 81. 📠 05 65 33 71 18. @ roumegouse@relaischateaux.fr 🍴 b,l,d. **Rooms** 15. 🔧 ⭘ Dec to end March. 💳 AE, DC, MC, V. Ⓕ Ⓕ Ⓕ

GÉMENOS

Relais de la Magdeleine This gem of a hotel, occupying a handsome 18th-century *bastide* (country house), has been run with warmth by the same family since 1932. All the bedrooms, even the cheapest ones, are prettily decorated in rustic style, with fine furniture and paintings; bathrooms are spruce. You might come across a donkey in the garden.
⊠ 13420 Gémenos, Bouches-du-Rhône. **Map** p224 C4. 📞 04 42 32 20 16. 📠 04 42 32 02 26. 🍴 b,l,d. **Rooms** 24. 🛁 🔧 ⭘ Dec to mid-March. 💳 MC, V. Ⓕ Ⓕ

GRIMAUD

Le Coteau Fleuri You don't have to meet the cheerful owner to feel positive about this hotel. It happens the moment you enter the spacious interior with its polished tile floors and white walls, and smell the fragrance of fresh flowers. Rooms and food have a Provençal flavour.
⊠ Place des Penitents, 83360 Grimaud, Var. **Map** p225 E4. 📞 04 94 43 20 17. 📠 04 94 43 33 42. @ coteaufleuri@wanadoo.fr 🍴 b,l,d. **Rooms** 14. 🔧 ⭘ 2 weeks before Christmas, first 2 weeks Jan. 💳 AE, MC, V. Ⓕ Ⓕ

FIGEAC
Château du Viguier du Roy Central, but with a peaceful cloister and interior garden. Warm sophistication in a setting of 12th-century origins.
⊠ Rue Droite, 46100 Figeac, Lot. **Map** p222 C3. 📞 05 65 50 05 05. 📠 05 65 50 06 06. 🍴 b,l,d. **Rooms** 21. Ⓕ Ⓕ Ⓕ

FLOURE
Château de Floure Former Romanesque abbey with extensive grounds, a maze and a pool. Pleasing rooms and fine food add to its appeal.
⊠ 11800 Floure, Aude. **Map** p222 C4. 📞 04 68 79 11 29. 📠 04 68 79 04 61. 🍴 b,l,d. **Rooms** 17. Ⓕ Ⓕ

GIGONDAS
Les Florets A tempting menu is accompanied by wine from the owner's vineyards in this family-run restaurant. Terrific terrace; plain rooms.
⊠ Route des Dentelles, 84190 Gigondas, Vaucluse. **Map** p224 C2. 📞 04 90 65 85 01. 📠 04 90 65 83 80. 🍴 b,l,d. **Rooms** 15. Ⓕ Ⓕ

HAUT-DE-CAGNES
Le Cagnard A restored medieval house with a panoramic position by the town ramparts.
⊠ Rue sous Barri, Haut-de-Cagnes, 06800 Cagnes-sur-Mer, Alpes-Maritimes. **Map** p225 F3. 📞 04 93 20 73 21. 📠 04 93 22 06 39. @ cagnard@relaischateaux.fr 🍴 b,l,d. **Rooms** 28. Ⓕ Ⓕ Ⓕ

For key to symbols see backflap. For price categories *see p217*

GRIMAUD

Le Verger A low, pink house with white shutters, typical of the region, the Verger is decorated plainly but agreeably with country-style fabrics and furniture. A wisteria-covered terrace makes a perfect venue for summer dining. In the garden of lawns and hydrangeas, there are plenty of shady spots in which to escape the midday sun.
☒ Route de Collobrières, 83360 Grimaud, Var.
Map p225 E4. ☎ 04 94 43 25 93. FAX 04 94 43 33 92.
⊓ b,l,d. **Rooms** 8. ⌷ ◯ ◯ Nov to Easter.
✉ DC, MC, V. Ⓕ Ⓕ

LACAVE

Château de la Treyne The origins of this near-perfect fortified manor date back to the 14th century, but it was rebuilt 300 years later. It is set in parkland, clinging to a cliff above the Dordogne river. Guests today find a harmonious blend of ornate and comfortable furniture in intimate rooms. Excellent regional food.
☒ Lacave, 46200 Souillac, Lot. **Map** p222 C3.
☎ 05 65 27 60 60. FAX 05 65 27 60 70.
@ treyne@relaischateaux.fr ⊓ b,l,d. **Rooms** 14. ▤ ⌷ ◯ ◯ mid-Nov to Easter. ✉ AE, DC, MC, V. Ⓕ Ⓕ Ⓕ

LACABARÈDE

Demeure de Flore Shielded from the road by a wooded garden, the 19th-century house may not be anything to write home about architecturally, but it certainly is once you look inside. Many of the bright rooms have floor-to-ceiling windows, and painstaking care has gone into their furnishing. Snack lunches by the poolside are sheer bliss.
☒ 106 Route Nationale, 81240 Lacabarède, Tarn.
Map p223 D4. ☎ 05 63 98 32 32. FAX 05 63 98 47 56.
⊓ b,l,d. **Rooms** 11. ⌷ ◯ ◯ Feb. ✉ MC, V. Ⓕ Ⓕ

LACAVE

Hôtel du Pont de l'Ouysse Tranquillity is guaranteed as the road leading to the hotel is a cul-de-sac. In warm weather, dining on the beautiful terrace that overlooks the river, sitting under a canopy of leafy trees and surrounded by shrubs, is magical. The seasonal menu features local produce.
☒ Lacave, 46200 Souillac, Lot. **Map** p222 C3.
☎ 05 65 37 87 04. FAX 05 65 32 77 41.
@ PONT.OUYSSE@wanadoo.fr ⊓ b,l,d. **Rooms** 13. ▤ ⌷ ◯ ◯ mid-Nov to March. ✉ AE, DC, MC, V. Ⓕ Ⓕ

HOSSEGOR
Les Huitrières du Lac The restaurant offers a lake view and suitably fishy menu. The view is shared by some of the large, simple rooms.
☒ 1187 avenue du Touring Club, 40150 Hossegor, Landes. **Map** p222 A4. ☎ 05 58 43 51 48.
FAX 05 58 41 73 11. ⊓ b,l,d. **Rooms** 9. Ⓕ

LALINDE
Le Château Perched above the river, this mini chateau with a crop of turrets has comfy new rooms, a snug *salon* and established restaurant.
☒ 1 rue de Verdun, 24150 Lalinde, Dordogne.
Map p222 B3. ☎ 05 53 61 01 82. FAX 05 53 24 74 60.
⊓ b,l,d. **Rooms** 7. Ⓕ Ⓕ

MAUZAC
La Métairie Amid meadows and pine woods, is this tastefully done-up, creeper-clad farmhouse. Seductive pool and terrace; kind staff.
☒ Millac, 24150 Mauzac, Dordogne. **Map** p222 B3.
☎ 05 53 22 50 47. FAX 05 53 22 52 93. ⊓ b,l,d.
Rooms 10. Ⓕ Ⓕ

MIRMANDE
La Capitelle Old stone house with a great vista from the ramparts. Public rooms have vaulted ceilings, bedrooms are elegant and colourful.
☒ Le Rempart, 26270 Mirmande, Drôme. **Map** p224 B1.
☎ 04 75 63 02 72. FAX 04 75 63 02 50.
@ capitelle@wanadoo.fr ⊓ b,l,d. **Rooms** 11. Ⓕ

LLO

Auberge Atalaya This rough-stone inn blends so well with the environment that it's hard to say where the craggy landscape stops and its walls begin. It has the double bonus of skiing on the doorstep in winter and hiking in summer. The rustic interior has polished wood and stone walls in the dining room; bedrooms are cosy.
🗵 Llo, 66800 Saillagouse, Pyrénées-Orientales.
Map p222 C5. ◖ 04 68 04 70 04. ⒻAX 04 68 04 01 29.
Ⅱ b,l,d. **Rooms** 13. ⛰ ⑧ ⬤ early Nov to late Dec.
⬤ MC, V. Ⓕ Ⓕ

MADIÈRES

Château de Madières Spectacularly situated, teetering on the edge of a cliff above the Vis gorge, is this 14th-century fortress. Its rugged exterior masks a comfortable hotel, lovingly restored by the Brucys. It has an alluring galleried *salon*, and bedrooms where white walls are offset by strongly coloured furnishings.
🗵 Madières, 34190 Ganges, Hérault. **Map** p223 D4.
◖ 04 67 73 84 03. ⒻAX 04 67 73 55 71.
@ madieres@wanadoo.fr Ⅱ b,l,d. **Rooms** 10.
⛰ 🍴 ⑧ ⬤ Nov to Easter. ⬤ AE, MC, V. Ⓕ Ⓕ Ⓕ

MALATAVERNE

La Domaine du Colombier A watering place for pilgrims to Santiago de Compestela, this imaginatively converted stone house is an ideal stopover, being near the *autoroute*. But travellers will not want to leave. There are flowers everywhere – on the terrace, tables, even on fabrics – and the Barettes are wonderful hosts.
🗵 Route de Donzère, 26780 Malataverne, Drôme.
Map p224 B2. ◖ 04 75 90 86 86.
ⒻAX 04 75 90 79 40. Ⅱ b,l,d. **Rooms** 23.
⑧ ⬤ Never. ⬤ AE, DC, MC, V. Ⓕ Ⓕ Ⓕ

LA MALÈNE

Manoir de Montesquiou More like a castle than a manor and dating from the 15th century, this family-run establishment has a lurid history and a dramatic site between sheer rocks in the Gorges du Tarn. Inside, dark wood furniture and rich fabrics complete the picture. Some bedrooms are in the turrets, some have extravagant four-poster beds; all very attractive.
🗵 48210 La Malène, Lozère. **Map** p223 D3.
◖ 04 66 48 51 12. ⒻAX 04 66 48 50 47. Ⅱ b,l,d.
Rooms 12. ▤ ⑧ ⬤ Nov to Apr. ⬤ DC, MC, V. Ⓕ Ⓕ

MONTFERRAT

La Calanco Attentive yet unobtrusive service and superior bedrooms in a 16th-century house with a secluded setting. Dinner on request.
🗵 Rue du docteur Rayol, 83131 Montferrat, Var.
Map p225 E3. ◖ 04 94 70 93 10. ⒻAX 04 94 70 91 49.
Ⅱ b,d. **Rooms** 6. Ⓕ

MONTICELLO, CORSICA

A Pasturella Village life centres around the bar of this simple charming hostelry, where you will find delightful bedrooms and hearty food.
🗵 Monticello, 20220 l'Ile-Rousse, Haute-Corse.
Map p223 F5. ◖ 04 95 60 05 65. ⒻAX 04 95 60 21 78.
Ⅱ b,l,d. **Rooms** 12. Ⓕ

MONTIGNAC-LASCAUX

Château de Puy Robert Plush furnishings and fine food at a neo-Renaissance Relais et Châteaux.
🗵 Route de Valojoulx, 24290 Montignac-Lascaux,
Dordogne. **Map** p222 B3. ◖ 05 53 51 92 13.
ⒻAX 05 53 51 80 11. @ puyrobert@relaischateaux.fr
Ⅱ b,l,d. **Rooms** 38. Ⓕ Ⓕ Ⓕ

MONTSALVY

Auberge Fleurie At the core of this unpretentious inn are its two cheerful dining rooms, with their red gingham tablecloths, bright copper and gleaming wood dressers.
🗵 Place du Barry, 15120 Montsalvy, Cantal. **Map** p222 C3.
◖ 04 71 49 20 02. Ⅱ b,l,d. **Rooms** 13. Ⓕ

For key to symbols see backflap. For price categories *see p217*

MAUROUX

Hostellerie Le Vert A side door leads into this 17th-century former farmhouse, now a compelling small hotel with exposed beams and stone walls. The bedrooms are attractive to return to at the end of a day out. The Philippes, a charming couple, work hard to ensure that guests have a perfect stay.

☒ Mauroux, 46700 Puy-l'Evêque, Lot.
Map p222 C3. 📞 05 65 36 51 36.
FAX 05 65 36 56 84. 🍽 b,l,d. **Rooms** 7. 🖼 🎛
⬤ mid-Nov to mid-Feb. 💳 AE, MC, V. Ⓕ

MIMIZAN

Au Bon Coin du Lac The ever-cheerful and efficient Madame Caule warmly greets guests at her little stone-and-wood lakeside hotel. Monsieur Caule has gained a Michelin star and widespread renown for his gastronomic cooking. His speciality is seafood; it is served with due deference in the pretty, light dining room.

☒ 34 avenue du Lac, 40200 Mimizan, Landes.
Map p222 A3. 📞 05 58 09 01 55.
FAX 05 58 09 40 84. 🍽 b,l,d. **Rooms** 8.
🎛 ⬤ Feb. 💳 AE, DC, MC, V. ⒻⒻ

MEYRUEIS

Château d'Ayres Peace reigns in this handsome chateau set within the Cevennes national park. A splendid garden of mature cedars, oaks and sequoias is just one of its attributes. Others are wood-panelled rooms with superb antiques and paintings, and a menu of mouthwatering Languedoc specialities.

☒ 34 avenue du Lac, 48150 Meyrueis, Lozère.
Map p223 D3. 📞 04 66 45 60 10. FAX 04 66 45 62 26.
@ alliette@wanadoo.fr 🍽 b,l,d. **Rooms** 27. 🖼 🎛
⬤ late Nov to late March. 💳 AE, DC, MC, V. ⒻⒻ

MOUGINS

Les Muscadins The American owner has filled this appealing whitewashed hotel with antiques from the houses of *Muscadins* (18th-century fops) – hence the name. With a tropical garden and terrace with spectacular views, it is hard to resist. Bedrooms are sophisticated, and the Mediterranean cuisine is highly regarded.

☒ 18 bd. Courteline, 06250 Mougins,
Alpes-Maritimes. **Map** p225 E3. 📞 04 92 28 28 28.
FAX 04 92 92 88 23. 🍽 b,l,d. **Rooms** 8. ▤ 🎛
⬤ Never. 💳 AE, DC, MC, V. ⒻⒻⒻ

MOUDEYRES

Le Pré Bossu This thatched stone cottage is set in fields and full of old-fashioned rural charm: wood floors, dressers, lace. Serious gourmet food.

☒ 43150 Moudeyres, Haute-Loire. **Map** p224 A1.
📞 04 71 05 10 70. FAX 04 71 05 10 21. 🍽 b,l,d.
Rooms 10. ⒻⒻ

MOUGINS

Le Mas Candille Terracotta flagstones, plain white walls and oak beams are typical of this 18th-century former farmhouse.

☒ Bd Rebuffel, 06250 Mougins, Alpes-Maritime.
Map p225 E3. 📞 04 93 90 00 85. FAX 04 92 92 85 56.
🍽 b,l,d. **Rooms** 23. ⒻⒻⒻⒻ

NAJAC

L'Oustal del Barry A neat inn on the main square of a stunning village; a welcoming place which takes its cooking and wine very seriously.

☒ Place du Bourg, 12270 Najac, Aveyron.
Map p222 C3. 📞 05 65 29 74 32. FAX 05 65 29 75 32.
@ oustal@caramail.com 🍽 b,l,d. **Rooms** 20. Ⓕ

NANS-LES-PINS

Domaine de Châteauneuf Provençal-style 18th-century country house with lavish decoration.

☒ Au Logis de Nans, 83860 Nans-les-Pins, Var.
Map p224 C4. 📞 04 94 78 90 06. FAX 04 94 78 63 30.
@ chateauneuf@relaischateaux.fr 🍽 b,l,d.
Rooms 30. ⒻⒻⒻⒻ

MOUSTIERS-STE-MARIE

La Bastide de Moustiers White-clad chefs collecting fresh vegetables and herbs from the garden are a common sight at Alain Ducasse's beautifully converted 17th-century *bastide*. With its exemplary cooking and its subtle decoration, the place is a celebration of Provence.
☒ La Grisolière, 04360 Moustiers-Ste-Marie, Alpes de Haute-Provence. **Map** p225 D3.
📞 04 92 70 47 47. **FAX** 04 92 70 47 48.
@ bastide@i2m.fr **⊞** b,l,d. **Rooms** 7. 🖥 ⛲ 🛎
🌑 Never. 🗲 AE, DC, MC, V. 🅕🅕🅕

OLARGUES

Domaine de Rieumégé This is a hotel to suit every pocket, with accommodation ranging from simple, antique-filled bedrooms, to a luxury room and suite sharing a private pool. The stone house is set in the Haut Languedoc national park. The old barn makes a lovely dining room, and a fire warms the cosy *salon*.
☒ Route de St-Pons, 34390 Olargues, Hérault.
Map p223 D4. 📞 04 67 97 73 99. **FAX** 04 67 97 78 52.
⊞ b,l,d. **Rooms** 14. ⛲ 🛎 🌑 Nov to Apr.
🗲 AE, MC, V. 🅕🅕

NAJAC

Hôtel Longcol A remote wooded valley of the Aveyron gorges shelters this ancient fortified farm. Owner Fabienne Luyckx's passion for Asian art is reflected in the bronzes, carvings and studded doors that fill the house. A professional hotelier, she takes the kitchen and cellar seriously but keeps prices low.
☒ La Fouillade, 12270 Najac, Aveyron. **Map** p222 C3.
📞 05 65 29 63 36. **FAX** 05 65 29 64 28.
@ longcol@relaischateaux.fr **⊞** b,l,d. **Rooms** 17.
🖥 🛎 🌑 mid-Nov to Easter. 🗲 AE, MC, V. 🅕🅕

PAUILLAC

Château Cordeillan-Bages Lovers of wine flock to this graceful *bordelais* château with its own vineyard; the wine list is extensive, of course, but it also hosts Ecole du Bordeaux wine courses. Public rooms have an English country house feel, while the bedrooms are the ultimate in designer chic.
☒ Route des Châteaux, 33250 Pauillac, Gironde.
Map p222 B3. 📞 05 56 59 24 24. **FAX** 05 56 59 01 89.
@ cordeillan@relaischateaux.fr **⊞** b,l,d. **Rooms** 25.
🛎 🌑 early Dec to Feb. 🗲 AE, DC, MC, V. 🅕🅕🅕

NOVES

Auberge de Noves Not an *auberge*, but a sophisticated manor with a warm ambience.
☒ Route de Châteaurenard, 13550 Noves, Bouches-du-Rhône. **Map** p224 B3. 📞 04 90 24 28 28.
FAX 04 90 24 28 00. @ noves@relaischateaux.fr
⊞ b,l,d. **Rooms** 23. 🅕🅕🅕

ORNAISONS

Relais du Val d'Orbieu The former mill has a large garden, pool and enviable wine cellar. Most of the airy bedrooms are in modern extensions and have their own terraces.
☒ 11200 Ornaisons, Aude. **Map** p223 D4. 📞 04 68 27 10 27. **FAX** 04 68 27 52 44. **⊞** b,l,d. **Rooms** 20. 🅕🅕

PIOLENC

Auberge de l'Orangerie Entrance to the lively, distinctively decorated village inn is through an overgrown courtyard.
☒ 4 rue de l'Ormeau, 84420 Piolenc, Vaucluse.
Map p224 B2. 📞 04 90 29 59 88. **FAX** 04 90 29 67 74.
@ orangerie@wanadoo.fr **⊞** b,l,d. **Rooms** 5. 🅕

PONT-DE-L'ARN

La Métairie Neuve The charming former farmhouse retains some of its original features: rafters, tiled floors and stone walls.
☒ Pont-de-L'Arn, 81660 Mazamet, Tarn.
Map p222 C4. 📞 05 63 97 73 50. **FAX** 05 63 61 94 75.
⊞ b,d. **Rooms** 14. 🅕

For key to symbols see backflap. For price categories see *p217*

PEILLON-VILLAGE

Auberge de la Madone A twisting mountain road leads up to this appealing *logis*, where the Millo family welcome their guests with warmth and courtesy. Set just outside the village walls, the hotel offers a dining terrace, an organic Provençal restaurant and pleasant rooms (those in the annexe are cheapest).

✉ 06440 Peillon-Village, Alpes-Maritimes. **Map** p225 F3. 📞 04 93 79 91 17. 📠 04 93 79 99 36. 🍴 b,l,d. **Rooms** 20. 🛁 🌑 2 weeks Jan, mid-Oct to mid-Dec. 🅾 MC, V. ⓕⓕ

LE PÖET-LAVAL

Les Hospitaliers Owner Yvon Morin used to be an art dealer, which explains the many original pieces adorning this former stronghold. Spectacular views can be had from various vantage points; best are the terrace, pool and top-floor *salon*. Service in the restaurant, where one son cooks and the other is *sommelier* (wine master), is superb.

✉ 26160 Le Pöet-Laval, Drôme. **Map** p225 D2. 📞 04 75 46 22 32. 📠 04 75 46 49 99. 🍴 b,l,d. **Rooms** 24. 🏊 🛁 🌑 mid-Nov to March. 🅾 AE, DC, MC, V. ⓕⓕ

PLAN-DE-LA-TOUR

Mas des Brugassières Just 8km (5 miles) north of the resort of Ste-Maxime and set among vineyards, this comfortable *mas* has a friendly feel. Although it was built in the 1970s, the roof and floor tiles and the solid, wooden furniture are all traditional. The best bedrooms are those that have doors on to the fertile garden.

✉ Plan-de-la-Tour, 83120 Ste Maxime, Var. **Map** p225 E4. 📞 04 94 43 72 42. 📠 04 94 43 00 20. 🍴 b. **Rooms** 14. 🏊 🛁 🌑 Nov to mid-March. 🅾 MC, V. ⓕⓕ

LE PONTET-AVIGNON

Auberge de Cassagne Bungalow bedrooms in spruce grounds are done out in exuberant Provençal style. The *auberge* itself is a mellow old house and its location a leafy suburb. Chef Philippe Boucher is a protégé of the renowned Paul Bocuse, with his own reputation and Michelin star.

✉ 84130 Le Pontet-Avignon, Vaucluse. **Map** p224 B3. 📞 04 90 31 04 18. 📠 04 90 32 25 09. @ cassagne@wanadoo.fr 🍴 b,l,d. **Rooms** 40. 🏠 🏊 🍴 🛁 🌑 Never. 🅾 AE, DC, MC, V. ⓕⓕⓕ

PORQUEROLLES

Auberge des Glycines This informal hotel in the port is brightly painted both inside and out, and set around a tree-filled courtyard.

✉ Place d'Armes, 83400 Porquerolles, Var. **Map** p225 D5. 📞 04 94 58 30 36. 📠 04 94 58 35 22. 🍴 b,l,d. **Rooms** 13. ⓕⓕⓕ

ILE DE PORT-CROS

Le Manoir Bedrooms in this handsome 19th-century manor have antiques and vistas over the fertile island. Good seafood.

✉ Ile de Port-Cros, 83400 Hyères, Var. **Map** p225 E5. 📞 04 94 05 90 52. 📠 04 94 05 90 89. 🍴 b,l,d. **Rooms** 23. ⓕⓕⓕⓕ

PORTO-VECCHIO, CORSICA

Hôtel Belvédère Indulge in a spot of contemporary luxury, including a pool, private beach and rooms in the grounds.

✉ Route de la Plage de Palombaggia, 20137 Porto-Vecchio, Corse-du-Sud. **Map** p223 F5. 📞 04 95 70 54 13. 📠 04 95 70 42 63. 🍴 b,l,d. **Rooms** 19. ⓕⓕⓕⓕ

PORTO-VECCHIO, CORSICA

Grand Hôtel de Cala Rossa Glamorous modern hotel by the beach. Bedrooms are airy.

✉ Cala Rossa, 20137 Porto-Vecchio, Corse-du-Sud. **Map** p223 F5. 📞 04 95 71 61 51. 📠 04 95 71 60 11. @ calarossa@relaischateaux.fr 🍴 b,l,d. **Rooms** 53. ⓕⓕⓕⓕ

PORQUEROLLES

Mas du Langoustier Set on this unspoilt island, with no cars, the hotel is surrounded by its own extensive pine woods. Their scent wafts up to the original *mas* and modern building opposite, which houses the best of the bedrooms. There are two restaurants serving first-class food.
⊠ 83400 Porquerolles, Var. **Map** p225 D5.
(04 94 58 30 09. FAX 04 94 58 36 02.
@ langoustier@compuserve.com ▥ b,l,d. **Rooms** 51.
▯ ◑ mid-Oct to May. ⊠ AE, DC, MC, V. ⒻⒻⒻⒻ

PUYMIROL

Les Loges de l'Aubergade In a region not noted for its gastronomy, august cook Michel Trama offers outstanding food, wine and cigars in the ancient home of the Counts of Toulouse. Set around a patio, with a Jacuzzi at its centre, the modern rooms are done up with style.
⊠ 52 rue Royale, 47270 Puymirol, Lot-et-Garonne.
Map p222 B3. (05 53 95 31 46. FAX 05 53 95 33 80.
@ aubergade@relaischateaux.fr ▥ b,l,d.
Rooms 10. ▤ ▯ ◑ mid-Feb to mid-March.
⊠ AE, DC, MC, V. ⒻⒻⒻⒻ

PORTICCIO, CORSICA

Le Maquis It started life some 50 years ago as a beach café; today it's a fashionable hotel with elegant rooms, its own beach, two swimming pools (one indoors, one out) and a tennis court (floodlit at night). The rooms are luxurious and face the sea, and some have their own terraces. The restaurant specializes in shellfish.
⊠ 20166 Porticcio, Corse-du-Sud. **Map** p223 F5.
(04 95 25 05 55. FAX 04 95 25 11 70. ▥ b,l,d.
Rooms 27. ▩ ▯ ◑ early Jan to early Feb.
⊠ AE, DC, MC, V. ⒻⒻⒻ

REILLANNE

Auberge de Reillanne This unpretentious country house hotel – parts of which date from the 12th century – is set amid fields, just outside the village, and has views towards the Lubéron massif. Its seven beamed bedrooms are huge, with little furniture and no televisions, but rows of books. Cooking is based on fresh local ingredients.
⊠ 04110 Reillanne, Alpes-de-Haute-Provence.
Map p224 C3. (04 92 76 45 95. ▥ b,d. **Rooms** 7.
▯ ◑ Never. ⊠ MC, V. Ⓕ

RAZAC D'EYMET

La Petite Auberge A cosy farmhouse run by English in French style. Guests can play with a giant chess set in the garden; pool.
⊠ 24500 Razac d'Eymet, Dordogne. **Map** p222 B3.
(05 53 24 69 27. FAX 05 53 27 33 55. ▥ b,l,d.
Rooms 7. Ⓕ

ROANNE

Troisgros The legendary family-run restaurant has a suitably glossy dining room and high-tech bedrooms.
⊠ Place de la Gare, 42300 Roanne, Loire. **Map** p221 E5,
p223 D2. (04 77 71 66 97. FAX 04 77 70 39 77.
@ troisgros@relaischateaux.fr ▥ b,l,d. **Rooms** 19.

ROCAMADOUR

Les Vielles Tours A medieval *gentilhommerie* with a snug *salon* in the turret and large, pleasing bedrooms. Lunch on request.
⊠ Lafage, 46500 Rocamadour, Lot. **Map** p222 C3.
(05 65 33 68 01. FAX 05 65 33 68 59.
@ roger.zozzoli@wanadoo.fr ▥ b,d. **Rooms** 17. ⒻⒻ

ROCHEGUDE

Château de Rochegude A lavish Relais et Châteaux in a 12th-century fortress: palatial rooms, gourmet cuisine and fine wines.
⊠ 26790 Rochegude, Drôme. **Map** p223 D4.
(04 75 97 21 10. FAX 04 75 04 89 87. @ rochegude@
relaischateaux.fr ▥ b,l,d. **Rooms** 29. ⒻⒻⒻⒻ

ROCAMADOUR

Domaine de la Rhue A skilful conversion of a 19th-century stable block has created a calm B&B with handsome evidence of its origins and flexible accommodation. Some of the country-style bedrooms have kitchenettes and their own garden entrances, making them ideal for families.
✉ La Rhue, 46500 Rocamadour, Lot. **Map** p222 C3.
📞 05 65 33 71 50. FAX 05 65 33 72 48.
@ domainedelarhue@rocamadour.com 🍴 b.
Rooms 12. 🔁 🌢 🌑 Nov to Easter. 🅔 MC, V. ⒻⒻ

ST-ETIENNE-DE-BAÏGORRY

Hôtel Arcé The Arcé family have been in charge here for five generations, and it is their hospitality that gives the hotel its special charm. In a pretty Basque village at the foot of the Pyrenees, it boasts a fabulous riverside location and a glorious dining terrace shaded by leafy chestnut trees.
✉ 64430 St-Etienne-de-Baïgorry, Pyrénées-Atlantiques.
Map p222 A4. 📞 05 59 37 40 14. FAX 05 59 37 40 27.
🍴 b,l,d. **Rooms** 23. 🔁 🌢 🌑 mid-Nov to mid-March.
🅔 MC, V. ⒻⒻ

ST-CIRQ-LAPOPIE

La Pélissaria A 13th-century house clinging to a hillside in a captivating medieval village. The eccentric layout means that, from street-level, stairs lead down to the light bedrooms, many with terrific views over the Lot river. Dinner, courtesy of hostess Madame Matuchet, is both delicious and innovative, and served in a gracious room with beams.
✉ St-Cirq-Lapopie, 46330 Cabrerets, Lot. **Map** p222 C3.
📞 05 65 31 25 14. FAX 05 65 30 25 25. 🍴 b,d.
Rooms 10. 🔁 🌢 🌑 mid-Nov to Apr. 🅔 MC, V. ⒻⒻ

ST-JEAN-DU-BRUEL

Hotel du Midi-Papillon Fans of this old rural posting inn have grown so numerous that bookings must be made months in advance. The welcoming Papillons continue a tradition of innkeeping of 150 years' standing. The food, all home-grown, home-reared or home-baked, is irresistible; prices are low.
✉ 12230 St-Jean-du-Bruel, Aveyron. **Map** p223 D4.
📞 05 65 62 26 04. FAX 05 65 62 12 97.
🍴 b,l,d. **Rooms** 19. 🔁 🌢 🌑 mid-Nov to Easter.
🅔 MC, V. Ⓕ

ROQUEFORT-LES-PINS
Auberge du Colombier The charm of this low-built white *mas* lies in its heavenly large garden of tall trees and a pool.
✉ 06330 Roquefort-les-Pins, Alpes-Maritimes.
Map p225 E3. 📞 04 92 60 33 00. FAX 04 93 77 07 03.
🍴 b,l,d. **Rooms** 20. ⒻⒻ

ROUSSILLON
Mas de Garrigon This modern hotel, built in traditional Provençal style, is run on house party lines. Lunch can be taken by the pool.
✉ Route de St-Saturnin d'Apt, Roussillon, 84220 Gordes, Vaucluse. **Map** p224 C3. 📞 04 90 05 63 22.
FAX 04 90 05 70 01. 🍴 b,l,d. **Rooms** 9. ⒻⒻⒻ

ST-CYPRIEN
L'Abbaye Walls and floors of delicate local stone throughout this enchanting hotel set in lush gardens, with a pool and tidy bedrooms.
✉ 24220 St-Cyprien, Dordogne. **Map** p222 C3.
📞 05 53 29 20 48. FAX 05 53 29 15 85. 🍴 b,l,d.
Rooms 24. ⒻⒻ

ST-EMILION
Le Logis des Remparts Sit beneath a parasol or swim in the pool in the peaceful garden of this ancient stone-built house, now a cosy B&B.
✉ 18 rue Guadet, 33330 St-Emilion, Gironde.
Map p222 B3. 📞 05 57 24 70 43. FAX 05 57 74 47 44.
🍴 b. **Rooms** 17. ⒻⒻ

ST-MARTIN-VALMEROUX

Hostellerie de la Maronne Beyond a garden of lawns and trees lies the empty rolling countryside of the Auvergne, making this smartly decorated, grey-stone Relais du Silence a true haven. Madame De Cock's ambitious menu is accompanied by a tantalizing wine list.
⊠ Le Theil, 15140 St-Martin-Valmeroux, Cantal. **Map** p223 D3. (04 71 69 20 33. FAX 04 71 69 28 22. @ hotelmaronne@cfi15.fr ▮ b,l,d. **Rooms** 21. ▦ ▮ ● Nov to March. ☒ AE, DC, MC, V. ⓕⓕ

ST-PAUL-DE-VENCE

Le Hameau A path bordered by lemon trees leads to this attractive white 1920s villa with red-tiled roofs. The scented garden of flowers and shrubs is the scene of unmissable breakfasts. Bedrooms are in rustic Provençal style; many have terraces or balconies. Overseeing all are the dedicated Huvelins.
⊠ 528 route de la Colle, 06570 St-Paul-de-Vence, Alpes-Maritimes. **Map** p225 F3. (04 93 32 80 24. FAX 04 93 32 55 75. ▮ b. **Rooms** 17. ▤ ▮ ● mid-Nov to Christmas, mid-Jan to mid-Feb. ☒ MC, V. ⓕⓕ

ST-PAUL-DE-VENCE

La Grande Bastide The Laloums' restoration of this country house combines new design with original materials such as local wood and stone. The 11 pastel-painted bedrooms are jazzed up with flamboyant Provençal prints. The result is an alluring B&B where guests feel instantly at home.
⊠ 1350 route de la Colle, 06570 St-Paul-de-Vence, Alpes-Maritimes. **Map** p225 F3. (04 93 32 50 30. FAX 04 93 32 50 59. ▮ b. **Rooms** 11. ▤ ▮ ● Never. ☒ AE, DC, MC, V. ⓕⓕⓕ

ST-RÉMY-DE-PROVENCE

Château des Alpilles Nothing jars in this refined 19th-century manor house of pale stone, where bay trees flank the front door. The antique-laden *salons* feature moulded ceilings and mosaic floors; the Provençal bedrooms are spacious. Food can be eaten by the pool in summer.
⊠ Route Départementale 31, 13210 St-Rémy-de-Provence, Bouches-du-Rhône. **Map** p224 B3. (04 90 92 03 33. FAX 04 90 92 45 17. @ chateau.alpilles@wanadoo.fr ▮ b,d. **Rooms** 20. ▤ ▦ ▮ ● early Jan to late Feb. ☒ AE, DC, MC, V. ⓕⓕⓕ

ST-FÉLIX-LAURAGAIS
Auberge du Poids Public Michelin-starred restaurant in a village inn, with sublime food, rustic dining room and comfortable rooms.
⊠ 31540 St-Félix-Lauragais, Haute-Garonne. **Map** p222 C4. (05 61 83 00 20. FAX 05 61 83 86 21. ▮ b,l,d. **Rooms** 10. ⓕ

ST-JEAN-DE-LUZ
La Fayette Red brick and arches typify the Dutch architecture of this modest, family-run hotel. Jolly rooms; pavement dining terrace.
⊠ 18-20 rue de la République, 64500 St-Jean-de-Luz, Pyrénées-Atlantiques. **Map** p222 A4. (05 59 26 17 74. FAX 05 59 51 11 78. ▮ b,l,d. **Rooms** 18. ⓕ

ST-JEAN-DE-LUZ
Le Parc Victoria The 19th-century villa is a model of style and correct housekeeping.
⊠ 5 rue Cepé, 64500 St-Jean-de-Luz, Pyrénées-Atlantiques. **Map** p222 A4. (05 59 26 78 78. FAX 05 59 26 78 08. @ parcvictoria@relaischateaux.fr ▮ b,l,d. **Rooms** 12. ⓕⓕⓕ

ST-PAUL-DE-VENCE
La Colombe d'Or Elegantly rustic, with garden, pool and a marvellous art collection. Picasso and friends were habitués.
⊠ Place de Gaulle, 06570 St-Paul-de-Vence, Alpes-Maritimes. **Map** p225 F3. (04 93 32 80 02. FAX 04 93 32 77 78. ▮ b,l,d. **Rooms** 26. ⓕⓕⓕⓕ

For key to symbols see backflap. For price categories see p217

ST-SAUD-LACOUSSIÈRE

Hostellerie St-Jacques A cheerful ivy-clad village inn, whose exterior gives little hint of what lies beyond: beautiful gardens, full of colour, sloping down to a pretty pool. The airy bedrooms and large summery bar/dining room have been decorated with care. The cooking doesn't disappoint. In summer, breakfast can be taken in the garden. There are several family rooms.
⊠ 24470 St-Saud-Lacoussière, Dordogne. **Map** p222 B2.
[05 53 56 97 21. FAX 05 53 56 91 33. ⊪ b,l,d.
Rooms 24. ⊞ ⊕ ● mid-Nov to Apr. ⊠ MC, V. Ⓕ

SALON-DE-PROVENCE

L'Abbaye de Ste-Croix The highlight at this 12th-century former monastery is the Michelin-starred food, eaten in a charming, rustic dining room. The former cells house the bedrooms, but there's nothing Spartan about them now. A huge open fireplace warms the vaulted sitting room.
⊠ Route du Val-de-Cuech, 13300 Salon-de-Provence, Bouches-du-Rhône. **Map** p224 A4. [04 90 56 24 55.
FAX 04 90 56 31 12. @ saintecroix@relaischateaux.fr
⊪ b,l,d. **Rooms** 24. ⊞ ⊕ ● Nov to mid-March.
⊠ AE, DC, MC, V. ⒻⒻⒻ

LES STES-MARIES-DE-LA-MER

Mas de la Fouque The exclusive Spanish-style ranch has an idyllic location beside a lagoon, where guests can glimpse flamingoes, egrets or the famous white horses of the Camargue. It's smart and luxurious yet family-run and friendly.
⊠ Route du Petit Rhône, 13460 Les Stes-Maries-de-la-Mer, Bouches-du-Rhône. **Map** p224 A4.
[04 90 97 81 02. FAX 04 90 97 96 84.
@ masdelafouque@francemarket.com ⊪ b,l,d.
Rooms 13. ▤ ⊞ ⊕ ● Nov to late Mar.
⊠ AE, DC, MC, V. ⒻⒻⒻⒻ

SARE

Hôtel Arraya Set on the main square of an archetypal Basque village, the 16th-century house was once a hostel for pilgrims to Santiago. It has an austere and off-putting façade, but inside lies an inn of great character and charm. Every corner and room is filled with polished pieces of fine local furniture. Adventurous cooking is a bonus.
⊠ 64310 Sare, Pyrénées-Atlantiques. **Map** p222 A4.
[05 59 54 20 46. FAX 05 59 54 27 04.
@ hotel@arraya.com ⊪ b,l,d. **Rooms** 21.
⊕ ● mid-Nov to late Mar. ⊠ AE, MC, V. ⒻⒻ

ST-PAUL-DE-VENCE

Les Orangers At the edge of the village, overlooking orange groves, is this chic, flower-filled Provençal farmhouse; impeccably kept.
⊠ Chemin des Fumerates, 06570 St-Paul-de-Vence, Alpes-Maritimes. **Map** p225 F3. [04 93 32 80 95.
FAX 04 93 32 00 32. ⊪ b. **Rooms** 10. ⒻⒻ

ST-RÉMY-DE-PROVENCE

Domaine de Valmouraine A farmhouse and lovely garden, stylishly converted to plush hotel.
⊠ Petite Route des Baux, 13210 St-Rémy-de-Provence, Bouches-du-Rhône. **Map** p224 B3. [04 90 92 44 62.
FAX 04 90 92 37 32. @ domdeval@wanadoo.fr
⊪ b,l,d. **Rooms** 14. ⒻⒻⒻ

ST-SERNIN-SUR-RANCE

Hôtel Carayon People flock from far and wide to sample Pierre Carayon's excellent cuisine. The riverside hotel offers great value for money.
⊠ Place du Fort, 12380 St-Sernin-sur-Rance, Aveyron.
Map p222 C4. [05 65 98 19 19. FAX 05 65 99 69 26.
@ carayonhotel@wanadoo.fr ⊪ b,l,d. **Rooms** 60. Ⓕ

ST-TROPEZ

La Ponche In the old town, an arty yet chic hotel in daring colours, where the seafood is superb. Overlooks a small fishing port and beach.
⊠ 3 rue des Remparts, 83990 St-Tropez, Var.
Map p225 E4. [04 94 97 02 53. FAX 04 94 97 78 61.
@ laponche@nova.fr ⊪ b,l,d. **Rooms** 18. ⒻⒻⒻⒻ

Sauveterre-de-Béarn

Hôtel du Vieux Pont A spectacular position on medieval arches above the Gave d'Oloron river makes this hotel exquisitely romantic. Rooms are pleasing and light, and a relaxed air prevails, encouraged by the genial English owners. To cap it all, the terrace is floodlit at night.
Rue du Pont de la Légende, 64390 Sauveterre-de-Béarn, Pyrénées-Atlantiques. **Map** p222 B4.
05 59 38 95 11. FAX 05 59 38 99 10.
paulwilliams5@csi.com b,l,d. **Rooms** 7.
Never. MC, V. (F)

Target

Château de Boussac A chateau with all the accoutrements – moat, lake, park and magnificent rooms filled with Louis XV furniture – but none of the formality. Despite the grand setting, the charming Marquis and Marquise de Longueil welcome guests like old friends. The Marquis works on the estate as well as helping to cook the delectable dinners, eaten *en famille*.
Target, 03140 Chantelle, Allier. **Map** p223 D2.
04 70 40 63 20. FAX 04 70 40 60 03. b,d.
Rooms 5. Nov to Feb. AE, MC, V. (F)(F)(F)

Seillans

Hôtel des Deux Rocs A model hotel: an 18th-century house with blue shutters and a civilized air in a ravishing medieval village. Madame Hirsch's sure touch is evident in the decoration, which varies between the traditional in the public rooms and the dashing in the bedrooms. Breakfast in the cobbled square is a real treat.
Place Font d'Amont, 83440 Seillans, Var.
Map p225 E3. 04 94 76 87 32. FAX 04 94 76 88 68.
b,l,d. **Rooms** 15. Nov to Apr. MC, V. (F)(F)

Touzac

La Source Bleue The main joy of staying in this quiet cluster of old paper mills, is the chance to walk by the willow-fringed Lot river or in the sizeable park. Fruit from the kitchen garden features in dishes which are served in a fittingly rustic room. Of the bedrooms, it is the ones in the attic that score highest on charm.
Moulin de Leygues, Touzac, 46700 Puy-l'Evêque, Lot.
Map p222 C3. 05 65 36 52 01. FAX 05 65 24 65 69.
sourcebleue@wanadoo.fr b,l,d. **Rooms** 16.
Jan to Apr. AE, DC, MC, V. (F)

Salles-Curan

Hostellerie du Levezou A warm welcome and fine food await visitors to this 14th-century castle, set in a picturesque hill village.
Rue du Château, 12410 Salles-Curan, Aveyron.
Map p223 D3. 05 65 46 34 16. FAX 05 65 46 01 19.
b,l,d. **Rooms** 12.

Sarlat

Hostellerie de Meysset Pine woods surround this long white house in the heart of Périgord Noir. Not surprisingly, the food is regional.
Route des Eyzies, 24200 Sarlat, Dordogne.
Map p222 C3. 05 53 59 08 29. FAX 05 53 28 47 61.
b,l,d. **Rooms** 26. (F)

Séguret

Domaine de Cabasse In rugged country, an appealing Swiss-run inn with its own vineyard.
Route de Sablet, 84110 Séguret, Vaucluse.
Map p224 B2. 04 90 46 91 12. FAX 04 90 46 94 01.
cabasse@avignon.pacwan.net b,l,d.
Rooms 12. (F)(F)

Soustons

La Bergerie A pristine whitewashed house with trim grounds and a restful air; it's no hardship that the set dinner is obligatory.
Avenue du Lac, 40140 Soustons, Landes.
Map p222 A4. 05 58 41 11 43. FAX 05 58 41 21 61.
b,d. **Rooms** 12. (F)

For key to symbols see backflap. For price categories *see p217*

TRÉMOLAT

Le Vieux Logis Wine and pigs once filled the dining room of this complex of farm buildings – a far cry from today's epitome of country chic, even though it has been home to the Giraudel-Destords for 400 years. Four-poster beds grace the rooms, antiques fill the *salon*'s every nook, and superb classic-modern cuisine is on offer.
✉ 24510 Trémolat, Dordogne. **Map** p222 C3.
☎ 05 53 22 80 06. **FAX** 05 53 22 84 89.
@ vieuxlogis@relaischateaux.fr 🍴 b,l,d. **Rooms** 24.
Never. AE, DC, MC, V. ⒻⒻⒻⒻ

VALENCE

Pic Despite the illustrious reputation of the restaurant, there isn't a hint of snobbery here. And though the great former owner Jacques Pic is dead, his son and daughter continue to create original dishes in their classic setting, as well as managing the more modest L'Auberge du Pin. Bedrooms are stunning.
✉ 285 avenue Victor-Hugo, 26001 Valence, Drôme.
Map p224 B1. ☎ 04 75 44 15 32. **FAX** 04 75 40 96 03.
@ pic@relaischateaux.fr 🍴 b,l,d. **Rooms** 15.
Never. AE, DC, MC, V. ⒻⒻⒻ

TRIGANCE

Château de Trigance You have to scale 100 rocky steps to gain access to this fabulous 11th-century castle, perched on a limestone peak. Owned by the Thomases for more than 20 years, it is a painstaking re-creation of the Middle Ages, with stone-vaulted dining room and canopied beds. Breakfast is taken on the battlements.
✉ 83840 Trigance, Var. **Map** p225 E3.
☎ 04 94 76 91 18. **FAX** 04 94 85 68 99.
@ trigance@relaischateaux.fr 🍴 b,l,d. **Rooms** 10.
Nov to late March. AE, DC, MC, V. ⒻⒻ

VENCE

Château du Domaine St-Martin A stone's throw from the Matisse chapel, this former Templar stronghold is one of France's most expensive hotels. Bills will be several thousand francs, but devotees claim its sumptuous luxury and faultless service are worth it.
✉ Avenue des Templiers, 06140 Vence, Alpes-Maritimes.
Map p225 F3. ☎ 04 93 58 02 02. **FAX** 04 93 24 08 91.
@ st-martin@webstore.fr 🍴 b,l,d. **Rooms** 35.
late Oct to early Apr.
AE, DC, MC, V. ⒻⒻⒻⒻ

TORNAC
Les Demeures du Ranquet The farmhouse restaurant, set in oak woods, is first class. The ten bedrooms are lush.
✉ Route de St-Hippolyte, Tornac, 30140 Anduze, Gard.
Map p223 D4. ☎ 04 66 77 51 63. **FAX** 04 66 77 55 62.
@ ranquet@mnet.fr 🍴 b,l,d. **Rooms** 10. ⒻⒻ

TOURTOUR
L'Auberge St-Pierre The 16th-century building is a manor rather than an inn, with rooms that have a medieval flavour. Food is fresh from the farm.
✉ Tourtour, 83690 Salernes, Var. **Map** p225 D4.
☎ 04 94 70 57 17. **FAX** 04 94 70 59 04. 🍴 b,l,d.
Rooms 16. ⒻⒻ

VAISON-LA-ROMAINE
Hostellerie Le Beffroi Old stone, beams and gleaming tiles abound in two hilltop houses.
✉ Rue de l'Evêché Haute Ville, 84110 Vaison-la-Romaine, Vaucluse. **Map** p224 B2. ☎ 04 90 36 04 71.
FAX 04 90 36 24 78. @ lebeffroi@wanadoo.fr
🍴 b,l,d. **Rooms** 22. ⒻⒻ

VÉNASQUE
Auberge la Fontaine A classy restaurant with a bistro and five elegantly 'rustic' apartments.
✉ Place de la Fontaine, Vénasque, 84210 Carpentras, Vaucluse. **Map** p224 B2. ☎ 04 90 66 02 96.
FAX 04 90 66 13 14. @ Fontvenasq@aol.com
🍴 b,l,d. **Rooms** 5. ⒻⒻ

Vence

La Roseraie A garden of palms, oleander and orange trees envelops this B&B, a *belle époque* villa of palest pink. Inside it has a lived-in feel, with walls covered in straw hats, dried flowers and old photos. Madame Ganier's artistic touch is evident in the summery Provençal-style bedrooms. There is a pleasant pool.
✉ Avenue Henri Giraud, 06140 Vence, Alpes-Maritimes. **Map** p225 F3. ☎ 04 93 58 02 20. [FAX] 04 93 58 99 31. [@] rvilla5536@aol.fr 🍴 b. **Rooms** 12. 🏊 🌳 ● Never. 💳 AE, MC, V. ⒻⒻ

Villeréal

Château de Ricard An immaculate country house with manicured gardens, where even the ivy covering the façade looks perfect. Welcome extras include a library, billiard room and laundry. Interior decoration is the owners' forte, borne out by the chic rooms. A delicious dinner is served four nights a week.
✉ Route de Beaumont, 47210 Villeréal, Lot-et-Garonne. **Map** p222 B3. ☎ 05 53 36 61 02. [FAX] 05 53 36 61 65. 🍴 b,d. **Rooms** 5. 🏊 🌳 ● Nov to May. 💳 Not accepted. ⒻⒻ

Vialas

Hôtel Chantoiseau In the craggy landscape of the Cévennes, this 17th-century former post house boasts the most exciting restaurant for miles; here, mouthwatering Michelin-starred specialities are created by chef Patrick Pagès. Bedrooms are comfortable and well-kept if a trifle small, with splendid views.
✉ 48220 Vialas, Lozère. **Map** p223 D3. ☎ 04 66 41 00 02. [FAX] 04 66 41 04 34. 🍴 b,l,d. **Rooms** 15. 🏊 🌳 ● mid-Oct to mid-Apr. 💳 AE, DC, MC, V. ⒻⒻ

Ydes

Château de Trancis The miniature Italianate chateau looks as if it has been transported from the banks of the Loire river, but in fact dates only from the 20th century. The interior is in keeping with the exterior, and has been fabulously furnished with antiques and rugs strewn on the polished floors. A charming Dutch couple run the place along house-party lines.
✉ 15210 Ydes, Cantal. **Map** p222 C3. ☎ 04 71 40 60 40. [FAX] 04 71 40 62 13. 🍴 b,d. **Rooms** 10. 🏊 🌳 ● Never. 💳 AE, DC, MC, V. ⒻⒻ

Vézac

Manoir de Rochecourbe A manor which has been in the Roger family for generations and, with its grand tower staircase, looks the part.
✉ Vézac, 24220 St-Cyprien, Dordogne. **Map** p222 C3. ☎ 05 53 31 09 84. [FAX] 05 53 28 59 07. 🍴 b,d. **Rooms** 6. ⒻⒻ

Vieux-Mareuil

Château de Vieux-Mareuil The ivy-clad walls of this 15th-century château mask an appealing hotel with bright rooms and smiling service.
✉ Route Angoulême-Périgueux, 24340 Vieux Mareuil, Dordogne. **Map** p222 C2. ☎ 05 53 60 77 15. [FAX] 05 53 56 49 33. 🍴 b,l,d. **Rooms** 14. Ⓕ

Villeneuve-lès-Avignon

Hôtel de l'Atelier Built in the 16th century for a cardinal, a haven of calm with a delightful shady courtyard just outside the city centre.
✉ 5 rue de la Foire, 30400 Villeneuve-lès-Avignon, Gard. **Map** p224 B3. ☎ 04 90 25 01 84. [FAX] 04 90 25 80 06. 🍴 b. **Rooms** 19. Ⓕ

Vitrac

Auberge La Tomette A cheerful village inn among chestnut groves, with a rustic panelled dining room and spotless modern bedrooms.
✉ 15220 Vitrac, Cantal. **Map** p222 C3. ☎ 04 71 64 70 94. [FAX] 04 71 64 77 11. [@] latomette@wanadoo.fr 🍴 b,l,d. **Rooms** 15. Ⓕ

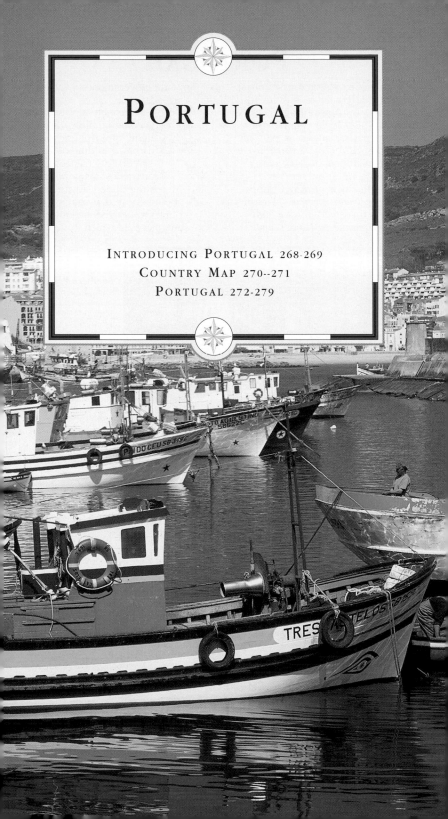

PORTUGAL

PORTUGAL

SOME OF PORTUGAL'S most enticing places to stay are the grand but crumbling country houses which have opened their doors to paying guests as part of the *Turismo de Habitaçao* scheme. Choose between an apartment in a palace, a guest room in a *quinta* (manor house), or a *casa rustica* – a farm cottage converted into a self-catering apartment. There's also the government-run *pousada* network whose members offer a reliably high standard of accommodation, often in highly atmospheric or old historic buildings such as converted castles and monasteries. Many *pousadas* have the added advantage of being located in parts of the country otherwise lacking inter-sting places in which to stay.

Castelo de Bom Jesus, a neo-Gothic 'castle' above Braga, page 272

PORTUGAL, REGION BY REGION

PORTUGAL CAN be divided into three regions: northern, central and southern.

Northern and Central Portugal

The granite-based Minho region is green from the masses of rain it receives. This is an agricultural area, and it's not at all unusual to see oxen pulling a cart, or women washing clothes in a water tank by the side of a country lane. There is plenty of accommodation in manor houses and farmhouses. The wild Atlantic coast at Viana do Castelo, and the fascinating historic towns of Barcelos and Guimarães, have a mix of *pousadas* and small, family-run guesthouses.

In the Douro valley, a steep gorge is flanked by terraced hillsides planted with vines which produce the region's port wine. Porto is the main city of the region. Places to stay include an Art Nouveau city-centre palace and a discreet, luxury 1940s hotel.

Inland, the old province of Trás-os-Montes is remote and mountainous, with the little- visited Beira Alta and Beira Baixa to the south. In the Beira Litoral, to the west, beautiful beaches of fine sand are pounded by Atlantic breakers; there are hotels in the resort of Póvoa de Varzim and near Aveiro.

The Ribatejo and the more interesting Estremadura which it flanks, encompass the coast all the way to Lisbon. There are attractive beach resort hotels, hill top castle *pousadas* (at Obidos and Setúbal), Coimbra with its ancient university, and the impressive palaces – and palace hotels – of Sintra and Estoril.

Southern Portugal

One of the most beautiful and little-known regions of Portugal is the Alentejo, an undulating landscape of grid-formation olive groves and cork oak forests. Here the *pousada* network comes into its own, with those at Evora and Vila Viçosa among the best. The Alentejo's Atlantic coast is a favourite among travelling surfers. There is a *pousada* with stunning panoramic views at Santa Clara-a-Velha.

The Algarve is now so built up that some travellers avoid it on principle. The exception is the area around Tavira, and the extreme west towards Sagres, where there are some great small guesthouses and villas.

Also included in this section are the islands of Madeira and the Azores. The latter may be difficult to reach (flights leave from Lisbon), but they are ideal places for getting away from it all, and for whale-watching. Accommodation is simple and atmospheric.

HIGHLIGHTS

HOTELS ILLUSTRATED on these introductory pages are by no means our only highlights. Unforgettable places also include Hotel Guincho at Cascais (page 273), a former sea fort; the Quinta da Alfarrobeira, a relaxed Algarve villa at Lagos (page 274); the Casa de Sezim, a relaxing and chic privately owned manor house with guest rooms in Guimarães (page 274); and the Convento de São Francisco, a cliff top monastery at São Miguel in the Azores (page 278).

FOOD AND DRINK

THERE ARE MORE than 365 recipes for *bacalhau* (salted codfish), the Portuguese national dish, so if you wish, you can eat it a different way every day of the year. People either love it or hate it, but it can be very good, especially cooked with chickpeas, olive oil and parsley. Other specialities are based on fish, often baked with potatoes and tomatoes in an earthenware dish. There are also simple meat dishes such as grilled rabbit, and more sophisticated ones such as steak in Madeira sauce. Often, people find that the simple country dishes are the most delicious.

Portuguese wines can be excellent, and their styles illustrate the country's wild variations in climate: acidic *vinho verde* and luscious ports, for instance, come from neighbouring regions. The deep reds of the Douro and Dão whites are also worth seeking out, along with the fruity southern reds.

Lunch runs from 1–3pm; dinner from 8pm to midnight, though all the *pousada* restaurants close promptly at 10pm. As part of the cover charge, you'll be brought a dish of savouries such as black pudding, grilled cheese and marinated olives.

BEDROOMS AND BATHROOMS

IF YOU want twin beds, ask for them specifically when booking. Unlike some other countries, double does mean a double – there's no sliding down the gap between two single mattresses pushed together. Most bathrooms are en suite and have a shower

and bath combined. In some simple guesthouses bathrooms are shared.

OTHER PRACTICAL INFORMATION

SOME OF the *pousadas* in historic buildings have just a few rooms which fill quickly; Lisbon's hotels and popular places on the coast are also often full at peak times.

Breakfast is usually buffet-style, a spread of juices, breads and preserves, fruit, cheese, cold meats, cake and sometimes wine. Eggs, bacon and sausage are often provided in the *pousadas*.

Portuguese housekeeping standards mean that even the simplest place is usually spotlessly clean, and service extremely polite.

Note that signposting can be non-existent in rural areas, and in town centres there are complex one-way systems. Faxing ahead for a locator map is often worthwhile. But ask anyone the way, and they will invariably take great trouble to help you.

Language English is often not spoken – or understood.

Currency The Portuguese *escudos*, written as 'pte' after the amount; or sometimes as a '$' sign (eg 100$00) or simply as 'esc'.

Shops Generally open 10am–7pm Mon–Fri, but many close for lunch or if business is slack, and, in Lisbon, for all of August. Some open 10am–1pm on Saturdays. Sunday opening is an alien concept. Banks are open 8:30am–3pm Mon–Fri.

Tipping A 10 per cent tip is the norm in restaurants; tipping taxi drivers is not obligatory, unless they have been particularly helpful.

Telephones Public call boxes are few. They take coins or

Santa Marinha, Guimarães' *pousada*, page 274

phonecards. You can make use of the phone in almost any bar. It will be metered, and charged by the unit. For calls within Portugal, dial the entire nine-digit number including the first digit of the area code. To call Portugal from the UK (or the US), dial 00 351 (011 351).

Public holidays 1 January; Good Friday; 25 April (Anniversary of the Revolution); 1 May; 6 June (Corpus Christi); 10 June (Camões Day); 15 August; 5 October (Republic Day); 1 November; 1 December (Independence Day); 8 December (Feast of Immaculate Conception), 25 December.

USEFUL WORDS

Breakfast	*Pequeño-almoço*
Lunch	*Almoço*
Dinner	*Jantar*
Free room?	*Tem algum quarto livre?*
How much?	*Quanto?*
Single room	*Quarto individual*
Double room	*Quarto de casal*

PORTUGAL PRICE BANDS

OUR PRICE bands refer, as elsewhere in this guide, to the cost of a standard room in high season. Breakfast is usually included in the room price. Prices quoted tend to include all taxes.

$	under 14,000pte
$$	15,000–25,000pte
$$$	26,000–35,000pte
$$$$	over 36,000pte

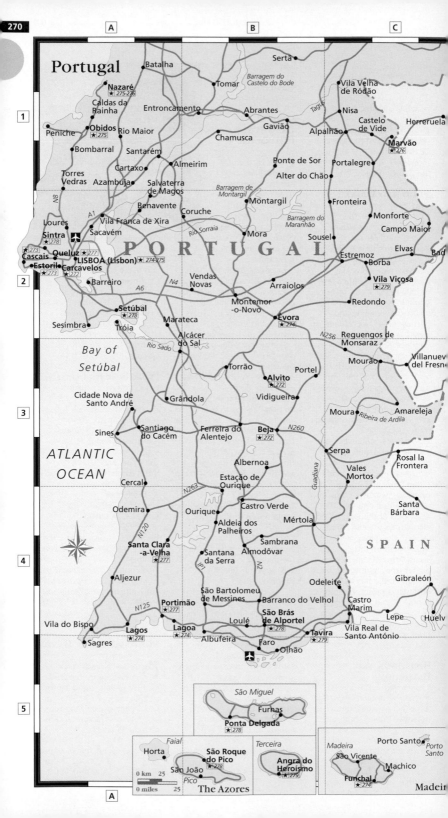

Portugal

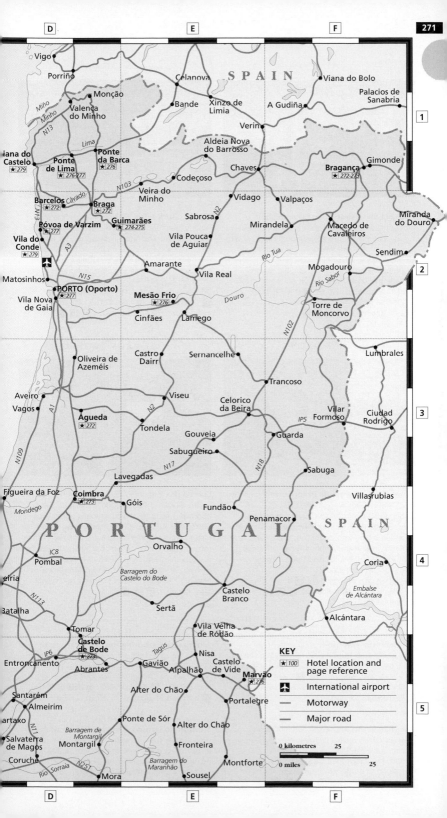

Alvito

Pousada do Castelo A life-sized knight in armour stands guard at reception – appropriate for this castle which looks as though it has come straight out of a picture book. The stylish rooms are large; some have original stone-arched and mullioned windows overlooking the village. Outside, peacocks stalk the grounds and pool.
✉ 7920 Alvito. **Map** p270 B3. ☎ (284) 48 53 43. FAX (284) 48 53 83. @ info@pousadas.pt
🍴 b,l,d. **Rooms** 20. ▤ ≋ ❀ ● Never.
💳 AE, DC, MC, V. $$$

Braga

Castelo Bom Jesus This neo-Gothic 'castle' was built as a family house in the 1790s on a hill above Braga. The family it was built for made much of their fortune in Brazil, so the murals in the dining room show views of their sugar plantation in Manaus. An attractive – albeit rather formal – place to stay.
✉ Tenoes Bom Jesus, 4700 Braga. **Map** p271 D2.
☎ (253) 67 65 66. FAX (253) 67 76 91. @ charmhotels@mail.telepac.pt 🍴 b,l,d. **Rooms** 13. ≋ ❀ ● Never.
💳 AE, MC, V. $$

Barcelos

Quinta do Convento da Franqueria Englishman Piers Gallie produces some 30,000 bottles of vinho verde a year on this estate, owned by his family since 1965. The 16th-century building was once a convent. Rooms are furnished with classic furniture in restful style; there's also a lounge with games and books. An ancient spring now feeds the swimming pool.
✉ 4750 Barcelos. **Map** p271 D2. ☎ (253) 83 16 06.
FAX (253) 83 22 31. 🍴 b. **Rooms** 5. ≋ 🍸 ❀
● Nov-Apr. 💳 AE. $$

Carcavelos

Quinta das Encostas This estate house is owned by the Count of Paço d'Arcos. The suite-sized bedrooms have period bathrooms; guests share a number of *salons* with the family. Visit the private chapel with a model of baby Jesus in the Count's former cradle, and the vast kitchens still used by caterers for wedding parties most weekends.
✉ Largo de Vasco d'Orey-Sassoeiros, 2775 Carcavelos.
Map p270 A2. ☎ (21) 457 00 56. FAX (21) 458 26 47.
🍴 b. **Rooms** 3. ≋ ❀ ● Sat, Sun.
💳 Not accepted. $$

Agueda

Pousada São Antonio A good motel-type stopover not far from the A1 motorway, with pool, tennis court, and 'grandma's house' feel.
✉ 3750 Agueda. **Map** p271 D3. ☎ (234) 52 32 30.
FAX (234) 52 31 92. @ info@pousadas.pt
🍴 b,l,d. **Rooms** 13. $$

Beja

Pousada de São Francisco Serene former convent which retains it Gothic chapel. The cloister has been glassed in.
✉ 7800 Beja. **Map** p270 B3. ☎ (284) 32 84 41.
FAX (284) 32 91 43. @ info@pousadas.pt
🍴 b,l,d. **Rooms** 35. $$$

Braga

Albergaria Senhora-a-Branca A city-centre hotel with large bedrooms and a roof terrace; good selection of restaurants in Braga's old town.
✉ 58 Largo da Senhora-a-Branca, 4710 Braga.
Map p271 D2. ☎ (253) 26 99 38. FAX (253) 26 99 37.
🍴 b. **Rooms** 21. $

Bragança

Moinho do Canico There is plenty of fishing to be had near this old watermill, now a guesthouse furnished in country style. Peaceful setting.
✉ Av. Abade de Bacal, Ponte de Castrelos, 5300 Castrelos, Bragança. **Map** p271 F1. ☎ (273) 32 35 77.
🍴 b. **Rooms** 2. $

CASCAIS

Casa de Pergola There's something of the English manor house about this busy guesthouse in central Cascais, with its mantel clocks, wood-panelled sittingroom ceiling and tea and scones in the afternoon. The pretty front garden is not really for lounging, but rooms are comfortable and have a personal feel. The cafés, restaurants and harbourfront of Cascais are close by.
☒ Avenida Valbom 13, 2750 Cascais. **Map** p270 A2.
📞 (21) 484 00 40. FAX (21) 483 47 91. 🍴 b. **Rooms** 10.
◉ Jan, Feb. 🚫 Not accepted. ⑤⑤

ESTORIL

Amazonia Lennox Each of the vast bedrooms are named after golf courses (St Andrews, Muirfield, and so on) and antique clubs and trophies decorate the walls; appropriate for a hotel near some great courses. The interiors are decorated with bold colours and specially commissioned furniture in keeping with the 1930s' architecture.
☒ Rua Eng Álvaro Pedro de Sousa 5. **Map** p270 A2.
📞 (21) 468 04 24. FAX (21) 467 08 59. 🍴 b,l,d. **Rooms** 34.
🖥 🏊 ⑧ ⌖ ◉ Never. 🚫 AE, DC, MC, V. ⑤⑤

CASCAIS

Villa Cascais This small harbourfront hotel creates a cocoon of soft white carpets and soothing interiors that you won't want to leave. And you don't have to: the excellent restaurant has great views of the port, and the fashionably decorated bedrooms are inviting. The rooftop sunbathing deck is for guests' use only.
☒ Rua Fernandes Tomás 1, 2750 Cascais.
Map p270 A2. 📞 (21) 486 34 10. FAX (21) 484 46 80.
🍴 b,l,d. **Rooms** 10. 🖥 📺 ⑧ ◉ Never.
🚫 AE, DC, MC, V. ⑤⑤⑤

ESTORIL

Hotel Palácio Much business is mixed with pleasure here, but there's a relaxed atmosphere, a great pool and lawn for sunbathing and plenty of golf nearby. Bedrooms have heavy dark furniture and lots of mirrors. The service recalls the days in the early 1900s when the hotel was a popular stop among deposed European royalty.
☒ Rua do Parque, 2769 Estoril. **Map** p270 A2.
📞 (21) 468 04 00. FAX (21) 468 48 67. @ palacioestoril@ mail.telepac.pt 🍴 b,l,d. **Rooms** 162. 🖥 🏊 ⑧
◉ Never. 🚫 AE, DC, MC, V. ⑤⑤⑤⑤

BRAGANÇA
Pousada de São Bartolomeu A modern *pousada* with blonde-wood furnishings and views across the valley to Bragança castle and village.
☒ 5300 Bragança. **Map** p271 F1. 📞 (273) 33 14 93.
FAX (273) 32 34 53. @ info@pousadas.pt
🍴 b,l,d. **Rooms** 28. ⑤⑤⑤

CASCAIS
Hotel Guincho This former sea-fort (now a five-star hotel) is surrounded by ocean on three sides. Ask for a room with four-poster and open fire.
☒ Estrada do Guincho, 2750 Cascais. **Map** p270 A2.
📞 (21) 487 04 91. FAX (21) 487 04 31. 🍴 b,l,d.
Rooms 29. ⑤⑤⑤

CASTELO DE BODE
Pousada de São Pedro An homage to hydro-electric power, this relaxing *pousada* is close to a dam and large reservoir, good for windsurfing.
☒ 2300 Tomar. **Map** p271 D4. 📞 (249) 38 11 59.
FAX (249) 38 11 76. @ info@pousadas.pt
🍴 b,l,d. **Rooms** 29. ⑤⑤⑤

COIMBRA
Hotel Quinta das Lagrimas A discreet yet bright 18th-century palace with suitably grand hallway and bedrooms.
☒ Santa Clara, 3040 Coimbra. **Map** p271 D4.
📞 (239) 44 16 15. FAX (239) 44 16 95. @ lagrimas@ relaischateaux.fr 🍴 b,l,d. **Rooms** 39. ⑤⑤⑤

For key to symbols see backflap. For price categories see p269

Guimarães

Pousada de Santa Marinha This former convent is now dedicated to earthly pleasures. The 12th-century building is monumental, but retains a human scale thanks to homely lounges with worn velvet furniture, the wood-lined summer balcony, and the fountains dotted around the hallways. Try to book a cell-like room with four-poster bed in the old building.
✉ 4800 Guimarães. **Map** p271 D2. ☎ (253) 51 44 53. [FAX] (253) 51 44 59. @ info@pousadas.pt 🍴 b,l,d. **Rooms** 51. ▤ ♣ ● Never. 💳 AE, DC, MC, V. $$$

Lagos

Quinta da Alfarrobeira A relaxed Dutch couple bought this farmhouse in 1996, and now rent out two self-contained cottages and occasionally a guest room in their own house. Set back from the sea, this is the perfect place to lounge by the pool, go for cycle rides, or read under the giant alfarrobeira tree.
✉ Estrada de Palmares-Odeáxere, 8600 Lagos. **Map** p270 A4. ☎ (282) 79 84 24. [FAX] (282) 79 96 30. 🍴 None. **Rooms** 1 room, plus 2 cottages. ≋ ♣ ● Never. 💳 Not accepted. $

Lagoa

Almansor A modern, upmarket hotel with some Moorish touches to the decoration, set next to a beautiful rocky cove. It's a busy place; facilities include indoor and outdoor pools and a beauty salon. There is live music and entertainment each night. Bedrooms are a gentler affair, with airy sea views and Portuguese print fabrics.
✉ Praia do Carvoeiro, 8400 Carvoeiro, Lagoa. **Map** p270 A4. ☎ (282) 35 80 26. [FAX] (282) 35 87 70. @ almansor@mail.telepac.pt 🍴 b,l,d. **Rooms** 293. ▤ ≋ ♣ ● Never. 💳 AE, DC, MC, V. $$$

Lisbon

As Janelas Verdes The small 18th-century palace hotel has the facilities of a much larger place. There's a beautiful courtyard garden and an antique-packed lounge to relax in, 24-hour room service and business facilities. In the stairwell is a portrait of writer Eça de Queirós, who in one of his novels based a fictional home on this house.
✉ Rua das Janelas Verdes 47, 1200 Lisboa. **Map** p270 A2. ☎ (21) 396 81 43. [FAX] (21) 396 81 44. @ jverdes@mail.telepac.pt 🍴 b. **Rooms** 17. ▤ ● Never. 💳 AE, DC, MC, V. $$$

Evora

Pousada dos Lóios Evora is one of Portugal's highlights, and this *pousada* – a former convent turned luxury hotel – is in the old town centre.
✉ 7000-804 Evora. **Map** p270 B2. ☎ (266) 70 40 51. [FAX] (266) 70 72 48. @ info@pousadas.pt 🍴 b,l,d. **Rooms** 32. $$$

Evora

Quinta de Espada Surrounded by cork oaks, this farm estate rents out several cottages. There is an honesty bar and a small pool.
✉ Estrada de Arraiolos, 7001 Evora. **Map** p270 B2. ☎ (266) 73 45 49. [FAX] (266) 73 64 64. 🍴 b;d by arrangement. **Rooms** 7. $

Funchal, Madeira

Vila Cantareira do Monte This island guest house is at the heart of an old manor house, set on a mountain 365m (1,200ft) above the bay.
✉ Caminho do Monte 150d, 9050 Funchal, Madeira. **Map** p270 C5. ☎ (291) 780 00 00. [FAX] (291) 780 00 08. 🍴 b;d at owner's restaurant nearby. **Rooms** 6. $

Guimarães

Casa de Sezim A grand manor house; guest rooms are chic and full of character, with Murano glass chandeliers and dark wooden floors.
✉ Santo Amaro, 4800 Guimarães. **Map** p271 D2. ☎ [FAX] (253) 52 31 96. 🍴 b;d on request. **Rooms** 9. $$

LISBON

Four Seasons Ritz With contemporary tapestries and assured decoration, this is one of Portugal's best and biggest hotels. Service is excellent, but despite the grandeur, there is no affectation. Regular guests say that breakfast – with its choice of Edward VII, Japanese or Continental menus – is the best meal in the panoramic restaurant.
Rua Rodrigo da Fonseca 88, 1093 Lisboa.
Map p270 A2. (21) 383 20 20. FAX (21) 383 17 83.
b,l,d. **Rooms** 282. Never.
AE, DC, MC, V. $$$$

NAZARÉ

Quinta do Campo This very grand private home is still a working farm, and the garden can be a bit noisy, but the Quinta is a place well worth seeking out. Rooms vary: some have brass bedsteads and azulejos-tiled bathrooms, others floral fabrics and 1920s' baths; all have a special atmosphere, as do the sitting rooms and library.
Valado dos Frades, 2450 Nazaré. **Map** p270 A1.
(262) 57 71 35. FAX (262) 57 75 55. b.
Rooms 8, plus 7 apartments. Never.
Not accepted. $$

LISBON

Quinta Nova da Conceiçao Waking to the sound of cocks crowing in the morning, you could forget that this small guesthouse is only 12 minutes by metro from central Lisbon. Guests live with the family and their lively dogs in a house full of ancient objects and stained glass. The tiled breakfast room was once a grand aviary; outside is a lush garden and sheltered pool.
Rua da Cidade de Rabat 5, São Dom de Benfica, 1500 Lisboa. **Map** p270 A2. FAX (21) 778 00 91. b.
Rooms 2. Never. AE, DC, MC, V. $$

OBIDOS

Pousada do Castelo This hotel is located inside the Manueline palace of an ancient castle encircling the whitewashed village of Obidos (which only those with nerves of steel should attempt to drive through). At dusk the coach parties evaporate and you can enjoy in peace the amazing view from the ramparts. The bedrooms, restaurant and bar are enjoyably creaky and old.
2510 Obidos. **Map** p270 A1. (262) 95 91 05.
FAX (262) 95 91 48. @ info@pousadas.pt b,l,d.
Rooms 9. Never. AE, DC, MC, V. $$$

GUIMARÃES
Paço de São Cipriano Romantic souls will love the sage-green tower room with Sleeping Beauty bed; this palace with rooms for rent has plenty else too, from topiary garden to swimming pool.
Tabuadelo, 4800 Guimarães. **Map** p271 D2.
FAX (253) 56 53 37. b. **Rooms** 6. $$

GUIMARÃES
Pousada Nossa Senhora de Oliveira
A popular historic-centre *pousada*, done out in Gothic style. Excellent food.
Apartado 101, 4801 Guimarães. **Map** p271 D2.
(253) 51 41 57. FAX (253) 51 42 04.
@ info@pousadas.pt b,l,d. **Rooms** 16. $$

LISBON
Britânia Restored in 1997 to its former glory from the Art Deco era, when it was built to Cassiano Branco's designs. No restaurant, but a clubby bar.
Rua Rodrigues Sampaio 17, 1150 Lisboa.
Map p270 A2. (21) 315 50 16. FAX (21) 315 50 21.
@ britania.hotel@mail.telepac.pt b. **Rooms** 30. $$

LISBON
Lisboa Plaza A classic hotel in the town centre, grand and old-fashioned, with very helpful staff. Owned by the same family since 1953.
Tv. Salitre/Av. Liberdade, 1250 Lisboa. **Map** p270 A2.
(21) 346 39 22. FAX (21) 347 16 30. @ plaza.hotels@
mail.telepac.pt b,l,d. **Rooms** 106. $$

For key to symbols see backflap. For price categories see p269

Ponte de Lima

Casa de Outeiro With its oil paintings, Oriental rugs and ancient library and lounge smelling of woodsmoke and leather-bound books, Casa de Outeiro abounds in faded grandeur. It is owned by the same family as the nearby Quinta do Sanguerinho (see below). Rooms have ancient beds and terracotta- and black-tiled floors; there's also a self-contained apartment.
✉ 4990 Ponte de Lima. **Map** p271 D1. ☎ (258) 94 12 06. [FAX] (258) 74 14 44. 🍴 b. **Rooms** 3, plus 1 apartment. 🍃 ● Never. 💳 AE. $

Ponte de Lima

Quinta de Pomarchão Choose between formally furnished self-catering apartments or rustic cottages on this large but slightly crumbling estate. It has been in the same family for 500 years; the owners' apartments – which guests may well get to see if they are invited in for an *aperitivo* – are crammed with family photos, *objets d'art*, armour and other heirlooms.
✉ Arcozelo, Ponte de Lima 4990. **Map** p271 D1. ☎ (258) 74 17 42. [FAX] (258) 74 27 42. 🍴 b. **Rooms** 10 apartments and cottages. 🏊 🍃 ● Never. 💳 AE. $$

Ponte de Lima

Casa das Pereiras Large, ancient house in the old town. The dark landing – with its own altar – is lit by a stone window in the shape of a Maltese Cross. The hall and lounge – a mix of 1970s' sofas and suits of armour – can be chilly, but the bedrooms are well heated and atmospheric, with panelled ceilings and carved wooden beds; modern bathrooms.
✉ Largo das Pereiras, 4990 Ponte de Lima. **Map** p271 D1. ☎ (258) 94 29 39. 🍴 b,l,d. **Rooms** 3. 🍃 ● Never. 💳 Not accepted. $

Ponte de Lima

Quinta do Salguerinho At the end of a narrow granite lane and drive lined with acanthus plants and arum lilies, in a rambling garden, are these two cottages. The wood-built *alpendre* serves as a summer house and winter suntrap, and there are plenty of games and space for children. Rooms are traditionally furnished.
✉ Lugar do Salguerinho Arcozelo, 4990 Ponte de Lima. **Map** p271 D1. ☎ (258) 94 12 06. [FAX] (258) 74 14 44. @ turihab@mail.telepac.pt 🍴 b. **Rooms** 5. 🏊 🍃 ● Never. 💳 AE. $

Marvão

Pousada de Santa Maria A warm, friendly mountain-top *pousada* by the border with Spain. Restaurant has great views but so-so food.
✉ Rua 24 de Janeiro 7, 7330 Marvão. **Map** p270 C1, p271 E5. ☎ (245) 932 01. [FAX] (245) 934 40. @ info@pousadas.pt 🍴 b,l,d. **Rooms** 29. $$

Mesão Frio

Pousada do Solar da Rede This 18th-century manor house in the Douro wine region is now a beautifully restored *pousada*. Own vineyard.
✉ Santa Cristina, 5040 Mesão Frio. **Map** p271 E2. ☎ (254) 89 01 30. [FAX] (254) 89 01 39. @ info@pousadas.pt 🍴 b,l,d. **Rooms** 31. $$$

Nazaré

Hotel Praia This no-frills hotel is included for its central location in a lively resort. Bedrooms are modern and have balconies, some with sea views.
✉ Av. Vieira Guimarães 39, 2450 Nazaré. **Map** p270 A1. ☎ (262) 56 14 23. [FAX] (262) 56 14 36. 🍴 b,l,d. **Rooms** 40 (50 more being built). $$

Ponte da Barca

Torre de Quintela A friendly, family-owned farm estate with guest rooms, billiards table, vineyards and its own chapel. Closed Nov-March.
✉ Nogueria, 4980 Ponte de Barca. **Map** p271 D1. ☎ (258) 45 22 38; mobile 0936 566 08 62. 🍴 b; l,d on request. **Rooms** 3. $

Portimão

Quinta Rosa de Lima This simple villa makes a pleasant change from the chain hotels of the Algarve, and is close to the beach, restaurants and nightlife of Praia da Rocha. The land by the villa – covered by vineyards and trees – belongs to the owners, so will never be built on. Inside, furniture is simple and rustic. Guests may use the pool at the nearby Penina hotel.
✉ Estrada da Torre, 8500 Portimão. **Map** p270 A4.
☎ (282) 41 10 97. 🍴 b. **Rooms** 4. ❦ ● Dec.
💳 Not accepted. $

Queluz

Pousada Dona Maria I In 1995 this *pousada* opened in what were once the servants' quarters for the royal palace opposite; you may still get to witness the arrival of delegates on state occasions. Inside, the huge, high-ceilinged rooms are traditionally furnished with great flair; radios have speakers in the bathrooms. Makes a good base for Lisbon, 5km (3 miles) away.
✉ 2745 Queluz. **Map** p270 A2. ☎ (21) 435 61 58.
[FAX] (21) 435 61 89. @ info@pousadas.pt 🍴 b,l,d.
Rooms 26. ≡ ● Never. 💳 AE, DC, MC, V. $$$

Porto (Oporto)

Casa de Marechal The urbane hotel was built in 1940, and show tunes of the era accompany the Dry Martinis at the bar. Dependability and discretion are the watchwords: the restaurant arranges private dinners for heads of state and others wanting to keep a low profile. The bedrooms have everything, from Jacuzzi to port.
✉ Avenida da Boavista 2652, 4100 Porto.
Map p271 D2. ☎ (22) 610 47 02. [FAX] (22) 610 32 41.
🍴 b,l,d. **Rooms** 5. ≡ 🍸 ❦ ● 3 weeks Aug, Christmas and New Year. 💳 AE, DC, MC, V. $$

São Brás de Alportel

Pousada de São Brás Set back from the scrum of the Algarve's coastal strip, this *pousada* is a short drive from the port of Tavira with its restaurants and beaches. It's an unpretentious place, with bright and cheerful fabrics in the (small) rooms, a good pool and well-maintained tennis court and a pile of magazines in the bar.
✉ 8150 São Brás de Alportel. **Map** p270 B4.
☎ (289) 84 23 05. [FAX] (289) 84 17 26. @ info@pousadas.pt 🍴 b,l,d. **Rooms** 33. ≡ 🏊 🍸 ❦
● Never. 💳 AE, DC, MC, V. $$

Ponte de Lima

Casa das Torres This family-run 18th-century manor house has some guest rooms opening onto the terrace and swimming pool; there's also table tennis, billiards and a bar.
✉ Lugar de Arribão, Facha, 4990 Ponte de Lima. **Map** p271 D1. ☎ [FAX] (258) 94 13 69. 🍴 b. **Rooms** 4. $

Porto (Oporto)

Hotel Castor A decent, central, inexpensive place to stay – rare for Porto – with a marble foyer, eclectic furnishings, and Italian restaurant.
✉ Rua das Doze Casas 17, 4000-195 Porto.
Map p271 D2. ☎ (22) 537 00 14. [FAX] (22) 536 60 76.
🍴 b,l,d. **Rooms** 63. $

Porto (Oporto)

Infante Sagres In central Porto, an Art Nouveau feast for the eyes, with stained glass stairwell and lounges filled with *chinoiserie*. Plainer bedrooms.
✉ Praça D. Filipa de Lencastre 62, 4050 Porto.
Map p271 D2. ☎ (22) 200 81 01. [FAX] (22) 205 49 37.
🍴 b,l,d. **Rooms** 74. $$$

Póvoa de Varzim

Luso-Brasileiro An unpretentious hotel built in 1910 in the middle of the action in one of northern Portugal's popular beach resorts.
✉ Rua dos Cafés 16, 4490 Póvoa de Varzim.
Map p271 D2. ☎ (252) 69 07 10. [FAX] (252) 69 07 19.
🍴 b,l,d. **Rooms** 62. $

For key to symbols see backflap. For price categories see p269

SANTA CLARA-A-VELHA

Pousada de Santa Clara Balconies and terraces make the most of the hilltop location, which gives a 360-degree view of forests, hills and man-made lake. The main attraction is the setting, but the standard of the accommodation is high. Don't miss the chance to eat here: the chef has won an award for her regionally inspired dishes.
☒ 7665 Santa Clara-a-Velha. **Map** p270 A4.
☎ (283) 88 22 50. FAX (283) 88 24 02. @ info@pousadas.pt ⑪ b,l,d. **Rooms** 19. ▤ ⛱ ◐
◐ Never. ▣ AE, DC, MC, V. ⑤⑤

SINTRA

Casa Miradouro The Swiss owner of this red-and-white striped house just outside the centre of Sintra has lavished care and attention on each of the light, airy rooms; many have great views in two directions, to the Pena Palace on the hill and towards the sea. There's also a comfortably furnished sitting room, large enough that you don't feel crowded out by other guests.
☒ Rua Sotto Mayor 55, 2710 Sintra-Vila. **Map** p270 A2.
☎ (21) 923 59 00. FAX (21) 924 18 36. ⑪ b. **Rooms** 6.
◐ ◐ A few weeks Jan, Feb. ▣ AE, DC, MC, V. ⑤⑤

SETÚBAL

Pousada de São Filipe Bedrooms are in the former dungeons, but there are no ghosts here – or so they say. This is one of the nicest *pousadas* close to Lisbon, and is especially interesting in summer when there are *fado* nights (*fado* is a mix of blues and flamenco). The restaurant is a good place to start the evening before going on to the packed bar scene of Setúbal below.
☒ 2900 Setúbal. **Map** p270 A2. ☎ (265) 52 38 44.
FAX (265) 53 25 38. @ info@pousadas.pt ⑪ b,l,d.
Rooms 16. ▤ ◐ ◐ Never. ▣ AE, DC, MC, V. ⑤⑤⑤

SINTRA

Palacio Seteais Escapists will love this 18th-century pleasure palace on a hill above Sintra; it's now a five-star hotel exuding well-being and contentment. There are plenty of tapestries and plush fabrics but the pastoral wall-paintings and pale wood floors keep everything light. Terraces make the most of the splendid views.
☒ Rua Barbosa du Bocage 10, 2710-517 Sintra.
Map p270 A2. ☎ (21) 923 32 00. FAX (21) 923 42 77.
@ hpseteais@mail.telepac.pt ⑪ b,l,d. **Rooms** 30.
▤ ⛱ ⑪ ◐ ◐ Never. ▣ AE, DC, MC, V. ⑤⑤⑤⑤

PICO

Casa das Barcas A low-fronted black-and-white house with traditionally furnished rooms and a garden; there is fishing and diving nearby.
☒ Cais do Pico, 9940 São Roque do Pico, Azores.
Map p270 B5. ☎ (292) 64 27 33/64 27 35.
FAX (21) 352 35 85. ⑪ b. **Rooms** 3. ⑤⑤

SÃO MIGUEL

Convento de São Francisco Sleep in an antique bed in front of an open fire in this 17th-century island monastery.
☒ Vila Franca do Campo, São Miguel, Azores.
Map p270 B5. ☎ (296) 58 35 32. FAX (21) 352 35 85.
⑪ b. **Rooms** 10. ⑤⑤

SINTRA

Estalagem de Colares Dedicated owner Cristina de Sousa's country inn is surrounded by vineyards, and has a good regional restaurant.
☒ Colares, 2710 Sintra. **Map** p270 A2.
☎ (21) 928 29 40. FAX (21) 928 29 83. ⑪ b,l,d.
Rooms 12. ◐ Never. ▣ AE, DC, MC, V. ⑤⑤

SINTRA

Quinta de Capela This elegant 16th-century farmhouse has antique-filled rooms, polished terracotta floors, and a sauna and small gym.
☒ Estrada de Monserrate, 2710 Sintra. **Map** p270 A2.
☎ (21) 929 01 70. FAX (21) 929 34 25. ⑪ b.
Rooms 7, plus 3 apartments. ⑤⑤⑤

Tavira

Quinta do Caracol A collection of whitewashed buildings connected by steps and passageways, this quinta has the look of a small village. The accommodation consists of two-bedroomed apartments with brick floors, print fabrics, and a small kitchen and sitting area; outside, an old water tank has been turned into a pool. Dinner is based on the best produce at market that day.
✉ São Pedro, 8800 Tavira. **Map** p270 B4.
☎ (281) 32 24 75. [FAX] (281) 32 31 75. 🍴 b,d. **Rooms** 14.
≋ ☕ 🌳 ● Never. 💳 Not accepted. [$][$]

Vila do Conde

Quinta São Miguel de Arcos This old farmhouse has been operating as a guesthouse since 1997. The hunting rifle over the fireplace, the antique beds and bright spreads, and the homely sitting room set the rustic style. There's a good restaurant in the village nearby. Not much English is spoken, except by the owners' son Antonio who lives a few miles away.
✉ Rua da Igreja 209, Vila do Conde, 4480 Arcos.
Map p271 D2. ☎ [FAX] (252) 65 20 94.
🍴 b. **Rooms** 3. ≋ 🌳 ● Never. 💳 Not accepted. [$]

Viana do Castelo

Casa Santa Ana The spotless rooms with antique beds, wood floors, and drawn-threadwork curtains each have a private terrace or balcony, the latter with view of the sea. In the garden you can sit out under a pergola and catch the scent of orange blossom, and the gentle sound of a fountain trickling into the old stone water tank, now home to several goldfish.
✉ Lugar da Armada, 4900 Afife. **Map** p271 D1. ☎ (258) 98 17 74. [FAX] (258) 98 17 74. @ stana@softhome.net
Rooms 6. 🍴 b,d. ≋ 🌳 ● Never. 💳 Not accepted. [$]

Vila Viçosa

Pousada Dom João IV The lavishly restored hotel was originally a convent for the ladies of the noble Bragança family. It has kept the best of the old – including frescoed side chapels – and merged them with a contemporary take on cloisters and kitchen garden. The whole place is stylish but very relaxing; the food is excellent.
✉ 7160 Vila Viçosa. **Map** p270 C2. ☎ (268) 98 07 42. [FAX] (268) 98 07 47. @ info@pousadas.pt
🍴 b,l,d. **Rooms** 36. ☰ ≋ 🌳 ● Never.
💳 AE, DC, MC, V. [$][$][$]

Tavira

Convento de Santo Antonio High 17th-century convent walls hide the nearby housing estate from the garden and swimming pool. The monastic-style bedrooms have fireplaces.
✉ Atalaia 56, 8800 Tavira. **Map** p270 B4.
☎ [FAX] (281) 32 56 32. 🍴 b. **Rooms** 6. [$][$]

Terceira

Quinta do Barcelos This island guesthouse is homely, with whitewashed walls, exposed beams, and beds with patchwork quilts.
✉ Terra do Pão 2, São Mateus, 9700 Angra do Heroismo, Terceira, Azores. **Map** p270 B5. ☎ (295) 64 26 84.
[FAX] (295) 64 26 83. 🍴 b; book d. **Rooms** 6. [$]

Viana do Castelo

Pousada do Monte Santa Luzia A grand hotel built in 1903 on a hill above town, where the air is scented by pine needles. Bedrooms are large.
✉ 4900 Viana do Castelo. **Map** p271 D1.
☎ (258) 82 88 89. [FAX] (258) 82 88 92. @ info@pousadas.pt 🍴 b,l,d. **Rooms** 47. [$][$][$]

Vila Viçosa

Casa de Peixinhos A manor house guesthouse with antiques, leather armchairs and the Passanha family's coat of arms over the fireplace. Dinner by arrangement (book 24 hours ahead).
✉ 7160 Vila Viçosa. **Map** p270 C2. ☎ (268) 98 04 72.
[FAX] (268) 88 13 48. 🍴 b. **Rooms** 9. [$][$]

For key to symbols see backflap. For price categories *see p269*

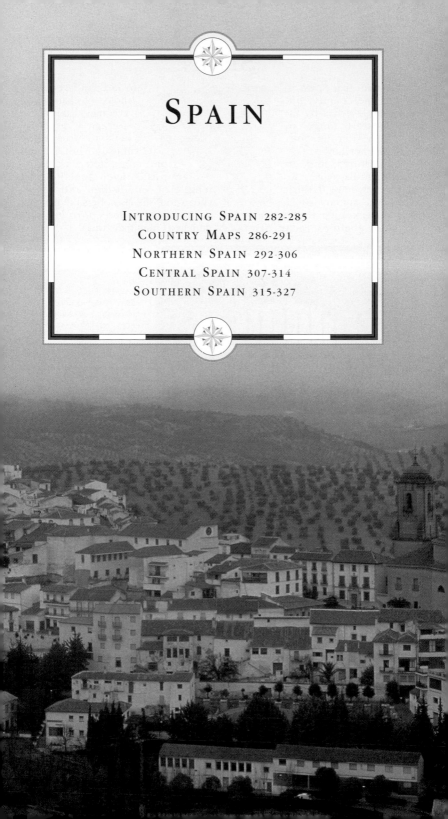

SPAIN

SPAIN

IT IS SAID that Spain is not one country, but several. It has by far the greatest range of landscapes in Europe, four distinct languages, many cultures, and, in Madrid and Barcelona, two of Europe's most dynamic cities. The country which was once known for its high-rise package ghettoes today offers a broad and eclectic choice of characterful accommodation; from former monastic cells to dream-like Gaudíesque hotels, and from converted castles to farmsteads. Even Tenerife, that temple of 'pile-it-high and sell-it-cheap' tourism, also offers the traveller a stunningly-sited *parador* and numerous rural hideaways.

Hotel San Gil, page 325, one of Seville's most striking buildings

SPAIN REGION BY REGION

SPAIN DIVIDES roughly into six regions and two major cities.

Northwest Spain

The long beaches and green, rural landscapes of Galicia, Asturias and Cantabria are a world away from package-holiday Spain. The region varies enormously in its landscapes, from the mountains and valleys of the Picos de Europa, to Spain's little-known fjord country, the Rias Baixas. Here, *casas rurales*, or country holiday homes (page 284), are very popular. The city of Santiago de Compostela, its great cathedral for centuries the goal of pilgrims, has both luxurious and spartan accommodation for its many thousands of visitors.

Northeast Spain

From the Atlantic and Bilbao in the west, Northeast Spain runs through the Basque country, Navarra, La Rioja, Aragon, the Pyrenees and northern Catalonia to reach the Mediterranean.

By contrast to Bilbao's exuberantly new-wave Guggenheim Museum, San Sebastian is long-established as the most elegant and fashionable of all the Spanish seaside resorts. It offers an interesting, wide range of accommodation and some very fine luxury hotels. Walkers in the the Pyrenees are less pampered, with *refugios*, basic mountain huts, and more comfortable *residencias-casa de payés*, as *casas rurales* are called in these parts.

Eastern Spain

Spain's eastern coastline is the land of the Costas, from Brava in the north to Blanca in the south. Long stretches (though by no means the whole coastline) are marred by fast-buck holiday developments, but step just a little way back from the beach bars and discos and normal service is quickly resumed.

Barcelona

Rivalling or surpassing Madrid in many aspects, Barcelona may officially be number two in Spain, but it is *numero uno* as far as most visitors are concerned. Its Old Town oozes an ancient and salty atmosphere but the city is probably best know for its Modernist architecture, some of the most original of which comes from the stable of the hugely-talented Antoni Gaudí. Barcelona has some superb

The Real at Santander, page 304, built for a king's entourage

visitor attractions, great bars and a buzzing nightlife. The city's most characterful hotels are on or just off Spain's most famous street, Las Ramblas.

Central Spain
Taking in the provinces of Castilla Y León, Castilla-La Mancha and Extremadura, the sun-scorched central plateau (*meseta*) surrounding Madrid is the Spain of Cervantes' Don Quixote and El Cid: epic landscapes dotted with picturesque windmills and imposing castles. A deep sense of history permeates the region, captured in the awe-inspiring Gothic cathedrals of Burgos and León, the stunningly-preserved medieval capital of Toledo, the perfect Renaissance architecture of Salamanca and the fairy-tale towers of Segovia's castle.

To the west is wild and parched Extremadura, Spain's most remote area. It receives relatively few foreign visitors, but Cuenca, with its famous hanging houses, the marvellous Roman city of Mérida and the Gothic-Renaissance buildings of Cáceres make the trip well worthwhile. Government-run hotels, or *paradores* (page 284), offer some of the best places to stay in the Central region.

Madrid
Not nearly as attractive nor as visitor-friendly as Barcelona, Madrid is a large modern capital, chiefly visited for its world-class museums and art galleries. However, it also has Spain's best shopping, excellent bars, and the country's most frenetic nightlife. In Madrid, accommodation is largely functional, with location rating higher than character.

Andalucia
This is the Southern Spain of popular imagination – flamenco, bullfighting, sherry, white cubist villages (*pueblos blancos*) and fields of sunflowers. It is also an enormously varied region, from desert in the east to the vast watery Doñana National Park in the west, with the snow-topped Sierra Nevada mountains, the historic city of Granada and long golden beaches nearby. In the historic Moorish-influenced cities of Granada, Seville and Córdoba, Andalusia boasts three of Spain's most beautiful and popular tourist destinations. Literally all kinds of accommodation are found in Andalucia, with the emphasis switching in recent years from coastal to rural.

The Islands
The Canaries and the Balearics have long been a byword for cheap, packaged tourism. There are exceptions however, the most striking being the northwest coast of Mallorca, which now features some of Spain's finest country house properties. Peace and quiet and individual rural accommodation can also be found in the beautiful, lesser-known Canary Islands of La Palma and La Gomera.

Highlights

HOTELS ILLUSTRATED on these introductory pages are by no means our only highlights. Other high points include the splendid Ritz in Madrid, page 311; the charming Castillo el Collado, page 299; Almud, page 303, a stable block converted into a B&B with exquisite taste; and luxurious Finca Buen Vino, page 320.

Rural Tourism

A POLICY OF *AGROTURISMO* or *turismo rural* (rural tourism) has been embraced by the Spanish government to help convert *fincas* (farms or estates) into country holiday homes known as *casas rurales*. Properties vary in size and may be in the wilds or just a mile or two from a busy resort. Owners usually accept just a few visitors at one time. Facilities and atmosphere vary greatly. Most allow for self-catering. What all *casas*

Hotel El Montiboli, La Vila Joiosa, page 327

Canoeing, organized by the Posada de Sigueruelo, page 313

rurales should have in common is that they offer peaceful surroundings, an insight into local culture and some degree of personal service. They are most numerous in Northern and Central Spain, and in Catalonia, where they are called *casa de pagès* or *casa de payés*. They are also becoming common in Galicia and Cantabria (*casas de labranza*) and in Andalucia.

MONASTIC CELLS

SPAIN HAS A LONG tradition of offering rooms to pilgrims and travellers. See, for example, page 298. Nowadays this form of hospitality is extended to tourists in some 150 monasteries and convents. A cell can consist of anything from a room almost as spartan as it sounds, deep in the heart of a monastery, to a charming

Parador de Hondarribia, page 229

converted apart-ment with its own garden.

Cells are most often found in Benedictine and Cistercian monasteries and convents in rural towns and villages, or around such cities as Burgos, León, Madrid and Segovia. Some of these stipulate married couples only, others have single-sex restrictions, and in others you will be expected to help with the washing up and to tidy your room.

PARADORES

SPAIN'S MOST NOTABLE hotel grouping is the state-run chain of *paradores* (*parador* means inn or stopping place). The most famous are housed in stunning historic buildings: former palaces, castles, royal hunting lodges, monasteries and so on. All are furnished and decorated in strictly vernacular style and should offer local cuisine of a high standard. But there are also modern, functional *paradores*, deliberately sited where there is (or was) a dearth of other satisfactory accommodation. The advantages of this type of *parador* are usually a splen-did location and views worth travelling miles to enjoy.

Paradores started as a cheap form of lodging, but they are now expensive and many have been overtaken by converted properties offering similar, but better-value accommodation. More-over, as government-run hotels, they can lack the personal touch and warmth of welcome.

FOOD AND DRINK

SPANISH CUISINE is as varied as its many regions. In the north is abundant fish and seafood from the Atlantic; the mountains and hills provide hams, sausages and game, which are often combined with beans to form hearty stews (a recurring theme throughout the country). The Basque Country, with its orientation towards the sea, is recognised as the gastronomic centre of all Spain.

In Madrid and the central region, game is plentiful and one-pot meat-and-pulse stews are generally the order of the day. Suckling pig and lamb, sausages and other pork dishes are common. *Cocido madrileno*, a slow-simmered stew of beef, chicken, ham, pork belly, chickpeas plus various other items, is the regional favourite.

The cuisine of both south and east coasts is mainly Mediterranean, but influenced by the Moors who introduced olives, oranges, almonds, saffron and rice. The last of these two are in Spain's most famous dish, *paella*, which has many ingredients, includ-ing seafood, chicken, rabbit and pork.

Catalonia's sophisticated and inventive combinations include fish and seafood stews and classic *romesco* sauce (red peppers, tomatoes and chillies).

Fried fish is the food of the south, with *fritura de pescados* (deep-fried squid and fish) a favourite with both visitors and locals. By contrast, some of Spain's best *jamón serrano* (cured ham) comes from the mountains of Andalucia.

Gazpacho, a chilled raw soup based on tomatoes, cucumber and peppers, is a Spanish culinary classic, as are *tapas*. Originating in Andalucia, but served all over Spain, *tapas* are snacks whose name stems from the traditional bartender's practice of covering a glass with a saucer or *tapa* (cover) on which was placed a bite-sized morsel. *Tapas* are nowadays eaten as snacks or combined to make up a full meal. Classic *tapas* include *tortilla* (potato omelette), *albondigas* (meatballs), cured ham, cheese, olives and many types of fish and seafood

La Rioja is the country's most prestigious wineproducing region, while the Pinedès region of Catalonia is the home of sparkling wine, or *cava*, as well as producing highquality still wines. Sherry is Spain's great vinous invention, named after Jerez de la Frontera in Andalucia, where it is still made.

The lavish Bobadilla at Loja, page 321, makes a Moorish 'village'

BEDROOMS AND BATHROOMS

DOUBLE BEDS are sometimes provided as conventional doubles as in Britain and the USA; sometimes as two singles pushed together. If you want a double, ask for a *cama de matrimonio*.

OTHER PRACTICAL INFORMATION

BOOK WELL in advance for hotels in Madrid, Barcelona and in any resort in high season. During Spain's festivities (including Easter Week) rooms are impossible to get, or charged at outrageously inflated prices.

Spanish breakfasts tend to be simple – coffee, rolls and fruit juice. *Paradores,* however, increasingly offer wide-choice buffet breakfasts. Lunch is traditionally the main meal of the day, starting around 1pm. Dinner is served late in the evening, around 9pm (earlier in tourist resorts); in summer, restaurants may open past midnight as people eat dinner later and later. At weekends, restaurants tend to be filled at lunchtime by large and boisterous family groups.

Language Spanish (Castillian) is the national language; you may also come across Catalan,

Gallego (in Galicia) and Euskera (in the Basque Country). English is spoken widely in tourist centres and most, but not all, large towns.

Currency The Spanish *peseta*, written as 'Pta'.

Shops Traditionally open 10–2pm and 5–8pm, Mon–Fri, and on Saturday morning. In resorts they may open all day and at weekends.

Tipping The Spanish rarely tip waiters more than 5 per cent, simply rounding up the bill. It is usual to tip tour guides and taxi drivers 10 per cent, and to leave a small amount for chambermaids.

The Maria Cristina, page 303

Telephoning Spanish phone numbers have no zero in front of the area code. To call Spain from the UK dial 00 34; from the US, 011 34, then the full number.

Public holidays 1 January; 6 January; Maundy Thursday, Good Friday and Easter Sunday; 1 May; 15 August 15; 12 October 12; 1 November; 6 December; 25 December.

USEFUL WORDS

Breakfast	*Desayuno*
Lunch	*Comida*
Supper	*Cena*
Free room?	*¿Habitacion libre?*
How much?	*¿Cuánto?*
Single	*Habitación individual*
Double	*Un habitación doble*

SPAIN PRICE BANDS

SPANISH HOTELS are officially classified by stars, from one to five. Don't be distracted: our price bands are simpler and refer to the price of a standard double room in high season, almost always excluding breakfast. Hotels rarely quote prices exclusive of VAT; other unexpected extras are rare.

Ⓟ	up to 12,000Pta
ⓅⓅ	12,000Pta–20,000Pta
ⓅⓅⓅ	20,000Pta–28,000Pta
ⓅⓅⓅⓅ	over 28,000Pta

Spain

Ortigueira
Cervo
Figueras del Mar
★ *297*

Ferrol **Neda**
★ *301*
Fene
Viveiro
Ribadeo
N634
Villalonga
★ *306*
Lu
A CORUÑA
S

Carballo
Betanzos
Villalba
N634
Taramundi
★ *303*

A Toxa (Toja)
★ *305*
N640
Rábade
Figueras
★ *297*

C552
Santiago de Compostela
★ *302,304*
A9
N547
Melide
LUGO
Can
del I

Muros
Cornide
★ *296*
Ulla
A6
Villablin

Vilagarcía de Arosa
★ *306*
La Estrada
Lalín
Embalse de Belesar
Villafranca
del Bierzo
A

Ribeira
Chantada
Escairón
★ *296*
Ponferr

Cambados
PONTEVEDRA
★ *300*
Carballiño
Monforte
Castr
los Polv

ATLANTIC OCEAN
VIGO
A52
OURENSE
Puebla de Trives
★ *299*

Ponteareas
N540
Xinzo de Limia
A52
A Gudiña
A52

Bayona
★ *294*
N550
Monção
A52

A Guarda (La Guardia)
★ *298*
Miño
Valença do Minho
Miño
Verín
★ *305*

Viana do Castelo
Lima
N101
Chaves
Bragança
N212
Alca

Braga
N2

Guimarães

N15
Rio Tua
Vila Real
Rio Sabof

Matosinhos
PORTO (Oporto)
Douro
Lamego
Torre de Moncorvo
Em. Alt

Vila Nova de Gaia

A1
Oliveira de Azeméis

Aveiro
Viseu
Celorico da Beira
Ciudad-Rodrigo
★ *308, 30*

Vagos
IP5
Guarda
Vilar Formoso
La Alb
★
Emba Gabriel

PORTUGAL

Figueira da Foz
Mondego
Coimbra

Pombal
Coria
Embalse de Alcántara
Plaser

Leiria
Barragem do Castelo do Bode
Castelo Branco

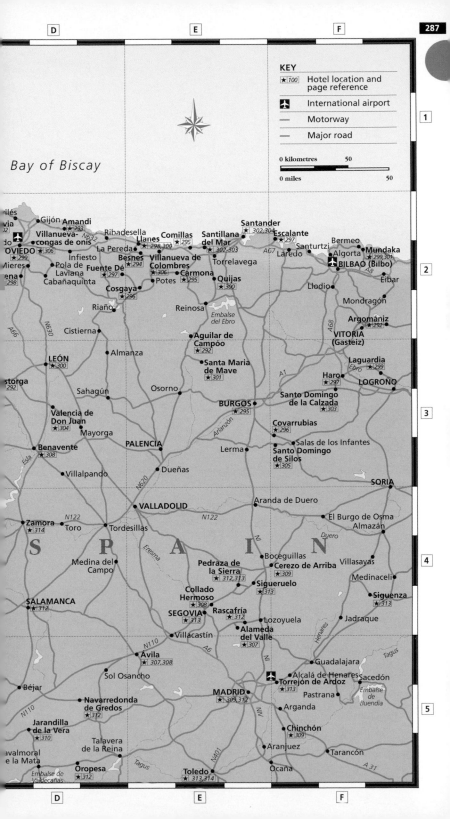

KEY

★ *100* Hotel location and page reference

✈ International airport

— Motorway

— Major road

0 kilometres 50

0 miles 50

Bay of Biscay

S P A I N

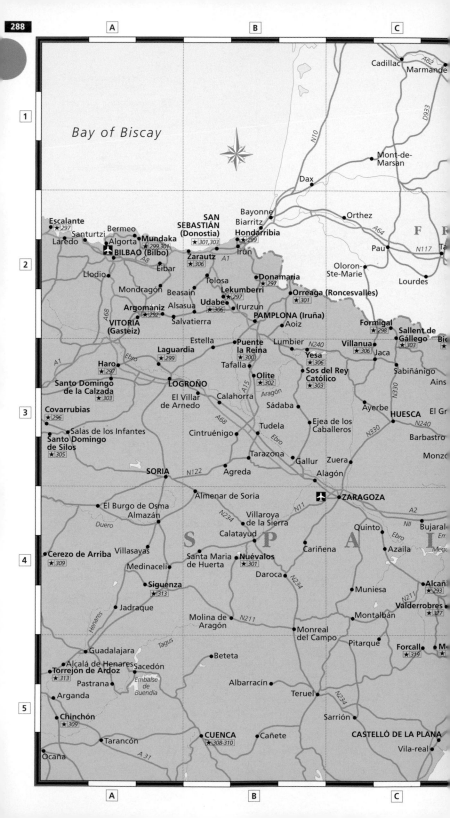

D · **E** · **F**

Cahors
Villeneuve-sur-Lot
Lot
Rodez
N106
Alés
N113
Moissac
Castelsarrasin
Albi
N88
Millau
Montpellier
Castres
N9
Frontignan
A62
A68
TOULOUSE
Sète
Auch
Muret
Mazamet
Béziers
A9
Agde
N **C** **E**
N113 Castelnaudary
A61
Saverdun
Carcassonne
Narbonne
Lannemezan
D117
Foix
Limoux
A9
Val d'Aran
Perpignan
...asque ★294
Baquèira-Beret ★293
Viella ★305
Arties ★292
N230
ANDORRA LA VELLA
Puigcerdà
Pont de Molins ★300
La Garriga ★298
Manages ★301
Bolvir ★295
Camprodon ★295
NII
...s ★4
La Seu d'Urgel ★305
Llannars ★298
Figueres
Castello de Ampurias ★296
Tremp ★304
C1313
Berga
N152
Peratallada ★299
Torrent ★305
GIRONA
Palafrugell ★303
Aigua Blava ★292
S' Agaro ★303
...us
Peramola ★302
Bassella
Segre
Cardona ★295
Vic
Santa Cristina d'Aro ★303
Viladrau ★305
Sant Feliu de Guixols
...Benabarre
C1411
Ponts
Artesa de Segre
Manresa
A7
Blanes
Alfarràs
Cervera
Granollers ★298
A19
LLEIDA
Tàrrega
Igualada
Sabadell
Mataró
KEY
L'Espluga de Francoli ★296,297
Vilafranca del Penedès
Valldoreix
Badalona
BARCELONA ★293,294
★100 Hotel location and page reference
...a
Montblanc
Valls
Sitges
El Prat de Llobregat
✈ International airport
N
Reus
A7
Cubelles ★296
Vilanova i la Geltru ★305
— Motorway
TARRAGONA
— Major road
Ebro
0 kilometres 50
0 miles 50

Balearic Islands
Pollença ★322
Cala Saint Vicenç ★316
Alcúdia
Campanet ★316
Amposta
Sóller ★326
Orient ★322
Cala Ratjada
Sant Carles de la Ràpita
Valldemonsa ★327
Deià ★310
Binissalem ★317
Vinaròs
Port d'Andratx ★323
Palma de Mallorca ★322
Randa ★323
Mallorca
San Miguel ★324
Eivissa
Menorca
MEDITERRANEAN
Ibiza ✈ ★321,324,325
SEA
Formentera
0 kilometres 50
0 miles 50

D · **E** · **F**

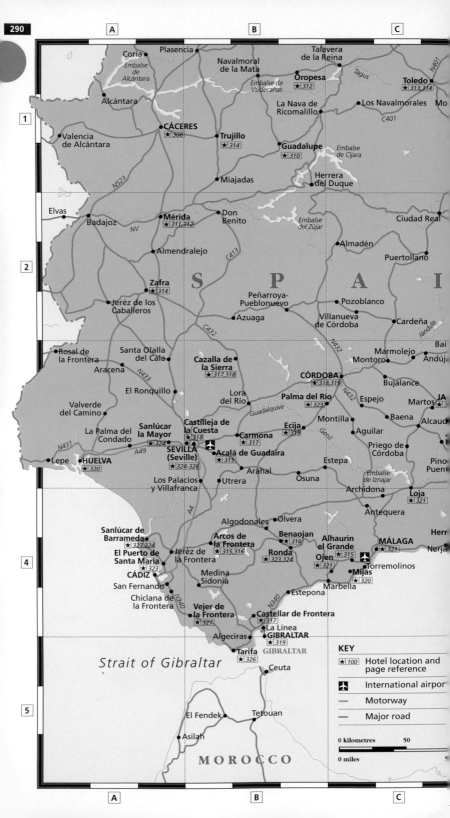

D | E | F

ranjuez • Tarancón • **CUENCA** ★ 308-310 • Cañete

CASTELLÓ DE LA PLANA
Vila-real •

Ocaña

A 31

Embalse de Alarcón

Alarcón ★ 307

N330

Lliria • • Sagvnt

1

El Toboso • • Mota del Cuervo
Pedro Muñoz
ncia • Alcázar de San Juan
• Villarrobledo

A-111

✈ **VALENCIA** ★ 327
Torrente •

Tomelloso
La Roda

Júcar

L'Alcúdia •
• Alzira

niel

• Manzanares
La Solana

Albacete •

N430
Almansa •

Gandía
Xátiva ★ 327

Denia ★ 319

agro
• Valdepeñas

N322

N301

Villena •

Castell de Castells ★ 317

Moraira ★ 321

Villanueva de los Infantes

Hellín •

Yecla •

Alcoy • **Penaguila** ★ 323

Benidorm •

N

Jumilla •

Elda •
San Juan de Alicante •

La Villa Joiosa ★ 327

2

arolina

N322

Embalse del Cenajo

ALICANTE (Alacant)

Segura

Los Marines

Cieza •

Moratalla •

Archena ★ 315

Elche ✈ ★ 319

• **Tabarca** ★ 326

res
uadalimar

• Villacarrillo

Caravaca de la Cruz •

Mula •

Orihuela •

Ubeda ★ 326,327

Cazorla ★ 318

Alcantarilla •

MURCIA ★ 321

Torrevieja •

16
• Jódar • Quesada

Huéscar •

Alhama de Murcia •

N332

• Baeza

Totana •

A92

Lorca •

Mazarrón • • Cartagena

3

A92
• Guadix

Albox •

Aguilas •

N334

ANADA ★ 319,320

N340

MEDITERRANEAN

• **Sierra Nevada** ★ 326

Bubión ★ 317

Turre • • **Mojacar**
★ 326 ★ 320

SEA

Orgiva ★ 322

Berja •

Pechina ★ 322

otril *N340*
Adra •

ALMERÍA

4

Gualchos •

San Jose ★ 323

The Canary Islands

0 kilometres 50
0 miles 50

• **Barlovento** ★ 316

Los Llanos de Aridane •
• Santa Cruz de la Palma
• Brena Baja

La Palma
Fuencalience •

Puerto de la Cruz •

San Cristobal de la Laguna •

Santa Cruz de Tenerife •

5

La Gomera

San Sebastián de l Gomera ★ 324

Tenerife

Las Palmas de Gran Canaria •

Santa Maria de Gufa •

Tafira Alta • • Telde

El Hierro
• Valverde

San Nicolas de Tolentino •

Gran Canaria

Frontera •

Melilla •

D

NORTHERN SPAIN

GALICIA • ASTURIAS • CANTABRIA • BASQE COUNTRY
NAVARRA • ARAGON • LA RIOJA • CATALONIA

W*ITH ITS ATLANTIC climate, the north coast is surprisingly green. The Pyrenees make a wonderful setting for rustic retreats, and, to the east, there are a few still unspoilt fishing villages on the Costa Brava. Northern Spain offers a vast choice of accommodation, from mountain hideaways, village inns and country mansions to palaces and converted monasteries, seaside villas and resort hotels. The great selection from the state-run parador network ranges from crenellated hilltop castles with vaulted rooms to handsome modern buildings. In Barcelona, the principal city of the north, are many large hotels, some ultra-modern, others with simpler old-world charm.*

AGUILAR DE CAMPÓO	AIGUA BLAVA

Monasterio de Santa María la Real Typical of the region's Romanesque architecture, this mellow stone, timbered Cistercian monastery has been thoughtfully converted. Much of the original craftsmanship has been preserved, with duplex bedrooms in the old dormitories and a barn of a restaurant.
⊠ Avenida Cervera s/n, 34800 Aguilar de Campóo, Palencia. **Map** p287 E2. ☎ (979) 122000. ☎ (979) 601122. @ fundacion@jet.es ▮ b,l,d. **Rooms** 18. ▮ ● Christmas. ☎ MC, V. ℗

Aigua Blava A hotel that puts a tasteful slant on the idea of the holiday village. It is located over pine-covered cliffs and flower-filled gardens, at the head of a picturesque creek, and its group of pristine whitewashed buildings contain everything you could possibly need.
⊠ Playa de Fornells, 17255 Aigua Blava, Gerona. **Map** p289 F3. ☎ (972) 622058. ☎ (972) 622112. @ hotelaiguablava@aiguablava.com ▮ b,l,d. **Rooms** 89. ▮ ▭ ▯ ▮ ● early Nov to late Feb. ☎ AE, DC, MC, V. ℗℗

ARGÓMANIZ
Parador de Argómaniz An ideal stopover, a handsome old building with a cavernous dining hall and sober, well-equipped bedrooms.
⊠ Carretera N1, 01192 Argómaniz, Alava. **Map** p287 F2, p288 A2. ☎ (945) 293200. ☎ (945) 293287. ▮ b,l,d. **Rooms** 53. ℗℗

ARTIES
Besiberri Modern variation on the Swiss chalet theme, complete with balconies. Cosy, and family-run, it provides all the necessary comforts after a hard day on the ski slopes.
⊠ El Fuerte 4, 25599 Arties, Lérida. **Map** p289 D2. ☎ (973) 640829. ☎ (973) 644260. ▮ b. **Rooms** 17. ℗

ARTIES
Parador Don Gaspar de Portolá By the smart ski resort of Baqueira-Beret, a parador littered with hunting trophies and comfy chairs.
⊠ Carretera de Baqueira, 25599 Arties, Lérida. **Map** p289 D2. ☎ (973) 640801. ☎ (973) 641001. ▮ b,l,d. **Rooms** 57. ℗℗℗

ASTORGA
Gaudí Excellent *tapas* are served in the bar of this elegant modern hotel (marble floors, chandeliers) on the main square.
⊠ Plaza Eduardo de Castro 6, 24700 Astorga, León. **Map** p286 D3. ☎ (987) 615654. ☎ (987) 615040. ▮ b,l,d. **Rooms** 35. ℗℗

ALCAÑIZ

Parador de Alcañiz A hill castle, 12th-century but remodelled some 600 years later, which combines the romance of the past – Gothic walls, cloisters, medieval murals - with the comforts of the present – white-walled bedrooms with carved furniture and tiled floors. Generous meals are served in a massive beamed dining hall.
⊠ Castillo Calatravos s/n, 44600 Alcañiz, Teruel. **Map** p288 C4. **(** (978) 830400. **FAX** (978) 830366. **††** b,l,d. **Rooms** 12. 🗐 🖲 ◉ mid-Dec to early Feb. 🗲 AE, DC, MC, V. ⓟⓟ

AMANDI

La Casona de Amandi At the foot of the Asturias, yet only ten miles from the beaches, La Casona has the look and feel of a much-loved home. Surrounded by a huge flower-packed garden, it has several small sitting rooms inside, with good antique furniture, where you can always find a corner to yourself. Bedrooms are large and, like their bathrooms, well equipped.
⊠ Amandi, 33300 Villaviciosa, Asturias. **Map** p286 D2. **(** (98) 5890130. **FAX** (98) 5890129. **††** b. **Rooms** 9. 🖲 ◉ Never. 🗲 MC, V. ⓟⓟ

BAQUEIRA-BERET

Royal Tanau At Spain's most elegant ski resort, a swanky five-star hotel: salons with rug-strewn floors and luxurious bedrooms.
⊠ Carretera de Beret s/n, Naut Aran, 25598 Baqueira-Beret, Lérida. **Map** p289 D2. **(** (973) 644446. **FAX** (973) 644344. **††** b,l,d. **Rooms** 30. ⓟⓟⓟ

BARCELONA

Arts Sophisticates flock to this 44-storey minimalist building. Rooms and duplexes, with views of city and sea, top the luxury scale.
⊠ Marina 19-21, 08005 Barcelona. **Map** p289 E4. **(** (93) 2211000. **FAX** (93) 2211070. **@** info@harts.es **††** b,l,d. **Rooms** 455. ⓟⓟⓟⓟ

BARCELONA

Claris A Neo-Classical façade masks a dazzling interior of pillars and sweeping marble floors, and at the top is a rooftop pool. It is not all uncompromising modernity though: Roman mosaics decorate walls and some bedrooms have Chesterfields and antiques. There is also a small museum of Egyptian treasures.
⊠ Pau Claris 150, 08009 Barcelona. **Map** p289 E4. **(** (93) 487 6262. **FAX** (93) 215 7970. **@** claris@derbyhotels.es **††** b,l,d. **Rooms** 120. 🗐 🚿 🍴 🖲 ◉ Never. 🗲 AE, MC, V. ⓟⓟⓟⓟ

BARCELONA

Condes de Barcelona In the heart of the 'Modernisma' or Art Nouveau area, this sleek, glossy hotel attracts an equally slick and glossy clientele. It occupies two 19th-century former palaces, facing each other across a quiet side street. A roof terrace, plunge pool and tempting restaurant are bonuses.
⊠ Paseo de Gracia 75, 08008 Barcelona. **Map** p289 E4. **(** (93) 488 2200. **FAX** (93) 488 0614. **@** cbhotel@ condesdebarcelona.com.es **††** b,l,d. **Rooms** 183. 🗐 🚿 🖲 ◉ Never. 🗲 AE, DC, MC, V. ⓟⓟⓟ

BARCELONA

Le Méridien The curved lines of the 1930s recur throughout this lavish four-star hotel. Despite its size, it is warm and welcoming.
⊠ Ramblas 111, 08002 Barcelona. **Map** p289 E4. **(** (93) 3186200. **FAX** (93) 3017776. **††** b,l,d. **Rooms** 206. ⓟⓟⓟⓟ

BARCELONA

Rivoli Ramblas Art Deco building and avant-garde design are combined in a great location. Spectacular views from the roof terrace.
⊠ La Rambla 128, 08002 Barcelona. **Map** p289 E4. **(** (93) 3026643. **FAX** (93) 3175053. **@** rivoli@alba.mssl.es **††** b,l,d. **Rooms** 90. ⓟⓟⓟⓟ

For key to symbols see backflap. For price categories *see p285*

BARCELONA

Duques de Bergara The airy foyer of this ornate Art Nouveau building has a distinctly Edwardian feel, with its imposing marble staircase, smart tiled floor and potted plants. Renovated in 1998, the decoration and furnishings are appealing thoughout. Suites have private terraces. The restaurant is Catalan.
⊠ Bergara 11, 08002 Barcelona. **Map** p289 E4.
((93) 301 5151. **FAX** (93) 317 3442. **@** cataloni@ hoteles-catalonia.es **⦶** b,l,d. **Rooms** 149. **▤ ▧ ▦ ▨**
● Never. **▨** AE, DC, MC, V. **ⓟⓟⓟ**

BARCELONA

Ritz The name alone conjures up an image of luxury and elegance, realized in each imposing salon and restaurant. Though splendid, it is not intimidating, largely due to the professional yet friendly staff. The Barcelona Ritz opened in 1919; both public rooms and bedrooms blend original fittings with modern facilities.
⊠ Gran Via de les Corts Catalanes 668, 08010 Barcelona. **Map** p289 E4. **(** (93) 318 5200. **FAX** (93) 318 0148.
@ ritz@ritzbcn.com **⦶** b,l,d. **Rooms** 125. **▤ ▨**
● Never. **▨** AE, DC, MC, V. **ⓟⓟⓟⓟ**

BARCELONA

Gran Hotel Havana The 19th-century façade belies the avant-garde design inside. The Havana has a great central location and a lively atmosphere. Live music is played each evening in the bar-lounge built around an atrium. Meticulous attention to detail is evident in the elegant bedrooms.
⊠ Gran Via de les Corts Catalanes 647, 08010 Barcelona. **Map** p289 E4. **(** (93) 4121115. **FAX** (93) 4122611.
@ hotelhavanasilken@bcn.servicom.es **⦶** b,l,d.
Rooms 145. **▤** ● Never. **▨** AE, DC, MC, V. **ⓟⓟⓟ**

BENASQUE

Hotel Ciria This central family-run hotel is one of the best in the popular skiing area of the Benasque valley. It has excellent facilities, and a warm, welcoming atmosphere nurtured by the caring Ciria family. Local lamb and game dishes are the specialities at the splendid restaurant, El Fogaril. The most attractive bedrooms are the ones in the eaves.
⊠ Avenida de los Tilos s/n, 22440 Benasque, Huesca.
Map p289 D3. **(** (974) 551612. **FAX** (974) 551686.
⦶ b,l,d. **Rooms** 42. ● Never. **▨** MC, V. **ⓟ**

BAYONA
Parador Conde de Gondomar Huge, with impressive amenities and a terrific site within a pre-Roman wall on the Monte Real peninsula.
⊠ 36300 Bayona, Pontevedra. **Map** p286 A3.
((986) 355000. **FAX** (986) 355076. **⦶** b,l,d.
Rooms 124. **ⓟⓟⓟ**

BAYONA
Villa Sol Antiques, pictures and books fill the tall rooms of this grand villa in a lush garden, home to the hospitable Rodriguez family.
⊠ Palos de la Frontera 12, 36300 Bayona, Pontevedra.
Map p286 A3. **(** (986) 355691. **FAX** (986) 356702.
⦶ b. **Rooms** 6. **ⓟⓟ**

BENASQUE
Aragüells In winter the lively bar/dining room is packed with locals and visiting skiers. Attic rooms are prettiest, but all have great views.
⊠ Avenida de los Tilos s/n, 22440 Benasque, Huesca.
Map p289 D3. **(** (974) 551619. **FAX** (974) 551664.
⦶ b. **Rooms** 19. **ⓟ**

BESNES
La Tahona A cobbled track ends at this quiet rural hotel with mountain views. Inside it has Spanish flair: all beams, whitewashed plaster walls and red tiles.
⊠ 33578 Besnes-Alles, Asturias. **Map** p287 E2.
(**FAX** (98) 5415749. **⦶** b,l,d. **Rooms** 19. **ⓟⓟ**

BOLVIR

Torre del Remei Up in the Pyrenean forest, Josep María and Loles Boix have created a winner in their stylish Belle Epoque summer palace. Exquisitely decorated with Grecian marble, Italian furniture and Tibetan carpets, it also boasts an exceptional restaurant and personal service. Golf, riding and mountain-climbing nearby.

Camí Reial s/n, 17463 Bolvir, Gerona. **Map** p289 E3. (972) 140182. **FAX** (972) 140449. @ t.remei@gro.servicom.es b,l,d. **Rooms** 10. Never. AE, DC, MC, V. ®®®®

CAMPRODON

Edelweiss Standing in the heart of a pretty Pyrenean town, with hills rising behind it, is this four-star hotel with a pleasing brick façade and balconied, white-shuttered windows. Inside are public rooms with panelled walls and ceilings, like large polished wooden boxes, dotted with tasteful reproduction furniture.

Carretera de Sant Joan 28, 17867 Camprodon, Gerona. **Map** p289 E3. (972) 740614. **FAX** (972) 740605. b,d. **Rooms** 21. Christmas. MC, V. ®®

BURGOS

Landa Palace The 1960s realization of a Gothic fantasy, described variously as charming and pretentious. Its origins lie in a 14th-century tower, bought by a restaurateur, who had it dismantled and rebuilt on the Madrid road. Around it, he built the rest: vaulted pool and dining room, spiral stairs and sumptuous suites.

Carretera Madrid km235, 09000 Burgos. **Map** p287 E3. (947) 206343. **FAX** (947) 264676. @ landapal@teleline.es b,l,d. **Rooms** 42. Never. MC, V. ®®®

CARDONA

Parador Duques de Cardona Commanding panoramic views in every direction, this mellow medieval fortress seems to grow out of the rocky hilltop. The interior is equally impressive, with a sense of period evoked through the solid oak furniture and rich fabrics. But the attraction for both locals and visitors is the imaginative regional cuisine served in the fine dining room.

Castillo s/n, 08261 Cardona, Barcelona. **Map** p289 E3. (93) 8691275. **FAX** (93) 8691636. b,l,d. **Rooms** 60. Never. AE, DC, MC, V. ®®

BIELSA

Parador del Monte Perdido In a remote valley of streams and stunning scenery is this modern parador with rustic rooms. In winter the focal point is the roaring open fire.

22350 Bielsa, Huesca. **Map** p288 C2. (974) 501011. **FAX** (974) 501188. b,l,d. **Rooms** 26. ®®®

BOLVIR

Chalet del Golf On a golf course and popular with enthusiasts, this newish chalet has an abundance of wood in snug rooms.

Devesa del Golf, 17520 Bolvir-Puigcerda, Gerona. **Map** p289 E3. (972) 880962. **FAX** (972) 880966. b,l,d. **Rooms** 26. ®®

CARMONA

Venta de Carmona A government-run house in a quaint village of unpaved streets and stone houses. A useful stopover.

Barrio del Palacio, 39554 Carmona, Cantabria. **Map** p287 E2. (942) 728057. **FAX** (942) 728057. b,l,d. **Rooms** 8. ®

COMILLAS

Casal del Castro Grand drawing rooms reflec the past of this 17th-century house in a beach resort popularized by King Alfonso XII.

San Jerónimo, 39520 Comillas, Cantabria. **Map** p287 E2. (942) 720036. **FAX** (942) 720061. b,l,d. **Rooms** 42. ®®

For key to symbols see backflap. For price cate

CASTELLO DE AMPURIAS

Allioli The charm of this 200-year-old Catalan farmhouse eclipses its less-than-ideal location in a dip below a main road. Inside, its character is enhanced with well-placed lamps, antiques and flowers, and huge hams hanging to dry over the snug bar. The beamed, whitewashed bedrooms have a country elegance and spotless bathrooms.
⊠ Urbanización Castellonou, 17486 Castelló de Ampurias, Gerona. **Map** p289 F3. ((972) 250320. FAX (972) 250300. ¶¶ b,l,d. **Rooms** 39. 🍴 🔲 ● Christmas to mid-Feb. 🗐 MC, V. ®®

COVARRUBIAS

Arlanza Ask for a room on the cobbled square and watch village life go by. An old nobleman's house, the Arlanza's dark, beamed interior is done out in rustic style, with a fine tiled staircase and modestly furnished bedrooms. Meals are the highlight: soup so hot that it has to be eaten with a wooden spoon, and local wild boar.
⊠ Plaza Mayor 11, 09346 Covarrubias, Burgos. **Map** p287 F3. ((947) 406441. FAX (947) 406359. @ arlanza@ctv.es ¶¶ b,l,d. **Rooms** 37. ● mid-Dec to mid-March. 🗐 AE, DC, MC, V. ®

CASTRILLO DE LOS POLVAZARES

Hostería Cuca la Vaina In this tranquil spot, only birdsong or the morning rooster are likely to disturb your peace. A new hotel in a little medieval town, it was purpose-built in stone, wood and glass to reproduce the local architecture. The result is harmonious and stylish. All the rooms are decorated differently; even corridors are brightened with plants or flowers.
⊠ Jardín s/n, 24718 Castrillo de los Polvazares, León. **Map** p286 C3. (FAX (987) 691078. ¶¶ b,l. **Rooms** 7. 🔲 ● Jan. 🗐 V. ®

CUBELLES

Llicorella This modern building, buffered from the outside world by manicured lawns, is as much a gallery for the owners' impressive collection of contemporary art as a sophisticated four-star hotel. Most of the plush bedrooms are in an annexe at the back. The highly regarded restaurant has a bias towards seafood.
⊠ San Antonio 101, 08880 Cubelles, Barcelona. **Map** p289 E4. ((93) 8950044. FAX (93) 8952417. ¶¶ b,l,d. **Rooms** 16. 🍴 ▦ 🔲 ● Never. 🗐 AE, DC, MC, V. ®®

CORNIDE

Casa Grande de Cornide A magnolia-filled garden with an enticing pool encircles this antique-filled old house, a gem of a B&B.
⊠ Calo, Teo, 15886 Cornide, A Coruña. **Map** p286 B2. ((981) 805599. FAX (981) 805751. ¶¶ b. **Rooms** 10. ®®

COSGAYA

Hotel del Oso A traditional-style house. The facade, with its flowered balconies and arched veranda, is as charming as the cosy rooms.
⊠ Carretera Potes-Fuente Dé, 39539 Cosgaya, Cantabria. **Map** p287 E2. ((942) 733018. FAX (942) 733036. **Rooms** 50. ®

ESCAIRÓN

Torre de Vilariño A 17th-century rustic stone house in an off-the-beaten-track village. Antonio García Beltrán is a genial host.
⊠ Fión 47, 27548 Escairón, Lugo. **Map** p286 B3. ((982) 452260. FAX (982) 452260. ¶¶ b,l,d. **Rooms** 9. ®

L'ESPLUGA DE FRANCOLÍ

Hostal del Senglar Simple, whitewashed hotel in a pretty garden. Food is hearty. The dining room doubles as a rural artefacts museum.
⊠ Plaza Montserrat Canals 1, 43440 L'Espluga de Francolí, Tarragona. **Map** p289 D4. ((977) 870121. FAX (977) 870012. ¶¶ b,l,d. **Rooms** 40. ®

DONAMARÍA

Donamaria'ko Benta In one of the least spoilt parts of the Pyrenees, on a secondary pilgrim route to Santiago, this rough-stone inn is a perfect retreat for jaded town dwellers in search of a rural idyll. It is a hospitable place, too. There are two sitting rooms, furnished with originality, and modest bedrooms in an annexe.

⊠ Barrio de la Venta 4, 31750 Donamaría, Navarra. **Map** p288 B2. **(** (948) 450925. **FAX** (948) 450708. @ donamariako@jet.es **₁₁** b,l,d. **Rooms** 5. 🗏 🚯 ● Never. 🗲 MC, V. ℗

FIGUERAS

Mas Pau Just outside Figueras, home to the Dali museum, stands this 17th-century farmhouse in mature grounds. The public rooms are done out in *modernista* style (Spanish Art Nouveau), with mirrors, wicker chairs and ferns; old photographs jostle for space on stone walls. The seven suites are restful in pink and grey.

⊠ Avinyonet de Puigventós, 17742 Figueras, Gerona. **Map** p286 C2. **(** (972) 546154. **FAX** (972) 546326. @ maspau@grn.es **₁₁** b,l,d. **Rooms** 7. 🗏 🏊 🚯 ● early Jan to Easter. 🗲 AE, DC, MC, V. ℗℗

ESCALANTE

San Román de Escalante A refined 17th-century house is the setting for this restaurant with rooms, plenty of class and a Michelin star. Guests who stroll in the lovely garden will encounter modern sculptures, while the period-style rooms are filled with paintings, old and new.

⊠ Carretera de Escalante-Castillo km2, 39795 Escalante, Cantabria. **Map** p287 F2, p288 A2. **(** (942) 677745. **FAX** (942) 677643. @ sanromanescalante@mundivia.es **₁₁** b,l,d. **Rooms** 10. 🚯 ● late Dec to late Jan. 🗲 AE, DC, MC, V. ℗℗

FIGUERAS DEL MAR

Palacete Peñalba This confection of a house, built in 1912 by a follower of Gaudí, is now a national monument. Signs of its eccentric Art Nouveau style are much in evidence: the curved double stairs to the entrance, the glazed and tiled atrium, and the original furniture that has been preserved. Meals can be taken in the owners' waterfront restaurant.

⊠ El Cotarelo s/n, 33794 Figueras del Mar, Asturias. **Map** p286 C2. **(** (98) 5636125. **FAX** (98) 5636247. **₁₁** b. **Rooms** 14. 🚯 ● Never. 🗲 AE, MC, V. ℗

L'ESPLUGA DE FRANCOLÍ
Masia del Cadet Family-run hotel with a warm welcome, hearty Catalan food, low prices and proximity to Poblet's fine monastery.

⊠ Les Masies de Poblet, 43440 L'Espluga de Francolí, Tarragona. **Map** p289 D4. **(** (977) 870869. **FAX** (977) 870496. **₁₁** b,l,d. **Rooms** 12. ℗℗

FUENTE DÉ
Parador Río Deva The stupendous panoramic setting, high in the Picos de Europa, makes up for the dull rooms at this modern parador.

⊠ 39588 Fuente Dé, Cantabria. **Map** p287 D2. **(** (942) 736651. **FAX** (942) 736654. **₁₁** b,l,d. **Rooms** 78. ℗℗

HARO
Los Agustinos The heart of the old monastery is the vast sitting room, its beamed ceiling crossed by arches. Plain bedrooms.

⊠ San Agustin 2, 26200 Haro, La Rioja. **Map** p287 F3, p288 A3. **(** (941) 311308. **FAX** (941) 303148. **₁₁** b,l,d. **Rooms** 62. ℗℗

LEKUMBERRI
Ayestaran This friendly hotel is split between summer and winter buildings. Inside both are simple but with welcoming rooms, crammed with good Basque furniture.

⊠ Aralarso, 31870 Lekumberri, Navarra. **Map** p288 B3. **(** **FAX** (948) 504127. **₁₁** b,l,d. **Rooms** 90. ℗

For key to symbols see backflap. For price categories *see p285*

FORMIGAL

Villa de Sallent There is no off-season for this hotel at the foot of a Pyrenean ski resort: in summer, it's a base for walkers. A modern building of stone and slate, it has a wood-panelled interior full of pine furniture that lends it a Scandinavian feel. The owners are restaurateurs so satisfying meals are guaranteed.

☒ Urbanización Formigal, 22640 Sallent de Gállego, Huesca. **Map** p288 C2. ☎ (974) 490223. 🖷 (974) 490150. 🍽 b,l,d. **Rooms** 41. 🅱 ◐ Never. 🗲 AE, DC, MC, V. ⓟⓟ

GRANOLLERS

Fonda Europa In a pleasant market town, behind a distinctive orange façade with blue and white panels, is this delightfully traditional Catalan hotel. It has been in the capable hands of the Parellada family since 1714. They have furnished the hotel with taste and refinement, and provide unfailingly courteous service.

☒ Anselm Clavé 1, 08400 Granollers, Barcelona. **Map** p289 E3. ☎ (93) 8700312. 🖷 (93) 8707901. 🍽 b,l,d. **Rooms** 7. 🗐 ◐ Never. 🗲 AE, DC, MC, V. ⓟⓟ

LA GARRIGA

Termes la Garriga In a spa town 35km (22 miles) north of Barcelona, this is ideal for the energetic or those keen to get into shape: there's a health centre with fitness programmes, a pool, bikes for guests' use and golf nearby. Even if keeping fit leaves you cold, the yellow-painted hotel with light, elegantly decorated rooms is a comfortable base. Children are not accepted.

☒ Banys 23, 08530 La Garriga, Barcelona. **Map** p289 F3. ☎ (93) 8717086. 🖷 (93) 8717887. **Rooms** 22. 🗐 ▦ 🍽 🅱 ◐ Never. 🗲 AE, DC, MC, V. ⓟⓟⓟⓟ

A GUARDA

Convento de San Benito Behind its simple exterior, the interior of this 16th-century convent has been restored with sympathy and flair. Reception is in the old portico, where ornate detailing has been preserved. Also intact are the cloister, fountain and turnstiles, which gave the nuns access to the outside world. The converted cells make charming bedrooms.

☒ Plaza de San Benito s/n, 36780 A Guarda, Pontevedra. **Map** p286 A3. ☎ (986) 611166. 🖷 (986) 611517. 🍽 b. **Rooms** 24. 🗐 🅱 ◐ Never. 🗲 AE, MC, V. ⓟ

LENA

Hostería del Huerna Modest mountain hotel, a favourite with *Madrileños* seeking a cheap weekend break. In winter, the snug salon has an open fire. Rather small bedrooms.

☒ Riopaso, 33630 Lena, Asturias. **Map** p287 D2. ☎ (98) 5496414. 🖷 (98) 5496431. 🍽 b,l,d. **Rooms** 30. ⓟ

LLANARS

Hotel Grèvol A well-equipped Pyrenean base, which reinvents the classic Tyrolean chalet.

☒ Carretera de Camprodon a Setcases s/n, 17869 Llanars, Gerona. **Map** p289 E3. ☎ (972) 741013. 🖷 (972) 741087. @ info@hotelgrevol.com 🍽 b,l,d. **Rooms** 36. ⓟⓟⓟ

LLANES

La Arquera Modern B&B with bright, cheerful exterior and mountain views, handy for the pretty port of Llanes and its beaches.

☒ La Arquera s/n, 33500 Llanes, Asturias. **Map** p287 E2. ☎ (98) 5402424. 🖷 (98) 5400175. 🍽 b. **Rooms** 13. ⓟⓟ

LLANES

Gran Hotel Paraiso In the lively main street close to the seafront, this contemporary hotel has standard rooms and small apartments ideal for families.

☒ Pidal 2, 33500 Llanes, Asturias. **Map** p287 E2. ☎ (98) 5401971. 🖷 (98) 5402590. 🍽 b. **Rooms** 22. ⓟ

HONDARRIBIA (FUENTERRABIA)

Obispo This elegant Renaissance house has been converted with restraint. The traditional stone and wood interior, set about with period furniture, has been softened by light, floral fabrics and each bedroom designed with style. There is a terrace with views over the bay, two sitting rooms and a cafeteria.

☒ Plaza del Obispo, 20280 Hondarribia, Guipúzcoa. **Map** p288 B2. ☎ (943) 645400. ℻ (943) 642386. @ bidasoa@camerdata.es ⬚ b. **Rooms** 17. 🔅 ⬤ late Dec to mid-Jan. 🅮 AE, MC, V. ⓟⓟ

HONDARRIBIA (FUENTERRABIA)

Parador de Hondarribia Everything about this 12th-century castle is simply stunning. Friendly staff, modern comforts and medieval architecture combine to produce a warmth and elegance with instant appeal. Each antique-filled room has its own character; a lovely courtyard invites relaxation. The parador needs no restaurant as the local selection is excellent.

☒ Plaza de Armas 14, 20280 Hondarribia, Guipúzcoa. **Map** p288 B2. ☎ (943) 645500. ℻ (943) 642153. ⬚ b. **Rooms** 36. ⬤ Never. 🅮 AE, DC, MC, V. ⓟⓟ

HONDARRIBIA (FUENTERRABIA)

Pampinot Expect a warm welcome in this 16th-century house at the heart of Hondarribia. The stone entrance hall sets off carefully chosen antiques; at the top of a beautiful columned staircase are the simpler bedrooms, some with frescoed ceilings. The Pampipot has no restaurant, but there are plenty nearby.

☒ Kale Nagusia 5, Apartado 93, 20280 Hondarribia, Guipúzcoa. **Map** p288 B2. ☎ (943) 640600. ℻ (943) 645128. ⬚ b. **Rooms** 8. ⬤ Nov. 🅮 AE, DC, MC, V. ⓟⓟ

LAGUARDIA

Castillo el Collado This unusual hotel represents one man's dream of a lifetime. Señor Javier spent ten years converting the *castillo* (fortified manor) and has furnished it with flair. All the bedrooms are differently done out with an appealing hint of decadence. There is a bar, smart restaurant and fine selection of Riojas in the cellar.

☒ Paseo El Collado, 01300 Laguardia, Alava. **Map** p287 F3. ☎ (941) 121200. ℻ (941) 600878. ⬚ b,l,d. **Rooms** 8. 🖩 🔅 ⬤ Never. 🅮 AE, DC, MC, V. ⓟⓟ

MUNDAKA

El Puerto A simple, traditional house with shady garden, much-loved by surfers who flock to this part of the Basque coast.

☒ Portu Kalea 1, 48360 Mundaka, Vizcaya. **Map** p287 F2, p288 A2. ☎ (94) 6876725. ℻ (94) 6876726. ⬚ b. **Rooms** 11. ⓟ

OVIEDO

Hotel de la Reconquista Sumptuous salons and bedrooms behind an impressive façade.

☒ Gil de Jaz 16, 33004 Oviedo, Asturias. **Map** p287 D2. ☎ (98) 5241100. ℻ (98) 5241166. @ Reconquista@hoteldelareconquista.com.es ⬚ b,l,d. **Rooms** 142. ⓟⓟⓟⓟ

PERATALLADA

Castell de Peratallada Medieval castle with splendid vaulted dining room and tented beds.

☒ Plaça del Castell, 17113 Peratallada, Baix Empordà, Gerona. **Map** p289 F3. ☎ (972) 634021. ℻ (972) 634011. @ casteperat@aplitec.com ⬚ b,l,d. **Rooms** 5. ⓟⓟⓟ

PUEBLA DE TRIVES

Casa Grande de Trives Limoges china, antiques and paintings fill the elegant interior of this distinguished 18th-century house.

☒ Marqués de Trives 17, 32780 Pobra de Trives, Orense. **Map** p286 B3. ☎ ℻ (988) 332066. ⬚ b. **Rooms** 7. ⓟⓟ

LAGUARDIA

Posada Mayor de Migueloa Great sensitivity shows in the conversion of this 17th-century stone mansion. Historically everything is of a piece, and beams, stone walls and floors, carpets and writing desks take you back to Spain's Golden Century. The owners, experts on Rioja, also produce delicious food.

⊠ Mayor de Migueloa 20, 01300 Laguardia, Alava. **Map** p287 F3. ((941) 121175. ℻ (941) 121022. ‖ b,l,d. **Rooms** 8. 🖩 ⚏ ⓪ ⬤ Never. 🗹 AE, MC, V. ℗℗

LLANES

El Habana This peaceful country hotel at the foot of the Sierra de Cuerra range simply bursts with character. Bedrooms are spacious. Some face the mountains; all have heated brick floors, antique furniture and modern bathrooms. Wander in the vast gardens, swim in the pool, or visit one of 30 local beaches.

⊠ El Pedroso s/n, 33509 La Pereda, Llanes, Asturias. **Map** p287 E2. ((98) 5402526. ℻ (98) 5402075. @ elhabana@ftpweb.com ‖ b,l,d. **Rooms** 10. ⚏ ⓪ ⬤ Never. 🗹 MC, V. ℗℗

LEÓN

Parador Hotel de San Marcos This 16th-century former monastery has a monumental Renaissance façade, a superb cloister and epic public rooms. Good pictures (ancient and modern), tapestries and excellent furniture dress the interior. One drawing room has a carved sandalwood ceiling. Most bedrooms are in a modern annexe, overlooking the gardens and river.

⊠ Plaza San Marcos 7, 24001 León. **Map** p287 D30. ((987) 237300. ℻ (987) 233458. ‖ b,l,d. **Rooms** 200. 🖩 ⓪ ⬤ Never. 🗹 AE, DC, MC, V. ℗℗℗

LLANES

La Posada de Babel Camelias and fruit trees flourish in the seclusion of the small park that surrounds this alluring hotel. It is housed in a striking modern building, the back of which is entirely glazed, bringing the garden inside. Inside, the style is traditional, with period furniture and paintings. One of the bedrooms is in a separate little cottage.

⊠ La Pereda, 33509 Llanes, Asturias. **Map** p287 E2. ((985) 402525. ℻ (985) 402622. ‖ b,l,d. **Rooms** 11. 🖩 ⓪ ⬤ Never. 🗹 AE, DC, MC, V. ℗℗

PONT DE MOLINS

El Molí This old mill, furnished with antique-shop bargains, has a fine restaurant and a few modestly priced bedrooms.

⊠ Carretera les Escaules, 17706 Pont de Molins, Gerona. **Map** p289 F3. ((972) 529271. ℻ (972) 529101. @ molipark@speedrom.es ‖ b,l,d. **Rooms** 8. ℗

PONTEVEDRA

Parador Casa del Barón Rooms are hung with tapestries and paintings at this refined yet welcoming parador in the old town.

⊠ Maceda s/n, 36002 Pontevedra. **Map** p286 A3. ((986) 855800. ℻ (986) 852195. ‖ b,l,d. **Rooms** 47. ℗℗

PUENTE LA REINA

Mesón del Peregrino Once a staging post for pilgrims to Santiago, now a stylish restaurant with rooms and a fine gastronomic reputation.

⊠ Carretera de Pamplona 11, 31100 Puente La Reina, Navarra. **Map** p288 B3. ((948) 340075. ℻ (948) 341190. ‖ b,l,d. **Rooms** 14. ℗℗

QUIJAS

Posada de La Torre de Quijas Antique-filled but child-friendly stone mansion – lots of books and toys are available.

⊠ Barrio Vinueva 76, 39590 Quijas, Cantabria. **Map** p287 E2. ((942) 820833. ℻ (942) 838050. ‖ b. **Rooms** 20. ℗

MARANGES

Can Borrell At the head of a valley near Andorra, in a picture-postcard mountain village nearly 1,500m (5,000ft) above sea-level, is this family-run farmhouse. Rooms have wonderful wood ceilings and beams; one has a breathtaking view. Service is friendly and personal, and the restaurant deserves its high local reputation.
☒ Retorn 3, 17539 Maranges, Girona. **Map** p289 E3. ☎ (972) 880033. ᴀ̲ᴄ̲ (972) 880144. @ info@canborrell.com ⦙⦙ b,l,d. **Rooms** 8. ◐ Mon-Fri early Jan to May. ✉ MC, V. ℗℗

NEDA

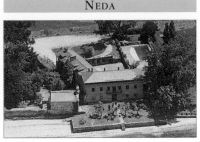

Pazo da Merced On the grassy bank of the Ría del Ferrol a handsome 17th-century house of dressed stone has been transformed by its architect owner into a stunning, homely B&B. Walls of ancient stone and glass abut, and antiques sit happily beside contemporary furniture. Polished wood floors gleam in the comfortable bedrooms.
☒ 15510 Neda, La Coruña. **Map** p286 B2. ☎ (981) 382200. ᴀ̲ᴄ̲ (981) 380104. ⦙⦙ b. **Rooms** 5. ⇆ ᵼᵼ ◑ ◐ Never. ✉ AE, DC, MC, V. ℗℗

MUNDAKA

Atalya Close to the fishing port of Mundaka, the Atalya is the best hotel on this stretch of coast, and as tranquil as the church and shoreline it overlooks. It is scrupulously maintained; rooms are rather small, but they are attractively done out and the beds are large. The aroma of fresh bread and coffee is an irresistible call to breakfast.
☒ Itxaropen Kalea 1, 48360 Mundaka, Vizcaya. **Map** p287 F2, p288 A2. ☎ (94) 6876888. ᴀ̲ᴄ̲ (94) 6876899. ⦙⦙ b. **Rooms** 15. ◑ ◐ Never. ✉ AE, DC, MC, V. ℗℗

NUÉVALOS

Monasterio de Piedra The centuries drop away as you walk the long, echoing corridors or climb the massive vaulted stairs of this 12th-century Cistercian monastery, transporting you back in time. Much of the original building is intact: cloisters, frescoes and alabaster windows that cast a dreamy opaque light. The former cells are now modern bedrooms.
☒ 50210 Nuévalos, Zaragoza. **Map** p288 B4. ☎ (976) 849011. ᴀ̲ᴄ̲ (976) 849054. ⦙⦙ b,l,d. **Rooms** 61. ⇆ ◑ ◐ Never. ✉ AE, DC, MC, V. ℗

RONCESVALLES (ORREAGA)

La Posada Views are of forests and mountains from this simple inn. Bedrooms have pretty floor tiles from Valencia. Food is robust
☒ Carretera de Francia s/n, 31650 Roncesvalles, Navarra. **Map** p288 B2. ☎ ᴀ̲ᴄ̲ (948) 760225. ⦙⦙ b,l,d. **Rooms** 18. ℗

SALAS

Castillo de Valdés-Salas Atmospheric castle redolent of the 16th century, with thick stone walls and cloisters around a paved courtyard.
☒ Plaza de la Campa s/n, 33860 Salas, Asturias. **Map** p286 C2. ☎ (98) 5832222. ᴀ̲ᴄ̲ (98) 5832299. ⦙⦙ b,l,d. **Rooms** 12. ℗

SAN SEBASTIÁN (DONOSTIA)

Hotel de Londres y de Inglaterra The grandeur of a bygone era is maintained in this white-stuccoed seafront hotel.
☒ Zubieta 2, 20007 San Sebastián, Guipúzcoa. **Map** p288 B2. ☎ (943) 426989. ᴀ̲ᴄ̲ (943) 420031. @ hotel.londres@nauta.es ⦙⦙ b,l,d. **Rooms** 145. ℗℗℗

SANTA MARÍA DE MAVE

Hostería El Convento A handsome medieval convent in orchards, abutting a lovely church. Accommodation is plain but comfortable.
☒ 34492 Santa María de Mave, Palencia. **Map** p287 E3. ☎ (979) 123611. ᴀ̲ᴄ̲ (979) 125492. @ convento@arrakis.com ⦙⦙ b,l,d. **Rooms** 25. ℗

For key to symbols see backflap. For price categories see p285

OLITE

PRAVIA

Parador del Príncipe de Viana Occupying part of an ancient castle, the former residence of the kings of Navarre, this parador has all the usual attributes: huge rooms, heavy furniture, tapestries and a baronial air. It also has a good kitchen. The bedrooms, in a rebuilt wing, are mundane compared to the rest of the building.

Plaza de los Teobaldos 2, 31390 Olite, Navarra. **Map** p288 B3. (948) 740000. FAX (948) 740201. b,l,d. **Rooms** 43. Never. AE, DC, MC, V.

Casa del Busto From the outside, there is little suggestion of the building's 16th-century origins as a minor palace. Inside, however, there is an abundance of handsome dark wood and stone, two inner tile-floored courtyards and a tangible sense of history. The bedrooms, beamed and furnished in regional style, are attractive and relaxing at modest prices.

Plaza del Rey Don Silo 1, 33120 Pravia, Asturias. **Map** p287 D2. (98) 5822771. FAX (98) 5822772. b,l,d. **Rooms** 27. Never. AE, MC, V.

PERAMOLA

QUIJAS

Can Boix Far from the crowds, a white, modern hotel with large well-equipped rooms, by the foot of the Roca del Corb and overlooking the green valley of the Río Segre. Joan Pallarès, the owner/chef, is a cheerfully visible presence who has a deft touch in his kitchen.

Can Boix s/n, 25790 Peramola, Lleida. **Map** p289 D3. (973) 470266. FAX (973) 470281. canboixperamola@cempresarial.com b,l,d. **Rooms** 29. mid-Jan to mid-Feb, 2 weeks Nov. AE, DC, MC, V.

Hotel Hostería de Quijas Gardens mature over time, and the one in which this 18th-century former palace is set has been well cared for over the past two centuries. Inside are antiques and uncovered stonework, with wooden beams and pillars in the dining room. The whole place is a haven of peace and quiet – especially if you have a room on the garden side.

39590 Quijas, Cantabria. **Map** p287 E2. (942) 820833. FAX (942) 838050. b,l,d. **Rooms** 19. late Dec to early Jan. AE, DC, MC, V.

SANTANDER

Romano This good-value B&B is conveniently close to the ferry terminal. Rooms are modestly furnished, but well maintained and with gleaming wood floors.

Federico Vial 8, 39009 Santander, Cantabria. **Map** p287 E2. FAX (942) 223071. b. **Rooms** 25.

SANTIAGO DE COMPOSTELA

Hostal Hogar San Francisco The style is mainly contemporary but elements such as the lovely beamed cloisters recall its monastic past.

Capillo de San Francisco 3, 15705 Santiago de Compostela. **Map** p286 B2. (981) 572463. FAX (981) 571916. b,l,d. **Rooms** 71.

SANTILLANA DEL MAR

Los Infantes Stone floors and vast carved chests, high beamed ceilings and chandeliers in this characterful 18th-century house.

Avenida Le Dorat 1, 39330 Santillana del Mar, Cantabria. **Map** p287 E20. (942) 818100. FAX (942) 840103. b,l,d. **Rooms** 30.

SANTILLANA DEL MAR

Posada Santa Juliana Beamed bedrooms share the town's medieval flavour. No public rooms, meals are served in the bar opposite.

Carrera 19, 39330 Santillana del Mar, Cantabria. **Map** p287 E2. (942) 840106. FAX (942) 840170. b,l,d. **Rooms** 6.

S'AGARÓ

Hostal de la Gavina With not one but two fine Costa Brava beaches on view from its perch on a promontory, this private palace has gradually become a public one. Wall-to-wall antiques include exquisite tapestries, and each room has a different style. The cuisine skilfully marries seafood with the best of local produce.
⊠ Plaza de la Rosaleda, 17248 S'Agaró, Gerona. **Map** p289 F3. █ (972) 321100. ☎ (972) 321573. @ gavina@eponet.es ❚❚ b,l,d. **Rooms** 73. 🗐 ⛲ 📺 🔊 ● mid-Oct to Easter. ⊠ AE, DC, MC, V. ℙℙℙℙ

SAN SEBASTIÁN (DONOSTIA)

Maria Cristina This grand hotel is a picture of elegance with its Louis XV and *belle époque* public rooms, yet the Maria Cristina is bang up to date behind the scenes. Bedrooms are light, fresh and meticulously kept. The stone-columned 'Easo' restaurant serves excellent Basque specialities. Service is excellent.
⊠ Oquendo 1, 20004 San Sebastián, Guipúzcoa. **Map** p288 B2. █ (943) 424900. ☎ (943) 423914. @ hmc@sheraton.com ❚❚ b,l,d. **Rooms** 136. 🗐 🔊 ● Never. ⊠ AE, DC, MC, V. ℙℙℙℙ

SALLENT DE GÁLLEGO

Almud Mariano Martín de Cáceres and his wife, María José, have converted an old stable block into a village B&B with exquisite taste. He is an architect and she has a passion for antiques. Her finds and family heirlooms fill the beautifully decorated yet homely rooms. A night here feels more like staying with friends than in a hotel.
⊠ Espadilla 3, 22640 Sallent de Gállego, Huesca. **Map** p288 C2. █ ☎ (974) 488366. @ hotel_almud@ctv.es ❚❚ b. **Rooms** 8. 🔊 ● Never. ⊠ AE, DC, MC, V. ℙ

SANTA CRISTINA D'ARÓ

Hotel Mas Torrellas This restored country house is a triumph of personality and keen pricing over pampering. Catalan vaultings support almost every ceiling. Bedrooms are neat and clean; try for one with a view. The cellar bar has wine barrels from every Spanish region.
⊠ Carretera Santa Cristina a Playa de Aro km1,713, 17246 Santa Cristina de Aró, Gerona. **Map** p289 F3. █ (972) 837526. ☎ (972) 837527. ❚❚ b,l,d. **Rooms** 18. 🗐 ⛲ 📺 🔊 ● late Oct to mid-Mar. ⊠ AE, DC, MC, V. ℙ

SANTILLANA DEL MAR
Siglo XVIII This manor outside the medieval town has been revamped in exuberant Baroque style with countless gilt mirrors. Pool.
⊠ Revolgo s/n, 39330 Santillana del Mar, Cantabria. **Map** p287 E2. █ (942) 840210. ☎ (942) 840211. ❚❚ b. **Rooms** 16. ℙ

SANTO DOMINGO DE LA CALZADA
Parador de Santo Domingo de la Calzada Built around an old pilgrims' hostel, a parador with a modern feel despite the stone vaulting.
⊠ Plaza del Santo 3, 26250 Santo Domingo de la Calzada, La Rioja. **Map** p287 F3. █ (941) 340300. ☎ (941) 340325. ❚❚ b,l,d. **Rooms** 61. ℙℙℙ

SOS DEL REY CATÓLICO
Parador Fernando de Aragón The food and the views are the attractions of this modern, rustic-style parador in a captivating hill village.
⊠ Arquitecto Sainz de Vicuña 1, 50680 Sos del Rey Católico, Zaragoza. **Map** p288 B3. █ (948) 888011. ☎ (948) 888100. ❚❚ b,l,d. **Rooms** 65. ℙℙ

TARAMUNDI
La Rectoral In a remote location in spectacular country, this attractive 18th-century stone house adheres to regional traditions in decoration and cooking.
⊠ 33775 Taramundi, Asturias. **Map** p286 C2. █ (98) 5646767. ☎ (98) 5646777. ❚❚ b,l,d. **Rooms** 18. ℙℙ

SANTANDER

Las Brisas For an elegant 19th-century villa at low prices, head for this yellow-and-white affair in a quiet area of Santander by the Sandinero beach. Jesús García, an English speaker, owns and runs this friendly hotel of 12 smallish but stylish bedrooms and smart bathrooms. Pleasant garden.

⊠ La Braña 14, 39005 Santander, Cantabria. **Map** p287 E2. 【 (942) 270991. ℻ (942) 281173. ⊞ b,d. **Rooms** 13. ◐ ● Never. ▣ AE, DC, MC, V. ℗℗

SANTIAGO DE COMPOSTELA

Parador 'Hostal de los Reyes Catolicós' Stroll in the cloisters of one of the four magical courtyards, as travellers have for 500 years, and you will feel a palpable sense of history. Europe's oldest hotel was opened in 1499 as a pilgrims' hostel. The façade is breathtaking, and salons and bedrooms rich and grand.

⊠ Plaza do Obradoiro 1, 15705 Santiago de Compostela, La Coruña. **Map** p286 B2. 【 (981) 582200. ℻ (981) 563094. ⊞ b,l,d. **Rooms** 136. ◐ ● Never. ▣ AE, DC, MC, V. ℗℗℗

SANTANDER

Real King Alfonso XIII used to summer in Santander and the Real was built in 1917 for his entourage. Today, its five stars should stand for location (it's on a spectacular site overlooking the bay), amenities, staff, atmosphere and an unstuffy elegance. You probably have to leave Cantabria to do better.

⊠ Paseo Pérez Galdós 28, 39005 Santander, Cantabria. **Map** p287 E2. 【 (942) 272550. ℻ (942) 274573. @ realsantander@husa.es ⊞ b,d. **Rooms** 123. ▤ ◐ ● Never. ▣ AE, DC, MC, V. ℗℗℗℗

SANTILLANA DEL MAR

PT Gil Blas This glorious manor of worn stone, with tiled roof and courtyard garden, is in perfect harmony with the medieval square in which it stands. It was built some 500 years ago as the Barreda Bracho family's country retreat, and the old house has great charm. Some rooms are in a new annexe opposite.

⊠ Plaza Ramón Pelayo 11, 39330 Santillana del Mar, Cantabria. **Map** p287 E2. 【 (942) 818000. ℻ (942) 818391. ⊞ b,l,d. **Rooms** 55. ▦ ◐ ● Never. ▣ AE, DC, MC, V. ℗℗

TORTOSA

Parador de Tortosa There are views from many vantages in this ancient Moorish castle; the best are from the pool on the ramparts.

⊠ Castell de la Suda s/n, 43500 Tortosa, Tarragona. **Map** p289 D4. 【 (977) 444450. ℻ (977) 444458. ⊞ b,l,d. **Rooms** 75. ℗℗

TREDÒS

Hotel de Tredòs A new stone and slate hotel, popular with skiers and mountaineers for its well-equipped bedrooms and friendly staff.

⊠ Carretera a Baqueira-Beret km 177.5, 25598 Viella, Lérida. **Map** p289 D3. 【 (973) 644014. ℻ (973) 644300. ⊞ b,d. **Rooms** 37. ℗℗

TREMP

Casa Guilla Rambling farmhouse run by Brits as a guesthouse: bedrooms in the old animal pens, bar in the stables and lounge in hayloft.

⊠ Santa Engràcia, 25636 Tremp, Lérida. **Map** p289 D3. 【 ℻ (973) 252080. @ casaguilla@ctv.es ⊞ b,l,d. **Rooms** 5. ℗

VALENCIA DE DON JUAN

Villegas II With only five bedrooms, the Villegas looks and feels like a private house. The fresh bedrooms all open out onto the shady garden with pool.

⊠ Palacio 17, 24200 Valencia de Don Juan, León. **Map** p287 D3. 【 (987) 750161. ⊞ b,l,d. **Rooms** 5. ℗

SANTO DOMINGO DE SILOS

Tres Coronas de Silos Santo Domingo is a classic Castillian village, renowned for its 900-year-old convent where Gregorian chants are still sung daily. This cosy family hotel, on the main village square, is in a large 18th-century house faithfully restored by local craftsmen, with snug rooms and a pleasing dining room offering regional dishes.

⊠ Plaza Mayor 6, 09610 Santo Domingo de Silos, Burgos. **Map** p287 F3. **(** (947) 390047. **FAX** (947) 390065. **¶** b,l,d. **Rooms** 16. **●** Never. **⊘** AE, MC, V. ⓅⓅ

LA SEU D'URGELL

El Castell Modern and luxurious, this 'Relais et Châteaux' hotel is refreshingly unaffected. Jaume and Ludi Tàpies have instilled their mountain retreat with a truly welcoming atmosphere. They have also won plaudits for the cuisine, which embraces Catalan and French regional dishes.

⊠ Carretera de Lérida a Puigcerdà km 129, 25700 La Seu d'Urgell, Lérida. **Map** p289 D3. **(** (973) 350704. **FAX** (973) 351574. **@** elcastell@relaischateaux.fr **¶** b,l,d. **Rooms** 38. **目** **≋** **◑** **●** Never. **⊘** AE, DC, MC, V. ⓅⓅⓅ

TORRENT

Mas de Torrent This inland island of serenity is only 8km (5 miles) from the smartest beaches of the Costa Brava. The Mas de Torrent is a hotel of taste, housed in a restored 18th-century farm with 20 family bungalows, and run by courteous, gentle people. Rooms are individually and exquisitely decorated. The restaurant is a gem.

⊠ 17123 Torrent, Gerona. **Map** p289 F3. **(** (972) 303292. **FAX** (972) 303293. **@** mastorrent@relaischateaux.fr **¶** b,l,d. **Rooms** 30. **目** **≋** **◑** **●** Never. **⊘** AE, DC, MC, V. ⓅⓅⓅⓅ

A TOXA

Gran Hotel de la Toja Islands make a special setting, and this hotel, sheltered off the Arosa estuary, is one of the nicest. It has magnificent views, gardens and pinewoods as well as facilities that distinguish the grand from the merely luxurious. The old half of the hotel is genuine Art Nouveau with a stunning staircase and stained glass windows. Staff are very welcoming.

⊠ 36991 A Toxa, Pontevedra. **Map** p286 A2. **(** (986) 730025. **FAX** (986) 730026. **¶** b,l,d. **Rooms** 197. **≋** **⛳** **◑** **●** Never. **⊘** AE, DC, MC, V. ⓅⓅⓅⓅ

VERÍN

Parador Monterrey Named after an imposing castle that sits on a nearby hilltop, this modern parador, built in local stone, has a leafy setting on its own hilltop plus a pool.

⊠ 32600 Verín, Orense. **Map** p286 B3. **(** (988) 410075. **FAX** (988) 412017. **¶** b,l,d. **Rooms** 23. ⓅⓅ

VIELLA

Parador Valle de Arán New parador where a picture window in the semi-circular lounge frames dramatic mountain scenery.

⊠ Carretera del Túnel, 25530 Viella, Lérida. **Map** p289 D2. **(** (973) 640100. **FAX** (973) 641100. **¶** b,l,d. **Rooms** 135. ⓅⓅ

VILADRAU

Hostal de la Glòria The Formatjes family have created a homely hotel in their classic Catalan house, decked out with copper pots and plates.

⊠ Torreventosa 12, 08553 Viladrau, Gerona. **Map** p289 E3. **(** (93) 8849034. **FAX** (93) 8849465. **¶** b,l,d. **Rooms** 22. Ⓟ

VILANOVA I LA GELTRÚ

César A pair of sisters are in charge of this highly regarded restaurant with rooms furnished with handpicked pieces.

⊠ Carrer Isaac Peral 8, 08800 Vilanova i la Geltrú, Barcelona. **Map** p289 E4. **(** (93) 8151125. **FAX** (93) 8156719. **¶** b,l,d. **Rooms** 32. ⓅⓅ

For key to symbols see backflap. For price categories see p285

UDABE

Venta Udabe When Javier Hernández Goñi and Laura Ganuza Tudela bought this inn, it was a ruin and they have worked extremely hard to restore it. In the garden of the traditional rustic building, they have added a pool. Dining is on the terrace in summer, and in winter there's a roaring fire. The superb food uses only the freshest ingredients.
⊠ Valle de Basaburúa, 31869 Udabe, Navarra.
Map p288 B2. [(948) 503105. ⏏ b,l,d. **Rooms** 8.
⌗ 🔌 ● mid-Dec to late Jan. ⊠ MC, V. Ⓟ

VILLANUEVA-CANGAS DE ONIS

Parador de Cangas de Onis Close to Covadonga, the site of the Christians' first victory over the Moors, and beside the River Sella, this welcoming gem of a hotel used to be the monastery of San Pedro de Villanueva. It has a magnificent courtyard, cloister and small church. The restaurant and rooms are in a new building.
⊠ 3500 Villanueva-Cangas de Onis, Asturias.
Map p289 D2. [(98) 5849402. ⬛ FAX (98) 5849520.
⏏ b,l,d. **Rooms** 64. 🎛 🔌 ● Never.
⊠ AE, DC, MC, V. ⓅⓅ

VILLAGARCÍA DE AROSA

Hotel Pazo O'Rial This attractively converted old manor house is set in beautiful gardens just where the Ría de Arosa opens out towards the Atlantic. Wooden beams, tiled floors and bare stone walls are standard, but here are softened by lace curtains and wool rugs. This is a busy fishing area, and the menu reflects local catches.
⊠ El Rial No 1, 36600 Villagarcía de Arosa Colombres, Asturias. **Map** p286 B3. [(98) 5412590.
⬛ FAX (98) 5412514. ⏏ b,d. **Rooms** 8. 🔌 ● Never.
⊠ MC, V. ⓅⓅ

VILLANUEVA DE COLOMBRES

La Casona de Villanueva In a quiet hamlet in magnificent countryside between the eastern end of Los Picos and the sea, is this 18th-century farmhouse. Inside are oak beams, comfy beds, furniture from past and present and practical bathrooms. Top-notch home cooking can be praised with the help of the resident dictionary.
⊠ 33590 Villanueva de Colombres, Asturias.
Map p287 E2. [(98) 5412590. ⬛ FAX (98) 5412514.
@ casonavillanueva@abonados.cplus.es ⏏ b,d. **Rooms** 8.
🔌 ● Never. ⊠ MC, V. ⓅⓅ

VILLALONGA

Pazo El Revel The lush garden (with a pool) almost encroaches on the covered terrace of this old Galician *pazo* with plain tiled rooms.
⊠ Camino de la Iglesia s/n, 36990 Villalonga, Pontevedra.
Map p286 C2. [(986) 743000. ⬛ FAX (986) 743090.
⏏ b. **Rooms** 22. ⓅⓅ

VILLANÚA

Faus-Hütte Visitors to this Alpine-style hotel are greeted by the glow of wood on floors and panelled walls and by congenial Señor Faus.
⊠ Carretera de Francia km 658.5, 22870 Villanúa, Huesca. **Map** p288 C3. [(974) 378136. ⬛ FAX (974) 378198. ⏏ b. **Rooms** 10. Ⓟ

YESA

Hospedería de Leyre A simple, peaceful hotel in beautiful country, set in an outbuilding of an important 11th-century Benedictine monastery.
⊠ Monasterio de Leyre, 31410 Yesa, Navarra.
Map p288 B3. [(948) 884100. ⬛ FAX (948) 884137.
⏏ b,l,d. **Rooms** 32. Ⓟ

ZARAUTZ

Karlos Arguiñano Seafood is the speciality at this chic, castellated beachfront restaurant with pretty rooms.
⊠ Mendilauta 13, 20800 Zarautz, Guipúzcoa.
Map p288 B2. [(943) 130000. ⬛ FAX (943) 133450.
⏏ b,l,d. **Rooms** 12. ⓅⓅⓅⓅ

CENTRAL SPAIN

CASTILLA Y LEON • CASTILLA-LA MANCHA
EXTREMADURA • MADRID

Towns and sleepy villages dot Central Spain's unspoilt landscape of mountains, lakes, olive trees, orchards and almond groves. As in the North, old buildings such as mills and castles, townhouses and country posadas, have been skilfully converted to hotels and paradors. For sheer size, there is little that can equal the

monumental castle parador at Sigüenza. But for romance, few places can compare with the former monastery at Chichón with its beautiful courtyard – a feature of so many Spanish buildings. The capital, Madrid, is set at the heart of the country. The city's hotels range from the gloriously restored Ritz to a peaceful 1930s villa with a pretty garden setting.

ALAMEDA DEL VALLE

ALARCÓN

La Posada de Alameda A popular refuge for the city-weary, this new *posada* has an incomparable setting in the Lozoya Valley, 90km (55 miles) north of Madrid. The large bedrooms have views over a varied, unspoilt landscape, encompassing mountains, lakes and almond groves. The walls are adorned with interesting modern pictures.
⊠ Grande 34, 28749 Alameda del Valle, Madrid.
Map p287 E4. **(** (91) 8691337. **FAX** (91) 8690163.
11 b,l,d. **Rooms** 17. **目 ▮ ●** Never.
⊠ AE, DC, MC, V. Ⓟ Ⓟ

Parador Marqués de Villena One half expects to see Don Quixote's horse Rosinante tethered by the courtyard well of this hilltop Moorish fortress. Behind the thick walls lie a vaulted dining chamber, a great hall which now doubles as sitting room and cafeteria, and bedrooms which echo the medieval theme.
⊠ Avenida Amigos del Castillo, 16213 Alarcón, Cuenca. **Map** p291 E1. **(** (969) 330315.
FAX (969) 330303. **11** b,l,d. **Rooms** 13. **▮ ●** Never.
⊠ AE, DC, MC, V. Ⓟ Ⓟ Ⓟ

LA ALBERCA

Las Batuecas The chestnut and cherry trees of the Sierra de Francia surround this impressive stone house. Covered terrace and grassy garden.
⊠ Carretera Las Batuecas, 37624 La Alberca, Salamanca.
Map p286 C5. **(** (923) 415188. **FAX** (923) 415055.
11 b,l,d. **Rooms** 27. Ⓟ Ⓟ

AVILA

Hostería de Bracamonte The walls of the cheerful bar are lined with photographs of the glitterati fans of this typical Castillian hotel, with its natural stonework and tapestry wallhangings.
⊠ Bracamonte 6, 05001 Avila. **Map** p287 E5. **(** (920) 251280. **FAX** (920) 253838. **11** b,l,d. **Rooms** 24. Ⓟ

AVILA

Gran Hotel Palacio Valderrábanos Through the important entrance, every beam and arch reeks of the past. Try for a room with a cathedral view.
⊠ Plaza Catedral 9, 05001 Avila. **Map** p287 E5.
((920) 211023. **FAX** (920) 251691. **11** b,l,d.
Rooms 73. Ⓟ Ⓟ

AVILA

Sancho de Estrada A medieval castle with thick stone walls, towers, coats of arms and an interior to match. Simple bedrooms compensate for their starkness with fabulous views.
⊠ Castillo de Villaviciosa, 05130 Avila. **Map** p287 E5.
(FAX (920) 291082. **11** b,l,d. **Rooms** 12. Ⓟ

For key to symbols see backflap. For price categories *see p285*

ALMAGRO

CÁCERES

Parador de Almagro Hand-painted signs ensure that guests don't get lost in this rambling modern building on the site of an old convent. Its rooms are arranged around 14 small quads. Painted ceilings, vivid tapestries and pottery add colour to the public rooms; bedrooms are simpler. There are flowers everywhere and a friendly ambience.
Ronda de San Francisco, 13270 Almagro, Ciudad Real. **Map** p291 D2. (926) 860100. FAX (926) 860150. b,l,d. **Rooms** 55. Never.
AE, DC, MC, V.

Meliá Cáceres The old town within the ramparts contains a host of fine mansions, built for generations of aristocrats. This serene hotel is in one of these mansions, a solid wooden door leading into a well-preserved, stylish interior, arranged around a courtyard. Vaulted stables make a wonderfully atmospheric bar.
Plaza de San Juan 11, 10003 Cáceres, Extremadura. **Map** p290 A1. (927) 215800. FAX (927) 214070. b,l,d. **Rooms** 86. Never.
AE, DC, MC, V.

AVILA

CÁCERES

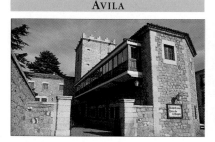

Parador de Turismo de Avila All that remains of the original 16th-century building is the tower, housing some small bedrooms, and the courtyard, shaded by a great pine. Bedrooms in the new part are larger and airier; some have four-poster beds, some fine views. The sun-trap terrace is an appealing place to relax.
Marqués Canales de Chozas 2, 05001 Avila. **Map** p287 E5. (920) 211340. FAX (920) 226166. b,l,d. **Rooms** 62. Never.
AE, DC, MC, V.

Parador de Cáceres A splendid 14th-century palace with a slender tower houses this elegant parador, its façade almost untouched since its foundation. Unlike many in the chain, the snug public rooms don't have massive proportions, and bedrooms are attractive in their simplicity. The inner courtyard is a delight, and the classic regional cuisine excels.
Ancha 6, 10003 Cáceres, Extremadura. **Map** p290 A1. (927) 211759. FAX (927) 211729. b,l,d. **Rooms** 31. Never. AE, DC, MC, V.

BENAVENTE

Parador Rey Fernando II de León The 12th-century castle keep survives as a drawing room with a wonderful *Mudéjar* coffered ceiling.
Paseo de Ramón y Cajal s/n, 49600 Benavente, Zamora. **Map** p287 D3. (980) 630300. FAX (980) 630303. b,l,d. **Rooms** 30.

CIUDAD RODRIGO

Conde Rodrigo A handsome 16th-century exterior hides a rather bland interior. There is, however, a good-value restaurant.
Plaza de San Salvador 9, 37500 Ciudad Rodrigo, Salamanca. **Map** p286 C5. (923) 461404. FAX (977) 461408. b,l,d. **Rooms** 35.

COLLADO HERMOSO

El Molino de Río Viejo Gorgeous old mill which stands amid poplars; the cosiest bedrooms are the ones in the eaves. Book well ahead.
Carretera N110 km 172, 40170 Collado Hermoso, Segovia. **Map** p287 E4. (921) 403063. FAX (921) 403051. b,l,d. **Rooms** 6.

CUENCA

Leonor de Aquitania An honest inn in the heart of the old town. The ground floor is flagstoned, walls bear tapestries and hunting trophies. Floral fabrics give the bedrooms an equally rural feel.
San Pedro 60, 16001 Cuenca. **Map** p288 B5. (969) 231000. FAX (969) 231004. b,l,d. **Rooms** 49.

CEREZO DE ARRIBA

Casón de la Pinilla This ranch-style hotel stands in open country on the outskirts of a sleepy village, minutes from the ski slopes of La Pinilla. In the restaurant, Sotomontero, the accent is on local specialities. In summer, breakfast and drinks are served on the long, balconied porch. With a playroom and activities ranging from riding to canoeing, the Casón caters to all ages.
⊠ 40592 Cerezo de Arriba, Segovia. **Map** p287 F4, p288 A4. 【 (921) 557201. **FAX** (921) 557209. 🍴 b,l,d. **Rooms** 9. 🔋 ● Nov. 🗲 AE, DC, MC, V. ⓟ

CHINCHÓN

Parador de Chinchón Soothe body and mind at this 15th-century former convent. Simple but elegant decoration includes the original frescoes on the main staircase; the internal courtyard is glorious. Outside are trees and flowers, bamboos and fountains, and a spectacular colonnaded swimming pool.
⊠ Avenida del Generalísimo 1, 28370 Chinchón, Madrid. **Map** p287 F5, p288 A5. 【 (91) 8940836. **FAX** (91) 8940908. 🍴 b,l,d. **Rooms** 38. 🔋 ● Never. 🗲 AE, DC, MC, V. ⓟⓟⓟ

CIUDAD RODRIGO

Parador Enrique II de Trastamara The whole of the 12th-century fortified town of Ciudad Rodrigo is a historical monument. This castle stands at the centre of the old town. Most of the rooms look inward towards the lovely enclosed gardens. Try for one of the bedrooms overlooking the Agueda river and the town.
⊠ Plaza del Castillo 1, 37500 Ciudad Rodrigo, Salamanca. **Map** p286 C5. 【 (923) 460150. **FAX** (923) 460404. 🍴 b,l,d. **Rooms** 27. 🔋 ● Never. 🗲 AE, DC, MC, V. ⓟⓟ

CUENCA

Parador Conventa de San Pablo This 16th-century former convent is perched dramatically above a gorge in the upper town, with rooms ranged around a calm courtyard. Staff are friendly and capable. Nearby is the Museum of Spanish Absract Art, in one of the 'Casas Colgadas' which literally hang over the gorge.
⊠ Paseo Hoz del Huécar s/n, 16001 Cuenca. **Map** p288 B5, p291 E1. 【 (969) 232320. **FAX** (969) 232534. @ cuenca@parador.es 🍴 b,l,d. **Rooms** 63. 🍴 🏊 🎾 🔋 ● Never. 🗲 AE, DC, MC, V. ⓟⓟⓟ

MADRID

Barajas Well outside the city centre, but conveniently near the airport, Barajas is a useful stopover hotel with a pool, gym and golf course.
⊠ Avenida de Logroño 205, 28022 Madrid. **Map** p287 E5. 【 (91) 7477700. **FAX** (91) 7478717. 🍴 b,l,d. **Rooms** 230. ⓟⓟⓟ

MADRID

Carlos V It looks like any other slick city hotel but, family-run with a caring staff, this one has a heart, as well as a beautifully furnished lounge.
⊠ Maestro Vitoria 5, 28013 Madrid. **Map** p287 E5. 【 (91) 5314100. **FAX** (91) 5313761. @ hotel.carlosv@ tsai.es 🍴 b. **Rooms** 67. ⓟⓟ

MADRID

Conde de Orgaz A modern hotel with well-appointed bedrooms, handy for the airport and the Campo de las Naciones Exhibition Centre.
⊠ Avenida Moscatelar 24, 28043 Madrid. **Map** p287 E5. 【 (91) 3884099. **FAX** (91) 3880009. 🍴 b,l,d. **Rooms** 91. ⓟⓟⓟ

MADRID

Emperatriz This large hotel with pale decoration and upholstered furniture manages to create an oasis of calm in the city centre.
⊠ López de Hoyos 4, 28006 Madrid. **Map** p287 E5. 【 (91) 5638088. **FAX** (91) 5639804. @ hotel.emperatriz@ mad.servicom.es 🍴 b,l,d. **Rooms** 158. ⓟⓟⓟⓟ

For key to symbols see backflap. For price categories *see p285*

Cuenca

Posada de San José Formerly the home of the painter Martinez del Mazo, this simple, charming hotel looks out over allotments and the cliffs of the Júcar gorge. For a view, book a room with a bathroom. Polished floors and furniture reassure you that this is a well-run house. The welcome is friendly, and so are the prices.
Julián Romero 4, 16001 Cuenca. **Map** p288 B5, p291 E1. (969) 211300. FAX (969) 230365. psanjose@arrakis.es b,d. **Rooms** 30. Never. AE, DC, MC, V.

Guadalupe

Parador Zurbarán Pilgrims used to shelter in this 18th-century hospital, and it still accommodates weary travellers. Orange trees shade an inner court where arcades lead to the salons and dining room. Bedrooms are attractively decorated; those in the modern building have outstanding views over monastery, village and mountains.
Marqués de la Romana 12, 10140 Guadalupe, Cáceres. **Map** p290 B1. (927) 367075. FAX (927) 367076. b,l,d. **Rooms** 40. Never. AE, DC, MC, V.

Guadalupe

Hospedería del Real Monasterio This is part fortress and part monastery. The Franciscans (still in residence) have created a hotel within their own walls. Gathered round a Gothic cloister are sitting rooms, a dining room and large bedrooms. The church has a splendid collection of paintings, including some by Zurbarán.
Plaza de Juan Carlos I, 10140 Guadalupe, Cáceres. **Map** p290 B1. (927) 367000. FAX (927) 367177. b,l,d. **Rooms** 47. mid-Jan to mid-Feb. MC, V.

Jarandilla de la Vera

Parador Carlos V It was at this remote fortified manor that Holy Roman Emperor Charles V spent his last nights before retiring to the monastery at Yuste in 1556. It is complete down to the towers and a drawbridge. The cool arcade, upper veranda and vast, comfortable rooms make you realize why the emperor chose this spot.
Avenida de García Prieto 1, 10450 Jarandilla de la Vera, Cáceres. **Map** p287 D5. (927) 560117. FAX (927) 560088. b,l,d. **Rooms** 53. Never. AE, DC, MC, V.

Madrid

Husa Princesa This modern five-star hotel has terrific amenities, from piano bar to aerobics room, and a great location for sightseeing.
Princesa 40, 28008 Madrid. **Map** p287 E5. (91) 5423500. FAX (91) 5423501. husaprincesa@husa.es b,l,d. **Rooms** 275.

Madrid

Mónaco The Mónaco is famous for putting up King Alfonso XIII in the early 1900s and for a stint as the city's most upmarket brothel. Today the old-fashioned furnishings look kitsch.
Barbieri 5, 28004 Madrid. **Map** p287 E5. (91) 5224630. FAX (91) 5211601. b. **Rooms** 32.

Madrid

Reina Victoria Ernest Hemingway stayed in this grand hotel, which has a plush modern interior, marble hall and comfortable rooms.
Plaza de Santa Ana 14, 28012 Madrid. **Map** p287 E5. (91) 5314500. FAX (91) 5220307. RUASUIC@trypnet.com b,l,d. **Rooms** 201.

Madrid

Santo Domingo A step from Plaza de España, a hotel of pastel tones, marble floors, deep carpets and trendy furnishings in differently styled rooms.
Plaza de Santo Domingo 13, 28013 Madrid. **Map** p287 E5. (91) 5479800. FAX (91) 5475995. sdomingo@stnet.es b,l,d. **Rooms** 120.

MADRID

Palace Haunt of the famous – from matadors to politicians – and the infamous (Mata Hari allegedly stayed here). The Palace matches the Ritz (see right) in grandeur; perhaps because it's much larger, service is not as personal. But it's worth a visit just to see the magnificent Art Nouveau rotunda with its Neo-Classical columns.
☒ Plaza de las Cortes 7, 28014 Madrid. **Map** p287 E5.
🄲 (91) 3608000. FAX (91) 3608100. @ palace1@mol.es
🍴 b,l,d. **Rooms** 440. 目 📺 🚻 🄾 Never.
🄴 AE, DC, MC, V. ⓅⓅⓅⓅ

MADRID

Ritz The Madrid Ritz has been tending to the whims of the wealthy since 1910, when it was built at the instigation of King Alfonso XIII. Public rooms are furnished with priceless carpets and tapestries, the spacious bedrooms with antiques. All this and faultless service make this Ritz one of Spain's top hotels.
☒ Plaza de la Lealtad 5, 28014 Madrid. **Map** p287 E5.
🄲 (91) 5212857. FAX (91) 5328776. @ reservas@ritz.es
🍴 b,l,d. **Rooms** 154. 目 📺 🚻 🄾 Never.
🄴 AE, DC, MC, V. ⓅⓅⓅⓅ

MADRID

La Residencia de El Viso If Madrid's large hotels leave you cold, try this delightful, good-value 1930s villa with a quiet garden. Once inside you can hardly believe that the location is so central. The bedrooms have co-ordinating fabrics; public rooms have high-backed chairs upholstered in red. Classic local dishes feature on the menu.
☒ Nervión 8, 28002 Madrid. **Map** p287 E5.
🄲 (91) 5640370. FAX (91) 5641965. @ info@estancias.es
🍴 b,l,d. **Rooms** 12. 目 🄾 🄾 Never.
🄴 AE, DC, MC, V. ⓅⓅ

MADRID

Santo Mauro Behind wrought-iron gates, an impressive, French-designed late 19th-century palace houses this luxurious hotel. With its stucco and original features intact, sophisticated modern furniture and decoration have been introduced to great effect, using marble, stained oak, wild silk and velvet.
☒ Zurbano 36, 28010 Madrid. **Map** p287 E5.
🄲 (91) 3196900. FAX (91) 3085477. @ santo-mauro@ ac-hoteles.com 🍴 b,l,d. **Rooms** 37. 目 🏊 📺 🄾
🄾 Never. 🄴 AE, DC, MC, V. ⓅⓅⓅⓅ

MADRID

Serrano A brutally modern façade masks a bright, exclusive hotel with period furniture and welcome personal touches.
☒ Marqués de Villamejor 8, 28006 Madrid.
Map p287 E5. 🄲 (91) 5769626. FAX (91) 5753307.
🍴 b. **Rooms** 33. ⓅⓅⓅ

MADRID

Suite Prado Specialist hotel with glossy modern apartments and room service. Baby-blue carpets and pastel armchairs are typical of the style.
☒ Manuel Fernández y González 10, Esq. Ventura de la Vega, 28014 Madrid. **Map** p287 E5. 🄲 (91) 4202318.
FAX (91) 4200559. 🍴 b. **Rooms** 18. ⓅⓅⓅ

MADRID

Wellington The bullfighting fraternity has long been associated with this genteel 1950s hotel. Top-floor bedrooms have private terraces.
☒ Velásquez 8, 28001 Madrid. **Map** p287 E5.
🄲 (91) 5754400. FAX (91) 5764164. 🍴 b,l,d.
Rooms 288. ⓅⓅⓅⓅ

MÉRIDA

Emperatriz A distinguished-looking granite mansion with a cloistered courtyard, vaulted dining room and two bars, one serving *tapas*.
☒ Plaza de España 19, 06800 Mérida, Badajoz.
Map p290 A2. 🄲 (924) 313111. FAX (924) 313305.
🍴 b,l,d. **Rooms** 42. ⓅⓅ

For key to symbols see backflap. For price categories *see p285*

MADRID

Villa Real In a building dating from 1900, the Villa Real is in the grand tradition of its neighbour the Palace (see p311) but is slightly kinder on the pocket – weekend rates are particularly reasonable. As well as more formal salons, there is an intimate bar. Service is carried out impeccably by a polite staff.
☒ Plaza de las Cortes 10, 28014 Madrid.
Map p287 E5. ☎ (91) 4203767. ℻ (91) 4202547.
@ info@derbyhotels.es 🍴 b,l,d. **Rooms** 115. 🗐 🖳
⬤ Never. 🄴 AE, DC, MC, V. ₧₧₧₧

OROPESA

Parador de Oropesa This feudal castle, built of sand-coloured stone in 1402, was the first castle to be converted into a parador in 1930. The interior is as impressive as the exterior, preserving original floors and vaulting. There are breathtaking views of the Sierra de Gredos and Tajo valley from the towers and terraces.
☒ Plaza del Palacio 1, 45560 Oropesa, Toledo.
Map p287 D5, p290 B1. ☎ (925) 430000.
℻ (925) 430777. 🍴 b,l,d. **Rooms** 48. 🗐 🏊 🚱
⬤ Never. 🄴 AE, DC, MC, V. ₧₧

MÉRIDA

Parador Vía de la Plata Though much of the building is modern, this parador's historical association is evident in many touches. It is full of Roman artefacts, its 16th-century chapel is now a sitting room and past the reception area is a cloistered courtyard. Upstairs, most of the large bedrooms overlook the Moorish gardens.
☒ Plaza de la Constitución 3, 06800 Mérida, Badajoz.
Map p290 A2. ☎ (924) 313800. ℻ (924) 319208.
🍴 b,l,d. **Rooms** 82. 🗐 🏊 🖳 🚱 ⬤ Never.
🄴 AE, DC, MC, V. ₧₧₧

PEDRAZA DE LA SIERRA

El Hotel de la Villa The walled medieval hilltop town, dominated by its castle, is a maze of higgledy-piggledy streets lined with beautifully preserved houses. In one of these is this stylish hotel, a stunning mix of the traditional and the contemporary. Its comfortable bedrooms are all different, with glossy well-equipped bathrooms.
☒ Calzada 5, 40172 Pedraza della Sierra, Segovia.
Map p287 E4. ☎ (921) 508651. ℻ (921) 508653.
🍴 b,l,d. **Rooms** 26. 🗐 🚱 ⬤ Never.
🄴 AE, DC, MC, V. ₧₧

NAVARREDONDA DE GREDOS
Parador de Gredos The exterior of this 1920s parador is stone, its interior wood. Massive rooms boast beams and hunting trophies.
☒ Carretera Barraco km43-Bejar, 05132 Navarredonda de Gredos, Avila. **Map** p287 D5. ☎ (920) 348048.
℻ (920) 348205. 🍴 b,l,d. **Rooms** 77. ₧₧

RASCAFRÍA
Santa María de El Paular Guests share this tasteful 14th-century monastery at the foot of the Sierra de Guadarrama with Benedictine monks.
☒ El Paular, 28741 Rascafría, Madrid. **Map** p287 E4.
☎ (91) 8691011. ℻ (91) 8691006. 🍴 b,l,d.
Rooms 58. ₧₧

SALAMANCA
Palacio de Castellanos Swish hotel in a 15th-century monastery, with a vaulted glass roof over the striking internal cloister.
☒ San Pablo 58-64, 37008 Salamanca. **Map** p287 D4.
☎ (923) 261818. ℻ (923) 261819. 🍴 b,l,d.
Rooms 62. ₧₧₧

SALAMANCA
El Rector An abundance of marble and stained glass, muted colours and a warm ambience lie in store behind the Renaissance-style façade.
☒ Paseo Rector Esperabe 10, 37008 Salamanca.
Map p287 D40. ☎ (923) 218482. ℻ (923) 214008.
@ hotelrector@teleline.es 🍴 b. **Rooms** 14. ₧₧

PEDRAZA DE LA SIERRA

La Posada de Don Mariano Televisions are only provided on request, as they would look too brash in the exquisitely decorated bedrooms. Each has its own character and is furnished in carefully chosen antiques. Avoid the rooms above the lively bar, whose ceiling is not solid enough protection against the noise.

☒ Mayor 14, 40172 Pedraza de la Sierra, Segovia. **Map** p287 E40. ☎ (921) 509886. ꜰᴀx (921) 509887. ⸝⸝ b,l,d. **Rooms** 18. ⸝ ⬤ Never. ⸝ AE, DC, MC, V. ⓟⓡ

TOLEDO

Hostal del Cardinal This beautiful house in central Toledo was a cardinal's summer home. Birds sing and fountains play in the Moorish garden, where dinner can be taken in the summer. Inside are handsome antiques and an elegant staircase. Room sizes vary; there is one small suite. The restaurant is next door.

☒ Paseo de Recaredo 24, 45004 Toledo. **Map** p287 E5, p290 C1. ☎ (925) 224900. ꜰᴀx (925) 222991. @ cardenal@macom.es ⸝⸝ b,l,d. **Rooms** 27. ⸝ ⸝ ⬤ Never. ⸝ AE, DC, MC, V. ⓟⓡ

SIGUERUELO

Posada de Sigueruelo A visit to this quiet village inn is to sample rural life at its best. In the rugged country that surrounds Sigueruelo, you can go hiking, cycling, riding or canoeing. The friendly staff at the Posada will organize it for you. On your return, the hotel's shady terrace and a drink will beckon. Rooms are small but have stone walls, beams, antiques and plenty of atmosphere.

☒ Badén 40, 40590 Sigueruelo, Segovia. **Map** p287 E4. ☎ ꜰᴀx (921) 508135. ⸝⸝ b,l,d. **Rooms** 6. ⬤ Never. ⸝ MC, V. ⓡ

TORREJÓN DE ARDOZ

La Casa Grande A farm founded in the 18th century by Empress Maria of Austria to supply the Imperial College makes a stunning hotel. Its massive beamed rooms are grandly decorated with antiques that once belonged to the Russian royal family. In the principal suite is a Baroque bed where Catherine the Great is alleged to have slept. The cavernous cellars are not to be missed.

☒ Madrid 2, 28850 Torrejón de Ardoz, Madrid. **Map** p287 F5. ☎ (91) 6753900. ꜰᴀx (91) 6750691. ⸝⸝ b,l,d. **Rooms** 9. ⸝ ⬤ Aug. ⸝ AE, DC, MC, V. ⓟⓡ

SEGOVIA

Infanta Isabel A handsome 19th-century townhouse opposite the cathedral, this B&B is furnished classically with flair.

☒ Plaza Mayor Isabel la Católica 1, 40001 Segovia. **Map** p287 E4. ☎ (921) 461300. ꜰᴀx (921) 462217. ⸝⸝ b. **Rooms** 27. ⓟⓡ

SEGOVIA

Los Linajes Tiled floors, beams and carved furniture produce a charming effect in this hotel nestling below the cathedral but with country views. Meals are in a cafeteria.

☒ Dr Velasco 9, 40003 Segovia. **Map** p287 E4. ☎ (921) 460475. ꜰᴀx (921) 460479. ⸝⸝ b,l,d. **Rooms** 53. ⓟⓡ

SIGÜENZA

Parador Castillo de Sigüenza Perched above the town, this huge medieval castle has a vast sitting room, snug bar and panoramic views.

☒ Plaza del Castillo, 19250 Sigüenza, Guadalajara. **Map** p287 F4, p288 A4. ☎ (949) 390100. ꜰᴀx (949) 391364. ⸝⸝ b,l,d. **Rooms** 81. ⓟⓡ

TOLEDO

María Cristina An old orphanage that preserves its heritage, this hotel and its dining room are especially popular at weekends and *fiestas*.

☒ Marqués de Mendigorria 1, 45003 Toledo. **Map** p287 E5, p290 C1. ☎ (925) 213202. ꜰᴀx (925) 212650. ⸝⸝ b,l,d. **Rooms** 73. ⓟⓡ

For key to symbols see backflap. For price categories see p285

TRUJILLO

Posada Finca de Santa Marta This country manor house, where oil and wine used to be produced, has been converted into a perfect rural getaway. Modern facilities blend sympathetically with the fabric of the building and the regional furniture, yielding bright, comfortable and attractive rooms.
⊠ Pago de San Clemente, 23003 Trujillo, Cáceres. **Map** p290 B1. **(** (927) 319203. **FAX** (91) 3502217. **@** henri@facilnet.es **⏹** b; d on request. **Rooms** 14. ⏹ ⏹ ⏹ Never. **⊠** AE, DC, MC, V. **℗**

ZAFRA

Parador de Zafra A 15th-century fortress with round towers conjures images from the days of the Conquistadors. Highlights are the stunning white marble patio, over which most of the large, appropriately furnished bedrooms look, and the magnificent staircase leading to them. The swimming pool in the walled garden is a delight.
⊠ Plaza del Corazón de María 7, 06300 Zafra, Badajoz. **Map** p290 A2. **(** (924) 554540. **FAX** (924) 551018. **⏹** b,l,d. **Rooms** 45. ⏹ ⏹ ⏹ ⏹ Never. **⊠** AE, DC, MC, V. **℗℗℗**

TRUJILLO

Posada de Trujillo Partly housed within the 16th-century convent of Santa Clara, and partly in a modern building, this parador has proved immensely popular. It's set in a maze of quiet streets yet has with views over the Extremadura countryside. Simple decoration does not signal lack of comfort.
⊠ Plaza Santa Beatriz de Silva 1, 10200 Trujillo, Cáceres. **Map** p290 B1. **(** (927) 321350. **FAX** (927) 321366. **⏹** b,l,d. **Rooms** 46. ⏹ ⏹ Never. **⊠** AE, DC, MC, V. **℗℗**

ZAMORA

Parador Condes de Alba y Aliste If you need a reason to go to Zamora this is it. A glorious Renaissance courtyard, with cloister below and enclosed galleries above, masks an interior perfectly in keeping with its 18th-century restoration. Half the rooms are in a new wing over a public pool (noisy at weekends). Service is friendly, informed and efficient.
⊠ Plaza de Viriato 5, 49001 Zamora. **Map** p287 D4. **(** (980) 514497. **FAX** (980) 530063. **⏹** b,l,d. **Rooms** 52. ⏹ ⏹ ⏹ ⏹ Never. **⊠** AE, DC, MC, V. **℗℗℗**

TOLEDO

Parador del Conde de Orgaz Contemporary hilltop parador, built sympathetically in local style, with a pool and great views over the city.
⊠ Cerro del Emperador, 45002 Toledo. **Map** p290 C1. **(** (925) 221850. **FAX** (925) 225166. **⏹** b,l,d. **Rooms** 76. **℗℗℗**

TOLEDO

Pintor El Greco This 17th-century house in the Jewish quarter, with colourful furnishings and modern comforts, makes an excellent base.
⊠ Alamillos del Tránsito 13, 45002 Toledo. **Map** p290 C1. **(** (925) 214250. **FAX** (925) 215819. **@** elgreco@estanciases.es **⏹** b. **Rooms** 33. **℗℗**

ZAFRA

Huerta Honda Window boxes overflowing with geraniums enliven this white villa with calm bedrooms, amusing decor and excellent food.
⊠ López Asme 30, 06300, Zafra, Badajoz. **Map** p290 A2. **(** (924) 554100. **FAX** (924) 552504. **⏹** b,l,d. **Rooms** 36. **℗℗**

ZAMORA

Hostería Real de Zamora Housed in a 16th-century palace of the Inquisition, comfortable tile-floored rooms are arranged around a pretty patio. Excellent Basque cuisine.
⊠ Cuesta de Pizarro 7, 49001 Zamora. **Map** p287 D4. **(** **FAX** (980) 534545. **⏹** b,l,d. **Rooms** 18. **℗**

SOUTHERN SPAIN
ANDALUCIA • MURCIA • VALENCIA
CANARY ISLANDS • BALEARIC ISLANDS

JUST A FEW KILOMETRES from the busy coast of Southern Spain and into the hills of Andalucia, is some of the country's most beautiful scenery – rolling hills, chestnut forests, olive and citrus groves. In this region, there are a number of handpicked hotels, some occupying historic buildings such as converted convents, others in airy modern houses. The fine cities of the South – Granada, Córdoba and Seville – all have small gems of hotels. Further north, in Alicante, hard by the concrete blocks of the Costa Blanca, is a hotel in Europe's largest palm grove. In the Balearic and Canary Islands, away from the tourist track, are some of the least spoilt settings for some of the most desirable hotels.

ALCAÑIZ

Parador La Concordia This 12th-century fortified monastery is monumental yet it has only 12 guest rooms. It's the former home of the Knights of Calatrava, who must have taken the furnishings when they left because little now is original. The grounds are open to the public so can be busy, but peace returns with nightfall.
☒ Castillo de los Calatravos, 44600 Alcañiz, Teruel. **Map** p288 C4. ☎ (978) 830400. ☒ (978) 830366. ⑪ b,l,d. **Rooms** 12. ⓦ ⬤ late Dec to Feb. ✉ AE, DC, MC, V. Ⓟ Ⓟ Ⓟ

ARCOS DE LA FRONTERA

Cortijo Faín Near Arcos de Frontera, a clifftop White Town teetering over the Guadalete valley, this delightful Andalusian manor is set with its gardens in the centre of a huge olive grove. The ten warmly furnished rooms of varying sizes have iron or brass bedsteads, and the calm public areas and library are dotted with paintings and antiques.
☒ Carretera de Algar, 11630 Arcos de la Frontera, Cádiz. **Map** p290 B4. ☎ ☒ (956) 231396. ⑪ b,l,d. **Rooms** 10. ▦ ⬚ ⓦ ⬤ Never. ✉ AE, DC, MC, V. Ⓟ Ⓟ

ALCALÁ DE GUADAIRA
Oromana This fine white house on the outskirts of Seville contains lofty communal rooms, a cosy bar and cool, pale bedrooms. Friendly staff.
☒ Avenida de Portugal, 41500 Alcalá de Guadaira, Sevilla. **Map** p290 B3. ☎ ☒ (95) 5686400. ⑪ b,l,d. **Rooms** 30. Ⓟ

ALHAURÍN EL GRANDE
Finca La Mota Acres of mature, grassy garden surround the large pool. Inside, the rooms are rustic. Unusually, the restaurant serves curries.
☒ Partido Urique, 29100 Alhaurín el Grande, Málaga. **Map** p290 C4. ☎ (952) 490901. ☒ (952) 594120. @ lamota@naptel.es ⑪ b,l,d. **Rooms** 16. Ⓟ

ARCHENA
Termas Flamboyant plasterwork, domes and arches decorate this comfortable spa hotel.
☒ Balneario de Archena, 30600 Archena, Murcia. **Map** p291 F3. ☎ (968) 670100. ☒ (968) 671002. @ reservas@balneario_archena_sa.es ⑪ b,l,d. **Rooms** 71. Ⓟ Ⓟ

ARCOS DE LA FRONTERA
El Convento Breakfast is served in the former convent's arched sacristy, lunch and dinner in the genial owners' restaurant a short walk away.
☒ Maldonado 2, 11630 Arcos de la Frontera, Cádiz. **Map** p290 B4. ☎ (956) 702333. ☒ (956) 704128. ⑪ b,l,d. **Rooms** 11. Ⓟ

For key to symbols see backflap. For price categories *see p285*

ARCOS DE LA FRONTERA

Hacienda El Santiscal This delightful restored 15th-century manor house is within sight of the white city of Arcos and has sweeping views out over the Arcos lake and the Santiscal mountains. The impressive list of local outings, activities and expeditions on offer ranges from ballooning to sherry tasting.

☒ Avenida del Santiscal 129, 11630 Arcos de la Frontera, Cádiz. **Map** p290 B4. ☎ (956) 708313. ⒻⒶⓍ (956) 708268. @ santiscal@gadesinfo.com 🍴 b,l,d. **Rooms** 12. 🖥 🏊 ♿ 🎍 ● mid to late Jan. 🗹 AE, DC, MC, V. ⓅⓅ

BARLOVENTO, LA PALMA

La Palma Romántica For keen stargazers, there's an observatory at this well-equipped Canary Island hotel, set between mountains and sea. It's worth negotiating the twisting road to this side of La Palma for the glorious scenery, the wildlife and the silence. Rooms are large; all have a balcony. A welcoming place.

☒ Las Llanadas, 38726 Barlovento, La Palma. **Map** p291 E4. ☎ (922) 186221. ⒻⒶⓍ (922) 186400. @ palmarom@lix.intercom.es 🍴 b,l,d. **Rooms** 41. 🖥 🏊 🎍 ♿ ● Never. 🗹 AE, MC, V. ⓅⓅ

BAEZA

Hospedería Fuentenueva The building's colourful history includes years as a women's prison, then as home to a judge. Now a lively, unconventional hotel, it is managed by a co-operative of five enthusiastic young people. The pleasing rooms retain their Moorish heritage; the public ones are often used for art exhibitions.

☒ Paseo Arca del Agua s/n, 23440 Baeza, Jaén. **Map** p291 D3. ☎ (953) 743100. ⒻⒶⓍ (953) 743200. 🍴 b,l,d. **Rooms** 12. 🖥 🏊 ♿ ● Never. 🗹 AE, DC, MC, V. ⓅⓅ

BENAOJÁN

Molino del Santo Not far from Ronda, where you can watch kestrels soaring below you, is a delightful mill on a scented mountainside. Converted by the English owner-managers, it makes a glorious hideaway. The rooms are simply and comfortably furnished; most have terraces overlooking the beautiful pool.

☒ Barriada Estación, 29370 Benaoján, Málaga. **Map** p290 B4. ☎ (95) 2167151. ⒻⒶⓍ (95) 2167327. @ molino@logiccontrol.es 🍴 b,l,d. **Rooms** 14. 🏊 ♿ ● Never. 🗹 AE, DC, MC, V. Ⓟ

ARCOS DE LA FRONTERA
Parador Casa del Corregidor An old magistrate's house with a spectacular clifftop setting and two terraces that take advantage of the vista.
☒ Plaza de España or del Cabildo, 11630 Cádiz. **Map** p290 B4. ☎ (956) 700500. ⒻⒶⓍ (956) 701116. 🍴 b,l,d. **Rooms** 24. ⓅⓅⓅ

CALA RATJADA, MALLORCA
Ses Rotges This captivating pink house is French-run and boasts one of the island's most highly regarded restaurants.
☒ Rafael Blanes 21, 07590 Cala Ratjada, Mallorca. **Map** p289 F5. ☎ (971) 563108. ⒻⒶⓍ (971) 564345. @ rotges@baleares.com 🍴 b,l,d. **Rooms** 24. ⓅⓅ

CALA SAINT VICENÇ, MALLORCA
Cala Saint Vicenç A handsome, well-run villa on the north coast, popular with families.
☒ Maresers 2, 07469 Cala Saint Vicenç, Mallorca. **Map** p289 F5. ☎ (971) 530250. ⒻⒶⓍ (971) 532084. @ calasaintvicenc@relaischateaux.fr 🍴 b,l,d. **Rooms** 38. ⓅⓅⓅ

CAMPANET, MALLORCA
Monnaber Nou This country estate hotel looks out over glorious hillsides. Facilities are first-rate.
☒ Possessió Monnaber Nou, 07310 Campanet, Mallorca. **Map** p291 F3. ☎ (971) 877176. ⒻⒶⓍ (971) 877127. @ monnaber@fehm.es 🍴 b,l,d. **Rooms** 25. ⓅⓅⓅ

BINISSALEM, MALLORCA

Scott's The discreet plaque outside this elegant English-owned merchant's house on the main square only hints at the unobtrusive luxury inside. It's meticulously decorated and furnished, the flowers are fresh, the beds a dream, and you can always find a quiet corner to yourself. Breakfast is to die for. Children over 12 only.

Plaza de la Iglesia 12, 07350 Binissalem, Mallorca. **Map** p289 F5. (971) 870100. FAX (971) 870267. scotts@bitel.es b. **Rooms** 16. Never. MC, V. ®®®

BUBIÓN

Villa Turística de Bubión Not a hotel but a complex of self-catering apartments, the Villa Turística consists of a cluster of low-rise houses built along traditional designs. Apartments are decorated with local textiles and ceramics, and each has a fireplace for chilly evenings. There is also a dining room/bar, and room service.

Barrio Alto, Bubión, Granada. **Map** p291 D4. (958) 763111. FAX (958) 763136. albujarr@ctub.es@igm.es b,l,d. **Rooms** 42 apartments. Never. AE, DC, MC, V. ®®®

CARMONA

Casa de Carmona A 16th-century palace in the heart of town, stylishly and faithfully restored, with opulent public rooms, a porticoed central patio and a delightful enclosed garden. The fabrics in the individual and well-equipped rooms set off the antiques. Outside, a shaded terrace gives a distant view of Seville. Top-class.

Plaza de Lasso 1, 41410 Carmona, Seville. **Map** p290 B3. (95) 4191000. FAX (95) 4190189. yolanda@cascadecarmona.com b,l,d. **Rooms** 30. Never. AE, DC, MC, V. ®®®

CARMONA

Parador Alcázar del Rey Don Pedro The original hilltop Moorish fortress was made into a palace for Don Pedro the Cruel. It is now an unashamedly efficient commercial hotel, making the most of the stupendous view. There is an attractive Moorish-influenced internal court, and the large public rooms are decorated with suits of armour and tapestry wallhangings.

Alcázar, 41410 Carmona, Seville. **Map** p290 B3. (95) 4141010. FAX (95) 4141712. b,l,d. **Rooms** 63. Never. AE, DC, MC, V. ®®®

LA CAROLINA
Hotel de la Perdiz This beamed hotel has the air of a hunting lodge: hunting trophies, huge hearths and solid furniture. Pretty garden.

Carretera N IV, 23200 La Carolina, Jaén. **Map** p291 D2. (953) 660300. FAX (953) 681362. b,l,d. **Rooms** 85. ®®

CASTELL DE CASTELLS
Pensión Castells Friendly *pension* in a quiet mountain village, run by the English owners. Guided walks, satisfying evening meals.

San Vicente 18, 03793 Castell de Castells, Alicante. **Map** p291 F5. FAX (96) 5518254. (969) 231004. b,d. **Rooms** 4. ®

CASTELLAR DE LA FRONTERA
Casa Convento La Almoraima A 17th-century hunting lodge built by the dukes of Medinaceli, this country house hotel has a fine rural setting.

Finca La Almoraima, 11350 Castellar de la Frontera, Cádiz. **Map** p290 B4. (956) 693002. FAX (956) 693214. b,l,d. **Rooms** 17. ®®

CAZALLA DE LA SIERRA
Hospedería de la Cartuja A haven of peace for artists who not only stay in this unusual, restored monastery, but also exhibit their work here.

Carretera Cazalla-Constantina, 41370 Cazalla de la Sierra, Seville. **Map** p290 B3. (95) 4884516. FAX (95) 4884707. b,l,d. **Rooms** 8. ®®

For key to symbols see backflap. For price categories *see p285*

CASTILLEJA DE LA CUESTA

Hotel Hacienda San Ygnacio The original buildings have been preserved in gleaming white around a large central courtyard dominated by four majestic palm trees. The rooms, with wrought-iron beds and rustic furniture, are not the height of style but are large and comfy. Palm and orange trees shade the pool.
⊠ Real 190, 41950 Castilleja de la Cuesta, Seville. **Map** p290 B3. 🄲 (95) 4160430. 🄵🄰🄷 (95) 4161437. 🄰 sygnacio@arrakis.es 🄷 b,l,d. **Rooms** 18. 🄴 ⊞ 🄸 ● Never. 🄴 AE, DC, MC, V. 🄟🄟🄟

CAZALLA DE LA SIERRA

Las Navezuelas In a broad valley in the hills north of Seville is this converted old olive mill, set on a large farm in a very pretty setting. It's a simple place, with a warm welcome, excellent home cooking and spotless rooms. There are cattle, sheep and goats on the farm, deer and wild boar in the woods and fish in the river.
⊠ Apartado 14, 41370 Cazalla de la Sierra, Seville. **Map** p290 B3. 🄲 (95) 4884764. 🄵🄰🄷 (95) 4884594. 🄰 navezuelas@arrakis.es 🄷 b,l,d. **Rooms** 8. ⊞ 🄸 ● early Jan to mid-Feb. 🄴 MC, V. 🄟

CAZALLA DE LA SIERRA
Posada del Moro Julia Piñero has lavished love and attention on her appealing hotel, furnishing rooms with carefully chosen pieces and pictures.
⊠ Paseo del Moro s/n, 41370 Cazalla de la Sierra, Seville. **Map** p290 C3. 🄲 🄵🄰🄷 (95) 4884858. 🄷 b,l,d. **Rooms** 15. 🄟

CAZORLA
Parador de Cazorla The architecture of this modern parador in the beautiful wooded landscape of the Sierra de Cazorla is based on a typical Andalusian *cortijo*.
⊠ Sacejo, 23470 Cazorla, Jaén. **Map** p291 D3. 🄲 (953) 727075. 🄵🄰🄷 (953) 727077. 🄷 b,l,d. **Rooms** 33. 🄟🄟

CÓRDOBA

Alfaros Córdoba was the Moorish capital and this large, well-appointed hotel reflects its mixed heritage in an otherwise modern décor. All its rooms are light and airy, the services are up-to-date and efficient, and the swimming pool is wonderful. Don't miss seeing the Mezquita, the mosque-cathedral, which is simply stunning.
⊠ Alfaras 18, 14001 Córdoba. **Map** p290 C3. 🄲 (957) 491920. 🄵🄰🄷 (957) 492210. 🄰 alfaros@igm.es 🄷 b,l,d. **Rooms** 133. 🄴 ⊞ 🄸 ● Never. 🄴 AE, DC, MC, V. 🄟🄟🄟

CÓRDOBA

Amistad Córdoba In the Barrio dela Judería, the old Jewish quarter with a synagogue to rival Toledo's, an opening in a Moorish wall reveals an excellent modern hotel. The public rooms are deliberately simple, with flashes of local colour. The sizeable bedrooms are more richly furnished and equipped. The service is impeccable.
⊠ Plaza de Maimónides 3, 14004 Córdoba. **Map** p290 C3. 🄲 (957) 420335. 🄵🄰🄷 (957) 420365. 🄷 b,l,d. **Rooms** 84. 🄴 ⊞ 🄸 ● Never. 🄴 AE, DC, MC, V. 🄟🄟

CÓRDOBA
Albucasis Tucked away in the Jewish quarter, this modern B&B offers comforts beyond the two-star norm. Its immaculate, air-conditioned interior blends contemporary and antique.
⊠ Buen Pastor 11, 14003 Córdoba. **Map** p290 C3. 🄲 🄵🄰🄷 (957) 478625. 🄷 b. **Rooms** 15. 🄟

CÓRDOBA
El Conquistador A modern building designed in Moorish style. Bedrooms are elegant; those at the front have views of the Mezquita. Quiet patio.
⊠ Magistral González Francés 15-17, 14003 Córdoba. **Map** p290 C3. 🄲 (957) 481102. 🄵🄰🄷 (957) 474677. 🄷 b. **Rooms** 102. 🄟🄟🄟

CÓRDOBA

Parador de Córdoba High above the heat of the city is this parador, built from the ruins of the summer palace built for Abderramán I. This is where Europe's first palm trees were grown. The building and decor are a fusion of Arabic and Andalusian, the rooms large and airy. The dining room is a showcase for regional dishes and wines.
⊠ Avenida de la Arruzafa s/n, 14012 Córdoba.
Map p290 C3. ☎ (957) 275900. ⅎₐₓ (957) 280409.
🍴 b,l,d. **Rooms** 94. 🎴 🏊 📱 ⬤ Never.
💳 AE, DC, MC, V. ®®®

ELX (ELCHE)

Huerto del Cura If you like palm trees, Elx has more of them than any other place in Europe. Hidden within its own palm grove, the Huerto del Cura offers quiet, modern rooms or bungalows scattered round the luxuriant garden. Rooms away from the pool are quietest. The restaurant offers regional and French cooking.
⊠ Porta de la Morera 14, 03203 Elx, Alicante.
Map p291 F2. ☎ (96) 5458040. ⅎₐₓ (96) 5421910.
🍴 b,l,d. **Rooms** 86. 🎴 🏊 📱 🚹 ⬤ Never.
💳 AE, DC, MC, V. ®®®

DEIÁ, MALLORCA

La Residencia This creeper-clad 16th-century manor house, set between the mountains and the sea by the unspoilt northwestern coast, is a delight. It's surrounded by tiered gardens and woodland, and filled with antiques, bright rugs and modern art. Rooms vary in size. The restaurant is one of the island's best.
⊠ Finca Son Canals, 07179 Deiá, Mallorca.
Map p289 F5. ☎ (971) 639011. ⅎₐₓ (971) 639370.
@ laresidencia@atlas_iap.es 🍴 b,l,d. **Rooms** 64. 🎴 🏊
🚹 📱 ⬤ Never. 💳 AE, DC, MC, V. ®®®®

GRANADA

América This delightful, modestly priced family-run hotel right next door to the Alhambra very swiftly becomes a home from home. Although quite small, the rooms are clean and cheerful with colourful woven bedspreads and curtains. They overlook the Alhambra's gardens or the patio where meals are served in summer.
⊠ Real de la Alhambra 53, 18009 Granada.
Map p291 D3. ☎ (958) 227471. ⅎₐₓ (958) 227470.
🍴 b,l,d. **Rooms** 13. 🎴 📱 ⬤ Dec to Mar.
💳 AE, DC, MC, V. ®®

CÓRDOBA

González In one of the Jewish quarter's narrow streets, this hotel has a cool marble interior and Moorish arches leading to a pretty flowery patio.
⊠ Manríquez 3, 14003 Córdoba. **Map** p290 C3.
☎ (957) 479819. ⅎₐₓ (957) 486187. 🍴 b,l,d.
Rooms 20. ®

DENIA

Rosa Parisian Michel Dessous has converted his modest *pension* into a fine villa with Florentine balconies. Some self-catering bungalows.
⊠ Congre 3, Las Marinas, 03700 Denia, Alicante.
Map p291 F2. ☎ (96) 5781573. ⅎₐₓ (96) 6424774.
🍴 b,l,d. **Rooms** 40. ®®

FORCALL

Palau dels Osset In the remote El Maestrat area, this 16th-century house on the porticoed main square is an oasis of rural comfort.
⊠ Plaza Mayor 16, 12310 Palau dels Osset, Castellón.
Map p289 C5. ☎ (964) 177524. ⅎₐₓ (964) 177556.
🍴 b,l,d. **Rooms** 20. ®

GIBRALTAR

The Rock Favoured by glitterati, this colonial-style hotel prides itself on its service. Stupendous views from its perch above the bay. The international dialling code for Gibraltar is 00350.
⊠ 3 Europa Road, Gibraltar. **Map** p290 B4. ☎ 73000.
ⅎₐₓ 73513. 🍴 b,l,d. **Rooms** 127. ®®®®

For key to symbols see backflap. For price categories *see p285*

GRANADA

Carmen de Santa Inés A beautiful old Arab house with a lovely patio is the setting for this small but perfectly formed bed and breakfast hotel, in the same ownership as the Palacio de Santa Inés (below). The nine bedrooms are cool and airy, and individually decorated. Those rooms that don't have views of the Alhambra overlook a varied garden.

⊠ San Juan de los Reyes 15, 18018 Granada. **Map** p291 D3. **(** (958) 226380. **FAX** (958) 224404. **Ⅱ** b. **Rooms** 9. **🌡 ◐** Never. **⌨** AE, DC, MC, V. **℗℗**

GRANADA

Parador San Francisco This immensely popular 14th-century former convent in the Alhambra's gardens is still a place of tranquillity. This is partly thanks to the superb views over the Generalife, the Albaicin and the snowy peaks of the Sierra Nevada. Inside, wooden saints stand in alcoves between finely furnished galleries, and there is plenty of space to relax. Book early.

⊠ Real de la Alhambra, 18009 Granada. **Map** p291 D3. **(** (958) 221441. **FAX** (958) 222264. **Ⅱ** b,l,d. **Rooms** 36. **🖫 🍴 🌡 ◐** Never. **⌨** AE, DC, MC, V. **℗℗℗℗**

GRANADA

Palacio de Santa Inés It is as elegant as its smaller sister, the Carmen de Santa Inés (see above), but the 'palace' has dark *caisson* ceilings, a picture-lined gallery and a slightly grander air. There are also some amazing fresco fragments attributed to Alejandro Mayner, a disciple of Rafael. All the stylish bedrooms are different.

⊠ Cuesta de Santa Inés 9, 18010 Granada. **Map** p291 D3. **(** (958) 222362. **FAX** (958) 222465. **Ⅱ** b. **Rooms** 13. **🖫 🌡 ◐** Never. **⌨** AE, DC, MC, V. **℗℗**

HUELVA

Finca Buen Vino Many people are drawn back to this haven of comfort in the Sierra de Aracena. Here, the air is pervaded with the scent of jasmin in summer and woodsmoke in winter. Rooms are very pretty and individual, there's crystal and linen at dinner (and sometimes a neighbour), and a pool with a seemingly endless view.

⊠ Los Marines, 21293 Huelva. **Map** p290 A3. **(** (959) 124034. **FAX** (959) 501029. **@** buenvino@ facilnet.es **Ⅱ** b,d. **Rooms** 6. **🏊 🌡 ◐** Aug, mid-Dec to early Jan. **⌨** AE, DC, MC, V. **℗℗℗**

GRANADA

Reina Cristina Poet and playwright García Lorca stayed in this refined 19th-century house with a glazed courtyard. Small but relaxing rooms.

⊠ Tablas 4, 18002 Granada. **Map** p291 D3. **(** (958) 253211. **FAX** (958) 255728. **@** clientes@ hotelreinacristina.com **Ⅱ** b,l,d. **Rooms** 43. **℗℗**

LA HERRADURA

Los Fenicios In one of the Costa del Sol's least built-up resorts, this hotel stands out from the crowd for its unusual architecture and unique lift.

⊠ Paseo Andrés Segovia, 18697 La Herradura, Granada. **Map** p290 C4. **(** (958) 827900. **FAX** (958) 827910. **Ⅱ** b,l,d. **Rooms** 42. **℗℗**

MIJAS

Club Puerta del Sol Sporty types will enjoy the tennis, pool and gym; others will love the views and garden of this chic horseshoe-shaped hotel.

⊠ Carretera Fuengirola-Mijas, 2965 Mijas, Málaga. **Map** p290 C4. **(** (95) 2486400. **FAX** (95) 2485462. **Ⅱ** b,l,d. **Rooms** 130. **℗℗**

MOJÁCAR

Mamabel's Run with much care and attention by Isabel Aznar and Jean Marie Rath, both lovers of art and antiquities. Sea views from terraces; delicious food. All the bedrooms are doubles.

⊠ Embajadores 5, 04638Mojácar, Almería. **Map** p291 E4. **(** **FAX** (9504) 72448. **Ⅱ** b,l,d. **Rooms** 9. **℗℗℗**

IBIZA TOWN, IBIZA

El Palacio At the top of a maze of steep streets lined with bougainvillea-clad houses, this classic mansion with an enclosed courtyard garden has been transformed into a paradise for film buffs. The bar has posters and other movie memorabilia, and every gorgeous room or suite is dedicated to a star – Garbo, Bogart, Monroe, James Dean.
⊠ Calle de la Conquista 2, 07800 Ibiza.
Map p289 E5. 🄲 (971) 301478. 🄵🄰🅇 (971) 391581.
@ etienne@ctv.es 🍴 b. **Rooms** 7. 🔊 🌑 Nov to Mar.
🄴 AE, DC, V. 🄟🄟🄟🄟

LOJA

La Bobadilla Set like an Andalusian village in its own huge grove of olive trees and Spanish oak, this is a gem that sets the standards by which other hotels are measured. Rooms are large, lavish, and rich in marble, silk and wood. Extras include two pools, a Turkish bath, and two fine restaurants supplied from the organic farm.
⊠ Finca La Bobadilla, 18300 Loja, Granada.
Map p290 C3. 🄲 (958) 321861. 🄵🄰🅇 (958) 321810.
@ info@labobadilla.com 🍴 b,l,d. **Rooms** 60. 🍴 ♨ 🄼
🄾 🌑 Never. 🄴 AE, DC, MC, V. 🄟🄟🄟🄟

JAÉN

Parador Castillo de Santa Catalina This impressive hill-top fortress, of the same vintage and style as the Alhambra, now looks benignly over a pretty valley filled with olive trees. Most of the rooms have balconies which share the view. Some furniture will excite 1960s fans, but there are also paintings and tapestries borrowed from the national collection.
⊠ Castillo de Santa Catalina, 23001 Jaén. **Map** p290 C3.
🄲 (953) 230000. 🄵🄰🅇 (953) 230930. 🍴 b,l,d. **Rooms** 45.
🍴 ♨ 🔊 🌑 Never. 🄴 AE, DC, MC, V. 🄟🄟🄟

MÁLAGA

Parador de Málaga-Gibralfaro The views are the prime asset of this parador, set in the peaceful gardens of the Gibralfaro far above the bustling port and summer heat of the city. Rooms are large and comfortable, with their own balconies. Summer dining is on a terrace and the bar, often busy with locals escaping the city, serves excellent snacks.
⊠ Monte de Gibralfaro, 29016 Málaga. **Map** p290 C4.
🄲 (952) 221902. 🄵🄰🅇 (952) 221904. 🍴 b,l,d. **Rooms** 38.
🍴 ♨ 🔊 🌑 Never. 🄴 AE, DC, MC, V. 🄟🄟🄟

MORAIRA

Swiss Hotel Moraira Exclusivity is the byword at this estate of smart villas set back from the sea. Lavish rooms, large pool.
⊠ Urbanización Club Moraira, 03724, Alicante.
Map p291 F2. 🄲 (96) 5747104. 🄵🄰🅇 (96) 5747074.
🍴 b,l,d. **Rooms** 25. 🄟🄟🄟

MORELLA

Cardinal Ram Heavy furniture highlights the character of this 16th-century mansion with its gleaming wood floors, beams and stone arches.
⊠ Cuesta Suñer 1, 12300 Morella, Castellón.
Map p289 C5. 🄲 (964) 173085. 🄵🄰🅇 (964) 173218.
🍴 b,l,d. **Rooms** 19. 🄟

MURCIA

Arco de San Juan The award-winning bold interior is tempered by fine antique furniture and a traditional façade. Near the cathedral.
⊠ Plaza de Ceballos 10, 30003 Murcia.
Map p291 F3. 🄲 (968) 210455. 🄵🄰🅇 (968) 220809.
🍴 b,l,d. **Rooms** 115. 🄟

OJÉN

Refugio de Juanar A comfortable rustic refuge in Marbella's wild hinterland, this hunting lodge offers snug rooms and robust regional cooking.
⊠ Sierra Blanca, 29610 Ojén, Málaga. **Map** p290 C4.
🄲 (95) 2881000. 🄵🄰🅇 (95) 2881001. 🍴 b,l,d.
Rooms 26. 🄟🄟

For key to symbols see backflap. For price categories *see p285*

ORIENT, MALLORCA

L'Hermitage In the mountainous interior of the island a 17th-century manor, cloister and new annexe cluster together amid citrus groves to form an appealing hotel. Rooms in the house have bags of character, those in the annexe have modern comforts. There are two snug lounges, a huge dining room and lovely terrace.

⊠ 07349 Orient, Mallorca. **Map** p289 F5. 📞 (971) 180303. **FAX** (971) 180411. @ info@hermitage_hotel.com ❚❚ b,l,d. **Rooms** 24. 🏊 🎮 🅾 🔴 Nov to Feb. 🖃 AE, DC, MC, V. Ⓟ Ⓟ Ⓟ Ⓟ

PALMA DE MALLORCA

San Lorenzo Pass through a wrought-iron gate on an old town street and, with the discovery of this hidden place, leave the cares of the world behind. The rooms are large, light and elegant with stylish bathrooms to match; two have their own roof terrace. A French Art Deco bar and a bougainvillea-hung garden complete the escape.

⊠ San Lorenzo 14, 07012 Palma de Mallorca. **Map** p289 F5. 📞 (971) 728200. **FAX** (971) 711901. @ sanlorenzo@fehm.es ❚❚ b. **Rooms** 6. 🏊 🅾 🔴 Never. 🖃 AE, DC, MC, V. Ⓟ Ⓟ

PALMA DE MALLORCA

Palacio Ca Sa Galesa This small, central 17th-century *palacio* offers stylish comfort with 20th-century amenities, and views of the bay and cathedral from its terrace. Oriental rugs dress wood floors and the comfy public rooms are set about with antiques. There is an indoor spa and outdoor summer pool. Free tea every afternoon.

⊠ Carrer de Miramar 8, 07021 Palma de Mallorca. **Map** p289 F5. 📞 (971) 715400. **FAX** (971) 721579. ❚❚ b. **Rooms** 12. 🏊 🎮 🅾 🔴 Never. 🖃 AE, DC, MC, V. Ⓟ Ⓟ Ⓟ Ⓟ

PALMA DE MALLORCA

Son Vida Ever since this 13th-century castle was turned into a luxury hotel in 1961, it has attracted the rich and famous, from Haile Selassie and Zsa Zsa Gabor to the Spanish royal family. Within the splendid building are all the facilities you would expect and more; outside is a glorious subtropical park and a golf course.

⊠ Castillo Son Vida-Raixa 2, 07013 Palma de Mallorca. **Map** p289 F5. 📞 (971) 790000. **FAX** (971) 790017. @ hsonvida@balears.net ❚❚ b,l,d. **Rooms** 171. 🖥 🏊 🎮 🅾 🔴 Never. 🖃 AE, DC, MC, V. Ⓟ Ⓟ Ⓟ Ⓟ

ORGIVA

Taray Bedrooms here are huge and modestly priced. Lovely garden of olives and orange trees, ideal walking and riding countryside beyond.

⊠ Carretera Tablate-Albuñol, 18400 Orgiva, Granada. **Map** p291 D4. 📞 (958) 784525. **FAX** (958) 784531. ❚❚ b,l,d. **Rooms** 26. Ⓟ

PALMA DE MALLORCA

Born This old mansion was originally the Marquis of Ferrandell's town base. Magnificent staircase and chandeliers, palm-planted courtyard.

⊠ Sant Jaume 3, 07012 Palma de Mallorca. **Map** p289 F5. 📞 (971) 712942. **FAX** (971) 718618. ❚❚ b. **Rooms** 29. Ⓟ Ⓟ

PECHINA

Balnearo de Sierra Alhamilla Roman baths survive at this 18th-century spa hotel. Bedrooms are traditional, with arched ceilings and double doors. The tiled dining room is barrel-vaulted.

⊠ 04259 Pechina, Almería. **Map** p291 E4. 📞 (950) 317413. **FAX** (950) 160257. ❚❚ b,l,d. **Rooms** 19. Ⓟ

POLLENÇA, MALLORCA

Formentor This ritzy hotel is set on a stunning promontory. It boasts its own beach and a famous buffet lunch.

⊠ Playa de Formentor, 07470 Pollença, Mallorca. **Map** p289 F5. 📞 (971) 899100. **FAX** (971) 865155. @ formentor@fehm.es ❚❚ b,l,d. **Rooms** 127. Ⓟ Ⓟ Ⓟ Ⓟ

PALMA DEL RÍO

Hospedería de San Francisco Bedrooms in this converted 15th-century Franciscan monastery are the former cells. They have few luxuries but plenty of character, bedspreads woven by nuns and hand-painted basins. There is a comfy sitting room, beamed bar and huge dining hall, though the summer venue for meals is the lovely cloister.
⊠ Avenida Pío XII 33, 14700 Palma del Río, Córdoba. **Map** p290 B3. **(** (957) 710183.
📠 (957) 710732. ⫟ b,l,d. **Rooms** 24. 🗐 🕪
⬤ Never. 🗷 AE, DC, MC, V. ℗

PORT D'ANDRATX, MALLORCA

Villa Italia Built in the 1920s by an eccentric Italian for his lover, Villa Italia is now patronized by a steady stream of glitterati. Marble floors, linen sheets, stucco ceilings, round baths, Roman capitals, personal service and a host of other hand-made details keep them coming. If it's all too much, retreat to the beautiful garden.
⊠ Camino Sant Carles 13, 07157 Port d'Andratx, Mallorca. **Map** p289 F5. **(** (971) 674011.
📠 (971) 673350. ⫟ b,l,d. **Rooms** 16. 🗐 ⫟ 🕪
⬤ Never. 🗷 AE, DC, MC, V. ℗℗℗℗

PENÁGUILA

Mas de Pau A valley of olives and almonds in the Sierra de Aitana is the setting for this rural house. Part of its appeal is a gorgeous pool with glazed roof and wrap-around windows, that allows you to swim and admire the view all year. Staff are attentive and polite, but bedrooms are cramped – especially those on the second floor.
⊠ Carretera Alcoi-Penáguila km 9, 03815 Penáguila, Alicante. **Map** p291 F2. **(** (96) 5513111.
📠 (96) 5513109. ⫟ b,l,d. **Rooms** 12. ⫟ 🕪
⬤ Never. 🗷 MC, V. ℗

EL PUERTO DE SANTA MARÍA

Monasterio San Miguel This large Baroque building was built in the 18th century by the Duke of Medinaceli to house the Clarisas Capuchinas order of nuns. It is now a smart, busy hotel with antique art and modern facilities. It is a popular venue for concerts and conferences – the former chapel can seat 600.
⊠ Calle Larga 27, 11500 El Puerto de Santa María, Cádiz. **Map** p290 A4. **(** (956) 540440. 📠 (956) 542604.
@ monasterio@jale.com ⫟ b,l,d. **Rooms** 150.
🗐 🕪 ⬤ Never. 🗷 AE, DC, MC, V. ℗℗℗

RANDA, MALLORCA

Es Recó de Randa Old stone house in a peaceful village, now a restaurant with rooms. Ask for a bedroom with a view of the mountains.
⊠ Font 13, 07629 Randa, Mallorca. **Map** p289 F5.
((971) 660997. 📠 (971) 662558. ⫟ b,l,d.
Rooms 14. ℗℗℗

RONDA

Reina Victoria The parador has eclipsed its position as Ronda's grandest hotel, but it enjoys a clifftop setting with matchless views.
⊠ Jerez 25, 29400 Ronda, Málaga. **Map** p290 B4.
((95) 2871240. 📠 (95) 2871075. ⫟ b,l,d.
Rooms 89. ℗℗℗

SAN JOSÉ

San José This eccentric yet charming hotel has large semi-circular windows in the sitting room, through which a tempting sandy beach is visible.
⊠ Correo s/n, 04118 San José, Almería. **Map** p291 E4.
((950) 380116. 📠 (950) 380002. ⫟ b,l,d.
Rooms 8. ℗℗

SANLÚCAR DE BARRAMEDA

Los Helechos This early 20th-century Andalusian building, restored in 1992, has quiet, comfortable rooms that provide a refuge in a central location.
⊠ Plaza Madre de Dios 9, 11540 Sanlúcar de Barrameda, Cádiz. **Map** p290 A4. **(** (956) 361349.
📠 (956) 369650. ⫟ b. **Rooms** 66. ℗

RONDA

Parador de Ronda Ronda is one of Spain's most spectacularly situated cities and this purpose-built parador has an incomparable spot, teetering precipitously above the Tajo gorge. If you can, book a top-floor suite – they have balconies and spectacular views – and watch the birds at close range. The dining room has a solid reputation.
☒ Plaza de España 1, 29400 Ronda, Málaga.
Map p290 B4. ☎ (95) 2877500. ⒻⒶⓍ (95) 2878188.
🍴 b,l,d. **Rooms** 78. 🍽 🏊 🎙 🌑 Never.
🅰 AE, MC, V. ⓅⓅⓅ

SAN SEBASTIÁN, GOMERA

Parador de la Gomera High above the main town of this volcanic island, where Columbus made his last stop before America, the parador is full of maritime mementoes. The decoration is exemplary: polished wood floors, rugs, potted plants, pitched beamed roofs, and furniture that gleams in the spacious bedrooms.
☒ 38800 San Sebastián de La Gomera, Santa Cruz de Tenerife. **Map** p291 E5. ☎ (922) 871100.
ⒻⒶⓍ (922) 871116. 🍴 b,l,d. **Rooms** 58. 🏊 🍽 🎙
🌑 Never. 🅰 AE, DC, MC, V. ⓅⓅⓅ

SAN MIGUEL, IBIZA

Hacienda Na Xamena The focal point of this glamorous clifftop *hacienda* is its terrace and pool overlooking sea and pine-wooded hills. Inside, dazzling white curved walls are offset with touches of vivid blue, terracotta, stone and wood to create a haven of understated luxury.
☒ Apartado 423, Na Xamena, 07815 San Miguel, Ibiza. **Map** p289 E5. ☎ (971) 334500. ⒻⒶⓍ (971) 334514.
@ htl.hacienda@vic.servicom.es 🍴 b,l,d.
Rooms 63. 🍽 🏊 🎙 🌑 Nov to mid-Apr.
🅰 AE, DC, MC, V. ⓅⓅⓅⓅ

SANLÚCAR LA MAYOR

Hacienda de Benazuza Unlike many other large hotels, this *hacienda* has not sacrificed its soul. The buildings span diverse cultures and centuries, from the thousand-year-old Arabic enclosing wall to a 16th-century Spanish coat of arms. Public rooms in rich ochres and reds have Moorish ceilings.
☒ Virgen de las Nieves, 41800 Sanlúcar La Mayor, Seville. **Map** p290 A3. ☎ (95) 5703344. ⒻⒶⓍ (95) 5703410.
@ hbenazuza@arrakis.es 🍴 b,l,d. **Rooms** 44. 🍽 🏊 🎙
🌑 Never. 🅰 AE, DC, MC, V. ⓅⓅⓅⓅ

SANLÚCAR DE BARRAMEDA

Posada de Palacio This unconventional, homely B&B occupies a fine house near the sherry *bodegas* in the old town. Stone-tiled courtyard.
☒ Caballeros 11, 11540 Sanlúcar de Barrameda, Cádiz.
Map p290 A4. ☎ (956) 364840. ⒻⒶⓍ (956) 365060.
🍴 b. **Rooms** 13. Ⓟ

SANLÚCAR DE BARRAMEDA

Tartaneros An inviting cafeteria in Art Nouveau style occupies most of the ground floor, while antiques and curiosities furnish the other rooms.
☒ Tartaneros 8, 11540 Sanlúcar de Barrameda, Cádiz.
Map p290 A4. ☎ (956) 362044. ⒻⒶⓍ (956) 360045.
🍴 b. **Rooms** 21. Ⓟ

ST ANTONIO DE PORTMANY, IBIZA

Pikes Its setting amid pine woods draws a smart crowd to this stylish mansion. Five-star amenities are combined with informality.
☒ Camino Sa Vorera, 07820 Sant Antonio de Portmany, Ibiza. **Map** p289 E5. ☎ (971) 342222. ⒻⒶⓍ (971) 342312.
🍴 b,l,d. **Rooms** 26. ⓅⓅⓅ

SEVILLE

Alfonso XIII Sumptuous mock Moorish palace was built for an exhibition in 1929. Exotic gardens outside, grand rooms and formal service within.
☒ San Fernando 2, 41004 Seville. **Map** p290 B3.
☎ (95) 4222850. ⒻⒶⓍ (95) 4216033. 🍴 b,l,d.
Rooms 146. ⓅⓅⓅⓅ

SANTA EULALIA DEL RÍO, IBIZA

Les Terrasses A traditional Ibizan house, done out with panache by a Frenchwoman, Françoise Pialoux. The house, bedrooms (in a converted farm building), two pools and gardens are on different levels. Peaceful nooks and crannies give it the intimacy of a private villa.
⊠ Apartado 1235, Carretera de Santa Eulalia, 07800 Santa Eulalia del Río, Ibiza. **Map** p289 E5.
((971) 332643. ̄FAX̄ (971) 338978.
@ lesterrasses@interbook.es ⊞ b,l,d. **Rooms** 7.
▤ ♒ ⑧ ⬤ Never. ⋐ MC, V. ⑦⑦⑦

SEVILLE

Patio de la Cartuja The residential hotel version of Patio de la Alameda (see below left) is similar in almost every respect, even down to the furnishings. The two are run under the combined name 'Patios de Sevilla'. The Cartuja has a long terrace, dotted with tables, chairs and parasols, and balconies decorated with geraniums.
⊠ Lumbreras 8-10, 41002 Seville.
Map p290 B3. ((95) 4900200. ̄FAX̄ (95) 4902056.
@ patios@bbvnet.com ⊞ b. **Rooms** 34. ▤ ⑧
⬤ Never. ⋐ AE, DC, MC, V. ⑦⑦

SEVILLE

Patio de la Alameda For people who relish their independence, this handsome building has been converted into 22 pleasant one-bedroom apartments. Each has a sitting room and kitchen and can accommodate up to four people. There's a daily maid service; if you don't feel like cooking, there are plenty of local restaurants and bars.
⊠ Alameda de Hércules 56, 41002 Seville.
Map p290 B3. ((95) 4904999. ̄FAX̄ (95) 4900226.
@ patios@bbvnet.com ⊞ b. **Rooms** 22. ▤ ⬤ Never.
⋐ AE, DC, MC, V. ⑦⑦

SEVILLE

San Gil Classified as one of the hundred most interesting buildings in the city, the San Gil marks the careful restoration of an early 1900s mansion. A wealth of original detail remains, including a striking tiled entrance and enclosed garden with fountains, palms, an ancient cypress and original mosaics. The cool bedrooms have crisp lines and wrought-iron furniture.
⊠ Parras 28, 41002 Seville. **Map** p290 B3.
((95) 4906811. ̄FAX̄ (95) 4906939. ⊞ b,l,d. **Rooms** 39.
▤ ♒ ⑧ ⬤ Never. ⋐ AE, DC, MC, V. ⑦⑦

SEVILLE

Casas de la Judería A maze of suites (some self-catering), separated by tiled courts with potted plants and fountains, comprise this historic hotel.
⊠ Callejón de las Dos Hermanas 7, 41004 Seville.
Map p290 B3. ((95) 4415150. ̄FAX̄ (95) 4422170.
⊞ b. **Rooms** 57. ⑦⑦

SEVILLE

Ciudad de Sevilla Designed for the Exposition of 1927, the hotel has a light, modern interior.
⊠ Avenida Manuel Siurot 25, 41013 Seville.
Map p290 B3. ((95) 4230505. ̄FAX̄ (95) 4238539.
@ ciusev.recep@ac.hoteles.com ⊞ b,l,d.
Rooms 94. ⑦⑦⑦⑦

SEVILLE

Doña María A brand new hotel behind an old façade, with Andalusian decoration, a glorious patio overflowing with plants and a rooftop pool.
⊠ Don Remondo 19, 41004 Seville. **Map** p290 B3.
((95) 4224990. ̄FAX̄ (95) 4219546. ⊞ b.
Rooms 68. ⑦⑦

SEVILLE

Murillo A treasure trove of antiques, from ornate screens to a sedan chair, in a handsome town house at the heart of the Barrio de Santa Cruz.
⊠ Lope de Rueda 7 & 9, 41004 Seville.
Map p290 B3. ((95) 4216095. ̄FAX̄ (95) 4219616.
⊞ b,l,d. **Rooms** 57. ⑦⑦

SEVILLE

Taberna del Alabardero The poet José Antonio Cavestany once lived in this 19th-century mansion in the heart of the city. Now it's a restaurant with rooms, elegantly decorated and specializing in a hybrid Basque-Andalusian cuisine. Breakfast, tea or drinks can be taken in the romantic central court with a stained-glass roof. Chic bedrooms with wood floors and chintz fabrics.
⊠ Zaragoza 20, 41001 Seville. **Map** p290 B3.
📞 (95) 4560637. FAX (95) 4563666. 🍴 b,l,d. **Rooms** 7.
🛏 🔔 🍷 ◐ Aug. 🗐 AE, DC, MC, V. ⓅⓅ

TURRE

Finca Listonero Restaurateurs Graeme Gibson and David Rice run this farmhouse in the hills above the unspoilt Almería coast. It has been stylishly converted and seamlessly extended, and functions along house-party lines. The setting is peaceful but sandy beaches, golf, tennis, riding and walking are all within easy reach. Daily menu of international dishes.
⊠ Cortijo Grande, 04639 Turre, Almería.
Map p291 E4. 📞 FAX (950) 479094. 🍴 b,d. **Rooms** 6. 🌊
🍷 ◐ Never. 🗐 MC, V. ⓅⓅ

SIERRA NEVADA

El Lodge After a long day on the piste, you can ski to the door of this modern chalet and relax in a Jacuzzi bath with a view of the surrounding peaks. It is one of Spain's premier ski hotels, built of Finnish pine, warm and soundproofed, with a comfy sitting room, a bar flaunting ski mementoes and snug log-cabin-style bedrooms.
⊠ Balcón de Pradollano s/n, 18196 Sierra Nevada, Granada. **Map** p291 D4. 📞 (958) 480600.
FAX (958) 480506. 🍴 b,l,d. **Rooms** 20. 🌊 🍴 🍷
◐ Never. 🗐 AE, DC, MC, V. ⓅⓅⓅⓅ

ÚBEDA

Palacio de la Rambla This 16th-century mansion in the centre of town, ancestral home of the Marquesa de la Rambla, makes a unique, historic B&B. Its heart is a beautiful ivy-clad Renaissance patio, around which are the four most interesting bedrooms, furnished with antiques and engravings. Breakfast is served in the salon.
⊠ Plaza del Marqués 1, 23400 Úbeda, Jaén.
Map p291 D3. 📞 (953) 750196. FAX (953) 750267.
🍴 b. **Rooms** 8. 🍷 ◐ mid-July to mid-Aug.
🗐 AE, MC, V. ⓅⓅ

SEVILLE

Los Seises Art Deco motifs inject style into elegant pastel rooms in this 16th-century palace which preserves a Roman mosaic and Arab well.
⊠ Segovias 6, 41004 Seville. **Map** p290 B3.
📞 (95) 4229495. FAX (95) 4224334. 🍴 b,l,d.
Rooms 43. ⓅⓅⓅ

SÓLLER, MALLORCA

Ca N'aí This captivating old Mallorcan house nestling in a valley scented with the fragrance of oranges, is popular for its first-rate restaurant.
⊠ Camí de Son Puça 48, 07100 Sóller, Mallorca.
Map p289 F50. 📞 (971) 632494. FAX (971) 631899.
🍴 b,l,d. **Rooms** 11. ⓅⓅⓅ

ILLA DE TABARCA

Casa del Gobernador This 18th-century colonial mansion, once the governor's house, wouldn't look out of place in the pirate haven of Tortuga.
⊠ Arzola s/n, 03138 Illa de Tabarca, Alicante.
Map p291 F2. 📞 FAX (96) 5114260. 🍴 b.
Rooms 14. Ⓟ

TARIFA

Hurricane Wind from the Straits of Gibraltar produces great windsurfing here. This hotel in an innovative building is where most surfers stay.
⊠ Carretera N340, Tarifa, 11380 Hurricane, Cádiz.
Map p290 B5. 📞 (956) 684919. FAX (956) 680329.
🍴 b. **Rooms** 33. ⓅⓅ

ÚBEDA

Parador Condestable Dávalos Eyecatching blue-and-white tiles on the façade announce this refined parador. Its glorious courtyard is set with tables and chairs and bursting with greenery. This is a friendly place, particularly evident in the tile-floored public rooms; bedrooms, some of which lead off a glazed gallery, do not disappoint.
☒ Plaza de Vázquez de Molina 1, 23400 Úbeda, Jaén. **Map** p291 D3. 🄲 (953) 750345. 🄵🄰🄷 (953) 751259. 🍴 b,l,d. **Rooms** 31. 🃠 🎤 🄾 Never. 🃟 AE, DC, MC, V. ⓟⓟ

LA VILA JOIOSA (VILLAJOYOSA)

Hotel El Montíboli This brightly luxurious hotel has carefully not grown past its ability to deliver a warm welcome to every guest. It is set on its own little headland. Below the hotel is a pool with a view, and down by the beach is another pool with a little lunch-time restaurant. Choose between a room with terrace and a bungalow.
☒ 03570 La Vila Joiosa, Alicante. **Map** p291 F2. 🄲 (96) 5890250. 🄵🄰🄷 (96) 5893857. 🄰 montiboli@ alc.servicom.es 🍴 b,l,d. **Rooms** 53. 🃠 🎤 🍴 🄾 🄾 Never. 🃟 AE, DC, MC, V. ⓟⓟⓟ

VALLDEMOSSA, MALLORCA

Vistamar On cliffs near the pretty port of Valldemossa is this lovely old villa, now a comfortable country hotel with a penchant for modern art. The beamed rooms are cool and attractive. The sea, though close, is unreachable on foot, but the pool is panoramic.
☒ Carretera Andraitx km 2, 07170 Valldemossa, Mallorca. **Map** p289 F50. 🄲 (971) 612300. 🄵🄰🄷 (971) 612583. 🄰 info@vistamarhotel.es 🍴 b,l,d. **Rooms** 16. 🃠 🎤 🄾 Nov to Jan. 🃟 AE, DC, MC, V. ⓟⓟⓟⓟ

XÁTIVA

Hostería Mont-Sant The small Mont-Sant is superbly located above the town and below the castle, and has spectacular views of both from each of the attractive rooms. Its grounds are surrounded by architectural remains dating back to the 12th century. The restaurant's regional dishes can be eaten inside or al fresco.
☒ Subida al Castillo s/n, 46800 Xátiva, Valencia. **Map** p291 F2. 🄲 (96) 2275081. 🄵🄰🄷 (96) 2281905. 🄰 montsant@servidex.com 🍴 b,l,d. **Rooms** 7. 🃠 🃠 🍴 🄾 🄾 early Jan to mid-Feb. 🃟 AE, DC, MC, V. ⓟⓟ

TURRE

El Nacimiento Off the tourist track, this farmhouse has been turned into a guesthouse by its genial organic farmer owners. You can taste the fruit of their labours at meals.
☒ Cortijo El Nacimiento, 04639 Turre, Almería. **Map** p291 E4. 🄲 (950) 528090. 🍴 b,l,d. **Rooms** 4. ⓟ

VALDERROBES

Torre del Visco This simple, peaceful refuge overlooking the Tastavins valley is very homely; breakfast is eaten in the farmhouse kitchen.
☒ Apartado 15, 44580 Valderrobes, Teruel. **Map** p288 C4. 🄲 (978) 769015. 🄵🄰🄷 (978) 769016. 🍴 b,l,d. **Rooms** 12. ⓟⓟ

VALENCIA

Ad Hoc Brickwork and beams are incorporated into the modern interior of this 19th-century old quarter building with maximum effect.
☒ Boix 4, 46003 Valencia. **Map** p291 F1. 🄲 (96) 3919140. 🄵🄰🄷 (96) 3913667. 🄰 adhoc@nexo.net 🍴 b,l,d. **Rooms** 28. ⓟⓟ

VEJER DE LA FRONTERA

Convento de San Francisco Remnants from its days as a convent are preserved in this friendly hotel, as well as Roman and medieval finds.
☒ La Plazuela, 11150 Vejer de la Frontera, Cádiz. **Map** p290 B4. 🄲 (956) 451001. 🄵🄰🄷 (956) 451004. 🍴 b,l,d. **Rooms** 24. ⓟ

For key to symbols see backflap. For price categories see p285.

ITALY

ITALY

ITALY'S BEST places to stay are often at the very cheap or the very expensive end of the spectrum. Many cities offer little in between, but away from urban centres the choice is wider. Often old farm estates in beautiful countryside have been restored to incorporate guest accommodation. Some of the two-star *pensioni* are truly excellent, run by hardworking owners: their hospitality and cooking can be unique. For glamour, head for a top hotel in a historic building – even if your budget restricts your stay to one night. Whether it's in the centre of Milan, deep in the countryside, surrounded by vineyards or on a fortified hill top, chances are it will be unforgettable.

Villa d'Este, Lake Como, page 343, a beautiful hotel with romantic grounds and a glittering interior

ITALY REGION BY REGION

IN THIS GUIDE, Italy has been divided into three areas: Northern Italy, Central Italy and Southern Italy.

Northern Italy
This is the wealthiest part of the country. The business lunch and the corporate weekend keep some very good hotels and restaurants in business, from Milan – centre of the textile and fashion trade – to Bologna, the medieval city at the heart of Italy's version of silicon valley. Venice, sinking under the weight of its visitors, has a few good-value places to stay, but only if you know the score; and, of course, it has its famous, luxury canalside *palazzi* – at a price.

Perhaps the most interesting experiences are provided by the small historic towns such as Ravenna, Bergamo and Parma, with their artistic and architectural treasures, and hotels that exude bonhomie and which serve up classic North Italian cooking. But don't overlook the Italian lakes of Como, Orta and Maggiore: they have a wistful, old-fashioned appeal with one or two glorious *grande dame* hotels.

The mountainous northern-most parts of Italy were acquired at the beginning of the 20th century, from what used to be southern Austria, Slovenia and parts of France. Alpine-style chalet guest-houses with balconies full of geraniums, and dumplings on the menu, are an incongruous feature in these parts.

The Adriatic coastline is flat, with grill-pan sunbathing and genuinely warm hospitality. On the opposite side of the country is the Ligurian Riviera. Here is the smart resort of Portofino; the former fishing village with its mini-scule harbour is for many travellers a must-see-and-be-seen-at stopover. Its hotel prices are off the top end of the scale, but you can always visit for the day and then stay in nearby Santa Margherita or Rapallo, which offer much better value.

Central Italy

Florence is one the highlights of many a modern grand tour. Its outstanding places to stay include a palace in the hills outside town. For fewer crowds, head for the walled towns such as Lucca, or go east towards Umbria or even little-visited Le Marche (The Marches'), where there are some fine country hotels near the medieval cities of Arezzo and Sansepolcro.

The island of Sardinia is said to have the clearest water for snorkelling and scuba diving. Choose between the glitzy Costa Smeralda or quieter, and more beautiful backwaters.

Rome and its province of Lazio could keep you busy for weeks, and there are plenty of choices of lodgings, with a mix of one-stars and classic grand Italian hotels in the centre and more spacious places with gardens in the outer districts.

On the other side of the country, the Abruzzo and Molise are empty, mountainous quarters from which thousands have emigrated over the past 200 years. Hotels are sparse and itineraries need planning.

Southern Italy

The landscape becomes dramatically rugged on the Amalfi peninsula south of Naples. Here there's a choice between excellent family-run *pensioni* or luxury *palazzi* in villages such as Ravello. The islands of Ischia and Capri in the Bay of Naples have accommodation in every price band, and are at their

Venice's Danieli, page 356 – in a famed location overlooking the lagoon

best in early spring before the holiday crowds arrive.

Puglia, in the 'heel' of Italy, has become fashionable among Italians, as have the Aeolian islands and Pantelleria. There are many villas for rent here, but few recommendable hotels. Sicily is a different world, with palm trees, citrus groves and volcanic beaches. There are some great places to stay here, though, again, not in large numbers. We believe we have featured the most

captivating, from the fashionable resort of Taormina to the capital, Palermo.

HIGHLIGHTS

HOTELS ILLUSTRATED on these pages are by no means the only highlights. Other favourites include the Baia d'Oro in Gargnano (page 346), for its fabulous setting on Lake Garda; the Salivolpi farmhouse hotel in Castellina in Chianti (page 360), perfect for family holidays; Rome's Hassler (page 367), a luxurious experience in old-world living; and the charm-ing Bellevue Syrene in Sorrento (page 379), for its stunning cliff top setting.

FOOD AND DRINK

EATING OUT is one of the obvious pleasures of a holiday in Italy, and the regional differences add to the experience – however, there are so many that it's impossible to begin to do them justice here.

The remarkable La Posta Vecchia, Palo Laziale, page 365

Villa Franca, Positano, page 378 with great views of the plunging Amalfi coastline

Northern dishes tend to be pork, veal and dairy based, with creamy sauces. In the south, vegetables and fish predominate, and many pasta dishes are accompanied by 'raw' sauces in which tomatoes, for example, are sweated with garlic and oil for just a few moments so that the freshness of the ingredients comes through. Among the many highlights of Italian cooking are Milanese risotto, coloured by saffron and flavoured with rosemary and the juices from a veal roast; and fresh mozzarella from around Naples, which spills cream from its centre when you cut into it.

For some of the best places for local delicacies, look out for the '*Agriturismo*' signs, usually a crossed knife and fork. Cheese, salami, homemade pasta, honey and

Villa Franca, Positano, page 378

other farm produce can be enjoyed in delightful, simple surroundings.

A *ristorante* is usually quite a formal place, with ranks of knives and forks and often a business clientele. The more informal *osteria* serves regional specialities, though the term is being highjacked by smarter establishments. The *birreria* (pubs) and *vineria* (wine bars) often offer meat and local cheese-based snacks (a snack is a *merenda*). The most enjoyable *trattorie* are the local, family-run places where the absence of a written menu, or a set menu with no choices, is usually a sign that the food will be simple, but unpretentious and delicious.

Space doesn't permit more than a brief sketch of Italian wine. Among the oustanding regions are Tuscany (for Brunello di Montalcino and Vino Nobile di Montepulciano); Friuli; and Le Langhe, a little-known region of Piemonte in Northern Italy (for the weighty Barolos and the earthy Barberas).

When eating out, most Italians order a bottle with a label only on special occasions. The norm is to have a carafe of house wine (usually local and perfectly quaffable). Ask for *un quarto* (quarter) or *un mezzo* (half) litre.

Lunch is generally from 12:30–3pm; dinner from 8–11pm or midnight, often followed by a stroll around the piazza, a coffee or a visit to a *gelateria* (ice-cream parlour).

Dinner starts with *antipasto* (seafood salad, or a selection of salami), followed by *il primo* (pasta or a soup) and on to the main business of *il secondo* (the meat or fish course). Vegetables (*contorni*) are ordered separately. Dessert (*dolci*) usually comes from the trolley. Most places make a cover charge (*pane e coperto*) and may also add a 10 per cent service charge. Take your receipt (*ricevuta fiscale*) when you leave the restaurant, or you can be subject to an on-the-spot fine; this strange law was introduced as an attempt to cut down on tax evasion.

BEDROOMS AND BATHROOMS

THE (potentially embarrassing) Italian word for a double bed is a *matrimoniale*. If you don't specify this, twin beds are automatically allocated. However, you can ask for these to be made up as a double if all the *matrimoniales* are taken. Make it clear if you want a room with en suite bathroom (*con bagno*); there are different

Stately Principe di Savoia in Milan, page 349

price tariffs for rooms with shared facilities. A shower is a *doccia*. Most places have showers and baths combined.

OTHER PRACTICAL INFORMATION

You'll OFTEN find air-conditioning in hotels, but heating in anything but the depths of winter should not be taken for granted.

Language Italians are good linguists. English, French and German are widely spoken, especially in tourist areas.

Currency The Italian *lira* (plural *lire*), written as 'L' before the amount in figures.

Shops Open 8 or 9am–12:30 or 1pm Mon–Sat, and then from 3:30–7 or 8pm. Museum times tend to follow the same pattern. In northern cities, businesses and some shops are open through the day. Shops are closed on Sunday except in tourist resorts, but usually you'll find a *pasticceria* (essentially, a delicatessen) open first thing in the day for essentials.

Tipping Waiters don't rely on tips in the same way as in other European countries (if lucky, they will get a share of the profits), but Italians usually round up the bill.

Telephoning Many hotels, especially the unassuming kind, make no profit from phone calls their guests make – a pleasant change from other European countries. As well as public call boxes (which take coins and phone-cards – called a *scheda telefonica*), in most big towns there are Telecom Italia offices with private phone booths – handy for long-distance calls.

To make a phone call within Italy, always dial the full pre-fix, even for a local number. To call Italy from the UK, dial 00, then the international dialling code 39; then dial the number, including the initial zero; from the US, 001 39.

Public holidays 1 January; 6 January; Easter Monday; 25 April (Liberation Day); 1 May; 15 August (Ferragosto, or Assumption); 1 November (All Saints); 8 December (Immaculate Conception); 25 and 26 December.

USEFUL WORDS

Breakfast	*Prima colazione*
Lunch	*Pranzo*
Dinner	*Cena*
Free rooms?	*Camere libere?*
How much?	*Quant'è?*
A single	*Una camera singola*
A double	*Una camera doppia*

ITALY PRICE BANDS

MOST HOTEL prices vary according to whether it's low or high season. The maximum price is displayed (by law) on the back of the room's door.

Our price bands refer as usual to the price of a standard double room with bathroom in high season.

Breakfast is usually included in the price quoted; local taxes can creep in as an extra at any time, especially in the historic or 'art' cities.

Ⓛ	under L200,000
ⓁⓁ	200,000–L325,000
ⓁⓁⓁ	L325,000–L450,000
ⓁⓁⓁⓁ	above L450,000

The lobby of the Four Seasons, Milan, page 348

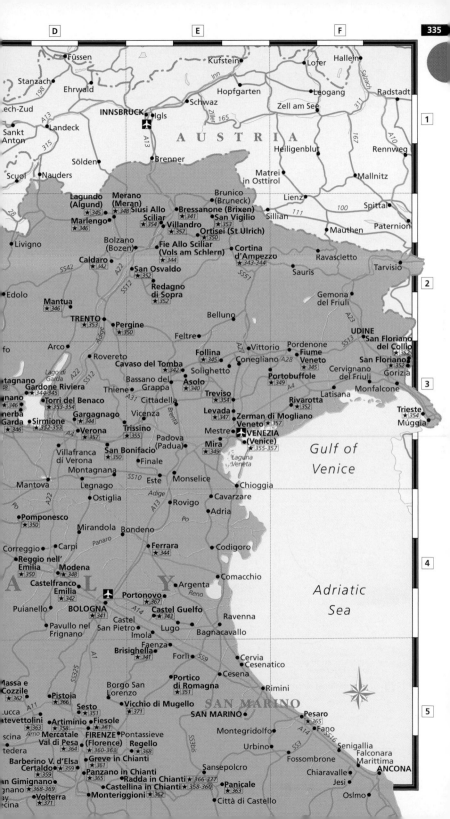

Livorno

Barberino Val d'Elsa ★ 361
Certaldo ★ 359
San Gimignano ★ 368-369
Volterra ★ 371 Lecchi in Chianti ★ 363
Greve in Chianti ★ 361
Panzano in Chianti ★ 365
Radda in Chianti
Poggibonsi
Castellina in Chianti ★ 358,350
Monteriggioni ★ 362
Monte San Savino ★ 364
Sansepolcro
Panicale ★ 363
Città di Castello
Arezzo

Rosignano Solvay

Cecina

Pievescola ★ 366
Sovicille ★ 370
Siena ★ 370
Castelnuovo Berardenga
San Benedetto ★ 368
San Gimignano ★ 368-369
Sinalunga ★ 370

Pomarance

Cortona ★ 361
Umbertic

San Vincenzo

Massa Marittima

Montefollonico
Pienza ★ 362
Monticchiello ★ 364
Bagno Vignoni ★ 363
Sarteano ★ 369
Cetona ★ 361

Castiglione del Lago
Castel del Piano Umbro
Fontignano ★ 363

Lago Trasimeno

Cenerer ★ 359
PER

Torgiano ★ 371
Canalicchio di Collazzone ★ 360
Monte Castello di Vibio ★ 362

Piombino

Elba

Follonica

Roccastrada

Ombrone

S2

Portoferraio ★ 360
Capolivieri
Lacona ★ 359

Punta Ala ★ 366

Grosseto

Scansano ★ 370

San Lorenzo Nuovo

Prato ★ 367
Orvieto

Toc
Titagnano ★ 371
Asproli ★ 359

Giglio ★ 361

Giglio

Giannutri

Orbetello
Porto Ercole ★ 367

Montalto di Castro

Tarquinia

Manciano

Lago di Bolsena

Montefiascone

Viterbo
Vetrella

SS3

Nar

Ame

I

Civita Castellana

Civitavecchia

A12

Lago di Bracciano

Cerveteri

Palo Laziale ★ 365

VATICAN CITY
ROMA (R ★ 366-3

Tevere

Tyrrhenian Sea

An

KEY

★ 100 Hotel location and page reference

✈ International airport

— Motorway

— Major road

0 kilometres   25

0 miles   25

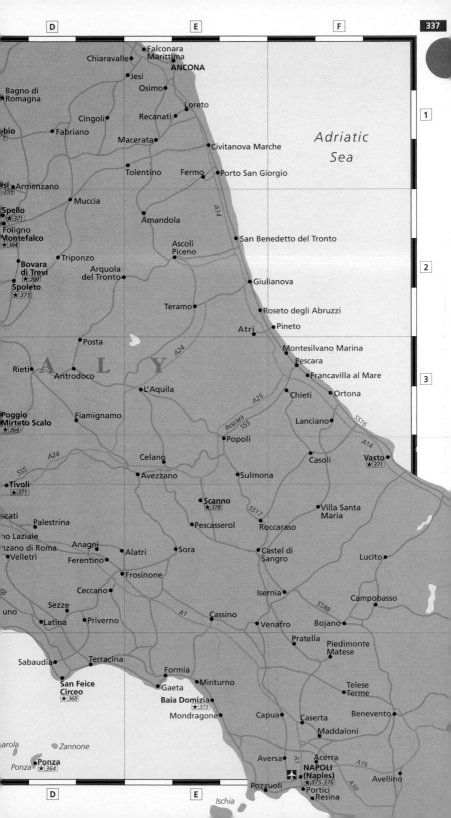

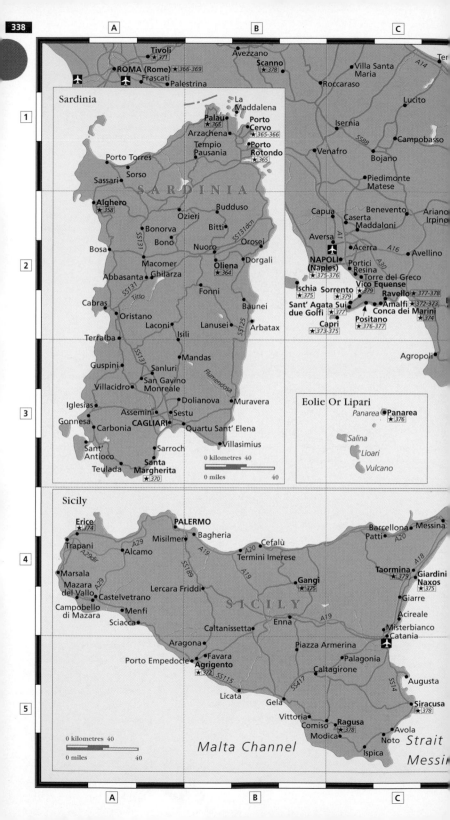

NORTHERN ITALY

PIEDMONT • VALLE D'AOSTA
LIGURIA • LOMBARDIA • VENETIA • EMILIA-ROMAGNA

*T*HE *NORTHERN THIRD OF Italy encompasses a rich diversity of landscapes, from the high jagged peaks of the Alps and the Dolomites, through the lakes of Lombardy, to two strips of Mediterranean coast and the great Veneto plain. There is a similarly wide choice of types of hotel. In the mountains are traditional Alpine and Tyrolean* *chalets, simple and homely; lakes such as Como, Maggiore and Garda are the setting for some of the most romantic hotels, both luxury and budget, in Italy; and the Veneto plain has its share of Palladian villas and other aristocratic houses turned into hotels. Also well served are the great cities of the north, most notably Milan and the incomparable Venice.*

ARGEGNO

ASOLO

Belvedere Simple and good value, in a dreamy position on the shores of Lake Como. Although rooms are small, they all have private facilities (shower or bath) and the best have wonderful lake views. The lady of the house is Scottish – hence the tartan bar. Her Italian husband is an accomplished home cook, and eating out on the terrace is a special pleasure.
⊠ Via Milano 8, 22010 Argegno, Como. **Map** p334 C2.
📞 031 82 11 16. 🅵🅰🆇 031 82 15 71. 🍴 b,l,d. **Rooms** 16.
🔵 🔘 mid-Nov to mid-March. 🃏 Not accepted. ⓁⓁ

Villa Cipriani In a beautiful medieval hilltop village this former home of poet Robert Browning is a sophisticated hotel with a heart, a jewel of the ITT Sheraton group. Bedrooms are gracious (try for an 'exclusive' or terrace room) and there is a charming garden with commanding views. The hotel is popular with wedding parties.
⊠ Via Canova 298, 31011 Asolo, Treviso. **Map** p335 E3.
📞 0423 95 21 66. 🅵🅰🆇 0423 95 20 95.
@ gianpaolo_burattin/ittsheraton.com 🍴 b,l,d.
Rooms 31. 🍽 🔵 🔘 Never. 🃏 AE, DC, MC, V. ⓁⓁⓁⓁ

ASOLO

Al Sole In a superb position, perched above Piazza Maggiore, a cool, modern, sophisticated hotel with plenty of luxurious touches.
⊠ Via Collegio 33, 31011 Asolo, Treviso. **Map** p335 E3.
📞 0423 52 81 11. 🅵🅰🆇 0423 52 83 99.
@ sole@prometeo.com 🍴 b. **Rooms** 23. ⓁⓁⓁ

BELLAGIO

La Pergola Tucked away in tiny Pescallo, just to the south of Bellagio, is this rustic, old-fashioned, family-run hotel with a splendid view.
⊠ Piazza del Porto 4, Pescallo, 22021 Bellagio, Como.
Map p334 C2. 📞 031 95 02 63. 🅵🅰🆇 031 95 02 53.
🍴 b,l,d. **Rooms** 10. Ⓛ

BERGAMO

Agnello d'Oro Tall, narrow inn on a tiny square in the city's medieval core. Cosy restaurant; the bright bedrooms verge on the basic.
⊠ Via Gombito 22, 24129 Bergamo. **Map** p334 C3.
📞 035 24 98 83. 🅵🅰🆇 035 23 56 12. 🍴 b,l,d.
Rooms 20. Ⓛ

BERGAMO

Gourmet Eating in fine weather on the shady terrace is a main attraction at this *città alta* restaurant-with-rooms. Bedrooms are large and light, with above-average bathrooms.
⊠ Via San Vigilio 1, 24129 Bergamo. **Map** p334 C3.
📞 🅵🅰🆇 035 437 30 04. 🍴 b,l,d. **Rooms** 10. ⓁⓁ

BELLAGIO

Florence The handsome 18th-century building occupies a prime position in Bellagio, pearl of Lake Como. An arcaded terrace makes a welcoming entry to the attractive foyer, with its beamed and vaulted ceiling and stone fireplace. Bedrooms have a similar rustic charm, with antiques and pretty fabrics. Excellent value.
⊠ Piazza Mazzini 46, 22021 Bellagio, Como.
Map p334 C2. 🔲 031 95 03 42. **FAX** 031 95 17 22.
@ hotflore@tin.it. 🍴 b,l,d. **Rooms** 38. 🔌
● mid-Oct to mid-April. 🅾 AE, DC, MC, V. Ⓛ Ⓛ

BOLOGNA

Corona d'Oro 1890 The name refers to the year in which the early 14th-century building became a hotel. Its wooden gallery and some Renaissance ceilings are still intact. The handsome, light-filled entrance hall was embellished with an Art Nouveau frieze supported on columns. Bedrooms are modern and well-equipped.
⊠ Via Oberdan 12, 40126 Bologna. **Map** p335 D4.
🔲 051 23 64 56. **FAX** 051 26 26 79.
@ hotcoro@tin.it. 🍴 b,l,d. **Rooms** 35. 🔳
● Aug. 🅾 AE, DC, MC, V. Ⓛ Ⓛ Ⓛ

BELLAGIO

Hotel du Lac A stone's throw from the Florence (see above) this is another popular Bellagio hotel, with a delightful setting on the piazza, a welcoming atmosphere and high standards of housekeeping and cooking. At breakfast you will find real marmalade and real orange juice; lunch or dinner on the lakeside terrace is a delight.
⊠ Piazza Mazzini 32, 22021 Bellagio, Como.
Map p334 C2. 🔲 031 95 03 20. **FAX** 031 95 16 24.
@ dulac@mbox.vol.it. 🍴 b,l,d. **Rooms** 48. 🔳🔌
● Oct to Apr. 🅾 MC, V. Ⓛ Ⓛ

BRESSANONE (BRIXEN)

Elephant In a pretty town, Tyrolean in character, an old inn named after a beast which stabled here during a journey over the Alps for the amusement of Emperor Ferdinand of Austria. The style is one of old-fashioned comfort, with smart corridors and impressive public rooms. Bedrooms are less characterful. Excellent food.
⊠ Via Rio Bianco 4, 39042 Bressanone, Bolzano.
Map p335 E2. 🔲 0472 83 27 50. **FAX** 0472 83 65 79.
@ elephant.brixen@acs.it 🍴 b,l,d. **Rooms** 44. 🔳🔌
● Nov; mid-Jan to mid-Mar. 🅾 AE, DC, MC, V. Ⓛ Ⓛ

BOLOGNA
Orologio Above-average breakfasts and views over Piazza Maggiore are the plus points, along with well-equipped, well-lit bedrooms.
⊠ Via 1V Novembre 10, 40123 Bologna. **Map** p335 D4.
🔲 051 23 12 53. **FAX** 051 26 05 52. @ hotoro@tin.it
🍴 b. **Rooms** 31. Ⓛ Ⓛ

BRESSANONE (BRIXEN)
Dominik Ideal for the fitness-conscious, with pool complex and skiing nearby. Airy, with light-filled rooms, and set amid lawns and terraces.
⊠ Via Terzo di Sotto 13, 39042 Bressanone, Bolzano.
Map p335 E2. 🔲 0472 83 01 44. **FAX** 0472 83 65 54.
@ dominik@pas.dnat.it 🍴 b,l,d. **Rooms** 28. Ⓛ Ⓛ Ⓛ

BRISIGHELLA
Relais Torre Pratesi Massive, sturdy early 16th-century tower and adjoining farmhouse. Carefully restored and elegantly furnished.
⊠ Via Cavina 11, Cavina, 48010 Brisighella, Ravenna.
Map p335 E5. 🔲 0546 845 45. **FAX** 0546 845 58.
🍴 b,l,d. **Rooms** 7. Ⓛ Ⓛ

CAMOGLI
Cenobio dei Dogi In a beautiful park overlooking the bay, a sober luxury hotel, formerly a summer palace of Genoa's *doges*.
⊠ Via Cuneo 34, 16032 Camogli, Genova.
Map p334 B4. 🔲 0185 72 41. **FAX** 0185 77 27 96.
@ cenobia@promix.it 🍴 b,l,d. **Rooms** 107. Ⓛ Ⓛ Ⓛ

BREUIL-CERVINIA

Hermitage Here Alpine charm comes with a sophisticated veneer, as befits a luxury hotel – this is a real haven, especially after a day's hard skiing. Bedrooms are spacious; the cosiest are the top-floor rooms with sloping beamed ceilings. The Matterhorn is ever-present, both in paintings and in all its glory, through the windows.
☒ 11021 Breuil-Cervinia, Aosta. **Map** p334 A2. 📞 0166 94 89 98. **FAX** 0166 94 90 32. @ hermitage@ relaischateaux.fr 🍽 b,l,d. **Rooms** 36. ▤ ▩ 📺 ⬚ ⬚
⬤ Apr to July; Sept to Nov. ⬙ AE, DC, MC, V. ⓁⓁⓁ

CALDARO

Leuchtenburg Swim, fish and sail on Lake Caldaro (or Kalterer See) from this homely, unpretentious *pensione* beneath the ruins of Leuchtenburg castle. In the white-painted, low-arched tavern, guests take hearty breakfasts and three-course dinners of regional dishes. Bedrooms have painted furniture and tiled floors.
☒ Campo di Lago 100, 39052 Caldaro, Bolzano. **Map** p335 D2. 📞 0471 96 00 93. **FAX** 0471 96 01 55. @ pensionleuchtenburg@iol.it 🍽 b,d. **Rooms** 19. ⬚
⬤ Nov to Easter. ⬙ MC, V. Ⓛ

BREUIL-CERVINIA

Neiges d'Antin This welcoming mountain hotel in the shadow of the Matterhorn was once the family home of its hands-on owners, the Biches. Excellent local cuisine and wines are served in the comfortable, beamed dining room. Home-made jams are a highlight of breakfast.
☒ Frazione Cret-Perrères, 11021 Breuil-Cervinia, Aosta. **Map** p334 A2. 📞 0166 94 87 75. **FAX** 0166 94 88 52. @ hotel.neigesantan@cervinia.alpcom.it
🍽 b,l,d. **Rooms** 28. ⬚ ⬤ May to June, Oct to Nov.
⬙ MC, V. ⓁⓁ

CANNERO RIVIERA

Cannero Overlooking the quiet resort's ferry landing stage, this is a modest and friendly hotel, in the the same capable family since the early 1900s. Downstairs, terraces and big windows make the most of the setting. Of the well-kept bedrooms, those at the front have the view, while those at the back are quieter.
☒ Via Lungo Lago 2, 28821Cannero Riviera, Verbania. **Map** p334 B2. 📞 0323 78 80 46. **FAX** 0323 78 80 48. @ hotelcannero@gse.it 🍽 b,l,d. **Rooms** 40. ▩ ⬚
⬤ Nov to Mar. ⬙ AE, DC, MC, V. ⓁⓁ

CANNOBIO

Pironi At the heart of this unspoilt lakeside village, an arcaded medieval building, beautifully preserved yet with all modern comforts.
☒ Via Marconi 35, Cannobio, Novara. **Map** p334 B2.
📞 0323 706 24. **FAX** 0323 721 84.
@ hotel.pironi@cannobio.net 🍽 b. **Rooms** 12. ⓁⓁ

CASTELFRANCO EMILIA

Villa Gaidello Club The 'club' consists of just three pleasantly furnished suites at a lovely 18th-century farmhouse amid peaceful grounds.
☒ Via Gaidello 18, 41013 Castelfranco Emilia, Modena. **Map** p335 D4. 📞 059 92 68 06. **FAX** 059 92 66 20.
🍽 b,l,d. **Rooms** 3. ⓁⓁ

CAVASO DEL TOMBA

Locanda Alla Posta Handsome inn with an unfussy restaurant serving inventive dishes, and large, plain, light bedrooms. Very good value.
☒ Piazza XIII Martiri 13, 31034 Cavaso del Tomba, Treviso. **Map** p335 E3. 📞 0423 54 31 12. 🍽 b,l,d.
Rooms 7. Ⓛ

COGNE

Bellevue In a picturesque French-speaking valley; much Alpine decoration, but very comfortable.
☒ Rue Grand Paradis 22, 11012 Cogne, Aosta.
Map p334 A3. 📞 0165 748 25. **FAX** 0165 74 91 92.
@ hotelbellevuecogne@netvallee.it 🍽 b,l,d.
Rooms 32. ⓁⓁⓁ

CASTEL GUELFO

Locanda Solarola The innovative and much-praised cuisine (Michelin star) is the main draw to this very individual establishment, the creation of Antonella Scardovi and Valentino Parmiani. Meals are served in an attractive beamed dining room, with the homely kitchen open to view. Bedrooms are lacey and Edwardian in character.
Via Santa Croce 5, 40023 Castel Guelfo, Bologna. **Map** p335 E4. 0542 67 01 02. FAX 0542 67 02 22. @ solarola@imola.queen.it b,l,d. **Rooms** 15. Jan, Mon. AE, MC, V.

CERNOBBIO

Villa d'Este When the flash and the famous come to Lake Como, they usually head for historic Villa d'Este. Built in 1568 by Cardinal Tolomeo Gallio, it saw many illustrious visitors before becoming a hotel in 1873. Its glittering interior and romantic grounds are the setting for many sporting and leisure activities. The food is suitably sumptuous.
Via Regina 40, 22012 Cernobbio, Como. **Map** p334 C2. 031 34 81. FAX 031 34 88 44. @ info@villadeste.it b,l,d. **Rooms** 166. Nov to Feb. AE, DC, MC, V.

CASTELROTTO

Cavallino d'Oro This hostelry on the central square dates back to 1393. It is full of character; its two panelled *Stübe* make charming dining rooms, serving excellent local cuisine, while public rooms are distinguished by finely carved furniture. Pretty painted furniture in some bedrooms, splendid four-poster beds in others.
Piazza Kraus, 39040 Castelrotto, Bolzano. **Map** p334 A4. 0471 70 63 37. FAX 0471 70 71 72. @ cavallino@cavallino.it b,l,d. **Rooms** 22. mid-Nov to mid-Dec. AE, DC, MC, V.

CHAMPOLUC

Villa Anna Maria The village of Champoluc is the main community of a steep-sided valley beneath the mighty Monte Rosa. This 1920s chalet-style villa on a wooded hill is a quiet, charming place: wood panelling, simple but cosy furnishings and country decorations. Not all the bedrooms have a private bathroom.
Via Croues 5, 11020 Champoluc, Aosta. **Map** p334 A2. 0125 30 71 28. FAX 0125 30 71 28. @ htl.annamaria@netvallee.it b,l,d. **Rooms** 20. Never. MC, V.

COLOGNE FRANCIACORTA

Cappuccini Former hilltop monastery, decorated with a fitting simplicity and restrained elegance. Often used for conferences and weddings.
Via Cappuccini 54, 25033 Cologne Franciacorta, Brescia. **Map** p334 C3. 0307 15 72 54. FAX 0307 15 72 57. b,l,d. **Rooms** 7.

CORTINA D'AMPEZZO

Ancora Stylish and sophisticated, with a large, popular terrace for drinks and tea. Personable, energetic owner, Flavia Sartor. Good food.
Corso Italia 62, 32043 Cortina d'Ampezzo, Belluno. **Map** p335 E2. 0436 32 61. FAX 0436 32 65. @ hancora@sunrise.it b,l,d. **Rooms** 64.

CORTINA D'AMPEZZO

Francheschi Park A twin-turretted, imposing hotel with a pleasantly traditional and very comfortable interior. A good choice for families.
Via Cesare Battisti 86, 32043 Cortina d'Ampezzo, Belluno. **Map** p335 E2. 0436 86 70 41. FAX 0436 29 09. b,l,d. **Rooms** 49.

COURMAYEUR

La Grange Good-value B&B in a renovated old barn; bright, cosy interior and warm atmosphere. Excellent breakfasts. Restaurant close by.
Strada La Brenva, Entrèves, 11013 Courmayeur, Aosta. **Map** p334 A2. 0165 86 97 33. FAX 0165 86 97 44. b. **Rooms** 23.

CIOCCARO DI PENANGO

Locanda del Sant' Uffizio Its position in the Monferrato hills and the willing but informal service make this converted 15th-century monastery a truly relaxing place. Some of the bedrooms have terraces opening onto the garden, which, with its pool, makes a quiet oasis. Get in training for the multi-course *menu degustazione*.
✉ 14030 Cioccaro di Penango, Asti. **Map** p334 B3. 📞 0141 91 62 92. 📠 0141 91 60 68. 🍴 b,l,d. **Rooms** 40. 🏊 🎱 ⬤ 3 weeks Jan, 3 weeks Aug. 💳 DC, MC, V. Ⓛ ⓁⓁ

ERBUSCO

L'Albereta The soft hills and vineyards of around Erbusco offer an ample supply of ingredients for an indulgent break, especially if you prefer your comforts with a contemporary, suave touch. Rooms in the 19th-century villa are chic and comfortable. The cuisine, by Gualtiero Marchesi, has gained him two Michelin stars.
✉ Via Vittorio Emanuele 11, 25030 Erbusco, Brescia. **Map** p334 C3. 📞 030 776 05 50. 📠 030 776 05 73. @ albereta@terramoretti.it 🍴 b,l,d. **Rooms** 44. 🍴 🎱 ⬤ 3 weeks Jan. 💳 AE, DC, MC, V. ⓁⓁⓁ

CORTINA D'AMPEZZO

Menardi The Menardi family opened their hotel in 1836. Since then, it has gained balconies adorned with cheerful window-boxes, an extra line of rooms sprouting from the roof, and an annexe. Furnishings are somewhat dated, but the standard of food, service and welcome is high.
✉ Via Majon 110, 32043 Cortina d'Ampezzo, Belluno. **Map** p335 E2. 📞 0436 24 00. 📠 0436 86 21 83. @ hmanardi@sunrise.it 🍴 b,l,d. **Rooms** 51. 🎱 ⬤ Oct to mid-Dec, mid-Apr to mid-June. 💳 AE, DC, MC, V. ⓁⓁⓁ

FIE ALLO SCILIAR (VOLS/SCHLERN)

Turm A solid former courthouse in which you will find typical, yet stylish, Tyrolean hospitality. Bedrooms vary in size, but are all different, with regional furniture and somewhere cosy to sit. You might find a ceramic stove in one, naive paintings in another. The apartments are good value, as is the elegantly presented food.
✉ Piazza dell Chiesa 9, 39050 Fie Allo Sciliar, Bolzano. **Map** p335 E2. 📞 0471 72 50 14. 📠 0471 72 54 74. @ turmwirt@cenida.it 🍴 b,l,d. **Rooms** 34. 🏊 🍴 🎱 ⬤ Nov to March. 💳 MC, V. ⓁⓁ

COURMAYEUR

Palace Bron A tall, smartly furnished hotel (Oriental rugs, chandeliers) set above the town in a grassy garden. Great views of Mont Blanc.
✉ Via Plan Gorret 41, 11013 Courmayeur, Aosta. **Map** p334 A2. 📞 0165 84 67 42. 📠 0165 84 40 15. 🍴 b,l,d. **Rooms** 27. ⓁⓁⓁ

FERRARA

Locanda Borgonuovo In the heart of this old city, a friendly, personally-run guesthouse. Simple rooms, generous breakfasts. Bicycles available.
✉ Via Cairoli 29, 44100 Ferrara. **Map** p335 E4. 📞 0532 21 11 00. 📠 0532 24 80 00. 🍴 b. **Rooms** 4. Ⓛ

GARDONE RIVIERA

Villa del Sogno Breathtaking views over Lake Garda, from this romantic, luxurious villa and its exotic gardens. Spacious, light bedrooms.
✉ Via Zanardelli 107, 25083 Gardone Riviera, Brescia. **Map** p335 D3. 📞 0365 29 01 81. 📠 0365 29 02 30. @ sogno@mail.gsnet.it 🍴 b,l,d. **Rooms** 32. ⓁⓁⓁⓁ

GARGAGNAGO

Foresteria Serego Alghieri On the vast Casal dei Ronchi estate, superb self-catering apartments.
✉ 37020 Gargagnago di Valpolicella, Verona. **Map** p335 D3. 📞 (045) 770 36 22. 📠 (045) 770 35 23. @ serego@easynet.it 🍴 b. **Rooms** 8 apartments for 2,3 or 4 people. ⓁⓁ

Finale Ligure

Punta Est Finale Ligure is one of the pleasanter resorts along this stretch of Italian Riviera, and the Punta Est is its most notable hotel. It comprises an old villa standing high above the coastal road on a rocky promontory, augmented by a modern annexe. Breakfast, served on bone china, is taken in a bright, canopied room.
Via Aurelia 1, 17024 Finale Ligure, Savona.
Map p334 B4. (019) 60 06 12. FAX (019) 60 06 11.
b,l,d. **Rooms** 39. Oct to Easter.
AE, MC, V. ⓁⓁⓁ

Follina

L'Abbazia This special hotel, in a village graced by an enchanting Cistertian abbey, consists of two buildings: a 17th-century *palazzo* and a charming little Art Nouveau villa. Rooms in both are decorated with great flair. Eat in the hotel's romantic restaurant, or at the superb Da Gigetto in Miane. Free admission to Asolo golf club.
Via Martiri della Liberta, 31051 Follina, Treviso.
Map p335 E3. 0438 97 12 77. FAX 0438 97 00 01.
@ info@hotelabbazia.it b,d. **Rooms** 24.
Never. AE, DC, MC, V. ⓁⓁ

Fiume Veneto

L'Ultimo Molino The 17th-century building is one of the last working mills in the area; though not used since the 1970s, the three wooden wheels are set in motion each evening. Inside, original character is preserved, and pretty fabrics are teemed with rustic furniture and elegant lighting. Bathrooms are sparkling and well-equipped.
Via Molino 45, 33080 Fiume Veneto, Pordenone.
Map p335 F3. 0434 95 79 11. FAX 0434 95 84 83.
@ flonder@punta.it b,d. **Rooms** 8.
10 days Jan, 10 days Aug. AE, DC, MC, V. ⓁⓁ

Gardone Riviera

Villa Fiordaliso Built in 1902 and once home to Gabriele d'Annunzio and later to Mussolini's mistress Claretta Petacci, the lakeside villa is sumptuously decorated. The huge Claretta suite has a magnificent marble bathroom. The restaurant, which spills out into the garden, serves superb food; good wine list.
Corso Zanardelli 132, 25083 Gardone Riviera, Brescia.
Map p335 D3. 0365 20 158. FAX 0365 29 00 11.
b,l,d. **Rooms** 7. Jan to mid-March.
AE, DC, MC, V. ⓁⓁⓁ

Ghiffa

Park Hotel Paradiso Atmospheric early 1900s villa in a pretty Lake Maggiore village. Ask for a lakeside room with balcony or garden.
Via Guglielmo Marconi 20, 28055 Ghiffa, Novara.
Map p334 B2. 0323 595 48. FAX 0323 598 78.
b,d. **Rooms** 20. ⓁⓁ

Iseo

I Due Roccoli Beautifully situated in wooded grounds above Lake Iseo, with very comfortable rooms and suites. Relais du Silence.
Via Silvio Bonomelli, 25049 Iseo, Brescia.
Map p334 C3. 030 982 29 77. FAX 030 982 29 80.
@ relais@idueroccoli.com b,l,d. **Rooms** 13. ⓁⓁ

Lagundo (Algund)

Der Pünthof A medieval farmhouse is at the core of this hotel, encircled by orchards and vines. The most appealing rooms are in the square tower.
Via Steinach 25, 39022 Laguno, Bolzano.
Map p335 D2. 0473 44 85 53. FAX 0473 44 99 19.
b,d. **Rooms** 18. ⓁⓁ

Laigueglia

Splendid Vaulted ceilings and a well testify to the monastic origins of this neat hotel. A bonus is the small garden, with pool, where drinks are served.
Piazza Bardaro 3, 17020 Laigueglia, Savona.
Map p334 B5. 0182 69 03 25. FAX 0182 69 08 94.
b,l,d. **Rooms** 45. ⓁⓁ

For key to symbols see backflap. For price categories *see p333*

GARGNANO

Baia d'Oro To appreciate the fabulous setting of this gaily painted hotel, arrive by boat. From the romantic terrace, you can almost dip your hand into Lake Garda and enjoy simply cooked fresh fish. The bedrooms are not to everyone's taste, with shiny fabrics and mirrored glass bedheads, but they are comfortable, with new bathrooms.
⊠ Via Gamberera 13, 25084 Gargnano, Brescia.
Map p335 D3. ⟨ 0365 71 171. **FAX** 0365 72 568.
🍴 b,l,d. **Rooms** 13. 🔊 ● mid-Nov to mid-March.
🔲 Not accepted. ⒧⒧

GARLENDA

La Meridiana This smart country house hotel is inland from the Riviera, in attractive grounds opening onto countryside, with a large pool. Most of the accommodation is in air-conditioned suites, airy and bright with modern fabrics; less expensive double rooms too. Noted restaurant.
⊠ Via Ai Castelli 11, 17033 Garlenda, Savona.
Map p334 A4. ⟨ 0182 58 02 71. **FAX** 0182 58 01 50.
@ meridiana@ab.infocom.it 🍴 b,l,d. **Rooms** 32.
🔲🍴🔊● Nov to mid-March.
🔲 AE, DC, MC, V. ⒧⒧⒧⒧

GARGNANO

Villa Giulia Rina Bombardelli has gradually upgraded her late 19th-century villa from humble *pensione* to three-star hotel, but has managed to retain the feel of a private guesthouse. The airy public rooms include an elegant dining room with Murano chandeliers and gold walls. Favourite bedrooms are those in the eaves.
⊠ Viale Rimembranza 20, 25084 Gargnano, Brescia.
Map p335 D3. ⟨ 0365 710 22. **FAX** 0365 727 74.
@ hvgiulia@gardanet.it 🍴 b,l,d. **Rooms** 27. 🔲🔊
● mid-Oct to week before Easter. 🔲 AE, DC, MC, V. ⒧⒧

ISOLA DEI PESCATORI

Verbano Lacking the grandeur of adjacent Isola Bella, this tiny fishing island on Lake Maggiore nevertheless has plenty of local colour, as does the large villa occupying one end. Its restaurant is the *raison d'être* – home-made pastas are a speciality. But there are also simple, old-fashioned bedrooms with balconies and beautiful views.
⊠ Via Ugo Ara 2, 28049 Isola dei Pescatori, Stresa, Novara. **Map** p334 B3. ⟨ (0323) 30 408.
FAX (0323) 33 129. 🍴 b,l,d. **Rooms** 12. 🔊 ● Jan, Feb.
🔲 AE, DC, MC, V. ⒧⒧

MANERBA DEL GARDA

Villa Schindler Set among olive trees and cypresses, a late 18th-century villa with a romantic atmosphere. Art courses available.
⊠ Via Bresciana 68, 25080 Manerba del Garda, Brescia.
Map p335 D3. ⟨ 0365 65 10 46. **FAX** 0365 55 48 77.
@ villaschindler@tin.it 🍴 b. **Rooms** 9. ⒧

MANTUA

Broletto Neat, straightforward accommodation in a renovated 16th-century townhouse. Unbeatable location at the heart of the city.
⊠ Via Accademia 1, 46100 Mantova. **Map** p335 D2.
⟨ 0376 22 36 78. **FAX** 0376 22 12 97. @ broletto@tin.it
🍴 b. **Rooms** 16. ⒧

MANTUA

San Lorenzo Marvellous views of aristocratic Mantua from the terrace of this plush, ornately furnished hotel, opened in 1967.
⊠ Piazza Concordia 14, 46100 Mantova. **Map** p335 D2.
⟨ 0376 22 05 00. **FAX** 0376 32 71 94.
@ hotel@hotelsanlorenzo.it 🍴 b. **Rooms** 41. ⒧⒧

MARLENGO

Oberwirt Public rooms are typically Tyrolean, with carved furniture and nick-nacks. Bedrooms are much plainer. The food is the highlight.
⊠ Via San Felice 2, Marlengo, 39020 Merano, Bolzano.
Map p335 D2. ⟨ 0473 44 71 11. **FAX** 0473 44 71 30.
@ oberwirt@dnet.it 🍴 b. **Rooms** 45. ⒧⒧

IVREA

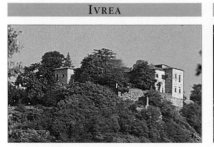

Castello San Giuseppe On an isolated hill with commanding views, this *castello* was originally a monastery before becoming a Napoleonic fort. Its atmosphere remains far more reflective than military. The hotel is centred round a peaceful inner garden with ornamental pond and shady trees. Bedrooms are rustically stylish, the best with frescoed ceilings.
⊠ 10010 Chiaverano d'Ivrea, Torino. **Map** p334 A3.
☎ 0125 42 43 70. FAX 0125 64 12 78. 🍴 b,d.
Rooms 16. 🛏 🔘 Never. 🅰 AE, DC, MC, V. Ⓛ Ⓛ

LENNO

San Giorgio A path lined with potted plants leads through lawns to the lakeside terrace of this large, atmospheric 1920s villa on the shores of Lake Como. Inside, spacious public rooms are filled with flowers, antiques and ornate mirrors. Bedrooms have a pleasantly dated feel but are very comfortable, with heavenly views.
⊠ Via Regina 81, Tremezzo, 22019 Lenno, Como.
Map p334 C2. ☎ 0344 40 415. FAX 0344 41 591.
🍴 b,l,d. **Rooms** 29. 🛏 🔘 Oct to Apr.
🅰 AE, MC, V. Ⓛ Ⓛ

LEIVI

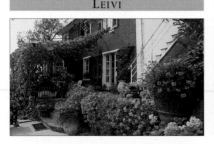

Ca'Peo Generous seasonal menus and wines chosen from 350 vintages have ensured a wide reputation for Franco and Melly Solari's rambling farmhouse restaurant. The attractive bay-windowed dining room enjoys magnificent views over the bay and hills east of Portofino. In addition, there are modern, airy apartments in an annexe in which to stay.
⊠ Via dei Caduti 80, 16040 Leivi, Genova. **Map** p334 C4.
☎ 0185 31 96 96. FAX 0185 31 96 71. 🍴 b,l,d.
Rooms 5 apartments. 🛏 🔘 Nov. 🅰 AE, MC, V. Ⓛ Ⓛ

LEVADA

Gargan Excellent dinners (home-made pasta and bread) are one of the attractions of this charming farm guesthouse. On the ground floor, a series of interconnecting dining rooms are elegantly furnished with antiques, lace curtains and pictures on white walls. Bedrooms have pretty wrought-iron bedsteads and floors strewn with rugs.
⊠ Via Marco Polo 2, 35017 Levada di Piombino Dese, Padova. **Map** p335 E3. ☎ 049 935 03 08.
FAX 049 935 00 16. @ agargan@tin.it 🍴 b,l,d.
Rooms 6. 🛏 🔘 Jan, Aug. 🅰 Not accepted. Ⓛ

MILAN
Antica Locanda Leonardo The trendy interior is a cross between Philippe Starck and a teenager's bedroom. Friendly service. Rare city garden.
⊠ Corso Magenta 78, 20121 Milano. **Map** p334 C3.
☎ 02 46 33 17. FAX 02 4801 9012. @ leo's.loc@cnn.it
🍴 b. **Rooms** 23. Ⓛ Ⓛ

MILAN
Antica Locanda di Solferino In the arty Brera district, an eccentric great aunty's country house. Paisleys, huge wardrobes, 1970s bathrooms.
⊠ Via Castelfidardo 2, 20121 Milano.
Map p334 C3. ☎ 02 657 01 29. FAX 02 657 13 61.
🍴 b. **Rooms** 11. Ⓛ Ⓛ

MILAN
Pierre Milano Smoothly run hotel, stylish and calm – and expensive. Rooms mix the occasional antique into contemporary design.
⊠ Via de Amicis 32, 20123 Milano. **Map** p334 C3.
☎ 02 7200 0581. FAX 02 805 21 57. 🍴 b,l,d.
Rooms 49. Ⓛ Ⓛ Ⓛ Ⓛ

MILAN
Spadari Contemporary, very central boutique hotel, with one-off furniture. Deluxe doubles have lovely balconies; standard rooms are small.
⊠ Via Spadari 11, 20123 Milano. **Map** p334 C3.
☎ 02 7200 2371. FAX 02 861 184. 🍴 b,l.
Rooms 38. Ⓛ Ⓛ Ⓛ

MALEO

Albergo del Sole This fine inn, noted for its simple but delicious regional dishes, is now run by the son and daughter of Franco Colombani who created it. The building displays the same robust restraint as the cooking. The bedrooms all have individual high points and good bathrooms; those above the dining room are traditionally furnished, those in the annexe more modern.
⊠ Via Trabattoni 22, 26847 Maleo, Milano. **Map** p334 C3. (0377 58 142. FAX 0377 45 80 58. ¶¶ b,l,d. **Rooms** 8. 🔞 ● Jan, Aug. 🗪 AE, MC,V. Ⓛ Ⓛ

MERANO (MERAN)

Villa Tivoli It's almost in countryside, surrounded by a terraced garden filled with more than 2,000 plant varieties. The interior is cool and chic, spacious and light; bedrooms all have south-facing balconies. The mountainous breakfast buffet could probably see you through to the excellent dinner.
⊠ Via Verde 72, 39012 Merano, Bolzano. **Map** p335 D2. (0473 44 62 82. FAX 0473 44 68 49. @ villati@pass.dnet.it ¶¶ b,l,d. **Rooms** 23. 🚌 🔞 ● mid-Nov to mid-March. 🗪 AE, DC, MC, V. Ⓛ Ⓛ

MERANO (MERAN)

Castel Fragsburg The setting's the thing at this 300-year-old former hunting lodge with commanding views of the Texel massif. The long, wisteria-covered terrace, seemingly suspended over the mountainside, is a lovely place on which to eat or drink. Bedrooms all have carved pine furniture, pretty country fabrics and balconies.
⊠ Via Fragsburg 3, 39012 Merano, Bolzano. **Map** p335 D2. (0473 24 40 71. FAX 0473 24 44 93. @ info@fragsburg.com ¶¶ b,l,d. **Rooms** 18. 🚌 📷 🔞 ● Nov to Easter. 🗪 Not accepted. Ⓛ Ⓛ

MILAN

Four Seasons This serene former monastery is only a few steps from Milan's main shopping street. It exudes confidence, *joie de vivre*, the smell of a business deal. Everything is of the highest quality, from the Frette bedlinen and underfloor heating in the marble bathrooms to the 220 staff who cater to every whim. Lovely, understated decor; fabulous food.
⊠ Via Gesu 8, 20121 Milano. **Map** p334 C3. (02 77 08 81. FAX 02 77 08 50 00. ¶¶ b,l,d. **Rooms** 98. 🖳 📷 🔞 ● Never. 🗪 AE, DC, MC, V. Ⓛ Ⓛ Ⓛ Ⓛ

MODENA

Canalgrande Stylish, peaceful villa set in lovely gardens in the city centre. Neoclassical, stuccoed reception rooms; vaulted cellar restaurant.
⊠ Corso Canalgrande 6, 41100 Modena. **Map** p335 D4. (059 21 71 60. FAX 059 22 16 74. @ info@canalgrandehotel.it ¶¶ b,l,d. **Rooms** 79. Ⓛ Ⓛ

MONFORTE D'ALBA

Giardino – Da Felicin Standing among hills and vineyards, a family-run restaurant-with-rooms. Good food, fine wines, light, spacious bedrooms.
⊠ Via Vallada 18, 12065 Monforte d'Alba, Cuneo. **Map** p334 A4. (0173 782 25. FAX 0173 78 73 77. ¶¶ b,l,d. **Rooms** 12. Ⓛ Ⓛ

MONTAGNANA

Aldo Moro Useful address within this handsome town's superb rectangle of medieval walls: a smart restaurant with modern, efficient rooms.
⊠ Via Marconi 27, 35044 Montagnana, Padova. **Map** p335 D3. (0429 813 51. FAX 0429 828 42. ¶¶ b,l,d. **Rooms** 25. Ⓛ

ORTA SAN GIULIO

Olina A highly enjoyable restaurant, with warm-toned, comfortable bedrooms (some with tiled floors and wooden ceilings) in an annexe.
⊠ Via Olina 40, 28016 Orta San Giulio, Novara. **Map** p334 B2. (0322 90 56 56. FAX 0322 90 56 45. ¶¶ b,l,d. **Rooms** 8. Ⓛ

MILAN

Principe di Savoia A colourful stained-glass ceiling in the winter garden is one of the period features of this stately evocation of the late 1890s/early 1900s. Bedrooms are superbly elegant, but you may prefer the breathtaking new Presidential Suite, complete with Pompeian-style swimming pool. The downmarket location is a drawback.
✉ Piazza della Repubblica 17, 20124 Milano.
Map p334 C3. ☎ 02 623 01. [FAX] 02 659 58 38.
🍴 b,l,d. **Rooms** 299. ▤ ≋ 🍸 🌿 ● Never.
💳 AE, DC, MC, V. ⓁⓁⓁⓁ

MONTEROSSO AL MARE

Porto Roca Along a beautiful, almost inaccessible strip of coastline, Monterosso (which can be reached by car) is the largest of the stunning Cinque Terre perched villages, and Porto Roca is by far the best hotel. Sitting on a headland, it's chief assets are the wonderul views (make sure your room has one) and a glorious terrace.
✉ Via Corone 1, 19016 Monterosso al Mare, La Spezia.
Map p334 C5. ☎ 0187 81 75 02. [FAX] 0187 81 76 92.
@ portoroca@portoroca.it 🍴 b,l,d. **Rooms** 43. ▤ 🌿
● Nov to mid-March. 💳 AE, MC, V. ⓁⓁⓁ

MIRA

Villa Margherita Less than a half-hour drive from Venice, this polished hotel is also well-placed for visits to the stately villas of the Brenta Canal. Nowadays the flat landscape is more industrial than rural, but this former country villa is all sophistication, with particularly attractive public rooms and a well-regarded restaurant.
✉ Via Nazionale 416, 30030 Mira, Venezia.
Map p335 E3. ☎ 041 426 58 00. [FAX] 041 426 58 38.
@ hvillam@tin.it 🍴 b,l,d. **Rooms** 19. ▤ 🌿
● Never. 💳 AE, DC, MC, V. ⓁⓁⓁ

MONZA

Hotel de la Ville Monza is synonymous with fast cars, but it also has a Neoclassical Villa Reale, surrounded by a lovely park. This fine hotel overlooks it. Owned for three generation by the Nardi family, it is dignified and traditional, full of oak panelling, Chinese vases and mahogany furniture. Its Derby Grill restaurant is renowned.
✉ Viale Regina Margherita 15, 20052 Monza, Milano.
Map p334 C3. ☎ 039 38 25 81. [FAX] 039 36 76 47.
@ delavill@tin.it 🍴 b,l,d. **Rooms** 55. ▤ ● 3 weeks Aug; Christmas and New Year. 💳 AE, DC, MC, V. ⓁⓁⓁ

ORTA SAN GIULIO

Orta Pleasantly old-fashioned, spacious central hotel with an endearingly shabby façade. Around the corner, its terrace overhangs Lake Orta.
✉ 28016 Orta San Giulio, Novara. **Map** p334 B2.
☎ 0322 902 53. [FAX] 0322 90 56 46. 🍴 b,l,d.
Rooms 35. ⓁⓁ

PARMA

Torino Quiet yet in the heart of the city, close to all the main sights, and with the bonus of a private garage. Rooms are clean, small and plain.
✉ Via Mazza 7, 43100 Parma. **Map** p334 C4.
☎ 0521 28 10 47. [FAX] 0521 23 07 25.
🍴 b,l,d. **Rooms** 35. ⓁⓁ

PARMA

Villa Ducale A Neoclassical mansion house approached through a flower-filled garden. Several bedrooms have small terraces.
✉ Via del Popolo 35, 43100 Parma. **Map** p334 C4.
☎ 0521 27 27 27. [FAX] 0521 78 07 56.
@ villaducale@pntn.it 🍴 b. **Rooms** 28. ⓁⓁ

PORTOBUFFOLE

Villa Guistinian Unstuffy, but not cosy: rooms are of awesome dimensions. Elaborate suites in the main house, simpler rooms in the old stables.
✉ Via Giustiniani 11, 31019 Portobuffole, Treviso.
Map p335 F3. ☎ 0422 85 02 44. [FAX] 0422 85 02 60.
🍴 b,l,d. **Rooms** 43. ⓁⓁ

ORTISEI (ST ULRICH)

Uhrerhof Deur The peace is broken only by the sound of ticking clocks (the name means 'House of the Clocks'). This traditional chalet is set in a tucked-away hamlet. Outside, a grassy garden with wonderful views; inside, bright, simple, immaculate rooms with plenty of homely details. There are also four apartments and, in the basement, a surprisingly smart health complex.
✉ Bulla, 39046 Ortisei, Bolzano. **Map** p335 E2.
📞 0471 79 73 35. **FAX** 0471 79 74 57. 🛏 b,d. **Rooms** 11.
🍴 🔊 ● Nov, 2 weeks after Easter. 💳 MC, V. Ⓛ Ⓛ

PERGINE

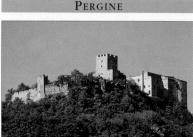

Castel Pergine For novelty, good value and fun this medieval hilltop fortress is hard to beat. Past and present co-exist in a friendly, mildly offbeat atmosphere. Age-worn steps and vaulted chambers lead to the airy lobby. Bedrooms, while not luxurious, are furnished with simple good taste. Strolls round the ramparts are a highlight.
✉ 38057 Pergine, Valsugana, Trento. **Map** p335 D2.
📞 0461 531158. **FAX** 0461 531329.
@ castelpergine@valsugana.com 🛏 b,d. **Rooms** 21.
🔊 ● Nov to Easter. 💳 AE, MC, V. Ⓛ

PEDEMONTE

Villa del Quar The owner lives in the fine main villa, her luxury hotel occupies the east wing. Public rooms are memorable: a galleried sitting room, and two dining rooms resplendent in silk, gilt and Murano glass. Bedrooms are more restrained, with opulent bathrooms. The lovely pool sparkles invitingly in the garden.
✉ Via Quar 12, 37020 Pedemonte, Verona.
Map p334 A2. 📞 045 680 06 81. **FAX** 045 680 06 04.
@ delquar@relaischateaux.fr 🛏 b,l,d. **Rooms** 22.
📋 ≋ 🔊 ● Jan to Mar. 💳 AE, DC, MC, V. Ⓛ Ⓛ Ⓛ

POMPONESCO

Il Leone Once flourishing, Pomponesco is today a shadow of its fomer self, although the old town has a certain faded charm. Here one finds Leone, little changed since 1630, with a coffered ceiling and frescoes in its lofty dining room. The place is renowned for robust regional cooking. Bedrooms are modern in contrast, but comfortable.
✉ Piazza 1V Martiri 2, 46030 Pomponesco, Mantova.
Map p335 D4. 📞 0375 860 77. **FAX** 0375 86 770.
🛏 b,l,d. **Rooms** 9. 🍴 🔊 ● Jan.
💳 AE, DC, MC, V. Ⓛ Ⓛ

REGGIO NELL'EMILIA

delle Notarie In the centre of town, a calm, elegant hotel with mainly spacious rooms and suites. Good restaurant serving local specialities.
✉ Via Palazzuolo 5, 42100 Reggio nell'Emilia.
Map p335 D4. 📞 0522 45 35 00. **FAX** 0522 45 37 37.
🛏 b,l,d. **Rooms** 40. Ⓛ Ⓛ

REGGIO NELL'EMILIA

Posta The austere façade of this comfortable hotel in the historic centre hides an embellished rococo interior. Full of charming flourishes.
✉ Piazza del Monte 2, 42100 Reggio nell'Emilia.
Map p335 D4. 📞 0522 43 29 44. **FAX** 0522 45 26 02.
🛏 b. **Rooms** 43. Ⓛ Ⓛ

SAN BONIFACIO

Relais Villabella The core of this former rice mill is a smart, well-regarded restaurant. Elegant public rooms, equally elegant bedrooms.
✉ Villabella, 37047 San Bonifacio, Verona.
Map p335 D3. 📞 045 610 17 77. **FAX** 045 610 17 99.
🛏 b,l,d. **Rooms** 9. Ⓛ Ⓛ Ⓛ

SAN FEDELE D'INTELVI

Villa Simplicitas A saffron-coloured 19th-century villa in a rural setting high above the lakes and their bustle. Old-fashioned in a charming, tasteful way. Welcoming, relaxed staff, good food.
✉ 22028 San Fedele d'Intelvi, Como. **Map** p334 C2.
📞 **FAX** 031 83 11 32. 🛏 b,l,d. **Rooms** 10. Ⓛ Ⓛ

PORTICO DI ROMAGNA

PORTOFINO

Al Vecchio Convento The stylishly rustic
dining room, at the back of the house, is the
main focus; here Signor Cameli cooks traditional
dishes with flair. A stone staircase leads to the
bedrooms, also traditional and decorated with
classy simplicity. Handsome antiques include
some particularly splendid bedsteads.
⊠ Via Roma 7,47010 Portico di Romagna, Forli.
Map p335 E5. ▊ 0543 96 70 53. ▊ 0543 96 71 57.
@ vecchioconvento@mail.asianet.it ▊ b,l,d. **Rooms** 15.
⬤ Never. ▊ AE, DC, MC, V. ⓁⓁ

Splendido One of Italy's most famous hotels,
dripping in chic, where languid elegance is the
order of the day – as well as a deep pocket for
paying the bill. It is set on the hillside over the
harbour, with a wonderfully sited swimming pool
and a glitzy terrace on which to see and be seen.
⊠ Viale Baratta 16, 16034 Portofino, Genova.
Map p335 B4. ▊ 0185 26 95 51. ▊ 0185 26 96 14.
@ reservations @splendido.net ▊ b,l,d. **Rooms** 69.
▊ ▊ ▊ ▊ ▊ mid-Jan to mid-March.
▊ AE, DC, MC, V. ⓁⓁⓁⓁ

PORTOFINO

RANCO

Eden In chic, crowded Portofino, hotel rooms are
at a premium, and the Eden is one of the few
modest establishments. It's a tiny place, in a
narrow street near the waterfront, whose shaded
garden makes a quiet enclave. Bedrooms and
bathrooms are small but spotless. There is no
sitting room, but a trattoria-style dining room
and a terrace overlooking the garden.
⊠ Vico Dritto 18, 16034 Portofino, Genova.
Map p334 B4. ▊ 0185 26 90 91. ▊ 0185 26 90 47.
▊ b,l,d. **Rooms** 12. ⬤ Never. ▊ AE, DC, MC, V. ⓁⓁ

Il Sole di Ranco The Brovelli family opened
their inn on the shores of Lake Maggiore in 1850;
today it is a smart restaurant (two Michelin stars)
with rooms. Carlo Brovelli cooks, aided by his
son. Dining on the vine-covered terrace is a
delight. Bedooms are mainly contemporary
suites, ranging in size and price.
⊠ Piazza Venezia 5, 21020 Ranco, Varese.
Map p334 B2. ▊ 0331 97 65 07. ▊ 0331 97 66 20.
@ ivanett@tin.it ▊ b,l,d. **Rooms** 15. ▊ ▊
⬤ Jan to mid-Feb. ▊ AE, DC, MC, V. ⓁⓁⓁ

SAN FLORIANO
Obereggen Modest chalet, just yards from ski
lifts, with a cosy bar and good food. Plump duvets
add a touch of comfort to the simple rooms.
⊠ Via Obereggen 8, San Floriano, 39050 Nova Ponente,
Bolzano. **Map** p335 F3. ▊ 0471 61 57 22.
▊ 0471 61 58 89. ▊ b,d. **Rooms** 12. Ⓛ

SESTO
Berghotel Tirol A modern chalet in a very
pretty town, overlooking classic Alpine scenery.
Pine-furnished, efficient, hospitable.
⊠ Via Monte Elmo 10, Moso, 39030 Sesto, Bolzano.
Map p335 D5. ▊ 0474 71 03 86. ▊ 0474 71 04 55.
@ info@berghotel.com ▊ b,l,d. **Rooms** 44. ⓁⓁ

SAN VALBURGA D'ULTIMO
Eggwirt The traditional *stübe* (dating from 1611)
is the heart of this excellent value, family-oriented
gasthof. Less personal bedrooms; superb views.
⊠ 39016 San Valburga d'Ultimo, Bolzano. **Map** p334 C2.
▊ 0473 79 53 19. ▊ 0473 79 54 71.
@ eggwirt@rolmail.net ▊ b,l,d. **Rooms** 20. Ⓛ

SESTRI LEVANTE
Grand Hotel Villa Balbi Swanky pink palace
with spacious bedrooms (the best are in the 18th-
century core). Heated seawater pool in garden.
⊠ Viale Rimembranza 1, 16039 Sestri Levante, Genova.
Map p334 C4. ▊ 0185 429 41. ▊ 0185 48 24 59.
▊ b,l,d. **Rooms** 99. ⓁⓁⓁⓁ

REDAGNO DI SOPRA

Zirmerhof The dimly lit hall with intricate wood carving, old fireplace and ticking grandfather clock, sets the tone at this mountain hotel. The place has a cosy, homely atmosphere. Rooms vary in size, but are all attractive, with traditional furniture. Good local cooking and wine list.
☒ 39040 Redagno di Sopra, Bolzano. **Map** p335 E2.
☎ 0471 88 72 15. ℻ 0471 88 72 25.
@ info@zirmerhof.com ⌷ b,l,d. **Rooms** 31.
Nov to Christmas, mid-Jan to mid-Feb, mid-March to mid-May. ✉ AE, DC, MC, V. ⓁⓁ

RIVAROTTA

Villa Luppis A rambling building, in the Luppis family since the 1800s. Rooms include a long, dreamy dining room, all pale pink and white, with antique furniture, silver and fresh flowers. Long corridors lead to well-furnished bedrooms with king-size beds. The fine old park contains a pool and fitness centre. Minibus to Venice.
☒ Via San Martino 34, 33087 Rivarotta, Pordenone. **Map** p335 F3. ☎ 0434 62 69 69. ℻ 0434 62 62 28.
@ hotel@villaluppis.it ⌷ b,l,d. **Rooms** 21.
Never. ✉ AE, DC, MC, V. ⓁⓁⓁ

SAN FLORIANO DEL COLLIO

Golf Hotel The name, referring to its nine-hole golf course, conjures up a modern sporting hotel. In fact it forms part of ancient Castello Formentini, and the interior is tastefully decorated with family furniture and pictures. The Formentini family's restaurant is close by. An excellent address in an area almost devoid of notable hotels.
☒ Via Oslavia 2, 34070 San Floriano del Collio, Gorizia. **Map** p335 F3. ☎ 0481 88 40 51. ℻ 0481 88 40 52.
@ romantic@t-online.de ⌷ b. **Rooms** 15.
Dec to March. ✉ AE, DC, MC, V. ⓁⓁⓁ

SAN OSVALDO

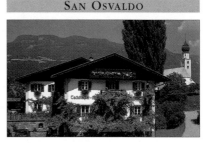

Gasthof Tschötscherhof The narrow road from Siusi leads through meadows, orchards and vineyards to this idyllic chalet farmhouse. Its white painted façade is almost obscured by clambering vines and tumbling geraniums. Inside: an old *stübe*, with gently ticking clock and rough wood floor, and neat bedrooms (some with balconies) without frills.
☒ San Osvaldo 19, 39040 Siuisi, Bolzano. **Map** p335 E2.
☎ ℻ 0471 70 60 13. ⌷ b,l,d. **Rooms** 8.
Dec to March. ✉ Not accepted. Ⓛ

SESTRI LEVANTE
Miramare Huge arched windows make the most of the view at this pink, shuttered house on Baia del Silenzio. Cool and contemporary.
☒ Via Cappellini 9, 16039 Sestri Levante, Genova. **Map** p334 C4. ☎ 0185 48 08 55. ℻ 0185 410 55.
@ hrm.miramare@rainbow.it ⌷ b,l,d. **Rooms** 43. ⓁⓁ

SIRMIONE
Villa Cortine Palace Luxury headland hotel with fabulous exotic gardens, dotted with fountains and statuary. The 1950s extension is unfortunate.
☒ Via Grotte 6, 25019 Sirmione, Brescia. **Map** p335 D3.
☎ 030 990 58 90. ℻ 030 91 63 90.
@ info@villacortine.com ⌷ b,l,d. **Rooms** 49. ⓁⓁⓁⓁ

SORISO
Al Sorriso Michelin two-star restaurant whose dining room is a picture of elegance. Rooms more ordinary (and affordable) than you might expect.
☒ Via Roma 18, 28018 Soriso, Novara. **Map** p334 B3.
☎ 0322 98 32 28. ℻ 0322 98 33 28. ⌷ b,l,d.
Rooms 8. ⓁⓁ

TORINO (TURIN)
Conte Biancamano Central hotel whose public rooms are decorated, with a touch of faded grandeur, with chandeliers and paintings.
☒ Corso Vittorio Emanuele 11 73, 10128 Torino.
Map p334 A3. ☎ 011 562 32 81. ℻ 011 562 37 89.
@ cbhtl.to@iol.it ⌷ b. **Rooms** 27. ⓁⓁ

SAN VIGILIO

SESTRI LEVANTE

Locanda San Vigilio An air of exclusivity pervades this hotel, set idyllically on its own lush Lake Garda headland. Right on the lake is the elegant dining room, with ceramic stove and sideboards displaying plates and bottles. You can also eat on a flowery arched veranda. Bedrooms in the main house are particularly lovely.
☒ San Vigilio, 37016 Garda, Verona. **Map** p335 E2.
📞 045 7256688. **FAX** 045 725 65 51.
@ sanvigilio@gardanews.it 🍴 b,l,d. **Rooms** 14. ❂
● Nov to Easter. 🗲 AE, DC, MC, V. ⒧⒧⒧⒧

Helvetia This charming hotel with a warm, personal atmosphere is distinguished by its pristine white façade and pretty yellow awnings. Signor Pernigotti devotes himself wholeheartedly to his hotel and its guests, and provides all sorts of unexpected extras (including bicycles). Excellent buffet breakfast served on the terrace.
☒ Via Cappuccini 9, 16039 Sestri Levante, Genova.
Map p334 C4. 📞 (0185) 41 175. **FAX** (0185) 45 72 16.
@ helvetia@rainbownet.it 🍴 b. **Rooms** 24. ❂
● Nov to Feb. 🗲 MC, V. ⒧⒧

SAUZE D'OULX

SIRMIONE

Il Capricorno The busy ski resort of Sauze d'Oulx attracts a fairly smart Italian clientele, winter and summer, as well as foreign skiers. This chalet hotel makes a good base, being cosily traditional, with rough beams and hand-made furniture, and set in an isolated position on the wooded slopes above the village. Good cooking.
☒ Case Sparse 21, Le Clotes, 10050 Sauze d'Oulx, Torino.
Map p334 A3. 📞 0122 85 02 73. **FAX** 0122 85 00 55.
🍴 b,l,d. **Rooms** 8. ❂ ● May to mid-June, mid-Sept to Nov. 🗲 MC, V. ⒧⒧

Grifone Very good value. The Grifone restaurant serves excellent fresh fish and a mouthwatering selection of *antipasti*. Its terrace overlooks both Lake Garda and the ramparts of Sirmione's *castello*, as well as a scrap of sandy beach. And it has simple, inexpensive rooms: basic but clean. Those on the top floor have the best views.
☒ Vicolo Bisse (Via Bocchio) 5, 25019 Sirmione, Brescia.
Map p335 D3. 📞 (030) 91 60 14. **FAX** (030) 91 65 48.
🍴 b,l,d. **Rooms** 16. ❂ ● Nov to Easter.
🗲 Not accepted. ⒧

TORINO (TURIN)
Turin Palace Dating from 1872, the city's most impressive hotel, with sumptuous, modernized rooms decorated with antiques.
☒ Via Sacchi 8, 10128 Torino.**Map** p334 A3.
📞 011 562 55 11. **FAX** 011 561 21 87. 🍴 b,l,d.
Rooms 125. ⒧⒧⒧

TORINO (TURIN)
Villa Sassi In the hills just outside the city, a beautiful and luxurious 17th-century villa with many original features. Individual bedrooms.
☒ Via Traforo del Pino 47, 10100 Torino.
Map p334 A3. 📞 011 898 05 56. **FAX** 011 898 00 95.
🍴 b,l,d. **Rooms** 17. ⒧⒧⒧

TORRI DEL BENACO
Europa Happy, welcoming and good value 1950s villa decorated in the rather drab style of the period. Pretty garden for outdoor dining.
☒ Via Gabriele d'Annunzio 13-15, 37010 Torri del Benaco, Verona. **Map** p335 D3. 📞 045 722 50 86.
FAX 045 629 66 32. 🍴 b,l,d. **Rooms** 18. ⒧

TRENTO
Accademia Sophisticated town hotel in an attractive medieval house. Clean white lines are enlivened by vibrant rugs and antique pieces.
☒ Vicolo Colico 4-6, 38100 Trento. **Map** p335 D2.
📞 0461 23 36 00. **FAX** 0461 23 01 74. 🍴 b,l,d.
Rooms 43. ⒧⒧

SIUSI ALLO SCILIAR

Bad Ratzes Set in a clearing surrounded by dense forest, this family-orientated hotel at first looks disconcertingly modern and anonymous. But the warmth of its owners, the Scherlins, gives it heart. The decor is conventional and a bit dated, but there are extensive public rooms, including a playroom, and bedrooms are comfortable.
⊠ Bagni di Razzes, 39040 Siusi allo Sciliar, Bolzano.
Map p335 E2. 📞 FAX 0471 70 61 31. 🍴 b,l,d.
Rooms 48. 🏊 🏋 🔱 ● Apr to mid-May, Nov to mid-Dec. 🚫 Not accepted. Ⓛ Ⓛ

TORINO (TURIN)

Victoria This modern, practical hotel in the heart of the shopping district is lifted far from the rut by its imaginative interior, its warmth of welcome, and its excellent value for money. It's quietly situated, with public rooms and some bedrooms overlooking a verdant garden. Each bedroom is differently done out, and very becoming; public rooms are equally attractive.
⊠ Via Nino Costa 4, 10123 Torino. **Map** p334 A3.
📞 011 561 19 09. FAX 011 561 18 06. 🍴 b. **Rooms** 96.
📺 ● Never. 🅰 AE, MC, V. Ⓛ Ⓛ

SORAGNA

Locanda del Lupo An extremely comfortable place to stay, in an area without many good addresses. This rather grand 18th-century coaching inn, in a small town near Cremona, was originally noted as a restaurant. It still serves interesting dishes, and has spacious bedrooms simply yet harmoniously furnished with antiques.
⊠ Via Garibaldi 64, 43019 Soragna, Palma.
Map p334 C4. 📞 0524 59 71 00. FAX 0524 59 70 66.
@ locanda@polaris.it 🍴 b,l,d. **Rooms** 46. 📺
● Aug, Christmas. 🅰 AE, DC, MC, V. Ⓛ Ⓛ

TORRI DEL BENACO

Gardesana Dining off the freshest of fish on the first-floor terrace of this comfortable hotel is a delight: it makes the perfect vantage point for watching harbour life in the pretty Lake Garda fishing village. The building itself has a long history, though the interior is modernized. The spruce bedrooms are thoughtfully equipped.
⊠ Piazza Calderini 20, 37010 Torri del Benaco, Verona.
Map p335 D3. 📞 045 72 25 411. FAX 045 72 25 771.
@ gardesana@easynet.it 🍴 b,l,d. **Rooms** 34. 📺 🔱
● Nov, Dec. 🅰 AE, DC, MC, V. Ⓛ

TREVISO

Campeol Across the street from the owners' atmospheric restaurant, Beccherie. Plain, spacious rooms with views of old Treviso; good bathrooms.
⊠ Piazza Ancillotto 8-ll, 31100 Treviso. **Map** p335 E3.
📞 0422 566 01. FAX 0422 54 08 71. 🍴 b,l,d.
Rooms 14. Ⓛ

TRIESTE

Duchi d'Aosta On the city's main square, a neo-Renaissance palace whose interior exudes the dignity and grandeur of a bygone age.
⊠ Piazza Unita d'Italia 2, 34100 Trieste. **Map** p335 F3.
📞 040 760 00 11. FAX 040 36 60 92. 🍴 b,l,d.
Rooms 55. Ⓛ Ⓛ Ⓛ

VALNONTEY

Petit Dahu In a little hamlet near Cogne, in the Gran Paradiso National Park, a tiny, homely hotel made up of two old stone-built houses. The owner can act as hiking guide; his wife cooks.
⊠ 11012 Valnontey, Aosta. **Map** p334 A3.
📞 FAX 0165 74 146. 🍴 b,d. **Rooms** 8. Ⓛ

VALSOLDA

Stella d'Italia The delightful shaded terrace juts right out onto Lake Lugano, offering lovely views. Ask for a room in the old wing of the hotel.
⊠ Piazza Roma 1, San Mamete, 22010 Valsolda, Como.
Map p334 C2. 📞 0344 68 139. FAX 0344 68 729.
@ stelladitalia@mclink.it 🍴 b,l,d. **Rooms** 35. Ⓛ Ⓛ

TRISSINO

VENICE

Relais Ca' Masieri The restaurant is set in a fine old shuttered mansion, with a shady terrace on which to dine in fine weather. It's no penance to eat indoors, however: the dining room is charming, decorated with delicate 18th-century frescoes. The food is delightful too. The contemporary bedrooms (some small, one huge) are in an adjacent old building.
Via Masieri 16, 36070 Trissino, Vicenza. **Map** p335 E3. 0445 49 01 22. FAX 0445 49 04 55. b,l,d. **Rooms** 8. late Jan to mid-Feb. AE, DC, MC, V. LL

Bisanzio For those who value uncomplicated comfort and convenience rather than character, this is a pleasant, quiet hotel set back from the Riva degli Schiavoni. The reception area is spacious and streamlined, with sitting areas and a bar. Best of the bedrooms are those with private terraces and rooftop views, and the family rooms (with foldaway bunks).
Calle della Pieta, Castello 3651, 30122 Venezia. **Map** p335 E3. 041 520 31 00. FAX 041 520 41 14. b. **Rooms** 43. Never. AE, DC, MC, V. LLL

VENICE

VENICE

Accademia A longtime favourite Venice *pensione*, the Accademia is loved for its rare garden setting (roses and fruit trees, canalside patio). Inside the shuttered 17th-century mansion, bedrooms have been renovated to a good standard with inlaid wood floors and antiqued mirrors. The public rooms are plainer, although the finely furnished first-floor landing still delights.
Fondamenta Bollani, Dorsoduro 1058, 20123 Venezia. **Map** p335 E3. 041 521 01 88. FAX 041 523 91 52. b. **Rooms** 30. Never. AE, DC. MC, V. LL

Bucintoro This simple, old-fashioned, family-run *pensione* has fabulous views from every room. Some, such as Nos 1 and 11, have windows overlooking both San Giorgio Maggiore and San Marco, and are much in demand by artists. No 4 has a large bed, airy curtains, and the lagoon waters gently lapping below. All rooms are plain, clean and light. Basic breakfasts.
Riva San Biagio, Castello 2135, 30122 Venezia. **Map** p335 E3. 041 522 32 40. FAX 041 523 52 24. b. **Rooms** 28. Never. Not accepted. LL

VARENNA

Hotel du Lac The bedrooms are small, but dinner on the terrace of this friendly hotel, by the side of Lake Como, is memorable.
Via del Prestino 4, 23829 Varenna, Lecco. **Map** p334 C2. 0341 83 02 38. FAX 0341 83 10 81. b,l,d. **Rooms** 18. LL

VENICE

Agli Alboretti Simple, spotless bedrooms with tiny bathrooms near the Accademia. Breakfast in summer under a pergola on the rear terrace.
Rio Terra Foscarini, Dorsoduro 884, 30123 Venezia. **Map** p335 E3. 041 523 00 58. FAX 041 521 01 58.
@ alborett@gpnet.it b,d. **Rooms** 19. LL

VENICE

Ai Santi Apostoli Lovely third-floor *palazzo* apartment transformed into an elegant B&B. Stylish sitting room and spacious bedrooms.
Strada Nova, Cannaregio 4391, 30131 Venezia. **Map** p335 E3. 041 521 26 12. FAX 041 521 26 11. b. **Rooms** 11. LLL

VENICE

Hotel des Bains The setting for *Death in Venice*, still evocative of that *belle époque* period. Rare swimming pool in landscaped setting. Also tennis.
Lungomare Marconi 17, Lido, 30126 Venezia. **Map** p335 E3. 041 526 59 21. FAX 526 01 13. b,l,d. **Rooms** 191. LLLL

For key to symbols see backflap. For price categories see p333

VENICE

Gritti Palace As Somerset Maugham wrote, there are few greater pleasures than taking a drink on the Gritti's terrace at sunset, watching Salute church bathed in colour. Before bed, he advised, glance at the portrait of Doge Andrea Gritti, who, after a tumultuous life, spent his last years here in peace. A fine hotel which captures the spirit of Venice.
☒ Campo Santa Maria del Giglio, San Marco 2467, 30124 Venezia. **Map** p335 E3. ☎ 041 79 46 11. **FAX** 041 520 09 42. 🍴 b,l,d. **Rooms** 93. 🗎 🎼
⬤ Never. 🗐 AE, DC, MC, V. Ⓛ Ⓛ Ⓛ Ⓛ

VENICE

Piccola Fenice Right by La Fenice theatre, now restored after a fire, and sister hotel to the well-known Fenice et des Artistes. Here you will find spacious suites for up to six people, perfect for families. Bathrooms are prettily tiled and have generous basins; furniture is attractive; and there are facilities for making breakfast. The topmost apartment has a little terrace with rooftop views.
☒ Calle della Madonna, San Marco 3614, 30124 Venezia. **Map** p335 E3. ☎ **FAX** 041 520 49 09. 🍴 b. **Rooms** 7 suites. 🗎 🌑 Jan. 🗐 AE, DC, MC, V. Ⓛ Ⓛ Ⓛ

VENICE

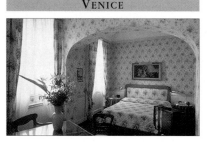

Londra Palace This venerable hotel can claim to be in the top league. Public rooms are cool and elegant, with good food served in the romantic dining room. Front bedrooms (the hotel boasts 100 windows onto the lagoon) have matchless views, and the quality of furniture and original paintings is impressive.
☒ Riva degli Schiavoni, Castello 4171, 30122 Venezia. **Map** p335 E3. ☎ 041 520 05 33. **FAX** 041 522 50 32. @ info@hotellondra.it 🍴 b,l,d. **Rooms** 53. 🗎 🎼
⬤ Never. 🗐 AE, DC, MC, V. Ⓛ Ⓛ Ⓛ Ⓛ

VENICE

Quattro Fontane A wide, shady terrace encircles this 150-year-old mock-Tyrolean building. There's plenty of character here, with charmingly decorated reception rooms filled with mementos of the owners' travels. Bedrooms in the main house are individual; those in the annexe are more streamlined, with gaily painted bathrooms.
☒ Via Quattro Fontane 16, 30126 Lido, Venezia. **Map** p335 E3. ☎ 041 526 02 27. **FAX** 041 526 07 26. @ quafonve@tin.it 🍴 b,l,d. **Rooms** 58. 🎼 🌑 Nov to Easter. 🗐 AE, DC, MC, V. Ⓛ Ⓛ Ⓛ

VENICE

Danieli This palace became a hotel in 1822, thereafter housing a raft of famous figures. Avoid, if you can, a room in the 1940s wing.
☒ Riva degli Schiavoni, Castello 4196, 30122 Venezia. **Map** p335 E3. ☎ 041 522 64 80. **FAX** 041 520 02 08. 🍴 b,l,d. **Rooms** 235. Ⓛ Ⓛ Ⓛ Ⓛ

VENICE

Locanda Ca' Foscari Budget one-star hotel, a cut above the norm. Modest but pristine bedrooms; some have their own bathroom.
☒ Calle della Frescada, Dorsoduro 3888, 30123 Venezia. **Map** p335 E3. ☎ 041 71 04 01. **FAX** 041 71 08 17. 🍴 b. **Rooms** 11. Ⓛ

VENICE

Locanda Sturion If you can conquer the steep stairs, you will find plush, handsomely decorated bedrooms, two of which overlook Grand Canal.
☒ Calle del Sturione, San Polo 679, 30125 Venezia. **Map** p335 E3. ☎ 041 523 62 43. **FAX** 041522 83 78. @ locandasturion@tin.it 🍴 b. **Rooms** 11. Ⓛ Ⓛ

VENICE

Raspo da Ua For local colour and little money, plus the chance to enjoy Burano at night minus the crowds, a restaurant with simple rooms.
☒ Via Galuppi 560, 30012 Burano, Venezia. **Map** p335 E3. ☎ 041 73 00 95. **FAX** 041 73 03 97. 🍴 b,l,d. **Rooms** 5. Ⓛ

VENICE

La Residenza There are drawbacks to staying in this grand Gothic *palazzo* – including the dubious smell that sometimes pervades the entrance hall and the muted atmosphere at breakfast. But for a modest two-star, it has a deliciously immodest setting, with a vast, lavishly stuccoed Baroque hall. Some of the rooms are quaintly old-fashioned. ⊠ Campo Bandiera e Moro, Castello 3608, 30122 Venezia. **Map** p335 E3. ℂ 041 528 5315. FAX 041 523 88 59. 🍴 b. **Rooms** 14. ▤ ● Never. 🗲 AE, MC, V. ⓁⓁ

VERONA

Gabbia d'Oro In this stylish hotel you will find an attention to detail rarely encountered. The decorative flair and individuality of the owner, Signora Balzarro, is evident from the moment you enter. Public rooms include a vibrant orangery, complete with Romeo and Juliet, a pair of parrots. The bedrooms are suitably romantic. ⊠ Corso Portoni Borsari 4a, 37121 Verona. **Map** p335 D3. ℂ 045 800 30 60. FAX 045 59 02 93. @ gabbiadoro@easynet.it 🍴 b. **Rooms** 27. ▤ 🅱 ● Never. 🗲 AE, DC, MC, V. ⓁⓁⓁⓁ

VENICE

Venetian Apartments London-based specialists offering a wide selection of apartments from cosy studios to luxurious *palazzos*. In a city where hotels are booked months in advance, this is a delightful and cost-effective way to become part of its fabric. Enjoy, if only for a short time, the domestic pleasures of being *un veneziano*. ⊠ 408 Parkway House, Sheen Lane, London SW14 8LS. ℂ (0181) 878 1130. FAX (0181) 878 0982. @ venice@dircon.co.uk 🍴 None. **Rooms** apartments sleeping from 1 to 12. ● Never. 🗲 MC, V. ⓁⓁ–ⓁⓁⓁⓁ

VERONA

Torcolo This B&B is an inexpensive option at the heart of lively Verona. Owner Silvia Pommari extends a warm welcome and her staff are helpful. Bedrooms vary, displaying several styles – 18th-century, Art Nouveau, modern. Most have somewhat cramped bathrooms; the best have separate shower cubicles. In summer, breakfast is served in the little off-street courtyard. ⊠ Vicolo Listone 3, 37121 Verona. **Map** p335 D3. ℂ 045 800 75 12. FAX 045 800 40 58. 🍴 b. **Rooms** 19. ▤ 🅱 ● mid to end Jan. 🗲 AE, MC, V. ⓁⓁ

VENICE
Serenissima A stone's throw from St Mark's, with simple but pretty bedrooms and many attractive modern paintings on white walls. ⊠ Calle Goldoni, San Marco 4486, 30124 Venezia. **Map** p335 E3. ℂ 041 520 00 11. FAX 041 522 32 92. 🍴 b. **Rooms** 37. ⓁⓁ

VERONA
Colomba d'Oro Slick central hotel where a muralled foyer evokes Renaissance Verona. Some bedrooms are traditional in style, others modern. ⊠ Via Cattaneo 10, 37121 Verona. **Map** p335 D3. ℂ 045 59 53 00. FAX 045 59 49 74. 🍴 b. **Rooms** 51. ⓁⓁⓁ

VILLANDRO
Steinbock Bedrooms are beamed, with new pine beds and plump white duvets. The restaurant is noted for its regional Tyrolean dishes. ⊠ Santo Stefano 38, 39043 Villandro, Bolzano. **Map** p335 E2. ℂ 0472 84 31 11. FAX 0472 84 34 68. 🍴 b,l,d. **Rooms** 16. Ⓛ

ZERMAN DI MOGLIANO VENETO
Villa Condulmer For the price of a three-star hotel in Venice you can stay in this impressive 18th-century villa only 20 minutes' drive away. ⊠ Via Zermanese 1, 31020 Zerman di Mogliano Veneto, Treviso. **Map** p335 E3. ℂ 041 45 71 00. FAX 041 45 71 34. 🍴 b,l,d. **Rooms** 48. ⓁⓁ

CENTRAL ITALY
TUSCANY • UMBRIA
LE MARCHE • ABRUZZO • LAZIO • SARDINIA

WITH THE CAPITAL, Rome, at its core, Central Italy contains a range of beautiful landscapes and towns rich in culture and history, including ancient palaces, churches and towers. Tuscany in particular offers a wealth of memorable hotels, ranging from hilltop hamlets converted for the purposes, to atmospheric pensioni in Florence and Siena. Umbria and the Marche offer some wonderful rural retreats in their gentle, pastoral countryside. The glossy island of Sardinia, included in this section, has plenty of luxury seaside haunts, plus a few simpler alternatives. If Rome is your destination, then the very best of hotels, from inexpensive to top-of-the-range, are described here.

ALGHERO, SARDINIA

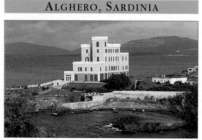

Villa Las Tronas Aloof on its rocky promontory, this castellated 19th-century folly has a grand interior and businesslike staff. Request a sea view (which costs extra) to avoid looking out onto Alghero's apartment blocks. Alghero's old town is nearby, and handy for morning espresso or cappuccino; breakfast here is not a strong point.
⊠ Lungomare Valencia 1, 07041 Alghero, Sardinia.
Map p338 A2. **[** 079 98 18 18. **FAX** 079 98 10 44.
⊞ b,l,d. **Rooms** 29. 🗐 🏊 🍴 🛈 🌑 Never.
🗐 AE, DC, MC, V. ⓁⓁⓁ

ARTIMINIO

Paggeria Medicea Terracotta pantiles, cool arcades and a formal garden characterize this hotel in a village near Florence. Created from the servant's wing of a 16th-century Medici villa, it is imbued with an understated elegance. Dinner is served on a terrace overlooking vineyards; food is Tuscan with a Renaissance flavour.
⊠ Viale Papa Giovanni XXIII, 59015 Artiminio, Firenze.
Map p335 D5. **[** 055 871 80 81. **FAX** 055 871 80 80.
@ artiminio@ten.it **⊞** b,l,d. **Rooms** 37. 🗐 🏊 🍴 🛈
🌑 Never. 🗐 AE, DC, MC, V. ⓁⓁⓁ

ASSISI
Santa Maria degli Ancillotti Hilltop retreat set in olive groves and vineyards. Excellent two-room suites with mini kitchens and terraces. Charming family. Pool, bikes, table tennis, archery.
⊠ Sterpeto 42, 06086 Assisi, Perugia. **Map** p337 D1.
[**FAX** 075 803 97 64. **⊞** b,d. **Rooms** 8. ⓁⓁ

ASSISI
Subasio Assisi's grand hotel, somewhat elderly, but splendidly sited near the Basilica, with a panoramic terrace and vaulted dining room.
⊠ Via Frate Elia 2, 06081 Assisi, Perugia.
Map p337 D1. **[** 075 81 22 06. **FAX** 075 81 66 91.
⊞ b,l,d. **Rooms** 65. ⓁⓁ

CASTEL DEL PIANO UMBRO
Villa Aureli Two self-catering apartments for 4-6 people in the magical home of Count Serego Alighieri, little altered since the 1700s. Pool.
⊠ Via Cirenei 70, 06071 Castel del Piano Umbro, Perugia. **Map** p336 C1. **[** 075 514 04 44.
FAX 075 514 94 08. **Rooms** 2 apartments. ⓁⓁ

CASTELLINA IN CHIANTI
Belvedere di San Leonino A 15th-century stone house, with well-equipped rooms, garden, terrace and pool. Good value. Siena 15km (11 miles).
⊠ Loc. San Leonino, 53011 Castellina in Chianti, Siena.
Map p336 B1. **[** 0577 74 08 87. **FAX** 0577 74 09 24.
⊞ b,d; l by arrangement. **Rooms** 28. Ⓛ

ASPROLI

Poggio d'Asproli This elegant stonebuilt farmhouse is the home of hotelier and artist Bruno Pagliari. Some of his work, mixed in with antiques, decorates the house. The sitting room has a huge fireplace and inviting sofas, and along one side of the room is a terrace for eating out on or just absorbing the peace. Bedrooms are similarly restful.
☒ Asproli, 06059 Todi, Perugia. **Map** p336 C2.
🇨 FAX 075 803 97 64. 🍴 b,d. **Rooms** 8.
≋ 🖊 ● Christmas. 🅔 Not accepted. ⓁⓁ

BAGNO VIGNONI

Posta Marcucci If you're exploring the countryside around Siena, this hotel in a small spa town is worth seeking out for its service (friendly and solicitous), and the reliable, traditional cuisine. The breakfast on the terrace is particularly good. Another treat is the open-air thermal pool in a quiet corner of the garden.
☒ Via Ara Urcea 43, 53020 Bagno Vignoni, Siena.
Map p336 B2. 🇨 0577 88 71 12. FAX 0577 88 71 19.
@ hotel@postamarcucci.it 🍴 b,l,d. **Rooms** 46.
≋ 🍴 🖊 ● mid-Jan to mid-Feb. 🅔 AE, DC, MC, V. Ⓛ

ASSISI

Umbra Just off Assisi's main square a row of old houses, some dating back to medieval times, have been connected to create a hotel with the feeling of a private home. There's a terrace, covered by a pergola, for dining out on. The public rooms are elegant; bedrooms are simpler, and some have lovely countryside views.
☒ Via degli Archi 6, 06081 Assisi, Perugia. **Map** p337 D1.
🇨 075 81 22 40. FAX 075 81 36 53. @ umbra@
mail.caribusiness.it 🍴 b,l,d. **Rooms** 25. 🖊 ● mid-Nov to
mid-Dec; mid-Jan to mid-March. 🅔 AE, DC, MC, V. ⓁⓁ

BARBERINO VAL D'ELSA

Il Paretaio A country estate with an unpretentious 17th-century farmhouse at its heart. Many guests come for the horse riding. Inside, bedrooms are rustic, with equestrian prints, worn terracotta floors and whitewashed walls; one of the nicest is in the old dovecot. Meals are communal, eaten round a long larchwood table.
☒ San Filippo, 50021 Barberino Val d'Elsa, Firenze.
Map p335 D5, p336 B1. 🇨 (055) 805 92 18.
FAX (055) 805 92 31. @ ilparetaio@tin.it 🍴 b,l. **Rooms** 6.
≋ 🍴 🖊 ● mid-Jan, Feb. 🅔 Not accepted. Ⓛ

CASTELNUOVO BERARDENGA
Relais Borgo San Felice A hamlet on the wine estate has become a luxurious hotel, with a swimming pool discreetly tucked away.
☒ San Felice, 53019 Castelnuovo Berardenga, Siena.
Map p336 B1. 🇨 0577 35 92 60. FAX 0577 35 90 89.
@ borgofelice@flashnet.it 🍴 b,l,d. **Rooms** 45. ⓁⓁⓁⓁ

CENERENTE
Castello dell'Oscano An 18th-century 'medieval' castle in a steep pine forest. Some rooms are in the less atmospheric Villa Ada next door.
☒ 06134 Cenerente, Perugia. **Map** p336 C1.
🇨 075 69 01 25. FAX 075 69 06 66. @ oscano@krenet.it
🍴 b,d. **Rooms** 20. ⓁⓁⓁ

CERTALDO
Osteria del Vicario The approach through modern Certaldo is discouraging, but press on to the old town and this simple, well-priced inn.
☒ Via Rivellino 3, 50052 Certaldo Alto, Firenze.
Map p335 D5, p336 B1. 🇨 FAX 0571 66 82 28. 🍴 b,l,d.
Rooms 11. Ⓛ

ISOLA D'ELBA
Capo Sud Island complex of little villas in a quiet spot with fine bay views. Rooms are modern and simple, scattered among trees and *macchia*, the hilly scrubland which covers much of the island.
☒ Lacona, 57037 Elba, Livorno. **Map** p336 A2. 🇨 0565
96 40 21. FAX 0565 96 42 63. 🍴 b,l,d. **Rooms** 40. ⓁⓁ

For key to symbols see backflap. For price categories *see p333*

BOVARA DI TREVI

Casa Giulia There's a three-day minimum stay at this red-brick country villa, but that's no hardship as it's a good base for Assisi, Perugia, Spoleto and Todi. The owners are welcoming, and their private collection of antique cameras, old toys and *objets d'art* give a personal touch. Bedrooms are plain but comfortable.

Via Corciano 1, 06039 Bovara di Trevi, Perugia. **Map** p337 D2. 0742 782 57. FAX 0742 38 16 32. b, dinner on request. **Rooms** 6. Never. Not accepted.

CASTELLINA IN CHIANTI

Salivolpi For a farmhouse holiday in Chianti country at a much lower price that many of the nearby 'hamlet' hotels, Salivolpi is a sound choice. The guesthouse comprises two low old stone farmhouses and a new bungalow in a large garden on the edge of the village. The neat bedrooms contain huge old carved beds. Breakfast is an abundant feast.

Via Fiorentina, 53011 Castellina in Chianti, Siena. **Map** p336 B1. 0577 74 04 84. FAX 0577 74 09 98. b. **Rooms** 19. Never. MC, V.

CANALICCHIO DI COLLAZZONE

Relais il Canalicchio In the countryside 40km (25 miles) south of Perugia, a hilltop village has been turned into a stylish hotel complete with gym, sauna and billiard room. Grinding stones and local ceramics are much in evidence, and there are antiques too in the public rooms. Some bedrooms have private terrace gardens.

Via della Piazza 13, 06050 Canalicchio, Perugia. **Map** p336 C2. 075 8707325. FAX 075 8707296. relais@ntt.it b,l,d. **Rooms** 26. Never. AE, DC, MC, V.

CASTELLINA IN CHIANTI

Tenuta di Ricavo A whole hamlet abandoned in the 1950s has now been converted into a hotel that's owned and run by the Scotoni and Lobrano families. It's very well done out, with large, whitewashed vaulted rooms and a jumble of old rather than antique furniture. The 'Black Sheep' restaurant is popular with non-residents.

Località Ricavo, Castellina in Chianti 530011, Siena. **Map** p336 B1. 0577 74 02 21. FAX 0577 74 10 14. ricavo@ricavo.com b,d. **Rooms** 23. Nov to Easter. MC, V.

ISOLA D'ELBA

Villa Ottone Across the bay from Portoferraio, in leafy grounds close to the sea, is this polished hotel whose main building is an 18th-century villa.

Ottone, 57037 Portoferraio, Elba, Livorno. **Map** p336 A2. 0565 93 30 42. FAX 0565 93 32 57. villaottone@overture.it b,l,d. **Rooms** 80.

FIRENZE (FLORENCE)

Hotel Annalena A traditional *pensione* with solid comforts and a huge drawing room. Bedrooms vary in size; acceptable bathrooms.

Via Romana 34, 50125 Firenze. **Map** p335 D5. 055 22 24 02. FAX 055 22 24 03. annalena@ hotelannalena.it. b. **Rooms** 20.

FIRENZE (FLORENCE)

Grand Early 1900s *palazzo* whose winter garden lobby is especially evocative. Bedrooms, frescoed with Renaissance scenes, have all modern luxury.

Piazza Ognissanti 1, 50123 Firenze. **Map** p335 D5. 055 28 87 81. FAX 055 21 74 00. b,l,d. **Rooms** 107.

FIRENZE (FLORENCE)

Royal Hotel This B&B hotel is cool and elegant, and its large, peaceful garden and parking spaces are a huge plus. Bedrooms are functional; some are small. Good value for money.

Via delle Ruote 52, 50124 Firenze. **Map** p335 D5. 055 48 32 87. FAX 055 49 09 76. b. **Rooms** 40.

CETONA

La Frateria di Padre Eligio Film-maker Anthony Minghella stayed here to revise a script; others come here on retreat (there are no TVs, phones, radios or newspapers) or simply on honeymoon or holiday. A religious community runs the place, but the ambience is not ascetic: expect wonderful food and beautifully furnished, candlelit rooms.
Convento di San Francesco, 53040 Cetona, Siena.
Map p336 C2. 0578 23 80 15. FAX 0578 23 92 20. frateria@ftbcc.it b,l,d. **Rooms** 7. Jan. AE, MC, V.

CORTONA

Relais Il Falconiere Owner Riccardo Baracchi was born in this small villa. His wife, Silvia, is also from the area and is the chef. Their excellent restaurant attracts diners from a wide area – the food really is special. Vaulted bedrooms are traditionally furnished. The pool overlooks a hillside of cypress trees and olives.
Località San Martino, 52044 Cortona, Arezzo.
Map p336 C1. 0575 61 26 79. FAX 0575 61 29 27. falconiere@relaischateaux.fr b,l,d. Rooms12. Never. AE, DC, V.

FIESOLE

Bencistà The Bencistà was built as a monastery in the 14th century and has polished tile floors, tall windows, gleaming furniture and an air of serenity, yet bills itself modestly as a *pensione*. Bedrooms have whitewashed walls and solid old furniture; some have glorious views over Florence and the Tuscan hills. A set menu is offered for dinner, which starts promptly at 7.30pm.
Via B da Maiano 4, 50014 Fiesole. **Map** p335 D5. FAX 055 591 63. bencista@uol.it b,l,d. **Rooms** 42. Never. Not accepted.

FIESOLE

Villa San Michele This villa was designed by Michelangelo, and if the antiques look as though they are from the 17th century that's because they probably are. Grandeur and authenticity is San Michele's hallmark. One of the many pleasures is taking breakfast in the *loggia*, looking across green hillsides to Florence below.
Via Doccia 4, 50014 Fiesole. **Map** p335 D5. 055 594 51. FAX 055 59 87 34. villasanmichele@firenze.net b,l,d. **Rooms** 40. mid-Nov to mid-March. AE, DC.

FIRENZE (FLORENCE)
Tornabuoni Beacci On the elegant prime shopping street, a long-established *pensione* with old-world atmosphere. Rooftop terrace.
Via de Tornabuoni 3, 50123 Firenze.
Map p335 D5. 055 26 83 77. FAX 055 28 35 94. b. **Rooms** 28.

ISOLA DEL GIGLIO
Pardini's Hermitage Smartly modern island villa with balconied bedrooms, reached from Giglio Porto by boat, car and donkey, or an hour's walk.
Cala degli Alberi, 58013 Giglio, Grosseto.
Map p336 A3. 0564 80 90 34. FAX 0564 80 91 77. b,l,d. **Rooms** 11.

GREVE IN CHIANTI
Castello di Uzzano Medieval castle, transformed over the centuries into an elegant country villa. The attractive apartments surround a courtyard.
Via Uzzano 5, Greve in Chianti, 50022 Firenze.
Map p335 D5, p336 B1. 055 85 40 32. FAX 055 85 43 75. b,l. **Rooms** 6 apartments.

GUBBIO
Villa Montegranelli A severe exterior contrasts with the light 18th-century style of the spacious public rooms. The villa is popular for functions.
Monteluiano, 06040 Gubbio, Perugia. **Map** p337 D1. 075 922 01 85. FAX 075 927 33 72. b,l,d. **Rooms** 21.

FIRENZE (FLORENCE)

Excelsior Florence's grandest hotel is made from two 19th-century houses that stand next to the River Arno. Its fabulous interiors abound in oil paintings, marble staircases, statues and stained glass windows. The rooms are spacious and old-fashioned in style; many have good views over the river. It is closer to the train station than to the city centre.
☒ Piazza d'Ognissanti 3, 50123 Firenze. **Map** p335 D5.
☎ 055 26 42 01. ℻ 055 21 02 78. 🍴 b,l,d.
Rooms 192. ● Never. 💳 AE, DC, MC, V. Ⓛ Ⓛ Ⓛ

FIRENZE (FLORENCE)

Morandi alla Crocetta This house just behind the archaeological museum was a brothel in Medici times, then a convent. Owner Kathleen Doyle Antuono has lived here since the 1920s, and now runs her first-rate hotel with her two sons. There are many special touches, from frescoed rooms to phones in the bathrooms.
☒ Via Laura 50, 50121 Firenze. **Map** p335 D5.
☎ 055 234 47 47. ℻ 055 248 09 54.
@ welcome@hotelmorandi.it 🍴 b. **Rooms** 10. 🗐
● Never. 💳 AE, DC, MC, V. Ⓛ Ⓛ

FIRENZE (FLORENCE)

Loggiato dei Serviti This vaulted hotel is airy and calm, and is set in a traffic-free square by the Ospedale degli Innocenti. The decoration is spare and elegant, with carved wooden bedheads and a few well-chosen pieces of furniture. The place is popular with visiting art historians so book well in advance. Breakfast is very good.
☒ Piazza della SS Annunziata 3, 50122 Firenze.
Map p335 D5. ☎ 055 28 95 92. ℻ 055 28 95 95.
@ loggiato_serviti@italyhotel.com 🍴 b. **Rooms** 29.
🗐 ● Never. 💳 AE, DC, MC, V. Ⓛ Ⓛ

FIRENZE (FLORENCE)

Porta Rossa Italy's second oldest hotel, dating from 1386, is a purposeful, bustling and civilized place. Leather couches and stained glass decorate the vaulted reception area. Bedrooms are comparatively plain but are large; it's worth asking for the tower suite with its views over town. Best of all is the hotel's central location, close to Piazza della Signoria.
☒ Via Porta Rossa 19, 50100 Firenze. **Map** p335 D5.
☎ 055 28 75 51. ℻ 055 28 21 79. 🍴 b. **Rooms** 85.
💳 AE, DC, MC, V. Ⓛ

MASSA E COZZILE

Villa Pasquini Little has changed here since the 19th-century. Once the retreat of an aristocratic family; bought intact by the present owners.
☒ Via Vacchereccia 56, Margine Coperta, 51010 Massa e Cozzile, Pistoia. **Map** p335 D5. ☎ 0572 722 05.
℻ 0572 91 08 88. 🍴 b,d. **Rooms** 12. Ⓛ

MONTE CASTELLO DI VIBIO

Fattoria di Vibio All is effortless simplicity and relaxed elegance at this 18th-century farmhouse.
☒ Località Buchella-Doglio 9, 06057 Monte Castello di Vibio, Perugia. **Map** p336 C2. ☎ 075 874 96 07.
℻ 075 878 0014. @ fattoriadivibio@cronos.it
🍴 b,l,d. **Rooms** 10. Ⓛ Ⓛ

MONTEFOLLONICO

La Chiusa The restaurant, an old olive oil mill, is the centrepiece, but great care has been given to the bedrooms and suites. Superb bathrooms.
☒ Via della Madonnina 88, 53040 Montefollonico, Siena. **Map** p336 B1. ☎ 0577 66 96 68. ℻ 0577 66 95 93.
🍴 b,l,d. **Rooms** 12. Ⓛ Ⓛ Ⓛ

MONTERIGGIONI

San Luigi Farmhouse country hotel in vast, lush grounds. Copious buffet meals, pool, tennis.
☒ Località Strove, Via della Cerreta 38, 53030 Monteriggioni, Siena. **Map** p335 D5, p336 B1.
☎ 0577 30 10 55. ℻ 0577 30 11 67. 🍴 b,l,d.
Rooms 34, plus 5 apartments. Ⓛ Ⓛ

FIRENZE (FLORENCE)

Torre di Bellosguardo This 16th-century villa with tower rests on a hill overlooking the city, just south of the Porta Romana. It aims to be a home from home and what makes the place special is the affable owner Giovanni Franchetti. Bedrooms are large and solidly furnished. There is a minimum two-night stay at weekends.
☒ Via Roti Michelozzi 2, 50124 Firenze. **Map** p335 D5.
𝄞 055 229 81 45. **FAX** 055 22 90 08. 🍴 b,l.
@ torredibellosguardo@dada.it 🍴 b,l. **Rooms** 16.
▤ ⬚ ⚲ ● Never. ☑ AE, DC, MC, V. ⓁⓁⓁⓁ

FONTIGNANO

Villa di Montesolare The Iannarones run this 18th-century villa hotel along houseparty lines, offering simple meals using fresh ingredients. They have restored the formal garden, and another 'secret' garden behind it. Some rooms are in the converted farmhouse with its own pool down the hill. Minimum stay three days.
☒ Località Fontignano, 06070 Fontignano, Perugia.
Map p336 C2. 𝄞 075 83 23 76. **FAX** 075 83 54 62.
@ info@villadimontesolare.it 🍴 b,l,d. **Rooms** 20.
⬚ 🍽 ⚲ ● Never. ☑ AE, DC, MC, V. ⓁⓁ

FIRENZE (FLORENCE)

Villa Cora A pleasure palace on the outskirts of Florence, this Renaissance-style 19th-century mansion was once the home of Baron Oppenheim and later Napoleon's wife Empress Eugenia. The formal interior includes ceilings encrusted with stucco, Murano glass chandeliers and regally draped beds.
☒ Viale Niccolò Machiavelli 18, 50125 Firenze.
Map p335 D5. 𝄞 055 229 84 51. **FAX** 055 22 90 86.
@ villacora@explorer.it 🍴 b,l,d. **Rooms** 48. ⬚ ⚲
● Never. ☑ AE, DC, MC, V. ⓁⓁⓁⓁ

LECCHI IN CHIANTI

San Sano The village's old watchtower forms the core of this hotel, with bedrooms in the former village houses, each connected by courtyards, passageways and stone steps. The dining room is in the former stables. Guest rooms are rustic in style, but stay the right side of overly countrified, and have modern bathrooms.
☒ San Sano, 53010 Lecchi in Chianti, Siena.
Map p336 B1. 𝄞 0577 74 61 30. **FAX** 0577 74 61 56.
@ hotelsansano@chiantinet.it 🍴 b,d. **Rooms** 12. ⬚ ⚲
● mid-Nov to mid-March. ☑ AE, DC, MC, V. ⓁⓁ

MONTEVETTOLINI

Villa Lucia Informal yet elegant farmhouse B&B run by Italian-American Lucia Vallera. Shady garden and terraces, small pool.
☒ Via dei Bronzoli 144, 51010 Montevettolini, Pistoia.
Map p335 D5. 𝄞 **FAX** 0572 62 88 17. 🍴 b; d on request.
Rooms 7, plus 1 apartment for 2. ⓁⓁ

MONTICCHIELLO DI PIENZA

L'Olmo An old farmhouse with beautifully decorated double room, suites (two with terraces), and apartment. Delicious breakfasts.
☒ Podere Ommio 27, 53020 Monticchiello di Pienza, Siena. **Map** p336 B1. 𝄞 0578 75 51 33.
FAX 0578 75 51 24. 🍴 b,d. **Rooms** 7. ⓁⓁⓁ

PANICALE

Le Grotte di Boldrino This former *palazzo* hewn into Panicale's walls is small and intimate. The decor juxtaposes new with old.
☒ Via Virgilio Cappari, 06064 Panicale, Perugia.
Map p335 E5, p336 C1. 𝄞 075 83 71 61.
FAX 075 83 71 66. 🍴 b,l,d. **Rooms** 11. Ⓛ

PERUGIA

Brufani The public rooms of this exclusive 1880s hotel were painted by Lillis, the German interior designer. Some bedrooms have spectacular views.
☒ Piazza Italia 12, 06100 Perugia. **Map** p336 C1.
𝄞 075 573 25 41. **FAX** 075 572 02 10. @ brufani@ italyhotel.it 🍴 b,l,d. **Rooms** 24. ⓁⓁⓁ

MERCATALE VAL DI PESA

Salvadonica Olive oil and wine are still produced on this large farm estate. The guest rooms are in a couple of huge farmhouses; there are also ten apartments in the grounds. It's an easy drive into Florence; there are many alternative distractions on site, including horseriding, billiards, tennis and football.
☒ Via Grevigiana 82, 50024 Mercatale Val di Pesa, Firenze. **Map** p335 D5. **(** 055 821 80 39.
FAX 055 821 80 43. **@** salvadonica@tin.it **ᴙ** b. **Rooms** 5.
🌊 ᴙ 🛁 ● Nov to Feb. 🗲 AE, DC, MC, V. Ⓛ Ⓛ

MONTEFALCO

Villa Pambuffetti A rose-pink brick villa located between Assisi and Perugia, with views of the Umbrian hills. Owners Alessandra and Mauro Angelucci have preserved the original 1920s' interiors, decorated with Tiffany lamps and cane chairs; the bathrooms are in authentic period style but with modern plumbing and fittings.
☒ Via della Vittoria 20, 06036 Montefalco, Perugia.
Map p337 D2. **(** 0742 37 94 17. **FAX** 0742 37 92 45.
@ villabianca@interbusiness.it **ᴙ** b,d. **Rooms** 15.
🍴 🏊 🌊 🛁 ● Never. 🗲 AE, DC, MC, V. Ⓛ Ⓛ Ⓛ

MONTE SAN SAVINO

Castello di Gargonza The village, abandoned earlier this century, has now been turned into a place to stay. It's not strictly a hotel (most accommodation is in the village houses let by the week), but the place is informal and good value. There are basic rooms for a one-night stop, with breakfast in the old oil-pressing house.
☒ Gargonza, 52048 Monte San Savino, Arezzo.
Map p336 B1. **(** 0575 84 70 21. **FAX** 0575 84 70 54.
@ gargonza@teta.it **ᴙ** b. **Rooms** 7, plus 25 houses. 🌊
🛁 ● 3 weeks Nov, 3 weeks Jan. 🗲 AE, DC, MC, V. Ⓛ Ⓛ

OLIENA, SARDINIA

Su Gologone This low white villa in the wooded foothills of the Supramonte mountains has guest rooms with whitewashed walls and tiled floors. Despite the large number of rooms, it feels small and personal, and the area is extremely peaceful. Food is extremely good; Sard specialities include spit-roasted suckling pig.
☒ Oliena, 08025 Nuoro, Sardinia. **Map** p338 B2.
(0784 28 75 12. **FAX** 0784 28 76 68.
@ golgone@tin.it **ᴙ** b,l,d. **Rooms** 77. 🍴 🌊 ᴙ 🛁
● Nov to Feb, except Christmas. 🗲 AE, MC, V. Ⓛ Ⓛ Ⓛ

PIENZA

Il Chiostro di Pienza Half the rooms in this stylishly converted monastery overlook the cloister, the rest have serene hill views.
☒ Corso Rosellino 26, 53026 Pienza, Siena.
Map p336 B1. **(** 0578 74 84 00. **FAX** 0578 74 84 40.
ᴙ b,l,d. **Rooms** 29. Ⓛ Ⓛ

PISA

Royal Victoria Original features at this dignified 1840s hotel include exquisite *trompe l'oeil* drapery. Rooms vary in size and style; all are fairly basic.
☒ Lungarno Pacinotti 12, 56126 Pisa.
Map p334 C5. **(** 050 94 01 11. **FAX** 050 94 01 80.
ᴙ b. **Rooms** 48. Ⓛ Ⓛ

POGGIO MIRTETO SCALO

Borgo Paraelios Immaculately executed country club-style hotel. Individually furnished rooms and suites are spread around gardens and courtyards.
☒ Valle Collicchia, 02040 Poggio Mirteto Scalo, Rieti.
Map p337 D3. **(** 0765 262 67. **FAX** 0765 262 68.
@ borgo@fabaris.it **ᴙ** b,l,d. **Rooms** 15. Ⓛ Ⓛ Ⓛ Ⓛ

ISOLA DI PONZA

Cernia On this alluring island, close to Chiaia di Luna beach and the pretty port, an airy holiday hotel. The best rooms have terraces.
☒ Via Panoramica, 04027 Isola di Ponza, Latina.
Map p337 D5. **(** 0771 80 99 51. **FAX** 0771 80 99 54.
ᴙ b,l,d. **Rooms** 50. Ⓛ Ⓛ Ⓛ

PALAU, SARDINIA

Capo d'Orso This relaxed hotel is only a short boat ride away from the busy Costa Smeralda, but miles away in spirit. The life of the place revolves around two white slivers of beach, the pool and a series of shaded terraces. Rooms are in a low-rise block unremarkable in style, but each has a balcony or terrace facing the sea.
☒ Località Cala Capra, 07020 Palau, Sardinia.
Map p338 B1. ☎ 0789 70 20 00. FAX 0789 70 20 09.
🍽 b,l,d. **Rooms** 60. 🗏 🏊 🍴 ⊘ ◐ early Oct to late April. 🅶 AE, DC, MC, V. ⓁⓁ

PANZANO IN CHIANTI

Villa le Barone This 16th-century villa in the countryside south of Florence is run along the lines of a house party, with honesty bar and a 'reception' in the form of a visitor's book. Rooms have the feeling of a private home furnished with personal effects. There are two sitting rooms and a pool with a view to lounge by.
☒ Via San Leolino 19, 50020 Panzano in Chianti, Firenze.
Map p335 D5, p336 B1. ☎ 055 85 26 21.
FAX 055 85 22 77. 🍽 b,l,d. **Rooms** 28. 🗏 🏊 🍴 ⊘ ◐ Nov to March. 🅶 AE, MC, V. ⓁⓁⓁ

PALO LAZIALE

La Posta Vecchia The artworks and antiques in this seaside mansion, lapped by the Tyrrhenian sea, were chosen by former owner John Paul Getty. It is probably Italy's most remarkable hotel. During building work, the foundations of a Roman villa were discovered; they can now be viewed through glass panels in the floor.
☒ 00055 Palo Laziale, Ladispoli. **Map** p336 C3.
☎ 06 994 95 01. FAX 06 994 95 07. @ postavec@caerenet.it 🍽 b,l,d. **Rooms** 17. 🗏 🏊 ⊘ ◐ mid-Nov to mid-March. 🅶 AE, DC, MC, V. ⓁⓁⓁⓁ

PESARO

Villa Serena There's no haughtiness at the villa of the Pinto family – or to give them their full title, the counts Pinto de Franca y Vergaes. The polished interior with its old master paintings exudes simplicity and calm, and good food is served in a down-to-earth atmosphere. Bedrooms range from antique-packed to faded gentility.
☒ Via San Nicola 6/3, 61100 Pesaro. **Map** p335 F5.
☎ 0721 552 11. FAX 0721 559 27. @ rapinto@flashten.it 🍽 b,l,d. **Rooms** 10. 🏊 ⊘ ◐ first 2 weeks Jan. 🅶 AE, DC, V. ⓁⓁⓁ

PORTO CERVO, SARDINIA
Balocco On the island's Costa Smeralda, a stylishly rustic modern hotel in lush gardens, close to the chic harbour of Porto Cervo.
☒ Via Liscia di Vacca, 07020 Porto Cervo, Sassari, Sardinia. **Map** p338 B1. ☎ 0789 915 10.
FAX 0789 915 10. 🍽 b. **Rooms** 34. ⓁⓁⓁ

PORTO CERVO, SARDINIA
Capriccioli An affordable family-run villa-type hotel close to a pretty beach. The Ristorante Il Pirate is the focus of the rustic establishment.
☒ Capriccioli, 07020 Porto Cervo, Sassari, Sardinia.
Map p338 B1. ☎ 0789 960 04. FAX 0789 964 22.
🍽 b,l,d. **Rooms** 40. ⓁⓁⓁ

PORTO CERVO, SARDINIA
Le Ginestre Little luxury villas among trees and flowering shrubs. Most of the rooms have balconies with sea views.
☒ 07020 Porto Cervo, Sassari, Sardinia. **Map** p338 B1.
☎ 0789 92 030. FAX 0789 940 87. 🍽 b,l,d.
Rooms 80. ⓁⓁⓁ

PORTO ROTONDO, SARDINIA
Sporting An oasis of luxury in tastefully simple neo-rustic buildings scattered around a promontory. Strong yachting contingent.
☒ Olbia, 07026 Porto Rotondo, Sassari, Sardinia.
Map p338 B1. ☎ 0789 340 05. FAX 0789 343 83.
@ sporthot@tin.it 🍽 b,l,d. **Rooms** 27. ⓁⓁⓁⓁ

PIEVESCOLA

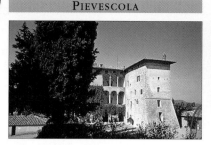

Relais La Suvera This 16th-century fortified villa once belonged to film-maker Luchino Visconti. Although he may not have had anything to do with the canopied beds and elaborate decorative style worthy of a film set, you feel he would have approved. The place is fun, sybaritic, romantic – and expensive.
⊠ Pievescola, 53030 Siena. **Map** p336 B1.
📞 0577 96 03 00. 📠 0577 96 02 20.
🍴 b,l,d. **Rooms** 35. 🛗 ❄ 📺 🎧 ⬤ Nov to March.
💳 AE, DC, MC, V. ⓁⓁⓁⓁ

PORTO CERVO, SARDINIA

Pitrizza On a headland surrounded by sapphire water, Pitrizza is a collection of villas, scattered through a garden leading to a small beach and seawater pool. Its strong point is the way it has combined peace and sociability – it's quiet but there's also a clubhouse with lively bar/restaurant.
⊠ Porto Cervo, 07020 Sassari, Sardinia. **Map** p338 B1.
📞 0789 93 01 11. 📞 0789 93 06 11.
@ reso66pitrizza@itsheraton.com 🍴 b,l,d.
Rooms 51. 🛗 ❄ 📺 🎧 ⬤ mid-Oct to Apr.
💳 AE, DC, MC, V. ⓁⓁⓁⓁ

PISTOIA

Villa Vannini This part of Tuscany has relatively few great places to stay, so this attractive villa is particularly welcome. It is managed by the welcoming owner Maria-Rosa Vannini. The excellent cuisine is based on Tuscan specialities; pre-dinner drinks are served on the terrace under cedar trees. Bedrooms are furnished in floral fabrics and with good furniture.
⊠ Villa di Piteccio, 51030 Pistoia. **Map** p335 D5.
📞 0573 420 31. 📠 0573 263 31. 🍴 b,l,d. **Rooms** 8. 🎧
⬤ Never. 💳 Not accepted. ⓁⓁ

PORTO CERVO, SARDINIA

Romazzino One of Europe's grandest beach hotels, the Romazzino has exclusive use of a white-sand bay. The hotel is on the large side but has the feel of a smaller place; families will feel comfortable. There are Moorish touches to the decoration, and service and food are top class. Large swimming pool
⊠ 07020 Porto Cervo, Costa Smeralda, Sardinia.
Map p338 B1. 📞 0789 97 71 11. 📠 0789 962 58.
🍴 b,l,d. **Rooms** 91. 🛗 ❄ 📺 🎧 ⬤ mid-Oct to late Apr.
💳 AE, DC, MC, V. ⓁⓁⓁⓁ

PUGNANO
Casetta delle Selve Nicla Menchi, the characterful owner of this elevated farmhouse B&B, has created an interior stunningly different from the norm. Great breakfasts.
⊠ 56010 Pugnano, San Giuliano Terme, Pisa.
Map p334 C5. 📞 📠 050 85 03 59. 🍴 b. **Rooms** 6. Ⓛ

PUNTA ALA
Piccolo Hotel Alleluja This is the smallest and most inviting of the exclusive hotels in this chic yachting-and-boutique town.
⊠ Via del Porto, 58040 Punta Ala, Grosseto.
Map p336 A2. 📞 0564 92 20 50. 📠 0564 92 07 34.
🍴 b,l,d. **Rooms** 38. ⓁⓁⓁⓁ

RADDA IN CHIANTI
Podere Terreno Old farmhouse guesthouse with views of vines and olive groves and great home cooking. Minimum stay two days.
⊠ Via Terreno 21, Volpaia, 53017 Radda in Chianti, Siena. **Map** p335 D5, p336 B1. 📞 📠 0577 73 83 12.
🍴 b,d. **Rooms** 7. ⓁⓁ

ROME
Condotti The comfy sofas in the glossy foyer are the only place to lounge. There is a frescoed breakfast room. Bedrooms are harmonious.
⊠ Via Mario De'Fiori 37, 00187 Roma. **Map** p336 C4, p338 A1. 📞 06 679 46 61. 📠 06 679 04 57.
@ hotelcondotti@italyhotel.com 🍴 b. **Rooms** 17. ⓁⓁⓁ

PORTO ERCOLE

PRATO

Il Pellicano This terracotta villa by the sea combines the best of a luxury hotel (great service and fine seafood cuisine) with an easygoing atmosphere and contemporary decoration. There's swimming off the flat rocks, and you don't have to move from the poolside to choose from a huge array of antipasti.

Cala dei Santi, 58, 58018 Porto Ercole, Grosseto. **Map** p336 B3. 0564 85 81 11. FAX 0564 83 34 18. @ info@pellicanohotel.com b,l,d. **Rooms** 41. Nov to March. AE, DC, V. ⒧⒧⒧

Villa Rucellai Potted lemon trees and clipped topiary characterize this country villa on the outskirts of industrial Prato. It has been in the Rucellai Piqué family since 1740 and is evidently a family home, but guests are free to use the grand hall and sitting room. Breakfast is taken at a communal table. Bedrooms are simple, but comfortable and full of personality.

Via di Canneto 16, 59100 Prato. **Map** p336 C2. 0574 46 03 92. b. **Rooms** 13. Never. Not accepted. ⒧⒧

PORTONOVO

RADDA IN CHIANTI

Emilia At this modest clifftop villa a short drive from the small resort of Portonovo, rooms are angled so that most have a sea view. Inside are some stupendous wall coverings – an illustrious band of 20th-century artists have paid for a stay here by donating a work. The food is very good, with fish a speciality.

Via Poggio 149a, 60020 Portonovo, Ancona. **Map** p335 E4. 071 80 11 45. FAX 071 80 13 30. @ info@hotelemilia.com b,l,d. **Rooms** 33. Nov to March. AE, DC, MC, V. ⒧⒧

Relais Fattoria Vignale This hotel has an appealingly domestic feel, decorated with muted colours, fresh flowers, oil paintings and standard lamps. Breakfast is served on the terrace or in the vaulted breakfast room. The 'taverna' on-site does snacks, and there's a very good restaurant – also called the Vignale – a short walk away.

Via Pianigiani 15, 53017 Raddi in Chianti, Siena. **Map** p336 B1. 0577 73 83 00. FAX 0577 73 85 92. @ vignale@chiantinet.it b. **Rooms** 29. 8-26 Dec; 6 Jan-25 March. AE,MC,V. ⒧⒧⒧

ROME
Hassler Above the Spanish Steps, with fabulous views from the roof terrace, restaurant and suites. Host to Europe's glitterati in its *dolce vita* days.

Piazza Trinità dei Monti 6, 00187 Roma. **Map** p336 C4. 06 69 93 40. FAX 06 67 89 91. b,l,d. **Rooms** 100. ⒧⒧⒧⒧

ROME
Lord Byron Originally a monastery, now a small, lavishly furnished hotel in the residential district of Parioli.

Via de Notaris 5, 00197, Roma. **Map** p336 C4. 06 361 30 41. FAX 06 322 04 05. @ info@ lordbyronhotel.com b,l,d. **Rooms** 37. ⒧⒧⒧⒧

ROME
Raphael Cloaked in ivy, and set back from Piazza Navona, with a startlingly theatrical foyer behind its discreet façade. Lovely roof terrace.

Largo Febo 2, 00186 Roma. **Map** p336 C4. 06 68 28 31. FAX 06 687 98 93. @ info@ raphaelhotel.com b,l,d. **Rooms** 71. ⒧⒧⒧⒧

ROME
Villa del Parco In a peaceful area a 20-minute bus ride from the centre of Rome. Inside, all is elegant and tranquil. Bedrooms vary in size.

Via Nomentana 110, 00161 Roma. **Map** p336 C4. 06 4423 77 73. FAX 06 4423 75 72. @ villaparco@ clink.it b. **Rooms** 24. ⒧⒧

REGGELLO

Villa Rigacci A 15th-century hilltop farmhouse with ivy-covered façade, open fires in winter, and tiled, stone-flagged and archwayed interiors. It makes a great bolthole close to Florence (30km/ 23 miles away). Furniture is highly polished and antique; bedrooms are mostly spacious; and food is a mix of international and French cuisine.
⊠ Vággio 76, 50066 Reggello. **Map** p335 E5.
📞 055 865 67 18. FAX 055 865 65 37. @ hotel@ villarigacci.it 🍴 b,l,d. **Rooms** 23. 🔲 🏊 🎤 🛗 ● Never.
🏧 AE, DC, MC, V. Ⓛ Ⓛ Ⓛ

ROME

Hotel dei Borgognoni Potted palms, Oriental ceramics and a modern decorative style combined with Old Master paintings make this smooth professional hotel a cool haven in the heart of the city. If you have the choice, go for a first-floor room with its own small terrace, furnished with tables, chairs and a parasol. Close to the Trevi Fountain and the Spanish Steps.
⊠ Via del Bufalo, 00187 Roma. **Map** p336 C4.
📞 06 69 94 15 05. FAX 06 69 94 15 01. 🍴 b.
Rooms 50. 🔲 ● Never. 🏧 AE, DC, MC, V. Ⓛ Ⓛ Ⓛ Ⓛ

ROME

Hotel Eden Extensively refurbished in1994, Eden is unashamedly status-conscious, flaunting its designer labels and its famous guests – among them have been actors Tom Cruise and Nicole Kidman. Decoration is a mix of neutral shades, oil paintings and openfires. The Michelin-starred terrace restaurant looks out over Rome's rooftops.
⊠ Via Ludovisi 49, 00187 Roma. **Map** p336 C4.
📞 06 47 81 21. FAX 06 482 15 84. @ reservations@ hotel-eden.it 🍴 b,l,d. **Rooms** 112. 🔲 🍽 🛗 ● Never.
🏧 AE, DC, MC, V. Ⓛ Ⓛ Ⓛ

ROME

Hotel Carriage This hotel is located in a street of designer clothes shops near Piazza di Spagna, has an airy roof terrace, feels pleasantly small and is professionally run. The boudoir style decoration of the public spaces (lots of gilt and towering floral arrangements) is tempered a little in the bedrooms, which are white and blue with solid repro-French furniture.
⊠ Via della Carrozze 36, 00187 Roma. **Map** p336 C4.
📞 06 699 01 24. FAX 06 678 82 79. 🍴 b. **Rooms** 22.
🔲 🛗 ● Never. 🏧 AE, DC, MC, V. Ⓛ Ⓛ Ⓛ

SAN BENEDETTO

Il Rosolaccio A hilltop farmhouse well restored by an English couple, Steven and Nathalie Music. Also self-catering apartments. Pool.
⊠ San Benedetto 34, 53037 San Gimignano, Siena.
Map p336 B1. 📞 0577 94 44 65. FAX 0577 94 44 67.
@ music@rosolaccio.com 🍴 b. **Rooms** 6. Ⓛ

SAN FELICE CIRCEO

Punta Rossa In a secluded setting above an exposed, rocky shore, a pleasant holiday hotel in the form of a mini village. Suites are very large.
⊠ Via delle Batterie 37, Quarto Caldo, 04017 San Felice Circeo, Latina. **Map** p337 D5. 📞 0773 54 80 85.
FAX 0773 54 80 75. 🍴 b,l,d. **Rooms** 34. Ⓛ Ⓛ Ⓛ

SAN GIMIGNANO

L'Antico Pozzo A 15th-century house in the middle of town, beautifully restored in 1990 and furnished with fine, simple taste.
⊠ Via San Matteo 87, 53037 San Gimignano, Siena.
Map p336 B1. 📞 0577 94 20 14. FAX 0577 94 21 17.
@ info@anticopozzo.com 🍴 b. Ⓛ Ⓛ Ⓛ

SAN GIMIGNANO

Il Casolare di Libbiano Country seclusion combined with proximity to San Gimignano and Siena at this tastefully furnished old farmhouse. Pool; good food.
⊠ Libbiano, 53037 San Gimignano, Siena. **Map** p336 B1.
📞 FAX 0577 94 60 02. 🍴 b,d. **Rooms** 6. Ⓛ Ⓛ

ROME

Hotel d'Inghilterra This used to be the guest accommodation for the Torlonia palace and a regal air survives, with antique mirrors and classically decorated rooms. It's in a great spot close to the Spanish Steps and Trevi fountain. Some of the more expensive rooms have their own terrace. Rates do not include breakfast.
⊠ Via Bocca di Leone 14, 00187 Roma. **Map** p336 C4. 🅲 06 699 81. 🖻 06 699 222 43. @ reservation-har@charminghotels.it 🍴 b,l,d. **Rooms** 105. ⬤ Never. 🖃 AE, DC, MC, V. ⓁⓁⓁⓁ

ROME

Sole al Pantheon In an unbeatable location opposite the Pantheon, this ancient building has been a hotel since 1467. It is distinctively and imaginatively decorated, with white leather seating and tiled floors lending a glamorous tone to the public areas. The bedrooms are all different. Bar and a leafy enclosed terrace.
⊠ Piazza della Rotonda, 00186 Roma. **Map** p336 C4. 🅲 06 678 04 41. 🖻 06 69 94 06 89. @ hotsole@flashnet.it 🍴 b. **Rooms** 25. ▤ ⓪ ⬤ Never. 🖃 AE, DC, MC, V. ⓁⓁⓁ

ROME

Majestic A beautiful wrought iron 'cage' lift and many mirrors and fittings survive from the 1880s when this classic, old-world hotel was built. There are bougainvillaea and olive trees in pots on the terraces, eight sizes of bed, a formal restaurant and a late-night brasserie with live jazz. Double-glazing keeps traffic noise to a minimum.
⊠ Via Veneto 50, 00187 Roma. **Map** p336 C4. 🅲 (06) 482 80 14. 🖻 (06) 488 09 84. @ hotelmajestic@flashnet.it 🍴 b,l,d. **Rooms** 96. ▤ ▧ 🍴 ⓪ ⬤ Never. 🖃 AE, DC, MC, V. ⓁⓁⓁⓁ

SAN GIMIGNANO

Casale del Cotone A former hunting lodge 2km (1 mile) north of San Gimignano, this is now a classy farmhouse-style B&B. Bedrooms are airy and refined, furnished with just one or two interesting pieces; the sitting areas and breakfast room are done out in the same mix of rustic and antique style. In summer, breakfast is served in the garden. Snacks available.
⊠ Località Cellole 59, 53037 San Gimignano, Siena. **Map** p336 B1. 🅲 0577 94 32 36. 🍴 b. **Rooms** 6, plus 2 apts. ⓪ ⬤ Nov to Jan. 🖃 Not accepted. Ⓛ

SAN GIMIGNANO
Relais Santa Chiara Just outside the town gates, a pleasant modern hotel offering comfort and convenience. Pool; private parking.
⊠ Via Matteotti 15, 53037 San Gimignano, Siena. **Map** p336 B1. 🅲 0577 94 07 01. 🖻 0577 94 20 96. @ rsc@cyber.data.it 🍴 b. **Rooms** 41. ⓁⓁⓁ

SAN GIMIGNANO
Le Renaie Modest sister hotel to the nearby Villa San Paolo, with lower prices. Peaceful location, pool and access to San Paolo's tennis courts.
⊠ Pancole, 53037 San Gimignano, Siena. **Map** p336 B1. 🅲 0577 95 50 44. 🖻 0577 95 51 26. 🍴 b,l,d. **Rooms** 25. ⓁⓁ

SAN GIMIGNANO
Villa San Paolo A hillside villa set in terraced gardens with tennis courts and pool. Intimate lounges; pretty bedrooms, gleaming bathrooms.
⊠ Strada per Certaldo, 53037 San Gimignano, Siena. **Map** p336 B1. 🅲 0577 95 51 00. 🖻 0577 95 51 13. 🍴 b. **Rooms** 18. ⓁⓁ

SARTEANO
Le Anfore Tastefully decorated old farmhouse guesthouse in unspoilt countryside. Spacious bedrooms; three are suites. Pool, tennis, riding.
⊠ Via di Chiusi 30, 53047 Sarteano, Siena. **Map** p336 C2. 🅲 0578 26 58 71. 🖻 0578 26 59 69. 🍴 b,d. **Rooms** 10. ⓁⓁ

SANTA MARGHERITA, SARDINIA

Is Morus This Mediterranean take on a country-house hotel is in a blissfully quiet corner of the island, far from any resorts. Bedrooms are white and uncluttered; some in the main building have sea views. There are also villas in the wooded garden. The private beach is a few steps away – the water can be weedy but is crystal clear.
⊠ Santa Margherita di Pula, 09010 Pula, Sardinia.
Map p338 A3. **(** 070 92 11 71. **FAX** 070 92 15 96.
†† b,l,d. **Rooms** 101. 🎦 🎴 🍴 🔋 ⬤ Jan to Apr.
🗎 AE, DC, MC, V. ⓁⓁⓁ

SIENA

Villa Scacciapensieri This villa lies just north of the city, close enough to hear church bells tolling. The bedrooms are a mix of styles: some suites are full of antiques, simpler rooms have painted country furniture. Breakfast and dinner are served outdoors, under the pergola. The Nardi family are very helpful hosts.
⊠ Via di Scacciapensieri 10, 53100 Siena. **Map** p336 B1.
(0577 414 42. **FAX** 0577 27 08 54. **@** villasca@tin.it
†† b,l,d, **Rooms** 32. 🎴 🍴 🔋 ⬤ Christmas, Jan to mid-March. 🗎 AE,DC,MC,V. ⓁⓁ

SIENA

Certosa di Maggiano A former Carthusian monastery on the outskirts of Siena now makes a restfully pampering hotel. The elegant cloisters date from the 14th century. Excellent modern cuisine is served in vaulted arcades round the central courtyard, in a ceramic-packed room inside, or next to the swimming pool.
⊠ Via Certosa 82, 53100 Siena. **Map** p336 B1.
(0577 28 81 80. **FAX** 0577 28 81 89.
@ certosa@relaischateaux.fr **††** b,l,d. **Rooms** 17.
🎴 🍴 🔋 ⬤ Never. 🗎 AE, DC, MC, V. ⓁⓁⓁⓁ

SINALUNGA

Locanda dell'Amorosa A working farm is the setting for this upmarket inn. Bedrooms, in the main house and in stone outbuildings on the estate, are simple, with whitewashed walls, tiled floors, and gleaming bathrooms. Dinner is served in the old stable block and food is a modern rendition of traditional Tuscan specialities.
⊠ 53048 Sinalunga, Siena. **Map** p336 B1.
(0577 67 94 97. **FAX** 0577 63 20 01. **††** b,l,d.
Rooms 17. 🎦 🔋 ⬤ mid-Jan to end Feb.
🗎 AE, DC, MC, V. ⓁⓁⓁ

SCANSANO

Antico Casale Captivating hotel in the coastal Maremma. Pretty bedrooms, terrace with views over a green, unspoilt valley. Riding offered.
⊠ Castagneta, 58054 Scansano, Grosseto. **Map** p336 B2.
(0564 50 72 19. **FAX** 0564 50 78 05. **††** b,l,d.
Rooms 15. ⓁⓁ

SIENA

Palazzo Ravizza A charming family run *pensione* in the best tradition. Rooms have lovely views over the Tuscan landscape. Pretty dining room.
⊠ Pian dei Mantellini, 53100 Siena. **Map** p336 B1.
(0577 28 04 62. **FAX** 0577 22 15 97. **††** b,l,d.
Rooms 36. ⓁⓁ

SOVICILLE

Borgo Pretale A group of grey stone houses clustered round a massive watchtower, artfully transformed into a stylish hotel.
⊠ Pretale, 53018 Sovicille, Siena. **Map** p336 B1.
(0577 34 54 01. **FAX** 0577 34 56 25. **@** borgopret@
ftbcc.it **††** b,l,d. **Rooms** 35. ⓁⓁⓁ

SOVICILLE

Borgo di Toiano A hamlet-turned-hotel, its terraces dotted with roses, its interiors restful and uncluttered. Ask for a room with a view. Pool.
⊠ Toiano, 53018 Sovicille, Siena. **Map** p336 B1.
(0577 31 46 39. **FAX** 0577 31 46 41. **††** b.
Rooms 10. ⓁⓁ

SPOLETO

Gattapone Built in the 1960s by the present owner's father, this hotel is a mix of knowingly retro pieces and high-tech extras. Regular guests include musicians at the local jazz festival and creative companies running seminars, but the architecture and stunning clifftop location above the village have a wide appeal.
☒ Via del Ponte 6, 06049 Spoleto, Perugia.
Map p337 D2. 🝑 0743 22 34 47. **FAX** 0743 22 34 48.
@ gattapone@mail.caribusiness.it 🍽 b. **Rooms** 16.
⬤ Never. 🃏 AE, DC, MC, V. Ⓛ

VASTO

Villa Vignola A small seaside hotel in a resort on the Abruzzo coast, with a big commitment to service. The decoration of the white clifftop villa has some Moorish influences though the style of bedrooms is a hybrid of Mediterranean and English country-house styles. The restaurant is strong on fish, with specialities such as squid-ink risotto and peppers stuffed with white fish.
☒ Vignola, 66054 Vasto Marina, Chieti. **Map** p337 F3.
🝑 0873 31 00 50. **FAX** 0873 31 00 60. 🍽 b,l,d.
Rooms 5. 🔋 ⬤ Never. 🃏 AE, DC, V. ⓁⓁ

TORGIANO

Le Tre Vaselle This wonderful village hotel is owned by the winemaking Lungarotti family – sampling some of their wine at dinner is a must. The sitting rooms are marked by huge fireplaces, stripy furniture, card tables and a grand piano. Rooms are in annexes next to the main building. Breakfast is lavish. Professional service.
☒ Via Garibaldi 48, 06089 Torgiano, Perugia.
Map p336 C2. 🝑 075 988 04 47. **FAX** 075 988 02 14.
@ 3vaselle@3vaselle.it 🍽 b,l,d. **Rooms** 61. 🟰 ♨ 🍽 🔋
⬤ Never. 🃏 AE, DC, MC, V. ⓁⓁ

VICCHIO DI MUGELLO

Villa Campestri This square Renaissance villa on a hillside south of Vicchio is one of the area's few good places to stay. Bedrooms are grand; some are in the main house, others in a farmhouse next door. Public rooms mix tapestries with Art Nouveau stained glass. The restaurant is popular with wedding parties at weekends.
☒ Via di Campestri 19, 50039 Vicchio di Mugello, Firenze.
Map p335 D5. 🝑 055 849 01 07. **FAX** 055 849 01 08.
@ villa.campestri@villacampestri.it 🍽 b,d. **Rooms** 25.
♨ 🔋 ⬤ Jan to March. 🃏 AE, DC, V. ⓁⓁ

SPELLO
La Bastiglia Smartly restored old mill-house with panoramic views from nearly all its rooms. Some are suites with private terraces.
☒ Piazza Valle Gloria 7, 06038 Spello, Perugia.
Map p337 D2. 🝑 0742 65 12 77. **FAX** 0742 30 11 59.
🍽 b,l,d. **Rooms** 22. Ⓛ

TITIGNANO
Fattoria di Titignano A simple rural guesthouse on a working farm estate in superb countryside. Battered rustic style with hints of former elegance.
☒ Titignano, 05010 Orvieto, Terni. **Map** p336 C2.
🝑 0763 30 8 22. **FAX** 0763 30 80 02. 🍽 b,d.
Rooms 17. Ⓛ

TIVOLI
Adriano Restaurant-with-rooms next to Hadrian's Villa. Elegant dining room; swanky bedrooms. Pretty garden and lovely adjacent park.
☒ Villa Adriana 194, 00010 Tivoli, Roma. **Map** p337 D4, p338 A1. 🝑 0774 38 22 35. **FAX** 0774 53 51 22. 🍽 b,l,d.
Rooms 10. ⓁⓁ

VOLTERRA
Villa Nencini Old-fashioned stone country hotel on the edge of town. Some bedrooms and bathrooms are cramped.
☒ Borgo Santo Stefano 55, 56048 Volterra, Pisa.
Map p335 D5, 336 A1. 🝑 0588 863 86.
FAX 0588 806 01. 🍽 b,l,d. **Rooms** 37. ⓁⓁ

For key to symbols see backflap. For price categories see p333

SOUTHERN ITALY

CAMPANIA • CALABRIA
BASILICATA • PUGLIA • SICILY

THERE IS ALMOST no end of opportunities for outdoor activities in the magnificent landscapes of southern Italy. The region as a whole is liberally endowed with wildlife and a rich array of ancient archaeological remains, not least those of the Romans at Pompei and those of the Greeks in Sicily. The cuisine, too, with its eclectic heritage and diversity of tastes, provides the excuse to dawdle on the coast or in the rustic mountain villages. Though good hotels are not so thick on the ground as in the rest of the country, the choice includes some of the very best, particularly along the stunning Amalfi coast. In contrast is the south's capital, the anarchic metropolis of Naples, which should not be missed.

AGRIGENTO, SICILY

AMALFI

Foresteria Baglio della Luna A sturdy medieval tower is at the core of this peaceful country hotel, which offers superb views of Agrigento's Valley of the Temples. The building has been sympathetically restored to retain much of the original structure; ancient walls surround the garden. Fine food, home-produced wine.
☒ Contrada Maddalusa, 92100 Agrigento, Sicilia.
Map p338 B5. ☎ 0922 51 10 61. FAX 0922 59 88 02.
@ bagliodel@orc.it ⑪ b,l,d. **Rooms** 24. ▤ ▮
● Never. ▨ AE, MC, V. ⓁⓁⓁ

Luna Convento In the 12th century, St Francis of Assisi chose this glorious spot on the cliff above a Saracen tower for a monastery. His cloister remains, together with some of the medieval buildings, but even the modern additions are charming at this luxurious historic hotel, owned by the same family since 1825.
☒ Via P Comite 33, 84011 Amalfi, Salerno.
Map p338 C2. ☎ 089 87 10 02. FAX 089 87 13 33.
@ luna@amalficoast.it ⑪ b,l,d. **Rooms** 45. ▨ ▮
● b,l,d. ▨ AE, DC, MC, V. ⓁⓁⓁ

ALBEROBELLO

Dei Trulli In pleasant pine-shaded grounds, several conical-roofed *trulli* are joined to form freestanding apartments with small veranda.
☒ Via Cadore 32, 70011 Alberobello, Bari.
Map p339 E2. ☎ 080 432 35 55. FAX 080 432 35 60.
@ htrulli@inmedia.it ⑪ b,l,d. **Rooms** 28. ⓁⓁ

AMALFI

Cappuccini Convento Converted 12th-century monastery with a superb clifftop location. Many bedrooms have private balconies.
☒ Via Annunziatella 46, 84011 Amalfi, Salerno.
Map p338 C2. ☎ 089 87 18 77. FAX 089 87 18 86.
@ cappuccini@amalfinet.it ⑪ b,l,d. **Rooms** 54. ⓁⓁⓁ

ALTOMONTE

Barbieri Modern lakeshore hotel with great views of Altomonte, a superb restaurant and modest but comfortable rooms.
☒ Via San Nicola 30, 87042 Altomonte, Cosenza.
Map p339 D3. ☎ 0981 94 80 72. FAX 0981 94 80 73.
⑪ b,l,d. **Rooms** 30. Ⓛ

AMALFI

Lido Mare Small B&B hotel on Amalfi's Piazza del Duomo. Some of the arched, whitewalled bedrooms have views over the sea.
☒ Largo Ducci Piccolomene 9, 84011 Amalfi, Salerno.
Map p338 C2. ☎ 089 87 13 32. FAX 089 87 13 94.
⑪ b. **Rooms** 15. Ⓛ

AMALFI

Santa Caterina Built in the 1930s, this sumptuous hotel on the coast road just outside Amalfi combines attractive décor with superb views, fine dining and impeccable service. Ask for one of the freestanding villas in the surrounding lemon groves. A private lift leads down the cliff to the pool and beach.

⊠ Strada Statale Amalfitana 9, 84011 Amalfi, Salerno. **Map** p338 C2. 📞 089 87 10 12. 🖷 089 87 13 51. @ s.caterina@starnet.it 🍴 b;l,d (not Jan, Feb). **Rooms** 66. 🗏 ≋ 🍴 🛇 ● Never. 🗲 AE, DC, MC, V. ⓁⓁⓁⓁ

CAPRI

Luna This old-fashioned seaside hotel's many pluses more than make up for the slightly overblown décor. The Luna has what must be one of the best locations on the island, perched on the cliffs of the south coast. Views from the spacious rooms are exhilarating. The pool is large by local standards.

⊠ Viale Matteotti 3, 80073 Capri, Napoli. **Map** p338 C2. 📞 081 837 04 33. 🖷 081 837 74 59. @ luna@capri.it 🍴 b,l,d. **Rooms** 50. 🗏 ≋ 🛇 ● Nov to Easter. 🗲 AE, DC, MC, V. ⓁⓁⓁ

BAIA DOMIZIA

Della Baia Antiques and modern furniture are blended with books, plants and flowers to create a homely atmosphere at this modern seafront hotel, run by three sisters. The bedrooms all have balconies and there are lounge chairs on the veranda and lawn for sun worshippers. The home-cooked food is good.

⊠ Via dell'Erica, 81030 Baia Domizia, Caserta. **Map** p337 E5. 📞 0823 72 13 44. 🖷 0823 72 15 56. 🍴 b,l,d. **Rooms** 56. 🗏 🍴 🛇 ● Oct to mid-May. 🗲 AE, DC, MC, V. ⓁⓁ

CAPRI

Pensione Quattro Stagione This flower-filled village house near the Marina Piccola is the closest thing in Capri to a traditional *pensione*. The rooms are comfortable, the views from the bougainvillea-shaded terrace lovely, and dinner (on request) a lively taste of Italy. Rates are extremely reasonable, so book well ahead.

⊠ Via Marina Piccola 1, 80073 Capri, Napoli. **Map** p338 C2. 📞 🖷 081 837 00 41. 🍴 b,d. **Rooms** 12. ● Nov to mid-March. 🗲 MC, V. Ⓛ

CAPRI

Grand Hotel Quisisana Capri's most luxurious and expensive hotel opened as a sanatorium in 1845. Excellent facilities, magnificent views.

⊠ Via Camarelle 2, 80073 Capri, Napoli. **Map** p338 C2. 📞 081 837 07 88. 🖷 081 837 60 80. @ info@quisi.com 🍴 b,l,d. **Rooms** 150. ⓁⓁⓁⓁ

CAPRI

Punta Tragara Smart, cubelike Le Corbusier building hanging dramatically over the cliff.

⊠ Via Tragara 57, 80073 Capri, Napoli. **Map** p338 C2. 📞 081 837 08 44. 🖷 081 837 77 90. @ hotel.tragara@capri.it 🍴 b,l,d. **Rooms** 35, plus 15 apartments. ⓁⓁⓁⓁ

CAPRI

La Scalatinatella Two villas with a lavish collection of Oriental furniture. All bedrooms are junior suites. Pool-side restaurant (lunch only).

⊠ Via Tragara 10, 80073 Capri, Napoli. **Map** p338 C2. 📞 081 837 06 33. 🖷 081 837 82 91. 🍴 b,l. **Rooms** 30. ⓁⓁⓁⓁ

CAPRI

Villa Krupp Lenin and Gorky once lived in this serene clifftop villa, which is now a simple, popular family-run hotel. Bright, spacious rooms.

⊠ Viale Matteoti 12, 80073 Capri, Napoli. **Map** p338 C20. 📞 081 837 03 62. 🖷 081 837 64 89. 🍴 b. **Rooms** 12. Ⓛ

CAPRI

Villa Brunella The setting's the thing here: this attractive modern hotel is built on steep terraced slopes among lemon groves, with fabulous sea views and large grounds. The spacious rooms make the most of the light and views, as do the large dining terrace and the pool. But be prepared to climb lots of steps to and from the bedrooms.
⊠ Via Tragara 24A, 80073 Capri, Napoli. **Map** p338 C2.
【 081 837 01 22. FAX 081 837 04 30. @ villabrunella@
capri.it 🍴 b,l,d. **Rooms** 8. 🗐 AE, DC, V Ⓛ Ⓛ Ⓛ

ERICE, SICILY

Moderno Modernity is relative in ancient Erice, but this charming hotel has skillfully blended a 19th-century building with contemporary design and traditional Sicilian crafts. The bedrooms are spacious, the restaurant serves an excellent, wide-ranging menu and the view from the roof terrace over the tiles is delightful.
⊠ Via Vittorio Emanuele 63, 91016 Erice, Trapani, Sicilia. **Map** p338 A4. 【 0923 86 93 00.
FAX 0923 86 91 39. @ moderno@tin.it 🍴 b. **Rooms** 41.
● Never 🗐 AE, DC, MC, V. Ⓛ

ERICE, SICILY

Elimo In the centre of the old hill village of Erice, in the same street as the Moderno (see above right), is this picturesque medieval house. It has been brought up to modern standards, with attractive public rooms and individually designed bedrooms, but retains much of its character. Courtyard and roof terrace for idle hours.
⊠ Via Vittorio Emanuele 75, 91016 Erice, Trapani, Sicilia. **Map** p338 A4. 【 0923 86 93 17. FAX 0923 86 92 52.
@ elimoh@comeg.it 🍴 b,l,d. **Rooms** 21. ● Never.
🗐 AE, DC, V. Ⓛ Ⓛ

FASANO

La Silvana Fasano is a good place from which to explore *trulli* country, with many examples of the conical-roofed stone houses in the area, and this modern, family-run hotel makes a good base. Many of the spacious, plainly furnished rooms have views; most have a private bathroom. Popular local restaurant.
⊠ Viale de Pini 87, 72010 Selva di Fasano, Brindisi. **Map** p339 F2. 【 080 433 11 61.
FAX 080 433 19 80. @ htlfierra@mail.media.it 🍴 b,l,d.
Rooms 18. ● Never. 🗐 V. Ⓛ Ⓛ

CAPRI

Villa Sarah Small modern hotel, set in its own vineyards and orchard, with well-kept rooms and delightful terraced gardens. Very reasonable prices.
⊠ Via Tiberio 3/A, 80073 Capri, Napoli. **Map** p338 C2.
【 081 837 78 17. FAX 081 837 12 15. @ demgiu@
mbox.caprinet.it 🍴 b. **Rooms** 20. Ⓛ Ⓛ

CETRARO

Grand Hotel San Michele An imposing villa with huge grounds and several small houses. Kitchen gardens supply the excellent restaurant.
⊠ Loc. Bosco 8/9, 87022 Cetraro, Firenze. **Map** p339 D4.
【 0982 910 12. FAX 0982 914 30. @ sanmichele@
antares.it 🍴 b,l,d. **Rooms** 73. Ⓛ Ⓛ Ⓛ

CISTERNINO

Villa Cenci Choose between rooms in the cool white villa or those in the traditional *trulli*. Home-grown vegetables and wine.
⊠ Via per Ceglie Messapica, 72014 Cisternino, Brindisi.
Map p339 F2. 【 080 444 82 08. FAX 080 444 82 08.
🍴 b,l,d. **Rooms** 25. Ⓛ Ⓛ

CONCA DEI MARINI

Belvedere Stay here for the setting, with fabulous views of the Amalfi Coast, and a lift down the cliff to the seawater pool and beach.
⊠ Strada Statale 163, 84010 Conca dei Marini, Salerno.
Map p338 C2. 【 089 83 12 82. FAX 089 83 14 39.
🍴 b,l,d. **Rooms** 36. Ⓛ

GANGI, SICILY

Tenuta Gangivecchio The Tornabene family have made a peaceful, secluded retreat of their converted 13th-century monastery, now run as a restaurant-with-rooms. Inside are tiled floors, whitewashed walls and beamed ceilings. The classic Sicilian food, using homegrown almonds, walnuts and herbs, is mouthwatering.
⊠ C da Gangivecchio, 90024 Gangi, Sicilia.
Map p338 B4. 📞 0921 68 91 91. **FAX** 0921 68 91 91.
@ gangivecchio@stonline.it 🍴 b,d. **Rooms** 10.
▤ 🏊 🍴 🏋 🛇 2 weeks end July. 🛋 MC, V. Ⓛ Ⓛ

ISOLA D'ISCHIA

La Villarosa In the centre of the little island town of Ischia, a few steps from the harbour and lido, a jungle of a garden surrounds this low-key spa hotel. Inside, a traditional country house atmosphere prevails, with elegant bedrooms (many with balconies) and antique-furnished salons. Dining terrace with fine rooftop views.
⊠ Via Giacinto Gigante 5, 80077 Porto d'Ischia, Napoli.
Map p338 B2. 📞 081 99 13 16. **FAX** 081 99 24 25.
@ hotel@lavillarosa.it 🍴 b,l,d. **Rooms** 43. 🏊 🍴 🏋 🛇
🛇 Nov to March. 🛋 AE, DC, MC, V. Ⓛ Ⓛ

GIARDINI-NAXOS, SICILY

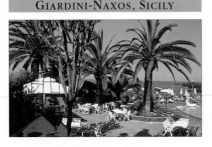

Arathena Rocks Away from the crowds by the sands of the busy resort but right on the rocky seafront, is this friendly family-run hotel. It's a delightful place, with seafront gardens and large pool with bar, cheerful balconied bedrooms (many with views of Mount Etna) and public rooms bright with ceramics.
⊠ Via Calcide Eubea 55, 98035 Giardini-Naxos, Sicilia.
Map p338 C4. 📞 0942 513 49. **FAX** 0942 516 90.
🍴 b,l,d. **Rooms** 49. 🏊 🏋 🛇 Nov to March.
🛋 DC, MC, V. Ⓛ Ⓛ

MARATEA

La Locanda delle Donne Monache This restored monastery in the centre of the seaside village offers many pleasures, including a charming garden, pool, private beach and a boat. Inside, the foyer's flamboyance gives way to modern chic in the bedrooms. The restaurant specializes in regional Italian cuisine.
⊠ Via Carllo Mazzei 4, 85046 Maratea, Potenza.
Map p339 D3. 📞 0973 87 74 87. **FAX** 0973 87 76 87.
🍴 b,l,d. **Rooms** 30. ▤ 🏊 🏋 🛇 Nov to March.
🛋 AE, DC, MC, V. Ⓛ Ⓛ Ⓛ

FASANO
Masseria Marzalussa Fortified 17th-century farmhouse in olive and citrus groves. Pool, shady courtyards, excellent regional cuisine.
⊠ Calle da Pezze Vicine 65, 72015 Fasano, Brindisi.
Map p00 000. 📞 080 441 37 80. **FAX** 080 441 37 80.
🍴 b,d. **Rooms** 7. Ⓛ Ⓛ Ⓛ

ISOLA D'ISCHIA
Il Monastero Charming *pensione* built into the walls of the 14th-century islet castle. Book well ahead; its good food, reasonable prices and superb views make it very popular.
⊠ Castello Aragonese 3, Ischia Ponte, 80077 Napoli.
Map p338 B2. 📞 081 99 24 35. 🍴 b,d. **Rooms** 22. Ⓛ

MONÓPOLI
Il Melograno Coolly sophisticated farmhouse hotel, set among olive and lemon groves.
⊠ Contrada Torricella 345, 70043 Monópoli, Bari.
Map p339 E2. 📞 080 690 90 30. **FAX** 080 74 79 08.
@ melograno@melograno.com 🍴 b,l,d. **Rooms** 37.
Ⓛ Ⓛ Ⓛ

NAPLES
Grande Albergo Vesuvio Elegant 1880s hotel with one of Naple's finest restaurants and wonderful views of the Castel dell'Oro.
⊠ Via Partenope 45, 80121 Napoli. **Map** p337 F5,
p338 C2. 📞 081 764 00 44. **FAX** 081 764 44 83.
@ info@vesuvio.it 🍴 b,l,d. **Rooms** 181. Ⓛ Ⓛ Ⓛ Ⓛ

For key to symbols see backflap. For price categories *see p333*

MARATEA

Santa Venere Splendidly set amid lawns and trees which sweep down to the rocky shore on the edge of Maratea, the low, arcaded Santa Venere exudes an air of quiet sophistication. The spacious, tastefully furnished rooms all have a terrace or balcony with views of this startlingly beautiful, wild stretch of coast.
☒ Via Fiumicello di Santa Venere, 85040 Maratea, Potenza. **Map** p339 D3. **(** 0973 87 69 10. FAX 0973 87 76 54. @ santavenere@labnet.it **Ⅱ** b,l,d. **Rooms** 40. 🗐 🛇 ● Oct to Apr. 🗲 AE, DC, MC, V. ⓁⓁⓁ

NAPLES

Santa Lucia The impeccably upmarket Santa Lucia, set overlooking the bay and the Castel dell'Oro, is one of the best-known hotels in southern Italy. The public rooms are opulently decorated with frescoes, marble, stucco and antiques; the bedrooms are only marginally less elaborate. The service and cuisine are flawless.
☒ Via Partenope 46, 80121 Napoli. **Map** p337 F5, p338 C2. **(** 081 764 06 66. FAX 081 764 85 80. @ reservations@santalucia.it **Ⅱ** b,l,d. **Rooms** 110. 🗐 ● Never. 🗲 AE, DC, MC, V. ⓁⓁⓁⓁ

MARATEA

Villa Chesa Elite This lavish Art Nouveau confection of ochre and cream stucco is perched high on the clifftop, with dizzying views over one of Italy's most spectacular stretches of coast. Excellent cuisine and carefully chosen antiques and paintings reflect the best of life during the heyday of the Grand Tour.
☒ Via Timponi 46, 85041 Acquafredda di Maratea, Potenza. **Map** p339 D3. **(** 0973 87 81 34. FAX 0973 87 81 35. @ villacheta@labnet.it **Ⅱ** b,l,d. **Rooms** 20. 🛇 ● Never. 🗲 AE, DC, MC, V. ⓁⓁ

PANAREA

Hotel Raya Modern and stylish, this cascade of pink and white bungalows stretches down from the island village to the sea. Inside, ethnic art from Polynesia, Africa and Asia abounds. All rooms have sea views and terraces; the open-air restaurant overlooks the port. No young children.
☒ Isole Eolie o Lipari, San Pietro, 98050 Isola Panarea, Messina. **Map** p338 C3. **(** 090 98 30 13. FAX 090 998 31 03. @ htlraya@netnet.it **Ⅱ** b,d. **Rooms** 36. 🛇 ● mid-Oct to mid-Apr. 🗲 AE, DC, MC, V. ⓁⓁ

NAPLES

Miramare In an Art Nouveau villa, a charming seafront hotel offering small but well-furnished rooms, a roof garden and bar.
☒ Via Nazario Sauro 24, 80132 Napoli. **Map** p337 F5, p338 C2. **(** 081 764 75 89. FAX 081 764 07 75. @ hotelmiramare@tin.it **Ⅱ** b. **Rooms** 31. ⓁⓁⓁ

NAPLES

Paradiso Good rooms, excellent food, and a stunning location in peaceful Posillipo area, with the whole bay and city spread out at your feet.
☒ Via Catullo 11, Posillipo, 80122 Napoli. **Map** p338 C2. **(** 081 761 41 61. FAX 081 761 34 49. @ paradiso.na@ bestwestern.it **Ⅱ** b,l,d. **Rooms** 74. ⓁⓁⓁ

OTRANTO

Albania Stylish modern hotel, ultra-efficient and spotlessly clean, with light and airy rooms and a seafood restaurant.
☒ Via S Francesco di Paola 10, 73028 Otranto, Lecce. **Map** p339 F3. **(** 0836 80 11 83. **Ⅱ** b,l,d. **Rooms** 10. ⓁⓁ

POSITANO

Albergo Casa Albertina A popular town-centre hotel, imaginatively decorated with local crafts. Bedrooms have sea views.
☒ Via Colono 36, 84017 Positano, Salerno. **Map** p338 C2. **(** 089 87 53 18. FAX 089 81 17 84. **Ⅱ** b. **Rooms** 19. ⓁⓁ

PARGHELIA

Baia Paraelios Holiday-camp style, but without the razzmatazz. This attractive, child-friendly hotel on the far southern toe of Italy consists of 72 small bungalows, sprawled across a wooded hill by a picture-postcard bay of white sand and dazzling blue sea. There are three pools, an open-air bar and a seaside terrace dining room.
⊠ Fornaci, 88035 Parghelia, Catanzaro. **Map** p339 D5.
📞 0963 60 00 04. FAX 0963 60 00 74. 🍴 b,l,d.
Rooms 72 bungalows. 🏊 🅿 ● Oct to Apr.
💳 AE, DC, MC, V. ⒧⒧⒧

POSITANO

San Pietro Unabashedly catering for the jetset, the San Pietro is an architectural masterpiece, merging imperceptibly into the cliff face east of Positano. Each individually designed room has a flower-laden terrace, and even the bathrooms have magnificent views. Superb gourmet cuisine completes a sumptuous package. Private beach.
⊠ Via Laurito 2, 84017 Positano, Salerno. **Map** p338 C2.
📞 089 87 54 55. FAX 089 81 14 49. @ spietro@starnet.it
🍴 b,l,d. **Rooms** 62. 📺 🏊 🅿 ● Nov to Apr.
💳 AE, DC, MC, V. ⒧⒧⒧⒧

POSITANO

Miramare Set on a steep hill just west of the main beach, a series of old fishermen's houses now make up this delightful small hotel. All the bedrooms have private, sea-facing terraces and spacious bathrooms. Another terrace has been glassed in, with bougainvillaea hanging from the ceiling, to form a splending breakfast room.
⊠ Via Trara Genoino 25-27, 84017 Positano, Salerno.
Map p338 C2. 📞 089 87 50 02. FAX 089 87 52 19.
🍴 b. **Rooms** 18. ● Nov to March.
💳 AE, MC, V. ⒧⒧

POSITANO

Le Sirenuse An 18th-century *palazzo* still run by its aristocratic owners, the Sirenuse has expanded to include more rooms and a web of private and public terraces, but still manages to retain house-party charm and exclusivity. Delightful Venetian and Neapolitan furniture complements original ceramics. First-class gourmet cuisine.
⊠ Via Colombo 30, 84017 Positano, Salerno.
Map p338 C2. 📞 089 87 50 66. FAX 089 81 17 98.
@ info@sirenuse.it 🍴 b,l,d. **Rooms** 64. 📺 🏊 🍴
● Never. 💳 AE, DC, MC, V. ⒧⒧⒧⒧

POSITANO

Palazzo Murat This haven of tranquillity in the town centre boasts 17th-century decoration and antique furnishings, and a profusion of flowers.
⊠ Via dei Mulini 23, 84017 Positano, Salerno.
Map p338 C2. 📞 089 87 51 77. FAX 089 81 14 19.
🍴 b. **Rooms** 28. ⒧⒧⒧⒧

RAVELLO

Palumbo A lovingly restored 12th-century *palazzo*, with lavish décor and superb food. Past guests include Wagner, DH Lawrence and JFK.
⊠ Via San Giovanni del Toro 28, 84010 Ravello, Salerno.
Map p338 C2. 📞 089 81 81 81. FAX 089 85 89 00.
@ info@palazzosasso.com 🍴 b,l,d. **Rooms** 24. ⒧⒧⒧

RAVELLO

Villa Maria A charmingly restored villa with terrace views and shady gardens. Some facilities shared with modern Hotel Giordano next door.
⊠ Via Santa Chiara 2, 84010 Ravello, Salerno.
Map p338 C2. 📞 089 85 72 55. FAX 089 85 70 71.
@ villamaria@villamaria.it 🍴 b,l,d. **Rooms** 17. ⒧⒧

SANT'AGATA SUI DUE GOLFI

Don Alfonso The only Michelin three-star in southern Italy, with a few rooms attached.
⊠ Corso Sant'Agata 11, 80064 Sant'Agata Sui Due Golfi, Napoli. **Map** p338 C2. 📞 081 878 00 26.
FAX 081 533 02 26. @ donalfonso@syrene.it 🍴 b,l,d.
Rooms 3. ⒧⒧

For key to symbols see backflap. For price categories *see p333*

POSITANO

Villa Franca It's a long, hard climb from the beach back up to the Villa Franca, but it is worth it. Its position gives it stunning views over the town and along the Amalfi Coast. The bedrooms are charming, using traditional painted ceramics alongside crisp blue and white to mirror the sun and Mediterranean beyond. Roof terrace.

⊠ Viale Pasitea 318, 84017 Positano, Salerno.
Map p338 C2. 089 87 56 55. FAX 089 87 57 35.
@ hvf@starnet.it b,d. **Rooms** 29.
Never. AE, DC, MC, V. Ⓛ Ⓛ Ⓛ

RAVELLO

Caruso Belvedere The rooms are surprisingly plain, but this is more than made up for by the views, the clifftop terrace and the sumptuous public rooms with their patterned tiled floors, frescoes and 19th-century art. The Caruso family pride themselves on personal service and the quality of their regional cuisine.

⊠ Piazza Giovanni del Toro 2, 84010 Ravello,
Salerno. **Map** p338 C2. 089 85 71 11.
FAX 089 85 73 72. b,l,d. **Rooms** 23. Never.
AE, DC, MC, V. Ⓛ Ⓛ Ⓛ

RAGUSA, SICILY

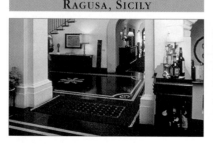

Eremo della Giubliana In tranquil rolling farmland, this 15th-century fortified convent now makes a glamorous hideaway hotel. It has been beautifully modernized yet retains much of its original structure, with splendid archways and pitch and limestone floors. Local produce and wines make up the bulk of the fine menu.

⊠ km 9, Contrada Giubiliana SP per Marina di Ragusa, 97100 Ragusa, Sicilia. **Map** p338 C5.
0932 66 91 19. FAX 0932 62 38 91. b,l,d.
Rooms 12. Never. AE, MC, V. Ⓛ Ⓛ

SIRACUSA, SICILY

Grand Hotel This is a truly grand hotel, with an imposing circular marble staircase, gracious Art Deco rooms filled with fine art, Murano glass chandeliers and antique furnishings. There is a luxuriant indoor garden, and a roof garden restaurant with fine views of the harbour and the old town. All bedrooms have sea views.

⊠ Viale Mazzini 12, 96100 Siracusa, Sicilia.
Map p338 C5. 0931 46 46 00. FAX 0931 46 46 11.
b,l,d. **Rooms** 58. Never. AE, DC, MC, V.
Ⓛ Ⓛ Ⓛ Ⓛ

SAVELLETRI
Masseria San Domenico A fortified refuge-turned-country house, now an imposing hotel.
⊠ Litoranea 379, 72010 Savelletri di Fasano, Brindisi.
Map p339 F2. 080 482 79 90. FAX 080 482 79 78.
@ masseriasandomenico@puglianet.it b,l,d.
Rooms 31. Ⓛ Ⓛ Ⓛ

SCANNO
Mille Pini This neat, simple, friendly chalet sits at the foot of the chairlift up to Monte Rotondo, the highest point in the Apennines.
⊠ Via Pescara 2, 67038 Scanno, L'Aquila. **Map** p337 E4, p338 B1. 0864 743 87. FAX 0864 74 98 18. b,l,d.
Rooms 21. Ⓛ Ⓛ

SELVA DI FASANO
Sierra Silvana Comfortable country hotel consisting of a cluster of modern buildings around an imposing four-room *trulli*.
⊠ Via D Bartolo Boggia 5, 72010 Selva di Fasano, Brindisi.
Map p339 E2. 080 433 13 22. FAX 080 433 12 07.
@ htlsierra@mail.media.it b,l,d. **Rooms** 120. Ⓛ

SIRACUSA, SICILY
Domus Mariae A former convent in a quiet quarter, still run by Ursuline nuns, with an ornate chapel, modern furnishings and air of calm.
⊠ Via Vittorio Veneto 76, 96100 Siracusa, Sicilia.
Map p338 C5. 0931 248 54. FAX 0931 248 58.
b,l,d. **Rooms** 12. Ⓛ Ⓛ

SORRENTO

Bellevue Syrene The Syrene opened in 1824 and was a favourite stop of Empress Eugénie of France. It has fabulous views of the bay from its clifftop position, and its many charms include a salon devoted to original Dali paintings, a Pompeii-style dining room, a wisteria arcade, peaceful courtyards, local ceramics and frescoes.
⊠ Piazza della Vittoria 5, 80067 Sorrento, Napoli. **Map** p338 C20. 081 878 10 24. FAX 081 878 39 63.
@ bellevue@sorrentopalaca.it b,l,d. **Rooms** 73.
🍴 🏊 🛁 ⬤ Never. 🖃 AE, DC, MC, V. ⓁⓁⓁⓁ

TAORMINA, SICILY

Villa Belvedere The simple but stylish Belle Epoque hotel has commanding views of town, sea and mountain. Other pluses are pretty flower gardens, attractive public rooms and a tantalising pool deck surrounded by giant palms. The rooms are clean and bright; some have private terraces.
⊠ Via Bagnoli Croci 79, 98039 Taormina, Messina, Sicilia. **Map** p338 C4. 0942 237 91.
FAX 0942 62 58 30. @ hotbelve@tao.it b.
Rooms 50. 🍴 🏊 🛁 ⬤ mid-Nov to mid-Dec, mid-Jan to mid-March. 🖃 AE, DC, MC, V. ⓁⓁ

TAORMINA, SICILY

San Domenico Palace In the heart of historic Taormina is this supremely luxurious former monastery. It caters unashamedly to the international jetset, and its beautiful cloisters and rooms are filled with art pieces. Other attractions are and enchanting garden, excellent sea views, and a wonderful restaurant.
⊠ Piazza San Domenico 5, 98039 Taormina, Messina, Sicilia. **Map** p338 C4. 0942 237 01. FAX 0942 62 55 06.
@ san-domenico@thi.it b,l,d. **Rooms** 109. 🍴 🏊 🛁
⬤ Never. 🖃 AE, DC, MC, V. ⓁⓁⓁⓁ

TAORMINA, SICILY

Villa Ducale A ten-minute walk from Taormina leads to this hotel with panoramic views from all rooms. Built by the grandparents of the current owners, it is carefully and interestingly furnished, with no two rooms alike. There is even a library for those who want to while away lazy hours on the flower-bedecked terrace.
⊠ Via Leonardo da Vinci 60, 98039 Taormina, Messina, Sicilia. **Map** p338 C4. 0942 281 53. FAX 0942 287 10.
@ villaducale@tao.it b. **Rooms** 13. 🍴 🛁
⬤ 20 Nov to 20 Dec. 🖃 AE, DC, MC, V. ⓁⓁⓁ

SORRENTO

La Badia A friendly family hotel with great charm and views over town, in a converted monastery set among olive and citrus groves.
⊠ Via Nastro Verde 8, 80067 Sorrento, Napoli. **Map** p338 C2. 081 878 11 54. FAX 081 807 41 59.
🍴 b,l,d. **Rooms** 20. Ⓛ

SORRENTO

Grand Hotel Excelsior Vittoria Two elegantly furnished 19th-century villas and a 1920s Swiss chalet. Stunning clifftop terrace and lush gardens.
⊠ Piazza T Tasso 34, 80067 Sorrento, Napoli. **Map** p338 C2. 081 807 10 44. FAX 081 877 12 06
@ exvitt@exvitt.it 🍴 b,l,d. **Rooms** 110. ⓁⓁⓁⓁ

STILO

San Giorgio A handsome 17th-century cardinal's palace, now a family-run village hotel, with fine views and a lively atmosphere.
⊠ Via Citarelli 8, 89049 Stilo, Reggio di Calabria. **Map** p339 E5. 0964 77 50 47. FAX 0964 62 93 06.
🍴 b,l,d. **Rooms** 14. Ⓛ

VICO EQUENSE

Capo la Gala Almost invisible modern hotel, carved from a series of terraces in the cliff-face, with bland rooms but a homely atmosphere.
⊠ Via Luigi Serio 7, Capo la Gala, 80069 Vico Equense, Napoli. **Map** p338 C2. 081 801 57 58.
FAX 081 879 87 47. 🍴 b,l,d. **Rooms** 18. ⓁⓁⓁ

For key to symbols see backflap. For price categories see p333

GREECE

GREECE

S MALL HOTELS of character are quite a new phenomenon in Greece: most have been in operation for little more than ten years, and many are in traditional buildings which have been in the same family for generations and have been lovingly restored. Greece has a very rich vernacular architecture – among the many choices we list are a cave-like island cliff dwelling, an 18th-century bandit chieftain's tower, a Venetian townhouse and a mountain mansion. Most Greek hotels are family-run, friendly and in-formal, but with little emphasis on luxuries such as room service and ambitious food.

Oía Maria Villas, page 390, fabulously sited on the island of Santorini

GREECE, REGION BY REGION

G REECE CAN be divided into two obvious parts: mainland and the islands.

Mainland Greece
The Gulf of Corinth and the Corinth Canal slice Greece into two. The southern Peloponnese offers a wide range of landscapes, from rugged, treeless mountains to gentle farmland, lush valleys and sandy beaches. There are lovely small hotels in historic buildings in towns such as Yíthion and Návplion, in medieval fortresses like Monemvasiá, and in the tiny castles of the Máni region and the stone villages of Arkadia.

Central and northern Greece are equally varied. The capital, Athens, a huge urban sprawl, is short of hotels of distinction, as are other main towns, but there are unique places to stay throughout the mainland. Among them are the rugged, dry-stone-walled homes of the Zagoria villages and restored neo-classical mansions in small ports such as Galaxídi, near Delphi.

The Islands
Of the thousands of Greek islands, only some hundred are inhabited. These are divided into six groups, plus Crete, largest of all the islands and an administrative region in its own right. Closest to Athens are the tiny Argo-Saronic islands, popular with foreign visitors and Athenians escaping from the city. The group includes car-free Ydra, and Spétses with its choice of excellent small resort hotels.

The white villages, blue-domed churches and mountainous, arid landscapes of the Cyclades islands are among the best-known images of Greece. Despite the popularity of Mykonos, Páros and Santoríni, there are a number of charmingly simple places to stay, ideal for peace and quiet.

Tourism is still relatively new to the large, widely spaced islands of the North-east Aegean group, where most beds are in small, simple *pensions* and larger holiday hotels.

The Dodecanese group, close to the Turkish coast, includes tiny isles such as Sými along with larger neighbours such as Rhodes, which receives hundreds of thousands of visitors annually. Many of the most charming hotels are in impressively restored neo-classical houses.

The Sporades and Ionian islands are dominated by the package holiday market, with few hotels of real character. Kýthira, in the Ionian group, is the exception, with some attractive small hotels in its white-washed village capital.

Crete, Greece's largest island and most southerly, is almost a country in its own right. Many of its most interesting and attractive places to stay are in old Venetian-Turkish townhouses.

HIGHLIGHTS

THE HOTELS illustrated on these introductory pages are by no means the only highlights. Some of the most memorable places to stay in Greece include La Moara, in Nymfaía (page 391), run by one of the country's leading winemaking dynasties; Hotel Malvásia, within the fortress walls of Monemvasía (page 389); and the charmingly quirky Xenonas Karamarli in Makrinítsa (page 388).

FOOD AND DRINK

THE BEST GREEK FOOD is the simplest: fish straight from the net; fresh vegetables served as salad with wild thyme and oregano. Restaurants in tourist areas have multilingual menus but the food in places off the beaten track is often better. In smaller villages you will be invited into the kitchen to see what's simmering on the stove or waiting to be grilled.

Méze, a selection of dishes served simultaneously, is a Greek mainstay. As well as olives and strong-flavoured feta cheese made from goat's or sheep's milk, *méze* might include roasted peppers, grilled cheese, humous (a purée of chickpeas and sesame seeds), taramasalata (a dip made of cod roe), and little sausages.

Greek seafood – especially *astakós* (lobster), *garidhes* (shrimp) and *barboúnia* (red mullet) – is expensive and is usually priced according to weight. Meat is usually veal, lamb or chicken, sometimes game; goat meat is regarded as a delicacy to be reserved for special occasions. The traditional Greek salad, with tomatoes, onion, cucumber, olives, peppers and feta cheese, is a meal in itself. Dinner, usually eaten late, is the main meal of the day.

Greek wine has improved in recent years. Good-quality red, white and rosé wines are now available throughout Greece, in addition to the traditional retsina, a white wine flavoured with pine resin, not to everyone's taste.

Best Western Hotel Europa, near the ruins at Ancient Olympia, page 390

BEDROOMS AND BATHROOMS

IF YOU WANT a double bed, ask for it specifically when booking, as most rooms are twin bedded. Most hotels offer en suite WC and shower as standard.

Water is usually heated by solar power and electric water heaters; at the end of a long summer day water may be scaldingly hot.

OTHER PRACTICAL INFORMATION

BOOK AHEAD from June to September, when Greeks as well as foreign visitors take their holidays. Tourism is highly seasonal, and many hotels on the islands close from October until April. In small hotels, breakfast is often the only meal served.

Language English is very widely spoken, especially in the resort areas.

Currency The *drachma*, 'Dr'.

Shops Most open 8am–1pm, and from 5–8pm Mon–Sat.

Tipping Formal tipping is not customary, but leaving small change to round up the bill is not unusual.

Telephoning Phone booths take prepaid telecards. To phone within Greece, dial the full number. To phone Greece from Britain, dial the country code 00 30, then the number, omitting the initial zero; from the US, 011 30.

Public holidays 1 January; 6 January; Shrove Monday; 25 March; Good Friday; Easter Sunday and Easter Monday; 1 May; Whit Monday; 15 August; 28 October; 25 and 26 December.

USEFUL WORDS

THE SYSTEM of transliteration used here to represent Greek is the one used by the Greek government.

Breakfast	*Topro-ee-no*
Lunch	*Tome-see-mer-ya-no*
Dinner	*Totheep-no*
How much?	*Posokanee?*
Free room?	*E-che-teh*
	tho-ma-tee-a?
Single (room)	*Mo-na*
	krevat-ya
Double (with a double bed)	
	Thee-klee-no meh
	thee-plo dre-va-tee

GREECE PRICE BANDS

MAXIMUM ROOM RATES are displayed on each bedroom door. Discounts may be offered for longer stays. Greek hotels and guesthouses are classified in five categories, but don't be swayed by this. Our price bands, which refer to the price of a double room in high season, are simpler to use.

Ⓓ	below 15,000Dr
ⓓⓓ	15,000Dr–22,000Dr
ⓓⓓⓓ	23,000Dr–30,000Dr
ⓓⓓⓓⓓ	above 30,000Dr

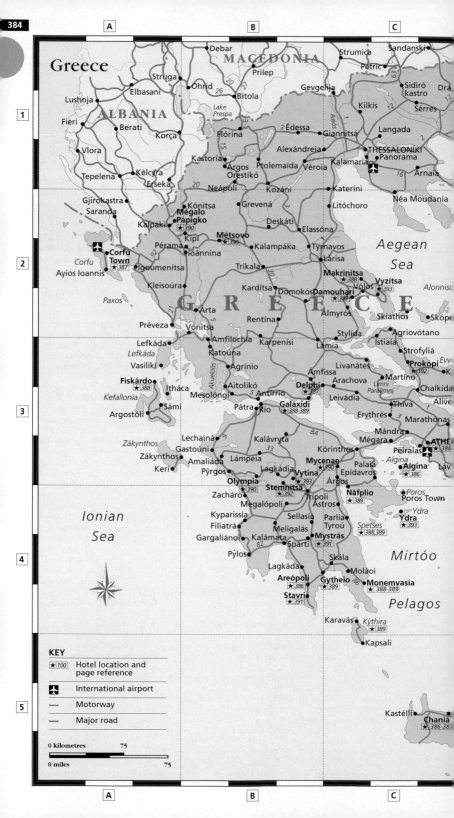

ATHENS

Andromeda Hotel A real find: a small boutique hotel, on a quiet side street 20-30 minutes' walk from Syntagma Square and the historic city centre. It is dotted with designer objects and antique carpets; its many amenities include laundry service and 24-hour room service. The restaurant serves Oriental and Polynesian specialities.
⊠ Timoleontos Vassou 22, 11521 Athens.
Map p384 C3. ▐ (01) 643 7302/4.
FAX (01) 646 6361. ▐▐ b,l,d. **Rooms** 30. 🖫
● Never. 🖴 AE, MC, DC, V. ⓓⓓⓓⓓ

ATHENS

John's Hotel Among the star features of the modern, medium-rise hotel are: its attractive Art Nouveau-style bar and foyer; a palm tree-studded garden and terrace; and a 15m (50ft) pool with waterfall. It is set in a residential suburb, close to the airport and some 30 minutes' drive to the city centre. Service is cool yet professional.
⊠ Pandoras 3 & Lazaraki, 16674 Glyfada, Athens.
Map p384 C3. ▐ (01) 894 6837/9. FAX (01) 898 0210.
▐▐ b,l,d. **Rooms** 68. 🖫 ♒ ▨ ● Never.
🖴 AE, MC, DC, V. ⓓⓓⓓⓓ

CHANIÁ, CRETE

Hotel Amphora The 13th-century building offers great views of harbour and fortress, old town rooftops, sea and mountains. Public areas and bedrooms are done out in traditional Cretan style, with wool rugs and amphorae, polished wooden floors, high panelled ceilings, blue-painted woodwork and pink walls. Excellent Euro-American style buffet breakfast.
⊠ Parodos Theotokopolou 20, 73100 Chaniá, Crete.
Map p384 C5. ▐ FAX (0821) 93224. ▐▐ b,l,d.
Rooms 45. 🖫 ● Never. 🖴 Not accepted. ⓓⓓⓓ

CHANIÁ, CRETE

Casa Delfino Suites This sensitively restored Venetian mansion is close to the bustling harbourside, yet its elegant studios are quiet and private. Rooms are extremely well-furnished, combining all mod cons (Jacuzzi, minibar) with classic style; rooftop views over the castle, out to sea, and inland to the White Mountains. Shady pebble-mosaic courtyard.
⊠ Theofanous 9, 73100 Chaniá, Crete. **Map** p384 C5.
▐ (0821) 84700. FAX (0821) 96500. ▐▐ b. 🖫
Rooms 20 studios. ● Never. 🖴 V. ⓓⓓⓓⓓ

AIGÍALI, AMORGÓS

Hotel Egialis This small family-run hotel perched on a hillside overlooks an excellent sandy beach which is a 10-minute walk away. Open-air terrace bar, pool and restaurant.
⊠ 84008 Aigíali, Amorgós. **Map** p385 E4. ▐ (0285) 73393. FAX (0285) 73395. ▐▐ b,l,d. **Rooms** 30. ⓓⓓ

AÍGINA

Aiginitiko Arhontiko An early-19th century mansion close to the pretty harbour. Rooms are creatively decorated with Venetian murals and furnished with antiques. Roof garden.
⊠ 18010 Aígina. **Map** p384 C3. ▐ FAX (0297) 24968.
▐▐ b,l,d. **Rooms** 12. ⓓⓓ

AREÓPOLI

Pirgos Kapetanakou Rooms in this unusual miniature 18th-century castle are comfortable but very plain, with polished wood floors, stone walls and minimal furniture.
⊠ 23062 Areópoli, Máni, Peloponnese. **Map** p384 B4.
▐ (0733) 51233. ▐▐ b. **Rooms** 5. ⓓⓓⓓ

ATHENS

Athenian Inn Clean, simply furnished rooms (some with air conditioning) in a quiet, fashionable location. Above-average breakfasts; friendly and efficient management.
⊠ Charitos 22, 10675 Athens. **Map** p384 C3. ▐ (01) 723 9552. FAX (01) 724 2268. ▐▐ b. **Rooms** 25. ⓓⓓⓓⓓ

CHANIÁ, CRETE

Hotel Nostos Archetypal picture-postcard Greece: down a charming narrow pedestrian street in the heart of the old town, is this café/bar/hotel, painted in bright blue, yellow and pink. Small round café tables, rush chairs and pots of flowers complete the picture. The studio rooms have gallery beds and balconies with great views of the castle and the mountains.
⊠ Zambeliou 42-46, 73113 Chaniá, Crete.
Map p384 C5. ☎ (0821) 94743. FAX (0821) 94740.
⨎ b. **Rooms** 12. ◯ Oct-Apr. ✉ V. ⓓⓓ

DAMOUCHARI

Hotel Damouchari This eclectically stylish rustic hotel, set close to a white pebble beach in a tiny fishing hamlet, is one of the nicest places to stay in all Greece. Rooms are colourfully painted and inventively furnished with antiques and curios from all over the Pilion region. Particularly attractive is the lounge and bar area. Owned and run by a very friendly husband-and-wife team.
⊠ Damouchari, Pilio. **Map** p384 C2. ☎ FAX (0426) 49840/41. ⨎ b. **Rooms** 4, plus 8 apartments. ⬤
◯ Oct-Apr. ✉ V (cash preferred). ⓓⓓ

CHANIÁ, CRETE

Suites Pandora A peaceful location on a quiet street is one of the attractions of this small collection of suites in a 19th-century mansion. Others are the views of the old town and boats in the harbour, the attractive courtyard and balconies, and the rooftop café terrace. Rooms are furnished in simple traditional style, with double brass beds and stone-flagged floors.
⊠ Lithinon 29, 73100 Chania, Crete. **Map** p384 C5.
☎ (0821) 43588. FAX (0821) 57864. ⨎ b.
Rooms 10 suites. ◯ Oct-Apr. ✉ V. ⓓⓓⓓ

FOLÉGRANDOS

Hotel Kástro The Kástro has been run by the same family for five generations. It's set on a quiet lane among traditional whitewashed cottages and enjoys breathtaking clifftop sea views. It's a long hike to the nearest swimming place, but the hotel is excellent value for money; it was fully refurbished in 1993. There's a roof terrace and a very attractive breakfast room.
⊠ Despo Danassi-Kallianta, 84011 Folégandos Town, Folégandos. **Map** p385 D4. ☎ FAX (0286) 41230. ⨎ b.
Rooms 12. ◯ Oct-Apr. ✉ Not accepted. ⓓⓓ

ATHENS
Marble House This friendly, efficient family-run hotel is at the end of a quiet cul-de-sac, within an easy walk of the Plaka. Excellent value.
⊠ Zinni Anastasiou 35, 11471 Athens.
Map p384 C3. ☎ (01) 923 4058. FAX (01) 922 6461.
⨎ b. **Rooms** 16. ⓓⓓ

CORFU TOWN, CORFU
Hotel Bella Venezia Central, Neo-Classical building, originally a bank, with tasteful high-ceilinged rooms. Secluded inner courtyard.
⊠ Zampeli 4, 49100 Corfu Town, Corfu. **Map** p384 A2.
☎ (0661) 46500. FAX (0661) 31749. ⨎ b,l,d.
Rooms 32. ⓓⓓ

DELPHI
Hotel Acropole A modern, family-run hotel with plain décor but good facilities, friendly management and balconies with superb views.
⊠ Filellinon 13, 33054 Delphi. **Map** p384 B3.
☎ (0265) 82675. FAX (0265) 83171. ⨎ b.
Rooms 42. ⓓⓓ

ERMOÚPOLI, SYROS
Esperance Rooms and Studios Elegant town house hotel; air-conditioned rooms furnished with simple elegance. Friendly manager.
⊠ Akti Papagou & Floegandrou 1, 84100 Ermoúpoli, Syros. **Map** p385 D4. ☎ (0281) 81671. FAX (0281) 85707.
⨎ b. **Rooms** 20. ⓓⓓ

GALAXÍDI

Ganimede Hotel This charming *pension*, run by the friendly Italian owner, occupies a traditional 19th-century sea captain's house. Some rooms have elaborate painted, coffered wooden ceilings, others are plain and simple. The courtyard with fountain, vines and flowers is a delightful place to enjoy Brunello's excellent breakfasts and evening aperitifs.
☒ 33052 Galaxídi. **Map** p384 B3.
📞 (0265) 41328. FAX (0265) 42160. 🍴 b,l,d.
Rooms 8. 🛋 ⬤ Nov. 🎫 V. ⓓ

MAKRINÍTSA

Xenonas Karamarli Each room in this lovingly restored 18th-century mansion is different and imbued with style. The delightful decor includes mock-Byzantine frescoes, carved wooden furniture and old rugs. All rooms are en suite. Admire the panoramic view over the town of Volos and the Gulf of Volos from the terrace café, where breakfast, drinks and *meze* are served.
☒ 37011 Makrinítsa, Pílio. **Map** p384 C2.
📞 (0428) 99570. FAX (0428) 99779. 🍴 b.
Rooms 9. ⬤ Never. 🎫 AE, DC, MC, V. ⓓⓓⓓⓓ

KOUNOUPSA, SPETSES

Hotel Nissia The Nissia features a palatial collection of villas designed in traditional local style, laid out around a splendid pool. The core of the hotel is a restored 19th-century building. Rooms are large and luxurious, with polished wooden floors and modern replicas of traditional furniture, and include a full kitchen. The pool has a separate children's section.
☒ 18050 Kounoupitsa, Spetses. **Map** p384 C4. 📞 Athens office (01) 346 2879. FAX (01) 346 5313. 🍴 b. **Rooms** 20, plus 10 suites. 🖥 🏊 ⬤ Never. 🎫 AE, MC, V. ⓓⓓⓓⓓ

MONEMVASÍA

Kellia Inn The Kellia was once a monks' dormitory and its rooms are appropriately plainly furnished. The monastery church is still outside, and both are overshadowed by the towering cliffs of Monemvasía. There's plenty of open space here with a big café terrace outside and a courtyard behind. The tourist office runs the inn in friendly but minimalist fashion.
☒ Kástro, 23070 Monemvasía , Laconia. **Map** p384 C4.
📞 (0732) 61520. FAX (0732) 617 6712. 🍴 b. **Rooms** 11.
⬤ Never. 🎫 V. ⓓⓓⓓ

FIRÁ, SANTORINI
Athina These simple, almost Spartan suites, built on three levels, overlook the caldera and feature a wonderful cliffside swimming pool.
☒ Kato Firá, 84700 Firá, Santorini. **Map** p385 D4.
📞 (0286) 24910. FAX (0286) 24913. 🍴 b.
Rooms 9 suites. ⓓⓓ

FIRÁ, SANTORINI
Enigma Apartments A simple yet elegant and quiet complex of small apartments built into the cliff face, with superb views out over the caldera.
☒ Enigma Apartments, 84700 Firá, Santorini.
Map p385 D4. 📞 (0286) 24024. FAX (0286) 24023.
🍴 b. **Rooms** 8. ⓓⓓⓓ

FIRÁ, SANTORINI
Homeric Poems Stylish, individually decorated suites partly built into the cliffside, each with its own terrace. Pool with a view and bar.
☒ Firostefani, 84700 Firá, Santorini. **Map** p385 D4.
📞 summer (0286) 24661, winter 0286 25025. FAX summer (0286) 24660, winter (0286) 23600. 🍴 b. ⓓⓓⓓ

FISKÁRDO, KEFALLONIÁ
Erissos This pretty two-storey village house has been attractively restored to offer simple rooms with balconies (nice harbour views) and kitchen facilities. Service is minimal.
☒ 28084 Fiskárdo, Kefalloniá. **Map** p384 A3.
📞 (0674) 41327 🍴 b by arrangement. **Rooms** 4. ⓓ

MONEMVASÍA

Lazareto Despite its rustic, traditional exterior the Lazareto is a modern hotel, set in grassy gardens. It is dramatically overlooked by the cliffs of Monemvasía and faces across the bay to Gefyra village and the mainland mountains; its attractive bar-terrace offers a fine place from which to admire the sunset. The characterful rooms are well equipped.
☒ 23070 Monemvasía, Laconia. **Map** p384 C4.
[(0732) 61991. FAX (0732) 61992. **11** b,l,d.
Rooms 14. 目 ♦ ● Never. ☑ V. ⓄⓄⓄ

NÁFPLIO

Hotel Byron A delightful owner-managed hotel in traditional buildings next to the 11th-century Venetian fortress, in the heart of the port. Rooms are simple but pretty, with polished wooden floors and some antique furniture. Most have fine views over the bay and across stone churches and tiled roofs; some have private terraces. There's also a very attractive café terrace.
☒ Platonos 2, 21100 Náfplio. **Map** p384 C4.
[(0752) 22351. FAX (0752) 26338. **11** b. **Rooms** 7.
目 ● Never. ☑ AE, MC, V. ⓄⓄ

MONEMVASÍA

Hotel Malvásia This unusual hotel is spread over three medieval Venetian buildings around the deserted ruined fortress town of Monemvasía. Each room is decorated in individual style, but all have polished wood or flagstone floors, traditional textiles and antique furniture. The best are in the original Malvásia Hotel building, where there is a bar/café.
☒ Kástro, 23070 Monemvasía, Laconia. **Map** p384 C4.
[(0732) 61323. FAX (0732) 61722. **11** b. **Rooms** 30.
● Never. ☑ V. ⓄⓄ-ⓄⓄⓄ

NTÁPIA, SPETSES

Zoë's Club A good choice for families: the attractive complex is on the outskirts of Ntápia and is very private and secluded. Its design – modern but influenced by the traditional architecture of the island – incorporates luxurious living rooms and full kitchens, terraces and balconies, flower-filled garden and a huge pool.
☒ Ntápia, Spetses. **Map** p384 C4. [(0298) 74447/8.
FAX (0298) 72841. **11** b,l,d. **Rooms** 22, 4 suites,
3 maisonettes. 目 ⊞ ♦ ● Oct-May.
☑ AE, V, MC. ⓄⓄⓄ

GALAXÍDI

Hotel Galaxa Delightful rooms in a traditional sea captain's house with great views of the harbour. Very friendly management.
☒ Eleftherias & Kennedy, Chirolakas, 33052 Galaxídi.
Map p384 B3. [(0265) 41620. FAX (0265) 42053.
11 b. **Rooms** 10. ⓄⓄ

GYTHEIO

Hotel Aktaion Neo-Classical style building right on the harbour; rooms are plain but comfortable, with high ceilings and modern furniture.
☒ Vas. Pavlou 39, 23200 Gytheio. **Map** p384 B4.
[(0733) 23500. FAX (0733) 22294. **11** b,l,d.
Rooms 22. ⓄⓄ

IKARÍA

Cavos Bay Hotel Modern but sensitively designed hotel on the edge of a pretty village with an excellent sandy beach. Fine views.
☒ 283310 Armenistis Rahes, Ikaría. **Map** p385 E4.
[(0275) 71381 FAX (0275) 71380 **11** b,l,d.
Rooms 40. ⓄⓄ

KYTHIRA

Hotel Margarita This grand 19th-century mansion, close to one of Greece's prettiest villages, is the island's finest hotel. Superb sea views but no balconies.
☒ 80100 Chora, Kythira. **Map** p384 C40. [(0735)
31711. FAX (0735) 31694. **11** b. **Rooms** 12. ⓄⓄⓄⓄ

For key to symbols see backflap. For price categories see p383

OÍA, SANTORINI

OLYMPIA

Caldera Villas This collection of cliff-edge cave-villas extends down several levels from the main street, close to the centre of Oía village and its many restaurants. There are fantastic views from the pool and terraces, where there is also a café and breakfast area. Rooms are in traditional dazzling white-and-blue décor; some have a refrigerator and kitchen facilities.
☒ 84702 Oía, Santorini. **Map** p385 D4. ☏ (0286) 71285/71525/71780/71781. FAX (0286) 71425. ⊞ b,l,d. **Rooms** 9. ⇌ ● Never. ⊟ Not accepted. ⒹⒹⒹ

Best Western Hotel Europa Don't worry, it doesn't feel like a chain hotel and is easily the best in Olympia. It is set just outside both the modern town and the ancient ruins, on a hillside above farmland and fertile countryside. There's an attractive pool and gardens with a taverna and a tennis court. Rooms are modern and lack character but have fine views. Good service.
☒ 27065 Ancient Olympia. **Map** p384 B3.
☏ (0624) 22650. FAX (00624) 23166. ⊞ b,l,d. **Rooms** 42. ⊟ ⇌ ⑧ ● Never. ⊟ AE, MC, V. ⒹⒹⒹ

OÍA, SANTORINI

RÉTHYMNO, CRETE

Oía Mare Villas Balanced on the edge of cliffs overlooking the caldera of Santorini this is one of the most magnificently sited accommodations in all Greece. The suites are in beautiful traditional-style buildings painted dazzling white, and simply but elegantly furnished, and there's a fabulous small pool with bar and terrace. Book well ahead (up to a year in advance).
☒ 84702 Oía, Santorini. **Map** p385 D4.
☏ FAX (0286) 71070. ⊞ b. **Rooms** 14 suites.
⇌ ● Nov-March. ⊟ V. ⒹⒹⒹ

Mythos Suites Hotel This 16th-century Venetian mansion is set on a quiet street in the picturesque old quarter of town, and is within easy walking distance of sights and beaches. It was painstakingly and tastefully restored in 1994, and great attention to detail has been paid in the lighting and decoration. There is a bright bar and breakfast area and sunny terraces.
☒ 12 Karaoli Square, 74100 Réthymno, Crete.
Map p385 D5. ☏ (0831) 53917. FAX (0831) 51036. ⊞ b. **Rooms** 10. ⊟ ⇌ ● Never. ⊟ Not accepted. ⒹⒹ

LÉFKES, PÁROS

Lefkes Village Set in 5 acres of grounds, the 'village' comprises 20 attractive, Neo-classical and Cycladic-style rooms round a pool, with a taverna and folk museum.
☒ 84400 Léfkes, Páros. **Map** p385 D4. ☏ (0284) 42398. FAX (0284) 41827. ⊞ b,l,d. **Rooms** 20. ⒹⒹⒹ

MEGÁLO PÁPIGKO

Nikos Saxónis Highly rated, fashionable getaway comprising a small complex of restored 18th-century stone houses with pretty gardens.
☒ 44016 Megálo Pápigko. **Map** p384 A2.
☏ (0653) 41615. FAX (0653) 41890. ⊞ b.
Rooms 8. ⒹⒹⒹ

MÉTSOVO

Egnatia Stone-built with a polished wood interior, this sturdy hotel offers great views of the Pindhos mountains in all directions.
☒ Tositsa 19, 44200 Métsovo. **Map** p384 B2.
☏ (0656) 41844. FAX (0656) 42110. ⊞ b,l,d. **Rooms** 37. ⒹⒹ

MYCENAE

Hotel Belle Hélène Schliemann This simple guesthouse hosted 19th-century archaeologists and still provides comfortable, peaceful lodgings.
☒ Christous Iouda, 21200 Mykínai. **Map** p384 C3.
☏ (0751) 76225. FAX (0751) 76179. ⊞ b,l,d. **Rooms** 8. Ⓓ

RÉTHYMNO, CRETE

Vecchio Hotel Apartments These attractive apartments provide excellent value. They are set in a quiet street in the heart of the old quarter; the building is new but decorated in pale blue and terracotta to fit the style of its medieval surroundings. The super pool is a real bonus. Rooms are simple and modern, well appointed and elegantly painted.
☒ Daliani 4, 74100 Réthymno, Crete. **Map** p385 D5.
☏ (0831) 54985. **FAX** (0831) 54986. ⸠⸠ b. **Rooms** 24.
▤ (extra charge). 🌊 ● Oct-Apr. ☑ V. Ⓓ Ⓓ

RHODES OLD TOWN, RHODES

San Nikolis Hotel The main building of this pretty bougainvillea-draped hotel oozes history and features two medieval arched rooms. Set on a cobbled street below the walls built by the Knights of St John, it overlooks the ruins of the Roman market. Rooms have all mod cons; some have a veranda, patio or balcony. Roof terrace and tree-shaded courtyard.
☒ Hippodamou 61, 85100 Rhodes. **Map** p385 F4.
☏ (0241) 34561. **FAX** (0241) 32034. ⸠⸠ b,l,d. **Rooms** 12, plus 8 suites. ▤ ● Never. ☑ AE, MC, V. Ⓓ Ⓓ

RHODES OLD TOWN, RHODES

Cava D'Oro Built into the ancient city walls, this was the residence of the Italian garrison commander during Italy's occupation of Rhodes (1912–45); it became a small hotel in 1987. It is a short walk to both the centre of the old town and the ferry harbour. Rooms are simply decorated but quiet and comfortable. There is a small courtyard for breakfast and drinks.
☒ Kisthinou 17, 85100 Rhodes. **Map** p385 F4.
☏ (0241) 36980. **FAX** (0241) 77332. ⸠⸠ b. **Rooms** 13.
● Nov-March. ☑ Not accepted. Ⓓ Ⓓ

STAVRI

Pirgos Tsitsiri Located in an ancient village and built around the old stronghold of one of the region's clan chieftains, this feels like a real bandit's hideout. The views over the mountains and across the Messinian Gulf are awesome. Rooms are simple and traditional with wooden floors and striped wool rugs and cushions.
☒ 23071 Stavri, Máni. **Map** p384 B4. ☏ May-Sept (0733) 56297, Oct-Apr (01) 685 8960.
FAX (01) 685 8962. ⸠⸠ b,l,d. **Rooms** 20. ▤ ▮
● Oct-Apr. ☑ Not accepted. Ⓓ Ⓓ

MÝKONOS TOWN, MÝKONOS
Belvedere Right in the heart of the Old Town, this luxury hotel features 40 rooms with all mod cons; there's even a gym and Jacuzzi. Fine views over the white cubic town houses.
☒ Rohari, 84600 Mýkonos. **Map** p385 D4. ☏ (0289) 5122. **FAX** (0289) 25126. ⸠⸠ b,l,d. **Rooms** 40. Ⓓ Ⓓ Ⓓ Ⓓ

MYSTRÁS
Hotel Byzantion Location makes this hotel: all rooms have a view of the castle. Comfortable and modern with good facilities, if a bit sterile.
☒ 23100 Neos Mystrás. **Map** p384 B4.
☏ (0731) 83309. **FAX** (0731) 20019. ⸠⸠ b,l,d.
Rooms 22. Ⓓ Ⓓ

NYMFAÍA
La Moara Owned by the Boutari winemaking family, this former watermill is now a luxury hotel with a superb wine bar and restaurant. Facilities include billiards and a library.
☒ 53078 Nymfaía, Florina. **Map** p385 D1. ☏ (031) 287626. **FAX** (031) 287401. ⸠⸠ b,l,d. **Rooms** 8. Ⓓ Ⓓ Ⓓ Ⓓ

OÍA, SANTORINI
Hotel Aethrio A beautiful complex of suites and rooms decorated with art, antiques and curios and set around a large pool. Great sea views.
☒ 84702 Oía, Santorini. **Map** p385 D4. ☏ summer (0286) 71040, winter (01) 9959 534. **FAX** summer (0286) 71930, winter (01) 9959 534. ⸠⸠ b. **Rooms** 20. Ⓓ Ⓓ

STEMNÍTSA

Trikolóneio This friendly, first-class guesthouse was created by knocking together two stone-built Arcadian highland mansions into one. It is set on the village square next to a church, with lots of flowers and greenery including a vine-shaded terrace. Rooms make much use of polished wood; all are en suite. The village is an ideal base for exploring the Loussios Gorge.

22024 Stemnítsa. **Map** p384 B3. (0795) 81297. FAX (0795) 81483. b. **Rooms** 20. Never. Not accepted.

SÝMI TOWN, SÝMI

Les Catherinettes This is one of the prettiest small hotels in all Greece, with polished wood floors, elaborately painted ceilings and dadoes, and tall windows overlooking the charming harbour. It is efficiently run by the friendly owner Julie and her daughter Marina. There is a good traditional taverna downstairs on the quayside; beaches are close by.

85600 Sými. **Map** p385 F4. FAX (0241) 72698. b,l,d. **Rooms** 6, 4 studios. Never. Not accepted.

SÝMI TOWN, SÝMI

Hotel Aliki Two steps from the sea, in a peaceful location only a few minutes from the Gialós harbour area, this pretty 19th-century sea captain's mansion is now a very well-run A-Class hotel. Rooms are en suite, and simply and comfortably furnished; ask for a balcony and sea view. There are café tables on the quayside and a comfortable bar and lobby area.

Akti G Gennimata, 85600 Sými. **Map** p385 F4. (0241) 71665. FAX (0241) 71655. b. **Rooms** 15. Oct to Apr. V.

SÝMI TOWN, SÝMI

Opera House A collection of blue-and-white Neo-Classical-style buildings house these cool, airy studios. Each has a large kitchen; all are traditionally furnished with wooden couches and colourful rugs. Bathrooms are functional. It's very quiet here, with tree-filled gardens and an attractive outdoor café-bar, though it's just a five-minute stroll to the harbour tavernas.

85600 Sými. **Map** p385 F4. (0241) 72034. FAX (0241) 72035. b. **Rooms** 32 studios. Nov to March. V.

OÍA, SANTORINI

Museum Hotel This historic mansion on the main street of this cliff-side village has panoramic views. Inside, rooms are artistically decorated and furnished.

Oía, Santorini. **Map** p385 D4. (0286) 71515. FAX (0286) 71516. b. **Rooms** 9 suites.

ORNOS, MÝKONOS

Kivotos Clubhotel Art and artefacts abound in this luxury resort built in Cycladic village-style around a gorgeous saltwater pool. Private beach.

84600 Ornos, Mýkonos. **Map** p385 D4. (0289) 24094. FAX (0298) 22844. b. **Rooms** 20, plus 4 suites.

PROKÓPI, EVVOIA

Candili Comfortable accommodation in the manor house and farmhouses of this magnificent private estate which offers courses in Greek cooking, painting, music and dance.

34004 Prokópi, Evvoia. **Map** p384 C3. (0227) 41381. FAX (0227) 41190. b,l,d. **Rooms** 32.

PSAROU, MÝKONOS

Mýkonos Blu This luxury complex in traditional style boasts unbeatable facilities, including two superb restaurants and range of watersports.

84600 Psarou, Platys Gialos, Mýkonos. **Map** p385 D4. (0298) 27780. FAX (0298) 27783. b,l,d. **Rooms** 102 bungalows.

VYTINA

Hotel Menalon The exterior features an imaginative and stylish use of decorative brickwork and lovely wooden balconies. Inside is a harmonious blend of traditional and modern; the walls are hung with paintings from the owner's collection of modern Greek painters. There is also an attractive courtyard. Service can be patchy however.
22010 Vytina, Arcadia. **Map** p384 B3.
(0795) 22217. FAX (0795) 22200. b. **Rooms** 51.
Never. Not accepted.

VYZÍTSA

Archontiko Blana A stone's throw from the main square of the peaceful village and shaded by giant plane trees, the mansion enjoys stupendous views west across the Gulf of Volos. Polished woodwork, shuttered windows and carved wooden doors impart local flavour; minibar fridges add a touch of luxury. Penthouse suite with a tiny sauna and whirlpool bath.
37010 Vyzítsa, Pílio. **Map** p384 C2.
(0421) 86840. FAX (0421) 43614. b. **Rooms** 4.
Never. Not accepted.

RÉTHYMNO, CRETE

Hotel Fortezza This modern, family-run hotel may be short on charm but it's long on facilities and has an excellent central location.
Melissinou 16, 74100 Réthymno, Crete.
Map p385 D5. (0831) 23828. FAX (0831) 54073.
b,l,d. **Rooms** 54.

VOLISSÓS, CHÍOS

Stélla Tsakíri A cluster of traditional stone houses, renovated by an Athenian sculptor and converted into comfortable suites, all with terraces, full kitchens and original features.
Plateia Pirgos, Volissós 82103, Chíos. **Map** p385 E3.
(0271) 21421. FAX (0271) 21521. **Rooms** 9.

YDRA

Hotel Bratsera Built in the 19th century as a sponge warehouse, the Bratsera is nowadays by far the best hotel on this fashionable artistic island and provides surprisingly good value. Rooms are a mix of traditional and modern, with built-in beds or antique brass-and-iron bedsteads, and equipped with fridge and TV. It has a lovely pool and its own restaurant.
18040 Ydra. **Map** p384 C4. (0298) 53971.
FAX (0298) 53626. b,l,d. **Rooms** 23.
Jan. AE, DC, MC, V.

YDRA

Ippokampos Hotel A friendly and unpretentious hotel, two steps from the harbourfront in the centre of traffic-free Ydra town. It is decorated in traditional white-and-blue painted woodwork; the flagstone courtyard is a mass of potted greenery and brilliant bougainvillea. The simply furnished rooms are bright and airy. There is a café-bar downstairs (music in the evenings).
18040 Ydra. **Map** p384 C4. (0298) 53453.
FAX (0298) 52501. b. **Rooms** 16. Oct-Apr.
Not accepted.

YDRA

Hotel Hydroussa In the village centre, a large, light and high-ceilinged traditional house. Attractive flower-filled courtyard.
Ydra Town, 18040 Ydra. **Map** p384 C4. (0298) 52400, 52217, 53193, 53580. FAX (0298) 52161.
b. **Rooms** 40.

YDRA

Hotel Miranda This traditionally furnished early 19th-century sea captain's mansion hosts an exceptional collection of art and antiques. Pleasant walled courtyard.
Ydra Town, 18040 Ydra. **Map** p384 C4. (0298) 52230. FAX (0298) 53510. b. **Rooms** 14.

Indexes

Each country featured in the guide has two indexes, one of hotel names, the other of hotel locations.

Hotel Names

In this index, hotels are arranged in order of the most distinctive part of their name; very common prefixes such as 'Albergaria' 'Albergo' 'Auberge', 'Gasthof', 'Gjestehus', 'Hostal', 'Hospedería' 'Hostellerie' 'Hostería', 'Hotel', 'Hôtellerie' 'Ostellerie', 'Pension' and 'Pensjonat', as well as definite and indefinite articles and common prepositions, such as 'à', 'de', 'de la', 'del', 'die', 'du','t', 'zum' and 'zur' are omitted or ignored in the alpha order.

Hotel Locations

In this index, hotels are listed by the name of the city, town or village they are in or near. Common prefixes, articles and prepositions are again ignored in the alpha order.

Austria

Hotel Names

Hotel Locations

Belgium and Luxembourg

Hotel Names

Hotel Locations

France

Hotel Names

Hotel Locations

Germany

Hotel Names

Landhotel, Der, Hotel, Gasthaus, Gasthof etc omitted

Hotel Locations

Great Britain

Hotel Names

Hotel Locations

Greece

Hotel Names

Ireland

Hotel Names

Hotel Locations

Italy

Hotel Names

Hotel Locations

The Netherlands

Hotel Names

Hotel Locations

Norway

Hotel Names

Hotel Locations

Portugal

Hotel Names

Hotel Locations

Spain

Hotel Names

El, La, Las omitted

Hotel Locations

Sweden

Hotel Names

Hotel Locations

Switzerland

Hotel Names

Acknowledgments

DORLING KINDERSLEY and DUNCAN PETERSEN gratefully acknowledge the help of hotels and other places to stay which provided help in preparing this guide; the national tourist offices of all the countries featured in the guide; Bill Bennett; Clara Inman and Stewart J. Wild.

We acknowledge with thanks hotels, individuals and tourist boards who provided photographs for publication in the guide. Also:

ANDALUCIA SLIDE LIBRARY: F. GALLARDO

CORBIS: Bob Krist 38-39; Charles & Josette Lenars 132-133.

EDMUND NAGELE: 10-11; 198-199.

TOM MACKIE: 184-185.

TONI SCHNEIDERS FOTOGRAFIE: Marco Schneiders 120-121.

TONY STONE IMAGES: Sylvain Grandadam 24-25; Stephen Studd 142-143.

READER'S QUESTIONNAIRE

HOW WAS YOUR STAY? We'd like to hear what you thought about the hotels you stayed in on your trip. What did you like about them? Did they meet your expectations? What improvements to their facilities or service would you recommend? Did you discover any new hotels we should consider for our next edition? Please cut out or photocopy this page and return it to: The Editorial Director, Travel Guides, Dorling Kindersley, 9 Henrietta Street, London WC2E 8PS, or contact us through www.dk.com

HOTELS STAYED IN ...

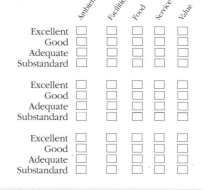

Hotel
Page No.
Comments

	Ambience	Facilities	Food	Service	Value
Excellent	☐	☐	☐	☐	☐
Good	☐	☐	☐	☐	☐
Adequate	☐	☐	☐	☐	☐
Substandard	☐	☐	☐	☐	☐

Hotel
Page No.
Comments

	Ambience	Facilities	Food	Service	Value
Excellent	☐	☐	☐	☐	☐
Good	☐	☐	☐	☐	☐
Adequate	☐	☐	☐	☐	☐
Substandard	☐	☐	☐	☐	☐

Hotel
Page No.
Comments

	Ambience	Facilities	Food	Service	Value
Excellent	☐	☐	☐	☐	☐
Good	☐	☐	☐	☐	☐
Adequate	☐	☐	☐	☐	☐
Substandard	☐	☐	☐	☐	☐

NEW HOTEL(S) I WOULD LIKE TO RECOMMEND ...

Name of Hotel
Country
Address & Telephone number
Comments

Name of Hotel
Country
Address & Telephone number
Comments

ABOUT YOU ...

Where did you buy this book?
☐ Bookshop
☐ Department store
☐ Other shop
☐ Online bookshop

Which newspaper(s) do you regularly read ...

How often do you travel abroad?
☐ Less than once every 2 years
☐ Once every 2 years
☐ Once a year
☐ More than once a year

Age
☐ Under 25
☐ 25 to 34
☐ 35 to 49
☐ 50 and above

If you took your children on holiday with you, what are their ages?
☐ 0 to 5 years
☐ 6 to 10 years
☐ 11 to 16 years
☐ over 16 years

TITLES AVAILABLE

THE GUIDES THAT SHOW YOU WHAT OTHERS ONLY TELL YOU

COUNTRY GUIDES

REGIONAL GUIDES

CITY GUIDES

TRAVEL PLANNERS

DK TRAVEL GUIDES CITY MAPS

DK TRAVEL GUIDES PHRASE BOOKS

CONTINUALLY UPDATED

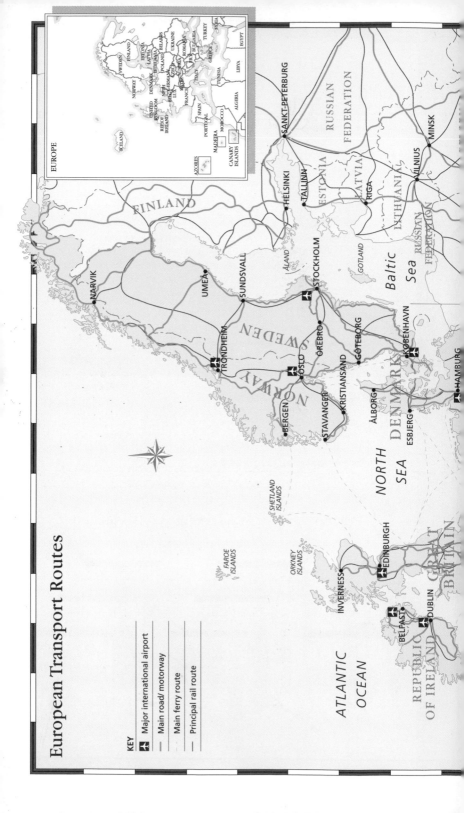

European Transport Routes

KEY

✈ Major international airport
— Main road/ motorway
⋯ Main ferry route
— Principal rail route

EUROPE

ICELAND

AZORES

MADEIRA

CANARY
ISLANDS

ATLANTIC
OCEAN

FAROE
ISLANDS

SHETLAND
ISLANDS

ORKNEY
ISLANDS

INVERNESS

EDINBURGH

GREAT
BRITAIN

BELFAST

DUBLIN

REPUBLIC
OF IRELAND

NORTH
SEA

NARVIK

NORWAY

TRONDHEIM

BERGEN

STAVANGER

OSLO

KRISTIANSAND

SWEDEN

UMEÅ

SUNDSVALL

ÖREBRO

STOCKHOLM

GÖTEBORG

KØBENHAVN

ÅLBORG

DENMARK

ESBJERG

HAMBURG

FINLAND

HELSINKI

TALLINN

ESTONIA

RIGA

LATVIA

LITHUANIA

VILNIUS

MINSK

RUSSIAN
FEDERATION

SANKT-PETERBURG

ÅLAND

GOTLAND

Baltic
Sea

RUSSIAN
FEDERATION